W9-DBS-991

BASIL OF CAESAREA

THE TRANSFORMATION
OF THE CLASSICAL HERITAGE

Edited by Peter Brown

PHILIP ROUSSEAU

BASIL OF CAESAREA

UNIVERSITY OF CALIFORNIA PRESS

Berkeley · Los Angeles · Oxford

University of California Press
Berkeley and Los Angeles, California

University of California Press, Ltd.
Oxford, England

© 1994 by
The Regents of the University of California

Library of Congress Cataloging-in-Publication Data

Rousseau, Philip.
    Basil of Caesarea / Philip Rousseau.
        p.   cm. — (Transformation of the classical heritage : 20)
    Includes bibliographical references and index.
    ISBN 0-520-08238-9 (alk. paper)
    1. Basil, Saint, Bishop of Caesarea, ca. 329–379. 2. Christian
saints—Turkey—Biography. 3. Bishops—Turkey—Biography.
I. Title. II. Series.
BR1720.B3R68   1994
270.2'092–dc20
[B]   93-3552
                                                                              CIP

Printed in the United States of America
9 8 7 6 5 4 3 2 1

For my parents

It is not names that save us,
but the choices we make.

Letter 257.2

CONTENTS

ABBREVIATIONS

Adul.	Basil *Ad adulescentes.*
B	*Regulae brevius tractatae = Short Rules.*
C	Yves Courtonne, editor of Basil's *Letters.*
CE	Basil *Contra Eunomium.*
D	Roy J. Deferrari, translator of Basil's *Letters.*
DSS	Basil *De spiritu sancto.*
Ep.	*Epistula(e).*
F	*Regulae fusius tractatae = Long Rules.*
GCS	*Die griechischen christlichen Schriftsteller der ersten Jahrhunderte.*
GNaz	Gregory of Nazianzus.
GNyss	Gregory of Nyssa.
HE	*Historia ecclesiastica.*
Hex.	Basil *Hexaemeron.*
Hom.	Basil *Homilia(e).* (The numbering of Basil's homilies is explained in the supplement to the Bibliography.)
Jones, *LRE*	A. H. M. Jones, *The Later Roman Empire, 284–602.* First published 1964. Reprinted in two paperback volumes. Oxford: Blackwell, 1986.
Laud.	Gregory of Nyssa *In laudem fratris Basilii.*
N	*Basilio di Cesarea, Discorso ai Giovani (Oratio ad adolescentes)*, ed. Mario Naldini.

Orat.   *Oratio(nes).*

PG   *Patrologia Graeca*, ed. J. P. Migne.

PL   *Patrologia Latina*, ed. J. P. Migne.

PLRE   *The Prosopography of the Later Roman Empire*, edited by
            A. H. M. Jones, J. R. Martindale, and J. Morris. Vol. 1,
            A.D. 260–395. Cambridge: Cambridge University Press,
            1971.

R   Rufinus's Latin translation of Basil's 'Rules'.

VMac.   Gregory of Nyssa *Vita s. Macrinae.*

PREFACE

This book makes no claim to exhaust the subject of Basil's thought and career. I have a narrower purpose in mind: to discover why he became a bishop, and in the process to explain how he found the opportunity; then to examine how he defined his task, and with what success. I do not roam over the social world of Cappadocia, nor do I pursue every allusion to classical and Christian antecedents. I am content to remain uncertain about some dates, provided my sense of Basil's development is not thereby called into question. I have no aspiration to be the man's definitive biographer.

I will confess that I thought Basil's reasonably well documented career would reveal a 'type', which would enable us to decide more generally what a fourth-century bishop might have been like. I have ended up thinking that he was probably rather odd, and not entirely successful. Yet there is something of general importance in that judgement. It seems not impossible that many bishops displayed the same quality, for the simple reason that none of them were clear about what 'being a bishop' might mean. Within the young Christian empire, with its fresh opportunities for status and influence among churchmen, there was still a variety of interpretation at work. The eccentricity and insecurity of Basil, therefore, might be typical in another way, warning us against suppositions based on subsequent formalities.

There is much to be said in Basil's favour. His address was direct, in the sermons especially, and carries more conviction than the ruminations of his brother Gregory. There is an urgency and enthusiasm to much that he said and wrote. At moments of theological profundity or exalted insight, he seems to have been agreeably unconscious of the effect he might create. Such qualities are easily distinguished from occasional lapses into conceit.

There is no point in being starry-eyed, however. In morality, he had high ideals; and his logical analysis of their implications could have inspired pessimism in some, and promised a bleak future in the lives of others. In that regard, he was at times himself the victim of his own intransigence. He could display also a lack of judgement and scruple, if he felt that loyalty or justice would undermine the interests of the Church— not often, but enough to make lasting enemies. His view of history and circumstance was coloured by the belief that God would test any virtue to the limit of endurance. He called the resulting tension 'hope', which might not persuade every modern reader. Finally, the undoubted privilege of his birth and education made it constantly difficult for him to avoid disdain and condescension. Again, he normally mastered such temptations; but failure was frequent enough to provoke anger in others.

Given his uncompromising ardour and his social advantage, it might seem surprising that he could remain accessible—to us, as well as to his contemporaries—and even charming; a figure of obvious significance, instructive to the historian. He provides us with the chance to learn how we should study a bishop of that time. His letters and sermons in particular present a surprisingly full picture of an individual. We enter at once into a particular dialogue, which will later enable us to test generalities. His own personality outweighs by far, in the written record, the evidence for a history of ideas or a social survey of the age.

Certain idiosyncrasies stood out. First, in his search for the basis of morality and authority, he concentrated on the meaning that could be attached to human nature, allowing rightly balanced and inspired self-knowledge to persuade each person to virtue and order. Rank, whether civil or religious, and the written word, whether of Scripture or the law, made their claims to loyalty and respect only insofar as they reflected the truths of the inner life. The heroes of martyrdom, the Christian rulers of the empire, the bishops who presided over the churches, were all judged by the standards of an inner vision. Second, he shared the attachment of many Christians to what they regarded as authentic tradition. Παράδοσις, literally, 'the handing over (of gifts from the past) from one person to another', was one of his most commonly expressed ideals. In his case, however, the touchstones of accredited continuity were the enduring practices, formulae, and theological implications of Christian cult; and doctrine, in the sense of extended or speculative argument, had to be measured against the simpler antiquity of sacrament and creed. Third, he thought relentlessly in social terms. The religious community claimed lasting priority: pursued on their own, the spiritual efforts of the individual were not only precarious but without meaning. Basil quickly became, and always remained, a churchman in that literal sense. Fourth, he wished always to maximize the opportunities for generosity. That followed, obviously, from his social concern. He encouraged in his audience a sense of responsibility for others. Its simplest demonstration was economic: the support of the poor by the rich. Yet beneath that lay another obligation: the demand for mercy, forgiveness, sympathy, and support in the less tangible areas of moral and spiritual growth. Hence another characteristic emphasis: the 'building up of the Church'. His ascetic writings were particularly inspired by such a goal. Fifth, he depended on friendship; and, like many who feel such a need, he found it difficult to make friends and keep them. For that reason, he may have expected too much of the ones he had, placing at times an intolerable weight on their affection, and exaggerating the intensity of his own. It remains true, however, that he could not have achieved even his own limited success without the intellectual stimulus and moral counsel of some half a dozen close colleagues.

We can find, of course, such habits and faults in several figures of the period. What gave Basil's life its special quality was the combination and, indeed, the interdependence of all five elements—which is what I hope this book will illustrate. Such a conjunction of qualities explains also the significance of the man in relation to more general features of his own time. How could Christians develop the resources and techniques of the Greek language, in order to propagate their own moral vision, and to propagate it persuasively to as large an audience as possible? What particular past should one appeal to, when upholding the rights of tradition? What distinguished 'orthodox' Christianity from paganism, from the secular world, from rival interpretations of what Christianity might mean? How large a group could one possibly appeal to, when defending high spiritual and moral ideals? What type of person was best fitted to assume leadership within the Church, and to propose authoritative answers to all those questions? Basil made his distinctive reply to every one of them. In the process, he showed that he was fully aware of the strains and enthusiasms typical of the fourth-century Church as a whole. Yet he showed also that its sense of direction was constantly adjusted by the responses of individuals like himself.

That dialogue between widely expressed inquiry and tentative, personal solution reminds us how provisional Christianity still remained—in its ideas and institutions, in its conception of where it had come from and where it was going. We can at times be too unreflective in our use of terms like 'Arianism', 'monasticism', 'barbarian invasion', and 'Christian empire'. Such clear-cut definitions of policy and event were simply unavailable in the 370s. Theodosius would become emperor only at the end of the decade; Arianism was still 'undefeated', and identical in the eyes of many with Christianity itself; the practice of the ascetic life had settled into nothing approaching its later forms; and the prospect of a Gothic kingdom within the frontiers of the empire was probably beyond the bounds of anyone's imagination. Basil's career cannot be made to illustrate or explain any anachronistic tidiness. The real uncertainties of his life—his theological conservatism and compromise, his ambivalent relationships with those in power, his loosely structured experiments in asceticism, not to mention his recurrent gloom about the security of the orthodox cause—all arose from personal experience but all mirror exactly the sense of an uncertain future that was widespread at the time.

Those reflections have governed, I hope, the structure of my argument. The first three chapters identify the resources—family, education, ascetic devotion—that may have fostered in Basil an episcopal vocation. One might suppose that people with his background, his erudition, his spiritual enthusiasm were the types most likely to seek episcopal office; but I argue, in the end, that that was not obviously the case. Basil's sense of family, and his understanding of intellectual and moral seriousness, were coloured from an early stage by a consciousness of what the Church provided in support, opportunity, and obligation. The fourth chapter describes the period during which he was forced to make the more permanent decisions that governed his path in life—the period of his confrontation with the Arian leader, Eunomius. It was then that he expressed himself for the first time at length on the nature of the Church as he saw it. In chapter 5, I explore a series of relations between Basil and Caesarea, presenting a picture of the priest and bishop at work. In the following chapter, on the ascetic writings, I suggest we discover the inner life that went with that priestly and episcopal activity: the two have to be conjoined under the heading of ecclesiology, and ascetic endeavour is not to be thought of as separable from the public life of the Church. In chapter 7, I discuss Basil's relations with other churchmen in his region, which provide also the context in which to explore his failures and successes in friendship, mentioned above. Chapter 8 extends the inquiry even further, assessing his role in the Arian controversy more generally, with particular emphasis on the schism in the church of Antioch. In chapter 9, we turn inwards again, attempting to describe his view of human nature and destiny. We discover, I think, in doing so, long-standing convictions that were at work even during moments clouded, from an external point of view, by apparent disappointment or ineptitude.

The literature on Basil is enormous. I make no claim to have mastered it. Readers better informed than I am will easily discover unattributed opinions that have already been expressed by others. I have read carefully, however, often several times, everything that has survived of Basil's writings; and lack of originality on my part will be attributable frequently, I hope, to the limited range of judgements that can claim to depend on an honest reading of the texts. There are some books, however, that I will mention now, because they have been a constant guide in ways it would be tedious to acknowledge footnote by footnote. Paul Fedwick, *The Church and the Charisma of Leadership in Basil of Caesarea* (1979), deserves to be mentioned first, since—amazingly—it is the only substantial book on Basil to have appeared in English since W. K. Lowther Clarke, *St Basil the Great: A Study in Monasticism* (1913). Fedwick addresses questions very close to some of my own. On a few issues, we certainly disagree. More important, we approach Basil from different starting points, as I think will emerge. I am interested by development in Basil's life, about which I detect far less concern in Fedwick's work; and I would claim to make at once a broader and more integrated use of the texts at our disposal. However, it has been helpful to take for granted many of the dates and narratives presented in Fedwick's book, which have been augmented by his documentation (and by the contributions of participants) in the proceedings he edited in two volumes, *Basil of Caesarea: Christian, Humanist, Ascetic* (1981). Every modern student of Basil is dependent on two other important works: Stanislas Giet, *Les Idées et l'action sociales de s. Basile* (1941); and Jean Bernardi, *La Prédication des pères cappadociens* (1968). I have also depended frequently on Yves Courtonne, *Un Témoin du IVe siècle oriental: Saint Basile et son temps d'après sa correspondance* (1973); and Benoît Gain, *L'Église de Cappadoce au IVe siècle d'après la correspondance de Basile de Césarée* (1985). It goes without saying that I have had to take into account, both directly and indirectly, the dating provided by the works of, for example, F. Loofs, Marius Bessières, Emmanuel Amand de Mendieta, and Jean Gribomont, which are mentioned in the Bibliography. Introductions to modern editions of Basil's works, especially in French, offer rich and authoritative information, much of which I have also taken for granted. Klaus Koschorke, *Spuren der alten Liebe: Studien zum Kirchenbegriff des Basilius von Caesarea*, appeared as I was bringing my own work to a conclusion. I have read it with pleasure; but, rather than engage critically with so recent a production, I have preferred to allow our two books to seek their different fortunes side by side. It would have been even more difficult to take into account Robert Pouchet's *Basile le Grand et son univers d'amis* (Rome, 1992).

It needs to be said that many of the works mentioned above suffer from one or both of two major disadvantages. Sometimes they treat Basil in relation to his Cappadocian colleagues, Gregory of Nazianzus and Gregory of Nyssa. Beside these last, as a theologian and a stylist in particular, Basil can seem both disappointing and less significant and therefore fails to capture careful and sympathetic attention. At other times, the books in question appear more interested in social and political history and use Basil's works as sources of information for almost everything except himself. I prefer to concentrate on the individual, for reasons I have already declared and hope to justify.

It is a pleasure to mention other debts. My first, here as elsewhere, is to Peter Brown. He helped to form me as an historian, has offered me constant encouragement and support over thirty years, and has stimulated me no less than thousands of others by his written work. His conversation and correspondence I am still lucky enough to enjoy and ignorant enough to need. The book started life when I held a Visiting Professorship in History and Classics at the University of California, Berkeley; and I remember keenly the unstinting kindness of many colleagues in both Departments, as well as the vigour of my graduate students. More recently, I put the finishing touches to my main research while holding an Honorary Research Fellowship in the Department of History and Archaeology at the University of Exeter. I owe much to the kindness and generosity of Christopher Holdsworth, who invited me there, and to the exciting seminars held in the Department of Classics under Peter Wiseman. I wrote the main draft of the book while at the Institute for Advanced Study, Princeton; and I would like to thank in particular Christian Habicht, Glen Bowersock, and Giles Constable for making my Membership so enjoyable and productive. There can be few research centres that contrive so successfully to make writing a tranquil and efficient process, while providing at other moments the instant company of outstanding scholars. I was lucky to share those blessings with Alan Cameron and Garth Fowden, who answered several questions referred to in the text, and helped me in other ways less specific than a footnote can recognize. I must thank also my own University. Its Leave and Research Committees have been unremittingly generous over the years. I belong to a Department that is tolerant and agreeable, as well as distinguished in many fields. I am sure my other friends will allow me to single out Val Flint, who has always been at once warm and perceptive in her response to my work. I am indebted to Barbara Batt, who helped me considerably in the preparation of my

manuscript, and to Jonette Surridge, who designed my map and made it
ready for publication. Several people were kind enough to read a complete
draft of the book, helping me to improve its style and accuracy, while failing
to save me, I dare say, from obstinacy in rash opinion and undetected error:
particular thanks to T. D. Barnes and, once again, Garth Fowden. Finally,
I owe much to the University of California Press, especially to those whose
patience and precision helped me to achieve even greater clarity: Doris
Kretschmer, Mary Lamprech, and Marian Shotwell.

My dedication to my parents represents my own sense of παράδοσις,
felt perhaps more urgently in middle years. A link between one's academic
work and the rest of life is not always easy to establish, and probably not
always useful. I retain some hope that Basil has made me take the past
seriously; and I sense (as he might not) that traditions he held dear continue
to flourish among those whom I live with most closely.

Philip Rousseau
University of Aukland
September 1993

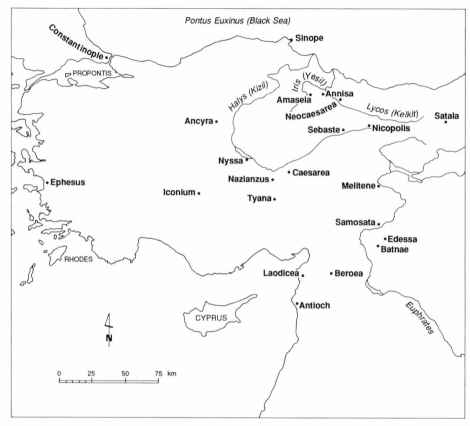

Map. Asia Minor and Syria.

· CHAPTER I ·

A CAPPADOCIAN FAMILY

Not before the moment of their death are we entitled to judge finally the shapes and tendencies of people's lives. Until we reach that point in our inquiry, we should pay Basil the compliment of holding in suspense our opinion as to what gave his life cohesion; for he was uncertain about that very question. He never gave the impression of having found a settled point of view—about himself or about his friends; about the world or about the responsibilities he had shouldered; even, perhaps, about his God.[1]

The career we seek to explain appears on the surface simple enough. Born around the year 330 (when the emperor Constantine was still alive), Basil belonged to a relatively prosperous and locally prominent family in Pontus, near the Black Sea coast of Asia Minor. He performed well as a student, first in Caesarea, then in Constantinople, and finally in Athens, where he spent some six years before leaving the city in 356. After a journey in Egypt, Syria, and perhaps other regions of the eastern empire, he returned to Pontus, where he practised the 'philosophic' or ascetic life in the company of relatives, friends, and disciples. Those events took place during the final years of the reign of the emperor Constantius

---

Cross-references occur in two forms: "chapter 1, n. 43," which refers to the note; and "chapter 1, at n. 43," which refers to the text.

1. It seems distracting, if not improper, to discuss in the opening paragraph of a biography the death of its subject. Suffice it to say here that I am aware of recent doubts about the date (traditionally 1 January 379), and discuss them in appendix 3 (which has particular reference to chapter 9). Meanwhile, we should bear in mind that Basil may have died as early as September 377.

(Constantine's last surviving son, who died in 361) and during the short reign of his cousin Julian (killed in a skirmish while campaigning in Persia in 363). By that time Basil had been ordained a priest. After hesitant engagements with church life and the continued pursuit of his ascetic interests in Pontus, he finally settled in Caesarea in 365. He became bishop of the city in 370. His career seems marked above all by involvement in the later stages of the Arian controversy (although he died well before the 'triumph of orthodoxy' at the Council of Constantinople in 381, held under the influence of a new emperor, Theodosius). Since the death in 373 of Athanasius, the heroic patriarch of Alexandria, Basil had inherited (in the eyes of some) the mantle of leadership in the struggle against the teachings of Arius and his successors. For most of his active life as a churchman, imperial power in the East was in the hands of the emperor Valens (appointed Augustus in 364 by his brother and western colleague, Valentinian, and killed at the battle of Hadrianople against the Goths in 378). Valens was a forceful patron of the Arian cause, and therefore (again, as some saw it) a symbolic antagonist, secular and heretical, for the saintly and learned bishop.

One rightly suspects the tidiness of that account. Its deceptively smooth contours are found, on closer inspection, to sport a rich forest covering of judgements and suppositions, which themselves obscure the ravines cut deep into its landscape. Were there no complexities to his family background? How do we know that his student years were even satisfying, let alone brilliant? Were the transitions from Athens to Pontus, from Pontus to Caesarea, as effortless as they can be made to seem? Does the battle against Arianism wholly exhaust the significance or tenor of his priestly career? Such are the questions that press immediately upon us.

One feature of the apparently straightforward biography is particularly striking. The restlessness of Basil's earlier years stands in contrast to the enduring commitment of his priesthood. Yet the events before 365 are taken as a natural preparation for the career that followed. Is the impression justified? Almost certainly not. So our immediate task is to show why. We have to examine the influence, during those early, supposedly formative years, of three sets of resources, upon which we might expect Basil to have drawn: his family background, his educational experience, and his ascetic enthusiasm. Can we relate them one to another in such a way as to bring Basil intelligibly, in our own eyes, to the brink of a lasting decision in 365? This chapter and the two that follow will address that question.

Basil is frequently presented in the context of his family, with an understandable emphasis on his prolific and influential brother, Gregory of Nyssa. The two are also associated with their mutual friend, Gregory of Nazianzus, under the label 'the Cappadocian fathers'. Basil's sister Macrina hovers just behind them in historians' eyes; and his mother (Emmelia), his grandmother (also called Macrina), and a host of relatives and ancestors form a dynasty of provincial privilege and devotion. Basil died before other more vocal members of this ménage, exposing himself thereby to their unreliable or calculated recollections. One thinks in particular of the funeral orations of the two Gregorys, and of his brother's *Life of Macrina*. Not only, therefore, has the family been taken as a framework of explanation for much in his life: the explanation put forward by the family itself has been allowed great weight.[2]

There is no doubt that family life could play an important part in the religious formation of Christians, just as it did in the formation of other attitudes, and in the choice of careers. Remarkably few of the well-known Christians of Basil's generation leap onto the historical stage straight from a completely pagan milieu. Christians had been breeding Christians for a long time. Almost a natural consequence of upbringing, baptism could sometimes be hard to resist, even if postponed to adult years on account of its less welcome demands. In other cases, it was associated with an experience of conversion; but conversion might

2. (a) Gregory of Nazianzus [henceforward GNaz] *Oratio* 43, *Patrologia Graeca* [henceforward *PG*] 36. 493–605. English translation by Leo P. McCauley ('On St. Basil the Great') in *Funeral Orations by Saint Gregory Nazianzen and Saint Ambrose*, pp. 27–99. That *oratio* was probably delivered in August or September of 381: Rosemary Radford Ruether, *Gregory of Nazianzus, Rhetor and Philosopher*, pp. 178f. (b) Gregory of Nyssa [henceforward GNyss] *In laudem fratris Basilii* [henceforward *Laud.*], *PG* 46. 788–817. English translation by Sister James Aloysius Stein in *Encomium of Saint Gregory Bishop of Nyssa on His Brother Saint Basil Archbishop of Caesarea*. This and GNaz's *oratio* were 'funeral orations' only in the loosest sense. (c) GNyss *Vita s. Macrinae* [henceforward *VMac.*], edited by Virginia Woods Callahan, in *Gregorii Nysseni opera*, 8:1 (Leiden: Brill, 1963): 370–414. Other important editions are by Pierre Maraval, *Grégoire de Nysse, Vie de sainte Macrine*; and by E. Gianarelli, *Vita di S. Macrina*. English translation by Virginia Woods Callahan in *Saint Gregory of Nyssa, Ascetical Works*, pp. 163–91. Woods Callahan provides no section numbers, either in her edition or in her translation, which makes reference difficult. I have used the section numbers provided by Maraval; and I refer to the page and line numbers of the Woods Callahan edition and to the page numbers of the Woods Callahan translation. In relation to Gregory of Nyssa's two works, Arnaldo Momigliano is, as always, memorable: 'While Macrina is brought near by a biography, Basil is made distant by a panegyric', 'The Life of St. Macrina by Gregory of Nyssa', p. 449.

have little to do with repudiating a pagan past and refer much more to withdrawal from a life of compromise and sin, and to acceptance of serious-minded dedication and self-denial. Martyrs and virgins, obvious symbols of radicalism and discontinuity in the Christian community, were also products of family life, nurtured within households that had come to accept heroism and self-abnegation as respectable careers. They represented a tradition not only established over a long period of time and carefully controlled and defined by the leaders of the Church but also untouched in many ways by the conversion and religious policies of Constantine.[3]

Basil's family belonged to that tradition. It possessed a religious memory reaching back in unbroken stages, through the Constantinian era, well into the third century. Basil's grandmother had known disciples of the great 'apostle' of Pontus, Gregory Thaumaturgus, founder of the nearby church of Neocaesarea.[4] Both his parents were Christians: 'the distinguishing characteristic of both his mother's and his father's family was piety'.[5] His father's family in particular had suffered disadvantage from the fact, in the years before Constantine's conversion. The parents were united by 'a common esteem of virtue'; and Gregory of Nazianzus later praised in particular those religious traits that marked them out as more than usually committed: 'their care of the poor, their hospitality toward strangers, their purity of soul achieved through austerity, the dedication of a portion of their goods to God'.[6] Their sons and daughters received a Christian upbringing; Macrina (born in 327) and Peter (born at least ten years later) perhaps more obviously than the others. Basil, Gregory, and Naucratius attended secular schools, following

3. A theme fully explored by Peter Brown, *The Body and Society: Men, Women, and Sexual Renunciation in Early Christianity*.

4. See Raymond Van Dam, 'Hagiography and History: The Life of Gregory Thaumaturgus'.

5. *Oratio* [henceforward *Orat*.] 43. 4, *PG* 36. 500B, tr. p. 30.

6. *Orat*. 43. 9, 505A, tr. p. 33. The hint of secure wealth is not to be ignored. Note the formal phrase ψυχῆς κάθαρσις ἐξ ἐγκρατείας. Concerning the father, both Gregorys were vague. Gregory of Nazianzus praised the whole family, not least because of their service to the empire, § 3; but about the elder Basil himself he said only that Pontus had 'put [him] forward at that time as its common teacher of virtue', § 12, tr. p. 36. Paul Fedwick, *The Church and the Charisma of Leadership in Basil of Caesarea*, p. 38, insists that he 'had no part in the contemporary political life'. That need not have ruled out local eminence based on landed wealth more than official status. The plateau farmland near Annisa, where the family was based, was fertile enough to supply the needs of any modest provincial ambition. See GNyss *VMac*. 5, 12, 20; ed. Woods Callahan, pp. 376, lines 19f.; p. 384, lines 14f.; p. 393, lines 3f.; tr. pp. 167, 172, 177. Further geographical details are discussed in chapter 3, n. 7.

in the footsteps of their father, himself a rhetor.[7] But the father's influence continued to bear the Christian mark: under his guidance, Basil was not only 'trained in general education' but also 'exercised in piety'.[8] After the father's death, his widow gradually adopted more formally a life of ascetic devotion.[9]

Constantine's patronage of the Christian religion naturally modified such family histories. A new future was assured to them, and their opportunities could be differently defined. To read a later account, such as that of Gregory of Nazianzus, is to gain the impression that such opportunities were shrewdly foreseen. The beneficiaries of toleration were often eager to justify the reticence and caution of forebears who had lived at a time when threats were greater. During the persecution of Maximin Daia, the last flare of hatred before miraculous tranquillity, Basil's relatives had prudently withdrawn to remote and wilder parts of Pontus, living roughly on the spoils of the hunt, and redefining heroism in the language of survival. Their story was 'but one chosen out of many, ... typical of the rest'. They joined a new band of 'athletes', men and women who 'survived their victory and did not succumb in their contests'. They became 'teachers of virtue for others—living martyrs, breathing monuments, mute proclamations [ζῶντες μάρτυρες, ἔμπνοοι στῆλαι, σιγῶντα κηρύγματα]'. In those simple phrases, fearful refugees were brilliantly transformed into pioneers of a new age.[10]

---

7. GNyss *VMac.* 3, 6, 8, 12; ed. Woods Callahan, pp. 373f.; p. 377, lines 11f.; p. 378, lines 12f.; pp. 383f.; tr. pp. 165, 167f., 171f. Socrates, even wiser after the event, makes a sharp distinction between the ascetic Peter and the learned Gregory, *Historia ecclesiastica* [henceforward *HE*] 4. 26, *PG* 67. 533Cf.

8. GNaz *Orat.* 43. 12.

9. So GNyss *VMac.* 11; ed. Woods Callahan, pp. 381f.; tr. pp. 170f. The process had been under way, however, for some time: see § 7, ed. pp. 377f., tr. p. 168. We shall have more to say about this in chapter 3, at nn. 8, 68. The elder Basil died sometime between 341 and 345, and Gregory may have felt the loss more keenly than Basil: Michel Aubineau, *Grégoire de Nysse, Traité de la virginité*, p. 44. I have taken Aubineau and Maraval (see n. 2) as the chief authorities on membership and chronology in the family. Reminders of the secular status and role of such figures are given by Christoph Klock, *Untersuchungen zu Stil und Rhythmus bei Gregor von Nyssa: Ein Beitrag zum Rhetorikverständnis der griechischen Väter*, esp. pp. 79, 104f.; and by Thomas A. Kopecek, 'The Social Class of the Cappadocian Fathers'. There is a useful review of Klock by Anthony Meredith: see the Bibliography.

10. GNaz *Orat.* 43. 5, 497B. Slightly at odds with that exalted image is their enthusiastic and entirely aristocratic indulgence in hunting, §§ 6f. Judicious avoidance of martyrdom was a well-established tradition by this period, represented most famously by Athanasius (although he fled from heretics rather than from pagans). Gregory of Nyssa referred to his grandparents as having been 'deprived of their possessions because of the confession of Christ', *VMac.* 20; ed. Woods Callahan, p. 393, lines 5f.; tr. p. 177.

Basil's own references to family ties were haphazard and indirect. He valued the heroic past, yet accepted the need to escape danger, and knew what it was to be 'long since instructed in the ways of God'. Such a combination of sensibilities provided Christians with a series of rich images, which might help them come to terms, for example, with the death of a son: 'Now is the opportunity at hand for you through patience to play the martyr's role'.[11] Basil's world was filled with men and women who shared that background—'children of confessors, and children of martyrs', as he called them on another occasion: 'Let each one of you employ his own kindred as examples for constancy on behalf of the true faith'.[12] In more prosaic terms, he acknowledged distant relationships in his own province and furthered as best he could the interests of obscure kindred—the 'many friends and relatives [φίλους καὶ συγγενεῖς] in my country' (including even the son of his old wet-nurse).[13] Such generous loyalty could interfere with other obligations. In promoting, for example, a priest to the bishopric of Satala, difficulties arose precisely because the man was a distant relative and childhood friend.[14] Basil's connections were so widespread that he found kin even among those he was less inclined to favour. Dealing with antagonism in Neocaesarea (where he naturally had family connections), Basil appealed to 'blood relationships . . . greatly conducive', as he put it, 'to an unbroken union and community of life'.[15] Clearly his relatives in the city had been disinclined to take the point.

Indeed, there is a great deal that calls into question any tranquil picture of family loyalty and mutual aid. The most famous instance, perhaps, concerned the strained relationship between Basil and his brother

11. *Homily* [henceforward *Hom.*] 327. 2; *Letter* [henceforward *Ep.*] 6. 2, tr. Roy J. Deferrari [henceforward D], 1: 41. For an explanation of the numbering of the *Homilies*, see the supplement to the Bibliography. In regard to the *Letters*, Deferrari's is the translation I almost always use, with only occasional adaptations. See also the translation by Sister Agnes Clare Way. The best available text is that edited by Yves Courtonne [henceforward C]. It is not insignificant that *Ep.* 6 (C 1: 19f.) is addressed to a mother: 'I know what the heart of a mother is', § 1, D 1: 39.

12. *Ep.* 240. 2, C 3: 63, D 3: 423/425.

13. *Ep.* 37, C 1: 80, D 1: 193. The letter implies that priesthood extends the obligations of kinship even further: 'I myself have been appointed to the position of a father [εἰς τὴν πατρικὴν τάξιν] by reason of this station to which the Lord has appointed me'. The theme is investigated further in chapter 5, at n. 154f.

14. *Ep.* 102. It is unlikely that the Poimenius involved, here and in *Ep.* 122, was the Poimenius of Sebasteia of *Ep.* 99, a theological opponent. The incident is treated further in chapter 8, at n. 62. For Basil's explicit opposition to the appointment of relatives in such circumstances, see *Ep.* 54.

15. *Ep.* 204. 2, C 2: 174, D 3: 157. The last phrase again carries us beyond the vocabulary of family life: see n. 13. The incident is discussed further below at n. 36 and in chapter 8, at nn. 28f.

Gregory. Basil faced opposition at the time of his consecration; and an uncle (also called Gregory), bishop of an unknown see, was among his critics. Gregory, his brother, attempted to hasten a reconciliation by forging three letters, apparently full of good wishes. The fraud was easily discovered, and Basil upbraided his brother with some force.[16] Of two other letters, from Basil to his uncle, the first suggests a close bond—'You have taken a father's place'—and reminds us of his prolonged exposure to the influence of his widowed mother, and of the extent to which family members may have furthered his clerical career.[17] The second letter stressed the importance of family: Basil hoped never 'to forget the ties of nature, and be set at enmity with my own kindred'. That sense of a family bond was interwoven also with the broader commandments of the Gospel:

> That we might not, as others have done, attach to our lives a melancholy story of a quarrel which divided the nearest and dearest from one another, a quarrel which ... would also be displeasing to God, who has defined the distinguishing mark of His disciples as perfect love.[18]

Whatever happened in the end between Basil and his uncle, the argument certainly made him wary of his brother. In 373 he was still complaining that he 'convenes synods at Ancyra, and in no way ceases to plot against us' (although he did admit that Gregory probably did so 'in his simplicity').[19] 'I know', he wrote on another occasion,

> that he is quite inexperienced [παντελῶς ἄπειρον] in ecclesiastical matters; and that although his dealings would inspire respect with a kindly man and be worth much, yet with a high and elevated personage, one

16. *Ep.* 58, C 1: 146, D 1: 359/361.

17. *Ep.* 59. 1, C 1: 147, D 2: 5. Basil was remarkably offhand in his only surviving allusion to his mother's death, in a letter to his friend Eusebius of Samosata, written in 371. The loss seems to have come almost as no more than the straw that broke the camel's back, after 'bodily ills, a tedious winter, vexatious affairs of business': 'and now [νῦν δὲ καί], as a result of my sins ...'! It is true that he then went on: 'I have been bereft of the only solace that I possessed, my mother'; but there was a certain sting in the tail, likely to have affected Macrina and Gregory among others, when he added: 'Forgive me for not having the patience to endure separation from a soul whose like I do not behold among those who are left behind [ἧς οὐδὲν ἀντάξιον ἐν τοῖς λειπομένοις ὁρῶ]', *Ep.* 30, C 1: 72, D 1: 175.

18. *Ep.* 60, C 1: 150, D 2: 11—written, it would seem, after the younger Gregory had made at least two of his blunders: see the final phrase, 'His words on a former occasion were not attested by the facts', C 1: 151, D 2: 13. Paul Fedwick, on the other hand, assures me that *Ep.* 59 was written after *Ep.* 60. Their order does not affect the point made here.

19. *Ep.* 100, C 1: 219, D 2: 185/187. He used the same phrase to Gregory himself, *Ep.* 58. On Gregory's 'helplessness' generally, see Jean Daniélou, 'Grégoire de Nysse à travers les lettres de saint Basile et de saint Grégoire de Nazianze'.

occupying a lofty seat, and therefore unable to listen to men who from
a lowly position on the ground would tell him the truth—what advantage
could accrue to our common interests from the converse of such a man
as Gregory, who has a character foreign to servile flattery?[20]

The judgement speaks volumes, not only about Basil's attitude to Gregory
himself but about the qualities he thought were useful in ecclesiastical
leadership. Nevertheless, he supported Gregory in his own conflict with
enemies of the orthodox party: his correspondence on that matter shows
how important he felt it was that Gregory's appointment to Nyssa should
not be thought of as owing anything to the favour of friends or relatives.[21]

Those random allusions scarcely provide us with a clear and full
picture of family feeling.   What other sources of information do we
have at our disposal?   Gregory of Nyssa's later impressions suggest that
divided opinion, not least in matters of religion, was a characteristic of
the family.   (We are reminded once again that an era of toleration could
open up more than one opportunity for a family that thought of itself as
Christian.)   His treatise De virginitate—an exercise in remote reflection,
heavily dependent upon Platonist philosophy—had little to say about the
role of virginity within the Church, for example, or about its relation to
sacramental practice.[22] It is true that his willingness to attempt the work in
370 or so probably reflects the fact that he was being drawn back at that time
into church affairs (and it may have been connected with his misplaced
attempts to reconcile Basil and the critics of his early episcopal conduct).
The almost academic detachment, on the other hand, is not altogether
surprising, bearing in mind that Gregory was married, and that he had
made an earlier and apparently firm decision, some seven years before,

20. Ep. 215, C 2: 207, D 3: 237/239.
21. Gregory was deposed in 375 and exiled in the following year: see Ep. 225, 231.
Contrast the situation of Gregory of Nazianzus, discussed in chapter 7. The phrase in Ep.
98 'my brother Gregory [τὸν δὲ ἀδελφὸν Γρηγόριον],' may refer to him, C 1: 213, D 2: 169.
22. Aubineau, Virginité, pp. 210f. Jean Gribomont, 'Le Panégyrique de la virginité,
œuvre de jeunesse de Grégoire de Nysse', suggests composition shortly after Basil's consecration; followed, with other useful comment, by Ton H. C. Van Eijk, 'Marriage and Virginity,
Death and Immortality', esp. pp. 230, 234–36. Gregory suggested that Basil had virtually
commissioned the work, and might more suitably have written it himself, De virginitate,
Preface 2. 18–20. See Reinhart Staats, 'Basilius als lebende Mönchsregel in Gregors von
Nyssa "De virginitate"'. Some textual details are discussed by Ezio Gallicet, 'Osservazioni
sul "De virginitate" di Gregorio di Nissa'.

to withdraw from ecclesial preoccupations and devote himself again to teaching. He deplored the sheer brutality of church politics and had welcomed the renewed opportunities in public life that followed upon the death of Julian in 363—all of which casts different light on Basil's feeling (quoted above) that his brother showed no stomach for the embattled life of a churchman, and certainly confirms that not every member of the family had been happy to espouse the traditions represented (as we are led to believe) by Emmelia and her other offspring.[23]

Many years later,[24] after he had experienced further changes and developments in his career, Gregory wrote a *Life* of his sister Macrina, who had died just a short while before, and after Basil himself.[25] The work provides us with one of the most important, but also one of the most tendentious, portraits of the family. Indeed, Macrina was presented as the guardian of the family history.[26] There is something very moving, and at the same time very suspicious, about the way in which the heroine, on her deathbed, tells her brother how he ought to regard the fortunes and aspirations of their ancestors, and how justly he may feel that the fame and status acquired by Basil and himself were a natural fulfilment and enhancement of that family past. We, in the twentieth century, possess what must be the major proportion of Basil's literary output, conveniently brought together in a single corpus; and we judge his character and significance accordingly. In the years just after his death, however, it was works like Gregory's *Life* that told a more immediate audience how they should think of the man. In the process, careful points were made, which Basil might not have regarded as central to his own view of his life's purpose, or, indeed, even fair.

The *Life* was designed to give prominence to the role of Macrina in the formation of Basil, as in other matters. She and the young Peter were presented as having been reared in a predominantly private and fervent atmosphere, while Basil, Gregory, and Naucratius, as we have seen, were

23. See Pierre Maraval, 'Encore les frères et soeurs de Grégoire de Nysse'; and Jean Daniélou, 'Le Mariage de Grégoire de Nysse et la chronologie de sa vie'. In addition to Macrina, Peter, and Naucratius, there may have been other sisters. *Ep.* 46 may have been addressed to one of them.

24. Certainly not before the end of 380, and possibly in 382 or 383: Maraval, *Vie*, p. 67.

25. Probably at the end of 379 or early in 380; possibly a few months later: Maraval, *Vie*, pp. 57–66. For rich commentary on the work, see Momigliano, 'Life of St. Macrina'. Gregory he characterizes as 'the most versatile and creative Christian biographer of the fourth century', p. 445; Macrina as 'the religious conscience of the family', p. 453.

26. GNyss *VMac*. 20: 'She took up the story of her life from infancy as if she were putting it all into a monograph [καθάπερ ἐπὶ συγγραφῆς πάντα καθεξῆς]'; ed. Woods Callahan, p. 392, lines 22f.; tr. p. 177.

formed within the more secular institutions of a traditional education. The distinction was not to endure. It was Macrina's declared hope and supposed achievement to take her most famous brother in hand, leading him to more radical devotion. Basil was presented by Gregory, after the completion of his education, as 'excessively puffed up by his rhetorical abilities and disdainful of all great reputations', considering himself 'better than the leading men in the district'.[27] His decision (shortly after his return to Cappadocia from Athens in 356) to embark upon a more ascetic career was presented as the result of Macrina's influence. To what extent that was true is hard to judge. The ideas and example of Eustathius of Sebaste, as we shall see, are normally thought to have been more important.[28] Naucratius had been persuaded, perhaps since 352, to adopt a way of life not dissimilar from that which Basil would later espouse, 'far from the noises of the city', devoted to hard work, self-sufficiency, and care of the old and infirm—all of which could be said to have borne the mark of Eustathius's influence.[29] At just about the time of Basil's return to Cappadocia, Macrina achieved a significant triumph, persuading her own mother to a more formal adoption of the ascetic life. By the time Basil joined them, there was quite a family group established in their lonely Pontus valley. Yet Basil kept his distance, establishing his ascetic retreat on the other side of the river.[30]

So there may have been, by the time Gregory came to write the *Life*, a received family history. Macrina was its guardian, and in some ways its guiding force. Basil's own career was seen to have developed within that context, very much under his sister's influence at important moments. Even as a bishop, so Macrina judged, he had fulfilled the long-standing aspirations and characteristics of his family. Yet Gregory felt obliged to hint also that not all members of the family thought alike at any given moment (and that included himself in his younger days): any sense of corporate identity and success was achieved only by dint of persuading various family members to change their minds and habits. When we combine those emphases and admissions in the

27. GNyss *VMac.* 6; ed. p. 377, lines 11f.; tr. p. 167. This passage will be examined again in chapter 2, at n. 63.

28. Although Macrina may already have told Basil something of Eustathius while her brother was still at Athens: Maraval, *Vie,* pp. 32, 52f.

29. GNyss *VMac.* 8; ed. Woods Callahan, pp. 378f., tr. pp. 168f. See Maraval, *Vie,* p. 52; Jean Gribomont, 'Eustathe le philosophe et les voyages du jeune Basile de Césarée', p. 124; and John Meyendorff, 'St. Basil, Messalianism, and Byzantine Christianity', esp. 221–25. The matter will recur in chapter 3, at n. 67.

30. See above, at n. 9, and Maraval, *Vie,* p. 53. Note the phrase in *Ep.* 223. 5 'in the village opposite, at my mother's [ἐπὶ τῆς ἀντιπέραν κώμης παρὰ τῇ μητρί μου]', C 3: 14 (in the apparatus), D 3: 303.

Life with what else we know about Basil's relatives, we can see that there could have been a variety of pasts and tendencies available to him, from which, as a young man, he might have been able to choose. Clerics and rhetors were just as prominent in his family circle as fanatical sisters.

———

Given the theoretical character of the *De virginitate*, one might expect to find in the *Life* a similar dimension. Yet Gregory of Nyssa, reflective theologian though he was, avoided seeing Basil within a merely intellectual tradition. He and Macrina were anxious to congratulate themselves on what they had achieved. They thought of their brother, explicitly, as 'great'. They did not regard him as merely an heroic ascetic. Yet it was his active career that inspired their admiration, not the originality of his thought.

Basil's own writings explain his brother's difficulty. Take, for example, the influence of Origen. No one can read Basil without detecting echoes of the great Alexandrian;[31] but how direct a dependence do those echoes suggest? One particular piece of evidence seems to place beyond doubt Basil's familiarity with Origen's works: he and Gregory of Nazianzus devoted considerable care to compiling, in their *Philocalia*, excerpts from his writings.[32] There, surely, is clear assurance that many apparently Platonist themes in Basil's thought came to him via the Christian master. But other patterns of influence, more closely associated with the interests of Gregory and Macrina, appear in the work. Among its excerpts is part of a letter supposedly from Origen to Gregory Thaumaturgus.[33] We may now doubt that Gregory was its recipient; but Basil and his friend clearly believed so.[34] Its presence in their compilation suggests that they may also

31. David Amand, *L'Ascèse monastique de saint Basile: Essai historique*, pp. 35f. (I shall always refer to this author, whose name appeared over the years in several different ways, by the more familiar Emmanuel Amand de Mendieta); Jean Gribomont, 'L'Origénisme de saint Basile'; Mario Naldini, *Basilio di Cesarea, Discorso ai Giovani (Oratio ad adolescentes)*, pp. 30–58; John M. Rist, 'Basil's "Neoplatonism": Its Background and Nature' (an exhaustive and crucial survey).

32. The significance of that undertaking will be examined further in chapter 3, at n. 91f.

33. *Philocalia* 13; ed. Robinson, p. 64. There is an English translation of this work by George Lewis entitled *The Philocalia of Origen*. See also *Origène, Philocalie 21–27, Sur le libre arbitre*, edited by Éric Junod.

34. For a complete disclosure of the required scepticism, see P. Nautin, *Origène, sa vie et son œuvre*, pp. 155f.; supported (with useful comment) by Éric Junod, 'Remarques sur la

have known an associated panegyric on Origen, thought to be the work of Gregory Thaumaturgus himself.[35]

The significance of those links—links between the Wonder-Worker and his imagined teacher, at least as believed in by the creators of the *Philocalia*—emerges in Basil's later correspondence. By that time, if not before, when he thought in terms of a 'theological' tradition, it stemmed from the great third-century bishop, even though associated with loyal members of his own family. In a long letter addressed to Neocaesarea, written in the first half of 376, he emphasized important connections:

> If sharing the same teachers contributes at all greatly to union, both you and we have not only the same teachers of God's mysteries, but also the same spiritual fathers who from the beginning have laid the foundations of your church. I mean the famous Gregory and all who, having succeeded in turn to his chair in your episcopate, one following the other like rising stars, have so walked in the same footsteps as to leave the marks of his heavenly administration visible to any who wish to see them.[36]

That tradition he then linked with his own family:

> And what indeed could be a clearer proof of our faith than that we were brought up by a grandmother, a blessed woman who came from amongst you? I mean the illustrious Macrina, by whom we were taught the sayings of the most blessed Gregory (as many as she herself retained, preserved to her time in unbroken memory), and who moulded and formed us while still young in the doctrines of piety.[37]

Only a few months before,[38] Basil had completed his *De spiritu sancto* and included in that work an even more detailed encomium of Gregory. His

---

composition de la "Philocalie" d'Origène par Basile de Césarée et Grégoire de Nazianze', and 'Particularités de la Philocalie'.

35. About that, of course, we cannot be certain. It is doubtful that the panegyric was the work of Gregory: Nautin, *Origène*, pp. 81f.; but see *Grégoire le Thaumaturge, Remerciement à Origène*, edited by Henri Crouzel (English translation, *Address to Origen*, by W. Metcalfe). Important guidance is provided by Van Dam, 'Hagiography and History'.

36. *Ep*. 204. 2, C 2: 173f., D 3: 157.

37. *Ep*. 204. 6, C 2: 178, D 3: 169. Both Gregory and his grandmother, although less directly connected, are mentioned (again in a letter addressed to Neocaesarea) in *Ep*. 210. 1, 3 of the same year. Fedwick, *Charisma*, p. 3, is eager to trace the influence of Origen upon Basil through those two figures.

38. See *Ep*. 231.

wish was to identify, again, an unbroken tradition of theological and cultic practice, reaching back to Gregory's day.[39]

The emphasis was not new. Several years before, when Neocaesarea had lost its bishop, Musonius, Basil declared in a letter of consolation: 'Beginning with Gregory, the great leader of your church, down to the present blessed departed one, [the Lord] has added one to the other, ever fitting them together like costly gems to a setting'. It was not just a matter of institutional continuity: 'Our friend [Musonius] produced nothing of his own, no discovery of modern thought [νεωτέρας φρενὸς εὕρημα], but ... he knew how to bring forth out of the hidden and goodly treasures of his heart "the oldest of the old store"'.[40] What was new, in the later letter, was the link asserted between Gregory and Basil's family. That link reappeared in a Life of the Wonder-Worker—written, like the Life of Macrina, by Gregory of Nyssa. We begin to suspect that the very reputation of the older Gregory, as appealed to by Basil and confirmed in lasting form by his brother, was seen as in some sense an heirloom, a tradition especially proper to the family itself: it represented a wish on their part to create a certain impression of their own past, and of their place in the past of the church in Asia Minor more generally.[41]

Yet the Life of Gregory provided only the vaguest impression of Origen's influence upon its hero. It may be that Gregory did not use—did not even know—the panegyric on Origen attributed to his namesake. (That may have been true of Basil, also, as we have admitted.) The evidence from silence is not conclusive: after the compilation of the Philocalia, even Basil made scarcely any direct reference to Origen.[42] One can adduce several explanations for that: his less speculative temperament; his wish to identify with even more ancient traditions; a certain suspicion attaching in

---

39. De spiritu sancto [henceforward DSS] 29 (§ 74). The most readily available edition is Basile de Césarée, Sur le Saint-Esprit, edited by Benoît Pruche. There is an English translation, St. Basil the Great on the Holy Spirit, by Blonfield Jackson, revised by David Anderson, using the text in PG 32. The work will be discussed in detail in chapter 7.

40. Ep. 28. 1, C 1: 66, D 1: 167, 161f. Compare the history attributed to Nicopolis in Armenia Minor: 'Your church, the nurse of piety, which we honour as the metropolis of orthodoxy, because of having been governed from of old by the most honoured men and the elect of God', Ep. 230, C 3: 36, D 3: 357/359.

41. That is not to say that the Life was complete invention: it was, rather, a calculated reinterpretation, for a literate audience, of oral traditions current in Gregory of Nyssa's own day, together with allusions to literary and cultic survivals. See Van Dam, 'Hagiography and History', which is preferable to the emphasis of Klock, Untersuchungen, p. 92, who sees Gregory as representing 'die Kontinuität der alexandrinischen Konzeption'; but note the caution (vis-à-vis Van Dam) of Momigliano, 'Life of St. Macrina', pp. 449f.

42. DSS 29 (§ 73). See Van Dam, 'Hagiography and History', 281f.; and Rist, 'Basil's "Neoplatonism"', p. 193.

some quarters to Origen himself. The *Philocalia* had ostentatiously avoided those sections of Origen's oeuvre that might have seemed to veer away from orthodoxy; and Basil and Gregory of Nazianzus would not have been the first to cloak Origen's thought in a respectable association with Gregory Thaumaturgus.[43] Broader, in any case, than a textual or theoretical dependence, Basil's later and deeper sense of tradition—a tradition to which his family was now made subordinate—was expressed in terms of an ecclesial history. It sprang from a bishop and proceeded through a line of bishops, with constant reference to the theological opinions and liturgical practices of those men. It concentrated on their pastoral impact, achieved not so much through the deployment of ideas as through the visible exercise of spiritual power. Beside the sophisticated conceits of Gregory's text, we shall be able, later, to place the practical uses to which Basil put that sense of heritage and discipleship as he struggled against the pretensions of rival leaders in the Church.

So we are faced with two sets of issues. First, how authentic a sense of the family's past was being created? Who controlled it? Who controlled, in particular, the way in which Basil was supposed to have been governed by it? Second, what was the relationship between the family component, in his sense of the past, and the ecclesial? The answer to those questions will tell us also when it was that Basil decided his family mattered: for a chronology is at stake, as much as the nature of the relationship to which he eventually admitted.

We noted earlier the modifications imposed upon Christian family history by the accession of Constantine, and by the subsequent official toleration of Christianity. Not only did Basil live after many of those modifications had taken place: he belonged to a generation that had come to appreciate the disadvantages and fragility of the Constantinian dispensation, especially when it came to the acceptable and proper relationships between politics and religion; between the instruments of policy, law, and administration, on the one hand, and the theological debates, cultic practices, and personal devotions, on the other, that were part and parcel of

<hr>

43. Nautin, *Origène*, p. 146. The matter will recur in chapter 3. It also had some relevance in Basil's relationship with Apollinarius of Laodicea (see *Ep.* 9), which will be discussed in chapter 7; but see also G. L. Prestige, *St. Basil the Great and Apollinaris of Laodicea*, pp. 17f.

religious life, pagan as well as Christian. The attachment of Constantius to the Arian cause would naturally have weighed heavily on a man loyal to the Council of Nicaea; but the supposed errors of the emperor may have contributed less to that misgiving than the political methods whereby he was able to intrude upon the belief and practice of the Church.[44] Although he may have seemed less directly an heir to the traditions and methods of Constantine and his immediate successors, the same misgiving could have been aroused by the emperor Valens. More paradoxically, a similar reaction might have been prompted by the religious policies of Julian, who in many ways attempted to govern in the pagan cause much as Constantine had governed in that of Christianity.[45]

In addition to those anxieties, engendered by toleration itself, Constantine had also made inevitable a change in the meaning of conversion. Just how much 'conversion to Christianity' there had been before Constantine, and what the phrase might refer to, are matters beyond the scope of this study; but once Christianity could be embraced without threat, 'conversion' became much more a matter of conformity than of brave eccentricity.[46]

44. The famous judgement of Ammianus bears repeating:

The plain and simple religion of the Christians he [Constantius] obscured by a dotard's superstition, and by subtle and involved discussions about dogma, rather than by seriously trying to make them agree, he aroused many controversies; and as these spread more and more, he fed them with contentious words. And since throngs of bishops hastened hither and thither on the public post-horses to the various synods, as they call them, while he sought to make the whole ritual conform to his own will, he cut the sinews of the courier-service. (21, 16. 18; tr. Rolfe, 2: 183/185)

For cautious reflection on this and other judgements, see E. D. Hunt, 'Did Constantius II Have "Court Bishops"?'. But T. D. Barnes, *Athanasius and Constantius: Theology and Politics in the Constantinian Empire*, has now provided us with a broader and comprehensive account. He has particular cautions to impart about Ammianus and Christianity: see pp. 166f. It is still useful to take note of Richard Klein, *Constantius II und die christliche Kirche*. Chief attention is paid to Constantius in the excellent essays in *L'Église et l'empire au IVe siècle*, edited by Albrecht Dihle.

45. The most useful recent guides are Polymnia Athanassiadi-Fowden, *Julian and Hellenism*; G. W. Bowersock, *Julian the Apostate*; and Robert Browning, *The Emperor Julian*. Julian will figure more prominently in chapter 2.

46. The literature on conversion—on the personal and social mechanics of changes in religious loyalty—has made remarkably little progress since A. D. Nock, *Conversion*. Ramsay MacMullen flaunts a characteristically jaundiced view in *Christianizing the Roman Empire*. More subtle are the reflections of Robert Markus, *The End of Ancient Christianity*. Robin Lane Fox, *Pagans and Christians*, offers less, for the period after Constantine, than the title might appear to promise. For judgements both shrewd and contentious, see Gerald Bonner, 'The Extinction of Paganism and the Church Historian'. Arnaldo Momigliano shows his customary flair and learning in 'Popular Religious Beliefs and the Late Roman Historians', emphasizing that 'intellectuals' both pagan and Christian maintained a desire

For those, therefore, who still wished to achieve or experience a marked shift in their religious lives, a moment of greater clarity and commitment (leaving aside, for the moment, the question of why they might have thought it necessary), baptism alone, even regular participation in the external life of the church, could no longer be enough: any prudent person who did not wish to fall foul of the law, or who hoped to improve the prospect of a successful career, would aspire to that much. An extra gesture would be called for; and that immediately posed the question whether more serious commitment was still a matter of some visible social declaration, or whether the new change of attitude had to take place at the level of one's inner life. Indeed, the problem of conversion, as we shall see in Basil's case, made it necessary to explore that very distinction, between religious society and the inner self.

There was bound to be, moreover, some tension between what one might have inherited through one's family (even if one called it Christianity) and what one felt obliged to achieve on one's own. The act of taking religion more seriously (which most often meant taking morality more seriously), the shaping of one's life according to some ideal of virtue, some ultimate goal, meant that one adopted a new attitude to one's past (which included one's biological past). Some aspects would need to be rejected, or at least turned in new directions. The resulting tension, between a received past and individual aspiration, mattered much more in the fourth century than any supposed 'conflict' between paganism and Christianity. It affected those born and bred as Christians (and one recalls again that few of the outstanding or ardent Christians known to us in that period were clearly identifiable as converts from a pagan background—except Constantine!); but it affected pagans also: for they were no less able or inclined to shift from one level of devotion to another.

---

to communicate with 'the masses', Christians succeeding for reasons not made entirely clear. (One must respect the contrasting evidence provided by Garth Fowden, 'The Pagan Holy Man in Late Antique Society'.) G. W. Bowersock's 'From Emperor to Bishop: The Self-Conscious Transformation of Political Power in the Fourth Century A.D.' is beguiling and helpful, but it skims over the period to which Basil belongs, between the death of Constantine and the career of Ambrose. Yvon Thébert, who indulges in analogous errors in 'À propos du "Triomphe du Christianisme" ', is willing to allow almost no originality to Christianity, save its capacity to mythologize its own past and its accidental fortune in proving attractive to the civil power. The argument undervalues the exclusively ecclesial motives for the 'encadrement des populations' and the disenchantment displayed by many Christian leaders vis-à-vis civil authorities after Constantine. My thanks to Peter Brown for introducing me to this paper and for discussing its emphases. He himself promises to build on earlier work in a forthcoming revision of the *Cambridge Ancient History*.

Set in such a context, the Christian family takes on rather a different appearance. Instead of being the precondition for a Christian life, handing on religion without question to the next generation, it becomes the precondition for the tension characteristic of a conversion experience: a social setting marked by suppositions and practices, against which the serious devotee might have felt it necessary later to react. It becomes possible to argue that the great upsurge of enthusiastic Christianity during the fourth century (documented most fully in the case of aristocratic exemplars, but alluded to at other levels of society) testified above all to a desire to escape from the style of Christianity that family traditions had in some instances come to represent.

The reason for raising such possibilities in relation to Basil is that he does seem to have acknowledged a need for conversion himself. One might have expected as much from the author of such famous and influential ascetic writings. Unfortunately, it is not easy to point to the moment of conversion itself. The obvious period of his life, it would seem, in which to look for such a change would be the months leading up to his practice of the 'philosophic' life in Pontus. Yet his own full account of that change occurred only in the writings and correspondence of later years. The same is true of more theoretical reflections in his ascetic writings. Similar caution would have to govern our interpretation of a striking passage in the *De spiritu sancto*, written in the early 370s. There he declared that imitating the death of Christ (an image traditionally associated with baptism) must include some break with the past: 'The first step required is to cut short the course of one's previous life'.[47] That little word 'first', however, placed immediately a wedge of time, however small, between commitment and baptism. Not every person, in the period after Constantine, even if eventually baptized, was likely to effect such a break at the early stage of a religious life. Basil may even have admitted that he found himself in the same situation, like thousands of other Christians in his day: 'Now while it may be that the Spirit does not offer strength to those totally unworthy, it does seem that he is present in some way to those once sealed [in baptism: ἅπαξ ἐσφραγισμένοις], awaiting the salvation that will come to them from a shift in the direction of their lives [ἐκ τῆς ἐπιστροφῆς]'.[48]

47. *DSS* 15 (§ 35).

48. *DSS* 16 (§ 40); ed. Pruche, p. 390. These particular passages are likely to have been drafted some time before the appearance of the work in its final form. Note the comparable opinion of Gregory of Nazianzus: baptism does not imply a sudden change of character, *De*

So when did Basil experience a conversion, and how was it related to his baptism in 357? Here we meet another puzzle. The only real 'biography' of Basil that we possess, from his own generation, is the funerary *oratio* of his former friend, Gregory of Nazianzus. That purported to describe a life of virtually unbroken development.[49] Gregory attached importance to Basil's Christian ancestors (although he shared with Macrina some difficulty in deciding which mattered most: their social prominence or their religious piety).[50] In his account of Basil's years at Athens, he stressed that they were already Christians.[51] In that way, he was able to suggest that the inclination towards the 'philosophic' life, which would mark also Basil's years of ascetic experiment after his return to Cappadocia, was already part of the 'Athens experience', not a reaction against it. In that, especially, the continuity resided: the idea of a clear break between Athens and Pontus (which was what the *Life* of Macrina suggested) was deliberately undermined. 'Athens, our studies together, our sharing of roof and hearth, the single spirit animating two people, the marvel of Greece, the pledge that we made that we would cast aside absolutely the world and live the coenobitic life for God, placing our words in the service of the one wise Word': so he remembered it in his own autobiographical sketch.[52] In the *oratio*, the vocabulary of philosophical dedication is exactly what one might expect from the scholastic environment they were about to leave: 'Philosophy was his pursuit, as he strove to break from the world, to unite with God, to gain the things above by means of the things below, and to acquire, through goods which are unstable and pass away, those that are stable and abide'.[53] That was not to say that going home was not seen as reaching out for something better;[54] but improvement did not lie in rejecting Athens, so much as in developing what had happened to them there. Indeed, significantly enough, Gregory did not mention the journey that Basil then undertook around the eastern empire, exploring ascetic possibilities, except in very general terms: 'voyages which were necessary and

---

seipso et de episcopis, lines 449f. This poem = *Carmina de seipso* 12, PG 37. 1166–1227. English translation by Denis Molaise Meehan, *Gregory of Nazianzus, Three Poems*.

49. See above, at n. 2.

50. GNaz *Orat.* 43. 4f. Compare GNyss *VMac.* 20; ed. Woods Callahan, p. 393, lines 3f.; tr. p. 177.

51. *Orat.* 43. 21.

52. GNaz *De vita sua*, line 476. This poem = *Carmina de seipso* 11, PG 37. 1029–1166. English translation in *Three Poems* (see n. 48). See also *Gregor von Nazianz, De vita sua*, with introduction, text, German translation, and commentary by Christoph Jungck.

53. GNaz *Orat.* 43. 13, tr. p. 38.

54. GNaz *De vita sua*, lines 259f.

in full keeping with his philosophical resolution'.[55] He proceeded more or less immediately to an account of Basil's ordination to the priesthood. In that way, he carried into effect the brief summary of Basil's life he had given in an earlier passage, calling him orator, philosopher, and priest.[56]

Now we have no more reason for believing Gregory of Nazianzus than we have for believing Gregory of Nyssa. To begin with, the *oratio* was by Gregory's own admission 'delivered' (the circumstances are unclear) some time after Basil's death: 'so long after the occasion, and after so many others have eulogized him in public and private'.[57] Perhaps Gregory had needed time to assess the significance of his subject, taking into account, no doubt, the other judgements to which he referred. We have to bear in mind, also, that Gregory had been seriously estranged from Basil, in ways to be described. It is hard to imagine that that did not have its effect, even on the more complimentary passages of his speech. Most important of all, when it came to describing any moment of radical change in Basil's life in the 350s, Gregory would have been forced to see it in relation to his own experience, at a period when the two men were more closely associated.

For Gregory had his own family heritage to contend with. He had come to be dominated by a father who seemed to move easily through phases of conversion, baptism, priesthood, and episcopate.[58] That was because of a long-standing εὐσέβεια, a religious dedication on his mother's side: while his father had 'fled the bondage of his father's gods', she was 'the daughter and the mother of the free'.[59] She had been 'from the

---

55. GNaz *Orat.* 43. 25, tr. p. 49.

56. GNaz *Orat.* 43. 13.

57. GNaz *Orat.* 43. 2, tr. p. 28. In Momigliano's estimation, 'Life of St. Macrina', p. 449, Gregory deliberately corrected the distancing effect achieved by Basil's brother in his panegyric.

58. See his *oratio* on his brother Caesarius (*Orat.* 7. 3), but especially the *oratio* on his father, delivered in 374 (*Orat.* 18. 5f., 12). Greek texts in *PG* 35. 756–87 and 985–1044 respectively; English translations by Leo P. McCauley in *Funeral Orations by Saint Gregory Nazianzen and Saint Ambrose*, pp. 5–25, 119–56. The elder Gregory had been an Hypsistarius, subscribing to a fire-worshipping cult with probable Persian connections. He was baptized in the mid-320s. Gregory emphasized the paradoxical closeness of the Hypsistarii to Christianity: 'By their way of life they anticipate the faith [τὴν πίστιν φθάνουσι] and only lack in name what they possess in attitude [τὸ ἔργον ἔχοντες]', *Orat.* 18. 6, *PG* 35. 992B, tr. p. 123. Basil appears to have known of comparable devotees, the Magousaioi: see *Ep.* 258. 4; Epiphanius *Expositio fidei* 13, *PG* 42. 804C, and Eusebius *Praeparatio evangelica* 6 (§ 275). Useful information is contained in P. Nautin, 'Epiphane', *Dictionnaire d'histoire et de géographie ecclésiastiques*, vol. 15, cols. 617–31. Conversation with Garth Fowden helped to clarify many of these connections.

59. GNaz *Orat.* 8. 4 (on his sister Gorgonia). Greek text in *PG* 35. 789–817; English translation by Leo P. McCauley in *Funeral Orations by Saint Gregory Nazianzen and Saint Ambrose*, pp. 101–18 (here p. 103).

beginning and by virtue of descent, consecrated by God, receiving piety as
a necessary heritage not for herself alone, but also for her children'.[60] Not
that all the children agreed about its significance: Gregory's brother, Caesarius, pursued a secular career;[61] and Gregory was long conscious of the
disturbing contrast between his own philosophical ideals and Caesarius's
worthy ambition and success.[62]

All those memories and obligations would have coloured the way
in which he accepted Christianity as an important component of the
experiences he shared with Basil during their years together at Athens and
immediately thereafter.[63] We have also to admit that, while he admired
the way of life that they shared for a while,[64] he did not follow his
friend home at once but continued to enjoy the Athenian way of life.
Nor, in the end, did he stay in Basil's company for long, even when
he was persuaded to join him in Pontus.[65] Such hesitations may have
induced regret, and even guilt, modifying in their own way his later
recollections.

Gregory, therefore, cannot be taken as entirely reliable in documenting
attitudes either to the influence of family or to conversion: the former, in
regard to Basil, seems to have been taken for granted by him, although
given less emphasis than Athens; and the latter appeared not at all. What
about Basil himself? He is equally confusing. During his first years
of ascetic experiment, he was, as we have seen, associated loosely with
members of his family, and perhaps subject to their influence. But the
connections appear in his writings only much later in his life: in his
correspondence at the time, there was little reference to family at all, and
certainly no suggestion that they had a major influence on the régime he
had come to adopt.

---

60. GNaz *Orat.* 7. 4, tr. p. 7. The speech was delivered in late 368 or early 369. I have
based my treatment of Gregory's life first on Ruether, *Gregory,* with reference back to Paul
Gallay, *La Vie de saint Grégoire de Nazianze.* His conclusions are usefully summarized in his
introduction to *Saint Grégoire de Nazianze, Lettres.* I shall refer to this edition throughout the
book; but note also Gallay's other edition of the letters, *Gregor von Nazianz, Briefe.* See also his
Grégoire de Nazianze.

61. And left a distracting set of problems behind him after his death: GNaz *De rebus
suis,* lines 117f., 220f. This poem = *Carmina de seipso* 1, PG 37. 969–1017. English translation by
Denis Molaise Meehan in *Three Poems* (see n. 48). Basil tried to help his friend in relation
to Caesarius's death: see *Ep.* 32. For dating problems, see Fedwick, *Basil,* 1: 13 n. 78.

62. GNaz *Ep.* 7. 9; ed. Gallay, 1: 10.

63. GNaz *Orat.* 43. 21; *De rebus suis,* lines 275f.; *De vita sua,* lines 112f., 119f.

64. GNaz *De rebus suis,* lines 261f., 482f.; *De vita sua,* lines 353f. That later period will be
studied fully in chapter 3.

65. GNaz *Orat.* 43. 24f. Again, more will be said in chapters 2 and 3.

Two later letters we have mentioned already.[66] The first appealed to a spiritual ancestry, shared with those whom he addressed, reaching back to Gregory Thaumaturgus. In that connection, as we have seen, he mentioned his grandmother Macrina, the great Gregory's admirer. He also made allusion to his sojourn in Pontus: 'Having travelled over many a land and sea, whomever we found walking according to the traditional rule of piety [τῷ παραδοθέντι κανόνι τῆς εὐσεβείας στοιχοῦντας], these we both listed as fathers and regarded as guides of our souls [καὶ πάτερας ... καὶ ὁδηγούς]'.[67] 'Fathers' as well as 'guides': the usefulness of those paragons now depended upon their place within a genealogy, a particular species of appeal to the past that Basil had brought into the argument by his reference to Gregory and Macrina. The enduring force of ancient ascetic practice owed its effect now to its place within a broader Christian history; one with which the narrower chronicle of his own family was also to be associated.

A second letter, written a few months later, made more explicit reference to the Pontus retreat:

> Because of my acquaintance with this region from boyhood (for here I was brought up by my grandmother), and because of my having remained here for the most part thereafter, when, ... learning that this was a suitable place for the study of philosophy on account of the quiet of its solitude, I passed a period of many successive years here, ... I, having obtained a brief breathing spell from the activities that press us, have gladly come to this remote spot.[68]

It is clear that by that time, in 376, the presence of family members had come to count for almost as much as the philosophical qualities of the region. A new context was being provided for old memories.

Most striking is the long letter Basil wrote in the middle of the previous year, setting out in detail his grievances against Eustathius of Sebaste. In the passage that concerns us here, Basil began with reference to his years at Athens, where he 'lavished much time on the vanity of the precepts of that wisdom made foolish by God'.[69] By such phrases, he created the impression that the biographical account which he then proceeded to develop was to be taken as describing a rejection of that Athenian experience. Moreover, in order to carry his account from the one phase to the other, he felt it necessary to allude to some dramatic, though very

66. *Ep.* 204 and 210; see above, nn. 36f.
67. *Ep.* 204. 6, C 2: 178, D 3: 169.
68. *Ep.* 210. 1, C 2: 190, D 3: 197. See also *Ep.* 216.
69. *Ep.* 223. 2, C 3: 10, D 3: 291/293.

vaguely described, conversion. His distaste for 'that wisdom made foolish by God' was not just a matter, therefore, of feeling that it squared poorly with a long-standing attachment to Christianity:

> When one day arising as from a deep sleep I looked out upon the marvellous light of the truth of the gospel, and beheld the uselessness of the wisdom 'of the princes of this world that come to nought', bemoaning much my piteous life, I prayed that there be given me a guidance to the introduction to the teachings of religion [χειραγωγίαν πρὸς τὴν εἰσαγωγὴν τῶν δογμάτων τῆς εὐσεβείας]. And before all things my care was to make some amendment in my character [διόρθωσίν τινα τοῦ ἤθους], which had for a long time been perverted by association with the wicked. And accordingly, having read the Gospel, and having perceived therein that the greatest incentive to perfection is the selling of one's goods and the sharing of them with the needy of the brethren, . . . I prayed that I might find some one of the brethren who had taken this way of life, so as to traverse with him this life's brief flood.[70]

Here we have all the elements of a conversion experience that can be found in so much religious literature of the period: a sudden clarity of vision, a sense of the need to reject one's past life, the inspiration of biblical texts, and a decision to embrace a generous poverty. None of them had appeared prominently in Basil's earlier accounts of that period of his life.

Basil went on, in his later letter to Eustathius, to refer also to his journey of ascetic exploration in the East; but now a new note was struck. He had admired the ascetics he had found, and he admitted that he 'perceived some in my fatherland trying to imitate the example of those men' (Eustathius included). But, by his own account, he was too trusting: 'I considered the things that were seen as indications of things that were invisible'. Unfortunately, 'the secret thoughts of each of us are unknown'. He had been willing enough to dismiss from consideration 'accusations about their teachings'. He had been, as he saw it, deceived. That feeling of disappointment, of having been cheated, a feeling directed chiefly against Eustathius himself, was now allowed to colour the whole period of his earlier asceticism. He virtually passed over it completely, hurrying at once, in his letter, to the period when 'we were called to the leadership of the Church'.[71]

70. *Ep.* 223. 2, C 3: 10, D 3: 291/293. By stressing a swift transition from enthusiasm to guidance, Basil betrayed the cautious conservatism one might expect in a mature churchman. Specifically excluded was any privileged knowledge upon which one could immediately rely for progress. See P. Aubin, *Le Problème de la conversion*, especially the contrast between pp. 93 and 104.

71. *Ep.* 223. 3, C 3: 11f., D 3: 295/297.

He also embarked upon another train of thought:

Granted that the rest of our actions are worthy of lamentation, yet this one matter I dare make boast of before the Lord, that I never held erroneous opinions about God, or, being otherwise minded, unlearned them later. Nay, the conception of God which I received in childhood from my blessed mother and my grandmother Macrina, this, developed, have I held within me [ταύτην αὐξηθεῖσαν ἔσχον ἐν ἐμαυτῷ].[72]

He immediately expanded the point: 'For I did not change from one opinion to another with the maturity of reason, but I perfected the principles handed down to me by them [ἀλλὰ τὰς παραδοθείσας μοι παρ' αὐτῶν ἀρχὰς ἐτελείωσα]'. That notion he continued to explore in the paragraphs that followed:

I consider that also in me the same doctrine has been developed through progress [τὸν αὐτὸν λόγον διὰ τῆς προκοπῆς ηὐξῆσθαι], and what now is mine has not taken the place of what existed in the beginning.... Through progress [ἐκ προκοπῆς] we observe a certain amplification [τινα αὔξησιν] of what we say, which is not a change from worse to better, but is a completing of that which was lacking, according to the increment of our knowledge [συμπλήρωσις τοῦ λείποντος κατὰ τὴν προσθήκην τῆς γνώσεως].[73]

We see in this single letter two biographies created. One contained a rejection of classical learning, a conversion, a search for guides and models, and a period of disappointment and frustration. The other appealed to long-standing family influence and the experience of gradual maturity within a Christian tradition.

———

Not only are those accounts hard to reconcile: they also fail to appear near the surface of Basil's writing in earlier years. Why did he suddenly, so much later in life, rewrite his past and reformulate the role played in it by family members, bringing them rather clumsily into the centre

72. *Ep.* 223. 3, C 3: 12, D 3: 299.
73. *Ep.* 223. 3, 5; C 3: 212, 14f.; D 3: 299, 305 (slightly adapted). Such phrases tell us much about Basil's view of development in Christian thought, which we shall have cause to touch upon more fully in later chapters. See in particular chapter 4, at nn. 109f. The significance of such passages in relation to Basil's thought more generally is discussed by Emmanuel Amand de Mendieta, 'The Pair ΚΗΡΥΓΜΑ and ΔΟΓΜΑ in the Theological Thought of St. Basil of Caesarea', pp. 130f.

of his new account? The clue lies in his fresh insistence on his own orthodoxy, and on that of his dead relatives; and the answer is made even clearer by the circumstances in which the later letters were written. It was not just that Basil had delayed, so to speak, the task of making sense of his life. He was attempting to score points over opponents in Neocaesarea, and to unravel from the central threads of his spiritual development the influence of his old mentor, Eustathius, casting them aside as irrevocably stained by the man's subsequent support of heresy. His difficulty with the church at Neocaesarea was partly the result of sheer rivalry between two sees—he might have claimed with justice at least a patronal influence, and they might have valued an independent dignity— and partly a matter of genuine fear on Basil's part that the community had fallen into doctrinal error (specifically, a form of Sabellianism). But the difficulty was complicated enormously by the fact that the city was close to his original ascetic retreat, where members of his own family were still living; that he had relatives in the city itself, who, together with other friends and acquaintances, had been intimately associated with his early years; and that Atarbius, the bishop, was a relative also. We can imagine how, in giving his own account of his family history, and of the position that it occupied within the history of the local church more generally, he was ruling out other dynastic claims, even within his own family—a further proof that that family was not entirely united in its view of what Christian tradition might demand or allow.

The implications are fundamental. Only at a late stage of his career, and under the pressure of controversy, did Basil place any emphasis on the importance of his family in his own development. The same may be said of his 'conversion', projected backwards to the years immediately following his return from Athens. The real conversion in Basil's life may well have been the experience that produced those later letters—the need to distance himself finally from Eustathius, and, in so doing, to reject a past that he had been happy hitherto to identify as his own: the great classical tradition of philosophic self-improvement, more particularly defined within the Church by leading ascetics such as Eustathius himself. Another tradition, now given central place, was the preservation of orthodoxy through a period of persecution (and, in his own life, through a variety of theological and clerical engagements), a persistent fidelity represented in addition by the continuity of his own family.

None of that will surprise us, when we come to explore more fully the tenor of Basil's thought. There is plenty of evidence to show that he attached more importance to individual determination than to the influence of family history and upbringing; and there is no reason to suppose that he had a less subtle view of his own spiritual growth. It was probably at exactly the period when he was writing to Neocaesarea and against Eustathius that he was able to admit to his own congregation that ancestry could not explain virtue. It was what each person did that counted, when apportioning praise; and, far from lying merely at the confluence of other streams, the exemplary Christian was himself a spring, an original source of spiritual beauty: πηγή ἐστιν ἀπὸ τῶν οἰκείων λαγόνων προχέουσα τὸ κάλλος.[74]

As far as antecedents were concerned, it was ecclesial ancestry that had come to dominate his mind. It was within that context that the more limited history of a family like his own was seen to operate. Tradition itself, παράδοσις, counted most, together with the loyalties tradition demanded. Basil's attachment to orthodoxy and his concern for the structure of the Church depended increasingly upon a broader sense of what παράδοσις might mean, allowing his own family's past to be no more than a striking paradigm. In his *De spiritu sancto*, just before the long passage already referred to, praising Gregory Thaumaturgus, Basil created exactly that sense of ecclesial pedigree and discipleship. He was defending his mildly idiosyncratic attachment to the formula 'with the Spirit' (as opposed to giving glory to Father, Son, *and* Spirit, which might have seemed better calculated to protect the Spirit's equality with the other two persons of the Trinity); and he explained: 'I received it from a man who spent a long life in the service of God, and by whom I was baptized and admitted to the ministry of the church'. The reference was to Dianius, an earlier bishop of Caesarea, by whom Basil had been baptized in 357 and ordained a reader in 360.[75] He then continued: 'I inquired on my own initiative whether any among the blessed ones of former times had used this phrase now open to criticism, and I found that there were many worthy of trust, both on account of their antiquity and of the precision of their understanding'.[76] That was the past he now felt he sprang from (writing in 375), and to which he was obliged as a son and heir. Again, the feeling was born of controversy, of a need to defeat an

---

74. *Hom.* 337. 2, *PG* 31. 592B. For the date (about 376), see Fedwick, *Basil*, 1: 10 n. 47. For other sermons that emphasize the undesirable influence of family, see *Hom.* 340. 9 ('certainly one of the first homilies preached by Basil', Fedwick, *Basil*, 1: 10 n. 50) and 345. 5 (which I also believe to be early).

75. See his praise of Dianius in *Ep.* 51. 1: 'From my earliest youth I was brought up with a love for Dianius, and I used to look up to the man. . . . When I reached the age of reason, then indeed I recognised him for what he was from his spiritual virtues', C 1: 132, D 1: 325.

76. *DSS* 29 (§ 71).

opponent, almost in defence of a philosophical school, extending over several generations.

The emphasis was echoed in his correspondence. Take, for example, a reference to Pope Dionysius, in a letter of 371 to Damasus, the contemporary bishop of Rome:

> The request we make is by no means a novel one, but, on the contrary, has been habitual not only with all the blessed and God-beloved men of the past, but also and especially with yourself [the bishops of Rome]. For we know through a continuous tradition [μνήμης ἀκολουθίᾳ], by the teaching received from our Fathers in answer to our questions and from letters which even to this day are preserved among us, that Dionysius, that most blessed bishop, who was pre-eminent among you both for the orthodoxy of his faith and for his virtue in general, was wont to visit our Church of Caesarea by letter, and to exhort our fathers by letter, and to send men to ransom the brethren from captivity.[77]

Such was the 'family' to which Basil felt he had transferred his allegiance; and he was able to accept a more personal family history only if it would serve the interests, or represent the virtues, of that broader, ecclesial society.

Many events and developments in Basil's life have been alluded to in this opening inquiry, and we shall have more to say about them all: his exploratory shifts from one style of life to another; his friendships and their failures; his relations with his family (the members of which were themselves very varied in temperament and experience); his vision of the Church; his sensitive defence of his own orthodoxy (which we may well view with suspicion also, entangled as it was in the slanted reappraisal of his past). Here, however, it is the reappraisal itself that claims immediate attention. Basil's life had none of the smooth inevitability implied by his brother and his friend. Certainly, a Christian family background cannot be taken as the simple antecedent of his later career. He may well have had difficulty identifying totally with the religious aspirations of his relatives—of his mother and sister in particular. He certainly faced several other crises of choice and identity in the course of his career—not least his decision to return permanently to the clerical life in 365, and his need to admit openly the breakdown of his friendship with Eustathius. We have begun to see also the way in which he responded to controversy, often producing in the process important new emphases; and the way in which he brought into the centre of his vision a sense of the history of the Church itself, which came to be for him the best guarantee of all that he associated with his own spiritual development. All point to the tasks of inquiry that lie ahead.

77. *Ep.* 70, C 1: 165f., D 2: 51.

· CHAPTER II ·

ATHENS

Having observed the extent to which a Christian family background had at best an ambiguous influence upon Basil's later life, let us subject to the same kind of inquiry his attitude to traditional classical education. We may begin with a working hypothesis: that his acquaintance with classical literature in general and his years of study at Athens in particular allowed him to recognize and resolve in his own way a fundamental problem. The heritage of Greek culture, and the commitment required of anyone who wished to be thought educated and to lay claim to resulting opportunities, were like dragons to be faced and fought with. Only after that confrontation could one embark upon an endeavour proper to oneself. Basil interpreted the problems involved in a specific way, revealed best by his insistence that actions counted for more than words.[1]

It mattered little, he thought, what might be going on in one's head, or even what one might be able to put into words: it was how one lived that marked one out as a person of virtue and significance. (To make such a choice was not necessarily to repudiate all traditional values, but rather to adopt one traditional position instead of another.) We shall see

---

1. Note how Gregory of Nyssa described the influence of Macrina upon Basil, after his return from Athens: he 'went over to this life full of labors for one's own hand to perform [πρὸς τὸν ἐργατικὸν τοῦτον καὶ αὐτόχειρα βίον]', *VMac.* 6; ed. Woods Callahan, p. 377, lines 17f.; tr. p. 167. The emphasis on πρᾶξις will recur in a variety of contexts; and it is worth noting at once what is not original in the idea: Aristotle's emphasis on ἠθικὴ ἀρετή, directing attention away from γνῶσις, is not far from the root of the matter, *Nicomachean Ethics* 1103b 26–29.

later how those ideals first achieved clear expression during Basil's early engagement in the Arian controversy. The change of perspective involved was to contribute to an even broader development in his life: a shift from text to cult, from a vision of himself as a dealer in words and documents to one as a builder of communities.

That is not to say that Basil was aware as yet of such a disposition in himself, during his years in what was one of the great centres of learning in the empire, between 349 and 355. A contrast between Athens and Jerusalem, between pagan learning and the teachings of the Gospel, had been made for a long time by at least some Christians. Its most famous expression, perhaps, came in the writings of Tertullian; but it coloured even the more optimistic confrontations between articulate Christians in the East and their pagan counterparts.[2] In relation to his actual years in Athens, we find no evidence for such a distinction in Basil's mind; for a solution to the contrast had also been set in place. Even forthright Christians of his own generation were able to come to terms with the content and method of the classical curriculum.[3] Basil blithely absorbed ancient philosophy, that of the Platonist school in particular, and sat at the feet of men praised later by the great pagan historian Eunapius, in his *Lives of the Sophists*.[4] We should not necessarily, in other words, see Basil during those years as embroiled in a conscious conflict between paganism and Christianity. Nor should we allow ourselves to be overshadowed by the presence and future impact of the emperor Julian. The influences we look for must be specific. What was the effect exercised by παιδεία, as it was called, by the traditional pattern of cultural formation, on Basil's image of himself and on his future development?

Athens laid claim to a long history of philosophical achievement, which gave its educational institutions, and indeed its whole civic com-

2. 'Quid ergo Athenis et Hierosolymis? Quid Academiae et Ecclesiae? ... Nobis curiositate opus non est post Christum Iesum', Tertullian *De praescriptionibus* 7; *Patrologia Latina* [henceforward *PL*] 1. 23–24.
3. Amidst an abundance of studies old and new, the following are particularly helpful: G. W. Bowersock, *Hellenism in Late Antiquity*; Averil Cameron, *Christianity and the Rhetoric of Empire: The Development of Christian Discourse*; Glanville Downey, 'Education and Public Problems as Seen by Themistius', and 'Education in the Christian Roman Empire: Christian and Pagan Theories under Constantine and His Successors'; Werner Jaeger, *Early Christianity and Greek Paideia*, and *Paideia: The Ideals of Greek Culture*; George Alexander Kennedy, *Greek Rhetoric under Christian Emperors*; and Henri-Irénée Marrou, *A History of Education in Antiquity*.
4. Eunapius *Lives of the Philosophers and Sophists*. The Loeb edition is numbered marginally according to the earlier text of Boissonade; and it is to these numbers I refer (e.g., B 483), adding the Loeb page number (e.g., W 466). For the background, see Robert J. Penella, *Greek Philosophers and Sophists in the Fourth Century A.D.: Studies in Eunapius of Sardis*, which by no means supersedes Fowden, 'The Pagan Holy Man in Late Antique Society'.

plexion, an unusual degree of stability and continuity. The reforms of Marcus Aurelius and the outstanding career of Herodes Atticus had marked a new beginning for the leaders of its various schools. That was not just a matter of ensuring a regular succession of 'professorial' appointments: veritable academic dynasties established themselves, reaching back to the time of Plutarch, and involving a close alliance between intellectual and civic leaders within the community.[5] Once we reach the relatively well documented period of philosophical activity in the late third and fourth centuries, a whole series of writers—Porphyry, Libanius, Himerius, and Eunapius especially—fill in for us some of the details of that lively tradition.[6]

A sense of illustrious antecedent was still forcefully felt in the time of Libanius, for example (he first went to Athens in 336). He remembered later having heard from an acquaintance a succinct and obviously widely repeated history of the great centre.[7] However, he found his own experience there disappointing (an impression confirmed by Eunapius), partly because of the disorder of student life, partly because he felt his ambition would be poorly served within 'so small a city'.[8] When he was actually offered a post in Athens, in 352, he turned it down.[9]

In spite of Libanius's personal misgivings, the evidence of continuity and of the city's enduring reputation makes it unwise to place too much weight on the physical decline that supposedly characterized Athens during the first part of the fourth century. Here we have another example of how difficult it sometimes is to integrate archaeological and literary evidence. Athens suffered physically an enormous setback when it was beset and extensively damaged by the Heruls, during their

5. See Fergus Millar, 'P. Herennius Dexippus: The Greek World and the Third-Century Invasions'. His introductory observations are especially useful, although there is less on the fourth century. T. D. Barnes, 'Himerius and the Fourth Century', is particularly important for its chronological clarity. See also John M. Dillon, 'Self-Definition in Later Platonism', pp. 65–69 (suggesting that Athens may not have been exclusively Platonist, and that 'Platonism' admitted of variety in any case).

6. Porphyry *Vita Plotini* (esp. 20. 39f.); of central importance in the case of Libanius is *Libanius' Autobiography (Oration I)*; for Himerius, *Himerii declamationes et orationes cum deperditarum fragmentis*. The long careers of Julian of Cappadocia and of Prohaeresius, covering together three-quarters of a century, offered Basil an extended tradition of his own. See the important survey by H. D. Saffrey and L. G. Westerink, 'L'École d'Athènes au IVe siècle'.

7. Libanius *Orat.* 1. 11.

8. Libanius *Orat.* 1. 18. See Eunapius *Lives* B 495 in W 520.

9. Libanius *Orat.* 1. 84f. For his opinions on the quality of teachers at Athens, see his reference at § 82 to 'imported corn'. His judgements were not echoed by Julian: see below, at nn. 25f.

violent foray into the Balkans in 267 and 268. It only very slowly recovered, in terms of its capacity to rebuild walls and public buildings, and then only over a more restricted area than had been occupied before that event.[10]

For that reason, it has seemed to some that the process of reconstruction would have been so slow as to have imposed upon the citizens the sense almost of a complete break with the past, or at least a feeling of retrenchment and atomisation (among the intellectual community in particular), which would have contrasted in their imaginations with the brighter days of Athens's glory.[11]

It is probably more appropriate, however, to believe that the developments we know of in the early years of the fifth century—philosophical self-confidence, architectural expansion, and Christian patronage—had deep roots in the century previous and point to an exciting atmosphere of revival, in which Basil (present in the city in the early 350s) could hardly have failed to share.[12]

We know a surprising amount about the tenor of student life in Athens during the fourth century. The impression given by Gregory of Nazianzus, in his *oratio* on Basil, is corroborated by reports in the writings of Libanius (referring mainly to the 330s) and of Eunapius (who went to Athens in late 364). Rowdy divisions in the student body seem to have been promoted mainly by boisterous loyalty to individual teachers and sprang almost inevitably from the structure of the academic community. Although the reputation of a teacher and the geographical origins of a student might determine allegiance on both sides, students were in practice, on their arrival, open market commodities; and rival gangs of established pupils attempted to capture, often by violence, further devotees for the masters they admired. Peer pressure then ensured that attendance at one master's lectures and discussions remained consistent; and newcomers were compelled to share in the violence shown to rival groups. The professors themselves were to some extent dependent upon the success of that system and therefore condoned the rough-and-tumble involved: on one occasion a professor was even arrested, as being no less responsible

10. Alison Frantz, *The Athenian Agora*. See especially pp. 8f. for decay, and pp. 8 and 19 for the endurance of paganism.

11. Alison Frantz, 'From Paganism to Christianity in the Temples of Athens', esp. p. 189; heavily indebted to Homer A. Thompson, 'Athenian Twilight: A.D. 267–600'.

12. See Garth Fowden's important review of Frantz's *The Athenian Agora*, 'The Athenian Agora and the Progress of Christianity'. Some additional points emerge in Alan Cameron, 'Iamblichus at Athens'. Dating in this latter paper is affected by T. D. Barnes, 'A Correspondent of Iamblichus'.

for urban unrest than his pupils.[13] It was to avoid potential disruption, according to Eunapius, that many classes were held in private houses; that is to say, in circumstances where access could be both limited and controlled.[14]

We know, from Gregory's account, that Basil experienced many disturbances of such a kind, and that he viewed them with as much disdain as had Libanius more than ten years before.[15]

Basil's chief teachers at Athens were Himerius and Prohaeresius, both treated at length in Eunapius's wonderful account of the intellectual life of his age.[16] Himerius, 'one of the most elusive writers of the fourth century',[17] studied at Athens until the early 340s. His movements thereafter appear to have been governed most by a desire to remain close to Libanius. He did not return to Athens until 352 (the moment when Libanius was considered for a chair and turned it down): so he was not in the city for the first two or three years of Basil's stay. In 361 he responded to the opportunity of Julian's accession to power, perhaps even to an imperial summons, and thus indulged what had long been recommended in his teaching, an inclination towards embroilment in public affairs.[18] One of his best-preserved speeches, delivered in honour of the *magister* Hermogenes in the early 370s, showed not only his own willingness to exercise his talent in public affairs but also, in his account of the career of Hermogenes himself, a natural progression (as he regarded it) from philosophy to the exercise of more public responsibilities.[19] Such an interpretation of intellectual discipline, expressed by a teacher acknowledged to have had some influence on Basil, will become more significant when we examine the tenor of the bishop's own life.

Prohaeresius was a more settled figure: he may be taken as a symbol of continuity in Athens, since he and his master Julian of Cappadocia covered between them a period of more than half a century. By the time Basil arrived at Athens, Prohaeresius was almost eighty years old. He also came from Asia, which, as Eunapius disclosed, explained why so

13. Eunapius *Lives* B 483 in W 468, and, more generally, B 485 in W 478.

14. Eunapius *Lives* B 483 in W 468. See also Libanius *Orat.* 1. 16, 19; *Ep.* 627.

15. GNaz *Orat.* 43. 16f.

16. Eunapius *Lives* B 494 in W 516f., B 485–93 in W 476–514. We shall explore later in the chapter the possibility that Basil studied for a while under Libanius in Constantinople. The dating adopted by Barnes, 'Himerius', pp. 210f., makes that possible (Libanius leaving Nicomedia for Constantinople in 349). For arguments more directly focussed upon Basil, see Paul Petit, *Les Étudiants de Libanius*, pp. 40f., 114f., 124f.

17. Barnes, 'Himerius', p. 207.

18. Eunapius *Lives* B 494 in W 516.

19. Barnes, 'Himerius', pp. 218f.

many of his pupils, Basil among them, were by origin from the same region of the empire. He was a Christian and became famous later for refusing to benefit from a personal exception made in his favour by Julian, after the emperor had forbidden Christians generally to teach publicly in the schools. The refusal may have rightly brought him honour; the invitation may have pointed to a weakness in his impact as a Christian, an impression reinforced by the silence of Gregory of Nazianzus (contrasting with heartfelt praise from the pagan Eunapius).[20]

Importance is commonly attached to the fact that Basil was studying in Athens at the time of Julian's own stay in the city in 355; and the assumption is readily made that the later emperor's subsequent declarations in favour of the pagan cause loomed large in Basil's life.[21] One might with more confidence suggest an impact of that sort on Gregory of Nazianzus, given the forcefulness of his two orations against Julian, composed shortly after the emperor's death; but even they are conceited in a technical sense, and carefully selective in their criticisms. Gregory's famous description of Julian, presenting a picture of nervousness, of arrogance, of inept and over-anxious self-display, was based, according to his own account, on close observation; but that need not imply personal association: so prominent a figure as the emperor's cousin would naturally draw interested attention to himself in a relatively small community.[22] Even when we take that factor into consideration, the attitude of the two friends at the time need not have been either as focussed or as deeply felt as it became under the impact of Julian's later policies. In his more mature years, Basil may have been swayed by Julian's harshness towards Caesarea, and perhaps also by his notorious prohibition of Christian teachers.[23]

20. Kennedy, *Greek Rhetoric*, p. 141.

21. An extreme example is the phrase of Alison Frantz, 'Pagan Philosophers in Christian Athens', p. 31: 'the fellow student and close friend' of Julian. See also Fedwick, *Charisma*, pp. 12f., as discussed in chapter 3, at n. 66.

22. The best available edition is that by Jean Bernardi, *Grégoire de Nazianze, Discours 4–5, Contre Julien*. Bernardi, while admitting that Gregory regarded Julian as a 'menace . . . sérieuse', suspected the value of his judgement. See his *La Prédication des pères cappadociens: Le prédicateur et son auditoire*, p. 10. Note also Alois Kurmann, *Gregor von Nazianz, Oratio 4, Gegen Julian: Ein Kommentar*. Kurmann gives a very full account of the factors governing judgement about dating (inclining to the earliest months of Valentinian's reign), pp. 6f. The book is usefully summarized in a review by Raymond Van Dam, which, nevertheless, places too much weight on Gregory's acquaintance with Julian. Gregory's description of Julian: *Orat.* 5. 23f. Browning, *Julian*, pp. 65f., stresses compatibility with the portrait given by Ammianus Marcellinus, 25, 4. 22.

23. We have no formal edict banning Christian teachers from the schools, only a vague declaration about morality: *Cod.Theod.* 13, 3. 5. However, Julian seems to have followed that up with an explanatory rescript, one version of which has survived in part, making it clear

On the whole, however, Julian's imperial career seems to have made much less impression on Basil than it did on Gregory and his family. He had embarked on a public career in the church well before Julian acceded to supreme power, and the changes in government policy set in train in 361 cannot have been the direct stimulus to a new sense of vocation.[24]

As for the years in Athens, Julian was there for only a few months and associated himself with a very different circle of teachers. Eunapius believed that he had gone to Athens solely to acquaint himself with the mysteries of Eleusis.[25] Certainly, he seems to have noted the fame and skill both of Himerius and of Prohaeresius, inclining to the former;[26] but there is no doubt that his chief enthusiasm was reserved for Priscus, whom Eunapius, as a consequence, treated with qualified respect, and who stayed thereafter in Julian's company, during his campaigns both in Gaul and in Persia, to the moment of the emperor's death.[27] Julian obviously retained a high regard for Athens, but it is surprising how little he said about it later. He saw the Athenians as 'most ambitious for honour and the most humane of all the Greeks'.[28] But his other direct allusions are in many ways rather condescending and reinforce the impression that he went to Athens seeking and finding what its most representative figures would have regarded as the least acceptable features of intellectual life in the city. Julian, like others we have mentioned, was aware of the city's traditions, but with a touch of disappointed nostalgia, harking back to 'the days when they employed their ancestral customs and lived in obedience to

---

that the law was interpreted to the disadvantage of Christians: see Julian *Ep.* 36 (Παιδείαν ὀρθήν); and Browning, *Julian*, pp. 168f. For the works of Julian himself, see *The Works of the Emperor Julian*, with an English translation by Wilmer Cave Wright. Ammianus Marcellinus was surprisingly harsh in his comments, 22, 10. 7; 25, 4. 20. For Julian's treatment of Caesarea (nothing to do with Basil personally), see chapter 5, at n. 220.

24. For a particularly clear assumption to the contrary, see Ann Moffatt, 'The Occasion of St. Basil's *Address to Young Men*'. Bernardi, however, is careful to argue that attitudes to Julian and attitudes to classical culture were not necessarily closely intertwined in the two friends' minds: see especially *Discours 4–5*, pp. 51f. The matter will be discussed further below, at n. 93.

25. Eunapius *Lives* B 475 in W 436.

26. Athanassiadi-Fowden, *Julian*, pp. 46f. Barnes, 'Himerius', p. 221, however, thinks Eunapius unreliable on that point. Julian *Ep.* 14 to Prohaeresius takes no opportunity to hint at previous intimacy.

27. Bowersock, *Julian*, is suggestive in saying very little about Julian's period in Athens. Browning, *Julian*, pp. 64f., emphasizes the concentration on Priscus. Eunapius provides most detail about Priscus in *Lives* B 481 in W 460f., which is ambiguous at best. Earlier, he admits that Priscus resisted some of Julian's flattery and ultimately escaped censure under Valens, B 477f. in W 444f., but does not hesitate to associate him in the same breath with less admired figures like Maximus.

28. Julian *Misopogon* 348BC; tr. Wright, 2: 451.

their own laws, as the inhabitants of a great and humane city'—all part and parcel, of course, of Julian's complete inability to see and respond to matters as they were.[29] As far as the present was concerned, all he could bring himself to admit was that 'neither from the Greeks has philosophy altogether departed'.[30]

Julian's selectivity reminds us how divided Athens was between different views of philosophy. That was not just a matter of varying schools with historically contrasting approaches: the subject of debate was the very purpose of education. The resolution of that issue, in Basil's experience as in anyone else's, mattered more than chance encounters with future emperors. The choices considered at the time have traditionally been symbolized by a contrast between Libanius, the great rhetor of Antioch, and Themistius, who made a more public career for himself at Constantinople. Dispute, for such it occasionally was, focussed on the relative merits of what we might call study for its own sake ('study' being taken to include both philosophical insight and its attendant self-discipline, together with literary learning and grace of style) and study placed at the service of public life. Libanius could be taken to represent the former, Themistius the latter, except that matters were complicated by a further contrast between the traditional values and social patterns of the *polis*, as defended by Libanius, and the ambitions and compromises attendant upon the service of the wider imperial power, happily accepted by Themistius in the capital city.[31] Libanius and Themistius made their greatest public mark in the decades after

29. Julian *Orat.* 3, 114D; tr. Wright, 1: 305.

30. Julian *Orat.* 3, 119; tr. Wright, 1: 316f. His *Letter to the Athenians* was probably one of a number of documents addressed to various cities at an important moment of self-justification (his final challenge to Constantius); and he praises the city's regard for justice more than its philosophy or culture. He must have found painfully ironic the admiration for Athens displayed by Constantine: 'During his whole life he honoured her in word and deed', *Orat.* 1, 8C; tr. Wright, 1: 21. See T. D. Barnes, *Constantine and Eusebius*, p. 72.

31. Two books above all provide useful background to the issue: Paul Petit, *Libanius et la vie municipale à Antioche au IVᵉ siècle après J.-C.*; and G. Dagron, *L'Empire romain d'Orient au IVᵉsiècle et les traditions politiques d'hellénisme: Le Témoignage de Thémistios*. See also Averil Cameron, *Rhetoric of Empire*, pp. 131f., and the introduction to Wayne A. Meeks and Robert L. Wilken, *Jews and Christians in Antioch in the First Four Centuries of the Common Era*. Themistius could plead, of course, that he was doing no more than showing devotion to his native city, entirely in the Hellenistic tradition championed by Libanius: see John Matthews (following Dagron), *Western Aristocracies and Imperial Court, A.D. 364–425*, pp. 116f., and Dagron himself, pp. 42f. Reflection on these and other issues is provided in two useful papers by Lawrence Daly, 'Themistius' Concept of *Philanthropia*' and 'Themistius' Plea for Religious Tolerance'; and by Glanville Downey, 'Philanthropia in Religion and Statecraft in the Fourth Century after Christ'. That *philanthropia*, however, had religious connotations also is stressed by John Whittaker, 'Christianity and Morality in the Roman Empire', pp. 217f.

Basil's years of study (and, indeed, both outlived him by many years). The contrasts, however, were claiming attention long before that (indeed, they were part of a cultural history dating back to the greatest orators of Greece in the fourth century B.C.). We have already seen a choice accepted in that regard by Himerius, both in his own career and in his praise of Hermogenes. Julian was conscious of the issue also (naturally enough, being an enthusiast in philosophy yet thrust upon a public stage) and could write later to former fellow students, urging them to remember that, while philosophy was entirely worthy of admiration, they should not 'despise the study of mere words or be careless of rhetoric'.[32]

While it may be dangerous to regard Eunapius as a typical commentator upon the intellectual scene, his *Lives of the Sophists*, reaching well back into the early fourth century, provide a suggestively full discussion of such problems. He emphasized the importance of deeds as well as words, when it came to assessing the depth and importance of philosophical discussion;[33] and, trying to 'rebuild the unity between life and thought', he admired those philosophers who were able to maintain a sense of reality by applying their wisdom in practical ways.[34] Indeed, the fundamental prejudices or principles that structured Eunapius's work were surprisingly similar to those adopted by Basil. There was a built-in sense of intellectual ancestry, and respect for tradition.[35] There was admiration for the asceticism specifically required as an accompaniment to a life devoted to philosophy. The way in which Eunapius described, for example, Porphyry's sojourn in Sicily, or Aedesius's temporary withdrawal from urban life, cannot but remind us of the path followed by Basil himself, who left Athens for remote contemplation in Pontus.[36] There was a respect for justice, to which Julian also appealed.[37] Finally, at the heart of philosophy as Eunapius understood it, we find an attachment to reason—accompanied, nevertheless, by deep suspicion of subtle

32. Julian *Ep.* 3, 441C; tr. Wright, 3: 7.

33. Eunapius *Lives*, Preface, B 452 in W 342.

34. Eunapius *Lives* B 471 in W 416f. (although he would have dissuaded them from embroiling themselves in the practice of the law). See Arnaldo Momigliano, *On Pagans, Jews, and Christians*, p. 175 (the quotation is from his 1985 paper, 'Ancient Biography and the Study of Religion in the Roman Empire').

35. Eunapius *Lives* B 453 in W 344.

36. For Porphyry, see Eunapius *Lives* B 456 in W 354f.; Aedesius enjoyed the tranquillity of a small estate (χωρίδιόν τέ τι περισκόπει), B 465 in W 392, and was then able to embark upon a more engaged mode of life, B 481 in W 462. See chapter 3, at n. 3.

37. Eunapius *Lives* B 458 in W 362, B 460f. in W 372f., B 481f. in W 462. For Julian, see especially Ammianus Marcellinus, 25, 4. 8f.

argument, which could as easily betray as defend the values that reason represented.[38]

All those principles would have been defined and defended in one way or another by the teachers with whom Basil came into contact. They were not exclusively Christian principles, although they prompted questions to which Christian answers were increasingly available. As central features of the intellectual life of the time, they place in a revealing light many of the points made by Gregory of Nazianzus in his account of the period. He mentioned, for example, the variety of teachers available to himself and his friend; their own readiness to seek in Christian circles the solutions to issues raised in secular or pagan circumstances; their dissatisfaction with Athens, in the sense that they regarded their long-standing Christianity as the most significant and valuable feature of their lives. Athens presented a challenge, in other words, to which (according to Gregory) they were already developing a Christian response. Yet the path they followed as a result, while Christian in form, was nevertheless governed also by their having recognized the issues and the challenge within the framework of traditional education. The answers were their own, the questions were not; and therefore the very style of their reply bore the mark of an alien inquiry.

The anxieties so far hinted at in general terms affected the academic community at the very level of the students' curriculum. First, there was the question of the texts that one should study, the methods one should employ in doing so, and the skills that one should expect to derive from the exercise—skills that would fit one for the role of teacher, lawyer, or administrator. Second, what type of education would support moral development, both in oneself and in those whom one might subsequently influence? Were the two tasks easy to reconcile? If not, which should take precedence?

As we have suggested, Christians were already addressing themselves in their own way to such topics of debate, even in centres of learning as traditional as Athens. After all, Julian's prohibition of Christian rhetors

---

38. Eunapius *Lives* B 475 in W 434. One must avoid, however, a certain naivety of judgement. Without emphasizing the matter explicitly, Eunapius gave prominence, in his *Lives*, to philosophers who resisted the attractions of Constantinople: see Matthews, *Western Aristocracies*, pp. 103–5.

shows that Prohaeresius was not isolated: there must have been others like him.[39] A suspicion of 'cleverness', and a corresponding desire for more practical formation, had already been expressed in Christian writings of the previous two generations, and not only by those who had turned their backs on *civilitas* more generally. There was, however, no 'official' Christian view. Church councils, for example, had yet to say much on the matter. Nor were there institutions dedicated to a specifically Christian form of education. There were no written works on the proper Christian attitude to traditional learning, such as Basil himself would later write, and Augustine in the West. The careers of scholars like Jerome and Rufinus lay in the future. The works of the great Alexandrian theologians, Clement and Origen, were exemplary rather than prescriptive and had operated originally within a segregated world of religious catechesis. While their solutions to a dialogue with pagan culture were absorbed into habits of thought (as in the case of Basil himself), their actual writings had come with time to cause some unease and would do so more and more as the fourth century progressed.

So Basil may have gone to Athens with some inclination to respond in a Christian way to the debates of the time—the natural result of his early formation—but it need not have been either distinct in his own mind or obvious to others. Already, during the year or so he had spent earlier in Constantinople, partly under the influence of Libanius, he could have started to resolve any tension between his Christianity and the classical curriculum. Gregory of Nyssa wrote on two later occasions to Libanius, making it clear that, although Basil had subjugated by then the worth of traditional learning to an appreciation of Scripture, he still spoke favourably of Libanius himself and acknowledged the importance of his influence.[40] Much may have been admitted in the process: both Sozomen and Socrates gained a clear impression that only after leaving Athens did Basil and Gregory of Nazianzus wean themselves from the seductions of classical philosophy and start to read widely in the writings of Origen.[41]

39. Implied by GNaz *Orat.* 43. 21.

40. GNyss *Ep.* 13. Gregory's own convictions were displayed further in *Ep.* 14, especially towards the end: namely, that genuine cultural treasures from the past remained available to all, regardless of whether people were always enlightened about the uses to which they might best be put. For the texts, see *Gregorii Nysseni epistulae*, edited by G. Pasquali.

41. Σοφιστεύειν δὲ ἢ δίκας ἀγορεύειν ὑπεριδόντες φιλοσοφεῖν ἔγνωσαν κατὰ τὸν τῆς Ἐκκλησίας νόμον, Sozomen *HE* 6. 17, § 1, lines 11f.; ed. Bidez, p. 258. See also Socrates *HE* 4. 26. Both writers stressed the link between their study of Origen and their opposition to Arianism, a matter to be explored in the following two chapters. Both also, mistakenly, stated that Basil studied under Libanius in Antioch, after leaving Athens.

One may be inclined to attach more weight to the witness of Gregory of Nazianzus himself. As we have seen, he was firm in his assertion that the two of them viewed their whole experience in Athens very much in the light of a prior attachment to Christianity. It has to be borne in mind that, even when he composed the *oratio* on Basil late in 381, Gregory was still very closely attached to the ideals that Athens had represented nearly thirty years before: 'Athens, the home of eloquence, Athens, a city to me, if to anyone, truly golden, patroness of all that is excellent'.[42] The same admiration recurred in his autobiographical poetry: 'The fame that goes with letters was the only thing that absorbed me. East and West combined to procure me that, and Athens, the glory of Greece'.[43]

But that attachment was justified by a certain submission to Christianity: 'I laboured much for a long time in the craft of letters; but even these too I laid prostrate before the feet of Christ in subjection to the Word of the great God';[44] 'I sought to turn bastard letters into the service of those that are genuine'.[45]

One is not surprised to find, therefore, in the *oratio* itself, some cautious distinctions:

> I take it all intelligent men agree that among human advantages education holds first place. I refer not only to our nobler form of it which disdains all the ambitious ornaments of rhetoric [πᾶν τὸ ἐν λόγοις κομψὸν καὶ φιλότιμον] and attaches itself only to salvation and the beauty of what is accessible to the mind [τοῦ κάλλους τῶν νοουμένων],[46] but also that external culture which many Christians by an error of judgment [κακῶς εἰδότες] scorn as treacherous and dangerous and as turning us away from God. ... We have adopted [from pagan usage] principles of inquiry and speculation [τὸ μὲν ἐξεταστικόν τε καὶ θεωρητικόν], while we have rejected whatever leads to demons, and error, and the abyss of perdition. And from such material we have drawn profit for piety, by learning to distinguish the better from the worse, and from its weakness we have made our own doctrine strong.[47]

42. GNaz *Orat*. 43. 14, tr. p. 38.
43. GNaz *De rebus suis*, line 96; tr. p. 28.
44. GNaz *De rebus suis*, line 98; tr. p. 28.
45. GNaz *De vita sua*, lines 113f.; tr. p. 80. 'Into the service of' does not quite reproduce the simple δοῦναι: Gregory's implication was that Christians were the true heirs of such 'letters' (hence τοῖς γνησίοις).
46. Here and below, I have adapted McCauley's translation. 'The beauty of spiritual contemplation' seems, here, unwarranted; and 'we have adopted', below, does more justice to ἐδεξάμεθα, making the association more active, more a matter of Christian choice, than McCauley's 'have received'.
47. GNaz *Orat*. 43. 11, tr. pp. 35f.

That is likely to have been a view that reflected not only feelings still strong in 381 but earlier experiences that Basil had not directly shared in, namely, Gregory's studies in Caesarea and Alexandria—just those centres in which Origen had achieved his great fusion of classical philosophy and biblical exegesis. It certainly coloured Gregory's subsequent view of matters Platonist.[48] Yet he presented Basil as following very much the same line of argument, even at the time: 'With him, eloquence was only an accessory [τὸ πάρεργον], and he culled from it only what would be helpful for our philosophy, since its power is necessary for the exposition of thought [ἐπειδὴ δεῖ καὶ τῆς ἐν τούτοις δυνάμεως πρὸς τὴν τῶν νοουμένων δήλωσιν]'.[49]

Such attitudes, on the part of both men, may explain why they were content to throw themselves wholeheartedly into the academic life of the city. Athens was, by Gregory's admission, 'harmful ... to the things of the soul'. Yet they felt confident: 'Our own experience there confirmed us in the faith'. They were like salamanders, dancing unharmed in the destroying fire.[50] Yet we know that Basil displayed less enthusiasm and greater caution. He had quickly shown signs of disillusionment, largely in the face of student rowdiness and faculty rivalries. Gregory attempted to reassure him: 'Culture is not a thing to be judged from a few brief experiences'. He was also quick to point out to the audience of his *oratio* that by this and other acts of encouragement he had bound Basil ever more closely to himself.[51] Yet Basil left Athens before Gregory did, and much against the wishes of his friend.[52] We recognize, therefore, that there are two ways of interpreting the picture that Gregory gives of their Christian lives at the time. 'The sole object of us both', he recalled, 'was virtue and living for future hopes, having detached ourselves from this world before departing from it'. That was a sentiment shared by many a pagan, who would have used the very same language.[53] 'Two ways were familiar to us',

48. Ruether, *Gregory*, pp. 19, 26f. See GNaz *Orat*. 7. 6, 9; 18. 31.

49. GNaz *Orat*. 43. 13, tr. p. 38. This was, however, a general observation, made before Gregory treated the Athens years specifically.

50. GNaz *Orat*. 43. 21.

51. GNaz *Orat*. 43. 18, tr. p. 43; see also *Orat*. 43. 17. Ruether, *Gregory*, p. 27 n. 8, presents Basil as 'clearly the leader'; Gregory admitted that only with reluctance. See also his *De vita sua*, lines 225f., even though Basil is there described as 'the great ornament of our generation', tr. p. 83—alluding, of course, to much more than his achievements in Athens. In the context of their years together in Athens, Barnes, 'Himerius', p. 221 n. 71, refers to Basil and Gregory as 'brothers'—a rare but mighty blunder!

52. GNaz *Orat*. 43. 24. See also his *De vita sua*, lines 225f.: Gregory was at first more willing to stay.

53. GNaz *Orat*. 43. 20, tr. p. 44. We shall explore that common ground between Christians and pagans more fully in chapter 3, at nn. 40f., 69f.

Gregory continued, 'the first and more precious leading us to our sacred buildings and the masters there [an odd allusion: πρὸς τοὺς ἱεροὺς ἡμῶν οἴκους, καὶ τοὺς ἐκεῖσε διδασκάλους]; the second and the one of less account, to our secular teachers [πρὸς τοὺς ἔξωθεν παιδευτάς]'.[54] They frequented both, in other words; and there was some analogy between the activities that took place in both, in spite of what may be an implied distinction between 'masters' and 'teachers'. And yet, he noted, 'our great concern, our great name, was to be Christians and be called Christians'.[55]

―――――――――

How reliably does that account describe for us the attitude of Basil himself at the time? Of his years in Athens, Basil wrote little. In an undatable sermon, he made scathing reference to the city, 'a school of impurity', suggesting that its influence at the time he spoke was likely to encourage in people a delight in intellectual novelty that would lead inevitably to heresy.[56] The dismissive tone of an early letter—'I left Athens, scorning everything there'[57]—obviously endured in his case more than admiration did in Gregory's. Immediately after his departure, Basil continued to regret that he could not bring Gregory quickly to his own point of view (although he did have some eventual success).[58] Later still, he felt that his studies at Athens had been a complete waste of time.[59]

If he held that opinion when he actually left in 355, he may have taken time to reach such a conclusion. After all, he had stayed in Greece for at least five years. More important, once returned to his native province, he may still have been prepared to try his hand at teaching, in the school at Caesarea.[60] (Gregory's narrative allows time;[61] and Gregory of Nyssa

54. GNaz Orat. 43. 21, tr. p. 45.
55. GNaz Orat. 43. 21, tr. p. 45.
56. Hom. 353. 8. The allusion was made in passing, thanks to a reference to Acts, which had provided the context for Tertullian's war cry (see n. 2 above).
57. Ep. 1, C 1: 3, D 1: 3. Note how the vocabulary of Sozomen echoed the words of Basil, ὑπεριδὼν τῶν ἐκεῖ: see n. 41 above.
58. I take that to be the implication of his complaint in Ep. 14. The context will be explored fully in chapter 3.
59. Ep. 223. 2. See also chapter 1, at nn. 69f. The nostalgic affection for a fellow student displayed in Ep. 271, if it does refer to shared experience in Athens, suggests no particular regard for the city itself.
60. Fedwick accepts that this is likely, and outlines the evidence, both in his Charisma, p. 135, and in Basil, 1: 6. One must respect, however, the doubts of Gribomont, 'Eustathe le philosophe', pp. 121f. Aubineau, Virginité, pp. 56f., is particularly helpful.
61. GNaz Orat. 43. 25.

said that he was taught by his brother in the city.)[62] It was Gregory of Nyssa who recalled that period in Basil's life, not only with admiration and gratitude but also with wry criticism: 'He was excessively puffed up by his rhetorical abilities [ὑπερφυῶς ἐπηρμένον τῷ περὶ τοὺς λόγους φρονήματι] and disdainful of all great reputations, and considered himself better than the leading men in the district'.[63]

Even when he had embraced a pastoral vocation, that tendency was not immediately corrected and seems to have provoked a painful tension in Basil the priest. Writing perhaps as early as 364 to his friend Leontius, an educated layman, he made a somewhat tortuous admission: 'The stain, as it were, that I have taken on by my tiresome association with the vulgar [τὸ οἱονεὶ ἐρρυπῶσθαι λοιπὸν τῇ κατακορίᾳ πρὸς ἰδιωτισμὸν ὄκνον] makes me naturally reluctant to address you sophists'.[64] At the very same period, he was suggesting that the ignorant could be left to their own devices, since they were beyond the reach of words.[65]

In much later work, too, one detects something akin to arrogance (a modern sensibility, perhaps, but close to Gregory's 'puffed up' disdain). Writing to one Martinianus on so ecclesiastical a matter as the administrative division of Cappadocia in 371, with its associated loss of influence for the metropolitan of Caesarea, Basil was well content to couch his appeal, obviously to a man of some literary distinction, in terms heavy with allusion to Homer, to history, and to a whole tradition of classical philosophy and writing. He cannot have been wholly unaware of the reflection upon his own experience, when he admitted that 'it is important as a proof of education "to have seen the cities of many men and to have learned their minds"'.[66] He included among the disasters consequent, as he saw it, upon the policy of Valens a decline in levels of culture and refinement; and that may not have been an argument entirely *ad hominem*:

> The gatherings of old, the orations, the conversations of learned men in the market-place, and all that formerly made our city famous, have left us; in consequence there is now less likelihood of a learned or an eloquent

62. GNyss *Ep.* 13. 4. See Gerhard May, 'Die Chronologie des Lebens und der Werke des Gregor von Nyssa', p. 53.

63. GNyss *VMac.* 6; ed. Woods Callahan, p. 377, lines 11f.; tr. p. 167.

64. *Ep.* 20, C 1: 50, D 1: 125 (C's slightly different text does not affect significantly D's translation). See GNaz *Orat.* 43. 55. There is, however, some irony in both passages.

65. Basil *Contra Eunomium* [henceforward *CE*] 2. 18. The most useful edition is *Basile de Césarée, Contre Eunome, suivi de Eunome, Apologie*, with introduction, text, translation, and notes by Bernard Sesboüé, in collaboration with Georges-Matthieu de Durand and Louis Doutreleau.

66. *Ep.* 74. 1, C 1: 172, D 2: 69, quoting Homer *Odyssey* 1. 3f.

man entering our Forum than that in former days in Athens men would appear in public who had been convicted of dishonour or were impure of hand.[67]

It will be vital to appreciate, however, the extent to which Basil rose above the limitations of his privileged education and of the rhetorical tradition that formed its base. Albeit with difficulty, he dedicated himself to the task of reaching beyond the erudite, the polished, the wealthy, and the powerful, who had gained their position through access to learning and clarity of expression.[68] Even the conventions celebrated and defended in the letter to Martinianus were brought to bear within a specifically Christian and religious context. Basil was asserting a close connection between educational standards and the ability to withstand heresy: 'for the danger is not slight that, since those in authority have been removed, the whole edifice will collapse'.[69]

The same concern lay behind a harsh sentiment expressed to his friend Gregory: 'We must remember that if we suffer unbridled mouths and uninstructed hearts [στόμασιν ἀχαλινώτοις καὶ καρδίαις ἀπαιδεύτοις] to prattle about whatever they please, ... not only shall we receive a false idea of the affairs of others, but they will do the same as to ours'.[70]

A new, religious attachment to traditional caution may explain the tone of many declarations. To someone within the circle of Gregory, for example, Basil appears to reassert the tastes of old: 'Although we do not

67. *Ep.* 74. 3, C 1: 175, D 2: 75. This letter is perhaps Basil's longest surviving reaction to Valens's reforms, and his most explicit request for help: see Thomas A. Kopecek, 'The Cappadocian Fathers and Civic Patriotism', p. 299. For Martinianus, who later became Prefect of the City of Rome, see *PLRE* 1: 564. *Ep.* 135 (written roughly at the same time) complains of a shortage of copyists in Cappadocia. Anxiety arising from the purely administrative changes involved will be referred to in several places below: see especially chapter 5, at nn. 159, 173f. A review of the policy, emphasizing 'secular' considerations, is provided by Stanislas Giet, *Les Idées et l'action sociales de s. Basile*, pp. 366f. See also A. H. M. Jones, *The Cities of the East Roman Provinces*, pp. 182f.

68. In what follows, I take issue with the view expressed succinctly (as more generally in several of his other works) by Ramsay MacMullen, 'The Preacher's Audience'. For Basil, in MacMullen's eyes, 'it was the rich that were ordinarily to be seen and addressed as such, or recognized through their possessions, slaves most signally but also grand houses and ... expensive education', p. 507; 'they [the preachers] have before them the city's leadership, the upper ranks, accompanied by their slaves', p. 510; after this the tone becomes affected by personal animus. My misgivings focus chiefly on the narrowness of MacMullen's selection in his nn. 9 and 10, and his unwillingness to recognize the special circumstances of many of his examples.

69. *Ep.* 74. 3, C 1: 175, D 2: 75.

70. *Ep.* 71, C 1: 167, D 2: 55f. Basil was criticizing ill-considered debate on the subject of the Holy Spirit. Deferrari has 'uneducated minds' where I have preferred 'uninstructed hearts'; but 'uneducated' is too narrow a word to describe the lack of formation here lamented.

say that we can lay any claim to elegance of style, yet by a sort of natural instinct we are charmed by it, and you who are graceful of speech attract us, even as men attract bees by the thrumming of a lyre'.[71] It was a rather different sense of refinement, however, that led him to suggest in a sermon (albeit an early one) that the hidden meanings so typical of proverbs in Scripture were discernible only to those 'more skilled', and that they in turn should not bandy their meaning about to those of more common cultivation.[72] It is easy to pick out a phrase like the following (this is Basil the mature bishop writing): 'Let him not prattle in a corner like a slave [δουλοπρεπῶς], but let him take his stand in the open and refute me freely [μετὰ παρρησίας]'.[73] Yet that freedom represented not only the confidence characteristic of an élite but also the dignity of a human soul cleansed and perfected, standing in the presence of its maker. Basil might have bemoaned, to an intimate group of ascetics, the fact that 'the many and simpler folk [τῶν πολλῶν καὶ ἀκεραιοτέρων], while acknowledging that we are being wronged, yet do not account to us as martyrdom our death for the sake of truth'.[74] He was expressing, nevertheless, the sorrow of a pastor, who felt that the 'many' were victims of the duplicity of others, and who had himself tried to rescue them.

What we observe, in all these examples, is the transference of valued distinctions—between knowledge and ignorance, between clarity and confusion—from one arena to another: from the ordered and respectful world of teacher and pupil in the secular schools (often disdainful of those outside their circle) to the Christian society represented by the word 'Church' (which also depended upon the preservation of authority, and on a clear understanding of who had the right to teach and of who was likely to possess the truth). In the course of the transference, the distinctions were modified, so that disdain was genuinely, if slowly, replaced by concern for spiritual welfare (touched, of course, by human weakness, and judged by canons we may not share). At the very least, we have to accept that Basil was making an honourable effort to maintain two sets of standards, or perhaps, more fairly, a synthesis of principles, both cultural and religious:

71. *Ep.* 323, C 3: 195, D 4: 271. The date of the letter is unfortunately not known.

72. Τὸ πεπαρρησιασμένον καὶ δεδημοσιευμένον τῆς διανοίας μὴ ἔχοντος: *Hom.* 340. 2; *PG* 31. 388C. For the date—'certainly one of the first homilies preached by Basil'— see Fedwick, *Basil*, 1: 10 n. 50, which is based, I presume, on the judgement of Bernardi, *Prédication*, p. 56.

73. *Ep.* 51, C 1: 133, D 1: 327. The context was entirely ecclesial. Compare *Ep.* 204. 4, with its disdainful reference to 'a hussy from the bake-shop [παιδίσκη μία τῶν ἐκ μύλωνος]', C 2: 176, D 3: 165: again, the focus was on the standards of debate proper to the Church.

74. *Ep.* 257. 1, C 3: 99, D 4: 33.

'If we have any claim to eloquence, most gladly shall we read the letters of an eloquent man; and if we have learned from Scripture how great is the good of love, of all worth do we regard correspondence with a man who loves us'.[75]

One of the most striking declarations on this topic from Basil's later years was a letter to Diodorus, the future bishop of Tarsus (significantly, therefore, to a man who stood at the beginning of a new tradition of formation and discipleship, developed within the confines of the Church).[76] Basil praised the 'simple and unlaboured style [τὸ τῆς λέξεως ἁπλοῦν τε καὶ ἀκατάσκευον]', which, he said, 'seemed to me to befit the purpose of a Christian, who writes not so much for display as for general edification [οὐ πρὸς ἐπίδειξιν μᾶλλον ἢ κοινὴν ὠφέλειαν]'.[77]

He was then able to point to ancient pagans who wrote in that useful way—Plato in particular.[78] The implication of an acceptable dependence on the part of Christians extended also to the traditional use of moral examples, 'the technical armory of evocation': 'So it is necessary also for us [i.e., just as it was for those older authors], ... if we introduce a character already well known to the world for rashness of conduct, to weave something derived from the quality of the character into the treatise'.[79] The skill was to be harnessed, therefore, to the task of moral formation.

The same point was made in a slightly later letter to an episcopal acquaintance: 'We use as a rule of life the commandment of the Lord and the pre-eminent examples of those blessed men whose nobility of soul

75. *Ep.* 194, C 2: 147, D 3: 86. Courtonne dates the letter to 375.
76. See Theodoret *HE* 4. 24f., where reference to Diodorus occurred exactly in the context of the fight against paganism, defending τὴν ἀποστολικὴν διδασκαλίαν (§ 4; ed. p. 262, lines 18f.). For the text, see *Theodoret, Kirchengeschichte*, edited by Léon Parmentier. English translation: *Ecclesiastical History ... by Theodoretus, Bishop of Cyrus*. See also Theodoret *Ep.* 58, edited by Yvan Azéma, *Théodoret de Cyr, Correspondance*, 2: 134f. Pierre Canivet, *Histoire d'une entreprise apologétique au V*e *siècle*, p. 37, doubts that Diodorus need have been literally the teacher of Theodoret. For the background, consult Frances M. Young, *From Nicaea to Chalcedon: A Guide to the Literature and Its Background*. Also useful is Richard Lim, 'The Politics of Interpretation in Basil of Caesarea's *Hexaemeron*', esp. pp. 352f.
77. *Ep.* 135. 1, C 2: 49, D 2: 307 (and 309 for what follows). Courtonne dates the letter to 373. Basil made his point also by his criticism of what he thought less successful in Diodorus's work, marred as it was 'with richer diction, with figures of divers kinds, and with charms peculiar to the dialogue', all of which 'by causing delay and waste of time disrupt the continuity of the thought and loosen the tension of the argumentative attack'—and again his anxiety was aroused by the demands and dangers of controversy within the Christian community.
78. *Ep.* 135. 1.
79. *Ep.* 135. 2, C 2: 50, D 2: 309/311. The earlier quoted phrase is that of Averil Cameron, *Rhetoric of Empire*, p. 84.

was especially shown in the face of adverse fortune'.[80] Here the exemplary figures were entirely Christian; and Basil evoked a tradition of education that was pursued much more within the Christian community itself:

> For a man who has already attained to such a degree of goodness, and who knows human nature both from daily experience and from spiritual training [ἐκ τε τῆς κατὰ τὸν χρόνον ἐμπειρίας καὶ ἐκ τῆς πνευματικῆς διδασκαλίας], it is fitting that the separation from near relatives [for he was writing to a man whose grandson had recently died] be not in all respects hard to endure.[81]

So the old literary tricks, as it were, could be reapplied by those whose interpretation of διδασκαλία drew upon other resources and represented other values. In the end, the actions of Jesus himself were veritable παιδεύματα: by imitating them, a Christian might become a vignette of humility also, marked by simplicity, honesty, and pleasantness of manner.[82]

We find other judgements about traditional learning in comparable religious contexts related to doctrinal controversy. In a letter to the bishops of the West, for example, written early in 372, Basil made a clear connection between traditional education and Arian error:

> The teachings of the Fathers are scorned; the apostolic traditions are set at naught; the fabrications of innovators are in force in the churches; these men, moreover, train themselves in rhetorical quibbling and not in theology [τεχνολογοῦσι λοιπόν, οὐ θεολογοῦσιν]; the wisdom of the world takes first place to itself, having thrust aside the glory of the Cross.[83]

An even more striking example occurred in his long letter of self-defence against Eustathius of Sebaste:

> Let there be an investigation as to whether the charge seem not due to the ignorance of the accuser rather than that the work is condemned through its own nature. For many good things do not seem to be so to those who do not possess a keen judgement of the mind [τοῖς τὸ κριτήριον τῆς διανοίας οὐκ ἀκριβὲς κεκτημένοις].... So also in the realm of literature I see the same thing often happening, whenever the critic falls short of the experienced skill of authors. For the critic of literature and the author ought to start out with about the same equipment ... but whoever wishes will straightway be a critic of letters, though he is unable to name his teacher or the time when he studied, and although he understand nothing at all, little or much, about letters. And I see that

80. *Ep.* 206, C 2: 183, D 3: 179.
81. *Ep.* 206, C 2: 182f., D 3: 179.
82. *Hom.* 329. 7.
83. *Ep.* 90. 2, C 1: 195f., D 2: 125.

in the utterances of the Spirit also, it has not been possible for every one to devote himself to the investigation of His words, but only for him who possesses the Spirit which gives discernment [ἀλλὰ τῷ ἔχοντι τὸ Πνεῦμα τῆς διαχρίσεως].... Therefore if our affairs are spiritual [πνευματικά], let him who wishes to judge our affairs show that he has the grace of spiritual discernment [ἔχοντα τὸ χάρισμα τῆς διαχρίσεως τῶν πνευματικῶν]. But if, as he himself falsely charges [so in other words the concession will be irrelevant], they are of the wisdom of this world [ἀπὸ τῆς σοφίας ... τοῦ κόσμου τούτου], let him show that he is experienced in the wisdom of this world.[84]

The distinctions here were very skilfully drawn. The context was carefully limited to πνευματικά, and any professional attachment to skill, accuracy, or technical formation was defended only in that context—as Basil expressed it to Diodorus, 'for general edification'. But it was professional, in this sense: that, just as those preoccupied with 'the wisdom of this world' had—or should have had—their disciplines and standards as critics, so also that desire for authenticity, experience, and insight, under the patronage of the Spirit, was to inform and protect the leaders of the Christian community.

Distinctions, again, were being at once transferred and modified. In order to appreciate the significance of that process, we need to look at Basil's own 'rhetoric'; at the way in which he allowed his homilies, for example, to be shaped only to a limited degree by traditional skills (without which, nevertheless, it would have been impossible even to compose or deliver them). He insisted that Christianity had its own rules for public declamation. As he expressed it in one sermon, 'The style of teaching proper to God knows nothing of the rules of panegyric [οὐκ οἶδεν οὖν ἐγκωμίων νόμον τὸ θεῖον διδασκαλεῖον]'.[85] Implied in such forthrightness was a fear that some in his audience expected oratory more akin to the exercises of the schools. The reason for his contrasting emphasis was, as he said himself, that a homily should prompt imitation (in this case, of a martyr's virtues). The opening section of the same sermon is littered with references to exemplary deeds, to imitation, to the need to feel inspired in practical ways to adopt a virtuous life.[86] Not only was a homily supposed

84. Ep. 204. 5, C 2: 177f., D 3: 165f.
85. Hom. 327. 2; PG 31. 492B. This sermon is to be dated to 373: Fedwick, Basil, 1: 10 n. 40.
86. Similar points were made in relation to the Forty Martyrs in Hom. 338. 1f., preached in the same year: Fedwick (again, following Bernardi, Prédication), Basil, 1: 10 n. 48. See also DSS 4 (§ 6): Scripture, in its characteristic way, is concerned more with usefulness than with expression. Gregory of Nazianzus is interesting on the persuasive power of the spectacular

to bring about such changes in behaviour: it was also an integral element of the Christian cult. Praising once again a martyr (probably in 376), Basil hoped that his audience would bring to their minds treasured memories of their own, sayings and anecdotes handed down in the community. Those memories, which constituted the truest act of praise, they were to share together in the public celebration of the festival (πάντα μοι συναγαγόντες, ἐγκώμιον ἐκ κοινοῦ ἐράνου πονήσατε). It is this sense of collusion between preacher and audience, of shared engagement in a common experience, that highlights most vividly the novelty of Basil's address, both in its motive and in its reach.[87]

It becomes apparent at once that Basil had embarked on something more complex than Christianized oratory: the whole 'atmosphere' of the homiletic occasion was coloured by its cultic context, and by the broader programme of moral transformation of which it formed but a part. The 'rhetoric' to which Basil now devoted himself was designed to affect behaviour as much as understanding. In the first place, he was pointing to the way in which the whole Church had experienced a shift in its view of history, and in its understanding of how history could achieve a pedagogic impact. Commenting on Psalm 45 (V 44), in which the queen 'forget[s] her] father's house', he made the verse apply to the Church itself; and the queen's change of residence referred to the way in which Christians had rejected worldly knowledge and skill, along with the pagan cult.[88] The point was made against a general background of criticism, which Basil willingly rehearsed in public addresses of this sort. In the early sermon discussed above, with its hint of enduring élitism, he could state, nevertheless: 'Poetry, rhetoric, sophistic inquiry take up an enormous amount of many people's time. They are false to the core. Poetry cannot survive without myth. Rhetoric cannot survive without cleverness of

---

(as opposed to oratorical declamation): *De seipso et de episcopis*, lines 238f. One is reminded of Jerome's report and apparent admiration of Gregory's skill, *Ep.* 52. 8.

87. *Hom.* 337. 1, *PG* 31. 589C. For the date, Fedwick, *Basil*, 1: 10 n. 47. Giet, *Idées*, pp. 246f., emphasizes the participation of the audience. Bernardi, *Prédication*, p. 12, is even more forceful, talking of 'une dimension collective toute nouvelle': 'L'orateur est au contraire [compared with 'l'écrivain'] confronté à son auditoire d'une façon si étroite que l'acte de prêcher est, dans une large mesure, *un acte collectif'* (italics mine). See Averil Cameron, *Rhetoric of Empire*, p. 79, on the homily as 'the hidden iceberg of Christian discourse': 'Through regular repetition and by continually drawing on and reinterpreting an increasingly familiar body of texts, [Christians] also constantly reaffirmed the essence of the faith and the constituents of membership of the Christian community'. James Marshall Campbell, *The Influence of the Second Sophistic on the Style of the Sermons of St. Basil the Great*, is exhaustive in its analysis but resigned to paucity in its conclusions.

88. *Hom.* 352. 10; see also 355. 2.

speech. Sophistry is nothing without false inference'.[89] What was required was moral perception, φρόνησις, which was 'capable of judging of what is to be done and what is not to be done'. Obviously that παιδεία (for he used the word) would have to be talked about; but 'words that carry truth, and spring from a healthy understanding, are simple, focussing upon one task, always treating the same issues in the same way [ἁπλοῦς ἐστι καὶ μονότροπος, τὰ αὐτὰ λέγων πάντοτε περὶ τῶν αὐτῶν]'.[90]

Colouring all those observations was the sense that a whole culture had had its day and was doomed now to extinction, or at least to transformation within a new society:

> Do you not see, in the teachings of the Gentiles, in that vain philoso-
> phy, how meagre, how inflated they are, when it comes to discoveries
> based upon them—in their abstract teaching, for example, in their moral
> programmes, in their natural philosophy, or in the esoteric teachings of
> their religious leaders—do you not see how the whole edifice has been
> scattered abroad and rendered good for nothing? The only truth now
> that has claim to public standing in the world is the truth of the Gospel.[91]

That transformation pressed urgently upon his audience. The pen of the writer, in Psalm 45 (V 44), moved rapidly across the page of time, so that all had come to hear the Gospel message and had rejected specifically the alternative wisdom that had stood them in stead hitherto.[92]

What we may rightly detect in those various quotations is a gradual movement, the adoption of a new point of view over a period of time. Confident rejection of the ancient culture (never total, in any case) came only slowly; and ambiguities persisted. Yet there was a clear shift—from obscure and conceited complexities of expression, and from the barrenness of vaunted intellectual discovery. It would be agreeable to discover a mo-ment of balance in Basil's life, when it tipped away from Athens towards Jerusalem; and our attention might naturally focus upon his pamphlet *Ad*

89. *Hom.* 340. 6. See n. 72 above.

90. *Hom.* 340. 6f. *PG* 31. 400.

91. *Hom.* 350. 7.

92. *Hom.* 352. 3f. Compare the reference in *Hom.* 353. 3 to the πατέρες τῆς ἀπολλυμένης σοφίας, *PG* 29. 421A. Christianity possessed an antiquity of its own: *Hom.* 340. 8, *DSS* 6 (§ 28). The 'transformation of rhetoric', in the sense explored here, will demand further attention: see chapter 4, where the matter is never wholly absent, especially at nn. 63f., 115f., 130f., 142f.; and chapter 5, at n. 138.

adulescentes (Πρὸς τοὺς νέους), which told young men 'how they might gain help from the words of the Hellenes'.[93]

Unfortunately, the *Ad adulescentes* is a work extremely difficult to date. It consistently veers away, as we shall see, from the mere study of literature towards an emphasis on morality. For that reason alone, it might be taken to stand at the point of reassessment we are looking for.[94] The moral emphasis, on the other hand, is not linked in any direct way with the institutionalized life of asceticism. That might suggest an early date; but, as we shall see, Basil was for a long time remarkably informal in his arrangement of the ascetic life, and broad in his address when recommending it.[95] It is also implied at several stages of the treatise that readers will be well acquainted with Christian life and practice, and with the contents of Scripture.[96] That would certainly incline us to associate the work with a period of pastoral responsibility, and in particular with Basil's need, when first appointed bishop, to defend his continuing emphasis on ascetic values.[97]

The possibility that he had originally addressed the work to his own nephews does not offer a great deal of assistance: their probable ages and

93. The edition made use of here is that by Naldini, *Basilio di Cesarea, Discorso ai Giovani*. See also N. G. Wilson, *Saint Basil on the Value of Greek Literature*; and *Saint Basile, Aux jeunes gens sur la manière de tirer profit des lettres helléniques*, edited and translated into French by Fernand Boulenger. English translation in *Saint Basil, The Letters*, 4: 379–435 (see chapter 1, n. 11).

94. There is no need to link its creation with Julian's move against Christian teachers—as if it might contain some acknowledgement of the emperor's justice! That proposal is put forward by Moffatt, 'Occasion': see n. 24 above. Wilson, *Value*, p. 9, is sceptical; Naldini, *Discorso*, p. 16, forcefully dismissive: both authors place the work much later in Basil's life. For more detailed argument, see Mario Naldini, 'Sulla "Oratio ad adolescentes" di Basilio Magno'. There is comment *ad rem* in Yves Courtonne, *Saint Basile et l'Hellénisme: Étude sur la rencontre de la pensée chrétienne avec la sagesse antique dans l'Hexaméron de Basile le Grand*, pp. 4f., 12f.

95. See chapter 6. Naldini, *Discorso*, pp. 10f., 18, makes the connection with asceticism but points also to the likelihood of a broader type of audience. Even in chapters 8 and 9 of the work, which discuss the practicalities of self-denial and simplicity of life, there is no allusion to a specifically monastic milieu.

96. In spite of a suggestion that a reading of Scripture is yet to come—at 2. 7 and 9, or 10. 1, for example—there is a clear implication of its priority as a source of inspiration acknowledged by writer and readers alike, at 7. 7f. For useful reflection on this tension, to be discussed shortly at greater length, see Boulenger, *Aux jeunes gens*, p. 25; Naldini, *Discorso*, p. 16; and Erich Lamberz, 'Zum Verständnis von Basileios' Schrift, "Ad Adolescentes" '.

97. So Gribomont, 'Panégyrique', pp. 251f., linking the work with Gregory of Nyssa's *De virginitate*. Naldini, *Discorso*, p. 12, confirms that view, although independently. I find this preferable to the connections made by Daniélou, 'Mariage de Grégoire de Nysse', p. 72, in relation to Gregory's treatise. See chapter 1, at nn. 22f., and chapter 5, at nn. 43, 62f., 76, 104f.

his style of address would still be compatible with his mature and even priestly years.[98]

Whatever the date, we can use the work as a species of multifocal lens. If we look along the axis, so to speak, of its relationship with the past, we see rich allusion both to classical texts and to Christian reflection upon them. Facing the text directly, we notice more the temperament of the writer, preoccupied with the moral formation of his readers. If we look then along another axis, leading to the future, we catch the voice of the pastor, familiar from the sermons and letters of his later years.

What of the work itself? We might be inclined to suppose that here above all we shall find a full discussion of the proper relationship between classical culture and the Christian faith. Yet that is not what leaps from the page. We are reminded that Christians of the period did not always think of themselves, in relation to pagan contemporaries, in quite such terms of contrast—their culture/our religion. It was not obvious that a Christian could simply take advantage of useful components in the established curriculum, while rejecting superstition. Traditional culture was still too much of a seamless web to make such distinctions either visible or easy.[99]

What the work does discuss, more intently, is whether it was possible to present a moral programme, a picture of the life of virtue, without an immediate appeal to Scripture. If so, what alternative materials were available to support such an exhortation? One has to say that Basil was not altogether honest in the answer he provided. Even posing the question in that way betrayed a possible tension between sources and goals, between the inherited teachings of the Church (preserved particularly in Scripture, and seen as instruments of moral formation) and the acquisition of the skills necessary in order to grow as a moral being. Was it possible to set out on a moral path that was identifiably Christian, without having first discovered and understood the treasures of the Christian past? Basil was not altogether successful in making a clean breast of the matter.

---

98. Boulenger, Naldini, and Wilson are all happy to include the nephews in Basil's audience, but insist also on a wider address. Basil himself does not seem to have found it difficult to embrace those other than his kin with a familial sense of concern: 'The Lord has set us in the second rank of fathers to Christians, having entrusted to us the moulding through religion [τὴν διὰ τῆς εὐσεβείας μόρφωσιν] of the children of those who believe in Him', Ep. 300, C 3: 174, D 4: 219. See below, at n. 130. Important details are provided by Moffatt, 'Occasion'; Aubineau, Virginité, p. 35 and n. 6; and Maraval, Vie, pp. 38f., and 'Encore les frères et sœurs de Grégoire de Nysse'.

99. A preliminary survey of pitfalls is usefully provided by Michele R. Salzman, '"Superstitio" in the Codex Theodosianus and the Persecution of Pagans'. General observations, useful in this context, are provided by Giet, Idées, pp. 217f.

He opened the treatise with a clear assurance that he had something different to offer: 'something of especial advantage to you', something 'that I myself have discovered'. He contrasted that with the blandishments of the traditional schools. He knew that he was addressing young men 'who each day resort to teachers and hold converse with the famous men of the ancients through the words which they have left behind them'. His own command was forthright: 'You should not surrender to these men once for all the rudders of your mind'.[100]

What was that discovery, that personal experience upon which Basil rested his teaching authority? It was simply that 'we ... in no wise conceive this human life of ours to be an object of value in any respect, nor do we consider anything good at all ... which makes its contribution to this life of ours only'.[101] That insight was to be associated with his having 'already been trained through many experiences', and having 'shared sufficiently in the all-teaching vicissitude of both good and evil fortune'.[102] The appeal was much more, in other words, to his conception of the 'philosophic life', and rather less, at that point, to any scriptural inspiration. Moreover, he had in mind experiences that his present audience was unlikely to appreciate: 'Just what this life is ... would be for the more mature [ἀκροατῶν] to hear'.[103] Subsequently he did bring Scripture into the picture: 'Now to that other life which lies beyond our present circumstances the Holy Scriptures lead the way, teaching us through mysteries [δι' ἀπορρήτων ἡμᾶς ἐκπαιδεύοντες]'. Yet those, too, his audience was not ready to appreciate: 'By reason of your age, it is impossible for you to understand the depth of the meaning of these'.[104]

---

100. Basil *Ad adulescentes* [henceforward *Adul.*] 1. 4, 6; tr. §§ 3, 5, p. 381. (Note that the section numbers within each chapter are not always the same in Naldini's edition as they are in the text accompanying the Loeb translation.) His readers were to see Basil himself, of course, in a different light (following Hesiod's advice, 'Excellent is he too who follows what is well indicated by others'); but he did supply also the preceding dictum, 'Best is the man who sees of himself at once what must be done'—an espousal of free choice that sprang, according to Naldini, *Discorso*, pp. 21, 48f., from the legacy of Origen. On the influence of Origen more generally, see also Naldini's 'Paideia origeniana nella "Oratio ad adolescentes" di Basilio Magno'.

101. *Adul.* 2. 1, tr. § 1, p. 381.

102. *Adul.* 1. 2; Naldini, *Discorso* [henceforward, in this context, N], p. 80; tr. § 1, p. 379. See Naldini's rejection, *Discorso*, p. 140, of 'conversion' as a proper translation of μεταβολή, arguing against Moffatt, 'Occasion', p. 76.

103. *Adul.* 2. 4, tr. § 3, p. 383.

104. *Adul.* 2. 6f.; N, pp. 84/86; tr. § 5f., p. 383. On the central place of Scripture in the treatise, see Naldini, *Discorso*, pp. 145f., 151f. The final phrase of *Ep.* 150 offers an equally neat summary of Basil's credentials as a teacher: 'Betake yourself to a man who both knows much

Straightway, therefore, we are made to face the tension already anticipated: Scripture was to reinforce moral values; but its reading lay unavoidably in the future, to be embarked upon only after a period of moral
growth. In the *Ad adulescentes*, it was the latter that earned most attention.
There seems to have been no suggestion, as there was in Basil's more
pastoral addresses, that Scripture had an absolute priority—awakening
the envy of pagans, and providing Christians with a means to judge the
moral content of the classical παιδεία.[105] Engagement with traditional literature was seen here as a necessary 'preliminary training',[106] although
it had in mind, of course, the future 'prospect of benefit with reference
to the care of our soul':[107] 'We also in the same manner must first ... be
instructed by these outside [i.e., pagan] means and then shall understand
the sacred and mystical teachings [of Christianity]'. Stages in time were
clearly expressed.[108]

So Basil came to view the classics not as an alternative path to growth
but as part and parcel of a Christian's formation. The challenge was to
achieve a morally fruitful association 'with poets and writers of prose'.[109]
Could Christians continue to find a use for such texts? Could they
contribute to the moral programme Christians wished to set in place?
Were they, rather, doomed to extinction? To pose such questions, and to
answer them in the pagans' favour, scarcely reflected embarrassment at
the enduring force of the ancient culture.

So, as soon as the tension was hinted at—the tension between Scripture
as a natural source of Christian formation and the discipline whereby formation was achieved—it was conveniently forgotten. Basil was content to
discover and defend 'some affinity [οἰκειότης] between the two bodies of
teachings'.[110] He used the image of fruit and leaves on a tree: ancient culture was the 'not unlovely' covering that offered 'protection' to Christian
fruit. Moses had been informed by the 'learning of the Egyptians', Daniel
by the 'wisdom of the Chaldaeans'.[111] Such learning and wisdom were
available still: the tree, in that sense, endured. There was no question of

---

from the experience of others, as well as from his own wisdom, and can impart it to those
who come to him', C 2: 75, D 2: 371.

105. *Hom.* 343. 1, 340. 8.
106. Προγυμναζόμεθα: *Adul.* 2. 7; N, p. 86; tr. § 6, p. 383.
107. *Adul.* 2. 8, tr. § 7, p. 385.
108. Προτελεσθέντες and τηνικαῦτα: *Adul.* 2. 9; N, p. 86; tr. § 8, p. 385.
109. *Adul.* 2. 8, tr. § 7, p. 385: 'A contest, the greatest of all contests, lies before us'.
110. *Adul.* 3. 1; N, p. 88; tr. § 1, p. 385.
111. *Adul.* 3. 2–4; N, p. 88; tr. §§ 2–4, pp. 385/387. Wilson, *Value*, p. 45, suggests that
the image of protection came from Aristotle.

some inevitable historical process, whereby pagan values were displaced by the message of the Gospel: each generation entered with confidence the same enclave of instruction, resting secure in the shade of the older learning.[112]

Having made that point, Basil offered cautious praise to poets, remaining wary of the prose writer's inclination to entertain, and of the inevitable falsity of rhetors. What called for attention were 'the deeds or words of good men', whom we should 'cherish and emulate'. Imitation of another's virtue was the central task.[113] There was, however, a deceptive shift in his logic: 'Since it is through virtue that we must enter upon this life of ours, and since much has been uttered in praise of virtue by poets, much by historians, and much more still by philosophers, we ought especially to apply ourselves to such literature'.[114] The acceptability of the classics at this stage of the argument depended upon an altogether prior sense of what 'virtue' might mean. The student was recommended merely to discover examples, which would support a set of moral values already acquired elsewhere.

That recommendation reflected attitudes characteristic of Basil's pastoral years:

> If a man has sweated much for the learning of letters, if he has directed the government of nations and cities, and if he emulates the great virtue of his forefathers, I consider it right and proper that his life be placed before us as an example of virtue [εἰς ὑπόδειγμα ἀρετῆς].

There we hear the self-confidence of the *Ad adulescentes*. But Basil and his correspondent, in this case, were operating within a world of relationships that depended upon more than that sense of heritage:

> However, as regards your disposition towards your children, you need not now give evidence of it merely by word, ... for you have ... exhibited something more than that natural affection which even irrational creatures give to their offspring; but you should also intensify your love,

---

112. Compare the attitude in *Hom.* 350, discussed above, at n. 90. Wilson, *Value*, p. 45, points to the contrasting views of Josephus and Philo, for whom older learning was inevitably superior and not merely preparatory.

113. *Adul.* 4. 2, tr. § 1, p. 387, and indeed passim. I am not sure that we have to see this, therefore, as a totally negative chapter, pace Naldini, *Discorso*, p. 158: the notion of identifying and imitating virtue establishes a fundamental principle. Here, as elsewhere, we should take note of Ernest L. Fortin's reference, 'Christianity and Hellenism in Basil the Great's Address *Ad Adulescentes*', to Basil's deceitful use of his examples, harnessed as they were to an entirely Christian mode of thought. Wilson, *Value*, p. 48, offers useful reflections on Stoic criticisms, and on 'the persuasive effect of stylistic grace or charm'.

114. *Adul.* 5. 1, tr. § 1, p. 393.

deliberately, of course, in proportion as you see that they are worthy of a father's prayers.[115]

In that transition from στοργή to ἀγάπη, from 'natural affection' to Christian love, we move from the world of, say, Plutarch (evoked in the same letter) to an economy of formation governed more by the principles of the Gospel.

That seems to have been the case also in the *Ad adulescentes*. Yet central values shifted their position from first principles to ultimate goals. Basil identified, on the basis of examples, the major characteristics of virtue: it was the one possession that could not be taken away; and it brought one as close as was possible to divine perfection. The former emphasis owed much to Cynic and Stoic influence and is no surprise;[116] but the latter suggestion—in this work above all, with its caution that 'least of all shall we give attention to them when they narrate anything about the gods'—is quite remarkable.[117]

Basil had brought the human and the divine very close to one another: 'When Heracles was quite a young man and was nearly of the age at which you yourselves are now', Virtue, 'withered and squalid', with her 'intense look', 'promised nothing dissolute or pleasant, but countless sweating toils and labours and dangers through every land and sea. But the prize to be won by these was to become a god [θεὸν γενέσθαι]'. The confidence, of course, was that of Origen, and of a Christian tradition that had reinforced in its own terms the tentative optimism of the ancient sources.[118]

From that point on, it was not the authors quoted but Basil himself who dominated the text. With a deft snippet from the *Odyssey*, he espoused deeds above words (an emphasis fundamental to his whole pastorate).[119] He warned his readers against anger, but now entirely in the light of the Gospel:

> Since these examples tend to nearly the same end as our own precepts [ταῦτα σχεδὸν εἰς ταὐτὸν τοῖς ἡμετέροις φέροντα], I maintain that it is of great value for those of your age to imitate them. For this example

115. *Ep.* 24, C 1: 60, D 1: 147/149.
116. *Adul.* 5. 9. See Naldini, *Discorso*, pp. 178f.
117. *Adul.* 4. 5, tr. § 4, p. 389. See Wilson, *Value*, p. 55.
118. *Adul.* 5. 16; N, pp. 100/102; tr. § 14, p. 399. The story comes from Prodicus via Xenophon *Memorabilia* 2, 1. 21. My thanks to Vivienne Gray for useful comment. Note the judgement of Naldini, *Discorso*, p. 182: 'uno dei "temi gloriosi" della teologia cristiana d'Oriente'. Compare the vivid and characteristic phrase of Gregory of Nazianzus, θεοῦ τε κτίσμα τυγχάνων, καὶ θεὸς εἶναι κεκελευσμένος, *Orat.* 43. 48, *PG* 36. 560A.
119. *Adul.* 6 passim.

of Socrates [from Plutarch] is akin to that precept of ours—that to him
who strikes us on the cheek we should offer the other cheek also.[120]

Here was a scriptural allusion that readers were expected to know and
understand: in which case, it seems, the reference to Plutarch made sense
only because they already knew in what direction his teaching was moving.
Not much of the 'mysteries' there.[121]

Basil did make a halfhearted admission at one point that he had lost the
thread of his original argument: 'Let us return again to the same subject of
which we were speaking at the beginning: we ought not to take everything
without exception, but only such matter as is useful [ὅσα χρήσιμα]'.[122] The
decision as to what was useful would be governed, however, by the goal in
mind. The whole of the chapter following revolves around the notion that
moral action is specified by the end in view, and that those who aspire to
virtue will do everything necessary, endure every hardship and discipline,
in order to reach that end. Words like σκοπός (the target) and τέλος
(the consummation) dominate the argument and determine the μελέται,
the practical exercises, that would guarantee progress and attainment.
Now those methods may well have reflected traditional teaching, Stoic in
particular;[123] but, when it came to defining the goal itself, Basil produced
only assumptions, which owed little to the examples adduced from ancient
texts. As one reads on, the underlying bourdon of Christian thought
becomes more and more obvious. The importance of self-knowledge, the
need for inner purification, the ideal of a freedom that rises above the
enslavement of property and fame—all occurred again and again in the
mature teaching of Basil and sprang directly and easily from the Christian
Platonist tradition by which he was so directly influenced.[124]

He made one last, pathetic attempt to regain his original drift; but
deceits were laid bare even more: 'Although we Christians shall doubtless
learn all these things more thoroughly in our own literature, yet for the
present, at least, let us trace out a kind of rough sketch, as it were, of what
virtue is according to the teachings of the pagans'.[125] By this stage, surely,

---

120. *Adul.* 7. 7f.; N, p. 106; tr. § 7, p. 405. This is the world of *Ep.* 24, clearly: see above, at
n. 114.

121. See above, at n. 104.

122. *Adul.* 8. 1; N, p. 110; tr. § 1, p. 407.

123. See Naldini, *Discorso*, pp. 195f.; Wilson, *Value*, p. 60.

124. Self-knowledge, *Adul.* 9. 6; purification, 9. 7; freedom, 9. 2. These achievements
are not limited to an ascetic life, but considered the only worthy goal of any human, 9. 5f.
Note how Naldini, *Discorso*, pp. 204f., rescues Basil from an unbiblical distaste for the body.

125. *Adul.* 10. 1; N, p. 130; tr. § 1, pp. 429/431.

the main question in a reader's mind would be, why? All Basil could say was that one ought to draw knowledge from whatever source was offered. Yet the study of those texts that one might therefore peruse was to be conducted in conjunction with continuing guidance: 'Of the things which in my judgment are best, some I have told you at this time, while others I shall continue to recommend to you throughout my whole life'.[126] How simply he lifted the treatise onto the broader plane of his pastoral duty. His final word was that readers should continue to seek advice; that they should not content themselves, in other words, with handbooks like this as they browsed among the shelves of past achievements:

> Whereas those who suffer from slight ailments go of themselves to physicians, and those who are attacked by more serious diseases summon to their homes those who will treat them; yet those who have reached the stage of melancholy that is absolutely beyond remedy do not even admit physicians when they call. Pray do not become afflicted in this last-named manner, characteristic of the men of the present time [and he was not thinking just of pagans], by avoiding those whose reasoning is sound.[127]

The final impression is of a work in some fundamental way inconclusive. It is disorganized, in that its logic is often shifting, and more often set in abeyance. It is deceitful, in that the texts referred to are mere objects of plunder, superficially useful, and interpreted out of context. It is narrowly addressed, to those susceptible to its sleights of hand; hardly suitable as a general treatise for broader sectors of the Christian community. Most important, it contains nothing that would surprise us in the writings and addresses of Basil's later years.

So we have to conclude that Basil consistently rejected, probably from the earliest period following his departure from Athens, the claims of the traditional curriculum. And the impression given by the *Ad adulescentes* is no different from that conveyed by his other statements during those years. For him, the whole educational edifice had already been dismantled, like a neglected temple, and was to be recycled within the fabric of a Christian building. Only what he had unconsciously absorbed from his Christian reading was allowed to remain unchallenged in the suppositions of his text.[128] The allusions to the classics that we find scattered elsewhere in

126. *Adul.* 10. 8; N, pp. 132/134; tr. § 7, p. 433.
127. *Adul.* 10. 9; N, p. 134; tr. § 8, pp. 433/435.
128. For crucial reflections, see Naldini, *Discorso*, pp. 29–58. His phrase on p. 51 sums up the matter: 'tema già platonico e presente nella pedagogia origeniana secondo la prospettiva e l'interiorità neotestamentarie'.

his writings have to be regarded as superficial reminiscences, calculated merely to impress his more literary friends.

The context within which we may reliably assess Basil's relationship with a younger generation in need of educational guidance is beautifully displayed in an undated letter to two young men:

> It is fitting assuredly that fathers should provide for their children, and farmers should care for plants or seeds, and that teachers should be solicitous for their pupils, especially when through natural ability they show in themselves the hope of better things. . . . But the solicitude we have for you is by so much the greater, and the hope we have for you is by so much the higher, as religion is higher than every art [ὅσον εὐσέβεια πάσης μὲν τέχνης]. . . . This religion, which was by us emplanted in your souls while they were still tender and pure and there nurtured, we pray we may behold advanced to full maturity and to timely harvests, your love of learning being assisted by our prayers [συλλαμβανομένης ἡμῶν ταῖς εὐχαῖς τῆς ὑμετέρας φιλομαθίας]. For you know full well that both our goodwill towards you and the co-operation of God are stored away in your minds, and when these are directed towards the right, then God, called the Co-operator, will be present even though unbidden, and every lover of God likewise, ready of his own accord to give instruction [καὶ πᾶς φιλόθεος ἄνθρωπος πρὸς διδασκαλίαν αὐτεπάγγελτος].[129]

There could be no more vivid evocation of a Christian παιδεία.

We may add as a postscript some impressions gained from letters between Basil and his old master Libanius.[130] Let us start with a letter from the rhetor:

> When you returned and dwelt in your fatherland [so this was written after Basil left Athens], I said to myself: 'What is our Basil doing now, and to what mode of life has he turned? Is he frequenting the courts, emulating the orators of old? Or is he making orators of the sons of wealthy fathers?' But when there came persons bearing the tidings that you were traversing

129. Ep. 294, C 3: 168f., D 4: 203/205.
130. It has to be a postscript, because doubts are bound to remain about the authenticity of those letters, even though some seem more likely to be genuine than others. A summary of possibilities, to which I have adhered, is given by Fedwick, Basil, 1: 5 n. 19. See also Marius Bessières, La Tradition manuscrite de la correspondance de s. Basile, pp. 165f. Stig Y. Rudberg, Études sur la tradition manuscrite de saint Basile, p. 20, agrees that the letters numbered 335–346 in the Basil collection are probably genuine, and 357 and 359 possibly so. There is useful information in R. Cadiou, 'Le Problème des relations scolaires entre saint Basile et Libanios'.

ways of life far better than these, and that you were considering how you might become more pleasing to God [ὅπως ἂν γένοιο Θεῷ μᾶλλον φίλος] rather than how you could amass wealth, I congratulated both you and the Cappadocians.[131]

Wishing to become a friend of God suggests conversion of a sort, involving a move away from the scholastic and rhetorical settings of Constantinople, Athens, and Caesarea. Libanius did not suggest, however, and would not have supposed, that rejecting a legal or teaching career, or status and monetary advantage, would necessarily amount to a rejection of classical culture. He made the same point in a later letter, praising 'that which you esteem above eloquence [ὃ δὴ πρὸ τῶν λόγων ἐπαινεῖς]—sobriety and the refusal to give over our souls to ignoble pleasures'.[132] The admission that morality counted for more (transcending λόγοι in this special sense) was in no way a repudiation of the chief fruits of education as Libanius understood it.

Indeed, he resisted any attempt on Basil's part to suggest the contrary. In a possibly genuine letter,[133] Basil described the character of a sophist, 'the peculiar quality of whose art is, as all men agree, the ability both to make great things small, whenever he so wishes, and to invest small things with greatness', although there would be 'something indescribably delightful in the language'.[134] He intended a contrast with himself:

We associate with Moses and Elias and such blessed men, who communicate their thoughts to us in a barbarian tongue [ἐκ τῆς βαρβάρου φωνῆς διαλεγομένοις ἡμῖν τὰ ἑαυτῶν], and it is what we learn from them that we give utterance to—in substance true, though in style unlearned [νοῦν μὲν ἀληθῆ, λέξιν δὲ ἀμαθῆ], as indeed these present words show.[135]

Libanius would have none of that:

---

131. *Ep.* 336. 1, C 3: 203, D 4: 289.

132. *Ep.* 346, C 3: 212f., D 4: 313. Fedwick now judges this letter spurious, with arguments to appear; but I use it to make a corroborative rather than an additional point. Compare Libanius *Ep.* 742 concerning Pompeianus: 'a noble and just man, who in no way despised poverty [ὁ πενίαν οὐδαμοῦ δυσχεράνας], who honoured genuine eloquence and rejected its opposite [ὁ λόγους τοὺς μὲν γνησίους τιμῶν, τοὺς δ' οὐ τοιούτους ἐλέγχων]'. For the text, see the edition by R. Foerster, *Libanii opera* (Leipzig: Teubner, 1871; reprint, Hildesheim: Olms, 1963), 10: 670. He may have intended a contrast with Himerius: Barnes, 'Himerius', p. 212.

133. If we can accept as genuine what looks like Libanius's reply, then at least the general drift of our surviving text is likely to be authentic.

134. *Ep.* 339, C 3: 206, D 4: 297/299.

135. *Ep.* 339, C 3: 207, D 4: 299.

You have made also your present letter, of which you speak ill, so beautiful that those who were present with us could not refrain from leaping to their feet when it was being read.... It was not possible, I think, for you to wrong the truth. And it would have been wronged, had you purposely written more poorly than you did instead of making use of your powers.

He went on to conclude: 'Of that which has always been ours and was formerly yours the roots not only remain but will remain as long as you live, and no lapse of time could ever excise them, not even if you should almost wholly neglect to water them'.[136] We know that in practice Basil had to admit as much.

From Libanius's point of view, therefore (and, if the letters are genuine, we have to accept that point of view, surely, as representative of the educated pagan class), Basil, in the period immediately following his return to Asia Minor, was seen to have reinterpreted, or to have turned to best advantage, the impressions he had received in the course of his exposure to the traditional curriculum; but (again, from Libanius's point of view) he was not indulging in any total or traumatic repudiation of the past. We ourselves are well able to observe, from his correspondence in particular, how he maintained the polish expected of any student.

The question remains, however, was Libanius sufficiently perceptive in his judgement of Basil's purposes? He displayed a pagan but friendly attitude; and we are fortunate in possessing his 'alternative' impression of what a traditionally educated Christian might have looked like. But does Libanius provide us with an accurate account of the tensions and contrasts affecting the polished and learned expression of a biblical culture? He was not unaware that Basil's approach to education was coloured by experiences and influences more deeply seated than those he had encountered at Athens or Constantinople. Was he entitled to suggest, therefore, that the 'philosophical' explorations and experiments that followed were no more than the natural continuation of much that Basil had learned from people like himself?

Any statement made by an educated person was bound to be marked by the tone and facility of the pagan past. Yet what has startled us in Basil's case—indeed, what has aroused suspicion—is the apparent ease with which he supposed he might marry the two: the biblical message and the classical voice. Was it that simple to combine Christian loyalty and rhetorical skill? Even if we suppose that the ecclesial heritage counted

136. *Ep.* 340, C 3: 208, D 4: 301/303. In another letter (numbered in the Foerster edition *Ep.* 1544) to the newly consecrated bishop Optimus, he interpreted the episcopal office as a fresh opportunity for rhetorical display (especially in § 2, ed. Foerster, 11: 561f.).

for more in Basil's case than family ties, could every Christian from such a background view with the same equanimity the enduring presence of erudition, style, and wit, when one claimed to be a disciple of Moses and Elias? It is time to examine more critically the 'philosophic' pose that left Libanius so undisturbed.

· CHAPTER III ·

THE PHILOSOPHIC LIFE

When Basil left Athens for his homeland in the summer of 355, he was returning to familiar surroundings and opportunities. Given his success at Athens, his experience in Constantinople as a pupil of Libanius, and the obvious learning and intelligence that would emerge in his later work, there was no reason why he should not have sought for himself a career at the highest levels of the eastern empire. Yet he chose not to do so, going first to Caesarea, and then to the family estate in Pontus.

The return to Caesarea might have been seen as the fulfilment of at least some secular expectations. Any city that had sent a prominent son to great centres of learning might hope that he would return to teach his fellow citizens: 'When he had gathered all virtue and knowledge into his single soul, as a great merchant ship gathers all kinds of freight, he set out for his own city to share with others the fine wares of his learning'.[1] And more than one city might claim that honour and that duty. Basil admitted later that Neocaesarea had had its eye on him during those years: 'Your city invited us to take charge of the youths, and an embassy of your men, the magistrates, came to see us'.[2] In accepting such an invitation, Basil would have been following in his father's footsteps: as

---

1. So Gregory of Nazianzus, concerning his brother Caesarius, who did go on to make a fine career for himself in Constantinople, *Orat.* 7. 8, tr. p. 10. Gregory's admiration, however, has to be balanced by the strictures he expressed in his *Ep.* 7: see chapter 1, at nn. 61f. A rhetor's career, even in a small centre, was rich in rewards, not least because of the exemptions it carried from curial duty. See Jones, *LRE* 1: 745 and n. 77; 2: 998 and n. 29.

2. *Ep.* 210. 2, C 2: 190, D 3: 199.

we know, the senior Basil had fulfilled some teaching role of note in the city and had supervised Basil's earliest education.[3] The son had made his mark, however, in Caesarea also (perhaps after his father's death in the early 340s), in 'this illustrious city of ours ... not less the metropolis of letters than of the cities which she rules ... [whose] characteristic mark ... is letters'.[4] So, nearly ten years later, Basil himself began to add to its reputation.[5] Among his pupils, as we have seen, was almost certainly his brother Gregory; and there was some irony, given later events, in the fact that Basil may have been chiefly responsible for launching Gregory upon a secular career, which was to keep him away from many of the pursuits of his own family (Basil's eventually included) for nearly fifteen years.[6]

Then came a change: in 357 or 358, Basil returned to Pontus. At some stage during the year or so before, he had undertaken a journey around the eastern Mediterranean and had been baptized by Dianius, the bishop of Caesarea: two experiences we shall discuss more fully in a moment. Now, withdrawn somewhat from the world, he began to practise an ascetic life.

Here was another kind of homecoming: for he did so in the company of his family, at Annisa, where they owned land.[7] We should recall, however, the divisions within that family: Basil, we know, did not simply join

3. GNaz *Orat*. 43. 12. One cannot help recalling Eunapius's description of Aedesius: 'He was extremely well born, but his family was not possessed of great wealth, and therefore his father sent him away from Cappadocia to Greece to educate himself with a view to making money, thinking that he would find a treasure in his son. But on his return, when he discovered that he was inclined to philosophy he drove him out of his house as useless', *Lives* B 461 in W 377. Basil's father, of course, did not live to face such disappointment. See chapter 2, at n. 36.

4. GNaz *Orat*. 43. 13. Libanius wrote favourably of the city: πόλις εὐδαίμων καὶ λαμπρὰ καὶ τοῦ δύνασθαι λέγειν ἐπιμελουμένη, *Orat*. 16. 14. See *Libanius, Selected Works*, ed. A. F. Norman, vol. 1, *The Julianic Orations*, p. 218. This emphasis on cultural quality may seem unbalanced or eccentric; but an urban centre in the fourth century was 'a civilized nucleus which provided a place of residence for the few who could afford to live away from the soil and offered facilities of various sorts to the rest' (R. P. Duncan-Jones, 'City Population in Roman Africa', p. 85).

5. For the evidence, and remaining doubts, see chapter 2, at nn. 40, 60f.

6. GNaz *Orat*. 43. 13, and see chapter 1, at n. 23, with further reference to Daniélou, 'Mariage de Grégoire de Nysse'.

7. The most reliable account of location, superseding earlier opinions, is considered to be that given by G. De Jerphanion in *Mélanges de la Faculté Orientale, Beyrouth* 5, 1 (1911): 333–54. I have used the summary of his views provided, with additional reflections, by H. Leclercq, 'Ibora'. See also Maraval, *Vie*, pp. 39f. The conclusion is that Annisa is now Sonusa or Uluköy, near the confluence of the Yeçil Irmak (the Iris) and the Kelkit Çayi (the Lycos); and that the Ibora is now the Iverönü. While Basil's own ascetic retreat (vividly described in *Ep.* 14: see below at nn. 19f.) was clearly situated in a steep, wooded valley, of which many run down in this district towards the coast, Annisa was close also to fertile, plateau country immediately to the south, attractive and profitable to any aspiring landowner.

a group calmly united in its view of what asceticism might mean. The apparent dominance of Macrina, to whom Gregory of Nyssa would later attribute so much influence and subtlety of thought, was exerted chiefly over her mother and achieved its effect only slowly. To a lesser degree, the much younger Peter may also have been moved by her example and advice. Gregory himself, as we have seen, made a distinction between the more obviously ascetic members of the family and those whose education in particular had followed a traditional and secular path—Basil, Naucratius, and himself.[8] Not that Macrina's ideas and régime should be thought of by contrast as 'monastic'.[9] She was intent, for the most part, upon the rearrangement of family activities in accordance with quite traditional patterns of female household asceticism, in which domination over servants was to be particularly rejected.[10] The only explicit reference to a visible régime, in Gregory's account, is to 'constant prayer and an unceasing singing of hymns'.[11] Gregory himself, however, for all his written admiration, had little contact with Macrina at that stage, or indeed with anyone else at Annisa. His relations with his mother were strained; and he seems for many years to have had little to do with the place. Certainly there is no evidence, significantly enough, that Basil tried to attract him there.[12]

As for Naucratius, he was soon removed from the scene, meeting his death in a hunting accident.[13] (His asceticism had features of its own that we shall examine below.) As far as family unity was concerned, there are

8. *VMac.* 6, 8, 12: see chapter 1, at n. 7. Maraval, *Vie*, p. 31, warns against exaggeration. By the time of Socrates, the distinctions seemed clear: ἀλλὰ Πέτρος μὲν τὸν μονήρη βίον Βασιλείου ἐζήλωσε· Γρηγόριος δὲ τὸ διδασκαλικὸν τοῦ λόγου, *HE* 4. 26; *PG* 67. 533C/536A.

9. Maraval, *Vie*, pp. 50f. and 90f., may be too schematic. Note his admission, pp. 69f.

10. *VMac.* 7: 'entering into a common life with her maids, making them her sisters and equals rather than her slaves and underlings'; ed. Woods Callahan, pp. 377f.; tr. p. 167. Maraval, *Vie*, p. 53, notes the persistence of the 'maison familiale'.

11. *VMac.* 11; ed. Woods Callahan, p. 382, lines 15f.; tr. p. 171.

12. Aubineau, *Virginité*, pp. 40, 56f., discusses later contacts. Obviously Gregory knew something of Cappadocian monasticism generally, as we can detect in his *De virginitate* 23. 6: see Aubineau, pp. 58f. Note also his reference to the large number of θυσιαστήρια in Cappadocia, *Ep.* 2. 9; ed. Pasquali, p. 16. But he was never formally involved in monasticism himself: May, 'Chronologie', pp. 62f., arguing against Daniélou, 'Mariage de Grégoire de Nysse', among others. Phrases in his *Ep.* 14—e.g., ἡμῖν συντυχεῖν—are too vague to imply a stay at Annisa like that of Gregory of Nazianzus. Nor did he go there during his exile: May, p. 54. But he certainly seems to have retained close contact with his brother Peter, after the death of Basil and Macrina: see the admiration expressed in *VMac.* 12; ed. Woods Callahan, pp. 383f.; tr. p. 172; and May, p. 57.

13. For Naucratius's way of life, see chapter 1, at n. 29. He was killed in the company of a servant, Chrysaphius, *VMac.* 9; ed. Woods Callahan, pp. 379f.; tr. p.169.

signs, for what they are worth, that Macrina and the young Peter did more to warm their mother's heart than Basil ever could.[14]

Nothing can disguise the fact that Basil kept his distance from all of them while in Pontus, living alone on the other side of the river.[15] There is no particular evidence that he had any influence in a reverse direction on Macrina's régime.[16] Gregory, his brother, in spite of his insistence on Macrina's importance, gave also the impression that Basil led an isolated life: 'He withdrew from the worldly show and began to look down upon acclaim through oratory and went over to this life full of labours for one's own hand to perform, providing for himself, through his complete poverty, a mode of living that would, without impediment, lead to virtue'.[17] It may not be entirely insignificant either that, once he had decided to embrace a public role in the church in 365, he rarely returned to that family group—perhaps no more than once.[18]

In the accounts dating from the period, we find far more evidence of association with people outside the family. Predominant, of course, was Gregory of Nazianzus. Letters between the two friends reflect a fair degree of initiative on Basil's part, and some hesitation on Gregory's. It is clear that Basil had begun his experiments in Pontus before Gregory finally returned from Greece, and that he tried to persuade Gregory to join him. It

14. *VMac.* 13; ed. Woods Callahan, pp. 384f.; tr. pp. 172f. See GNaz *Ep.* 5 for an account of Basil's mother rescuing him and his friend from their domestic ineptitudes.

15. He does mention, in his *Ep.* 223. 5, that he spent some 'days [πόσας δὲ ἡμέρας]' in his mother's company, when visited by Eustathius, C 3: 14 (in the apparatus), D 3: 303. The *Life of Macrina* is vague as to how far his mother had adopted an ascetic life by then: see tr. Woods Callahan, p. 167, for the period before Basil's arrival; a more definitive commitment, p. 168, appears to have come after, and Emmelia could still be described, even then, as 'rather worldly'. It is not clear what significance we should attach to the phrase 'in the village opposite [ἐπὶ τῆς ἀντιπέραν κώμης]' as a clue to Emmelia's whereabouts, tr. Woods Callahan, p. 168. See n. 7 above for the physical context. Further details will be discussed below.

16. Our impression in that regard will be governed in part by the degree of organization we think characteristic of Basil at the time—a matter to be pursued in chapter 6. The reflections of Maraval, *Vie*, pp. 54, 68f., are helpful meanwhile; and we should not imagine that Basil was any more organized.

17. *VMac.* 6; ed. Woods Callahan, p. 377, lines 15–19; tr. pp. 167f.; a passage already referred to in chapter 2, at n. 1.

18. *Ep.* 210 seems to have been written from the region in the middle of 376. Basil may have made two journeys in that year; but *Ep.* 216 and 217 must refer to the same occasions—'We also went as far as the little hermitage [τοῦ οἰκιδίου] of our brother ['Peter' does not appear in Courtonne's Greek]', C 2: 208, D 3: 239; and 'to visit relatives [τῶν ἐπιτηδείων]', C 2: 208, D 3: 241. The phraseology of *Ep.* 210. 1 itself may imply that such opportunities occurred rarely—'a brief breathing spell [βραχείας ἀναπνοῆς]', C 2: 190, D 3: 197. The only other possible occasion was during Basil's visit to Armenia in 373. See Benoît Gain, *L'Église de Cappadoce au IVᵉ siècle d'après la correspondance de Basile de Césarée*, p. 395.

is also clear that Gregory made two separate journeys to Basil's retreat. It is not so easy to interrelate the surviving letters with events in Gregory's life. His father was still alive when he returned, and bishop of Nazianzus. In a sense, Gregory had a forum ready made for his endeavours. Yet he does not seem to have identified or seized his opportunities with any degree of confidence. Eventually his father ordained him a priest, more or less forcibly, to help him in his pastoral tasks, now that he was an old man. Gregory was seized with grave doubts about his suitability for that task and sought refuge with Basil for a while; but he eventually went back to his home town and fulfilled the role chosen for him by his family and his fellow citizens.

It is worth surveying the letters that survive, in order to see how they relate to those events. We have two letters from Basil to Gregory: the first describes in idyllic terms his newfound retreat; the second is a longer and more theoretical account of his ascetic ambitions.[19] It is possible that the second letter was an attempt on Basil's part to explain himself more seriously, having heard from Gregory in response to the first. That would allow us to propose further that some surviving letters from Gregory to Basil were replies to the first of the pair we have mentioned. Three of Gregory's letters appear to fill the bill, openly poking fun at the eager harshness of Basil's life, although the last of the three becomes more serious.[20] The only trouble is that Gregory had clearly by that time been to Pontus; and Basil's second letter seems an oddly formal piece to send to someone who had recently shared with the writer the life it attempted to describe. Basil admitted that Gregory had yet to decide 'to live with us'; but he may have meant permanently, and he assumed also that any such decision by Gregory would be based on a knowledge of 'the nature of our surroundings'.[21] Nor is it entirely clear when Gregory's three letters were written. He agreed

---

19. *Ep.* 14 and 2, almost certainly written in that order. Another letter to Gregory, *Ep.* 19, is probably from this period, but too short and vague to tell us very much. (Fedwick, *Basil*, 1: 8 is happy to follow Courtonne in suggesting that it was written after Basil's ordination, but before his final settlement in Caesarea.) An edition of *Ep.* 2 is printed in Rudberg, *Études*. Basil's ability to wax eloquent about physical settings should not be underestimated: for two striking examples, which could easily refer to scenes in his native province, see *Hexaemeron* [henceforward *Hex.*] 2. 3; 4. 6. Full bibliographical details of this work are provided at the beginning of chapter 9.

20. GNaz *Ep.* 4, 5, and 6.

21. *Ep.* 2. 1, C 1: 5, D 1: 7.

on an earlier occasion that he had yet to keep a promise made in Athens to join Basil in the 'philosophic life'; and he referred to his obligations to relatives.[22] His next surviving letter implied that Basil was in Caesarea, involved in the pursuit of wealth and with public affairs (τρυφᾶτε δὲ καὶ πλουτεῖτε καὶ ἀγοράζετε).[23] That might suggest that both those earlier letters were written before Basil had gone to Pontus at all. Yet Gregory's chief modern biographer would date all the correspondence to 361 (both the earlier two letters and the three that do refer to the Pontus retreat).[24] That seems unacceptable, particularly since it brings the exchange of letters concerning Basil's ascetic experiments uncomfortably close to the period when both friends were considering ordination to the priesthood. Later letters from Gregory discuss that matter, as we shall see, in a new and obviously subsequent tone: the philosophic ideal had now become problematic, and Gregory had decided to accept the alternative responsibility, exhorting Basil to follow his example, return to Caesarea, and settle his differences with the bishop Eusebius (which we shall discuss below).[25]

These confusions and apparent incompatibilities are important, because we need to know how we should space out the references to events in Pontus, and how we should relate them to the more pastoral involvements of both men in Caesarea and Nazianzus. The following suggestions seem the most tenable.[26] Basil returned from Greece, taught briefly in Caesarea, travelled in the East, went back for a short while to Caesarea, and then decided to withdraw to Pontus. He invited Gregory, in a letter we do not possess, to join him (Gregory by this time having returned from Greece also). Gregory wrote his first two surviving letters, in effect refusing. (His next letter shows that he had decided to teach in some capacity.) Those letters must date from 357 or early 358. From Annisa, Basil then wrote the two letters we have mentioned (14 and 2), and Gregory eventually agreed to come. During their period together, the two men composed the *Philocalia*, and then Gregory decided to go back to his family. From Nazianzus, he wrote the three letters that described and commented upon the régime they had followed in Pontus. We should probably date those letters to 359: certainly well before Basil's ordination, and probably before a visit he made to Constantinople at the end of that year.[27] Basil was

22. GNaz *Ep.* 1. 1; ed. Gallay, 1: 1.
23. GNaz *Ep.* 2. 3; ed. Gallay, 1: 2.
24. So Gallay, followed by Ruether, *Gregory*, p. 29.
25. GNaz *Ep.* 8 and 19.
26. They are largely those repeated in Fedwick, *Basil*, 1.
27. He went to attend a church synod; and we shall discuss the circumstances fully in chapter 4, at nn. 8f.

then ordained a reader and returned to Pontus; Gregory was ordained a priest by his father, probably early in 362, and took temporary and brief refuge with Basil (for three months or so at the most). Basil was also ordained a priest during 362 (and we shall discuss to what extent Gregory's experience affected his attitude); but he settled in Pontus yet again, following an argument with the new bishop of Caesarea, Eusebius. It was during this second period of withdrawal that Gregory wrote other letters to Basil, reflecting on the significance of their priestly ordination, and discussing how it might be reconciled with their continuing pursuit of philosophy. In the end, he felt able—even obliged—to invite Basil more urgently to accept broader ecclesiastical responsibilities. This correspondence we may date more naturally to 364 or so: closer to the time, in 365, when Basil did finally return to Caesarea, after an absence of some eighteen months.[28]

The synopsis reveals several things. First, Basil's ascetic experiments in Pontus were constantly interrupted by what we might call ecclesial affairs. The interplay between them will demand more attention in a moment. Second, Gregory of Nazianzus was much less assured in his attachment to the philosophic life (as Basil currently interpreted it) and made up his mind to undertake a public career in the Church sooner than his friend. Third, Basil's two letters to Gregory and Gregory's three 'Pontus-related' letters in reply all date from the period before their ordinations. They provide, therefore, some impression of a period in their lives, albeit short, when they had a settled and shared idea of the Christian régime they wished to adopt. Perhaps at no other time were their feelings for one another so strong, recapturing something of their mutual regard and dependence in Athens, but giving it the intensity of a shared isolation. Many years later, wishing 'to honour an old friendship, to revere virtue, and to sympathize with those who labour', Basil interceded with the powerful on Gregory's behalf (in relation to difficulties Gregory had over his recently deceased brother's property); and he included the following revealing observations:

> It is an intolerable calamity that one so disinclined by nature or desire should be compelled to plead in cases at law, and that one vowed to

---

28. These are, once again, GNaz Ep. 8 and 19. Ep. 16, 17, and 18, addressed to Eusebius himself, have much to say on the same matter. Gregory may have been responding to a visit to Caesarea by Valens in 365, during which Eusebius was subjected to theological debate with Homoean churchmen in the emperor's entourage, and his inadequacy (in Gregory's eyes) was laid bare. See Hanns Christof Brennecke, *Studien zur Geschichte der Homöer*, pp. 212f., and chapter 5, at n. 8. Brennecke's work will be assessed more fully in chapters 4, 5, and 8.

poverty should be dunned for money, and that one who long ago deter-
mined to pass his life in seclusion should be dragged into the open and be
practised upon by demagogues.[29]

Gregory, for his part, in spite of later disagreements, long regarded Basil
as the person closest to him in his way of life, his teaching, and his high
philosophical ideals.[30]

<hr>

Among the many insights that this correspondence supplies, perhaps
the most instructive concerns the species of dependence and leadership
involved. From a distance of decades, the historians Socrates and Sozomen
thought they had a clear picture of what the two friends were attempting
to achieve. Both suggested that Basil founded ascetic communities of some
sort (ἀσκητήρια in Socrates, συνοικίας τε μοναχῶν πολλάς in Sozomen),
and that he did so as a teacher, intent not least on counteracting the
influence of Arians.[31] That would be to conflate too much the shifting
enthusiasms of Basil's long ascetic and pastoral career. Yet it does seem
possible that Basil quickly adopted, in the philosophic life as much as in the
teaching of rhetoric, the role of a master. Moreover, he influenced people
other than Gregory. His own brother, in the preface to his De virginitate,
described Basil as being 'the only one capable of teaching [παιδεύειν] such
things'.[32] Basil himself, rejecting later accusations brought against him at
Neocaesarea, wrote:

> We are being accused because we have men practised in piety [τῆς
> εὐσεβείας ἀσκητάς], who have withdrawn from the world [ἀποταξαμέ-
> νους τῷ κόσμῳ] and all earthly cares.[33] . . . I would count it worth my
> whole life to have these as my faults, and to have men with me and under

29. Ep. 33, C 1: 76, D 1: 185. The significance of the sentiment is not affected by doubts
over the dating of this letter and of the one preceding (to Sophronius). Fedwick, Basil, 1: 13f.,
is adamant that Gregory was by that time a bishop, as the texts can be taken to imply. The
phrases quoted, however, and the absence of any of the antagonism that arose over Gregory's
consecration to Sasima in 371, make it difficult to accept. On the other hand, Gregory was
able to enjoy periods of 'seclusion' after that time. See Ruether, Gregory, pp. 35–41.

30. GNaz Ep. 16. 4. Orat. 43 gives the same impression. In Ep. 58. 4, he admitted an
uninterrupted connection between their friendship at Athens and their more general and
lasting harmony of mind.

31. Note especially the use of ταῖς αὐτοῦ διδασκαλίαις in Socrates HE 4. 26, PG 67.
532A; and of τὰ πλήθη διδάσκων in Sozomen HE 6. 15, line 4; ed. Bidez, p. 258, lines 21f.

32. GNyss De virginitate, Preface, 2. 18–20; ed. Aubineau, p. 250; and see p. 31.

33. The vagueness of the vocabulary is arresting—in 376.

me as teacher [παρ' ἐμαυτῷ, ὑπ' ἐμοὶ διδασκάλῳ] who have chosen this life of asceticism.[34]

In a later account of those early years, Basil alluded to the same type of relationship:

Were not the most faithful of your disciples [τῶν σῶν μαθητῶν οἱ γνη-σιώτατοι—he was addressing Eustathius] in my presence the whole time? While visiting the brotherhoods [τὰς ἀδελφότητας ἐπισκεπτόμενος], and spending whole nights with them in prayer, always speaking and hearing opinions about God without contention, did I not furnish precise proofs of my own mind?[35]

It may not be wise to attach too formal a meaning to ἐπισκεπτόμενος; it is clear, moreover, that Basil was talking about Eustathius's disciples, not his own; and 'speaking and hearing opinions about God [λέγων καὶ ἀκούων ἀεὶ τὰ περὶ Θεοῦ]' does not necessarily suggest the activities of a teacher. Basil, in this letter, was more intent upon listing witnesses to his orthodoxy. However, Gregory of Nazianzus certainly mentioned other ascetics in the district (referring to the late 350s). In his more jocular letters, he made fun of the pretentious names that sprang to mind for their settlement: a place for thought, for solitude, and for the leisure that indispensably accompanied instruction (τοῦ φροντιστηρίου τε καὶ τοῦ μοναστηρίου καὶ τῆς σχολῆς).[36] He did not refer in the same breath to others who might have benefitted from such arrangements—indeed, he said that only hunters came near (although that, again, was part of the jest), and, in the letter following, that he and Basil coped rather badly on their own.[37] But when his tone became more serious, he mentioned explicitly 'brothers' who took their cue in the spiritual life from Basil himself (τίς ἀδελφῶν συμφυΐαν καὶ συμψυχίαν τῶν ὑπὸ σοῦ θεουμένων καὶ ὑψουμένων [sc. δώσει]); and he referred to the way in which the two of them were able to confirm in writing the pursuit of virtue—by 'written rules and regulations [ἣν ὅροις γραπτοῖς καὶ κανόσιν ἠσφαλισάμεθα]'.[38] Here, then,

34. *Ep.* 207. 2, C 2: 185, D 3: 185.
35. *Ep.* 223. 5, C 3: 14, D 3: 303/305. In relation to the point that follows, one should note that C gives only ἐπισκεπτόμενος, while D notes also ἐπιπορευόμενος in one MS—namely, Parisinus 1020 S. This last belongs to what Bessières, *Tradition manuscrite*, pp. 94f., called his BX family, which is marked by oddities but reaches back to the roots of the tradition. As a translator, C conforms to D with 'visiter', 3: 14.
36. GNaz *Ep.* 4. 3; ed. Gallay, 1: 3f.
37. *Ep.* 4. 5 and *Ep.* 5.
38. GNaz *Ep.* 6. 37; ed. Gallay, 1: 7. Note that *both* of them are described as writing in this way.

is slight evidence for association with and leadership of others. It reminds us that the solitude sought for was more from secular life than from human company as such. Even so, it would be dangerous to anticipate, and to see in this earliest period a clear step towards the establishment of formal monasticism, whether in organization or in legislation.[39]

The most we can suppose so far, then, is that Basil decided to pursue a more philosophic life on his family estate, where he inevitably had some association with members of his family, although not as close as one might suppose; that he attempted to attract the companionship of his old friend, but of no one else in particular; that he made some contact with disciples of Eustathius of Sebaste; and that he began to exert some slight influence of his own and took the first steps towards supplying written recommendations. Of the latter, his second letter to Gregory may well be an early example.

In all this, of course, Basil was moving in a well-established tradition. The very word 'philosophy' would have conjured up, for even the most traditionally educated person with pretentions to moral seriousness, exactly the kind of life Basil now proposed.[40] We have seen how Libanius

39. The whole matter will be discussed in detail in chapter 6. I view with caution the more precise confidence of Léon Lèbe, 'S. Basile: Note à propos des règles monastiques'. Nor can I detect in Basil's activities at this time 'la lutte aux côtés du prolétariat', which assumes too close an association between his own admirers and the disciples of Eustathius ('des pauvres et des sans-culture, . . . des marginaux, des cyniques, craints et méprisés') and reads back into this stage of Basil's life the charitable work later undertaken in Caesarea: Jean Gribomont, 'Un Aristocrate révolutionnaire, évêque et moine: S. Basile', pp. 183f.

40. Here we shall avoid a bibliography of all ancient culture. Much of relevance has been discussed in chapter 2, particularly in regard to Eunapius: see especially n. 4 and, more generally, n. 3. Philostratus's *Life of Apollonius of Tyana* and Iamblichus's *Life of Pythagoras* maintained the tradition. Useful points are made by Patricia L. Cox, *Biography in Late Antiquity: A Quest for the Holy Man*. Even more helpful is A.-M. Malingrey, '*Philosophia*': *Étude d'un groupe de mots dans la littérature grecque, des Présocratiques au IVe siècle après J.-C.* For Christian anxieties, see Marguerite Forrat's introduction to *Eusèbe de Césarée: Contre Hiéroclès*, edited by Édouard Des Places. Averil Cameron stresses the importance of a shared vocabulary, in ethics as in other matters, which enabled persuasion to gain its effect across the barrier between pagan and Christian, 'reaching into existing cultural territory', *Rhetoric of Empire*, p. 132; and see p. 41. Valuable also are the observations of Whittaker, 'Christianity and Morality', pp. 212f. In the specific matter of asceticism, Anthony Meredith, 'Asceticism— Christian and Greek', pp. 312–32, has important points to make. In particular, he defends the 'philosophical' nature of Basil's régime at this date—'philosophical' being understood in a sense proper to the broader ethical traditions of classical antiquity, p. 323.

regarded his retreat to Pontus as a continuation of his attachment to culture, rather than as an alternative to it.[41] Gregory of Nazianzus (who, together with Gregory of Nyssa, used the term φιλοσοφία much more frequently and consistently than did Basil) affirmed the same associations in a letter to the other great rhetor of the day, Themistius—referring to him as both 'the king of letters' and 'a man particularly deserving the title of philosopher'; 'a man of philosophic inclination', who would appreciate Plato's ideal of a marriage between reflection and power.[42]

There was also, in Basil's Pontic retreat, a touch of aristocratic ease, traditionally associated with reflection amid the amenities of one's own estate. For all his high moral tone, Basil was well able to conjure up that heritage also, when it suited him, or when it matched what he took to be the prejudices of his audience.[43] Writing from Pontus to the influential Candidianus, he congratulated him on a certain philosophic retirement of his own—'as Plato says, in a very "storm and surge" of affairs you "withdraw under the shelter of a strong wall", as it were, and contaminate your soul by no disturbance'[44]—and suggested with some flattery that his own 'tranquillity [ἄπραγμον, a precise equivalent of the Latin otium] can only be preserved by my being placed under your efficient protection'. The purpose of the letter is equally revealing. One of Basil's servants had died;[45] and

> a boorish fellow of our community [ἀνήρ τις ἄγροικος τῶν συνοικούντων ἡμῖν: he had some legal claim against the dead man] ... of a sudden, with certain desperadoes like himself, attacked my house, beat and pounded the women-servants who guarded it [τά τε γύναια τὰ φυλάττοντα], then broke down the doors, and carried off everything.[46]

41. Libanius Ep. 336. See chapter 2, nn. 130f.

42. GNaz Ep. 24. 1f.; ed. Gallay, 1: 32.

43. See his Ep. 14, for reference to 'the guests who join me in hunting', C 1: 44, D 1: 111—which recalls the misfortunes of Naucratius: see n. 13 above. Other evidence of family wealth and status has been discussed in chapter 1, at nn. 6f. Gregory of Nyssa described how, much later, Peter was able to relieve local famine from the resources of the family estate, VMac. 12; ed. Woods Callahan, p. 384, lines 14f.; tr. p. 172.

44. The reference is to Plato Republic, 6, 10 (496D): ζάλην τὰ παρόντα ἐνόμιζον καὶ πέτραν τινὰ ἐζήτουν ἢ κρημνὸν ἢ τειχίον, ὑφ' οἷς σκεπασθήσομαι. Both Themistius (Orat. 8, 104c; 24, 308a; 26, 326b) and Gregory of Nazianzus (Orat. 5, at PG 35. 534C) referred to the same passage. For Themistius, see Themistii orationes quae supersunt, edited by Heinrich Schenkl and Glanville Downey.

45. So, with Deferrari, I take the phrase οἰκέτου μου τελευτήσαντος.

46. Ep. 3. 2, C 1: 14, D 1: 27/29. The extract also shows that Basil could be embroiled in quite complex financial and legal relationships with such dependents. For Candidianus, see also GNaz Ep. 10.

Here we have not only a shared sense of privileged ease but also the picture of a household fully endowed with servants and property. (The letter probably dates from Basil's second period in Pontus, during and after 363.) There were plenty in his circle, then and later, who would have taken his circumstances for granted. Terentius, for example, after four years or so as *comes* and *dux* in Armenia, had retired from public affairs and had then been brought back to attend to matters in Antioch. Basil lamented at once: 'We were immediately disturbed (for the truth will be told), considering how contrary to your inclination it is, when once you had given up public affairs and had devoted yourself to the concerns of your own soul, to be compelled to return again to the same matters'.[47]

Similar points might be made about Basil's earlier travels in the East, undertaken before he decided to make use of the opportunities of the Pontus estate. Many with the time and money (for it was an adventure open chiefly to the élite) travelled at that time to the holy places of Palestine, which had been developed as centres of pilgrimage by the patronage and enthusiasm of Constantine. Their curiosity and privilege drew them also in the process to the developing centres of ascetic experiment in Egypt and Syria.[48]

Yet such a custom had ancient roots. A desire to travel in search of moral inspiration had motivated many a pagan long before and is illustrated for us in texts of the Pythagorean tradition and in the classical novel.[49]

There were specifically Christian features in Basil's experience, however, that call for closer attention. First, where did he go? The 'voyages' referred to by Gregory of Nazianzus appear to be catalogued in Basil's first surviving letter.[50] He described how he moved from Athens, past

47. *Ep.* 214. 1, C 2: 202, D 3: 227. Points made in chapter 2 have some relevance here, at nn. 64f.

48. For an admirable introduction, see E. D. Hunt, *Holy Land Pilgrimage in the Later Roman Empire, A.D. 312–460*; more recently, Peter W. L. Walker, *Holy City, Holy Places: Christian Attitudes to Jerusalem and the Holy Land in the Fourth Century A.D.* Maraval, *Vie*, p. 54 n. 3 gives some late evidence.

49. One thinks in particular of the journeys of Apollonius of Tyana, recounted in the *vita* by Philostratus. See n. 40 above; and Ewen Lyall Bowie, 'Apollonius of Tyana: Tradition and Reality'. Some impression of the complexity of the subject, and of the interconnections that have to be made, is excellently presented in compact form by John Matthews, 'Hostages, Philosophers, Pilgrims, and the Diffusion of Ideas in the Late Roman Mediterranean and Near East'. The theme takes on a Christian form most notably in the religious biographies produced by Jerome: see J. N. D. Kelly, *Jerome, His Life, Writings, and Controversies*, pp. 170f.; and Philip Rousseau, *Ascetics, Authority, and the Church in the Age of Jerome and Cassian*, pp. 133f.

50. GNaz *Orat.* 43. 25.

Constantinople, probably to Caesarea, then to 'Syria' and 'Egypt', where he remained at the time of writing (in Alexandria), intending to return home after some unspecified interlude.[51] The references and time frame are vague enough, although we know from his involvement in other events that the journey must have taken place over a period of a year or so during 356 and 357. Many years later, writing to Eustathius, he was slightly more explicit, making it apparent then that he had studied ascetic régimes in Coele-Syria, Palestine, Mesopotamia, and Egypt beyond Alexandria.[52] He produced virtually the same list of places in a contemporary letter to Neocaesarea.[53] We have no reason to doubt, therefore, that a study of the famous holy men of the East had been one motive for his journey, as well as the natural feeling that travel would be a philosophical instruction—he wished, no doubt, for his own sake too, 'to have seen the cities of many men and to have learned their minds'.[54] Yet he added: 'What superiority is there in seeing many men one by one over seeing one single person who has taken to himself the experience of all mankind?'[55] And what makes the question of moment is that, in that first surviving letter, he gives as the only motive for his journey a desire to follow the 'Eustathius' to whom the letter is addressed. Here, perhaps, was the 'single person' he had in mind; and there are sound reasons for supposing that it was indeed Eustathius of Sebaste.[56] Later on, when relations between them were strained, and Eustathius's earlier influence had become (in Basil's

51. *Ep.* 1.
52. *Ep.* 223. 2.
53. *Ep.* 207. 2; but he uses the odd word ἀκούω—'I hear that in Egypt there exists . . .', C 2: 185, D 3: 185. Jean Gribomont, *Histoire du texte des Ascétiques de s. Basile*, p. 86, was quite certain that Basil and the ascetics of Egypt knew nothing of one another. That led him to be critical of both W. K. Lowther Clarke, *St. Basil the Great: A Study in Monasticism*, and Amand de Mendieta, *Ascèse*. Amand de Mendieta, pp. 38f., was certainly quite mistaken in the connections he made between Basil and Pachomius: see Jean Gribomont, 'Saint Basile', p. 111. Clarke, pp. 116f., was also misled, though with some delicious anachronisms: 'It is hardly to be expected that a man of aristocratic family, fresh from a brilliant University career, and conversant with the ideals of European civilisation and culture, should wish to set up in his native land an exact reproduction of the life led by Egyptian peasants', p. 43. Fedwick, *Charisma*, pp. 23, 156f., has inherited the illusions. I retain the misgivings expressed in my *Pachomius: The Making of a Community in Fourth-Century Egypt.*, p. 77 n. 1. Insufficient attention has been paid to the fact that both Basil and Eustathius spent time in Syria and districts to the east, exploring a world brilliantly revealed to us in the early sections of Theodoret's *Historia religiosa*. Much that Theodoret described, made infamous by extreme and at times bizarre self-abnegation, alluded also to coenobitic organization, lay patronage, and episcopal control.
54. *Ep.* 74. 1, C 1: 172, D 2: 69. See chapter 2, n. 66.
55. *Ep.* 74. 1, C 1: 172, D 2: 69.
56. Gribomont, 'Eustathe le philosophe'.

eyes) tainted by heresy, he was less ready to put his former mentor in the centre of the picture. In 356, however, Basil may have regarded Eustathius in ways he later hoped a young protégé of his own would regard him: as 'someone to lead us by the hand and escort us safely over the briny billows of life', 'a great and experienced teacher'.[57] Those were exactly the phrases he recalled when he expressed his ultimately disappointed hopes in Eustathius: 'I prayed that there might be given me a guidance to the introduction to the teachings of religion. . . . I prayed that I might find some one of the brethren who had taken this way of life, so as to traverse with him this life's brief flood'.[58]

What did the influence of Eustathius represent? By the time Basil pursued him through the eastern provinces, Eustathius was already a bishop.[59] That matters enormously, for several reasons. First, the 'guide' that Basil had in his sights was not some heroic athlete of the desert but a man with pastoral responsibilities and a public reputation. Second, Eustathius's views on asceticism were no longer those for which he had originally been both famous and suspect. Third, he now wished in particular to incorporate the ascetic régime more obviously into the life of the Church as a whole.

Eustathius had long been involved, and in controversial ways, with the development of the ascetic life. We first hear of him as having been rebuked by his father, the bishop Eulalius, for dressing in a way unfitting for a cleric—the assumption being that Eustathius was already adopting an ascetic pose, not least in critical contrast to more generally accepted mores among the clergy. A fuller background is then provided in the canons of a council held at Gangra (perhaps as late as the mid-350s), which was concerned to counter the excesses of some of those associated with Eustathius. Most notable among those excesses were criticism of marriage and reluctance to celebrate the sacraments in churches. The

---

57. *Ep.* 150. 1, C 2: 71f., D 2: 363, addressed to Amphilocius. This letter was written just as Basil was beginning to fall out with Eustathius, and illustrates usefully an important moment of change in his status, from disciple to master. An edition of the text is printed also in Rudberg, *Études.*

58. *Ep.* 223. 2, C 3: 10, D 3: 293. The translation preserves both references to the sea but obscures slightly the parallel τοῦ χειραγωγήσαντος ἡμᾶς (*Ep.* 150) / χειραγωγίαν (*Ep.* 223).

59. For full accounts of Eustathius's life, see Jean Gribomont, 'Eustathe de Sébaste', *Dictionnaire de spiritualité,* vol. 4, pt. 2, cols. 1708–12, and 'Eustathe de Sébaste', *Dictionnaire d'histoire et de géographie ecclésiastiques,* vol. 16, cols. 26–33. More generally: F. Loofs, *Eustathius von Sebaste und die Chronologie der Basilius-Briefe: Eine patristische Studie;* and Giet, *Idées,* pp. 210f. Also helpful is Charles A. Frazee, 'Anatolian Asceticism in the Fourth Century: Eustathios of Sebastea and Basil of Caesarea'. Eustathius was certainly consecrated by 356. He will recur in chapter 4.

bishops were faced not just with an ascetic movement as such but with a zealous reform of the Church, regarded by the 'Eustathians' as too lax and grandiose, thanks to the influence of imperial toleration and patronage.[60] Eustathius himself, however, accepted the council's criticisms with humility and continued to pursue a career within the mainstream Church.[61] He gained in the process admiration for his personal sanctity and continued to exert a spiritual influence on religious enthusiasts; but an increasing gulf opened between himself and some who clung to more radical ideals—particularly his early disciple Aerius, who found it too restricting to work under Eustathius as bishop and reverted to a life in wilder country, marked by antagonism towards the clergy, towards too hierarchical a notion of church order, and towards growing emphasis on the cult of the dead pursued (in Aerius's eyes) at the expense of the living. Eustathius, by contrast, though judged eventually by some to have been unsound in his theology, continued to lead a life of undoubtedly acceptable virtue.[62]

Such was the model whom Basil had heard of already at Athens (perhaps Macrina had told him).[63] Such was the man he followed through the East (at the moment when Eustathius himself was establishing a clearer relationship between his ascetic ideals and his more formal responsibilities within the Church).[64] Such was the man who visited Basil at Annisa, and with whose disciples Basil happily mixed.[65] We are talking about a bishop; about a man who was also in the process of modifying his religious views, while maintaining a reforming spirit; about a man, above all, who wished to make the Church as much a force for social change as for cultic enthusiasm, and who certainly wished to inject into Christian experience a degree of moral seriousness that would affect public life as well as personal development.

Association, on Basil's part, with someone of that inclination places the whole of the 'Annisa period' in a much broader context and makes Basil's

---

60. See T. D. Barnes, 'The Date of the Council of Gangra'. He admits that the exact date is probably 'undiscoverable', p. 121, although he would opt for 355, p. 124; the chief point being that a date in the early 340s is not *demanded*. For the decisions of the council, see Carl Joseph Hefele, *Histoire des conciles*, tr. H. Leclercq, vol. 1, pt. 2, pp. 1029–45.

61. A point made clear by Sozomen *HE* 3. 14. See also his account in 4. 24f.

62. For a jaundiced but detailed account, to add to that of Sozomen, see Epiphanius *Panarion* 75. 1. 1.

63. So *Ep.* 1 implies. See Maraval, *Vie*, pp. 32, 52f.; Gribomont, 'Eustathe', *Dictionnaire de spiritualité*, col. 1709; Philip Rousseau, 'Basil of Caesarea: Choosing a Past', p. 50 and n. 35.

64. So Gribomont, especially in 'Eustathe', *Dictionnaire d'histoire et de géographie ecclé-siastiques*, col. 28.

65. *Ep.* 223. 5.

occasional forays into church affairs not only less surprising but also more significant.[66] It casts further light as well on the divisions within his own family. Some of them had fallen under Eustathius's influence before he became a bishop. Although orthodox in their views, they may have inclined more to the ideals of an earlier phase in the Eustathian tradition, with its emphasis on a poverty and chastity less visibly related to the life of the Christian community as a whole. That would have been true particularly of Naucratius, who seems more like (though not so extreme as) the malcontents who later followed Aerius away from Sebaste. He had withdrawn from society and yet devoted himself to the care of 'a group of old people living together in poverty and infirmity'.[67] Basil's mother, too, seems to have found his régime more attractive than that adopted by Basil himself and by Gregory.[68] What we may suspect, therefore, is that Basil (having followed Eustathius in the East, and having observed his conduct as a bishop) was responding to a later version of the man's philosophy. He would have felt, as a result, that his family had allowed themselves to espouse ideals that both he and his mentor now found inadequate.

What we begin to detect, therefore, are the roots of a major thrust in Basil's life: the search for a community, a brotherhood, within which to explore, develop, and defend fundamental elements of religious life. Such a community had to be ascetic in some sense and had to aim higher than the disputatious congregations of ambitious bishops. Yet neither world— whether of philosophical reflection or theological controversy and pastoral responsibility—could be abandoned entirely in favour of the other.

───────────

It took time, of course, for such ideas to flower. When we read closely the accounts that Basil wrote at the time, we can see that he was far from being clear in his own mind exactly what he was up to. He certainly would not have seen himself as moving with conscious clarity from a

66. The contrasting explanatory framework is that appealed to, for example, by Fedwick, *Charisma*, pp. 12f., which emphasizes the impact of Julian, not least upon issues of 'church' and 'state' (to use a potentially misleading vocabulary), as an incentive to such vocational shifts in Basil's life. See chapter 2, at n. 21.

67. GNyss *VMac*. 8; ed. Woods Callahan, p. 379, lines 6f.; tr. p. 169; and see the whole of §§ 8 and 9. On the similarity to Eustathian principles, see Maraval, *Vie*, p. 52; and Gribomont, 'Eustathe le philosophe', p. 124. Recall introductory comments made in chapter 1, at n. 29.

68. For her revealing grief at his death, see *VMac*. 9f.; ed. Woods Callahan, pp. 379f.; tr. pp. 169f.

secular career, revolving around the teaching of rhetoric, to an episcopal or priestly career, devoted to the incorporation of ascetic practice into the pastoral life of the Church, or to the careful orchestration of a sense of social responsibility. It would seem, rather, that the chief motor of change in his life at that time was a cautious assessment of personal loyalties (to his family, to Gregory, to Eustathius; and to others who will engage our attention in due time). Moreover, as we have seen already, the account given in his later letters was in no way the same as that given at the time. The differences affect as much the interpretation of asceticism as of the other influences supposedly shaping his life.

What has to be avoided, therefore, is wisdom after the event. Sozomen could happily record that Basil went to Pontus 'to be with the monks pursuing philosophy there', and that he and Gregory 'lived a life of philosophy according to the law of the Church [φιλοσοφοῦσι μοναχοῖς κατὰ τὸν τῆς 'Εκκλησίας νόμον]'.[69] Gregory of Nyssa likened Basil to Moses—among other things in his withdrawal to solitude, where he might, in philosophic guise, draw close to God [προσφιλοσοφῶν τῷ Θεῷ].[70] Modern authors have been equally hasty in their conflations: 'The pursuit of the philosophic ideal is nothing other than a mystical ascent towards Christ'.[71] We have to take into account other hints from the period. Even though writing after Basil's death, Gregory of Nazianzus could strike a more neutral and traditional note: 'Philosophy was his pursuit, as he strove to break from the world, to unite with God, to gain the things below, and to acquire, through goods which are unstable and pass away, those that are stable and abide'.[72]

What do we find, therefore, when we look more closely at those two letters from Pontus, addressed to Gregory of Nazianzus? In the first, the nature of Basil's new enterprise (as he himself perceived it) is betrayed by his phraseology. He had decided to bring an end to his 'wandering [τῆς πλάνης λήξομεν]'—and we should think here not only of his journey in the East but also of the whole series of discontented searchings for a satisfying

69. See Sozomen HE 4. 15, 17.

70. GNyss Laud., PG 46. 809BC.

71. So Maraval, Vie, p. 98 (translation mine). To be fair, the judgement is partly that of Gregory of Nyssa. Note that here, in contrast to the opinion of Sozomen, 'philosophy' did not mean monasticism in some strict sense. Macrina, as we have seen above (at n. 11), was noted for the simplicity of her life, and for her regular prayer and the singing of hymns. Basil, interestingly enough, is presented in the text much more as a person devoted to hard work: see above, at n. 17.

72. GNaz Orat. 43. 13, tr. p. 38. One valuable aspect of Amand de Mendieta's Ascèse is that it places Basil the ascetic firmly in the tradition of Hellenistic philosophy; see pp. vii, 14, 62. Recall the judgements of Averil Cameron in n. 40 above.

mode of life that had afflicted him since his departure from Athens, if not for longer. What he valued most about his proposed place of retreat was its 'tranquillity', which he contrasted with 'the disturbances of the city'. A choice had been made, therefore: to reject, or at least to escape from, the culture of city life itself. Basil attached to that decision an element of providential revelation;[73] and such feelings were to persist, even during his second long stay in Pontus:[74]

> For contemplation and the exercise of the mind, whereby we are joined to God, solitude is an excellent co-worker; and here, at the edge of the world, we enjoy a solitude abundant and bountiful, by the grace of that God who Himself has granted us the power to speak.[75]

When we turn to the second letter, written later in 358, we find that Basil's ideas had made a significant advance. Quite why he composed this little treatise (supposing that it was designed, in this form or in some earlier version, for Gregory himself) is not clear. It may be that the sheer variety of régime that characterized ascetic groups in Pontus—including those of his relatives and those inspired by Eustathius—had prompted Basil to some independent formulation of his own theories.

He began by apologizing for any impression he may have given that Pontus had attracted him merely by its scenic beauty. He assured Gregory that he had now begun to realize how merely leaving the preoccupations of city life did not guarantee moral progress: 'I have not yet been able to leave myself behind'. Much of the rest of the letter was devoted to working out the implications of that growing realism, and to assuaging attendant anxieties.[76] Interwoven with traditionally expressed misgivings about married life and political involvement was an emphasis on the need for interior tranquillity (ἐν ἡσυχίᾳ τὸν νοῦν ἔχειν), and for a withdrawal (ὁ χωρισμὸς ἀπὸ τοῦ κόσμου παντός) that would separate the ascetic not only from the world but from his own body (τῆς πρὸς τὸ σῶμα συμπαθείας τὴν ψυχὴν ἀπορρῆξαι). The task was seen in very negative terms—'to become

73. 'God showed me a spot exactly suited to my purpose and inclination [τῷ ἐμῷ τρόπῳ: D's 'taste' is a little insubstantial]', Ep. 14. 1, C 1: 42, D 1: 107.

74. After the synod of Constantinople, but before his priestly ordination: see n. 27 above.

75. Ep. 9. 3, C 1: 40, D 1: 101. This letter illustrates the growing impact of purely theological concerns upon Basil's pursuit of philosophy—a matter to be explored more fully in the next chapter.

76. Which makes it unfair to reduce the significance of the letter, as does Amand de Mendieta, Ascèse, p. 94: 'Toute pétrie de réminiscences classiques et œuvre d'un styliste délicat, elle n'entre guère dans les détails concrets de la vie ascétique, et se tient presque exclusivement sur le plan théorique des principes'.

as one without a city, without a home, without possessions or the love of friends'—culminating in a rejection of learning itself. Basil advocated a purging of one's inner being (what he called 'the unlearning [ἀπομάθησις] of the teachings which already possess it'), and the opening of the self to a whole range of new impressions 'engendered ... by divine instruction'. Solitude, therefore, was now a means rather than an end: a lonely retreat that would provide the circumstance in which such purging might be achieved—the dismissal, above all, of desire, anger, fear, and grief.[77]

What should strike us thus far is that, while Basil made Christian associations and displayed Christian beliefs, he had not yet fully related that Christianity to more traditional aspirations. The rounded deliberation of his major ascetic writings, perhaps even of the *Philocalia*, still lay in the future. All he wished to do at this stage was to protect from external distraction a simple ascetic programme (τὸ συνεχὲς τῆς ἀσκήσεως). Central expressions of that conviction retain, in the Greek, a surprisingly neutral flavour: 'The discipline of piety nourishes the soul with divine thoughts [ἄσκησις δὲ εὐσεβείας τὴν ψυχὴν τρέφει τοῖς θείοις διανοήμασι]'. Only afterwards did he make a series of vague Christian allusions—imitating the song of the angels; praying continuously to the creator—as if to justify with additional vocabulary a moral endeavour already hallowed and supported by tradition, and explicable psychologically on terms of its own.[78] Writing to a lay friend, Olympius, close by in Neocaesarea, he defended his solitude, his poverty, and his philosophy (ἐσχατία, πενία, and φιλοσοφία are mentioned verbatim) with playful but significant allusions to Zeno, Cleanthes, and Diogenes. It is unlikely that those were dishonest concessions to a correspondent who might not understand more Christian terminology: Olympius was a 'holy soul', living in the heartland of Christianized Pontus, for long a close friend, and well able to understand and intervene in the religious conflicts of Basil's later life.[79]

So it is worth dwelling on the formal antiquity of Basil's exposition. The goal of the ascetic was described first in classic phrases of the Platonist tradition: 'The mind [νοῦς] ... withdraws within itself, and of its own accord ascends to the contemplation of God [πρὸς τὴν περὶ Θεοῦ ἔννοιαν

77. All points from *Ep.* 2. 2; C 1: 6f.; D 1: 9, 11, 13. With time, the public utility of such self-possession would become more apparent, as in *Ep.* 112. 2 to the *praeses* Andronicus: 'Of those who, transcending the many through philosophy [φιλοσοφίᾳ], have abated their wrath, an immortal remembrance has been handed down to all time', C 2: 14, D 2: 217/219.

78. Those were points still being made much later by GNyss*VMac.* 11; ed. Woods Callahan, p. 382, lines 6, 15f.; tr. p. 171. See *Ep.* 2. 2, C 1: 7, D 1: 13.

79. *Ep.* 4; C 1: 15f.; D 1: 29, 31. See also *Ep.* 12, 13, 131, 211. Amand de Mendieta, *Ascèse*, p. 171, was anxious to play down the Stoic element.

ἀναβαίνει]. Then when it is illuminated without and within by that glory, it becomes forgetful even of its own nature'. That emphasis was reinforced in the closing phrases of the letter: 'Let one hour, the same regularly each day, be set aside for food, ... the ascetic devoting the remainder to the activities of the mind [ἐν τῇ κατὰ νοῦν ἐργασίᾳ]'. A passage on prayer expanded upon that vocabulary (in ways, however, that may have been more proper to Basil himself):

> Prayer is to be commended, for it engenders in the soul a distinct conception of God [τοῦ Θεοῦ ἔννοιαν]. And the indwelling of God [τοῦ Θεοῦ ἐνοίκησις] is this—to have God set firm within oneself through the process of memory [τὸ διὰ τῆς μνήμης ἐνιδρυμένον ἔχειν ἐν ἑαυτῷ τὸν Θεόν]. We thus become a temple of God [ναὸς Θεοῦ] whenever earthly cares cease to interrupt the continuity of our memory of Him [τὸ συνεχὲς τῆς μνήμης].[80]

What does seem even more peculiar to Basil himself is a preoccupation with social morality—a surprising shift, given earlier emphasis on solitude and personal perfection. The ascetic was now seen as endeavouring to overcome moral failings shared with others, with the purpose of remaining a social being, but of a different sort. That may be taken as one result of Basil's opening admission, 'I have not yet been able to leave myself behind'; and it may have reflected also the social ideals of Eustathius and his disciples. One should not flirt with women; one should not engage in idle conversation; one should not listen to poetry. The alternative virtues recommended—self-restraint, manliness, justice, and prudence—were also to some extent dependent for their fulfilment on the company of others. Long sections of the letter discuss the correct forms of conversation and the proper modes of dress and etiquette: scarcely any of them were likely to preoccupy a rough hermit. By following that path, the devotee, the σπουδαῖος, would learn 'to perform as he should the several duties of life'.[81]

If those concerns bring us closer to the mind of Basil himself, it is noteworthy that so Christian a resource as Scripture was introduced into the discussion only subsequently, as a gloss to the argument: 'A most important path to the discovery of duty is also [καί] the study

80. *Ep.* 2. 2, 4, 6; C 1: 8, 10, 12; D 1: 15, 17, 19, 23. Note the parallel phrase, τὸ συνεχὲς τῆς ἀσκήσεως, quoted above at n. 78. I have modified D in the interests of precision. We shall discover more about this 'memory of God' in chapter 6. A paper by John Whittaker, 'Plutarch, Platonism, and Christianity', is particularly helpful in this context, summarizing the Platonist tradition on many issues with a useful clarity.
81. *Ep.* 2. 2f., C 1: 8f., D 1: 15f.

of the divinely-inspired Scriptures'.[82] Moral propriety, therefore, was a destination distinct from, perhaps even logically prior to, the scriptural path by which it was to be reached. Appeal to the Scriptures themselves was additional and subsequent to the considerations that had gone before. Those Scriptures did provide 'the precepts of conduct'; but Basil had much more to say about 'the lives of saintly men' described within their pages—men who 'lie before us like living images of the way of life approved by God'. He continued: 'In whatever respect each one perceives himself deficient, if he devote himself to such imitation, he will discover there, as in the shop of a public physician, the specific remedy for his infirmity'.[83] The Scriptures offered the Christian, in other words, little that was different in pedagogical force from the moral exemplars of the classical canon that Basil would later describe in his *Ad adulescentes*.

One could not call these letters either simplistic or uncalculated. They were clearly written by a Christian; and they took for granted a context, shared by Basil and those to whom he wrote, marked by a variety of Christian aspirations. Yet he was happy also to express his new sense of ascetic purpose in predominantly traditional terms. It is true that the pursuit of the 'philosophic' life was a path familiar to Christians and had for a long time attracted specifically Christian commentary and interpretation. Yet that had not robbed the word 'philosophy' of broader connotations, acceptable to Christians but still part of the standard vocabulary and habitual patterns of thought current among those non-Christians who took seriously the definition and pursuit of moral virtue. What is more, many of those traditional connotations remain unqualified, even when they are central to Basil's exposition. When identifiable Christian vocabulary is introduced, while it is not entirely incidental to, or at odds with, the ascetic programme, it is to some extent superimposed upon it, not wholly integrated, not entirely necessary, whether in relation to motives or to models of behaviour.[84]

Nor did a more integrated approach come quickly or easily. The subtle juxtaposition of Platonism and the Psalms, falling effortlessly from a

82. *Ep.* 2. 3, C 1: 8, D 1: 15. There is some doubt about the καί (omitted in some MSS), but this passage does follow after the other points made. Basil's phrases linked the observation totally with what had come just before: πρὸς τὴν τοῦ καθήκοντος εὕρεσιν echoing καθηκόντως ἕκαστον ἐπιτελεῖν τῶν κατὰ τὸν βίον in § 2.

83. *Ep.* 2. 3.

84. See GNaz *De vita sua*, lines 296f., for the feeling that a retired life did not automatically contribute to a knowledge of Scripture. My judgements on *Ep.* 2 are different from, but not to be taken thereby as directly critical of, the shrewd judgements of Meredith, 'Asceticism', esp. p. 326.

bishop's pen, was a late achievement.[85] Even when Basil had begun to preach publicly to the Christian community, one can detect the difficulty with which he was still making unaccustomed connections. A sermon on jealousy, for example, descended only very slowly from philosophical generalities to some sense of social concern and remained sceptical about even the trustworthiness of the seemingly charitable.[86] However, the transition from word to action, already noted as a fundamental characteristic, did begin to make itself felt; and that must be one of the symptoms of change in Basil's ascetic aspiration. The spirit of prayer, therefore, that so obviously characterized his Pontus days, referred to by both the Gregorys, was likely, he would later admit, to be best reflected in what one actually did.[87] In a sermon that was certainly very early, he was able to affirm the central importance of ethics—that is, of behaviour, and of the pursuit of virtue—before distracting himself with a long and more academic definition of terms.[88] So the impulse to a more thorough Christianization of his ascesis seems to have been most directly connected with that sense of the need to act, and to act on behalf of others.

When we examine, therefore, the way in which Basil himself discussed his Pontus endeavours at the time, we find no sudden or straightforward path from the world of the Athenian scholar to the discipleship of an ascetic bishop. Eustathius had an influence, certainly; but from within, so to speak, as seen by Basil himself, that influence was not as clear in its implications as it might later become, or as it seemed in the eyes of others.

———————

Once we begin to see the 'Pontus period' as one of transition, we can make more sense of other ventures. Consider the composition of the *Philocalia*. In undertaking that task, Basil and Gregory continued to use intellectual disciplines developed in Athens; but the result was Christian in form, the fruit of a different and equally ancient religious tradition. One

85. See, for example, *Ep.* 213, where Basil prays 'that I may never, drowned in the unrealities of this world [τῇ φαντασίᾳ τοῦ βίου τούτου καταβαπτισθείς], become forgetful of God, who raises the needy from the earth [virtually a direct quotation from Psalm 113 (V 112)]', C 2: 201, D 3: 223/225.

86. *Hom.* 332, esp. §§ 5 and 6. For that reason, it would not surprise me if this sermon was early, as Bernardi felt, pace Fedwick, *Basil*, 1: 10 n. 43, with his appeal to Gribomont.

87. *Hom.* 334. 3.

88. *Hom.* 340. 1. It is hard to imagine how such a sermon might have been received. For the date, see Fedwick, *Basil*, 1: 10 n. 50: 'certainly one of the first homilies preached by Basil'.

might imagine that Gregory, nurtured by an episcopal father, would have had more specifically theological experience to draw upon; but the elder Gregory was not noted for theological learning, and his son was likely at that stage to have acknowledged such influence with some hesitation. As for Basil, quite apart from our doubt about the impact of his family in that period, it is unlikely that his current sense of the Christian past would have been based upon a detailed knowledge of theological writings. The gradual Christianization of his asceticism was achieved more by an appeal to Scripture than by obvious use of the writings of Origen. Yet we know that the two of them spent at least some of their time in Pontus extracting long passages from several of Origen's works, as well as from other sources such as Eusebius. They must have had copies with them.[89] What can explain that new enthusiasm?

Here we should consider a second experiment—Basil's journey in the East. It carried him not only in pursuit of Eustathius, and not only to the cells and monasteries of famous ascetics, but also to Alexandria, and surely also to Antioch: in other words, to the great centres of the 'Alexandrian school', where he might have been expected to discover not only the memory but also the surviving writings of Origen, and probably of his famous contemporaries and pupils. It was almost certainly a new experience. He was able to gain direct access to a corpus of theological ideas and no longer needed to depend on the more diffuse absorption of a religious tradition. He had been following, moreover, in Gregory's footsteps. Perhaps his friend, even at Athens, had shared with him his own less recent discovery of the sources of Christian philosophy.[90]

Yet what did he, and Gregory, do with that new source of information? They did not proceed to compose treatises or commentaries of their own: they simply, in a rather primitive way, collected bits and pieces from Origen's works, without any comment of their own whatsoever. The structure of the *Philocalia* offers clues to their motives.[91] The first fourteen sections are concerned largely with hermeneutics, in one sense or another: what should one make of the text of Scripture, and what tools are best calculated to help one in the task? Here were sections of Origen's work that could aid the two friends, and perhaps others, in the task of assessing how

89. Basil also possessed during that period writings of Dionysius of Alexandria and (probably) his contemporaries: *Ep.* 9. 2.

90. For Gregory's own travels, see *Orat.* 7. 6, 18. 31; Ruether, *Gregory*, p. 19.

91. This is very much the approach adopted by Junod, 'Particularités', p. 190, and in his introduction to *Origène, Philocalie*, pp. 11f. See also his 'Remarques', and Gribomont, 'Origénisme'. Lim, 'Politics of Interpretation', has useful points to make about both Antioch and Origen in Basil's works.

to relate their learning to the difficult tasks of mounting a scholarly and critical appreciation of the Bible, harnessing this new source of inspiration to the religious goals they had already set themselves. The next six sections, all from the *Contra Celsum*, show Origen addressing directly the problem of how to argue the Christian case against nonbelievers. They concern the purpose of apologetic and focus on the issues that were likely to cause pagans difficulty. The final seven sections are all concerned with human freedom, and its relation to the overriding purposes of God, taking into account both the individual's destiny and the resources made available by nature. Moral purpose and resignation in the face of adversity are, in these passages, much more to the fore.

It is by no means clear what the audience for the work might have been. It looks like a vade mecum of useful texts, to offer in response to different inquiries. It is unlikely that the two friends needed it for themselves, since they presumably had access to the full material: they would have had to analyze it very carefully, in order to make such precisely directed extracts. Did they have in mind the ascetics among whom they were living, and whom (by Gregory's account) Basil was beginning to influence? That depends on what one thinks their needs would have been. The passages on the use of Scripture and the formulation of the basis for a moral programme would obviously have had some significance. The more directly apologetic extracts (admittedly fewer in number) seem less usefully targetted. One thing is clear: it was not, in a strict sense, a creative exercise, nor particularly reflective: it was, on the contrary, highly practical in character, and obviously devoted to making available the central texts of a tradition, in a form that could be consulted quickly, prior to or even during some dialogue or confrontation. It will not be difficult to detect a connection with Basil's increasing willingness at that time to involve himself in public debate on religious matters, already hinted at in some of his letters, and to be explored more fully in the chapter that follows.

We should consider in the same context Basil's ordination—first as a reader, then as a priest. The chronology of that commitment to the clerical order is completely interwoven with his explorations in the ascetic life: each forces us to reassess the significance of the other. Let us recollect the sequence of events. Basil travelled in the East in 356 and 357. Probably in 357 he was baptized by Dianius of Caesarea. He then retired to Pontus and was joined by Gregory. In 359 or 360 he attended a synod in Constantinople. In the latter year he was ordained a reader by Dianius; but, suspecting among other things the orthodoxy of his bishop, he withdrew again to Pontus. It was there, early in 362, that Gregory joined him for the second time, having been just recently ordained by his father. Shortly after Gregory had returned to Nazianzus, Basil went back to Caesarea to be reconciled with Dianius on his deathbed; and he was ordained a priest by Dianius's successor, Eusebius. A year or so later, the two men became estranged, and Basil went for a third time to Annisa. He stayed there until 365 and then returned to Caesarea finally.

Two things should strike us at once. First, Basil was willing to leave his ascetic retreat in 359 in order to attend a church synod. Second, the rest of his time at Annisa was spent as an ordained minister. We should note also his recurrent inability to get on well with pastoral associates. So his ascetic life was combined not only with a growing sense of pastoral vocation but also with a growing interest in the religious conflicts that lay at the heart of church affairs at that time.

Now enough has been said about the influence of Eustathius of Sebaste to make all that hardly surprising. The ecclesiastical interest bears his mark, just as much as Basil's ascetic ideals. Although we have to be cautious about the antagonistic context in which the information is embedded, we remember also that, in his recollections addressed to Eustathius some ten years later, Basil referred to conversations with the bishop's disciples, which were as much on theological matters as they were about the pursuit of virtue—'always speaking and hearing opinions about God'.[92] Couple that with the excerpting of Origen, the hints in his letter to Maximus, and the writing of the *Contra Eunomium* (which we shall discuss at length in the next chapter), and a coherent pattern begins to emerge: Basil was not merely living out the more ascetic implications of a cultivated life but gradually feeling his way towards a public role in the Church, and towards a cautious identification of the party or parties with whom he wished to be associated.

The only trouble is that he does not say anything much about the experience, then or later. We have to draw on the reflections of Gregory of Nazianzus, in order to make full sense of what was afoot in their lives. That dependence on our part brings with it other inconveniences. We cannot automatically assume that Gregory was a reliable witness in regard to contemporary events, any more than he was later in regard to those past. We can take it for granted, on the other hand, that his attitudes to the priesthood were rather different from those of Basil— certainly if the pattern of his later career and statements is anything to go by. Fundamentally, Gregory never felt happy about the relation between the pursuit of philosophy, as he interpreted it, and engagement with

92. *Ep.* 223. 5, C 3: 14, D 3: 305. See above, at n. 35.

the pastoral life. Basil, by contrast, assessed the issue carefully over a period of some years, made a definite commitment, and stuck to it.[93] (It is helpful to compare with the views of both men the position adopted by Gregory of Nyssa, who, in spite of his own somewhat chequered career as a churchman, felt much happier in later years about his and his brother's vocations: 'Their philosophy was enhanced by the consecration'.)[94]

So what do we learn from Gregory of Nazianzus? The first text to note is his second *oratio*, in which he defended his decision to flee from Nazianzus, after his ordination. It is hard to believe that this was not a matter he discussed with Basil at Annisa, during those weeks in early 362. It is not impossible, indeed, that at least the bare bones of his pamphlet were drafted in Basil's company. The question is, of course, whether they reflect any of Basil's own views (before his own ordination).

The great bulk of the *oratio*, concerned with Gregory's reasons for flight, falls into four sections. In the first, he made incidental points calculated to seize attention: the Church was naturally divided into the leaders and the led, and he could not think of himself as a natural leader; current exemplars of church leadership did not awaken admiration; he was just on the verge of engaging finally with a life of quiet and withdrawal. The last assertion is hard to believe, put forward by a man who had tried the delights of Pontus and had decided not to persist. He does mention what may have prompted his inclination in the first place: a promise made during a moment of danger. He recalled the incident again, in his funeral oration on his father, identifying it with the experience of near shipwreck on his way from Alexandria to Athens.[95]

In the second section, he proceeded to deeper reflection. The important task in life was to develop a personal relationship with God. That was what religion was all about. Indeed, the whole of salvation history was devoted to proclaiming that such a relationship was possible, and to identifying the means by which it might be brought about.[96] Here was a judgement of extraordinary importance. Whatever degree of pastoral involvement Gregory was eventually willing to accept, it would still be dedicated largely to spiritual achievement at an individual level. We shall be forced to ask

93. We should avoid being forced to make a study of Basil into a study of Gregory as well; but we shall have several occasions to recall not only his hesitation over his own ordination in 362 but also his reaction to Basil's consecration as bishop (in chapter 5), and to his own forcible elevation to the see of Sasima (in chapter 7).

94. *VMac.* 14; ed. Woods Callahan, p. 385, line 21; tr. p. 173.

95. GNaz *Orat.* 2. 3, 8, and 6 respectively; and see also 18. 31, 37.

96. GNaz *Orat.* 2. 17f., 23f.

whether Basil, for all his apparently different path in life, was not far from the same opinion.

In the third section, Gregory returned to the scene about him and commented unfavourably on the temper of current controversy. One is tempted to ask whether he was able to face the sheer pressure of public debate, the virtual civil war that seemed to afflict the Church. He did show genuine anxiety about the effect that that war was having on ordinary people and on their capacity to take any speaker seriously.[97]

In the fourth section, he discussed the training required by the clergy in such circumstances. He emphasized their need for a thorough initiation into Scripture, an initiation that would demand as much effort as that devoted to a difficult, professional skill. Such training would take a long time, leaving only a few years in old age for responsible leadership; and it should be preceded in any case by a period of moral formation, without which genuine wisdom was unattainable.[98]

So long and repetitive a defence of his own withdrawal from the contest made it increasingly difficult for him to put forward any reasonable explanation of why he nevertheless did decide to go back to Nazianzus (for the pamphlet was clearly circulated after his return). To balance his many declarations of caution and unworthiness, he could adduce only his affection for the community, his sense of responsibility towards his parents, and his suspicion that perhaps, like Jonah, he was being called by God. Efforts to resist would be circumvented anyway, and his inadequacies would be efficiently counteracted by help from above. It boiled down in the end to obedience.[99] It has to be said that the petulance of his third *oratio*—I took the trouble to come back, but no one was willing to listen to what I said; I hope for better behaviour in future—calls the sincerity of the whole exercise into question. It bears little immediate relation to any feelings we have reason to expect in Basil.

In his *oratio* for his dead father, Gregory commented on the election of Eusebius as bishop of Caesarea. It will be useful to bear his views in mind when we read later his reflections on Basil's own elevation to the see; but they tell us something, also, about the circumstances in which Basil found himself, once he accepted ordination at Eusebius's hands. It was a time of

97. GNaz *Orat.* 2. 37f. For 'civil war'—ὁ πρὸς ἀλλήλους πόλεμος (*PG* 35. 489B)—GNaz *Orat.* 2. 79f.

98. GNaz *Orat.* 2. 49f., 71f. See also his *De seipso et de episcopis*, lines 199f.—the apostles may have been simple men; but the Scriptures demanded learning in reader and commentator alike—and n. 84 above.

99. GNaz *Orat.* 2. 102f., 106f. The note of affection and responsibility was sounded again much later, in *Orat.* 43. 25.

turbulence (and we think back to the observations of the second *oratio*). 'The city was naturally inclined to be especially factious in the matter because of the fervour of its faith', said Gregory, 'and the splendor of the see only increased the rivalry'. Not unnaturally, there was partisan support for this candidate and that, 'as usually happens in such cases, according as one chanced to be influenced by friendship for an individual or by piety towards God'.[100] Several factors carried weight, therefore; none of them, as we know, redeeming in Gregory's eyes: theological debate, ecclesiastical ambition, and an election that was at least mildly corrupt. Yet we also know that Basil was there at the time, that he stayed there afterwards, and that he was willing to be a priest in the service of the victor. That was not the whole story, however, and Gregory offers us other comment, more reassuring, perhaps, in the light it throws on Basil himself. In a letter to his friend, written in 362 (after Basil's ordination), Gregory expressed a sense of puzzlement (which we may link with the final passages of the second *oratio*): he did not really understand what the Holy Spirit was up to. There was no doubt in his mind, still, that there was some tension between the priesthood and the philosophic life, which by definition withdrew itself from view. He suggested, nevertheless, that they should both accept the office (and in effect both had, by this time) because of the pressure of heresy, and because of the faith that others had placed in them.[101] They were to join, as Basil later put it, 'the fellowship of men who obey the law of love and shun the peril of silence'.[102]

That link between their final surrender (as Gregory saw it) and the demands of theological controversy was even more clearly affirmed in letters Gregory wrote when trying to bring Basil back to Caesarea, after his falling out with Eusebius. Writing to Eusebius himself, he hinted that Basil had been ordained precisely to help his bishop in likely conflicts with theological opponents (although Valens, appointed emperor by his brother in the East only in 364, had yet to appear upon the scene as a fresh champion of the Arian cause). The tug-of-war between philosophy and pastoral involvement could still be felt; but he argued now that it would be unjust to enjoy the 'better part' while not accepting also the demands of the Gospel in respect to charity towards others. It was perhaps the first time

100. GNaz *Orat.* 18. 33, tr. pp. 146f.

101. GNaz *Ep.* 8. 3, 2, and 4. Basil *Ep.* 17 made the point that one did not have to be a priest in order to make an intellectual mark in the struggle against heresy; but the letter is of uncertain date.

102. *Ep.* 28. 3, C 1: 69f., D 1: 169. See above, at n. 65. What they were deciding, in practice, was to take on the role of preacher; and their cautious movements in that direction are usefully placed in the context provided by Bernardi, *Prédication*, pp. 371f.

in Gregory's treatment of the subject that the Gospel was brought into play in order to undermine the traditional demands of the philosophic life.[103] Gregory then wrote again to Basil himself, insisting forcibly that they both faced a moment of truth. It was essential that they come to the aid of the old bishop. Their courage would prove that their previous labours had not been for nothing. Engagement with affairs in Caesarea, in other words, could now be taken to represent the fulfilment of their ascetic fervour—they could give in to Eusebius καλῶς ... καὶ φιλοσόφως: with a philosophic propriety. The motive was clearly the defeat of heresy; and they should seek inspiration in the example of Bezalel—wise and skilful, and able to teach others his craft.[104]

The easiest way to judge how much all this tells us about Basil's own attitudes in his early years is to imagine where we would be without the evidence of Gregory. If we were forced to make do with Basil's 'Pontus letters', we would acquire a picture of traditional philosophical retirement, dressed to some extent in Christian colours, with associated allusion to Scripture. We would detect a growing interest in the Arian issue, which would be confirmed by our knowing that the *Contra Eunomium* was written at that time. We might read back some smaller hints expressed elsewhere.[105] Otherwise, we would have to explain to ourselves, without much help from Basil, how a disillusioned rhetor might turn into a committed priest. If we were to add the later encomia of the two Gregorys and the *Life of Macrina*, we might not be much the wiser. Gregory of Nazianzus, at that late stage, had very little to say about the Pontus period at all. The *Life of Macrina* is more informative, but not about the actual transition from ascetic experiment to pastoral action. As for Gregory of Nyssa's final *oratio* on Basil, the man had become so theologized a figure—the Moses of the age—as to arouse every historical suspicion.

Once we add the early letters and orations of Gregory, while we may not gain immediate or even totally reliable access to Basil's mind, we do acquire a fuller sense of context, and we can identify theoretical issues that the pair must have discussed together. Arianism and associated controversies lay at the heart of the matter: both men seem to have thought

103. GNaz *Ep.* 16, esp. § 8. Two other letters to Eusebius were chiefly concerned to remind the bishop that not all blame lay with Basil.

104. GNaz *Ep.* 19. 1, 4f.: σύστασις αἱρετικῶν κατατρέχει τὴν Ἐκκλησίαν. The reference to Bezalel is from Exodus 35.30f. Basil made a similar point to Gregory himself, when trying to gain his friend's support against theological enemies: they might achieve much, he said, 'living up to our old agreements and to the responsibility which we now owe to the churches', *Ep.* 71. 2, C 1: 167, D 2: 57.

105. As, for example, in the letter quoted in the previous note.

they had a responsibility and a talent that needed to be brought into play in the cause of orthodoxy. They were also concerned with the preparation of the clergy in general for such a task: priests should be armed, they thought, with carefully collected apologetic material, and should be well versed in Scripture, steeping themselves in a body of literature, just like any other members of the cultured class. Moreover, the two friends regarded periods of reflection and of self-discipline as a necessary part of that preparation. Even while he was still at Athens, Basil may have been thinking along such lines; Gregory, on the other hand, developed later a sense of vocation that was at once more intimate and more exalted, and that therefore proved more difficult to relate to the pastoral realities around him.

There is one further aspect of Basil's philosophical reflection that calls for our attention. With his departure from Athens, we begin to possess his own writings: it is at this point that the existing corpus of his letters begins. We are therefore in a position—although we have to be cautious, faced with a fair amount of literary formalism—to build up a picture of his inner life, of his shifting attitudes to experience, to opportunity, and to other personalities. We properly begin to look for signs of individual temperament.

One such sign is Basil's attitude to fate. It appears in the very first survival of his writings, his letter to Eustathius. Having given an account of the difficulties he had faced, catching up with his hero, he concluded:

> Is not all this the hand of Fate [ταῦτα οὐχ εἰμαρμένης ἔργα], as you yourself would say,[106] and the work of Necessity [ταῦτα οὐκ ἀνάγκης]? ... But, as I said, I have been put at ease by the receipt of your letter, and I no longer hold the same opinion. I now say that I ought to give thanks to God when He giveth benefits, and not be vexed with Him when He dispenseth them grudgingly.[107]

There are several instances of that conviction in Basil's early letters—indeed, the line of thought represented what was to become a theme in much of his later work. It sprang in part, without doubt, from his

106. Around this phrase, ὡς ἂν αὐτὸς εἴποις, has gathered the suspicion that the recipient was a pagan; but, as Gribomont, 'Eustathe le philosophe', argues and as the sequel shows, it was the recipient's letter to Basil that had confirmed an alternative, Christian, view. See above, at n. 56.

107. *Ep.* 1, C 1: 4, D 1: 7.

sense of philosophical vocation, and especially from Stoic teaching. It also reflected literary and intellectual convention.[108] By the same token, the very survival of convention offers proof that it continued to serve the needs of individuals at moments of bereavement or insecurity.[109] It is not just a matter of identifying a specifically Christian element in this or that passage: such elements, in Basil's case, were often completely interwoven with other traditions.[110] We need, rather, to highlight those nuances that allow us to recognize the personal feelings of the author.

That can be done. It is true that in classic examples of *consolatio*—his letters, for instance, to the parents of a young man recently dead—Basil did little more than fulfil the expectations of the genre. He was particularly anxious to counter a psychologically unwholesome indulgence in grief.[111] Even his Christian allusions were not always peculiar to himself and his circle. His appeal to the resurrection of Jesus (a particular way of defending the usefulness of hope) may have been based chiefly on non-Christian literary antecedents.[112] His sense of a need for courage may have led him to evoke the example of the martyrs; but his vocabulary recalls just as much the similar exhortations found in Plutarch or Seneca.[113] More idiosyncratic, perhaps, was the subtlety with which he discussed the achievement of harmony between λογισμοί and αἰτία, between the attitudes that one might bring to bear upon misfortune and the forces that actually caused it.[114] The same may be said of his notion of 'testing', as expressed to a bereaved mother: 'Now is the Lord making His test of your love for Him [τὴν δοκιμὴν ... τῆς πρὸς αὐτὸν ἀγάπης]'.[115] Equally personal was his belief that grief had to be shared: 'Above all I have this to urge—that you spare your partner in life; be a consolation one to the other'.[116] Basil ended this splendid letter as follows:

108. The tradition is explored and documented by Robert Clark Gregg, *Consolation Philosophy: Greek and Christian Paideia in Basil and the Two Gregories*. Specific letters of Basil are listed on p. 132. The tradition also influenced Basil's homiletic discourse: see, for example, *Hom.* 334. 4.

109. Gregg, *Consolation*, p. 145.

110. Gregg, *Consolation*, pp. 74, 131.

111. Gregg, *Consolation*, chap. 3, pp. 81–123, with a contrasting emphasis on ἀπάθεια. For the examples referred to here, see *Ep.* 5 and 6.

112. The Pauline texts alluded to are discussed by Gregg, *Consolation*, pp. 153f., and the Christian attitude generally, pp. 194f.

113. Gregg, *Consolation*, pp. 181f.

114. *Ep.* 5. 2. Compare 'that sober reason [τὸν λογισμὸν ... τὸν σώφρονα]', C 1: 17, D 1: 35, with 'a reason, incomprehensible to man [τις αἰτία ἀνθρώποις ἀκατάληπτος]', C 1: 18, D 1: 37.

115. *Ep.* 6. 2, C 1: 20, D 1: 41. Compare *Ep.* 101, C 2: 2, D 2: 189. The notion will recur.

116. *Ep.* 6. 2, C 1: 21, D 1: 43/45.

Therefore I do pray the Lord Himself so to touch your heart with His ineffable power [τῇ ἀφάτῳ αὐτοῦ δυνάμει] as to enkindle light in your soul by the exercise of good counsels [διὰ τῶν ἀγαθῶν λογισμῶν], that you may have within yourself the sources of your consolation [ἵν' οἴκοθεν ἔχῃς τῆς παραμυθίας τὰς ἀφορμάς].

Such phrases carry us far beyond literary dependence upon the *consolatio* tradition. The link between λογισμός and αἰτία (now δύναμις), between attitude and explanation, was to be achieved by the inner presence of God, described in the language of spiritual enlightenment, and leading to an independence worthy of a human being created by that same God.[117]

We have to note, also, the way in which Basil's philosophical reflection more generally provided the context within which those personal interpretations of the *consolatio* tradition were allowed to develop. A life of piety, he felt, was bound to involve one in 'the afflictions of this world'. It was the broader view that allowed hope its full effect, 'for hopes, which hold and weld together man's entire life, give consolation for the hardships which fall to the lot of each'.[118] So it was not just the bereaved who had to wage war against adversity, like well-trained athletes, but the lifelong ascetic also, 'running with an eye to the prize of his high calling'.[119] Even those who had escaped misfortune were to cultivate a certain fear, to 'preserve the same attitude of mind that we had at the moment of our perils': that was the moment when there would arise within them 'a feeling of repentance for the past, and then a promise regarding the future'.[120]

Here we touch upon the central nerve of the moral life, the conflated notions of conversion and of lifelong dedication to self-improvement, which had little to do with literary precedent or Stoic ἀπάθεια. Basil's attachment to the ascetic ideal had become firmly associated with the notion of coping with misfortune, and of doing so in the company of like-minded enthusiasts and visionaries. It was to impart to his whole life a characteristic amalgam of morbidity and optimism: the first was never absent but became a precondition, one might say, for the triumph of the second.

117. *Ep.* 6. 2, C 1: 21, D 1: 43/45.
118. *Ep.* 18, C 1: 48, D 1: 119. Basil's imagery is extraordinarily bold and strong: πάντα τὸν τῶν ἀνθρώπων βίον συνέχουσαι καὶ συγκροτοῦσαι. He used also the technical word for 'consolation', παραμυθοῦνται.
119. *Ep.* 23, C 1: 59, D 1: 143.
120. *Ep.* 26, C 1: 64, D 1: 157. Recall the promise made by Gregory of Nazianzus, as recounted in *Orat.* 18. 31, and referred to above, at n. 95. There is some irony in the fact that Basil's *Ep.* 26 was addressed to Gregory's 'secular' brother, Caesarius.

· CHAPTER IV ·

EUNOMIUS

Neither his family background nor his secular education nor his early engagement with the ascetic life was simple, therefore, in its effect on Basil's later career. The particular religiosity of his family seemed less attractive than traditions preserved elsewhere in the Church. The skills, standards, and tastes reflected in the schools of Athens reinforced a certain hauteur and increased his facility of thought and expression; but they were modified by an older and deeper loyalty to the values and techniques of Scripture. His taste for ascetic retirement in the classical tradition was challenged and interrupted by a sense of responsibility towards the controversial and pastoral needs of the Church. At all three levels, we detect the attraction of a long-standing option open to men of Basil's circumstance, bound by rules and antecedents of its own: membership of the clerical order. Almost at every turn, Basil sensed a growing loyalty to a group of men and a task within Christian society that family, scholarship, and self-discipline could only partially prepare him for.

At the time when Basil was making fundamental decisions about the direction of his life, church affairs in the East were still dominated by the Arian controversy. If he were to choose a career based upon a clerical vocation, any man of talent and ambition was bound to become embroiled in the intricacies of that debate. Following in Basil's steps, we enter upon an arena of church life that was immensely broad and complex. The economy of our own analysis will dissuade us from concentrating on theological issues—not because the theology was unimportant, but because historians exercise a particular species of patience, waiting to see what emerges from the dust of battle. Theological ideas will not tell us much about Basil, even though they may have been developing in Basil's head. We shall study the debate, rather, as a circumstance of his life, within which his own more personal sense of vocation, of the possibilities open to him, of necessary method, was able to take shape. There was a logic to the Arian conflict—a logic of style, of attack—that heightened, for its participants, the importance, the practical consequences, of its more theoretical components. So the question for us will be, what were people able to make of the opportunities of party rivalry and confrontation?

Historians have reasonably clear ideas about the vocabulary used by Arians and their opponents and about the chronology of their struggle: letters and treatises, council decrees and condemnations, the complaints of exiles and the subtleties of political intervention, all make such matters relatively plain.[1] Much more elusive are motives and effects. Justice demands that we start, at least, with the assumption that churchmen linked their convictions with a sense of pastoral duty. Many of them felt that right belief on the subject of the Trinity had a direct impact upon the salvation of souls—not just because conformity was a virtue in God's eyes, but because a correct judgement on the Trinitarian issue affected directly one's definition of the human person, one's understanding of human destiny and of the moral path by which it was to be fulfilled.[2]

There was, however, a political dimension, which has not always been happily handled. One outcome of Constantine's conversion and the

---

1. The bibliography of Arianism is enormous, and it would be futile to attempt a comprehensive account. The following major works have proved most useful: Robert Clark Gregg and Dennis E. Groh, *Early Arianism—A View of Salvation*; Robert C. Gregg, ed., *Arianism: Historical and Theological Reassessments*; Thomas A. Kopecek, *A History of Neo-Arianism*; Manlio Simonetti, *La crisi ariana nel IV secolo*; Christopher Stead, *Substance and Illusion in the Christian Fathers*; Rowan Williams, *Arius: Heresy and Tradition* (see the useful review by Robert Clark Gregg, in *Journal of Theological Studies* n.s. 40 (1989): 247-54); Rowan Williams, ed., *The Making of Orthodoxy*. In this last collection, R. P. C. Hanson, 'The Achievement of Orthodoxy in the Fourth Century A.D.', p. 144, makes the convincing point that the Arian controversy lasted for so long chiefly because the contestants were able to develop only slowly answers to the questions that Arius had raised; but it seems weak to say that they did so merely by 'a process of trial and error', p. 151. Barnes, *Athanasius and Constantius: Theology and Politics in the Constantinian Empire*, appeared after I had completed my work, although I was able to check some dates and appreciate its more general importance. I also found Brennecke, *Geschichte der Homöer*, very helpful. My thanks to T. D. Barnes for leading me to this work, which I confess had escaped me; and I only regret that Brennecke's arguments have not been as neatly folded into my own account as I would have liked. His views on Valens are most succinctly expressed on pp. 205f., 223, 239f., and on Basil on pp. 226f.

2. One of the central themes of Gregg and Groh, *Early Arianism*. Similar sympathy is displayed by Maurice Wiles, 'Eunomius: Hair-splitting Dialectician or Defender of the Accessibility of Salvation?'.

ensuing toleration of Christianity was that the emperor and his associates in government were able to impose upon the Church the political control in religious affairs that had hitherto been reserved for pagans. Initially enthusiastic, there were churchmen who reverted in time to a longer-standing unease, marked by opposition to civil authority, or at least by the refusal to accept its every edict. It was not just a question of keeping alive the spirit of the martyrs, although there were signs enough of that. Many bishops were drawn from provincial élites that had behind them a long tradition of cautiously failing to cooperate with the imperial authorities. One should not be surprised to find them maintaining that reserve.[3] We cannot simply reduce the Arian controversy to a species of strain in 'church-state relations'; but it was conducted against a civil background, and the fortunes of those engaged were often encouraged or impeded (depending on one's point of view) by political and social pressures. Moreover, the controversy expressed, if it did not actually create, tensions between cities themselves. Doctrinal purity, or its absence, was a useful stick with which to beat a local rival for eminence in influence, patronage, even wealth; and in that competition the friendship of the emperor could be a useful weapon. In that context, too, the arguments themselves had a direct effect. They were not merely an excuse for the continuity of old antagonisms: the answers that emerged at a theological level allowed those who aspired after power to articulate new histories for the status and influence they now claimed, and new definitions of the communities over which they expected to wield that power. Relationships with the central authorities of the empire were inevitably part of such a campaign.

Let us attempt, therefore, as plain a sketch as possible of the tangled Arian conflict. The Council of Nicaea in 325 had been designed to condemn what were perceived as the errors of Arius, and to dampen enthusiasm for his cause. In this it succeeded for a while. Subsequent depositions, however, altered affairs. Eustathius was ousted from Antioch in 330 and Marcellus from Ancyra in 336—the latter ploy betraying in particular a renewed fear of Sabellianism. Battle lines had been redrawn. Supporters of Arius were reasserting themselves, while opponents were attempting to shift the basis of their criticism. The prominence of Antioch and Ancyra in those disputes came to have a special significance in Basil's career: for it was in relation to those sees that many of his own loyalties

---

3. An aspect of the matter nicely brought out by Raymond Van Dam, 'Emperor, Bishops, and Friends in Late Antique Cappadocia', although we shall have occasion to question one or two points later.

were later to develop. Marcellus in particular (he did not die until 374), and Sabellianism more generally, would always arouse his anxiety. (A Sabellian position will exaggerate the divinity shared by Father and Son, thus clearly rejecting the Arian view, but to such an extent as to obscure any distinction between them.) Yet he came to accept the opinions and policies of Basil of Ancyra, successor to Marcellus. The latter, in exile, attracted the support of western bishops, confirmed by Julius of Rome at a synod in 340. Orthodoxy of that ilk, therefore, was beginning to abandon the middle ground (Athanasius of Alexandria, who owed much to the support of the West, would eventually identify with that tendency), and churchmen inclined to conciliation, and therefore to a vaguer theology, were willing to fill the vacuum. Basil of Ancyra belonged in such company.

Their first clear declaration of intent was made at a council held in Antioch in 341. The gathering was dominated by the policies of Eusebius of Nicomedia, the acknowledged and influential leader of those dedicated to avoiding or undermining the decisions of Nicaea. So it espoused a theology that was beyond doubt mildly Arian; but its debates were genuinely designed to achieve a new consensus by stating as little as possible. (We should note that Dianius of Caesarea was present.)[4] The council's efforts, however, were soon roundly rebuffed by another meeting, of western bishops, held at Sardica in 343. Those attending maintained the more intransigent position represented by Athanasius.

An escalation of the conflict became inevitable. No doubt those who sympathized with the Arian cause were held in check for a while by the caution imposed upon Constantius, under some pressure from his more orthodox brother Constans in the West. Yet the appointment of Leontius to the see of Antioch in 344 may be seen in part as a reaction to Sardica, and certainly as a more local shift in sympathy towards the Arian party. It was under the patronage of this new bishop that Aetius, 'Neo-Arianism's founding father', established himself in the city, along with his disciple Eunomius.[5] From 350 onwards, certainly, with Constans

---

4. Dianius seems to have been part of a small 'Cappadocian contingent': see Gustave Bardy, *Recherches sur Saint Lucien d'Antioche et son école*, p. 326. The council's espousal of the formula ἀπαράλλακτον εἰκόνα would be echoed in Basil's later reflections: see below, at n. 21. For interpretation along these lines, see Kopecek, *Neo-Arianism*, p. 80. Useful still is L. W. Barnard, 'East-West Conciliatory Moves and Their Outcome in the Period 341–351 A.D.', and, more generally, essays reprinted in his *Studies in Church History and Patristics*. The work of Bardy just referred to contains much information and reflection, not least on the prominence of Antioch, 'la véritable patrie spirituelle de l'arianisme', p. vi.

5. The phrase is Kopecek's, *Neo-Arianism*, p. 61. The church at Antioch will receive more particular attention in chapter 8.

dead and Constantius sole emperor, Arians enjoyed a decade of renewed vigour. The traditions set in train by Eusebius of Nicomedia were once again asserted at the first council held in Sirmium in 351. Churches in the West still felt able to reject that stance, at Arles in 353, and at Milan in 355. Yet the most unbending orthodox still found themselves ousted from their sees—further proof that they had placed themselves on a limb.

Their opponents in the East, meanwhile, showed signs of a nervous division. Some felt that the original genius of Arius had been betrayed by conciliar compromise. Aetius and Eunomius were the leaders here, protected by Leontius until his death in 357, and wedded to the notion that the Son was 'unlike' the Father (ἀνόμοιος—hence their being known as 'Anomoeans'). Basil of Ancyra on the other side, now supported by Eustathius of Sebaste, veered away from such extremes; and he and his supporters drew as close as they dared to Nicaea by calling themselves 'Homoiousians', because of their belief that the Son was 'of like substance' (ὁμοιούσιος) to the Father.[6] The more rigorous supporters of Nicaea believed that the Son was 'of the *same* substance' as the Father (ὁμοούσιος).

Such a division almost inevitably generated a new compromise of its own; and the situation in the East became enormously complicated, with Anomoeans to one side and Homoiousians to the other, a centre party emerging meanwhile, labelled 'Homoeans', because they were content, more or less, to say merely that the Son was 'like' the Father (ὅμοιος).

Because they valued harmony and peace more than the refinement of doctrinal formulae, the Homoeans came to dominate the 'unorthodox' scene for nearly twenty years. Their success was due in part to their alliance with Constantius and with Valens, neither of whom could tolerate the more extreme position of Aetius and his supporters. The chief landmarks of Homoean success were twin councils held at Seleucia and Ariminum in 359. (It was in response to their decrees that Jerome made his famous comment 'The whole world groaned, amazed to find itself Arian'.)[7] A degree of acceptance in the West, the favour of the emperor, and at least the beginnings of what would become the final ostracism of Aetius combined to inspire confidence among the Homoeans; and they made preparations

---

6. For their early attempt to gain the support of the Caesar Gallus, see Kopecek, *Neo-Arianism*, pp. 106f., and Brennecke, *Geschichte der Homöer*, p. 89; and for Eunomius's activities at this time, Kopecek, pp. 145f.

7. *Dialogus contra Luciferianos* 19, *PL* 23. 181C. The geographical extent of the perception undermines, of course, the amazement. Ariminum had originally opted for the Nicene formula ὁμοούσιος but was later constrained to accept the more general declarations of Seleucia.

for a gathering in Constantinople, towards the end of 359, which they hoped would secure their triumph.

It was at this point that Basil entered the picture, for he attended the gathering or was at least present in the city during some of its sessions. He was certainly aware of what was afoot. His brother Gregory may have been there with him.[8] It was also around this time that he allowed Dianius of Caesarea to ordain him a reader, thus committing himself in some degree to a clerical career. But why had he gone to Constantinople in the first place (leaving, in other words, his Pontic retreat)? Is it enough to suppose merely that he accompanied his bishop, Dianius?

We need to recognize that, alongside the apparently smooth progress of the Homoean party and the associated embarrassment of the more extreme Arians, another struggle was under way. During 357 and 358, when the Homoean formula was beginning to gain a following, Aetius and Eunomius appeared to strengthen their grip on the church in Antioch. The death of Leontius in 357 had robbed them of an important patron. His successor, Eudoxius, was at first discouraging, since he represented theologically the desire for compromise more characteristic of the 340s. However, Aetius brought him round. Other eastern churchmen, meanwhile, seemed disinclined to interfere.

It was those developments that aroused fresh alarm among the Homoiousians. George, bishop of Laodicea since 335, and originally a follower of Eusebius of Nicomedia, wrote to Macedonius of Constantinople and to Basil of Ancyra, suggesting that more needed to be done to counter the resurgent Anomoeans. Basil was in the process of organizing a synod at Ancyra (this was in 358); and the allies decided to use the occasion to mount their offensive. They wished to persuade the emperor that the concept ὁμοιούσιος (or rather their own subtle qualification, ὅμοιος κατ' οὐσίαν) was equivalent to the term by now espoused by the Homoeans, ὅμοιος κατὰ πάντα, 'like [the Father] in all things', but was much more likely to put an end to the errors rife in Antioch. Their synodal letter and delegation to Constantius had some success; and Aetius and Eunomius were even exiled for a time. It was the high point of the Homoiousian cause.

---

8. GNyss CE 1. 82, with the assertion that they did not mingle with the contenders. For the embarrassment thus disguised, see Kopecek, *Neo-Arianism*, p. 301. Gregory's treatise is best edited by Werner Jaeger. I shall not pursue here the debate about the timing and distinguishable sessions of this synod, since it does not affect our understanding of Basil's attitude. See Kopecek, pp. 303f.; Brennecke, *Geschichte der Homöer*, pp. 48f.; and L. R. Wickham, 'The Date of Eunomius's *Apology*: A Reconsideration', by whom I am wholly persuaded.

Present at Basil's synod, and prominent in the subsequent embassy to the emperor, was Eustathius of Sebaste—the very man whom our own Basil had just been following around the East; close to whose see he was now residing (at Annisa); with whom, indeed, he had been holding long spiritual conversations.[9] It is hard to believe that they did not discuss Eunomius's activities, both in Antioch and in Alexandria: he had been there at the time of their own travels. So between his earliest association with Eustathius around 356 and the production of his first major work on Trinitarian theology, the *Contra Eunomium*, Basil was in a perfect position to educate himself at first hand in the intricacies of the Arian conflict, and to do so in the company and under the influence of a man deeply engaged in the same dispute.

That engagement, on Basil's part as well, was not in the cause of extreme orthodoxy but in the company of the Homoiousians, and within traditions represented in the see of Ancyra. Basil of Ancyra's own views are therefore worth noting. He laid claim to a theological ancestry enshrined in a series of councils that would, in other eyes, fall into different camps: Antioch in 341, Sardica in 343, and Sirmium in 351. That it was possible to construct a pedigree of that sort shows we should not too easily adopt a Nicene (let alone an Athanasian) view of what orthodoxy represented. Basil also insisted that the place to start when trying to define the Trinity was with the baptismal formula reproduced in the Gospel of Matthew (28.19). Finally, he was firmly convinced that Scripture formed a unit, in which one part should always be read in the light of another.[10] Here was the tradition that our own Basil had now come to regard as orthodox. The significance of the baptismal formula and the unity of Scripture would certainly be central themes in his *Contra Eunomium*. It was to be a work written from a Homoiousian and Eustathian point of view.[11]

9. See chapter 3, at nn. 35f.

10. For this *professio fidei*, see Epiphanius *Panarion* 73. 12–22. For the text, see Karl Holl, *Epiphanius (Ancoratus und Panarion)*, vol. 3; alternatively, *PG* 42. 425–44. Also Joseph T. Lienhard, 'The Epistle of the Synod of Ancrya, 358: A Reconsideration'.

11. All this is to depart somewhat from the opinions of Stanislas Giet in 'S. Basile et le concile de Constantinople de 360', which shows too much anxiety for the preservation of Basil's theological purity and is too much swayed by his later reinterpretations. Just how close Basil may have been to his namesake of Ancyra was exhaustively explored by P. Maran in his *Vita Basilii*, 7. 1; reprinted, *PG* 29. 26f. No conclusion demands our believing, however, that Basil was present at the synod of Ancyra. See also the usefully broad survey of Joseph T. Lienhard, 'Basil of Caesarea, Marcellus of Ancyra, and "Sabellius"'.

We now have a much fuller explanation of why Basil was drawn to Constantinople. Whatever his loyalty to Dianius, he must have been stirred by the fact that the fortunes of Eustathius were now likely to hang in the balance. The Homoeans, since the synod at Ancyra, had achieved their own victory at Seleucia. Constantius had been prevailed upon to support a looser and apparently more scriptural formula: George of Laodicea and Basil of Ancyra were seen to have overreached themselves politically. Eunomius was poised to seize the leadership of the Arian cause, and to take the opportunity of the coming assembly in Constantinople to defend his theology and to exploit the divisions among his opponents. (His declarations were to take final form in his later *Apology*.) Sure enough, although Aetius was again exiled at Constantinople, Eustathius was also deposed, along with the bishops of Ancyra and Tarsus.[12] Macedonius of Constantinople was displaced by no less a person than Eudoxius of Antioch, the devious patron of Aetius. The new patriarch was prevailed upon to appoint Eunomius to the see of Cyzicus.[13] It was a dark moment. Basil had not waited to see the humiliation of those he admired, and withdrew from the city. Shortly afterwards, matters worsened further. Dianius, who had just set Basil upon his clerical path, was forced in the face of serious threats to subscribe to the synod's decrees.[14] Basil was later satisfied that his capitulation had been due to 'the simplicity of his heart', and that he never intended to repudiate the ancient decisions of Nicaea.[15] At the time, however, he felt obliged to withdraw once more to Pontus.[16]

12. For Basil's connections with Silvanus of Tarsus, see *Ep.* 47, 223. 5.

13. In this, as in other matters, I have followed the editors of the 'Sources chrétiennes' edition of Basil's *Contra Eunomium*—in this instance, accepting the account of Philostorgius, *HE* 5. 3, instead of the later date (366) demanded by Socrates, *HE* 4. 7. A contrary view is espoused by M. Spanneut, 'Eunomius de Cyzique'; but his account is nevertheless very useful.

14. Sozomen mentioned the threat of exile, a blow to one's reputation perhaps worse than physical torture, *HE* 4. 26, lines 2f.; ed. Bidez, p. 183. For a sense of shame in Basil that he had *not* experienced physical persecution, see *Ep.* 240. 2. Brennecke, however, *Geschichte der Homöer*, pp. 59f., emphasizes rightly that the decisions confirmed at Constantinople were subscribed to quietly by a majority of churchmen in the East, setting the seal on an ecclesiological tradition that Valens would inherit and defend; and see, more generally, pp. 202f.

15. *Ep.* 51. 2, C 1: 132, D 1: 327. The quoted phrase occurs in some MSS only.

16. Perhaps this was what Eunomius meant when he said later that Basil had 'run away', GNyss *CE* 1. 82, 119.

Two histories are thus unfolded: the first, that of Basil's association (partly ascetic) with Eustathius; the second, that of the theological and ecclesiological tradition within which he felt himself to move. They remained, however, difficult to separate entirely; and they changed in character as the years passed.

Basil was able to present the first with a reasonable degree of clarity in a letter of 377, addressed to churchmen in the West.[17] By that time, he felt obliged to characterize Eustathius as an out-and-out supporter of Arius himself—'numbered among his most faithful disciples'. The man had gained ordination at the hands of Hermogenes of Caesarea only by deceit (an unlikely story). The key to his gradual downfall thereafter had been, in Basil's eyes, his association with Eusebius, the early architect of the moderate Arian position. Basil described how Eustathius had sided at Ancyra against ὁμοούσιος and in favour of ὁμοιούσιος. He had attended subsequently the council at Seleucia, had tried to salvage his cause during the synod at Constantinople, had travelled to the West (after his deposition), and had managed to persuade Liberius to recommend his reinstatement. It was a tangled acount; but it gave a not wholly falsified picture of Eustathius's position around 360. The point is that, at the time, Basil had viewed him with a great deal more favour.

Also in the letter of 377, he gave his views on Apollinarius of Laodicea and on Marcellus of Ancyra. Three strands of concern, therefore, were wound together in his mind. Those associations had also been made at the time of the synod at Constantinople, but in different ways, with less obvious pain to himself. In a letter written at exactly the time he was composing the *Contra Eunomium*, Basil discussed authors he had been reading, including Dionysius of Alexandria, the pupil of Origen. He saw the Anomoean tendency reaching back that far: for he deprecated in Dionysius an excessive anxiety about the errors of Sabellius, which had inclined him too much to what Basil now regarded as a characteristically Arian position.[18] And indeed, in the early 360s, even though the new bishop of Laodicea was already set to become the leading Sabellian of his generation, Basil felt no little sympathy for Apollinarius. It was only in

---

17. *Ep.* 243, C 3: 121f., D 4: 89f. We shall discuss the wider context in chapter 8. It is worth noting here Gribomont's suggestion, 'Eustathe', *Dictionnaire d'histoire et de géographie ecclésiastiques*, cols. 29f., that Basil was actually present at Tyana, when Eustathius returned in apparent triumph from his appealing journey to the West (to be outlined in a moment). The possibility is supported, perhaps, by the phrase τὰ γράμματα τὰ διὰ τοῦ μακαρίου Σιλουανοῦ κομισθέντα ἡμῖν in *Ep.* 67 and makes his later recriminations all the more ironic, C 1: 160.

18. *Ep.* 9. 2.

later letters, like the one to the churchmen of the West, that he recast the role of Apollinarius in the Sabellian-Arian conflict. So also, in 373, in a declaration of faith he forced upon Eustathius, he presented Marcellus and Sabellius as the villains—villains towards whom Eustathius (albeit more consistent and probably more honest) was suspected by Basil of retaining some sympathy.[19]

Amidst those sleights of hand (which are no more than further illustration of Basil's readiness in the 370s to redefine the path he had taken in life), we need to focus our attention on the realities of the early 360s. Even then Basil was making theological adjustments. The *Contra Eunomium* itself we have to associate to some extent with the purposes of Eustathius. In 364, a synod was held at Lampsacus. It represented another Homoiousian attempt to revoke the decisions of Constantinople (and indeed of Ariminum), to restore the reputation of Macedonius (who by that time had died), and to revive the decrees made at Antioch in 341—all causes with which Basil was willing to identify. Eustathius attended the gathering. Basil's first major theological treatise, therefore, appears to have taken shape initially as notes dictated to Eustathius, when he talked with Basil en route to the meeting; notes that he could use against the Anomoean party.[20] But in the intervening years, Basil had developed new cautions of his own. In a contemporary letter, he expressed a continuing willingness to accept the term ὅμοιος, provided it was taken to mean ὅμοιος κατ' οὐσίαν, 'like in substance', and provided he was allowed to add yet another word, ἀπαραλλάκτως, 'without variation'. Those phrases taken together, he said, amounted to the ὁμοούσιος of Nicaea, to which he now began to pledge a firmer and more specific allegiance. The synod at Constantinople had watered things down by accepting merely ὅμοιος. He confessed, in other words, to a shift of emphasis: 'I have therefore myself adopted the phrase "of the same substance" [τὸ ὁμοούσιον], because I think that this term is less open to perversion'.[21] The adaptation is clear; but so also is the attachment to nuance. He was naturally ready to distance himself from

19. See *Ep.* 125. 1, and chapter 7, at nn. 30, 60. A useful theological account of Marcellus is provided by T. E. Pollard, 'Marcellus of Ancyra: A Neglected Father'; but he does not discuss Basil's attitudes.

20. *Ep.* 223. 5. Whether the copy sent to Leontius (see *Ep.* 20) represented the same stage of composition is hard to say. We should entertain the possibility that Leontius's copy was the only one to survive: Fedwick, *Basil,* 1: 10 n. 57. We may take with a pinch of salt Gregory of Nyssa's touching belief that Basil wrote the work only to regain the soul of Eunomius to the Church, *CE* 1. 4. For a discussion of Lampsacus, see Brennecke, *Geschichte der Homöer,* pp. 206f.

21. By which he meant, simply, that it would 'do less harm [ἧττον ... κακουργεῖσθαι]', *Ep.* 9. 3, C 1: 39, D 1: 99. Deferrari's translation makes nonsense of one point, by translating

both the simplicity and the vindictiveness of an assembly that had attacked a man he admired. That was not to say, however, that he was willing to abandon the Homoiousian party (which never ceased to assert its fidelity to the principles of Nicaea). The subtleties of this letter (to Maximus 'the philosopher') were still a far cry from later declarations.[22]

Other points emerge from the correspondence of the early 360s. First, a number of Basil's letters were addressed to lay people. Maximus provides an immediate example: he was a 'citizen of the world', enjoying a 'life of activity' (as opposed to 'contemplation and the exercise of the mind').[23] Origen, addressed only shortly afterwards, was also a layman, congratulated for his 'advocacy of the doctrine of the true religion'.[24] Leontius, who received a copy of the Contra Eunomium, was of similar status, 'honourable and upright'. He seems to have been prosperous and to have possessed an estate.[25] It is instructive to see how Basil could present to such a person both his theological interests and his exercise of the priesthood. He teased Leontius for being a sophist, fond of chatter for its own sake. He bemoaned his own 'tiresome association with the vulgar'. Leontius was left to judge whether his friend's work was more than 'child's play'. Yet Basil was willing to seek his serious criticism; and he presumed that Leontius would make use of the Contra Eunomium in opposition to heresy.[26] Theological interest and engagement in controversy on the part of the laity—teachers, landed proprietors, family men—challenges substantially the habitual presentation of the Arian conflict as a clerical affair. It implies also that more was at stake than truth and error: churchmen were competing for the allegiance of supporters from beyond their own professional order and may even have had occasion at times to regard the laity as rivals in the task of developing and propagating religious ideas. Basil continued to assume that men and women in the secular sphere would display some interest

---

τὸ ὁμοούσιον as 'likeness of substance'. For ἀπαραλλάκτως, see also Ep. 361, and Henri de Riedmatten, 'La Correspondance entre Basile de Césarée et Apollinaire de Laodicée', 59f.

22. As, for example, in Ep. 159. 1: 'As for us, then, to state it in a word, the creed of the Fathers who assembled at Nicaea has been honoured by us before all those formulated later, and in this the Son is confessed to be consubstantial [ὁμοούσιος] with the Father', C 2: 86, D 2: 395. Basil's continuing hesitancy in regard to Nicaea, during the early 360s, is stressed by Prestige, Basil and Apollinaris, p. 37, and taken up by Brennecke, Geschichte der Homöer, esp. pp. 226f. (although I am sceptical that Basil had in his sights the establishment of a 'nizänische Reichskirche' wholly analogous to the 'homöische Reichskirche' defended by Constantius and Valens). See also Brennecke, p. 242.

23. Ep. 9. 3, C 1: 40, D 1: 99/101.

24. Ep. 17, C 1: 47, D 1: 117.

25. Assuming that Ep. 35 referred to the Leontius addressed in Ep. 20.

26. Ep. 20, C 1: 50f., D 1: 125.

in theology, and in the intricacies of the Arian controversy in particular. He wrote on that subject with cautious and slightly condescending clarity to the daughters of a prominent general.[27] He responded more fully to the questions of a father and daughter, who seem to have been exposed to the pressure of religious opponents.[28] He could at least admire the 'zeal' of the *comes* Magninianus, amidst 'the din of men of that place [perhaps Neocaesarea], who do no deed but say things in order to slander us', though he declined in that instance to express any opinions in writing.[29] By that time, perhaps, Basil had gained confidence in his distinct vocation to the priesthood; but the examples from an earlier period show us to what extent he was working at the cusp of a social distinction within the Church, not entirely sure where his own sense of purpose would carry him.

A second point is related. In his letter to Maximus, Basil used a strange phrase, 'I have definitely decided not to make my own convictions public'.[30] It is true that the actual dictation of the *Contra Eunomium* may have been more than two years away; but it is hard to believe that Basil had not given the matter some earlier thought. Before penning his own response, he had obviously read the full version of Eunomius's *Apology* very carefully; and that may have appeared before the end of 361. Basil could have gained, in any case, a detailed impression of Eunomius's position while he was in Constantinople; he may even have heard viva voce an early version of the argument, delivered as an attempt to assuage the anxieties of Eudoxius, and of the emperor.[31] His declared reticence, therefore, may simply reflect a decision to limit the 'publication' even of the *Contra Eunomium* to personal friends like Leontius. On the other hand, there is nothing in the letter to Maximus to suggest that he positively did not wish his views to be bruited abroad. Whether they were, of course, is another matter again. Eunomius took many years to respond to the response and did so only in stages, in part after Basil's death. Was that because of hesitation on his part, or because the *Contra Eunomium* was not a widely circulated work? It is hard to judge.

27. *Ep.* 105.
28. *Ep.* 159.
29. 'Because I do not wish to leave behind me any work on the faith or to compose sundry creeds', *Ep.* 175, C 2: 111f., D 2: 457: this in 374, just before he completed his *De spiritu sancto.* For the spelling Magninianus, see *PLRE* 1: 533. He, too, had a pious daughter, mentioned in *Ep.* 325.
30. *Ep.* 9. 3, C 1: 39, D 1: 99. For τὰ ἑαυτῶν ἐγνωκότας, 'convictions' may be too definite, and Courtonne's 'difficultés' too insecure: perhaps 'the opinions I have so far formed', or 'those aspects which I feel I now understand'. One must remember that the letter was written after the synod at Constantinople, but before Basil's ordination to the priesthood.
31. Wickham, 'Date'.

We probably simplify matters too much if we see the choice as one between silence and outspokenness. Basil seems to have felt that one of the problems with the Arian dispute in his day was that people broadcast their opinions without any attempt to communicate with opponents, or to achieve and safeguard genuine unity. He criticized Athanasius of Ancyra, for example, because he had not been willing to send even a 'brief letter' on the dispute between them—'or, if you would not entrust such matters to writings, to have summoned me to your presence, [or, failing that] to employ one of those who are close to you and capable of keeping secrets as an agent of communication with us'.[32]   The choices form a little ecclesiology of their own: the apparently enclosed world of the letter-writing circle may have lain closer to the heart of Basil's Church than we might imagine.   In relation to the *Contra Eunomium*, therefore, and to the theological developments of earlier years, Basil's caution may have reflected rather more his uncertainty as to what position he should adopt, what allegiance he should declare, what style of engagement he should commit himself to.   It was the same dilemma he had discussed with Gregory: whether to join 'the fellowship of men who ... shun the peril of silence'.[33]   He was like the Maximus of another letter, 'giving up a great house and an illustrious family and changing over to the life of the Gospel, ... reflecting concerning himself on such questions as he naturally will—whence he arose and whither he is going'.[34]

The *Contra Eunomium* cannot be read, therefore, in abstraction from its varied context. It was bound to reflect the competing thoughts of a man intent upon defining his loyalties and grappling with the question of how to engage in church affairs more publicly. It seems a philosophical work; but Basil refused to deal with philosophical issues for their own sake. He seized upon the occasion to make clear a theological position he could adopt with consistence and integrity, and an image of the Church that that theology would support. To that extent, therefore, the work did not stand on its own. It invites association with the later *De spiritu sancto* (designed to make up for its shortcomings), and with a whole series of homilies and

---

32. *Ep.* 25. 2, C 1: 62, D 1: 153, written shortly after his consecration.

33. *Ep.* 28. 3, C 1: 69f., D 1: 169. See chapter 3, at n. 102. The 'perils', of course, were much more complicated; and we shall see Basil having to choose constantly between openness and caution (as well as between concern and disdain). Gregory felt the same way, warning Basil at one stage: καὶ δημοσίᾳ πᾶν τὸ λεγόμενον, πολύς τε περὶ αὐτὸν ὁ πόλεμος, *Ep.* 58. 10; ed. Gallay, 1: 75. This shows almost the inhibition of a Synesius. See below, at n. 96.

34. *Ep.* 277, C 3: 149f., D 4: 161. This was probably the Maximus addressed in *Ep.* 301, but not the Maximus of *Ep.* 9: see *PLRE* 1: 585, s.v. Maximus 22 and 25.

letters scattered through the remaining years of Basil's life. It provided an assured basis for Basil's lasting sense of churchmanship. The other documents, often echoing statements of the *Contra Eunomium* itself, form a series of allusions and confirmations that stretch like a comet's tail across the following years, drawing our eye constantly backwards towards this earlier source of energy and enlightenment.

Eunomius was a predominantly philosophical thinker and writer,[35] and it was inevitable that Basil should adopt a philosophical mode of argument in reply. So the reader must tread a philosophical path also; but the aim will be, for us as for Basil, to see beyond the intricacies of logic, and to detect the implications of the immediate debate for the structure of the Church and for the Christian life more generally. Not every detail need detain us here.[36]

Two themes, however, reward attention, because they allowed Basil to make points that reached beyond the bounds of Eunomius's essentially logical preoccupations. Those themes were, first, the relationship between time and eternity, and, second, the relationship between language and reality.

The problem of time had arisen even in the classic phrase, used perhaps by Arius himself, ἦν ὅτε οὐκ ἦν: 'There was [a time] when he was not'.[37] Should one combine this notion of the Son's 'not being' with a reference to time? Was it not more a matter of saying, simply, that one could conceive of the Son's 'not being'? Much of Basil's discussion revolved around this

---

35. Keeping in mind my limited goals, focussed on Basil, I have tried to avoid turning this account into a treatment of Eunomius himself. In addition to the editions of his work, a useful bibliography is provided by Milton V. Anastos, 'Basil's Κατὰ Εὐνομίου, a Critical Analysis', in Fedwick, *Basil*, 1: 70 n. 6. On the specific issue of the philosophical background, see Anastos, pp. 118f. and n. 170. The article as a whole provides a useful theological summary of the work, although it judges both Basil and his opponent from a partisan point of view. The broader issues discussed below are not, it seems to me, recognized, let alone explored. Wiles, 'Eunomius', p. 167, admits: 'The nature of the material from Eunomius' own pen, as well as the citations in polemical sources, is singularly ill-suited to reveal any deeper religious concerns'; and yet, rightly, he produces a sympathetic portrait of the Arian, who had pastoral as well as logical sensibilities.

36. For a few more technical additions, see my earlier essay, 'Basil of Caesarea, *Contra Eunomium:* The Main Preoccupations'.

37. Christopher Stead, 'The *Thalia* of Arius and the Testimony of Athanasius', esp. p. 29. Whatever Arius's intentions, and however strict one's approach, as a translator, to the words here bracketed, opponents rightly refused to ignore the temporal implications of ὅτε.

issue of whether there was a 'before' and an 'after' in relation to the Father's generation of the Son. Perhaps he created thereby as many problems as he solved.[38] His own solution was to fall back upon Scripture; in particular the opening of John's gospel, with its two phrases 'in the beginning' and 'was': the two notions, he said, had to be fused completely, so that one could not 'get behind' the first or separate it from the second.[39]

The appeal to Scripture was characteristic. It provided the only context within which the question at hand could acquire any urgency. One could not prompt religious sentiment, or safeguard religious values, simply by scoring logical points. Basil was especially anxious to maintain a correct link between time and eternity, between the created order and the divine; a link that would be based upon an accurate understanding of the Son and of his relationships (with human beings, just as much as with the Father). And only in the light of Scripture could one appreciate fully why the relationship of the Father with the Son was a matter of importance. Fatherhood, Basil argued, was of the essence of God.[40] To that extent, a relationship to the Father was as characteristic of mortals as it was of the Son himself.[41] That was why they called God 'our Father' also: not merely by analogy but in the truest sense.[42] The very meaning of the word 'father' was to be sought first in God, not read back into the divinity from the human experience of passionate procreation. It was the quality of 'being related' that claimed priority, and problems connected with the mode of generation were of less significance—indeed, they were, in the end, beyond understanding and should not even be discussed.[43]

---

38. *CE* 2. 11f., relating to Eunomius *Apol.* 15. 8–11 (V 7–9—see immediately below for explanation). In the 'Sources chrétiennes' edition of the *Apologia*, Basil's treatise is also printed, 2: 234–98, with French translation, 2: 235–99 (see chapter 2, n. 65). It is to the line numbers of this edition that I initially refer. See also *Eunomius: The Extant Works*, edited by Richard Paul Vaggione. Both books provide biographical commentary. The *Apologia* itself is printed on pp. 34–74 of Vaggione's work, with an English translation, pp. 35–75. References in brackets, of the style V 7–9, refer to the line numbers of this edition.

39. *CE* 2. 14: 'In the beginning was the Word [ἐν ἀρχῇ ἦν ὁ Λόγος]'.

40. *CE* 1. 5. Eunomius certainly seems to have rejected the senses that Basil would have applied to that relationship. For justified comment on Eunomius *Apol.* 9. 1–4 (V 1–3), see *CE* 1. 16.

41. *CE* 2. 10. The assertion was, of course, a risky one. See Gregg and Groh, *Early Arianism*, pp. 50f.

42. *CE* 2. 23.

43. *CE* 2. 20–22. The espousal of silence will recur. Basil felt it was a mistake to suppose that theologians always had all the λόγοι necessary to their specific tasks, *Hom.* 336. 7. More generally, he held consistently to the view that speculation merely generated fruitless controversy, *Hom.* 321. 1, 341. 7. See the points raised in n. 92.

What was Basil's chief concern in all this? He wanted to safeguard the notion of a vital God, a God who reached out to his creatures, a God who was characterized by his power (δύναμις) and his action (ἐνέργεια). In the passages of the *Contra Eunomium* just referred to, that vocabulary coloured entirely Basil's analysis both of generation and of creation and was made to affect also the responses of the worshipping creature.[44] The same considerations governed his handling of redemption, prompted by an examination of Acts 2.36. There Eunomius had found the apparently helpful phrase 'God has made him [i.e., Jesus; and the crucial word was ἐποίησεν, 'has made'] both Lord and Christ'. Basil argued that the passage referred only to the historical moment of self-emptying that marked the beginning of God's redemptive gesture. Luke was not making a statement about the nature of God in the strict sense (according to the canons of θεολογία) but was using, rather, the language appropriate to a description of God's activity within the created order (οἱ τῆς οἰκονομίας λόγοι). He was working, in other words, within the context of salvation. Terms like 'Lord' and 'Christ' had nothing to do with the οὐσία, the substance of the Son: they were ἐξουσίας ὄνομα, titles associated with power and action.[45]

So much for the first theme, concerning the relationship between time and eternity. When it comes to the second, the relationship between language and reality, we are faced more with a difference of epistemology. Basil outlined what he saw as his opponent's position fairly early in his own reply.[46] First, according to Eunomius, there was an inseparable correlation between the οὐσία, the intimate being of God, and the vocabulary used in referring to that οὐσία—for example, when one called God 'unbegotten' (ἀγέννητος). At the same time, a certain independence was also to be maintained: God remained ἀγέννητος, whether humans called him such or not. There was also (and this third point was not unconnected with the other two) a tendency on Eunomius's part to make understanding a

---

44. So the θεῖον βούλημα of the creative God, by the mediation of the Word, πρόεισιν εἰς ἐνέργειαν, *CE* 2. 21; and both εὐσέβεια and the Gospels themselves were charged with a δύναμις directly related to a correct understanding of such divine action, § 22. Note the link in *CE* 1. 5 between δύναμις and the ῥῆμα τοῖς εὐαγγελιζομένοις, and in *Hom.* 321. 6 between ἡ θεία δύναμις and the bodies of the holy. Behind these and similar emphases there always lurked the assertion of Paul: 'The kingdom of God does not consist in talk but in power [ἐν δυνάμει]', 1 Cor. 4.20. Not surprisingly, therefore, the emphasis was not wholly absent from Arian formulations; which made the precisions of Basil's argument all the more important: see Gregg and Groh, *Early Arianism*, pp. 91f.

45. *CE* 2. 3. The contrast between θεολογία and οἰκονομία will be discussed further below, at n. 71.

46. *CE* 1. 5: ὡς οὖν ἔχουσιν αἱ φωναὶ πρὸς ἀλλήλας, οὕτως ἕξουσι, φησί, καὶ αἱ δι' αὐτῶν σημαινόμεναι φύσεις (ed. Sesboüé, 1: 260).

matter merely of accurate expression. Consequently, language provided a reliable, even if transient, map of reality. Words were like frames in a film, a series of flashing images, miniature in themselves, even colourless, and certainly lacking depth or movement; but, set in motion by human discourse, confidently projected outwards upon the world, they could provide a picture entirely faithful to reality. To speak accurately, therefore, was to know profoundly.[47]

Basil described what he thus took to be a central aspect of Eunomius's argument chiefly so that he could put forward an alternative of his own.[48] Words, he said, had to be distinguished from thoughts. That enabled him to launch upon a broad discussion of διάνοια and ἐπίνοια—making thereby, roughly speaking, a distinction between the act and the content of thought, between understanding and idea. Διάνοια and ἐπίνοια represented an arena intermediate between words and things; and their effect was not only active but even creative. It was, according to Basil, within that intermediate arena that a concept like ἀγέννητος would properly find its place. The movements of an observing mind were at first immediate and confused. The processes of understanding broke the conglomerate and undefined impressions into parts: first into thoughts (νοήματα) and then into language itself.[49] The process was described as an ἐπενθύμησις: the thinker literally 'inserted' himself—specifically (to Eunomius's cost) between οὐσία, the substance, and ῥῆμα, the articulated word. And after

47. So, when talking of the Son, οὐσία and σημαινόμενον were, for Eunomius, the same. It was possible to say: ἐπαληθευούσης τῇ οὐσίᾳ τῆς προσηγορίας; the very noun penetrated through, as it were, to the οὐσία, CE 2. 6. Basil, in CE 2. 24, plucked from Eunomius Apol. 18. 17–18 (V 13–14) the phrase παρηλλαγμένων τῶν ὀνομάτων, παρηλλαγμένας ὁμολογεῖν καὶ τὰς οὐσίας (sc. ἐχρῆν), suggesting (quite rightly) a contradiction between this passage and 17. 7–10—although it is possible that Eunomius may have been more subtle, wishing to assert that, while different names must refer to different substances, the same name need not always refer to the same substance. Basil returned to the point in DSS 2 (§ 4). Expressed in these terms, the debate seems dry. Here as elsewhere, 'a sharp eye is needed to discern serious arguments among the numerous conceits and ploys' (Gregg and Groh, Early Arianism, p. 45). Basil's cautious distinctions, explored step by step below, led inevitably to his central assertion—that humans know and respond to the actions of God, rather than to his essence. Eunomius's position, by contrast, laid claim in the end to what Gregory of Nazianzus would later describe as 'unbridled contemplation [θεωρία γὰρ ἀχαλίνωτος]', Orat. 39. 8, PG 36. 344A. See Barnard, Studies in Church History, p. 293.

48. CE 1. 6, for much of what follows. Useful background reflections are provided by Frances M. Young, 'The God of the Greeks and the Nature of Religious Language', pp. 58f. A distinction in this matter between Basil and Athanasius (concerning αἱ οὐσίαι and αἱ λέξεις) is discussed by Gregg and Groh, Early Arianism, p. 25.

49. As he put it later, CE 2. 4, words were ὕστερα τῶν πραγμάτων, which meant that they were dependent as well as subsequent (taking advantage of a concession by Eunomius Apol. 17f.).

putting things into words, after expressing oneself, one's understanding was not lost with the passing sound and breath: the νοήματα remained, firmly embedded 'in the soul of the thinker'.[50]

What Basil had done was redefine the issue, and in a way enduringly characteristic of his own cast of mind. Instead of there being a problem about the relationship between language and reality, there was now a new doubt about the relationship between thought and expression. He retained grave doubts about the efficacy of words in any religious context— or perhaps better, he described their efficacy in ways that circumvented his own epistemological anxieties: 'Even when I wrote to your learned self [this was in a much later letter to Gregory of Nazianzus], I was not unaware that every theological expression [πᾶσα θεολογικὴ φωνή: so 'expression' in the most literal, physical sense] is inferior to the thought of the speaker [τῆς διανοίας τοῦ λέγοντος]'.[51] He made the same point in a sermon that was concerned with the generation of the Son: 'One has to observe, therefore, how far the word falls short of the truth'.[52] To Gregory, in the letter quoted, he immediately made a broader point: 'Speech, I presume, is naturally too weak a thing to serve perfectly the conceptions of our minds [τοῖς νοουμένοις]'.[53] There was even a moral dimension to that reserve: sins of the tongue, after all, were at once the easiest and the most devastating to commit.[54]

All such statements were made against a general background, a theory of anthropology and of human destiny that became the central theme of Basil's life. Perhaps one of its best expressions was a splendid sermon he preached on the phrase in Deuteronomy, πρόσεχε σεαυτῷ, 'Take heed for yourself'.[55] Language was to be seen as a providential gift of the creator, whereby people could open to one another hearts that might otherwise be

---

50. Note the phraseology, τὴν λεπτοτέραν καὶ ἀκριβεστέραν τοῦ νοηθέντος ἐπενθύμησιν—almost a parody of Eunomius's caution.

51. *Ep.* 7, C 1: 21, D 1: 45. For the late date, see Fedwick, *Basil,* 1: 13 n. 76.

52. *Hom.* 321. 2. The 'fall', ἀπόπτωμα, has almost a moral and tragic quality, *PG* 31. 1460B.

53. See n. 51.

54. *Hom.* 351. 9. Recall the primacy given to verbal etiquette in *Ep.* 2: see chapter 3, at n. 81. The written word caused even more problems. A lament from the middle years of his episcopate is typical: 'The living word makes for more effective persuasion, and it is not, like the written word, open to attack and subject to calumny', *Ep.* 212. 2, C 2: 199, D 3: 219. See below, at n. 95f.

55. In the general sense of 'Take care, lest you . . .', Deut. 15.9. See *Hom.* 319. 1f. for most of what follows. There are obvious connections with the *Hexaemeron,* which will be explored in chapter 9. For the text, see *L'Homélie de Basile de Césarée sur le mot "Observe-toi toi-même"*, edited by Stig Y. Rudberg. That this was an early sermon is affirmed by Bernardi, *Prédication,* pp. 67f.

sealed off. As he wrote at the time of the *Contra Eunomium* itself, 'Words are the images of the soul'.[56] But there was a dark side to the matter as well: human beings were thereby possessed of an inner world of thought, where sin could play at speed, unobserved, with whole areas of human experience sealed off from exterior moral control, thus infecting society, conversely, with the dangers of hypocrisy. Beneath the surface of those reflections lay an even broader theory of the Fall, whereby the simplicity of the human heart had been fractured by passion. Yet the very ambiguity, the potential breadth, of the word λόγος pointed to a path out of those difficulties: 'words' might create a problem; but 'reason' guaranteed its resolution (and λόγος conveyed both notions), enabling a person to shun sin and to embrace justice 'naturally [ἐκ φύσεως]'. The moral problem, therefore, was not *whether* one could articulate one's rationality but *how*.[57]

One should not be surprised to find the foretaste of an answer in the *Contra Eunomium*. It was not just a question of finding oneself, as an 'understander', interposed between word and substance. The whole process of response to reality started with sense experience (αἴσθησις); and sense experience did not engage with οὐσίαι anyway, but only with the individual properties of things. By introducing that point, Basil hoped to compel Eunomius to acknowledge what would happen to his Trinitarian vocabulary when it was forced to operate at the level of human experience; for all humans shared one οὐσία, just as did the Father and the Son, yet they were knowable also as separate beings, because it was individual properties that were first perceived and talked about.[58] The epistemological mechanics of the process were treated more fully in the second book of the work. Basil described how individual properties impinged upon the mind: 'They set in motion an active quality [ἐνέργεια] within intelligible things, they play within our souls like light, and they lead us to quick understanding [πρὸς τὴν ἐφικτὴν ταῖς διανοίαις σύνεσιν]'.[59] The implication was that the mind attended more to action than to substance, and therefore more to the 'how' of God's existence than to the 'what'.[60] People could

---

56. *Ep.* 9. 1, C 1: 37, D 1: 93: I feel that 'soul' rather than 'mind' offers a better rendering of ψυχή in this context.

57. *Hom.* 350. 8.

58. *CE* 2. 4. It was even possible to use the hallowed formula τὸ ὁμοούσιον in the slightly jarring context of τὸ ὁμοούσιον πάντων ἀνθρώπων. See also 2. 6. The point was repeated with reference to terms of relationship: they, too, were inapplicable to οὐσίαι, 2. 9.

59. *CE* 2. 28 (2: 120). The notions of ἐνέργεια and φῶς enabled him to make important connections later: see below, at nn. 78f.

60. *CE* 1. 8, 15. For further reflections on ἐνέργεια (and some misunderstandings on Basil's part), see 1. 24, 2. 31; Eunomius *Apol.* 23. 4f., 18f. (V 4f., 15f.).

talk about οὐσίαι, but such conversation was part of a process whereby they created for themselves fresh meanings. They moved sideways within the confines of language, rather than out towards reality. Theology, in that sense, was a second-degree activity, not a verbal description of an observable world.[61]

So a sharp eye counted for as much in Basil's theology as a keen mind. Engagement with the visible could respond even to silence—that silence characteristic of the created order, which had no need of words to make its point and did not demand words of those who attempted to understand it: 'In its very silence it cries aloud in witness to its maker and its lord, so that you may hurry forward to an understanding of the one who alone is wise'.[62] Here we begin to see how Basil unravelled the process whereby rationality became articulate—articulate in the sense that it could be expressed without being verbalized; for the correlate of silence was action, action in preference to speech. 'This is the knowledge of God, the keeping of God's commandments'.[63]

We discover in this series of philosophical arguments the roots of another great theme in Basil's teaching. In his sermon on the phrase 'Take heed for yourself', he explored further the relationship between observation and formative understanding. If people could acquire an accurate knowledge of themselves, he said, they would have at their disposal an immediate guide to the knowledge of God.[64] They did not have to look at the natural world in order to understand its creator[65] but would find the key to understanding within themselves. That was because each person was a cosmos in miniature—although what one observed within oneself was not the creator in person but the wisdom of the creator. The question was, of course, how could one come to 'know' one's inner self? Basil was ready to make his own answer: ἐκ

61. *CE* 1. 14.
62. *Hom.* 340. 3.
63. *Hom.* 337. 4. Basil linked the emphasis with the need for a verbal reticence about the nature of God, and about the meaning of John's words, 'In the beginning ...'. Σιωπή was a θεραπεία, a soothing antidote to the turmoil of inquiry. The context for the sermon was the more developed reflection on the Trinity that accompanied the composition of the *De spiritu sancto*: Fedwick, *Basil*, 1: 10 n. 47. The reader will rightly detect an echo of the points raised in chapter 2, at nn. 64f., stressing a pastoral dependence on more than traditional skill in speaking. The theme is developed further below, especially at nn. 115f., 130f., 142f.; and in chapter 5, at nn. 141f.
64. Κατανόησις in relation to ourselves, ἔννοια in relation to God, *Hom.* 319. 7; *PG* 31. 213D; Rudberg, *Homélie*, p. 35; but the distinction may not be important, since we have κατανόησις of God in *Hom.* 354. 6, *PG* 29. 445B.
65. This represented to some extent a modification of *Hom.* 340. 3: see above, at n. 62, and below, at n. 67.

τῶν ἐνεργειῶν γνωρίζεται μόνον, 'You know it only from the evidence of its activities'. Any advance beyond that entailed a shift from knowledge and logical argument in the normal sense to the realm of faith. The path was sketched out, therefore, with great care: first came knowledge of self generally, then an appreciation of the wisdom of the creator manifested in the activities of the soul, and finally the transition from insight to belief.[66]

That was not an isolated view. In a sermon concerned with Arianism, Basil offered the same exhortation to 'enter into the hidden places of [the] soul', where a person might learn what it meant to say that God was from the beginning, and that the Word came forth, and that he was nevertheless entirely one with God. Learning of such a sort would lead immediately to authentic worship.[67] In a sermon on Psalm 46 (V 45), Basil insisted that, unless one could see the works of God, no amount of thought would help. Even the most purified vision was still a vision of what God did, of his ἔργα.[68] In these passages, Basil provided the most relevant context for his frequent emphasis, here and in other homilies, upon the need to act: to regard action as the central expression of religious faith, the most appropriate response of the devotee to the observable providence of God.[69] They are passages that carry us from Basil's reflections on the nature of παιδεία to the pastoral task that he faced in his own church. Around the visible deed, whether of God or of one's fellow humans, revolved the rhetoric of Basil's ecclesial career, based not on description and analysis but on an alternative 'logic' of insight and reverent admiration.

The cohesion and momentum of his address depended on its association with a reading of Scripture, to which the *Contra Eunomium* gave central attention. Scripture loosened the logjam between thought and expression, and between word and deed. Scripture was the key to the way in which language functioned. It pointed, for example, as we have seen, to the original sense of the word 'father'. Observe, said Basil, what happens, if one thinks of Jesus as 'gate', 'way', 'bread', 'vine', 'shepherd', and 'light'. The full meaning of such expressions could not come merely

---

66. Note the two crucial phrases: first, ἀλλ' ἐν σεαυτῷ, οἱονεὶ μικρῷ τινι διακόσμῳ, τὴν μεγάλην κατόψει τοῦ κτίσαντός σε σοφίαν, PG 31. 213D/216A; Rudberg, *Homélie*, p. 35; and second, τῇ διανοίᾳ ἐπιτρέψας τὴν πίστιν, νοητὴν ἔχε τὴν περὶ αὐτοῦ κατάληψιν, 216A; Rudberg, p. 35. See below, at n. 80.

67. *Hom.* 343. 4. Note that the ἔξω with which the inner attention is contrasted (μὴ ἔξω διαβλέψῃ) is not the natural world but the world of argument (διὰ τῆς δεικτικῆς φωνῆς): PG 31. 481AB.

68. *Hom.* 353. 7. The passage is filled with words associated with νοῦς, θεωρία, οἰκείωσις τοῦ Θεοῦ, διάνοια; and yet ἔργα hold all together.

69. *Hom.* 327. 1, 334. 3, 337. 1., 338. 1.

from breaking down the simplicities of sense experience but must depend on the inclusion of a relationship (as with 'father'), a relationship to the believer.[70]

What the human person faced, as an observer and an understander, was a dynamic world, a world in which God reached out to the creature and expected the creature to reach back in turn. Language did not describe a static situation but offered comment upon a drama; and it was Scripture that illustrated most reliably the extent to which one had immediate access to actions rather than to an actor—above all, to the action of salvation. We have noted already Basil's comment on Eunomius's use of Acts 2.36: '[Luke] does not impart information to us in a theological manner, but deploys rather the language appropriate to the visible dispensation of the created order'.[71] Once more, it was the knowledge of properties that was under scrutiny.[72] Of course, revelation was involved, not least the revelation that there was a Father; but human beings had to begin their process of understanding with the Son.[73] Fatherhood took its origin in God; but knowledge of that truth began with knowledge of the Son, and knowledge not of his substance but of the Son perceived as an ἐξουσία, one acting in a way characteristic of God.[74]

To those reflections, Basil gave a final twist. The power and energy of God, moving outwards and downwards in the cosmos, contributed indispensably to the creature's understanding of what that movement meant. The Word—something addressed, and therefore heard—was a necessary condition for the very functioning of the mind. Yet the mind was able to acknowledge that there was an οὐσία 'beyond' the Word.[75] Basil happily accepted the apparent contradiction between the two statements—one suggesting a limitation in human understanding, the other transcendence. People had simply to trust that there was a correspondence between the way the mind went into action, the way it perceived, and the 'reality' created by God. That correspondence depended, so Basil believed, on the fact that Adam and Eve had been made in God's image. So the capacity to think and to talk was linked to the patterns of divine generation and cosmic creation. They became the condition rather than the object of understanding and speech.

70. *CE* 1. 7. See above, at nn. 41f. The same point occurs in *DSS* 8 (§ 17).
71. *CE* 2. 3 (2: 16). So one may distinguish between θεολογία and οἰκονομία: see above, at n. 45.
72. *CE* 2. 29.
73. *CE* 1. 26.
74. *CE* 2. 3.
75. *CE* 2. 16.

In the light of those assertions, we can make more sense of passages that connect the workings of the mind with what we might call the workings of the Trinity. The passionless generation of the Son by the Father should prompt one to recall the synchronic harmony between thought and the movement of the mind.[76] One's ability to know oneself represented a dialogue like that between Father and Son: a dialogue identified in itself with the person of the Spirit.[77] As in the Trinity, so in the mind, light was the chief analogue of life and insight.[78] Above all, the comparability of Father and Son, which Eunomius denied and which Basil insisted upon, kept open a path to the Father: a path of genuine knowledge; a path that led one to aspire without blasphemy to likeness to God.[79]

Those were all ideas with a long future in Basil's thought. One would expect an emphasis on enlightenment by the Spirit, given Basil's interest in later years; but, once noticed, it is more obvious in its presence elsewhere: in the contrast, for example, between πίστις and ἀπόδειξις, faith and logical argument,[80] and in the analogous activities of the Trinity and of the human mind. The last point was often expressed in some detail. John's use of the term 'Word', to proclaim the truth of the relationship between Father and Son, rested on the fact that a word comes from the mind, yet is passionless in a technical sense, and is above all an image of the one who gives it being. Just as with the Father, so with human speech: words present an image of the totality of one's understanding in the matter spoken of:

> For our own words are an offspring [γέννημα] of the mind, brought to birth without passion.... The mind remains undivided in its own substance, supporting the whole of our speech without falling short in

76. CE 2. 16.
77. CE 3. 4.
78. CE 2. 28.
79. CE 1. 26f., appealing to Matthew 5.48, and using, again, the pregnant phrase τῇ πρὸς τὸν Θεὸν τῶν ὅλων ὁμοιώσει.
80. Hom. 358. 1. See above, at n. 66. It is important not to make this too sharp a feature of Basil's thought (as does Fedwick, for example, in Charisma, p. 5). Whatever distrust of philosophical or rhetorical techniques we may find, it makes full sense only in the contexts already created here: worshipful response, Scriptural definition, action and example. Rationality, argument, and understanding were conducted or achieved, according to Basil, within an actively virtuous and believing community. In any case, ἀπόδειξις could not be excluded totally, even from the handling of Scripture: Ep. 263. 4. The same applied to κατάλυψις: Hom. 352. 5 (and see n. 67 above). These skills were rendered harmless when deployed within the boundaries of one's Christian culture: DSS 25 (§§ 58f.). The real problem was thirsting after novelty, DSS 17 (§ 42): see below, at n. 98.

any way; and the word comes forth enfolding within itself all the power of the mind that gave it being.[81]

Not surprisingly, it was when Basil wrote the *De spiritu sancto*, bringing to a firmer conclusion the arguments of the *Contra Eunomium*, that those ideas acquired greatest precision. He asserted without hesitation, in the later treatise, that the relation of the Spirit to the Father and the Son was analogous to the relationship of the human spirit to the human self as a whole.[82] He wrote even more vividly on the matter to his friend Amphilochius of Iconium: 'The mind that is tempered with the divinity of the Spirit [ὁ μέντοι τῇ θεότητι τοῦ Πνεύματος ἀνακραθεὶς νοῦς] is at last initiated into the great speculations'.[83] Another crucial letter, again to Amphilochius, summed up the implications of the *Contra Eunomium*. Commenting on a phrase in John's gospel—'No one has ever seen God; the only Son, who is in the bosom of the Father, he has made him known'— Basil asked what it was that the Son had 'made known': 'His substance or His power?' His power, clearly:

> The disciples, when did they worship Him? Was it not when they saw that creation was subject to Him? For from sea and winds that obeyed Him they knew His Godhead. Therefore from the activities is the knowledge, and from the knowledge is the worship. 'Do you believe that I can do this [referring now to a passage in Matthew]? I believe, Lord'; and he worshipped Him. Thus worship follows faith, and faith is strengthened by power.

And he concluded: 'We understand God from His power. Therefore we believe in Him whom we understand, and we worship Him in whom we believe'.[84]

81. *Hom.* 343. 3, *PG* 31. 477D/480A. The words omitted may make a vivid allusion to the circumstances of childbirth: οὔτε γὰρ τέμνεται, οὔτε μερίζεται, οὔτε ῥέει.

82. *DSS* 16 (§ 40). The vocabulary is notably precise: τὸ δὲ μέγιστον τεκμήριον τῆς πρὸς Πατέρα καὶ Υἱὸν τοῦ Πνεύματος συναφείας, ὅτι οὕτως ἔχειν λέγεται πρὸς Θεόν, ὡς πρὸς ἕκαστον ἔχει τὸ πνεῦμα τὸ ἐν ἡμῖν (2: 390). The *DSS* will be examined more fully in chapter 7.

83. *Ep.* 233, C 3: 40, D 3: 369.

84. *Ep.* 234. 1, C 3: 41, D 3: 375/377. See John 1.18 and Matthew 9.28 (in relation to which Basil's 'worshipped' is a gloss).

Beneath the philosophical surface of Basil's anti-Arian polemic, therefore, lay a movement back and forth in relations between God and humanity. The debates about time and eternity, and about thought and
word, dealt merely with the symptoms and mechanics of that deeper
cosmic rhythm. God was seen primarily as a being who was related to
others—to his Son, and to his creatures. In the face of that generous contact, he demanded a response that would extend beyond the mere attempt
to describe reality, divine or otherwise. Eunomius, as Basil presented him,
had wanted people to understand God with clear, purified minds.[85] Basil,
on the other hand, wanted them to recognize the generosity of God, by
acting in such a way as to demonstrate their corresponding trust and affection. Two related questions remained. How was that response (a matter of
deeds rather than of words) to be made both authentic and effective? Who
was to guarantee both the authenticity and the effectiveness? That Basil
should have raised the questions in the first place showed how far he had
moved from a trust in asceticism for its own sake. In answering them,
he explored two further themes that were to remain at the forefront of his
mind for the rest of his life: the themes of authority and worship.

Basil presented Eunomius, more or less fairly, as a man who rejected
majority opinion, rank, and mere priority in time as factors that could
be allowed to give an opinion authoritative weight, or to contribute to
reliable statements of doctrine.[86] In setting up an alternative position,
he also espoused the notion of 'tradition' (παράδοσις), but he gave it
the preeminent value—and with a nuance of his own, referring to 'the
tradition that has held sway among so many holy men throughout the
passage of time'. The chief characteristic of παράδοσις, in Basil's eyes, was
not the convincingness of its intellectual appeal but its antiquity and its
holiness. The latter quality was particularly important. Παράδοσις was not
just a collection of statements or ideas but a heritage passed from person to
person: so the character of the individuals involved counted for almost
as much as the truths that were handed on.[87] It was also an historical

85. See Eunomius *Apol.* 20. 5 (V 4f.), quoted at *CE* 2. 31: καθαρᾷ τῇ διανοίᾳ τὰς περὶ
τούτων ποιεῖσθαι κρίσεις (2: 128).
86. *CE* 1. 3 (especially at 1: 158), and see 2. 1f., together with Eunomius *Apol.* 4. 7–10
(V 6–9).
87. *DSS* 7 (§ 16). It is necessary, at this early stage, to be warned that Basil's sense of
antiquity (particularly when linked with the formulae of baptism, discussed at the end of this
chapter) may not have been fully justified historically. See the arguments of H. J. Carpenter,

process in a stricter sense, a matter of custom as much as of enduring logic.[88] For that reason, παράδοσις transmitted patterns of behaviour as well as of belief: 'There is the custom among us, which we can cite in defence of our position, a custom having the force of a law, because our ordinances have been handed down to us by holy men'.[89] Παράδοσις, therefore, was entirely related to the economy of action already discussed: deeds were to be carried out in the shadow of heritage.

It governed also the conduct of Basil himself, as one intent upon forming the behaviour of others: he became an example of παράδοσις in action. Writing to Amphilochius, Basil concluded a long description of his own programme of pastoral and ascetic formation with an invitation to Amphilochius to visit Caesarea in person, 'in order that you, guarding his [i.e., Basil's own] words carefully in your memory, might by the application of your own intelligence find out in addition whatever he left unsaid'. A clear distinction was thus made between what was handed on and what was to be added on the basis of personal experience and endeavour.[90] The final phrases of the letter present a vivid image of Basil the teacher, standing on the frontier between a received heritage and an audience awaiting formation—'a man who both knows much from the experience of others, as well as from his own wisdom, and can impart it to those who come to him'.[91]

The specific παράδοσις under discussion in the *Contra Eunomium* seemed by contrast almost entirely a matter of words; and that may explain some of the anxieties that Basil betrayed in his argument. Discussion turned first to the Fathers (for Eunomius had made some appeal to earlier writers—a potential embarrassment for Basil). Without actually quoting Eunomius yet, Basil asserted that his opponent had merely cobbled together a profession of faith 'from naive and woolly statements [ἐξ ἁπλῶν καὶ ἀδιορίστων λέξεων]'. He admitted that many of the Fathers had made such declarations—but not πρὸς ζητήσεις, in answer to questions, to challenges addressed against the orthodox position: rather, in the simplicity of their hearts (ἁπλῶς ... οὕτως ἐφ' ἑαυτῶν ... ἐν ἁπλότητι καρδίας).

'Creeds and Baptismal Rites in the First Four Centuries', about the novelties of fourth-century opinion, still accepted by J. N. D. Kelly in the third edition of his *Early Christian Creeds* (1972).

88. The point was made in several responses to Amphilochius: see, for example, *Ep.* 199. 21, with its contrast between 'reasoning' and 'custom', λόγος and συνήθεια, the former being 'not easy [οὐ ῥάδιος]', C 2: 158, D 3: 113.

89. *Ep.* 160. 2, C 2: 88, D 2: 401.

90. For an analogous point in relation to the *Ad adulescentes*, see chapter 2, at n. 100.

91. *Ep.* 150. 4, C 2: 75, D 2: 371. Basil pretended that this letter had been written by Amphilochius's friend, Heracleidas.

The implication was clear: authoritative statements within the Christian tradition were always likely to be controversial; that is to say, forged in the course of debate against the enemies of the truth. Personal reflections, of the sort to which Eunomius appealed, were perfectly in order but were not to be taken as 'for others'.[92]

That cautious distinction governed Basil's attitude to a great deal that had survived from the Church's past reflection. He complained in 376, for example, that his enemies in the region of Neocaesarea had attempted to mislead Anthimus of Tyana by quoting ambiguous statements about the Father and the Son from the *Exposition of the Faith* by Gregory Thaumaturgus, overlooking the fact that 'this was said, not dogmatically, but controversially [οὐ δογματικῶς ... ἀλλ' ἀγωνιστικῶς] in the dialogue with Aelianus'.[93] (It was a touchy example, of course, since Gregory, even by Basil's own admission, would have been regarded as the leading figure in the παράδοσις of the region.) He made a similar point in relation to his own bishop, Dianius, from whose hands he had received both baptism and ordination as a reader. Referring many years later to their estrangement after the synod of Constantinople, he defended himself against slanders that continued to focus on the incident: 'Tell me, did I anathematize the most blessed Dianius? For this is the charge they made against us. Where or when? In whose presence? On what pretext? Was it in bare words or in writing?'[94] The last point was the telling one. Basil was always careful to distinguish between what might be said and what might endure on the written page. In the context of yet another squabble, relating to his association with Apollinarius of Laodicea, he declared that 'we cannot be convicted from a work that we ourselves have hitherto published about faith, nor from such unwritten spoken words as we have ever openly uttered to the churches of God'; and the same applied to words 'spoken in private'.[95] Preaching and conversation were inevitably moments of danger; but (with luck) they would not survive to cause embarrassment or error. The written word represented a far less destructible vehicle, which one should protect as much as possible against seepage from speculative rumination or the hurried formulae of argument. Basil assumed that even his own mistakes were most likely to be found in written form: 'If our

92. *CE* 1. 4 (1: 162). Basil's suspicion of 'questions', in this sense, was constant (see below at n. 102f.); but he would not leave them hanging dangerously in the air, 'for there is danger of treason [προδοσίας], if one is not quick to answer the questions about God which those ask who love the Lord', *Ep.* 7, C 1: 22, D 1: 45/47; and see n. 114.

93. *Ep.* 210. 5, C 2: 195, D 3: 209.

94. *Ep.* 51. 1, C 1: 132, D 1: 323.

95. *Ep.* 223. 4, C 3: 13, D 3: 301.

error concern faith, let the treatise be shown to us'—as if to say, faith (and its naturally careful expression) was all one should expect to find exposed in a 'treatise'.[96]

Basil was afraid that many opinions, carelessly broadcast, might acquire the hard texture of heritage, when in fact they were no more than novel reflections. He made the point very forcibly in relation to Apollinarius (when his earlier regard had waned): 'By his facility in writing he has a tongue that suffices him for every subject' and 'has filled the world with his books'. Basil focussed in particular on Apollinarius's 'theological writings', constructed 'not out of Scriptural proofs, but out of human arguments'. Readers, as a result, became confused. They lost 'the ancient character of the true religion': 'intent on innovations', they 'turned aside to inquiries and contentious investigations'.[97] Basil reinforced the point elsewhere. He congratulated Egyptian colleagues on their 'zeal for orthodoxy in religion': 'Neither by multitude of books nor by subtlety of sophisms has the firmness of your heart been disturbed'. On the contrary, they 'recognised those who make innovations against the apostolic teachings', and would not consent 'to cover over by silence the harm that is being worked by them'.[98] Together with other themes we have touched upon, this contrast between what was ancient and apostolic and what was embraced merely for the sake of contentious novelty lay at the heart of Basil's view of church discipline.

Eunomius helped Basil to sharpen his view, because he illustrated an exactly contrary inclination. His error lay in setting his mind to work on the material of tradition, subjecting it to detailed criticism. He used the same word as Basil, παράδοσις, and was willing to accept the patristic heritage as a guide and touchstone (ὥσπερ τινὰ γνώμα καὶ κανόνα); but tradition was to be subjected to strict judgement.[99] Basil made hay of that position, saying that Eunomius was full of reverent praise one minute and full of 'criticism' the next. Why, he asked, should anyone wish to subject κανόνα to additions—that is, to his own painstaking comments?[100] It was through such analysis, criticism, and commentary that the most dangerous novelties were likely to arise. To pit one's more recent insights against the received wisdom of the past, 'the apostolic proclamation of faith [τὸ ἀποστολικὸν τῆς πίστεως κήρυγμα]', was to seek merely 'the popular

    96. *Ep.* 204. 5, C 2: 176, D 3: 165. Given what happened to Basil's own work at the hands of others, the bravura was ironic: see GNaz *Orat.* 43. 66. See n. 33.
    97. *Ep.* 263. 4, C 3: 124f., D 4: 97f.
    98. *Ep.* 265. 2, C 3: 128, D 4: 107f.
    99. Eunomius *Apol.* 4. 7–10 (2: 240) (V 6–9).
    100. *CE* 1. 4f.

novelty of the day [τὴν νῦν ἐπιπολάζουσαν καινοτομίαν]'.[101] Indeed, matters were worse than that: even to ask a question was to invite suspicion. The 'old-time blessedness of the churches' had been untouched by 'the malady of inquiry'.[102] Silence became almost a principle for Basil, a 'therapy', as we have seen:[103] 'Do not inquire into matters that lie beyond the bounds of discovery'.[104]

The attitude was by no means restricted to the *Contra Eunomium*. Writing to Gregory from Pontus, Basil had made the plea 'One should take heed not to be boorish in conversation, but to ask questions without contentiousness, and to answer without self-display'.[105] 'To ask questions without contentiousness' was precisely what controversialists in the wider Church seemed incapable of doing. Moreover, his exhortation was embedded in a long description of the practical life, the life of action, which he contrasted increasingly with a life of wordiness. Basil, of course, did answer questions and even encouraged them; but he did so with extraordinary care. Before launching into comment, for example, on the 'canons', for the benefit of his friend Amphilochius, he presented a neat vignette of the process he thought he was engaged in: 'Questions asked by a wise man, as it seems, make even a fool wise'. Basil felt, as a consequence, that he had 'become a more prudent administrator than before and wiser by this very questioning, learning many things that we do not know'. He admitted that, 'though we have never before taken up for study the questions you raise, we have been obliged to examine into them accurately, both to recall whatever we have heard from our elders, and independently to draw conclusions akin to what we have been taught'.[106] Here was a skilful attempt to interweave the advantages of personal reflection with a disciplined respect for what had been bequeathed. Basil reserved the keenest expression of his nervousness for the final section of the letter:

> I am surprised that you should demand of Scripture a schoolmasterly precision, and that you think we are forcing matters when we espouse an interpretation that produces the best possible clue to Scripture's meaning, instead of just translating accurately what is signified by the Hebrew words. But since we ought not to pass over indifferently questions stirred up by an inquiring person . . .

101. *Ep.* 105, C 2: 6, D 2: 199. See *DSS* 17 (§ 42).
102. *Ep.* 172, C 2: 107f., D 2: 447.
103. *Hom.* 337. 4. See n. 63.
104. *Hom.* 342. 3. See above, at n. 92.
105. *Ep.* 2. 5, C 1: 10, D 1: 19.
106. *Ep.* 188, intro.; C 2: 120f.; D 3: 5f.

(and he went on to offer some interpretation of a passage from Psalm 8).[107] It is not insignificant that Basil should have expressed those caveats to Amphilochius. In his introduction to the closely associated *De spiritu sancto*, Basil praised his friend for being a φιλομαθής, attending carefully to every φωνή, every individual word that concerned the nature of God. He congratulated him on not simply making inquiries, τὰς ἐρωτήσεις, pursued in the cause of conflict, but seeking τὸ ἀληθές, the truth. He pointed out that what gave even little words their importance was their δύναμις—literally, their power: the momentum, as it were, that carried the hearer or reader from sign to meaning.[108] So a process of interpretation lay at the centre of the exercise. We can see, as a result, how closely interwoven his epistemology and his ecclesiology had become. One read the texts handed down within the Church by exactly the same means, with exactly the same guidance, and subject to exactly the same discipline as governed one's 'reading' of the world of experience.

Basil wished, therefore, to control both the redeployment of ancient material and the insights and responses that naturally followed upon the reading of such material. In one sense, Christians had to content themselves with the formulae they had inherited. In another sense, they could bring experience to bear upon the texts. What they were not permitted to do was express them afresh in their own words—although, with caution and privacy, they could produce the occasional ad hoc statement of their own (which no one else was bound to regard as further παράδοσις).

The balance hoped for was likely to be difficult; but Basil walked that particular tightrope again and again. Recall his words to Eustathius of Sebaste. His 'conception of God' had 'developed'. 'I did not change', he wrote, 'from one opinion to another': 'I perfected the principles handed down to me'. 'The same doctrine has been developed [in me] through

107. *Ep.* 188. 15; C 2: 131; D 3: 45; but I have followed neither Deferrari's translation nor that of Courtonne (which appears quite contrary but is also obscure): what I have produced seemed to me assured partly in the light of discussion with Garth Fowden. The *Contra Eunomium* had anticipated the point made here. One could not escape from the authoritative παράδοσις by pretending to an insight that was prior to or 'behind' the Hebrew. Subsequent (and inspired) translators (the writers of the Septuagint) had blocked off such a loophole; and those who came after them were constrained (although entirely with confidence) to seek out meanings dependent on that hallowed text: CE 2. 7.

108. *DSS* 1 (§§ 1–2) (2: 250–56). He was talking about σημαινόμενα, as in the letter just quoted: words seen as pointing beyond themselves. The point is to be connected with his rejection of Eunomius's view, that there was a match between language and reality: see above, at n. 47; and note the allusion there also to the *DSS*.

progress'.[109] The concessions were at once generous and cautious. When the discussion was carried over into a more public domain, however, difficulties began to multiply. To the church of Antioch, in 373, Basil declared with confidence:

> As to creed, we accept no newer creed written for us by others, nor do we ourselves make bold to give out the product of our own intelligence [τὰ τῆς ἡμετέρας διανοίας γεννήματα παραδιδόναι], lest we make the words of our religion the words of man; but rather that which we have been taught by the holy Fathers do we make known to those who question us.[110]

The position seems straightforward. It appears to have been repeated in the careful letter drawn up by Basil, at the same time, for Eustathius of Sebaste to sign (in order to assure both Basil and others of his orthodoxy).[111] Yet two points were being made that betrayed the greater complexity of the situation. First, Basil said that those who wished to repudiate error should simply subscribe to a formula (in this case, of Nicaea—'The creed embodied therein suffices'), and that others should leave until the day of judgement the problem of whether an adequately corresponding submission had been made at the level of the heart. He then added:

> It is therefore fitting to receive them when they confess that they believe according to the words [κατὰ τὰ ῥήματα] set forth by our Fathers at Nicaea and according to the meaning disclosed by those words when soundly interpreted [καὶ κατὰ τὴν ὑγιῶς ὑπὸ τῶν ῥημάτων τούτων ἐμφαινομένην διάνοιαν].[112]

So tightly expressed a concession soon began to unravel under pressure. Controversies with Eustathius and others—concerned in part with a more 'developed' understanding of the Holy Spirit—forced Basil to make distinctions in relation to the very creed of Nicaea itself: 'This was not what that holy and God-beloved synod had in mind [ἐνόησεν]'—a remarkable claim to privileged information. Part of the point was that his enemies were inconsistent in their own interpretations: 'They employ the words

---

109. *Ep.* 223. 3, C 3: 12f., D 3: 299. He repeated the point later: 'Through progress a certain amplification is witnessed in what we say [ἐκ προκοπῆς τινα αὔξησιν ἐπιθεωρεῖσθαι], which is not a change from worse to better but is a completing of that which was lacking [συμπλήρωσις τοῦ λείποντος], according to the increment of our knowledge [κατὰ τὴν προσθήκην τῆς γνώσεως]', § 5, C 3: 14f., D 3: 305. See chapter 1, at nn. 72f.

110. *Ep.* 140. 2, C 2: 61, D 2: 335.

111. *Ep.* 125. The circumstances will be discussed fully in chapter 7.

112. *Ep.* 125. 1, C 2: 31, D 2: 261.

of the creed, like physicians, according to occasion, adapting it to their existing condition now in one way and now in another'. Even consistency was not in itself a sufficient basis for confidence. Basil felt obliged to add: 'But the rottenness of this sophistry it is not for me to prove [ἐλέγχειν] but for you to consider [νοεῖν]. For the Lord will give you understanding [σύνεσιν] to discover [γνωρίζειν] what is the straight doctrine and what is the crooked and perverted'. The original vocabulary needs careful attention, for Basil appears to have been advocating a direct, almost an inspired, understanding of conciliar decrees.[113]

When it came to deciding which interpretation to adopt, faced with ambiguity or silence in a text, Basil did hint at alternative sources of authority and confidence. On the specific issue of the Holy Spirit, Nicaea had expressed itself 'cursorily [ἐν παραδρομῇ] ... because at that time this question had not yet been agitated'. Yet the 'sense' of the doctrine (διάνοια) 'was unassailably inherent in the souls of the faithful'.[114] Here was another and no less extraordinary claim to privileged information: for the question had to be, how did Basil (or anyone else, for that matter) know what was going on in the souls of the faithful? Basil had his answer. Eunomius had apparently criticized him for being 'antagonistic to the opinions and recollections of the many'.[115] Certainly, in the *Contra Eunomium* as elsewhere, we can catch him in a posture of arrogance— dismissing the uninformed, for example, because they lay beyond the reach of words.[116] Eunomius, for all his pastoral ambitions, was by no means beyond criticism either: for he admitted that he had no intention of being tied down by 'the unreflective opinions of the majority'.[117] Basil threw that indifference back in his face, with carefully chosen words of his own: 'He does not think it necessary to take into account the simple and unstudied faith of the majority'.[118] We shall return to the contrast between

113. *Ep.* 226. 3, C 3: 26f., D 3: 337. We probably need to take into account, also, the specifically ascetic audience here addressed: an audience at once privileged and private.
114. *Ep.* 125. 3, C 2: 33, D 2: 267. In relation to the points raised in what immediately follows, note the phrase in *Ep.* 7 to Gregory of Nazianzus: 'Devote yourself entirely ... to those impulses which are implanted by God in your mind for the establishment of the good [ταῖς παρὰ τοῦ Θεοῦ ἐγγινομέναις τῇ διανοίᾳ σου ὁρμαῖς πρὸς τὴν ἀγαθοῦ σύστασιν]', C 1: 22, D 1: 47. The context was concerned with the way in which one should discuss the deposit of the faith: see nn. 51, 92.
115. GNyss *CE* 1. 94; ed. Jaeger, 1: 54.
116. *CE* 2. 18. See chapter 2, nn. 71f.
117. Eunomius *Apol.* 25. 1f. (2: 284) (V 1f.).
118. *CE* 3. 1 (2: 144). This confidence, echoing that of *Ep.* 125 quoted above, at n. 114, provides a crucial balance to passages where Basil was less willing to include 'the many'. Probably the most famous example occurs in *DSS* 27 (§ 66): 'That is the rationale behind maintaining an unwritten tradition, so that carelessness should not render the understanding

'unreflective' and 'unstudied'; but even more important was the distinction between 'opinions' and 'faith'. Basil was advocating a position based on creed rather than on reason, involving, on the one hand, a submission to formulae and, on the other, a correct, even inspired disposition of heart.

That explains why he may seem at times to have been divided between his suspicion of intellectual 'cleverness' and his demand that all believers aspire to a high degree of spiritual purity. Did he not, one might ask, simply substitute one élite for another? Writing to ascetics—to a section of the Christian community more directly under his influence, perhaps, and more likely to take its religion seriously—he commiserated with them that most people did not appreciate the doctrinal stand they were forced to take, 'our death for the sake of truth'.[119] He took for granted also their privileged insight: 'Our mind being enlightened by the Spirit looks up at the Son, and in Him as in an image beholds the Father'.[120] Yet this implied intimacy—between himself and them, and between them and God—was not an example of arrogance. Rather, it placed their specific vocation within a broader sphere of religious life. It made their conviction and their rigour more than a mere issue of erudite debate and linked it with every Christian's appropriate experience of God's influence, and of moral and spiritual development. The very breadth of the potential social context explains Basil's corresponding anxiety about people who seemed unaware of such responsibilities:

> I shall weep for the laity.... The ears of the more simple-minded are being turned away; already they have become accustomed to the heretical impiety. The nurslings of the Church are being brought up in the doctrines of ungodliness.... Baptisms are in the heretics' hands, attendance upon those who are departing this life, visits to the sick, the consolation of those who grieve, the assisting of those who are in distress, succour of all kinds, communion of the mysteries; all of these things, being performed by them, become a bond of agreement between them and the laity.

What the Arians had captured was the very cult of the Church. The laity's experience of ceremony and social ministration—the very context within

---

of teachings [δογμάτων] open to contempt among the many through constant intimacy [συνήθειαν]' (ed. Pruche, p. 484). For a contrastingly positive view of συνήθεια, see n. 88 above (in a context not wholly dissociated from this). Important background and discussion is provided by Amand de Mendieta, 'ΚΗΡΥΓΜΑ and ΔΟΓΜΑ', and The 'Unwritten' and 'Secret' Apostolic Traditions in the Theological Thought of St. Basil of Caesarea.

119. Ep. 257. 1, C 3: 99, D 4: 33.
120. Ep. 226. 3, C 3: 27, D 3: 339.

which the reception and interpretation of tradition had to take place—was now vitiated by 'a long-standing deception'.[121]

But what of this emphasis on the 'simple-minded', on the 'nurslings of the Church'? Was that not arrogant and élitist? Should not such apparent hauteur affect our understanding of Basil's preference for action over word?[122] Not necessarily. What he admired, what he thought of as the 'simple' antidote to false élitism, was a genuine openness, a readiness to say what one meant. That was what the Arians had done most to undermine: 'They concealed the malady deep in their hearts and uttered pious words or at least did not oppose what was expressed by us'.[123] It was not just that heretics were skilful and deceitful users of rhetorical skills (the *De spiritu sancto* is filled with that accusation, no less than the *Contra Eunomium*),[124] training themselves 'in rhetorical quibbling and not in theology [τεχνολογοῦσι λοιπόν, οὐ θεολογοῦσιν]'.[125] Rather, they did not discuss matters 'in order to build up their audience [πρὸς οἰκοδομὴν τῶν παρόντων]'.[126]

We are brought back, once again, to the broad interpretation placed by Basil upon the concept of a pastoral address. The image of a building was not chosen accidentally, for he was discussing virtues essential to the preservation of the social body. City or 'political' life, of whatever ideological complexion, was, he thought, impossible without sincerity. Otherwise, people turned public affairs into a mere theatre, wearing masks that bore no relation to their inner lives.[127] Only a perfect symmetry between heart and tongue could guarantee a corresponding symmetry in

---

121. *Ep.* 243. 4, C 3: 72f., D 3: 447. See chapter 8, nn. 129, 176. The emphasis brings together many threads here examined separately, and was neatly summarized in Gregory of Nazianzus's description of priests 'leading people by means of the divine mysteries [λαοὺς ἄγοντες ἐνθέοις τελέσμασι]', *De vita sua*, line 326; *PG* 37. 1052; tr. p. 86.

122. See above, at n. 117.

123. *Ep.* 204. 6, C 2: 179, D 3: 171.

124. *DSS* 3 (§ 5), 17 (§ 41), 18 (§ 47); to be compared with *CE* 2. 24. GNaz *Orat.* 18. 16 disparages those who conduct themselves τεχνικῶς, *PG* 35. 1005A; and in GNyss *In suam ordinationem*, the course of action criticized is συλλογίζεσθαι, *PG* 46. 549D.

125. *Ep.* 90. 2, C 1: 196, D 2: 125. Basil was careful, naturally, not to rule too much out of court: the Church needed people 'to tend the flock of the Lord with knowledge [μετ' ἐπιστήμης]', *Ep.* 92. 2, C 1: 200, D 2: 137; and careful argument was always important, *Hom.* 352. 5; *DSS* 25 (§§ 58f.). (Note, however, that the phrase from *Ep.* 92 does not occur in the earlier draft, *Ep.* 242, which is more certainly the work of Basil himself: see chapter 8, n. 122.) One is reminded of Jerome's advice: 'People look for learning in a priest. . . . A man innocent in his behaviour, but with nothing to say, may profit others by his example, but does them equal harm by his silence. The fury of wolves is frightened off by the way the dog barks', *Ep.* 69. 8. Basil's position was different, perhaps more subtle, but analogous.

126. *Hom.* 342. 2, *PG* 31. 1489C.

127. *Hom.* 330. 2. See, more generally, *Hom.* 340. 11.

the fabric of the community itself. With truth in one's heart and with lips free from guile,[128] one would be ready to achieve that symmetry. Inward understanding would guarantee personal progress, while wise words would offer aid to others; and in both cases deeds would follow, to confirm the spiritual grace.[129]

Basil realized also that he had to practise what he preached. So he presented consistency as at least one of the hallmarks of an honest teacher: 'Words that carry truth, and spring from a healthy understanding, are simple, focussing upon one task, always treating the same issues in the same way'.[130] To achieve as much was to achieve an exact proportion between one's own address and the expected character of the audience (which would be 'simple and unstudied [ἁπλοικῶς ... ἀνεπιτηδεύτως]'—echoing the very phrases of the Contra Eunomium).[131] Then, in one uncomplicated address (ἐκ μιᾶς ὁμολογίας), the preacher could lead that audience from learning to belief (πεπεισμένους ἔχων τοὺς διδαχθέντας).[132]

What we witness here is another transition from θεολογία to οἰκονομία, from theological reflection and argument to religious experience in the company of fellow believers.[133] It was the journey that Basil himself had made; and he would encourage others to make it again and again. As in the case of language, Scripture underpinned his argument: demanding, in this instance, a recognition of its central place in the life of the Church, its position of authority—it was, indeed, the paradigm of authority, as of παράδοσις. One had to respond to it, therefore, with all the subtleties of submission discussed above: openness to the influence of divine energy; readiness for action; a respectful reticence; a quest for illumination; a sense of a common destiny, of a tradition and of a purpose shared with others. Almost the opening assertion of the Contra Eunomium was the view that, in the face of the all-sufficient truth of the Gospel handed down to us by the apostles (and again, the language used was that of παράδοσις: τῇ δὲ παραδόσει τῶν ἀποστόλων), the best reaction was silence.[134] It is unlikely to have been accidental that the treatise virtually ended on the same note.[135]

128. *Hom.* 346. 3.
129. *Hom.* 354. 2. Compare the attitude of GNaz *De seipso et de episcopis,* lines 262f.: words should contain οὐδὲν πλέον (in the manner of the facile) but display in a straightforward way the salvation achieved within, *PG* 37. 1186.
130. *Hom.* 340. 7, *PG* 31. 400.
131. See above, at n. 118.
132. *Hom.* 341. 4.
133. See above, at n. 45.
134. *CE* 1. 1 (1: 140).
135. *CE* 3. 6. See *DSS* 27 (§ 66): Scripture, too, was marked by a silence of its own, not making every aspect of truth explicit.

The emphasis persisted. It was by one's very silence that one gave honour to the mysteries of the Trinity: σιωπῇ τιμάσθω ... σιωπῇ τιμήσωμεν.[136] Once again, one withdrew from discussion and entered the realm of worship: 'The Magi adore, while Christians argue'.[137] Scripture was handed down not just as a text but within the framework of the liturgy, and of its associated homilies. It was not just a question of thinking as you were taught to think. The very act of ministering the word to a community was like a saving gesture, built into the tradition itself; and fidelity to that tradition, constantly called to mind, would almost automatically bring salvation to the present generation.[138] The other public rituals of the Church, equally, were a species of heritage, providing a context for the hearing of the word. Rituals could undergo change—servile preservation of ancient forms was to be considered a defect—but they would still retain their accumulated patina of sanctity through being constantly 'understood in a pious and holy sense'.[139]

It was that view of things that gave Scripture its absolute character, its stance beyond the reach of misdirected curiosity and pretentious reexpression. The *Contra Eunomium* itself, of course, had particular points to make. Certain words, like ἀγέννητος (unbegotten), could be ruled out of court, simply because they did not appear in Scripture and were therefore unnecessary. To coin such a term was akin to blasphemy.[140] But the point made more broadly was that only Scripture provided the framework within which an understanding of God could operate. The meanings one might grasp or acknowledge within the sacred text would always be meanings proper to one who believed in God. We have seen already how, for Basil, the process worked. He emphasized a human awareness of the power and the activity of God and stressed the way in which the very vocabulary of Scripture brought the creature into a relationship with God.[141]

That was why access to truth, to put it simply, could occur only in the context of worship, which orchestrated the human response to revelation. To recognize religious authority, therefore, was not a matter of

136. *Hom.* 342. 4.
137. *Hom.* 321. 6.
138. *DSS* 19 (§ 50), 30 (§ 79). The vocabulary is particularly precise in this last passage, virtually the closing statement of the work: 'We, who have so powerful and so longstanding a companion to fight and speak out on our behalf [i.e., the Spirit], shall we shrink from the service of the word, preserved to our own day by the unbroken remembrance of that which was handed on by the fathers?'
139. *DSS* 29 (§§ 74f.). See also § 71.
140. *CE* 1. 5. Even the word ἐποίησεν in Acts did not justify intruding the associated but otherwise novel word ποίημα (creature), *CE* 2. 2. See above, n. 45.
141. See above, at nn. 44f., 72f.

assenting to statements but rather of seeing oneself bound as a believer to a revealing God. It was a relationship, moreover, genuinely available to those who might escape the reach of mere argument. Adoration brought an understanding of its own.[142]

Eunomius's chief fault, therefore, lay in not helping his audience to move into that scriptural arena, where they would be able to make correct suppositions about the meanings of words, and to adopt accordingly the correct posture vis-à-vis their creator.[143] He tried to fool the simple, instead of opening up for them a path for the δύναμις of God; that δύναμις that Basil would later discuss with Amphilochius, and that gave substance to the words of those who preached the Gospel.[144]

So we take the short step from acknowledgement to worship. Worship was not an alternative to understanding but its visible support, its warranty, the proof of its presence. Even Eunomius had recognized the distinction between statements based on a process of rational analysis and statements designed to acknowledge before God that he was what he was.[145] The second, however, was still too 'dry' a procedure for Basil's liking. He, too, would assert that, when people called God ἀγέννητος and ἄφθαρτος (unbegotten and immortal), they not only understood what the words meant but acknowledged at the same time that they were truly proper to God.[146] In his case, however, the accuracy of the declaration became much more obviously a gesture of obeisance and brought about the very fulfilment of religious hopes: 'It is not a question of finding out what God is [he used the term ἐξερεύνησις] but of acknowledging [ὁμολογία again] that he is: that is what brings you salvation'.[147]

142. Hom. 321. 2.
143. That was particularly important, of course, in the case of 'begetting language'. Eunomius could not escape from the distractions of human sexuality, whereas for Basil, as we have seen, 'fatherhood' gained its primary meaning from the relationship between the Father and the Son, as revealed in Scripture. See CE 2. 14, 23, and above, at nn. 40f.
144. CE 1. 7. See above, at nn. 44, 108.
145. The contrast being between τό τε κατ' ἐπίνοιάν τι λέγεσθαι and τὸ ἀποπληροῦν τῷ Θεῷ τὴν τοῦ εἶναι ὅ ἐστιν ὁμολογίαν, CE 1. 7 (1: 192).
146. Καὶ ἐπινοεῖσθαι τῶν ὀνομάτων τούτων ἑκάτερον, καὶ ὁμολογίαν—and note the repetition of Eunomius's word—εἶναι τοῦ κατ' ἀλήθειαν τῷ Θεῷ προσόντος, CE 1. 7 (1: 192).
147. CE 1. 14 (1: 224). ῾Ομολογία, as an attitude or response that gave worship almost the force of verbal assent, lay close to the root of Basil's conception of wisdom, insight, or

That Basil regarded worship as the link between text and audience, between doctrine and Church, is most vividly attested by his treatment of baptism.[148] The formulae of the sacrament had their uses, of course, in the conduct of controversy: they implied much about the relations between Father, Son, and Spirit, hallowed by ancient usage; and they made no concessions to such novelties as δημιουργός and ποίημα. But they carried one far beyond apologetic: 'Baptism is the seal of our faith [σφραγὶς τῆς πίστεως]; and faith means assenting to the divinity [θεότητος συγκατάθεσις]'.[149]

That emphasis enjoyed a long future in Basil's thought. The baptismal formula governed all thought and speech[150]—and in an open-ended way, for 'the "moment of baptism"' as he put it, 'extends throughout a person's life': without it, one would be robbed of enlightenment, which alone guaranteed inner balance and the knowledge of God.[151] Human nature itself, one might say, was to be defined, indeed was constituted, by a trinity. 'A thorough understanding of God the Father, the received tradition concerning the Word who was in the beginning with God, and the enlightenment brought about by the Holy Spirit': these were τὰ τοῦ ἀνθρώπου ἐξαίρετα, the very hallmarks of a human being.[152] That amalgam of knowledge, tradition, and enlightenment would be given, in addition, an historical momentum, as one moved from creation through the Incarnation to the fulfilment of one's own destiny.[153]

Those broader implications—for orthodoxy, for personal development, for the sense of human history—explain why Basil could set up the baptismal formula itself as the touchstone of communion within the

---

understanding. See Gain, *Église*, p. 333 n. 35 (with reference to Fedwick, *Charisma*, pp. 41f.), and also pp. 139f. See below, at nn. 157f.

148. One is tempted to make wholesale use of the *De baptismo*; and I am swayed towards acceptance of its reliability, not only by arguments in a recent edition but also by Gribomont, *Histoire*, pp. 307f. The latter supposed that our existing text represents at least the careful notes of a disciple; and he found the emphasis on a radical interpretation of Christian obligations, tending towards a universally applicable ascetic ideal, entirely typical of Basil himself—a matter to be discussed in chapter 6 (and see also appendix 2, n. 8). However, the plentiful clues to Basil's thought on the matter in indubitably genuine works make an appeal to the *De baptismo* a bonus rather than a necessity; and I have allowed room for a cautious scepticism. For the text (as edited by U. Neri), see *Basile de Césarée, Sur le baptême*, introduced, with French translation and notes, by Jeanne Ducatillon.

149. *CE* 3. 5 (2: 164). Fedwick, *Charisma*, pp. 79f., is too limited in his treatment of the link between formula and theology generally.

150. *DSS* 10 (§ 24).

151. *Hom.* 320. 1. For valuable comment on this sermon, see Jean Gribomont, 'Saint Basile, le Protreptique au baptême'.

152. *Hom.* 354. 6, *PG* 29. 445B.

153. *Ep.* 105, C 2: 6f., D 2: 199/201. See also *Ep.* 159, 175. All three letters were addressed to members of the laity: see the point made above at nn. 23f.

Church. It was to that formula that Eustathius of Sebaste was invited to subscribe, in phrases echoing directly the letters and sermons just referred to: 'We must be baptized as we have received the words of baptism, and we must believe as we are baptized, and we must give glory as we have believed, to the Father, the Son, and the Holy Ghost'.[154] But other important admissions were made. That transition—from tradition to rite, from rite to belief, from belief to worship—depended on correct interpretation: 'Unless the mind become free from confusions as to the proper ties of each, it is impossible for it to render the doxology to the Father and to the Son and to the Holy Ghost'.[155] How was one to achieve and maintain such clarity of mind, the basis for the authenticity of ritual?[156] Basil described with some subtlety, in the De spiritu sancto, the mutual reinforcements to be worked for:

> Belief and baptism form two modes of salvation, which remain in harmony with each other, and are impossible to separate. Belief is brought to perfection through baptism: baptism is set on a firm footing by belief.... Acknowledgement [ὁμολογία] comes first, leading to salvation; and baptism follows [a clear progression is implied: προάγει ... ἐπακολουθεῖ], setting the seal on our assent [συγκατάθεσιν].[157]

So ὁμολογία and συγκατάθεσις in the second sentence were intimately associated with 'belief' in the first; and their prior development gave authenticity to subsequent participation in ritual. The core of the experience might remain interior: 'Made holy, therefore, by the Spirit, we receive Christ as one who lives with us in our inmost selves [εἰς τὸν ἔσω ἄνθρωπον], and with Christ we receive the Father, who makes his dwelling place among the worthy'. But public declarations and ancient ceremonies were the visible signs of that hidden event: 'This bond [between God and creature] is made visible by the tradition of baptism and by the declaration of faith [καὶ ἡ παράδοσις τοῦ βαπτίσματος, καὶ ἡ ὁμολογία τῆς πίστεως]'.[158]

Those twin concepts, of 'tradition' (παράδοσις) and of 'declaration' (ὁμολογία), which have occurred several times, bring our analysis to a fitting conclusion: for they sum up so much that was central to Basil's

154. Ep. 125. 3, C 2: 33, D 2: 269. See above, at n. 19.
155. Ep. 210. 4, C 2: 194, D 3: 207.
156. The difficulty was analogous to that discussed above, at nn. 111f.
157. DSS 12 (§ 28) (p. 346).
158. Hom. 341. 5, PG 31. 609CD.

argument. The four issues emphasized here—time, language, authority, and worship—formed a logical basis or starting point, from which he was able to move beyond the agenda of debate presented by Eunomius. We find ourselves carried quickly from the consideration of theological formulae to a much broader vision of individual perfection, of church life, and of human history.

Those are the qualities that make the *Contra Eunomium* so important for our understanding of Basil's development. They illuminate, more specifically, the choices he made in the early 360s. The work is startling in the range of its concern and anticipates so much subsequent self-assurance. The analysis given here may appear at times abstract or remote; but only if we overlook its context. For the period before the appearance of the book, we have only the impression of varied resources and varied opportunities, cautiously assessed and explored. Once it comes into our hands, we discover in its author a man with clear ideas on many aspects of church life—its apparatus of authority, its historical tradition, its dependence on Scripture, its acceptance of the challenge to address and influence as wide an audience as possible.

The *Contra Eunomium* reveals the formation of a churchman. Its fundamental convictions were to last to the very end of Basil's life and awaken echoes at every level of his endeavour—in his desire to define and experience spiritual growth, to practise the ascetic life, to proclaim his faith in public oratory, and to engage in theological controversy. It points backwards also, forcing us to see in a new light the use that Basil made of family and provincial heritage, of education, of simplicity and self-discipline in the pursuit of philosophy. To produce reflection of such maturity demanded from an early stage a careful foresight. Basil cannot but have noticed that, in his society and time, the priestly career was a public and obvious option. But what kind of priesthood, and within what type of Church? Those were the questions that governed not only his movement from one setting to another but also his espousal of models, his acknowledgement of loyalties. Now, in this work, he had not only judged the mettle of the heretics but had armed himself for an even larger task of his own. He had established a trinity in his own life: he had found his voice, drawn up his message, and identified his audience. We can hardly be surprised to find that, only a few months after its completion, Basil was on his way back to Caesarea, to begin the final and uninterrupted phase of his pastoral life.

· CHAPTER V ·

CITY AND CHURCH

The year 365 was crucial in Basil's life. From that time onwards, he remained (as both priest and bishop) the chief pastor of Caesarea. He committed himself in the process to a city of great antiquity and strategic importance.[1] The land around Caesarea, sandy and liable in parts to flooding, was not particularly prosperous in agricultural terms, although famous for horse breeding. It lay, however, at the meeting point of almost every major road across Asia Minor (partly because only some thirty kilometres to the north stood one of the chief crossing points over the great river Halys—the modern Kizil Irmak). Westwards ran the old trade route to Ephesus and the Aegean. Northwest, across the river, one travelled to Ancyra, and beyond to Constantinople. To the northeast, along the southern bank of the Halys, the road ran to Sebaste, and ultimately to Nicopolis and Armenia beyond. Alternatively one could travel by an arduous

---

1. Three helpful works span more than a century of scholarship: J. A. Cramer, *A Geographical and Historical Description of Asia Minor* (1832); William Mitchell Ramsay, *The Historical Geography of Asia Minor* (1890); and Jones, *Cities* (2d ed., 1971). Cramer is quaint in both his interests and his style, but closely and explicitly wedded to the ancient texts: see especially 'Ancient Pontus', 1: 242–322, and 'Cappadocia and Armenia Minor', 2: 105–62. Ramsay is excellent on roads. Jones is authoritative, clear, and readily available: see 'Cappadocia', pp. 174–90. For other information on the broader historical background, I have used also John Garstang and O. R. Gurney, *The Geography of the Hittite Empire*; David Magie, *Roman Rule in Asia Minor to the End of the Third Century after Christ*; and Anthony D. Macro, 'The Cities of Asia Minor under the Roman Imperium'. For details about the army, see Stephen Mitchell, 'The Balkans, Anatolia, and Roman Armies across Asia Minor'; and Benjamin H. Isaac, *The Limits of Empire: The Roman Army in the East*.

road southeast, through Euphratensis, to Samosata on the Euphrates it-self. There were also roads north and south. In the latter case, the route provided the main access through the Cilician gates to the Mediterranean, and ultimately to Antioch. The road north was, for Basil, the road home: to Pontus and the family estates; but also to Sinope and the Black Sea. (One could make that journey also via Sebaste, and then northeast through Neo-caesarea.) In his own day, the position of the city between the eastern capi-tal and the Armenian and Syrian theatres would have meant the frequent passage of armies and the imperial entourage—both a cause of inconve-nience and an opportunity for access to power. In regard to the latter, much of the land around Caesarea belonged to the imperial fisc, which invited frequent contact with officials responsible to the court rather than to local provincial authorities. Basil's see stood also on a great geographical cusp, with the flat plains of Anatolia on one side and the mountains that reached eastwards into Armenia on the other. (The local situation of the city—a little further south than the modern Kayseri—made the contrast all the more vivid, with the snow-covered peak of Mount Argaeus rising abruptly behind it to a height of nearly four thousand metres.) Ancient kingdoms, for all those reasons, had made Caesarea their administrative centre, main-taining access to a variety of more populous and fertile districts, standing guard against the less predictable loyalties of mountain tribes, and survey-ing from a distance the trade of three great seas. No one living in the city could forget entirely the implications of that past; and the very presence, in more recent centuries, of imperial authority, together with memories of its imposition under Pompey and his successors, would bring to mind the enduring tensions between the Greek, Roman, and Armenian worlds. Moreover, only a century before, Goths from the north and Persians from the south had penetrated that imperial arena, following the paths of older enemies, and pillaging the very countryside around Caesarea.

To such a city, therefore, Basil now returned. What we need to discover is the species of consistency his dedication to the place might be taken to represent. Along what central axis did his pastorate move? To what extent were the churchmanship and the ecclesiology of the *Contra Eunomium* carried forward successfully in his career thereafter? In the attempt to answer such questions, let us explore first a more particular hypothesis. Did his initial years as a priest help him to set in place a lasting sense of direction? He tells us very little about those years: there is a striking gap in his collected letters.[2] Perhaps his technically subordinate position made

2. In Fedwick's chronology, *Basil*, 1: 11, only four letters can be ascribed to that period, and doubts of different sorts surround two of them.

it improper to write letters that might have been construed to represent the opinion of his church as a whole. Gregory of Nazianzus saw the period as one of preparation for his episcopate, marked by a sensitive respect for ecclesiastical discipline: 'He received the honour according to the law and order of spiritual advancement [and] recognized the laws of obedience'.[3]

The manner of his return to the city cannot be separated from the reasons for his departure in 363, after his disagreement with Eusebius. 'It is better', said Gregory later, 'to pass over in silence its origin and character'; but he referred to 'a natural antipathy' and suggested that some at least thought Eusebius's position to have been uncanonical, if not slightly unorthodox. He was more specific when it came to describing Basil's supporters: 'All the more select and wiser members of the Church were roused against Eusebius; since they are wiser than the multitude, they have separated themselves from the world and consecrated themselves to God. I speak of the Nazarites among us, who are especially zealous in such matters'. They were able to attract to their cause 'a considerable portion of the people, including some of lowly station and others of high rank'.[4] Gregory did not approve of the strain thus imposed upon the church, and he praised Basil for leaving the city, in order to prevent further discord.[5] It is clear that the admirers he left behind, however, were acceptable in Gregory's eyes because they were in some sense ascetic. We may detect a local attachment to the style of church life inspired by Eustathius.

Yet that cannot have been the whole story.[6] Even prior to Basil's exercise of the priestly ministry, there had been significant doctrinal tensions within the city; and the writer of the Contra Eunomium was unlikely to have viewed them with equanimity.[7] Gregory, we know, encouraged Basil to return as a gesture against heresy. Valens, after all, was now established in the East. With hindsight, Gregory made a confrontation between the two men one of the chief features of his posthumous portrait of Basil. Eusebius,

3. GNaz Orat. 43. 25, 33; tr. pp. 50, 55f. No doubt he was comparing Basil's attitude with current practice elsewhere.

4. GNaz Orat. 43. 28, tr. pp. 51f. For Eusebius, see also § 33: 'He had been newly installed in the see, while still breathing worldly air, and not yet adjusted to the things of the Spirit', tr. p. 56.

5. GNaz Orat. 43. 29: 'following our sincere counsels and exhortations', tr. p. 52. Recall the circumstances, discussed in chapter 3, at n. 100.

6. Gregory exaggerated the role of ascetics in church affairs—he made similar statements, as we shall see, at the time of Basil's consecration—and he always preferred to mix with 'companions of the better sort [σὺν ἀρείονι πομπῇ]', GNaz De rebus suis, line 462; PG 37. 1004; tr. p. 40.

7. GNaz Ep. 42. 2—οἳ ποτε ἐφεδρεύοντες, ed. Gallay, 1: 54.

by contrast, was made to seem inept and lacking in experience.[8] To his own friends, by the time of his consecration in 370, the outcome was beyond doubt, and entirely due to Basil's labours in recent years. Gregory's father, addressing all the social orders of the city, congratulated them on their new reputation for unity, τὴν ... χάριν τῆς ὁμονοίας. Only Basil's further promotion to bishop would ensure its survival.[9]

Orthodoxy was not his only concern. The disciple of Eustathius and the author of the *Contra Eunomium* was naturally interested in practical religion, in developing a sense of social responsibility among Christians. A catastrophic shortage of food throughout Cappadocia in 369 provided the perfect opportunity to make his point. The fullest account comes from Gregory of Nazianzus.[10] Basil made only passing allusion to the event; but three sermons, likely to date from this time, offer further comment.[11]

Gregory attributed the severity of the shortage to the fact that Caesarea was deep in the interior and lacked the exchange opportunities of communities nearer the coast. He pinpointed as a major cause of distress profiteering on the part of 'those who enjoy plenty'. Basil's role was to exploit his influence with 'magistrates and the most powerful men of the city'. 'By his word and exhortations he opened up the storehouses of the rich'. He also maintained control over the resulting redistribution of the food supply. He gathered those in need into one place, collected 'all kinds of food helpful for relieving famine', and proceeded (with the help of 'his own servants

8. GNaz *Orat*. 43. 33. For the confrontation with Valens, and with Arianism generally, see §§ 30f. GNaz *Ep*. 18. 2f. may suggest that Eusebius had taken Gregory's support of Basil, between 363 and 365, as a reflection on his own ability to cope with the pressures of the day. *Ep*. 19. 20, to Basil, describes the antidote. See chapter 3, at n. 28. Given the support that Valens gave Basil, in several regards, we have to interpret *Orat*. 43 with a cautious recognition of its high rhetorical tone: see Brennecke, *Geschichte der Homöer*, pp. 227f.

9. GNaz *Ep*. 41. 6 (ed. Gallay, 1: 52) and 9.

10. GNaz *Orat*. 43. 34–36, tr. pp. 56–59.

11. See *Ep*. 31: he had to linger in the city 'to attend to the distribution of aid', C 1: 73, D 1: 177. Compare the conduct of his brother Peter in similar circumstances: *VMac*. 12; ed. Woods Callahan, p. 384, lines 14f.; tr. p. 172. As presented by Palladius a generation later, Ephraem achieved fame and honourable status in Edessa by responding to the crisis of famine: *Lausiac History* 40. *Hom*. 322, 325, 336 are examined below. Gribomont, 'Aristocrate révolutionnaire', p. 184, sees Basil's efforts in 369 as part of a concerted plan to mobilize both popular and élite support for radical social change under his (eventual) episcopal leadership. One should not hasten either clarity of thought or practical achievement; but in the longer term, as we shall see, the argument makes some sense. The best and broadest context for economic developments in Cappadocia is provided by Evelyne Patlagean, *Pauvreté économique et pauvreté sociale à Byzance, 4e–7e siècles*. One of her major points, taken up below, is that whatever 'revolution' Christian charity represented took place within a context provided by traditional patterns of social dependence.

[τοῖς ἑαυτοῦ παισίν]') to serve simple meals—'cauldrons of pea soup and our salted meats'. Gregory was careful to add that he did so without profit to himself.

Basil's motives are not to be taken for granted. It would be unjust to doubt his 'sympathy for the afflicted'; but Gregory went further. Basil was not to be equated with Moses or Elias or even Joseph in Egypt, least of all with the feeder of the five thousand: 'Signs are for unbelievers, not for believers'.[12] 'He had in view', his former friend asserted, 'only one object: to win mercy by being merciful, and to acquire heavenly blessings by his distribution of grain here below'. 'His support of the needy' was displayed 'more often in cases of spiritual want': a telling point, 'for this', continued Gregory, 'is frequently a means of touching the soul and reducing it to subjection by kindness'.[13]

Do Basil's three sermons support that somewhat Victorian image of self-serving benevolence? If dated to 369, they were presumably among the 'words and exhortations [that] opened up the storehouses of the rich'.[14] Two of them, however, are weak and abstract, as responses to crisis; the last of the pair being the worst. No one, Basil suggested, was going to be inclined towards social justice unless he or she felt stimulated by the thought of eternal reward and punishment. Famine itself was clearly a punishment for sin. The rest of the address was concerned mainly with arguments in support of God's providence, and with an exhortation to remember that human destinies lay beyond the needs of the body. One was likely to have come away from such a discourse with little more than the feeling that God had chosen to make one the victim of misfortune.[15]

12. One suspects a dig at someone—perhaps even at Gregory of Nyssa, who, in his *Laus*, made those connections.

13. He made the point again, when winding up his account. Gregory of Nyssa also placed emphasis on this 'spiritualization' of Basil's social concern: καὶ σωματικῶς μὲν ἐν τῷ προαστείῳ κατεσκευάσατο, τοὺς πτωχοὺς τῷ σώματι, πτωχοὺς τῷ πνεύματι διὰ τῆς ἀγαθῆς διδασκαλίας εἶναι ποιήσας, ὥστε αὐτοῖς γενέσθαι μακαριστὴν τὴν πτωχείαν τῆς ἀληθινῆς βασιλείας προξενοῦσαν τὴν χάριν, PG 46. 809D. For reflection on the point, see W. K. Lowther Clarke, *Basil*, p. 100. Meredith, 'Asceticism', p. 325, suggests more broadly that a spiritual emphasis (as opposed, for example, to the endorsement of literal poverty) made moral recommendations attainable by persons in the lay state.

14. Chronological order is not easy to determine: see Bernardi, *Prédication*, pp. 60f. I would prefer the reverse of the numerical order (see n. 11 above); and there is support for the notion that *Hom.* 322 was preached in November. On the attitudes to wealth and property that emerge in these sermons, see Giet, *Idées*, pp. 96f.—although he may overemphasize the extent to which Basil defended private ownership.

15. *Hom.* 336. For additional comment on this sermon, see also Amand de Mendieta, *Ascèse*, pp. 146f.

A second homily was scarcely better.[16] Famine represented a test of endurance and an invitation to better behaviour, for it arose chiefly from indulgence in social and moral disorder. Basil offered, however, little practical advice. He exhorted his audience in a halfhearted way to invest at least some of their wealth in future rewards (by giving it to others). He contrasted non-Christians, who were quite good at coming to the rescue of those bound to them by ties of kinship, with the Christian community described in Acts, which practised genuine benevolence towards all. Apart from that, his hearers were encouraged to repent, leaving subsequent physical relief in the hands of God. There was just one hint of the immediate disaster: Basil admitted that the majority were now suffering for the sins of the few. Perhaps he wished to focus upon the profiteers the wrath of the disadvantaged, proving that he had some power over the masses as well as over the mighty.

It does rather look as if Basil was content to set his sights on spiritual matters, even in times of physical suffering. The third sermon, however (first in the current numbering, but possibly last in date of delivery), was a precisely articulated piece of social propaganda.[17] One would like to think that it represented Basil's more considered reaction to the events described by Gregory. He started, once again, by telling his listeners that they should endure with patience the visitations of God. At the same time, he assured the better-off that there was nothing wrong with economic success, which was no less the result of God's providence. That looks like reinforcement of the social status quo in the name of some higher hope. Yet he continued, in his address to the wealthy, by saying that success and prosperity should be oriented towards a generous life: riches were accumulated in order to be shared with others. At this point he began to explore an idea only lightly touched upon in the other two sermons. The possession of power demanded that one should regard one's fellows as one's equals. Control over the lives of others should make one realize that one could not afford to treat them any worse than oneself.[18] That may

16. *Hom.* 325.
17. *Hom.* 322.
18. See especially the juxtaposition of phrases in § 2: οἰκονόμος τῶν ὁμοδούλων ... ὡς περὶ ἀλλοτρίων βουλεύου τῶν ἐν χερσί, *PG* 31. 264C. A deep theology lay behind this use of ὁμόδουλος in *DSS* 20 (§ 51). The same notions were reflected in closely associated letters to Amphilochius—for example, '[the just man] is not inclined to the enjoyment of what is given but to its management [he is an οἰκονομικός]', *Ep.* 236. 7, C 3: 54, D 3: 405. See Giet, *Idées*, p. 31. While the paragraphs that follow veer away from the suggestion that, in the circumstances of 369, Basil was adopting an uninhibited egalitarianism, it is worth noting how close to such a position his calmer and more honest reflections would always draw him: at the very end of his life, he would still insist 'that to every man belongs by nature [κατὰ

have seemed odd to the rich, but only because equality was being held in abeyance, so to speak, by God's providence, so that those in need could demonstrate virtuous patience, and those in a position to alleviate need could practise generosity—both thereby gaining a rightful recompense. At the last judgement, the greatest villain would be not the thief but the ἀκοινώνητος, the person who would not acknowledge a common bond with all other human beings.

Basil was not attempting to subvert completely the existing social order. His point was that, by failing to recognize those truths, citizens were refusing to see what their current situation implied. Too many of the rich were living lives of fantasy.[19] They could not acknowledge, in particular, that current relations were only temporary, leaning inevitably towards some hitherto postponed state of fuller perfection. It was not just a matter of recognizing that loss here might be gain in heaven, but rather that heaven would see all one's social aspirations fulfilled: 'Then the whole people, standing about our common judge, will call you nourisher, benefactor, and all those other titles that attach to philanthropy'.[20] In other words the rich would, if they practised virtue, fare forever in exactly the way they had worked so hard to fare in this more transitory world. Here, surely, was a sermon likely to open a storehouse or two: impelling a change of heart by hinting just frequently enough at self-interest, even economic self-interest, and by rousing the emotions with those familiar symbols of social deference and dignity beloved of the δυνατώτεροι!

These ad hoc exhortations, which must have affected Caesarea's view of its new priest and future bishop, do not stand in isolation. Gregory's reference to a 'soup kitchen', and his account of how Basil 'assembled in one place those afflicted', call to mind the famous Basileiados, the 'new city'—a whole range of buildings for the care of the sick and the destitute, and for the distribution of surplus food to those in need.[21] One

---

τὴν φύσιν] equality of like honour [ὁμοτιμίας ἰσότης] with all men, and that superiorities in us are not according to family, nor according to excess of wealth, nor according to the body's constitution, but according to the superiority of our fear of God', *Ep.* 262. 1, C 3: 119, D 4: 85. See also n. 202 below.

19. Οὐ τὰ πράγματα βλέπουσιν, ἀλλὰ τὰ ἐκ πάθους φαντάζονται, § 4, *PG* 31. 269B.

20. ῞Οταν δῆμος ὅλος ἐπὶ τοῦ κοινοῦ κριτοῦ περιστάντες σε τροφέα καὶ εὐεργέτην καὶ πάντα τὰ τῆς φιλανθρωπίας ἀποκαλῶσιν ὀνόματα—a consolation reserved, of course, for the rich: § 3, *PG* 31. 265D. See also *Hom.* 339. 8 and *DSS* 13 (§ 29). In this way Basil made the traditional city, in Patlagean's words, *Pauvreté*, p. 21, 'une place de choix au don charitable'. Jörg Schlumberger, ' *Potens* and *potentia* in the Social Thought of Late Antiquity', pp. 96f., exaggerates the isolation of the *potens* at the last judgement.

21. GNaz *Orat.* 43. 35. The phrase 'new city' is Gregory's own; part of a full description, *Orat.* 43. 63 (for the phrase itself, see *PG* 36. 579C).

imagines that something of that system was already in place during the emergency of 369, and that the famine encouraged Basil to make more formal arrangements for the needy. The project must have taken, however, several years to develop fully.[22] Basil himself referred to the enterprise in three letters, which appear to provide us with a chronological framework.[23] In the first, to the governor Elias, Basil reported that he was 'already in action, being engaged meanwhile in getting our materials together'.[24] Yet he had just provided a full description of a church, residences, hospices, and workshops, which had already given rise to 'criticisms' and 'slanders'. What stage of development had the *Basileiados* reached? The traditional belief that this letter was written in 372 rests largely on a reference to Valens, who had 'allowed us', as Basil put it, 'to govern the churches ourselves'—a phrase taken to refer to a famous visit the emperor made to Caesarea at Epiphany that year. Yet Valens could have passed through Caesarea at least three other times since 370.[25] We need not attach episcopal significance to the word οἰκονομεῖν (which could mean just 'administer', rather than 'govern'); and Basil may have been alluding to the emperor's willingness on some other occasion (other than 372) to support his social benevolence with revenues and other resources from nearby imperial estates.[26]

The two other letters are addressed to Amphilochius. The first must predate his consecration as bishop of Iconium, which took place towards the end of 373. 'Heracleidas' (that is to say, Basil) is made to describe to his friend a 'poorhouse [πτωχοτροφεῖον]', distinct from but close to the city, which was visited regularly by the bishop. Its character seems to have been closely associated with the type of exhortations that took place there, which emphasized a life of poverty, generosity to those in need, and asceticism generally. There is little sign of the bustle and the deployment of resources suggested in the letter to Elias. The second letter to Amphilochius was an invitation to attend celebrations in honour of the

22. See Giet, *Idées*, pp. 417f.
23. *Ep.* 94, 150, 176 respectively, spaced out over a number of years: to Elias, the governor of Cappadocia, normally taken to have been written late in 372 (and see Kopecek, 'Civic Patriotism', pp. 302f.); to Amphilochius ('As if from Heracleidas'), written a few months later; and to Amphilochius again (now a bishop), in 375.
24. *Ep.* 94, C 1: 205, D 2: 151/153. For what follows, see also below, at nn. 173f. Why Basil should have written in such detail, yet with such caution, to a governor is well explored by Stefania Scicolone, 'Basilio e la sua organizzazione dell'attività assistenziale a Cesarea'.
25. Van Dam, 'Emperor, Bishops, and Friends', pp. 74f.
26. There is no doubt that Basil saw his letter to Elias as concerned chiefly with 'temporal affairs [περὶ πάντων τῶν κατὰ τὸν βίον μου πραγμάτων]'. For fuller details on the chronological problems involved, see appendix 1, pp. 349–351.

martyrs; and Basil added: 'Accordingly we urge you to arrive three days beforehand, in order that you may also make great by your presence the memorial chapel of the house of the poor [ἵνα καὶ τοῦ πτωχοτροφείου τὴν μνήμην μεγάλην ποιήσῃς τῇ παρουσίᾳ]'.[27] Considerable obscurity attaches to this phrase, since there is no clear indication of what a 'memorial' might have been in this case—whether a ceremony or a building (the Greek has nothing specifically indicating a 'chapel'). There seems little reason to suppose that the event represented the beginning or the completion of anything in particular. The 'poorhouse' of the letter from 'Heracleidas', however, seems to have been firmly established.[28]

The weight of the evidence, therefore, suggests that the *Basileiados* was sufficiently under way by 372 to attract the patronage of the emperor and to be described in some detail to Elias. It may well have been started as early as 370; and that certainly brings it close enough to the famine of 369 to make a connection assured. The crisis prompted Basil to apply principles of organization and morality clearly displayed in subsequent activities and institutions. The generally 'Eustathian' quality of the programme makes it likely that such ideas had been active in his mind for some time before that. In other words, such practical charity, for all our caveats about motivation, was quickly established as a feature of Basil's pastorate and simply continued across the years of his consecration as a bishop.[29]

We need to assess carefully the quality of the régime that was set in place. As far as later recollections were concerned, care of the sick predominated: Theodoret mentioned in particular those who were seriously ill.[30] Gregory of Nazianzus was naturally more detailed in his account. He described 'the care of the sick and the practice of medicine' as 'our

27. *Ep.* 176, C 2: 113, D 2: 461.
28. Giet, *Idées*, p. 421 n. 2, speaks of 'l'inauguration [presumably, from what he says, 'de l'hospice']', and he has the date wrong.
29. Eustathius may have had a more direct hand in the matter than appears on the surface of the evidence. Two shadowy figures, Basil and Sophronius, may have been sent by Eustathius to help run the *Basileiados*. Basil described his namesake as 'a guard of my life [φυλακτηρίου τῆς ἐμῆς ζωῆς]', *Ep.* 99, C 2: 24, D 2: 241, which may heighten the venom of his later reference to 'spies [φύλακας]': see below, at n. 65.
30. Οἳ τὸ σῶμα ἅπαν λελωβημένοι πλείονος ὅτι μάλιστα θεραπείας προσδέονται, Theodoret *HE* 4, 16; ed. Parmentier (as 4, 19.13), p. 245; *PG* 82. 1161CD. Sozomen is vaguer, with πτωχῶν ... καταγώγιον, *HE* 6, 34. 9; *PG* 67. 1397A; ed. Bidez, p. 291. Socrates is silent. For a poignant impression of what later became of the *Basileiados*, see the *Letters* of the fifth-century bishop Firmus of Caesarea, especially *Ep.* 12 (famine simply could not be coped with) and 43 (the inmates actually ran away!). My thanks to Peter Brown for bringing these texts to my attention. See *Firmus de Césarée, Lettres*, with introduction, text, translation, notes, and index by Marie-Ange Calvet-Sebasti and Pierre-Louis Gatier.

common intellectual avocation'.[31] He wrote of a 'common treasury of the wealthy, where superfluous riches, sometimes even necessities, thanks to the exhortations of Basil, are laid up. . . . There, sickness is endured with equanimity, calamity is a blessing, and sympathy is put to the test'. Allusion seems to be chiefly to lepers—'living corpses, dead in most of their limbs, driven away from their cities and homes'. All this is echoed in the briefer phrases of Theodoret. Basil himself 'greeted the sick like brothers', in sharp contrast to common attitudes, and was willing to engage in 'the dressing of their wounds'.[32]

Here we have two elements, therefore: the storage and distribution of surplus, and the care of the seriously ill, especially those likely to be outcasts on account of their afflictions. Gregory's descriptions add flesh to the bald phrases of the two letters to Amphilochius, with their reference to a 'poorhouse'. The letter to Elias, however, had gone even further. There was, to begin with, 'a house of prayer built in magnificent fashion' (which may or may not have anything to do with the 'memorial chapel' to which Amphilochius was invited three years later). There was 'a residence, one portion being a generous home reserved for the one in charge [οἴκησιν, τὴν μὲν ἐλευθέριον ἐξῃρημένην τῷ κορυφαίῳ], and the rest subordinate quarters for the servants of God's worship [τοῖς θεραπευταῖς τοῦ θείου] arranged in order'. The impression is very clerical. The buildings were substantial enough to be thought suitable for 'you magistrates yourselves and your retinue'. Basil then mentioned 'hospices for strangers, for those who visit us while on a journey, for those who require some care because of sickness'. All those people required 'nurses, physicians, beasts for travelling and attendants'. They needed equipment and places to work; 'still other buildings', therefore. Basil concluded: 'All of [these] are an ornament to the locality, and a source of pride [already] to our governor'. They certainly deserved the epithet used by Gregory of Nazianzus, the 'new city'.[33]

They would also have demanded considerable financial investment. In that context we should place the occasional pleas in Basil's correspondence for special concessions in respect of taxation and other civil obligations. Writing to the Prefect Modestus, no less, sometime during his episcopate, Basil asked specifically that his clergy be exempt from taxation

31. Τὸ κοινὸν ἡμῶν ἐμφιλοσόφημα, GNaz Orat. 43. 61, PG 36. 576B, tr. p. 79. See the general observations of Gain, Église, p. 421 n. 3.

32. GNaz Orat. 43. 63, tr. pp. 80f.

33. Ep. 94, C 1: 205f., D 2: 151. The term κορυφαῖος does not necessarily mean 'bishop' (as in Deferrari) and may more properly imply simply the leader of some group. Ep. 150. 3 describes Basil visiting the complex, 'according to custom', C 2: 74, D 2: 367.

en bloc.[34] He reminded Modestus that such a concession would 'confer a great benefit even upon the public revenues'.[35] We should not be surprised to find, therefore, general letters in the collection prepared for *chorepiscopoi* to present to financial officials, as a prelude to discussing with them 'the welfare of the poor'. Those officials were also invited to inspect 'the home for the poor [again, πτωχοτροφία, πτωχοτροφεῖον]', and to ensure that it, too, was exempt from tax assessment.[36] One gains the impression of a well-ordered system, with considerable economic ramifications, not limited by any means to Caesarea. One of the financial officials addressed above was himself the patron of a similar institution at Amaseia in Pontus;[37] and similar establishments are suggested by chance allusions elsewhere in Basil's letters.[38]

One other matter demands attention. Gregory of Nazianzus couched his description of the *Basileiados* in language that reached beyond mere charity. His account came immediately after a description of Basil's ascetic foundations; and he emphasized motives that transcended pity.[39] 'This to me', said Basil's friend, 'is the most wonderful achievement of all, the short road to salvation and the easiest ascent to heaven'. By despising our fellows, he said, we dishonour Christ; and 'in the misfortunes of others', he added, we 'consult well our own interests', because we 'lend to God the mercy of which we stand in need ourselves'. Much of what followed associated the gestures of charity with the development

34. Individual privileges would simply have been passed on to unclerical, perhaps even unworthy, relatives. 'We', on the other hand, 'give the relief which is derived from our immunity from taxation, not altogether to the clergy, but to those who are at any time in distress', *Ep.* 104, C 2: 5, D 2: 197.

35. *Ep.* 104, C 2: 5, D 2: 197. For evidence of fiscal efficiency and provincial prosperity in this period, see Jones, *LRE* 1: 146f.; more specifically on the issue raised here, see Kopecek, 'Civic Patriotism', pp. 300f.; and Patlagean, *Pauvreté*, p. 173.

36. *Ep.* 142 and 143. These are letters to *numerarii*. It is not entirely clear whether they are addressed to officials in the office of the Praetorian Prefect or at provincial level; but the intended recipients clearly had status and authority. See Jones, *LRE* 1: 450, 589, 592 (Praetorian Prefecture); 434, 450, 526, 594 (provinces).

37. *Ep.* 143.

38. *Ep.* 301, 315, and perhaps 313. In view of the generally 'Eustathian' character of some of these enterprises, it is interesting to recall Sozomen's reference to one Marathonius, a wealthy layman, employed in the Praetorian Prefect's office, who took the sick and the poor into his own home and was then persuaded by Eustathius to become an ascetic (τὸν ἀσκητικὸν βίον ἐπήνεσε). He eventually set up a monastery of some sort (συνοικίαν μοναχῶν) in Constantinople itself, *HE* 4, 27. 4; ed. Bidez, p. 184. Palladius devotes three chapters to Ancyra, describing how ascetics and laity could dedicate themselves specifically to the service of the poor and sick: *Lausiac History* 66–68.

39. In this connection we should recall the 'spiritual' gloss of Gregory of Nyssa: see above, at n. 13.

of a true humility in oneself. While recalling Gregory's reflections on Basil's conduct during the famine, the tenor of the *oratio* suggests also a connection (perhaps in Basil's mind as well) between the industrious generosity of the 'new city' and the pursuit of the serious life of self-improvement in a more or less organized form. A chance phrase in the letter to Elias may be of significance here. Writing of the τέχναι, the skills and (by implication) the resources necessary to support all those nurses, physicians, and attendants, Basil added that, while some were 'necessary for gaining a livelihood', others were 'such as have been discovered for a decorous manner of living [πρὸς εὐσχήμονα βίου διαγωγὴν]'.[40] That seems to point beyond a mere provision for the sick or the unemployed. If we turn, then, to the letter from 'Heracleidas', we find Basil making a very close connection between the 'poorhouse' where Heracleidas was supposedly lodging and the practice of asceticism. The whole letter was, indeed, an invitation to Amphilochius to share with the writer 'the way that is in accordance with Christ's polity [τῆς κατὰ Χριστὸν πολιτείας]', which he would not find 'wandering in the desert' among 'the caves and the rocks', but in Caesarea itself, where, in the person of Basil, he could avail himself of 'the aid which true men can give'.[41] One is not surprised to find, therefore, that the imaginary conversations between Heracleidas and Basil ranged beyond 'the subject of poverty' (seen here as a positive virtue) and covered such issues as surrendering the disposition of one's goods (following the evangelical precept) to a person of experience and status, and the question of 'how we should live day by day'.[42] All such references suggest that the 'new city' was seen as a centre of religious formation almost as much as a refuge for those in distress.[43]

40. *Ep.* 94, C 1: 206, D 2: 151.

41. *Ep.* 150. 1, 4; C 2: 71, 75; D 2: 361, 371. 'True men' is unnecessary (and not in the Greek): a simple contrast is being made between isolation and human company.

42. *Ep.* 150. 3, C 2: 74f., D 2: 367/369. Sozomen described the *Basileiados* immediately after a general reference to ascetics in Cappadocia, 'most of whom live together in houses in the towns and villages [ἐν πόλεσιν ἢ κώμαις]', *HE* 6, 34. 8f.; *PG* 77. 1397AD; ed. Bidez, p. 291.

43. But we should avoid too hasty a use of the word 'monastic', in contrast to Giet, *Idées*, pp. 422f.—an issue to be dealt with in the next chapter.

A vein of social concern, therefore, and of social experiment, is thus laid bare in Basil's early pastorate, together with characteristic conjunctions— relations with civil authorities, a coherent system of ecclesiastical administration, and the theory and organized practice of the ascetic life. Basil's view of what a church should be like, and of how his own authority and influence should be exercised within it, is already made clear. Care of the sick, provision for the needy, formation in asceticism, together with 'political' elements (the 'new city', 'Christ's polity', the engagement of élite support), heralded nothing less than a major social revolution, setting in place patterns of collaboration and of economic and political patronage that challenged directly the hypocrisy, corruption, and uncontrolled self-interest governing, in Basil's eyes, the society in which he had to operate.

It is not surprising, therefore, that those developments invited controversy. Basil recognized his need to respond to 'those who keep annoying your honest ears' (writing to Elias), and to 'the criticisms of the censorious'. Matters came to a head when he approached the moment of his election and consecration as bishop. Some regarded it as the inevitable outcome of his return to Caesarea. The misgivings of others (exacerbated, perhaps, by the improprieties that surrounded the election) were to undermine his status and effectiveness for at least the first few years of his episcopate.

The reasons that governed his return in 365 continued to govern the decisions made in 370. We have mentioned Gregory of Nyssa's unfortunate attempt to reconcile Basil with their uncle, who had opposed the appointment.[44] The letters Basil wrote as a result hint at the broader issues involved: 'Slanders are given room', 'Suspicions will necessarily ever increase for the worse', and 'Whole cities and peoples get the benefit, indirectly, of our misfortune'.[45] He was referring chiefly to the need to maintain a common front against heresy, which had been the argument brought to bear in 365 by Gregory of Nazianzus.[46]

It is to Gregory that we have to turn for the fullest account. That is a pity, for his funeral *oratio* was inevitably coloured by the circumstances of his own consecration (later than Basil's), which he deeply resented,

44. See chapter 1, at nn. 16f.
45. *Ep.* 59 passim, C 1: 147f., D 2: 5f.
46. See chapter 3, at nn. 101f. Giet, *Idées*, pp. 271f., gives a characteristically anecdotal account of Basil's difficulties in his first few years as bishop.

and which he felt that Basil had forced upon him.[47] He admitted that his friend's promotion 'was not effected without difficulty nor without the envious opposition of the bishops of the country and of the most vicious men of the city'. 'It was inevitable', he continued, 'that the Holy Spirit should be victorious, and the victory was truly a decisive one. For He roused up from distant parts to anoint him men celebrated and zealous for piety'.[48] Among them was Gregory's own father (Gregory the Elder, then bishop of Nazianzus), by that time frail and sick. Gregory's funeral oration on his father (delivered much nearer the time, in early 374) adds useful details.[49] He repeated his characteristic prejudice that most influence in such an affair should be allowed 'to the select and purest portion of the people, those concerned with the sanctuary, and the Nazarites among us'—in a word, clergy and ascetics. 'To them alone, or to them above all, should the right of making such appointments belong'—ruling out domination by 'the most wealthy and powerful', not to mention 'the impulse and rashness of the people'.[50] Those were not merely general observations but were provoked directly by the memory of 370.

To his account in the *oratio* on Basil, Gregory appended a careful apologia.[51] Although, as he observed, '[Basil's] philosophy squared with my own at that time', Gregory decided not to 'rush forward after his accession with great joy', because, 'since Basil's position was still painful and troublesome', he was afraid of 'jealousy' and 'the suspicion of arrogance'. In other words, his influence might have appeared improper at a delicate moment. Yet we know that Basil was anxious to have his companionship at such a trying time:

> The cause of the present state of affairs is one which I have long urged you not to permit to arise, but which I now through very weariness of repetition pass over in silence—the fact that we do not meet one another. For if we, living up to our old agreements and to the responsibility which we now owe to the churches, were in the habit of spending the greater part of the year together, we should not have given access to these calumniators.

---

47. The incident will be discussed in chapter 7. The relevant section is quite short: GNaz *Orat.* 43. 37, 39–40.

48. GNaz *Orat.* 43. 37. The phrases recall what we know of his views on the proper influences to be brought to bear in ecclesiastical appointments: see especially *De seipso et de episcopis*, lines 136–783.

49. GNaz *Orat.* 18. 35f.

50. GNaz *Orat.* 18. 35, tr. p. 149.

51. GNaz *Orat.* 18. 39.

'If you are merely seen', he added, 'you will stop [the enemy's] attack'.[52] Yet Gregory was surely wise to be cautious. He warned Basil forcefully about the jealousies and antagonisms that were bound to surround his consecration.[53] Not that he was anything other than delighted at his friend's success.[54] Indeed, he had more of a hand in it than the *oratio* suggests. He drafted, for example, letters from his own father, espousing Basil's cause. The elder Gregory's chief concern seems also to have been the keeping of heresy at bay.[55] But his letter to the bishops assembling for the election cannot disguise the fact that they were attempting to exclude the old man, precisely because he was a known supporter of Basil. They themselves had already made up their minds to find another candidate.[56] Even so, as Gregory's orations testify, his father played an important part. The correspondence suggests quite candidly that the election must have been very close, and conducted with a minimum of propriety.

So we can detect already the indignations that were likely to persist— quite apart from considerations of church law (although, given the pressures against orthodoxy at the time, it is unlikely that Basil would have survived the imputation of any serious infringements). Unease about his care of the needy and the ascetic life, the underhand influence of family and friends, and a certain naivety (easily interpreted as arrogance) all would have prompted opposition.

Gregory of Nazianzus was anxious to reject such accusations: 'He preferred to be charged with arrogance by a few men ... than to do anything contrary to reason or his own resolutions'—not immediately the best way of smoothing ruffled feathers.[57] It was easy enough to insist that 'the steadfastness and firmness and integrity of his character is, I imagine, what they have termed pride'; but Gregory betrayed, perhaps, the basic cause of the problem when he added: 'The vices are closely rooted beside the virtues and, in a certain sense, are next-door neighbours.

52. *Ep.* 71. 2, C 1: 167f., D 2: 57. We should note the allusion to heresy, as well as to the particular opposition Basil now faced. There is no doubt from the tone of this letter that Gregory was not yet a bishop; but I am not convinced that it has to be taken as an answer to Gregory's *Ep.* 58: see Fedwick, *Basil*, 1: 13 n. 75.

53. GNaz *Ep.* 40, esp. § 4.

54. GNaz *Ep.* 44. 5, 45. 1.

55. GNaz *Ep.* 41. 8, 42. 2. Involving Eusebius, the bishop of distant Samosata, was a particularly dangerous challenge to canonical practice. If Paul Devos, 'Saint Grégoire de Nazianze et Hellade de Césarée en Cappadoce', is right, the older Gregory may already have been nurturing Basil's successor, Helladius—a remarkable demonstration of persistent patronage.

56. GNaz *Ep.* 43. 1f., 5.

57. GNaz *Orat.* 43. 39, tr. p. 61.

And it is very easy for a man to be mistaken for what he is not by those
who are not well trained in such matters'.[58] If that was the best one could
say, more than ten years later, then there is good reason to suppose that
opinions were very heated in 370.

Basil, as we know, shook off with difficulty the conceits of an educated
man.[59] Now he was discovering that episcopal office could engender
conceits of its own. One is not overimpressed by a letter that brushed aside,
for example, an unknown layman's sense of grievance, accusing the bishop
of 'forgetfulness of friends' and the 'haughtiness which is engendered by
power'. Such anger may be explained in Basil's closing phrase 'Never
assume that a man's preoccupation with affairs is a sign of his character
or of malice'.[60] Basil's involvement, on a suddenly expanding scale, with
the pressures of Arianism, and his anxiety about the fragile network of
friendships that he was trying to build up with other bishops, could have
made him seem at times remote from more particular concerns. A devout
virgin of Caesarea, for example, had been compromised and slandered
by some schemer; and she felt that Basil had not done enough to protect
her, or to restore her reputation, 'on the ground that, when I should have
sympathized with her like a father, I was indifferent to so great an evil
and philosophized amid the sufferings of others [φιλοσοφῶ ἐν ἀλλοτρίοις
παθήμασιν]'.[61] Few phrases could have encapsulated so deftly the potential
distance between a bishop and those who looked to him for more than
dignity and effectiveness against distant enemies.

Even more galling, of course, was the fact that Basil did have a visible
group of supporters, whom he seems to have been ready enough to 'gather
about him in a vulgar and hotheaded way'.[62] The hotheadedness referred
as much to a style of religiosity as to diplomatic naivety. Many of Basil's
supporters would have been of an ascetic disposition. Both Gregorys were
anxious to stress that he maintained his dedication to the 'philosophic
life', despite his elevation to ecclesiastical office.[63] Writing to Eustathius
of Sebaste only a year or so after his consecration, he himself complained
that 'in this unhappy city' there was still forceful opposition from those
'who constantly express their contempt for the pious life and assert that
our pretended humility is but a trick to get ourselves trusted and a pose
intended to deceive'. 'The result is', he continued, 'that no mode of life is so

58. GNaz Orat. 43. 64, tr. p. 82.
59. See chapter 2, at nn. 64f.
60. Ep. 56, C 1: 143, D 1: 353.
61. Ep. 289, C 3: 160, D 4: 185.
62. GNaz Ep. 45. 2, with the added phrase 'as your opponents are likely to put it'.
63. GNaz Orat. 43. 38; GNyss VMac. 14; ed. Woods Callahan, p. 385, line 21; tr. p. 173.

suspected as vicious by the people here as is the profession of asceticism [τὸ ἐπάγγελμα τοῦ ἀσκητικοῦ βίου]'.[64] In his final, lengthy attack on Eustathius in 376, Basil even implied that 'sentinels and spies [φύλακας καὶ σκοπευτάς]' had been planted in Caesarea, in part, at least, to monitor such enthusiasms.[65] Ill feeling then spilled over into criticism of Basil's 'social work'. He complained to his friend Eusebius of Samosata about bishops who could only 'pretend to be in communion with us', not least 'on account of the opposition to good works [τῇ ... πρὸς τὰς ἀγαθὰς πράξεις ἐναντιώσει] which is fomented by the devil'.[66]

Such tensions were aggravated further by the Arian controversy. Barely six months a bishop, he was writing to Eusebius of Samosata about the troubles besetting the church in Antioch, and about the unsatisfactory 'orthodoxy' of the new bishop Demophilus at Constantinople.[67] To Meletius of Antioch himself, Basil could reflect: 'Everything here is full of distress, and my only refuge from my troubles is the thought of your Holiness'.[68] He was able to add to his list of 'troubles', not long afterwards, the division of his diocese by the emperor and the breakdown of his friendship with Eustathius. Challenges of such a sort may have seemed at times welcome escapes from more local opposition. Yet that opposition showed little sign of easing. Grievance flowed into grievance as the years passed. Gregory of Nazianzus seems facile and unconvincing when he recounts how Basil was able eventually to win over his critics. He could not hide the fact that 'the war with the bishops and their allies' involved a degree of 'ill will' that was 'long standing', based on 'the resentment they felt at his election'.[69] Basil himself knew that he was dealing with more than theological disagreement or canonical impropriety. Modestus, for example, was acting, he said, 'from peculiarly personal motives [ἰδιοπαθῶς]' in supporting his enemies.[70] Churchmen should maintain, he felt, doctrinal

64. Ep. 99, C 2: 24f., D 2: 243; but I am ready, with Courtonne, to substitute ταπεινο-φροσύνης for σωφροσύνης (which is only most tendentiously translated 'chastity'). The matter still rankled as far away as Neocaesarea some four years later: Ep. 207. 2.

65. Ep. 223. 3, C 3: 11, D 3: 297, which it seems reasonable to link with the grievances more particularly rehearsed in Ep. 99. See Gribomont, 'Eustathe', both Dictionnaire de spiritualité, col. 1709, and Dictionnaire d'histoire et de géographie ecclésiastiques, col. 30. It was ironic that such bitterness should have arisen in the context of his relationship with Eustathius.

66. Ep. 141. 2, C 2: 63, D 2: 341. Compare his complaint in an undated letter, perhaps reflecting the disenchantment of those years: 'For a man's life to be above slander is one of the most difficult things in the world, not to say an impossibility', Ep. 24, C 1: 59, D 1: 145.

67. Ep. 48. But he did not doubt Demophilus's genuine piety.

68. Ep. 57, C 1: 144, D 1: 355.

69. GNaz Orat. 43. 58, tr. p. 75.

70. Ep. 79, C 1: 181, D 2: 89.

unity, even when they had 'private reasons [ἰδίας ... ἀφορμάς] for differing with one another'.[71] What he deplored (and what he felt he faced) was a public challenge to unity mounted by those who, 'concealing their private enmities [τὰς ἰδίας ἔχθρας], pretend that they hate one another for religion's sake [ὑπὲρ τῆς εὐσεβείας]'.[72]

We should not underestimate the resulting strain. He wrote to his intimate supporter, Eusebius of Samosata, early in 374, after serious illness; and he confessed that, had he been better able to travel (he probably meant at the end of the summer of the previous year), he would have taken refuge with Eusebius himself: 'For I had decided to get out of the way of the missiles of the ecclesiastics because I had no means of protecting myself against the contrivances of my adversaries'.[73] We may believe, therefore, that a physical crisis he experienced during that winter was a matter of more than a diseased liver. He felt it necessary to have a complete rest, away from Caesarea. Although he was seizing ostensibly upon the opportunity of a thermal cure,[74] he needed more than warm waters: 'For I almost fell into suspicion of everybody, thinking that there was nothing trustworthy in anyone, because my very soul had been stricken by their treacherous wounds'.[75] Later, he reflected more calmly (in a letter to a civil official):

> It is not possible from afar off to see the providences of God, but through pettiness of spirit we men gaze at that which is at our feet.... You doubtless recall, for instance, how discontented we once were at the care which had been imposed upon us, how many friends we summoned in order that through them we might thrust spiteful treatment aside. For thus we called the matter.[76]

Whatever may have been the particular causes and symptoms of his failure and disappointment, there is no doubt that, well into the 370s, Basil remained unable to build upon the strengths of his family background, his education, and his engagement with the philosophic life. His arrival in Caesarea in 365 did not herald an unbroken career, during which he would be able to put into practice unchallenged his theological and moral principles. Some of his convictions were given new scope—the

71. *Ep.* 69. 2, C 1: 164, D 2: 47.
72. *Ep.* 92. 2, C 1: 200, D 2: 139; but the specific phrases may not be those of Basil: see chapter 8, n. 122.
73. *Ep.* 136. 2, C 2: 52f., D 2: 315.
74. *Ep.* 137, 138. 1.
75. *Ep.* 223. 3, C 3: 12, D 3: 297.
76. *Ep.* 313, C 3: 187, D 4: 251.

struggle against heresy; the concern for the poor and the sick. But other preoccupations would block his pastoral endeavours: the very manner in which he exercised authority; the strain he imposed on his friends, and his consequent search for new supporters; and the controversial way in which he interwove the ascetic life with the religious life of the Christian community more generally.

So the pursuit of the Arian controversy and the chronicle of Basil's social relations can hide a discontinuity and frustration and calls into doubt a consistent attention to principle. Basil is too easily seen as the hammer of theological error or as a typical member of the provincial élite—maintaining influential acquaintances, fighting for the eminence of his city, making lofty gestures of philanthropy. There are too many obvious fractures, even in Basil's own account of his development. They were formed above all by a certain ineptitude in his attempt to define and display the social diplomacy proper to his task as a bishop.

That task, although old, with a history of its own, was also new, in the sense that the fourth century presented new opportunities and new challenges unforeseen by the earliest architects of church leadership. Oddly enough, it is not easy to determine from Basil's own words how he regarded his role. That in itself may indicate the extent to which he learned more by experience than by articulated reflection. It is instructive, in this respect, to compare him with Gregory of Nazianzus.[77] His friend developed quite a detailed account of what priesthood meant to him, in his second *oratio*, yet failed almost immediately to make any success of a pastoral career. Basil, on the other hand, while content to allow his impressions to emerge indirectly, as in the *Contra Eunomium*, seems to have embarked at first upon his priestly career with unhesitating commitment. What was important to both of them, as we have already emphasized, was their prior association with a clerical society. They were not inventing roles for themselves but assessing cautiously whereabouts in an existing system they might best find their niche. While Gregory continued to distract or frustrate himself by attachment to 'philosophic' principle, Basil seized upon the example of Eustathius of Sebaste, and upon the opportunities presented by the Arian dispute.

77. See nn. 46 and 48 above.

Once he became a bishop, he made constant if indirect reference to the system over which he now presided, with its synods, its legal traditions, and its habits of administration. His letters to *chorepiscopoi* are good examples. Faced with virtual simony, Basil quoted Paul—'We and the churches of God have no such custom'—insisting that 'if you sell what you have received as a free gift, you will be deprived of all its grace'.[78] Still on the matter of ordinations, he made on another occasion even more specific allusion to inherited regulation—'the practice that has long been followed in God's churches'—and felt himself 'compelled to resort to the renewal of the canons of the Fathers'.[79] In a particular case, concerning the scandal created by a priest who shared his house with a woman (perhaps honorably, since he was seventy years old), Basil appealed to 'the canon put forth by our holy Fathers of the Nicaean Council', and placed the matter in a broad context: 'If you dare, without correcting your ways, to cling to your priestly office, you will be anathema to all the laity; and those who receive you will be excommunicated throughout the Church'.[80]

Such snippets of correspondence remind us how closely hedged about the conduct of church affairs had become, not only with rules and customs but also with expectations, and not only on the part of bishops. Some clergy may have travelled widely, as messengers on behalf of leading churchmen in that contentious age; but most of them led very circumscribed lives: 'For even if our clergy seems to be numerous, yet it is composed of men who are unpractised in travel, because they do not go trafficking nor follow the out-of-doors life, but generally practise the sedentary arts, deriving therefrom the means for their daily livelihood'.[81]

Basil's most extensive references to the binding customs of the Church occur in three long letters to his friend Amphilochius.[82] Although the context concerns the 'canons' of the Church, he felt able in a more intimate exchange to theorize on the nature of his office. Referring at one point to schismatics, he commented on the validity of their orders:

---

78. *Ep.* 53. 1, C 1: 138, D 1: 339/341, with allusion to 1 Cor. 11.16. See also *Ep.* 290. Henry Chadwick, 'The Role of the Christian Bishop in Ancient Society', p. 2, provides initial background. The context is usefully broadened by Van Dam, 'Emperor, Bishops, and Friends', pp. 62f., referring to the interplay between a network of friends and acquaintances and the demands of canon law.

79. *Ep.* 54, C 1: 139f., D 1: 343/345.

80. *Ep.* 55, C 1: 141f., D 1: 347f. The reference seems to be to the third canon of Nicaea.

81. *Ep.* 198. 1, C 2: 153, D 3: 101.

82. *Ep.* 188, 199, 217. He answers more theological questions for Amphilochius in several other letters.

Those who separated first had ordination from the fathers, and through the imposition of their hands possessed the spiritual gift; but those who had been cut off [i.e., excommunicated], becoming laymen, possessed the power neither of baptizing nor of ordaining, being able no longer to impart to others the grace of the Holy Spirit from which they themselves had fallen away.[83]

Concentration on the Holy Spirit was a common feature of Basil's letters to Amphilochius. It obviously lay at the heart of his image of priesthood. The priest was a person who had power within him, guaranteed by historical transmission, which he was then able to share with others. As he wrote on another occasion, those 'committed with the care of the churches' act 'through union in the Spirit [τῇ συνεργείᾳ τοῦ Πνεύματος] . . . and impress this source of their action upon [their] minds [ἐμβάλλεσθε τῇ διανοίᾳ τὴν ὁρμὴν ταύτην]'. To that extent, priesthood imposed a lasting programme of self-improvement.[84]

Amphilochius seems often to have been made privy to such reflections. The letter from 'Heracleidas' contained several important elements. It is true that the context referred most to formation in the ascetic life; but that was presented as part and parcel of a bishop's task. Basil saw himself, in relation to his hoped-for charge, as 'a great and experienced teacher', 'someone to lead us by the hand'. He painted a picture of himself instructing Heracleidas in the virtue of poverty, but within a system where 'it was not necessary to anyone to take upon himself the distribution of his goods, but only to commit this task to him to whom the management of the alms of the poor had been entrusted'. Amphilochius was invited to come to Caesarea to experience that guidance, Basil insisting in a characteristic way that 'teaching a Christian how he ought to live does not call so much for words as for daily example'. The bishop would be, therefore, 'a man who both knows much from the experience of others, as well as from his own wisdom, and can impart it to those who come

83. *Ep.* 188. 1, C 2: 123, D 3: 17.
84. *Ep.* 227, C 3: 30, D 3: 345. We should not demand of Basil too much tidiness of thought; but an apparent distinction between an 'official' view of priesthood and a 'charismatic' emphasis is not uncommon. See another comment addressed to Amphilochius, concerning a priest 'who through ignorance has been implicated in an unlawful marriage': 'For him who should heal his own wounds to bless another is unfitting. For benediction is the communication of sanctification [εὐλογία γὰρ ἁγιασμοῦ μετάδοσίς ἐστιν]. But how will he who does not possess this because of his transgression through ignorance impart it to another! Therefore let him bless neither publicly nor privately [μήτε τοίνυν δημοσίᾳ μήτε ἰδίᾳ]', *Ep.* 199. 27, C 2: 159, D 3: 117/119. The final phrase certainly suggests that the power of priesthood was not seen to reside merely in its public exercise.

to him'.[85] Once Amphilochius was himself a bishop, Basil felt able to give hardheaded advice. Better one good man in charge of affairs within a church than a number who might fail in their task 'and engender the practice of indifference among the laity'. The virtue to be sought consisted in this: to be 'a servant of God, a workman that needeth not to be ashamed, not considering the things that are his own, but those of the many, that they may be saved: who, if he knows himself unequal to the care, will take unto himself workers for the harvest'.[86]

Basil had built up his picture of priesthood, therefore, at a variety of levels: canonical precedent, spiritual power, practical guidance by word and example, and shrewd realism in the face of conflict. The practical and ad hoc nature of his observations makes it less surprising that his most vivid statements on the subject occurred when he was describing other worthy examples of the priestly office. He was, after all, a man guided by successful example, as he had been by Eustathius. Dianius was another figure who loomed large in his assessment of the traditions within which he himself hoped to operate.[87] Dianius 'looked like a man worthy of honour and reverence, with a manner befitting greatness, possessing in his appearance whatever is proper to holiness'. Such external qualities mattered; but Basil valued also 'the simplicity, nobility, and generosity of his character, and all the other qualities peculiar to the man—his gentleness of soul, his lofty spirit combined with mildness, his decorum, his control of temper, and his cheerfulness and affability mingled with dignity'.[88] Those qualities may seem desirable in any person with pretensions to superior virtue, but it was the combination of openness with stature that marked them out as proper to a church leader.

Basil penned that portrait when his experience of episcopacy was well developed. Two other descriptions were composed much closer to the

---

85. *Ep.* 150 passim, C 2: 71f., D 2: 361f.

86. *Ep.* 190. 1, C 2: 142, D 3: 71/73. The catena of scriptural allusions is typical. *Ep.* 191 was not addressed to Amphilochius but also contains interesting reflections on episcopal relations. 'We gave great thanks to God', wrote Basil, 'that we had found traces of an ancient charity [ἀρχαίας ἀγάπης] in the words of your epistle'. He went on to describe a Church now lost, in which bishops were not 'circumscribed city by city [κατὰ πόλεις περιγεγράμμεθα]' but were able to 'govern the churches by the old kind of love [τῷ ἀρχαίῳ εἴδει τῆς ἀγάπης], admitting as our own members those of the brethren who come from each part, sending forth as to intimate friends, and receiving in turn as from intimates [ὡς ἐπὶ οἰκείους ... πάλιν ὡς παρ' οἰκείων]', C 2: 144f., D 3: 79/81. Compare *Ep.* 203. 3.

87. See chapter 1, at n. 75, and chapter 4, at n. 94.

88. *Ep.* 51. 1, C 1: 132, D 1: 325. The translation of the first phrases is my own. The words γεραρὸς ἰδεῖν may indicate recollection of the Homeric prophet in Alexander's dream (Plutarch *Alexander* 26. 3), who was γεραρὸς τὸ εἶδος.

time of his own consecration: one of Athanasius, the recently deceased bishop of Ancyra, and one of Musonius, who had also died recently in Neocaesarea. Of Athanasius, Basil wrote: 'A mouth has been sealed which abounded in righteous frankness and gushed forth words of grace for the edification of the brotherhood'; and behind it, so to speak, were 'the counsels of a mind which truly moved in God'. The 'limbs of the Church', he said, had been 'knitted together by his superintendance as by a soul [οἷον ὑπὸ ψυχῆς τινός], and joined into a union of sympathy and true fellowship'.[89] Musonius was

> a bulwark of his native land, an ornament of the churches, a pillar and foundation of the truth, a firm support of the faith of Christ, a steadfast helper for his friends, a most formidable foe for his enemies, a guardian of the ordinances of the Fathers, an enemy of innovation; in his own person he showed forth the ancient character of the Church, so moulding on the model of the early organization, as after a sacred image, the form of the church under his charge, that those who were of his society seemed to live in the society of those who shone like stars two hundred years and more ago.[90]

Basil presented here a remarkable interplay between personal relations and public affairs, and a respect for past tradition. The loss of a voice is what the church would most lament, and of a sympathetic companion:

> Now your fairest garland has faded; your church is hushed, your assemblies are sad of countenance, the sacred synod yearns for its leader; the mystic words await their expounder, the children their father, the elders their comrade, those in authority their chief, the people their protector, those who lack sustenance their nourisher; as they all call him back by the names most appropriate to each, to help them each in their own distress, they raise each his own lament in terms fitting to himself.[91]

Reinforced here was the image of a man able to relate to his community at every level, playing a variety of roles, and becoming in the end the city's 'soul'.

Basil was identifying, of course, the roles he tried to take upon himself. It was a difficult image to live up to; and, by espousing such ideals, he

---

89. *Ep.* 29, C 1: 71, D 1: 173. Compare the unity of clergy and people at Chalcis, described in *Ep.* 222, and discussed more fully below at n. 144. On the soul as governor, see *Hom.* 340. 15 and *Ep.* 293. The interplay between spiritual and institutional 'government' is of great significance.

90. *Ep.* 28. 1, C 1: 66, D 1: 161.

91. *Ep.* 28. 2, C 1: 68, D 1: 165/167. Note the similar titles bestowed upon benefactors in *Hom.* 322. 3, as discussed above at n. 20, especially the use of τροφέα in both cases.

created for himself a virtual martyrdom during his episcopate. His letters are famously filled with references to his frequent ill health.[92] Only rarely do we obtain an objective view. Gregory of Nazianzus implied on one occasion, just before his own consecration, that Basil could feign illness when it suited him, chiefly when he wished to prompt sympathy, if not guilt, in others.[93] Genuine enough, however, was a particularly serious bout of liver problems in the winter of 373/374, which brought him, as he put it himself, 'to the very gates of death'.[94] The letters of that winter document a clear escalation of pain and danger. Basil began to see his whole life as one of sickness, sent above all as a punishment for sin and a trial of hope. He was now able to internalize the images of fate and endurance that he had used to console the bereaved in earlier years.[95] The readiness to see himself as about to 'breathe his last', in Gregory's phrase, persisted.[96] For a long time after his recovery, he continued to think of bodily weakness as having 'been with me from early manhood to my present old age, reared with me and chastening me in accordance with the just judgment of God'.[97]

Rather more sinister was the way he wove his illness into his sense of church history. A letter to Antioch illustrates the tendency well. He presented his sickness first as the result of church misfortune, and then as a sacrifice that would avert, like other forms of endurance, the anger of God. The language, again, echoed letters of consolation in a stricter sense, with hope holding pride of place. He even admitted that an end to trial might be in sight: 'Presently He will come who will take our part; He will come and not delay ... yet a little while, yet a little while'.[98] But the moral weight that accompanied such optimism was heavy indeed. Still in the throes of his major crisis, he wrote to Eusebius: 'In all this we, as well as others, are but feeling the effect of the general condition of affairs [τῆς κοινῆς καταστάσεως τῶν πραγμάτων], for the Lord has clearly

---

92. Gain, *Église*, pp. 397f., presents a list of illnesses. A letter to Eusebius of Samosata contains the interesting admission 'I never gained a command of language sufficient to enable me to describe clearly my varied and complex sickness' (although he promptly proceeded to mention 'fevers, dysenteries, and rebellions of my bowels'), *Ep.* 162, C 2: 95f., D 2: 419. Correspondents not incredulous would no doubt have felt grateful.

93. Ἀρρωστεῖν ἔδοξας καὶ ἀναπνεῖν τὰ τελευταῖα, GNaz *Ep.* 40. 2; ed. Gallay, 1: 49. It is interesting to hear that note sounded so early.

94. *Ep.* 141. 1, C 2: 63, D 2: 341.

95. *Ep.* 136 and 138 are particularly important examples. On fate and consolation, see chapter 3, at nn. 106f.

96. As in the final phrases of *Ep.* 198, written in 375.

97. *Ep.* 203. 1, C 2: 167, D 3: 143.

98. *Ep.* 140. 1, C 2: 61, D 2: 335; but the whole letter reflects the feeling.

abandoned us, seeing that we have grown cold in our love on account of the widespread increase of lawlessness [τοὺς διὰ τὸ πληθυνθῆναι τὴν ἀνομίαν ψύξαντας τὴν ἀγάπην]'.[99] Basil felt that he had a personal price to pay in all this: 'My recovery is being hindered for the most part by my discouragement, since all the symptoms of my disease recur as the result of my exceeding grief'.[100] He continued to play upon those feelings, as Gregory had implied, not without self-pity: 'How can this be otherwise than troublesome? How can it help making life painful for me, who hold as the one relief from the evils the frailty of my body, because of which I am convinced that I shall remain for no long time in this unhappy life'. That was written in 376: so he took a long time to shake off the sense of grievance and threat that had either accompanied or exacerbated his earlier brush with death.[101]

Loneliness, therefore, and opposition to both his theological and his ascetic ideals, contributed to a sense of weakness, frustration, and compromise, which undermined in their turn any clarity or confidence he may have had about the exercise of his priesthood and episcopate. How could such a man provide for other Christians the spiritual nourishment necessary to foster community life? How could he use to that same end the structures of the Church he had inherited? If Basil was to be the 'soul' of his own church, the source of 'sympathy and true fellowship', how could he extend his energies beyond his personal difficulties, to engage truly in the salvation of others?[102]

Gregory of Nazianzus was, perhaps unconsciously, ironic in his own judgement. Faced with the ravages visited upon 'the holy nation' by doctrinal discord, Basil was not, he said, one 'to lament misfortune in silence and merely lift up his hands to God', for he felt himself to be 'the guardian and protector of the community'. Yet the weakness that afflicted his charges applied no less keenly to himself: 'The prosperity or adversity of an individual is of no significance for the community, but when the community itself is in this or that condition, the individual is of necessity affected in the same way'.[103] Basil made the same point to

99. *Ep.* 141. 2, C 2: 64, D 2: 343.
100. *Ep.* 141. 2, C 2: 63, D 2: 341/343.
101. *Ep.* 212. 2, C 2: 200, D 3: 221.
102. This is, perhaps, the main point of discussion in Giet, *Idées.* Arthur Hilary Armstrong, 'Man in the Cosmos: A Study of Some Differences between Pagan Neoplatonism and Christianity', pp. 7f., in a characteristic moment of perception, regarded belief in salvation through community membership as the distinguishing hallmark of Christian thought *vis-à-vis,* for example, the Neoplatonist tradition.
103. GNaz *Orat.* 43. 41f., tr. pp. 62f.

Eusebius (again, in the midst of his illness): 'As for the interests of the churches—how they have gone to ruin and have been lightly sacrificed, while we, consulting our own personal safety, neglect the good of our neighbours and are unable to see even this, that the ruin of each of us is involved in the common disaster—why need I say a word?'[104] The woman who had complained to Basil about her compromised virtue symbolized exactly the tensions involved:

> Some take delight in slanders, because men by nature rejoice in recrimina-
> tions; others profess indeed to be indignant, but they have no sympathy;
> others are convinced that the slanderous abuse is true; others are in doubt,
> giving heed to the multitude of [my accuser's] oaths. And there is no one
> who sympathizes with me; but in truth I now realize my loneliness, and I
> bewail myself that I have no brother, no friend, no relative, no servant
> bond or free, no one at all to sympathize with me; and, as it seems, I find
> my single self to be more to be pitied than the whole city, in which there is
> so great scarcity of men who hate wickedness; they do not realize that the
> wanton violence committed against their fellows moves in a circle and
> will one day catch them.[105]

It could be argued that Basil was faced with a hopeless task, attempting to build a new ecclesial structure in the face of enduring social patterns inimical to the venture. Indeed, he may have been struggling against social conservatism in himself. Gregory of Nazianzus praised 'his independence [παρρησία] toward magistrates and the most powerful men in the city'; but his own brother described him as 'closely associated with Prefects, often in the company of generals, on easy terms with Emperors'.[106] Such ease of contact could bring admirable opportunity and yet compromise freedom. Both descriptions imply interaction; and one has to assess the precise nature of the relationships involved.

104. *Ep.* 136. 2, C 2: 52, D 2: 315.
105. *Ep.* 289, C 3: 160, D 4: 185. See above, at n. 61.
106. GNaz *Orat.* 43. 34, tr. p. 56; GNyss *Laus, PG* 46. 796D/797A. Patlagean, *Pauvreté*, pp. 31f., emphasizes churchmen's readiness, if not desire, to maintain the equilibrium of traditional social and political relationships. I am not sure that she has succeeded, in relation specifically to Basil, in describing accurately the balance between that tendency and his establishment of ascetic disciplines within the confines of the city: by the end of chapter 6, we shall have unravelled some of the issues. Brennecke, *Geschichte der Homöer*, pp. 227f., contrasts Basil's calm and helpful relations with the powerful, on the one hand, and the image presented later of a man oppressed by the mighty, on the other.

It takes but a moment to discover that his correspondence is littered with appeals to the eminent and refined. Some, naturally, were based on friendship.[107] Others seem more servile. 'The very act of writing to so great a man'—this was to the Prefect Modestus—'is most conducive to honour in the eyes of the discerning; for intercourse with men who are overwhelmingly superior to the rest of mankind affords the greatest distinction to such as are deemed worthy of it'.[108] In this instance, his appeal had been about tax relief for the clergy. Where the matter was more personal, Basil was cautious to make his approach with even greater hesitation and deference: 'I must earnestly beg pardon for troubling your Excellency in view of the magnitude of the office you hold'—this to a man whom he could count as a friend and supporter.[109] His patronage, however, was valued by others, and he took it for granted that he could enhance thereby his own status. If an ex-governor felt it worthwhile to harness the metropolitan of Caesarea to his cause, Basil was equally ready to end his plea on the man's behalf with unashamed self-interest: 'I beg your Grace to add something to your natural zeal for the good, and this on our account, that the man may know clearly the benefit derived from our intercession in his behalf'.[110]

Petition, therefore, was a natural duty, expected of a man in his position. 'I have written', he admitted to an unknown patron, 'about many who engage my interest, and in the future I shall write about still more. For neither can the supply of the needy fail, nor is it possible for us to refuse them the favour'.[111] A whole range of bargains was involved, in which Basil was not the least to gain. Even in the most obsequious letter, he could be surprisingly honest: 'We ought not to converse in the same manner with a physician as with any ordinary person, nor, obviously, with

107. For general examples that probably imply little more, see Ep. 15, 37, 111, 177, and 178 (which may allude to the treason trials initiated at Antioch by the emperor Valens and described by Ammianus Marcellinus, 29, 1–2: a reminder of how dangerous such petitions could be), and 179, 180, 192, 273, 275, 279, 308, and 312. As a background to all that follows, see Barnim Treucker, Politische und sozialgeschichtliche Studien zu den Basilius-Briefen. For the bishop as patron, see Chadwick, 'Role of the Christian Bishop', p. 8.

108. Ep. 104, C 2 4f., D 2: 195. See also Ep. 110. To a governor, who was also a friend, he could say (in jest) that he had stared in awe at the seal of his letter, 'as if it brought some state pronouncement'. In this case, Candidianus had not written ἀπὸ τοῦ σχήματος, according to his rank; but the joke reminds us how Basil might have reacted to a letter from an exalted stranger: Ep. 3. 1, C 1: 13f., D 1: 25/27.

109. Ep. 109, C 2: 10f., D 2: 209/211. The person on whose behalf Basil made the appeal is addressed in Ep. 107.

110. Ep. 149, C 2: 71, D 2: 361. See also Ep. 147 and 148.

111. Ep. 35, C 1: 78, D 1: 189. 'Petitioners', he grumbled on another occasion, 'are hard to satisfy', Ep. 309, C 3: 185, D 4: 247. Ep. 311 and 314 make the same point.

a magistrate in the same way as with a person in private station, but from the skill of the one and from the authority of the other we should try to derive some benefit for ourselves'.[112] 'I know that the first and greatest object of your Honour's zeal', he wrote on another occasion, 'is to favour the cause of justice in every way, and the second, to benefit your friends'— no contradiction being feared!'[113] The final phrases of a letter to the general Andronicus sum up matters beautifully:

> Although he had letters from many who were interceding for him, he considered the one from us to be more valuable than them all, having learned, I know not where, that a word from us was of weight with your Perfection. Therefore that he on his part may not be deceived in the hopes which he has placed in us, and that there may be for us some occasion for glorification before our people, be pleased, most illustrious master, to assent to our request.[114]

Those are not the words of a man nervous about his role as patron.

In what causes did Basil make his bids for favour? To the grandiose, he could speak with grandeur: 'As for me, as I strive earnestly for my country as a whole [ἐμοὶ δ' ὑπὲρ πατρίδος πάσης ἀγωνιῶντι], I must needs address to your Magnanimity this petition . . . that you stretch forth a helping hand to our fatherland now bowed to its knees'.[115]

He made not infrequent claims to such breadth of interest on behalf of 'our country [τῆς πατρίδος ἡμῶν]'.[116] 'Consider', he wrote to Sophronius, *magister officiorum*, 'that your whole country is addressing these words to you through our single voice [πᾶσαν οἴου τὴν πατρίδα διὰ μιᾶς τῆς ἡμετέρας φωνῆς]'.[117] Yet the favours asked in those instances were unusual in scale. In other contexts, πατρίς, fatherland, could represent a narrower

---

112. *Ep.* 84. 1, C 1: 187, D 2: 105.

113. *Ep.* 86, C 1: 190, D 2: 113. Note the expostulation in *Ep.* 137 'not that justice may be foiled', C 2: 54, D 2: 319; and the (albeit ironic) admission in *Ep.* 96 'for the fact that he was the most incorruptible man we know, and that he never granted a favour in violation of justice, we have passed over as of less significance than the man's other virtues', C 1: 209, D 2: 159.

114. *Ep.* 112. 3, C 2: 15, D 2: 221.

115. Again, to Modestus: *Ep.* 114, C 2: 5, D 2: 195.

116. *Ep.* 78, C 1: 180, D 2: 85/87. There is probably some connection with *Ep.* 77, and perhaps with *Ep.* 96, although the matter is more obscure. In the letter quoted here, Basil was apparently writing on behalf of Therasius, for whom see *PLRE* 1: 909; and also below, at n. 134.

117. *Ep.* 96, C 1: 209, D 2: 161. For Sophronius, a frequent addressee, see *PLRE* 1: 847f. He was *magister officiorum* from 369, certainly until 374, and came originally from Caesarea itself. On his predictable intimacy with Basil, see Treucker, *Studien*, p. 51. On the theme of πατρίς, see Giet, *Idées*, pp. 158f.

range of interests.[118] Seeking tax concessions (a not infrequent anxiety), Basil could start a letter to the relevant official with all the servility already described; could then suggest that he had in mind an opportunity for the man to display 'kindness', an opportunity 'through which it is possible to set upright again our country [ἡμῶν τὴν πατρίδα]'; but could come to the point at last, with a request related to the property of a friend, which was proving uneconomical because of the burden of tax imposed upon it.[119]

Basil obviously considered it perfectly natural to plead for those who were close to him: 'If you love me, as you do, it is, of course, your wish by all means in your power to relieve those also whom I regard as my own self'.[120] A whole network of persons, most of them devout, many of them economically supportive of Basil, were regarded by him as part of his 'family'; and their civil interests, therefore, were also very much his own.[121] A short letter to Modestus is worth quoting in full: Basil displayed deference, guarded his own reputation as a patron, and showed how totally interwoven were the worlds of private interest and public administration, for all the careful distinctions preserved between justice and friendship:

> Even though it is bold to bring petitions to so great a man by letter, nevertheless the honour which you have shown for us in the past takes the dread from our heart, and we take courage to write in behalf of men who, while related to us by kinship, are yet worthy of honour by reason of their integrity of character. Moreover, he who presents this letter of ours stands to me in place of a son. Since, therefore, he needs only your good-will to attain that which he seeks, deign to receive my letter, which the aforesaid offers you in place of a petition, and to grant him an opportunity to describe his situation and to converse with those who are able to assist him, to the end that by your command he may quickly obtain what he desires, and that it may be within my power to boast that there has been given me by the grace of God such a champion, who regards those who are related to me as his personal suppliants and clients.[122]

118. Take, for example, the obvious pettiness of *Ep.* 318, coupled with an appeal to αὐτὸ τὸ τῆς πατρίδος δίκαιον, C 3: 191.

119. *Ep.* 83, C 1: 186f., D 2: 101/103. See Kopecek, 'Civic Patriotism', pp. 300f.; and recall the broader context discussed above at nn. 35f.

120. In this case 'the presbyter of this place ... a foster-brother of mine [σύντροφος]', *Ep.* 36, C 1: 79, D 1: 191. See also *Ep.* 37, which we shall discuss again below at n. 155.

121. Certainly true of *Ep.* 36 and 37. See also *Ep.* 137, concerning 'the house of our most revered mother Palladia, whom not only the kinship of family binds to us, but also the goodness of her character has caused to be a second mother to us', C 2: 53f., D 2: 317/319. *Ep.* 303, 310, and 315 have points to add.

122. *Ep.* 280, C 3: 152f., D 4: 167/169.

Were such appeals successful? Sheer persistence suggests so.[123] Yet Basil had no illusions about the tortuous care needed to approach the great. He felt that his own brother Gregory, for example, would be seriously at a disadvantage if faced with 'a high and elevated personage, one occupying a lofty seat, and therefore unable to listen to men who from a lowly position on the ground would tell him the truth'.[124] He had, of course, experienced the same difficulty:

> The scarcity of replies received here renders scarce our letters to your Honour. For we count as proof that our letters bring annoyance to your Honour the fact that no answers are ever received to whatever we write on each occasion. But the thought of the multitude of the cases which encompasses you changes us again to the opposite opinion, and we have forgiveness for him who having so many duties in hand forgets us whom, even if one had nothing but leisure and quiet, it would not be easy to remember because of our humble station in life.[125]

It would be a grave error, however, to think that this correspondence illustrated nothing more than the obsequious and self-interested ploys of a provincial élite, subversive of justice and efficient administration. It betrayed constant effort, certainly, and frequent frustration—acceptable costs for those accustomed to status and influence, and familiar with the idiosyncrasies of the imperial system, within which public and private interests had long been contributing one to the other. But there was more than that to Basil's public role. He had status, too, within his own city, where the principles of the Gospel could present a novel challenge at every level. That city he could regard as the focus of another social network—'the mother of almost all the churches' and 'the centre of a great circle'.[126]

123. See *Ep.* 272—a most interesting letter, not least on the strains that status imposed upon friendship.

124. *Ep.* 215, C 2: 207, D 3: 239.

125. *Ep.* 317, C 3: 190f., D 4: 257/259. The words were but a prelude, however, to another confident request. Compare this with the peremptory tone to an *inferior* who does not reply, *Ep.* 331.

126. GNaz *Ep.* 41. 6; ed. Gallay, 1: 52. In relation to what follows, Fedwick, *Charisma,* p. 41, is not wholly successful in relating social reality to what he regards as Basil's 'general principles', and is content to suppose the bishop 'not always coherent', with 'somewhat incomplete and conflicting views', for which the only explanations are 'the difficult period of history in which he lived and the urge to serve the present hour in the most adequate manner'. A bishop's life in the 370s was at once more complicated and potentially more honourable than that. For a frank reluctance to discuss 'the relationship between church and empire during the reign of Valens', see *Charisma,* p. 37. Bernardi, *Prédication,* pp. 12, 335f., 352f., is anxious to use the sermons in particular as windows onto the social life of the local Christian community; but he ends on a note of pessimism, exaggerated in my view: 'Nous serons donc réduits aux seules ressources de la critique interne de textes dont nous n'avons

Not that he ceased to value the traditional features and virtues of city life. The development of crafts and skills, involvement in public affairs, the acquisition of property, travel from place to place—all were part of God's plan, part of the goodness of creation, a basis for optimism in life.[127] Accepted social categories could stand as models for the virtues expected of a Christian.[128] Such analogies were not designed to draw hearers away from the secular sphere. Virtue, correctly understood, would affect the quality of the civic milieu. Fasting, for example, included fasting from social discord.[129] In more general terms, Christians were to aim at the creation of a community marked above all by peace and order, εἰρήνη and εὐταξία.[130] Basil's homilies interposed no distinctly ecclesiastical form of behaviour between the practice of personal virtue and the achievement of social harmony: each simply supported and symbolized the other.

In making the point, he did show some deference towards the expectations of a lay audience. The letters of patronage, the appeals to civic imagery, all represented engagement with levels of experience and activity outside the narrow orbit of the clerical life. In particular, Basil could not escape from association with the powerful or with the civil administration. The allusions in his sermons to travel, property, entourage, and trade evoked the most familiar experiences of significant public figures.[131] A bishop would always depend on such people, among whom he had to live, and with whom he had to work, even in the cause of religion: he simply could not operate without them. That was why, when writing to a layman, he could inquire 'how it is with your practice of asceticism [τὸ τῆς

---

jamais la pleine assurance qu'ils nous apportent la parole même de leur auteur', p. 387. Since the argument in the rest of this chapter will continue to undermine tidy distinctions between the secular and the religious, I quote the succinct perception of Th. Nikolaou, 'Der Mensch als politisches Lebewesen bei Basilios dem Großen', p. 28: 'Basilios denkt nicht in den augustinischen Kategorien einer Gegenüberstellung des "göttlichen" und des "weltlichen" Staates. Ihn interessiert primär der Gottesstaat in der konkreten Gestalt der kirchlichen Gemeinde'.

127. *Hom.* 319. 6—although he does go on to praise also the more 'natural' simplicities of life: sleeping under the stars, for example. See the general acceptance of civic realities in *Hom.* 332. 1f. Averil Cameron, *Rhetoric of Empire*, pp. 82f., 188, sees such 'affirmation of the social order' as inseparable from public oratory, even in a Christian empire, although it was on the basis of such traditional assumptions that Christians themselves were then able to give new meaning to social categories. The long traditions within which Basil had to work are explored by Fergus Millar, 'Empire and City, Augustus to Julian: Obligations, Excuses, and Status'.

128. *Hom.* 319. 4, which refers to huntsmen, travellers, builders, stewards, shepherds, farmers, soldiers, and athletes. Similar connections are made in *Hom.* 320. 7.

129. *Hom.* 330. 10.

130. *Hom.* 330. 11, 331. 5.

131. *Hom.* 323. 2.

ἀσκήσεως]', and yet encourage a degree of involvement in local government: 'As regards security of life and all glory it is enough to be the ruler,
like your forefathers, of your own city'.[132] He could share with another
correspondent a 'love of letters' and the friendship of the great; express
admiration for a mutual lay acquaintance, for his 'superlative ability both
to discern a man's virtues and to make them known by speech'; and then
invite his friend to visit 'this old fireside of ours'—thus conjuring up a
world of easy access and refinement.[133] Such also were the people whom
he generously supported in his letters of appeal. The comradeship was
tempered, in other words, by obligation and risk: 'Though I have much
to say on various topics, I have put them off until our meeting, not judging
it safe [ἀσφαλές] to entrust such matters to letters'.[134] To a governor of
Cappadocia, he could praise φιλοσοφία, express a witty distaste for pick-
led cabbage, and toss off a couple of allusions to Homer.[135] Yet the same
man was addressed elsewhere with understated caution: 'that you may
learn from me by word of mouth those things which it does not become
me to write'.[136] Here we do no more than peep through a keyhole, into
a world in which Basil appears to move at one moment with unassuming
confidence, among social and cultural peers, and at another with every
sign of diffident dependence.

Yet Basil had proposals of his own to make, even to those whose
ancient habits of privilege he respected and partially shared. He wished
'to rule over a city as though it were a single household [κρατεῖν πόλεως
ὡς μιᾶς οἰκίας]';[137] and in the process he radically redefined what social
intercourse might mean within a Christian dispensation. He used existing
social forms, categories, and expectations that reached back centuries, in
order to create a world more recognizably his own. His task was to define
his proper audience, and to develop a mode of address that would help him
reach out to it intelligibly and constructively. He functioned as a member
of an élite; but it was an élite that he constantly strove to inspire with
his own ideals, so that they became coworkers in a Christian enterprise.

132. *Ep.* 116, C 2: 21, D 2: 233/235. See Petit, *Étudiants,* pp. 126f. A similar point is made
in *Ep* 294.
133. *Ep.* 64, C 1: 154, D 2: 21/23. See *Ep.* 72 for the same addressee.
134. *Ep.* 77, C 1: 179, D 2: 85. See above, at n. 116.
135. *Ep.* 186.
136. *Ep.* 187, C 2: 54, D 2: 319.
137. *Ep.* 299, C 3: 173, D 4: 217. In this letter to a *censor,* the ambition seems both secular
and less honourable than 'the inactive and tranquil life'; but, as Basil proceeds, it becomes
obvious that he values such commitment to public service: 'It will not escape our God, who
has set before us great rewards for good deeds', C 3: 174, D 4: 219.

'Through you', he wrote on one occasion, 'I address the entire city [δι' ὑμῶν γὰρ τῇ πόλει πάσῃ διαλέγομαι]'—perhaps one of his most characteristic utterances; and, in that very phrase, he turned the attention of the more sophisticated outwards, to face (as he did himself) the needs of their less cultivated fellows.[138]

The best support in such an undertaking was 'a truth-loving soul possessed of a sound judgment of affairs'.[139] Basil sought always the collaboration of men and women noted for 'remembering the orthodox' and for 'hospitality shown to ascetics'. He placed a high value on 'teachers' and 'champions of religion . . . capable of refuting the persuasive sophistry of heresy'.[140]

He had in mind a Church that formed a social whole; clergy and laity bound together in common loyalty and endeavour. Letters to Samosata provide vivid examples. To its clergy Basil exclaimed: 'The whole people of God do we greet through your Piety, those who enjoy dignities and civil magistracies, as well as all ranks of the clergy'.[141] Addressing the municipal council, Basil praised their 'zeal for good works' and exhorted them to 'stand about the shepherd of the Church'. Within that greater union, each would have a particular task, 'some different act performed on behalf of the Church of God'.[142] One might think that the situation in Samosata was exceptional, for their bishop Eusebius was at that time in exile; but Basil made the same point to other churches. To the people of Beroea in Syria, he expressed his joy at what he had heard 'not only of the care exercised by you who are entrusted with the service of the altar, but also of the concord of the whole people, and the magnanimous conduct of those who rule the city and administer its government, as well as their sincere piety toward God'.[143] To the church at Chalcis, he made the same broad address: 'both you the leaders of the Church, to whom the ministry of the altar has been entrusted, and every individual of the laity, and the more powerful among them'.[144] Finally, in a series

138. *Ep.* 204. 2, perhaps to the leading citizens of Neocaesarea, perhaps chiefly to its clergy, C 2: 174, D 3: 159. In either case, Basil pointed outwards to what was Ramsay MacMullen's 'audience', seen, I think, in a truer light: see chapter 2, n. 68.

139. *Ep.* 212. 1, C 2: 198, D 3: 217/219.

140. *Ep.* 305, C 3: 182, D 4: 237/239.

141. *Ep.* 219. 2, C 3: 3, D 3: 275. One is reminded of Basil's own situation in 370, when Gregory the Elder addressed on his behalf every social order in the city, GNaz *Ep.* 41. 9.

142. *Ep.* 183, C 2: 117f., D 2: 471/473.

143. *Ep.* 220, C 3: 4, D 3: 277. 'Your example has set many churches aright', C 3: 4, D 3: 279.

144. *Ep.* 222, C 3: 6f., D 3: 285. Basil gives here, as in *Ep.* 229, a very sensitive account of the mutual relations between clergy and laity. In a passage that dwells on the collaboration

of letters concerning the translation of a bishop from Colonia to Nicopolis, he reserved particular praise for the layman's role in church affairs: 'The management of the churches is in the hands of those who have been entrusted with their guidance, but they are strengthened by the laity'.[145] These last he addressed more directly: 'Although you were busy about public affairs you did not hold as secondary the affairs of the churches'.[146]

To the leading citizens of Nicopolis he gave a striking account of their intended role in support of the new bishop:

> Nothing so discountenances either rulers or the rest who may begrudge your peaceful state as harmony in affection for him who has been given to you, and the strength of your resistance. For it engenders in them despair of every wicked attack, if they see that neither clergy nor laity receive their schemes. Therefore what mind you have regarding the good man, make this public in the city; and to the people and to all who live in the country speak words that will strengthen their noble intentions, so that the genuineness of your love for God may be proclaimed among all.[147]

He could hardly have expressed more clearly the idea of a church in action, whose effectiveness depended on the fullest possible involvement of at least its leading lay members.

Given so high an ideal, both of unity and of engagement, Basil can be expected to have placed great emphasis on the preservation of this influential sector of his community. Not least important was the fact that ordinary people in the city were likely to be impressed by the conduct of those with power.[148] Letters of theological instruction have to be seen in that context.[149] That to the daughters of the *comes* Terentius, for example, with its nugget of catechesis, represented the all-important third element in his correspondence with lay persons, to be placed alongside familiarity among social equals and the exercise of patronage.[150] He also took it for granted that lay persons would be drawn into ecclesiastical disputes and

---

of churchmen and leading lay officials 'possessing the spark of the faith', Theodoret mentions explicitly the churches of Beroea and Chalcis, *Hist. relig.* 3 (Marcianus). 11; tr. Price, p. 42.

145. *Ep.* 230, C 3: 35, D 3: 357. The phrase παρὰ τῶν πεπιστευμένων was used constantly by Basil; and its further implications will be explored in the following chapter.

146. *Ep.* 228, C 3: 32, D 3: 349.

147. *Ep.* 230, C 3: 35f., D 3: 357. Note reference to 'all the laity who fear the Lord', *Ep.* 240. 3, C 3: 64, D 3: 427. The lay people of Caesarea itself were able to muster powerful support for their bishop: see GNaz *Orat.* 43. 58.

148. *Hom.* 344. 6. The 'lights of the world [τῶν λαμπτήρων τοῦ κόσμου]', oppressed by Arian rulers to the cost of 'the people [τοὺς λαούς]', may not have been only churchmen: *DSS* 30 (§ 77) (1: 524).

149. See chapter 4, at nn. 23f.

150. *Ep.* 105.

would require guidance accordingly. The same Terentius was presented with a long letter, late in 376, describing the dispute in the church at Antioch, its relations with the West, and Basil's own position in the Arian dispute. Terentius was obviously well informed, and interested. Basil was not afraid to add:

> I wish that your august Reverence might be persuaded of this, that you and everyone who, like you, has a care for the truth and does not condemn those who fight for the true faith, should wait for the lead to be taken in this union and peace by the champions of the churches [ἀναμένειν δεῖ καθηγήσασθαι ... τοὺς προστάτας τῶν 'Εκκλησιῶν], whom I consider as pillars and the foundation of the truth and of the Church.[151]

Those appealed to in the cause of some judicial or administrative issue, therefore, were approached just as often (how could it be otherwise, in an increasingly Christian society?) within the context of religious expectations and demands. A letter to Victor, *magister equitum* and ex-consul, provides a perfect example. He had 'anticipated our appeals on behalf of the Church, having done all that we could have asked'; and Basil added:

> In what you do you seek to win favour, not with men, but with God who has honoured you, who has given you some blessings in this present life and will give you others in the world to come, in recompense for your travelling His way with truth, keeping your heart unswerving in the orthodox faith from the beginning to the end.[152]

The overlap of worlds is beautifully summed up in a letter addressed (probably) to Junius Soranus. Soranus (who may also have been a relative of Basil) held a military post on the Danube frontier and was thoroughly informed on current events within Gothic society. He had a personal interest in church administration, and in particular in the cult of recent martyrs, such as Saba (martyred in 372). Basil could not but acknowledge the central position that such a person would hold within the Church:

> You surely remember, since by the grace of God you are faithful, the invocations of the Church—that we both make supplication for our brethren who are sojourning abroad, and offer prayers in the Holy Church for those who are enrolled in military service, and for those who speak out boldly for the sake of the name of the Lord, and for those who show the

---

151. *Ep.* 214. 4, C 2: 206, D 3: 235. See also *Ep.* 175, 211.
152. *Ep.* 152, C 2: 77f., D 2: 375. For Victor, see *PLRE* 1: 957f. See also *Ep.* 320 and 227.

fruits of the Spirit; and certainly in the greater number of these prayers, or even in all of them, we consider that your Honour also is included.[153]

That sense of incorporation, and in many cases of intimacy, led naturally to the development of a new sense of 'family'. The same group of people, the leaders of the committed laity, expected to be drawn into that kind of relationship with their bishop. The maligned virgin who felt herself a social outcast said, among other things, that Basil 'should have sympathized with her like a father [πατρικῶς αὐτῇ συναλγεῖν]'.[154] Basil saw himself in just such terms: 'I myself have been appointed to the position of a father by reason of this station to which the Lord has appointed me'.[155] Even when writing to a Praetorian Prefect, Basil described his client as standing 'in place of a son [ἐν υἱοῦ μοι τάξει καθέστηκεν]'.[156] Patrons in their turn were expected to behave in a special way towards those of their own faith:

It is incumbent on you, not only not to allow such things to be done, but also, with all your power, to prevent their being done, if possible against any man, but if such things must be, against any presbyter at least, or, of presbyters, against such as are of like mind with us and are journeying along the same road of piety.[157]

Clerical self-interest was not the only factor. Basil made striking claims to the pagan father of a recent young convert. First came a personal assertion:

The common law of all men makes those who are advanced in years common fathers, and the special law of us Christians [καὶ ἡμέτερος δὲ

153. *Ep.* 155, C 2: 80f., D 2: 383. For other reflections on this letter, see Maraval, 'Encore les frères et soeurs de Grégoire de Nysse', p. 165; and Peter Heather and John Matthews, *The Goths in the Fourth Century*. See also *Ep.* 165 and *PLRE* 1: 848. A point made by Matthews, *Western Aristocracies*, p. 195, in relation to Ambrose is clearly of analogous importance in our own context. He writes of 'the relations which might develop between individual members of the governing class, who without being fanatical Christians were yet interested in understanding their religion, and the men of the church whom they might come to regard as their spiritual guardians'. Such relations were, he says, 'an essential aspect of the process of Christianization'.

154. *Ep.* 289, C 3: 160, D 4: 185.

155. *Ep.* 37, C 1: 80, D 1: 193. The Greek terminology is interesting: καὶ αὐτὸς εἰς τὴν πατρικὴν τάξιν τετάχθαι διὰ τὸ σχῆμα τοῦτο εἰς ὃ ἔταξεν ἡμᾶς ὁ Κύριος. Σχῆμα stands out (as a reference to his priesthood or episcopate) amidst so much τάξις.

156. *Ep.* 280, C 3: 153, D 3: 167. See also *Ep.* 277, φίλτατε παίδων, C 3: 150; 319, ὁ υἱὸς οὗτος, C 3: 192; and the same theme in 73. 1, treated further below at n. 168. Amphilochius was probably a special case: *Ep.* 161, 'To a father's heart [πατρικοῖς σπλάγχνοις] every occasion is good for the embracing of a well-beloved child [τέκνον ἀγαπητόν]', C 2: 94, D 2: 415.

157. *Ep.* 87, C 1: 191, D 2: 115.

τῶν χριστιανῶν ἴδιος (sc. νόμος)] places us old men in the place of parents [ἐν γονέων τάξει] to the men of your years.

He then turned to the paternal rights of the correspondent himself:

> While we deem it right that you should demand his obedience in other respects—for he is responsible to you as to his body both by the law of nature and by this civil law according to which we are governed [καὶ τῷ πολιτικῷ τούτῳ (sc. νόμῳ) καθ' ὃν οἰκονομούμεθα]—yet as to his soul, since he brought it with him from a diviner source, we should consider it to be subject to another, and that there are due from it to God debts that have a priority over all.

The very existence of the letter suggests that Basil included himself in the phrase 'subject to another [ἄλλῳ ... ὑποκεῖσθαι]'; but he presented himself also as making 'the petition of your city', implying that the conversion had brought joy to a whole community, which was willing to regard the father also as thereby entering upon a new relationship of affection and shared good fortune.[158]

To interweave in that way the vocabulary of kinship and civic identity was skilful enough. Equally striking in its effect was the relation established between 'the special law of us Christians' and 'this civil law according to which we are governed', which, rather than creating an alternative, added to the meaning of νόμος, 'law'. Several of the passages quoted in the last section, referring to the Christian context within which traditional social roles were to be played out, seem to blur the boundary between what might nowadays be termed the secular and the religious worlds. This is because, in Basil's time and circumstance, such distinctions were still in the making. When he complained to high officials, for example, about the division of the province of Cappadocia, we might assume that he had at heart predominantly ecclesiastical interests. Yet he couched his appeal as if addressing a quite different set of issues, emphasizing in particular the consequent decline in the standards of learning for which Caesarea was famous, and the threat of general economic decay.[159] On other occasions, however, he approached officials as if they were conducting their duties within a framework entirely

158. *Ep.* 276, C 3: 148f., D 4: 157/159.
159. *Ep.* 74–76. See chapter 2, at nn. 66f., and below, at nn. 178f.

governed by Christian preoccupations: 'We are always very grateful to God and to rulers who have care over us, whenever we see the government of our country entrusted to a man who is first a Christian, then upright in character, and a strict guardian of the laws according to which we regulate human affairs'.[160]　Indeed, there were times when he seems to have suggested that church and state, as we might say, were virtually coterminous.　The newly consecrated Amphilochius, for example, exercised 'the ministry of the saints [τὴν λειτουργίαν τῶν ἁγίων]'; but those same saints were part of 'one people' and 'one Church', which meant that 'your fatherland both rejoices and is made happy by the dispensations of the Lord, and she does not believe that she has lost one man, but that through one man she has acquired whole churches'.[161]　It was the easy conjunction of 'people', 'Church', and 'fatherland' (λαός, ἐκκλησία, and πατρίς) that allowed a bishop, a person of predominantly religious status, to move into the secular sphere without embarrassment or hesitation.

One can understand, therefore, why Basil expected his own authority to penetrate every corner of society.　Excommunication, for example, 'proclaimed to the entire district', would make it clear that a miscreant 'must not be received in any of the ordinary relations of life [ἀπρόσδεκτον αὐτὸν εἶναι πρὸς πᾶσαν κοινωνίαν χρήσεως βιωτικῆς]'.　That does more to highlight an ominous and extensive influence than the mere fact that high officials would carry his letters for him, or that he could call upon armed support in his own defence against pressure from civil magistrates.[162]　Yet confusions and ambiguities persisted. Take, for example, the *Basileiados*. Basil admitted to the governor Elias that there was some overlap of perceived responsibilities. Elias rightly saw himself, in Basil's view, as 'competent single-handed to restore the works that have fallen into ruin, to people the uninhabited areas, and in general to transform the solitudes into cities'.[163]　Yet it was the bishop and his clergy who were saving the state

---

160. *Ep.* 225, C 3: 21, D 3: 321. See further below at n. 184. Whether the Demosthenes here addressed was the man who had afflicted Basil a few years before is not certain, although likely: see appendix 1, at n. 2. Recall the 'inclusion' of the world of Junius Soranus above at n. 153. Basil made to Amphilochius (and therefore as churchman to churchman) very legalistic points about the use of state or civil violence within the boundaries of Christian society: *Ep.* 188. 13, 217. 55.

161. *Ep.* 161. 1, C 2: 93, D 2: 413 (modified in the light of Courtonne).

162. *Ep.* 288, C 3: 158, D 4: 181. See *Ep.* 200, 215, 237; GNaz *Orat.* 43. 55f.—this last an instance of the claim to an independent system of justice, which we shall discuss in a moment.

163. *Ep.* 94, C 1: 206, D 2: 153.

money and taking upon themselves the task of advising civilian officials how they should organize public welfare.[164]

The most arresting instances of ambiguity occurred in the administration of justice. A bishop enjoyed certain legal rights in that regard, established since the time of Constantine.[165] It is by no means clear, however, from his own correspondence, whether Basil was either happy or consistent in their exercise. The case of the aggrieved virgin of Caesarea helps us to observe the interplay between civil and ecclesiastical intervention. Basil had already excommunicated the unattractive male involved; and that was designed in part to discourage vengeance. Now he confronted the problem of what to do in the face of further affronts. 'I have within my power', he wrote to a judicial official, 'some such decision as this—not to hand over the miscreants to the magistrates, yet neither to attempt to have them discharged if they have already been handed over'. He could preserve his independent authority, or he could let the secular law take its course. His chief worry, however, was a potential conflict of principles: 'Just as to hand them over is not kind [οὐ φιλάνθρωπον], so, on the other hand, to have them discharged is the act of one who supports wanton violence'.[166]

In another case, where a leading layman intended to bring to bear the full force of the law, faced with what he saw as insults on the part of his slaves, Basil urged a friend to calm the man's anger—a moral rather than an institutional stratagem. To the man himself, Basil was more specific: 'The fact is that the most befitting solution—the one which is capable of bringing you the greatest credit and is sufficient to enhance the dignity of my standing with my friends and contemporaries—would have been to entrust the punishment into our hands'. He then went on to disclose the distinctions he had in mind: 'A stern reprimand by us is no less effective in vindicating justice, nor is God's law held in slighter honour than the civil usages which play a part in the lives of men'. What did a 'stern reprimand' involve? Basil was vague: 'It would have been possible for them to be converted here in this place through the usages of our

---

164. *Ep.* 104 (making the point even to the Praetorian Prefect) and 194. Basil was concerned with practices well beyond the bounds of Caesarea: *Ep.* 143.

165. For the *audientia episcopalis*, see *Cod.Theod.* 1, 27. 1. This was, of course, a legislative concession and does not immediately inform us of resulting episcopal practice; but there is every evidence that many took advantage of the decision, which did more than all else, perhaps, to enhance the position of bishops in the Christian empire. See Chadwick, 'Role of the Christian Bishop', p. 6.

166. *Ep.* 289, C 3: 159f., D 4: 181f. See above, at nn. 61, 105, 154.

Church'.[167] The last phrase seems to link the whole process with an event or gesture occurring in the broader context of cult. Yet that was not to imply a soft option: 'and thus to set you free from the obligation of your oath, and at the same time themselves to pay the penalty commensurate with their crimes'.[168] On another occasion, when it seems that church officials had stolen or embezzled clothing destined for the poor, Basil assured a civilian officer:

> I have given orders to convert them in the discipline and correction of the Lord [ἐπιστρέψαι ἐν παιδείᾳ καὶ νουθεσίᾳ Κυρίου], for I think in the name of God I shall make them better for the future. For what the stripes of the court do not accomplish, this we have often known the fearful judgments of the Lord to effect.[169]

There was still little indication of what 'the fearful judgments of the Lord' would have looked like in practice, but all involved may have taken that knowledge for granted. Constant reference to anger and vengeance, and to the need for conversion and improvement, suggests very strongly that Basil was talking about a process of correction that operated entirely within the sphere of Christian worship and spiritual counselling, a combination of public shame and private exhortation.[170] He seems to have regarded the civil system, on the other hand, as harsh, preoccupied with punishment more than forgiveness or genuine changes of behaviour. 'Decisions rendered by magistrates do not bring even victory without loss', he noted; and 'contentious natures [αἱ φιλόνεικοι φύσεις]' exposed themselves in the courts at their peril. The reason, as he explained, was their

> folly and perversity of character, which give no heed to the counsels of others, but trust only in their own opinions and in the considerations which they happen to think of. And they happen to think of what they rejoice in, and they rejoice in what they wish. And he who thinks that

167. Ἐνταῦθα ἐπιστραφέντας τοῖς ἡμετέροις νομίμοις—place, effect, and means: all three are significant.

168. *Ep.* 73, C 1: 170f., D 2: 61f. The reference to Callisthenes' 'credit' and to Basil's 'dignity' recalls points made above at nn. 112f. Basil knew he was addressing a person of significance—'We value highly association with the best men [τῶν ἀρίστων ἀνδρῶν]'—but also one rightly in need of spiritual guidance, owing Basil 'the respect . . . of a son to a father'. See above, at n. 156.

169. *Ep.* 286, C 3: 156f., D 4: 177. Note that Basil admitted that 'the custody of such persons is a matter of concern to you yourself as one engaged in the business of the public'; and he had to conclude: 'If it seems best to you to refer this matter also to the Count, we have so much confidence in the justice and uprightness of the man that we permit you to do what you wish'. One suspects that he had little choice; and the admission was marked more by caution than by confidence.

170. We shall observe more of this technique in the following chapter.

what he wishes is profitable is not a safe judge of justice, but is like the blind being led by the blind.[171]

That series of opinions, varied or obscure though they may have been, casts light on a dramatic confrontation described by Gregory of Nazianzus. A civil judicial official had been trying to force marriage upon a distinguished widow; and 'she fled to the holy table and made God her protector against outrage'. Basil, apparently, 'had established laws for all in such cases'. It was taken for granted that he would 'raise his hand on behalf of the mercy of God and the law which commands respect for the altar'. The civil judge, however, was adamant: 'All must yield to my authority' (which would render Christians, in Gregory's eyes, 'traitors to their own laws'). Basil was eventually brought before the judge himself, and Gregory clearly enjoyed presenting the black-and-white confrontation of opposing polities. At this point the citizens, and in particular 'the imperial armorers and weavers', rushed to Basil's aid ('for in such circumstances these men are rather impetuous and are daring because of the freedom they enjoy').[172] One is suspicious, of course: the event represented for Gregory a climactic instance of Basil's 'war with the world'. One is alarmed, also: mob violence seems to have played as great a part as spiritual exhortation in gaining the bishop his point! It does confirm the view, however, that Gregory's audience would not have found it odd if conflicts of authority were a natural consequence of the exercise of episcopal responsibility.

Such anecdotes and examples help us to interpret also what is probably the most famous icon of confrontation between Basil and 'the world': his meeting with the emperor Valens on the feast of the Epiphany, 372. For Gregory of Nazianzus, whose account we have already explored, the event was another dramatic set piece; but elements of his story deserve further attention.[173] In the description of the liturgy itself, Basil and Valens become contrasting figures. Basil was like Samuel, 'a pillar attached to God and the altar ... with body and eyes and mind undisturbed'. Valens was impressed; this was a spectacle 'such as he had never seen before'.[174] In

171. *Ep.* 307, C 3: 183f., D 4: 241/243. See also *Ep.* 320.
172. GNaz *Orat.* 43. 56f., tr. p. 74. See above, at n. 162.
173. GNaz *Orat.* 43. 47f. (including a preliminary meeting with Modestus). For details of this and associated events, see above at nn. 24f.
174. GNaz *Orat.* 43. 52, tr. p. 70. The point was made also by Sozomen, *HE* 6, 16. 7; ed. Bidez, p. 257, lines 21f.; *PG* 67. 1333A; and by Theodoret, *HE* 4, 16. 11; ed. Parmentier (as 4, 19. 11), p. 245; *PG* 82. 1161BC.

the preceding conversation with Modestus, Basil daringly used the phrase 'my ... Sovereign [βασιλεὺς ὁ ἐμός]' to refer to God, in contrast to the emperor.[175] He did not fear exile, 'nor do I count as my own the land where I now dwell or any land into which I may be cast'.[176] At the same time, 'we are reasonable', he asserted, 'and more submissive than anyone else, for so the law prescribes [τοῦτο τῆς ἐντολῆς κελευούσης]'.[177]

Such an apparent emblem of distinctiveness has to be replaced firmly in its historical context. Gregory could not disguise the outcome of Basil's resolute response: the meeting was 'the beginning of our restoration'.[178] He was almost immediately entrusted with the task of reforming the church in Armenia, at a delicate point in Rome's relations with that kingdom, and with her rival for influence there, the newly aggressive empire of Persia.[179] A letter to the *comes* Terentius reported on the matter. Basil confused the course of his negotiations with the failure of his relationship with Eustathius of Sebaste; but the latter remained obviously incidental, and the main affair proceeded not too badly.[180] Then we have noted already the pleasure Basil expressed in his letter to Elias, that 'the great Emperor, on his part, ... has allowed us to govern the churches ourselves' (and probably supported the *Basileiados*). Valens remained hesitant about bringing too much pressure to bear upon a bishop who was firm in his views, certainly, but also efficient in his administration, and useful in the contacts he had been able to build up over a number of years, which he might now be persuaded to play upon to the advantage of the empire generally.[181]

175. GNaz *Orat.* 43. 48, PG 36. 560A, tr. pp. 67f. (where the word 'true' is a gloss).

176. GNaz *Orat.* 43. 49, tr. p. 68. Compare GNyss *Contra Eunomium* 1. 134, PG 45. 292C. Gregory emphasized even more Basil's displacement from any physical sense of place: *Laus* at PG 46. 797A, 816B. See also *Hom.* 346. 1.

177. GNaz *Orat.* 43. 50, PG 36. 561A, tr. p. 69 (where the word 'our' is a gloss).

178. GNaz *Orat.* 43. 53, tr. p. 71. As Gregory of Nyssa pointed out, Cappadocia survived: *Contra Eunomium* 1. 139f., PG 45. 293B–296A. Certainly, in relation to problems arising from the division of Cappadocia, Basil blamed other bishops more than he did Valens for its specifically ecclesial effects: *Ep.* 98. 2. Van Dam, 'Emperor, Bishops, and Friends', is corroborated.

179. That involvement we shall discuss further both in chapter 7 and (very fully) in chapter 8.

180. *Ep.* 99.

181. *Ep.* 94, C 1: 205, D 2: 151. See also *Ep.* 129. 2, 213. 2. That Valens *supported* Basil in some degree is a point made well by Van Dam, 'Emperor, Bishops, and Friends', pp. 57f. What was left to Caesarea, now at the centre of Cappadocia I, made it isolated as a πόλις but surrounded chiefly by imperial estates (much of the land dating back to royal property of pre-Roman days)—a point worth bearing in mind in relation to Valens's patronage of the *Basileiados*. See above, at nn. 24f. and 159, and chapter 2, at nn. 66f., together with Jones, *Cities*, p. 184.

Other references to the difficulties of the earlier 370s confirm an enduring confidence *vis-à-vis* the state. Some cases we have mentioned. To the clergy of Colonia (robbed, in a sense, of their bishop), Basil advised against an appeal to civil authority. It was foolish to say that 'failing of what we seek we shall have recourse to the courts': that would be to 'trust men with our affairs the chief aim of whose prayer is the catastrophe of the churches'. Anxiety about the appointment and dismissal of bishops was a church matter: 'Those who do not receive from the churches of God what is commanded by the churches "resisteth the ordinance of God"'.[182] Similarly in the case of Antioch, Basil told Terentius to 'wait for the lead to be taken by the champions of the churches'.[183] Perhaps the most brutal intrusion upon church affairs was launched by the *vicarius* Demosthenes. An early victim was Basil's own brother, arrested on charges of mismanaging church funds. Writing to Demosthenes himself, Basil was cautious and admitted that the state had some claims in the matter. Potential conflict of interest was restricted to the exercise of canonical regulations (governing in this case the conduct of Gregory's election), which should remain (naturally enough) the concern of the bishops themselves.[184] But Basil was not always so deferential. Demosthenes was the one, in his opinion, who confused the boundaries between civil and religious affairs. In particular, his use of civil fiscal burdens as a punishment to impose upon religious opponents was totally unacceptable.[185] No wonder Basil was alarmed at 'the monstrous and wicked men who have gained such control over the laity', and who 'make use of the power of government [τῇ ἐκ τῆς ἀρχῆς δυναστείᾳ] in accordance with their will'.[186]

How, then, should we represent to ourselves 'Christ's polity', as Basil called it, ἡ κατὰ Χριστὸν πολιτεία?[187] Influence and prestige were the chief

182. *Ep.* 227, C 3: 30f., D 3: 345/347.

183. *Ep.* 214, C 2: 206, D 3: 235. See above, at n. 151.

184. *Ep.* 225. See above, at n. 160; and also Theodoret *HE* 4, 16. 14; ed. Parmentier (as 19. 14), p. 245; *PG* 82. 1161D and 1164A.

185. *Ep.* 237. 2.

186. *Ep.* 239. 1, C 3: 59, D 3: 415; 248, C 3: 86, D 3: 481.

187. *Ep.* 150. 1, C 2: 71, D 2: 361. See above, at nn. 41f. For a more limited view of the authority Basil was able to command, both within and outside the Church, see Giet, *Idées*, pp. 152f., 173f. Giet was still using what must now be regarded as an outmoded distinction between 'church' and 'state': see pp. 356f. It is at this point especially that we should begin to feel sympathy with the emphases made by Fedwick, *Charisma*, pp. 12f.: it was not, perhaps,

forces at work. They underpinned both the language and the technique of politics in that age. The social sphere within which one hoped to be both patronal and impressive had to be extended ever outwards. For a man in Basil's position, there were no obvious theoretical limits to such an ambition. He could hope to include within the orbit of his own δυναστεία persons and institutions that we would regard as 'secular' or 'civil'. Indeed, they were regarded as such at the time. Yet at any given moment, for a variety of reasons (and the enmity bred by heretical opinion loomed large), other persons and institutions might seem to lie beyond the current limits of one's power. They demanded, at least for a time, a more cautious species of diplomacy. To that extent, therefore, the whole world was Basil's world. The influence he could exercise and the status he could enjoy may have been different from that of Modestus or Demosthenes, not 'secular' in that sense. Yet the persons and circumstances he hoped to touch and control were the objects of similar ambitions in those men also. It was not a matter of separate spheres of responsibility but of power contesting power in a single arena.

For Basil, the innermost enclave of that arena was his own city; and it was in his addresses to that city that he made clear his 'political' ambitions. The very acceptance of baptism involved, in his eyes, a promise to move from the worship of idols to the service of a living God. That meant setting up a new altar, in contrast to the old altar of pagan cult: an altar in the heart, upon which one sacrificed one's very self.[188] The emphasis was interior, but the rejected alternative was visible enough. Basil was always skilful at painting a picture of public life—its devotion to buildings, to processions, to demonstrations of social deference. Those he would then reject, in favour of service to the true king. He felt that city life in the old style, marked above all by sycophancy, was but one step beyond the morality of rural bandits and piracy at sea.[189] When he deployed scriptural images to describe the shift of loyalty required, the terms of the contrast implied a move on the part of Christians towards a differently defined

that Basil wished simply to be 'less dependent' on the state; but he was certainly engaged on a 'project of church reform on the pattern of the pre-Constantinian model or, better yet, of the apostolic community of Jerusalem'.

188. DSS 10 (§ 26), Hom. 358. 5. The intimacy of this new 'holy place', closely associated with the presence of the Holy Spirit, is discussed further in DSS 26 (§ 62). Compare the wonderful images in GNaz Orat. 43. 67. It is at this point we should recall the insistence of Bernardi, Prédication, p. 376: 'Ce sont les sermons des Cappadociens qui nous révèleront les aspects les plus essentiels de leur activité de pasteur'. He sets the scene of pastor and audience very well, pp. 364f.

189. Hom. 356. 4. See also 323. 7, 331. 5.

polity, rather than to no polity at all. To cross the Red Sea, as in Exodus, had been to escape literally from an undesirable political situation, an allegory for escape from the 'tyranny' of the devil.[190] Yet the community described in Acts was an acceptable model precisely because it extended one's understanding not only of harmony of spirit but also of generosity at a material level, which should reach well beyond the limits of pagan philanthropy, focussed on family and kin.[191]

So, when it came to defining the new polity, Basil could be quite hard-headed, even while admitting a transcendent dimension. Discussing, for example, 'the river whose streams gladden the city of God' (which represented in the first place the Holy Spirit), he was led to explore more formal descriptions. The city, he said, was in this case 'the church [or perhaps just 'the assembly', ἐκκλησία] of those who have their city [τὸ πολίτευμα] in heaven'. He then added that it might also be 'the whole body of intelligent creatures'. As if that were not entirely satisfactory (one suspects he had begun to think aloud at this point), he agreed that some people would think of a city as 'a stable system of government administered according to law [σύστημα ἰδρυμένον, κατὰ νόμον διοικούμενον]'; and he was willing enough to see that definition applied to the heavenly city as well.[192] In another sermon (impossible to date, unfortunately), he opted for the same 'secular' phraseology. Reflecting on the verse of the psalm, 'Who will bring me to the fortified city?', he asserted that the writer was 'probably talking about the church; and he calls it a city, because it is a system of government administered on a legal basis [τὸ σύστημα ... νομίμως οἰκούμενον]'.[193]

We will expect Basil, therefore, to have had as much to say about the visible aspects of a truly Christian polity as he did about the transcendent polity to come. Christians, by baptism, were called into the company of the angels; but it was still as 'fellow citizens', which allowed other associations to cluster around the experience of the sacrament: freedom from slavery, release from financial injustice. No audience consistently exposed to such exegesis could fail to understand that membership of such

190. *Hom.* 320. 2.
191. *Hom.* 325. 8—hardly a fair point! For broad comment on the model presented by the earliest Christian community, and its subsequent impact on church history, see Martin Hengel, *Acts and the History of Earliest Christianity.* The whole issue of finding a new social framework within which to define moral goals is splendidly handled by Jean Bayet, 'Science cosmique et sagesse dans la philosophie antique'. Note especially his allusion to decreasing dependence on 'l'étroit nationalisme d'une ville', and the corresponding search for alternatives, p. 503.
192. *Hom.* 353. 4, *PG* 29. 421CD. The sermon reflected at this point upon Psalm 46 (V 45). 4.
193. *Hom.* 355. 4, *PG* 29. 468B. In this instance, the reference was to Psalm 60 (V 59). 9.

a Church would have immediate social and economic consequences.[194] Even one's emotional life, in its corporate expression (as at moments of grief, for example), would look different.[195] The same applied to economic relations: 'Humans are political beings, used to living together. In their common experience of public life [ἐν δὲ τῇ κοινῇ πολιτείᾳ] and in their dealings one with another, they have to show a generosity directed towards improving the lot of those in need'.[196]

The chief visible or social sign that a necessary change had taken place in people's inner lives would be economic in form. Basil was confident that he addressed a Christian community, nourished from early years on the word of God; but not everyone had committed themselves to the obligations of the baptized. Indeed, many had accustomed themselves unwarrantedly to the generosity of the Church, without submitting to its sacramental discipline (an enlightening comment on the possible impact of the Basileiados).[197] As for the needs of others, those they simply failed to notice.[198] What they had to grasp, he felt, was that absence of generosity was a major sin. Its effect was visible and social. It brought about an imbalance in nature itself, and it engulfed the whole community in God's punishment: 'Peoples and cities share in these various misfortunes, which represent blows struck against an excess of evil'.[199] Even from a practical point of view, greed and oppression were destructive in a community, bringing in their train 'bad neighbours in the city, bad neighbours in the country'. Generosity, on the other hand, at least gained one friends and freed one from the gall of seeing one's hoarded wealth fall into undesirable hands after one's death.[200] But there was a specifically Christian economy, within which the opportunities for social virtue were expected most use-

194. *Hom.* 320. 3. See the comments of Gribomont, 'Protreptique'.

195. *Hom.* 328. 6.

196. *Hom.* 346. 6, PG 29. 261C. See Nikolaou, 'Der Mensch als politisches Lebewesen', which stresses how the famous Aristotelian phrase repeated here was interpreted entirely within the context of Christian obligations. To that extent Basil would have been able to criticize the πολιτεία of his own day as at odds with classical tradition.

197. *Hom.* 320. 1, 3. It is important to remember that high ideals and an elevated tone do not necessarily imply that a sermon was not addressed to a wide audience: see Bernardi, *Prédication*, pp. 33f., together with pp. 352f. and 364f. Sozomen created the impression of an almost totally Christian city, in the time of Julian; but his phraseology—οἰκήτορας, ὡς πανδημεὶ Χριστιανίζοντας—calls into question his intended implication as much as his accuracy: *HE* 5, 4. 2; ed. Bidez, p. 197.

198. *Hom.* 322. 4. See n. 17 above.

199. *Hom.* 336. 3: κοιναί τινές εἰσι πληγαὶ πόλεων καὶ ἐθνῶν, τοῦ κακοῦ τὴν ἀμετρίαν κολάζουσι, PG 31. 333B.

200. *Hom.* 323. 5 (πονηρὸς ἐν πόλει σύνοικος, πονηρὸς ἐν ἀγροῖς, ὁ πλεονέκτης, PG 31. 293B), 335. 6, 339. 3.

fully to occur. A wealthy man should see himself as 'a steward to his fellow slaves [οἰκονόμος τῶν ὁμοδούλων]'. He would find that, because of his own selflessness, he was hailed as 'the father of many children'. The resulting circulation of his wealth would make it grow. He would also be subscribing to a principle of equality, whereby the goods of this world that were destined for all would truly be shared by all.[201] Basil did not mince his words on this last point: 'All have one nature, this person and that ... all are related, all are brothers, all are the offspring of a single father'.[202]

Compromise there may have been, therefore: Basil would sugar his pill by promising that generosity would at least help towards an eternal reward.[203] But he was even more forceful in making a direct connection between generosity and the social effects without which it would have no meaning. When he described how a rich man might find himself applauded on Judgement Day, in exactly the way he expected to gain applause in the earthly city here and now,[204] the point was not made in the abstract. It is these people standing around you now, Basil would say, who will cry out to you then: 'You did not help us in our lifetime. Why should we help you now?'[205] He found it easy to present that final reckoning in terms familiar from the experience of local judicial proceedings, with frantic supporters, hostile witnesses, bombastic rhetors, and attempts at fruitless bribery.[206] Such an evocation of the familiar was designed to achieve more than a mere shift of attitude: behave now, Basil was saying, as you hope to behave then, for those circumstances of dependence and responsibility are not postponed indefinitely but press visibly upon your conscience in the city of today.

The two levels of appeal were a persistent feature of Basil's homiletic address. When discussing so simple a habit as calling Jesus 'the way', he had in mind a sense of movement, of progress on a journey, that involved both personal enlightenment and 'the exercise of justice'.[207] The ordained purpose of living in association with other Christians was to provide oneself with an appropriate setting within which moral development could be sustained. The Church nurtured people by its teaching, urging each one

---

201. *Hom.* 322. 2 (*PG* 31. 264C), 3 (265C), 5, 7. On ὁμόδουλος, see above, at n. 16.

202. *Hom.* 335. 2, *PG* 31. 1441A. *Hom.* 354. 1 makes the same point in the context of the Church. Fedwick, *Charisma*, pp. 1f., sees this last sermon as giving a total view of the Church.

203. See above, at nn. 15f., and in particular *Hom.* 322. 3, 325. 8.

204. *Hom.* 322. 3. See above, at n. 18.

205. *Hom.* 339. 8.

206. *Hom.* 323. 6.

207. *DSS* 8 (§ 18): τὴν γὰρ εἱρμῷ καὶ τάξει διὰ τῶν ἔργων τῆς δικαιοσύνης καὶ τοῦ φωτισμοῦ τῆς γνώσεως ἐπὶ τὸ τέλειον προκοπήν, ed. Pruche, p. 310.

towards baptism, towards 'intimacy with God [οἰκείωσις πρὸς Θεόν]'; but
it was the intimacy of those sharing a common household.[208] Closeness
to God, dwelling with God, made the Church 'the house of God [ὁ οἶκος
τοῦ Θεοῦ]'. A right to membership in that household would depend
upon a readiness to absorb its teaching, and to master one's passions,
but also upon 'an urbane deportment [ἀγωγὴν ἀστείαν]' and a taste for
asceticism.[209] Knowledge and enlightenment were to an important degree
the aim (such was the essence of Basil's anthropology);[210] but no single
mind, no individual, could achieve alone that degree of perception. One
needed the company of others. It was in a sense the Church as a whole
that gained a true knowledge of God.[211]

That might seem to address our earlier doubt about the possible relationship between a broadly focussed pastorate and individual salvation.[212]
But did Basil attach a lasting value to society as such, once its function as a
context for individual growth had been fulfilled? Were not the demands
of morality in the end individual and interior? The experience of social
life was made irretrievably painful, surely, by an almost epistemological
malaise: by people's inability to communicate with clarity, even to share
with others, their moral concern.

'The Church is an organization', declared Basil, 'precisely in so far as it
is made up of individuals [εἴπερ ἐκ τῶν καθ' ἕκαστον ἔχει ἡ ἐκκλησία
τὸ σύστημα]'.[213] Consequently, the phrase 'dedication of the church' (Basil
was preaching here on a feast of dedication) referred to 'that renewal of
the mind brought about by the Holy Spirit in those who, one by one, made
up the body of the church of Christ [τοῖς καθ' ἕνα τῶν συμπληρούντων
τὸ σῶμα]'.[214] Yet the organization, the σύστημα, did have a function of
its own. Basil was able to present an interior and very beautiful image

208. *Hom.* 320. 1, *PG* 31. 425A. See above, at n. 139.
209. *Hom.* 319. 3; *PG* 31. 204C, 205B.
210. *DSS* 15 (§ 35).
211. *Hom.* 351. 3, 352. 10.
212. See above, at nn. 102f. Useful reflections on the broader background to this
necessary balance are contained in Jean Pierre Vernant, 'The Individual within the City-State'.
213. *Hom.* 325. 8, *PG* 31. 328AB.
214. *Hom.* 349. 1, *PG* 29. 308A. The vocabulary recurs in the *Hexaemeron*: see, for example,
5. 6: καὶ τοὺς καθ' ἕνα ἡμῶν διὰ τῆς πίστεως ἐμπεφυτευμένους τῇ ἐκκλησίᾳ κλήματα
προσηγόρευσε [sc. ὁ Κύριος], ed. Giet, p. 304. There are classical antecedents. In *Hex.* 8.
4, for example, Basil showed how Aristotle created a direct line of development between
a collection of individuals and a united community, 'allowing the energies of each individual
to converge towards a common goal [thus making 'political life', in the technical sense,
applicable by analogy to the animal world: ἔστι δέ τινα καὶ πολιτικὰ τῶν ἀλόγων, εἴπερ
πολιτείας ἴδιον, τὸ πρὸς ἓν πέρας κοινὸν συννεύειν τὴν ἐνέργειαν τῶν καθ' ἕκαστον]',
ed. Giet p. 446. See chapter 9, at nn. 62, 75.

of the peace that the Christian life was designed to achieve; but he went on at once to suggest that the Church was held together by a structure akin to the bones and sinews of the body, which supported its weaker parts. That was what was meant by 'the bond of love and peace'.[215] Organization and individual needed one another.

Yet the liaison was not lasting or total. In one sermon, Basil discussed the terminology of Psalm 29 (V 28). On the one hand, we have 'tent';[216] and our tent is our body, which we have with us until death, and within which we offer up to God a genuine cult that nevertheless depends upon the moral discipline of good works. On the other hand, we have the *aula*, the 'temple' or 'holy place'.[217] This must refer in some way to the Church; but there is only one *aula*, heavenly and eternal.[218]

That shifting sense of where a person most genuinely offered worship to God, most effectively and lastingly entered into the presence of God, offers the clue to what might otherwise appear confused and ambiguous. The holy place, the place of cult in the fullest sense, was to be found at both levels: in the tent, and in the *aula*. It was not a matter of contrasting the individual and the corporate: it was a matter of recognizing the difference between 'Church now' and 'Church to come'. Because of an interplay of language, neither appeared stable in the eye of a human observer. The 'Church' at any one time was the place through which individuals passed on their way to God. Their very passing carried the Church forward also. Each contributed to the progress of the other. In a particularly fine sermon on Psalm 45 (V 44), Basil explored those difficult relationships at some length. The Church's beauty, like that of the bride in the poem, was 'within' (ἔσωθεν, as Basil's version had it). It was not acquired or preserved in order to gain the admiration of others. Yet that very point introduced a social note. People still needed to know whether there *was* a beauty, a spiritual quality within; and proof resided in the way that πρᾶξις, a pattern of behaviour, a visible response, followed upon the teaching of the word. Then Basil came to the passage 'You will make them princes in all the earth'. He avoided at once any glib triumphalism: genuine authority, he said, sprang from the self-possession and the inner control achieved by the holy ones. But the Church itself was involved in that victory: by siding with the traditions of the fathers,

215. *Hom.* 351. 10, 13 (*PG* 29. 384C).
216. The superscription of the psalm, in the version he used, contained the phrase ἐξοδίου σκηνῆς.
217. So he read the end of verse 2 of the psalm: προσκυνήσατε τῷ Κυρίῳ ἐν αὐλῇ ἁγίᾳ αὐτοῦ.
218. *Hom.* 348. 1f.

by adopting an ascetic mode of life, by remaining 'sons of the bride of Christ', Christians could share with the Church a dominion over the whole world. What finally gave the Church so enduring and universal a presence? What made it the place in which God was called constantly to mind? It was 'the declaration of the people [ἡ ἐξομολόγησις τῶν λαῶν]' (the voice of the *Contra Eunomium* once again).[219] To that extent, the people created the Church. They chose it as the framework within which to formulate their worship of God. It was, indeed, the instrument of their declaration.

Having heard the sermon, and having made their declaration of faith, the people would move at times to other phases of liturgical celebration. It is particularly in sermons proper to those occasions that we gain our fullest impression of cultic practice, and that the interwoven vocabulary of city and church was most carefully explored. Central are the sermons that focus on the cult of the martyrs. Basil had a particular interest in the cult of Eupsychius, a young married layman of distinguished birth who had been executed towards the end of Julian's reign in connection with the destruction of a temple dedicated to Fortune in Caesarea itself.[220] It is important that he should have focussed upon a hero so recent. It reminds us that death in defence of religious belief was not just a dim memory, lost in a glorious past. Basil held an annual synod at Caesarea in honour of Eupsychius (a church had been dedicated to his memory) and was easily

219. *Hom.* 352. 11f., *PG* 29. 409D-413D. See chapter 4, at nn. 147f.
220. See Sozomen *HE* 5, 11. 7f.; ed. Bidez, pp. 209f. Additional background is provided in *HE* 5, 4. 1f.; ed. Bidez, pp. 196f. If Sozomen is correct (and he may have admitted to uncertainty over details: συμβάλλω δέ, ed. Bidez, p. 210), Eupsychius was not the only person executed; and others were exiled. Libanius referred to the incident, with perhaps more trustworthy reticence: *Orat.* 16. 14. See *Libanius, Selected Works*, ed. Norman, 1: 218. Fiscal motives behind Julian's rigour are not to be underestimated. For important background, see Garth Fowden, 'Bishops and Temples in the Eastern Roman Empire, A.D. 320–435'; and Richard P. Duncan-Jones, *Structure and Scale in the Roman Economy*, p. 123. Ammianus sympathized with mistreated provincial *curiales* (specifically in the vicinity of Caesarea, during Julian's reign), while deploring the illegal methods employed by some to overcome their difficulties, 22, 9. 8f. Brennecke, *Geschichte der Homöer*, p. 154, emphasizes the Homoean pedigree of martyr stories dating back to Julian, a tradition highjacked (in the case of Eupsychius at Caesarea, remarkably quickly) by the supporters of Nicaea ('ohne daß die meisten Christen dabei einen Wechsel empfanden'). For Eupsychius, see Brennecke, pp. 150f., and for the martyr tradition more generally, pp. 114–57.

distressed if those invited did not attend.[221] He also took an interest in the return of the bodies or relics of those native to Asia Minor who had been martyred during the Gothic persecution.[222]

Basil was in no way exceptional in his devotion. Such an appeal to the heroic dead was widespread in the Church during the fourth century;[223] and memories of such a sort had been kept intensely alive within his own family, inspiring his mother in particular.[224]

The experience reached beyond pious recollection: Basil believed that contact with the bones of the dead placed one in touch with a source of holiness.[225] That focus helped to preserve in new circumstances the fervour of an older régime. Programmes of moral formation and techniques of emotional exaltation, which had inspired at least some Christians in periods of real danger, had now to be given new force, at a time when Christianity was not only tolerated but positively encouraged. 'You are', Basil told the clergy of Nicopolis, 'children of confessors, and children of martyrs, who strove unto blood against sin'.[226] Heroism was no longer what they themselves might have to expect, but a part of history, a reassurance that their own more modest trials were no more than a passing phase, incapable of undermining their cause completely. Yet 'life under discipline has something akin to those lives which have been made perfect by fortitude', and a carefully orchestrated recollection of the dead would help churchmen to impress such values on their people.[227]

221. *Ep.* 100, 142, 176, 252, 282; and note reference to a similar occasion at Phargamos, 'made illustrious by the glory of martyrs and by the largely attended synod held there every year', *Ep.* 95, C 1: 207, D 2: 155/157. For the perceived usefulness of such occasions, see *Hom.* 335. 5. Gregory of Nazianzus described some aspects of the celebrations in honour of Eupsychius in his *Ep.* 58. 7. For less desirable associations, see *Hom.* 324. 1, 8.

222. See n. 153.

223. It would be burdensome to provide a full bibliography. The following are obvious authorities: Hippolyte Delehaye, *Les Passions des martyres et les genres littéraires*; André Grabar, *Martyrium: Recherches sur le culte des reliques et l'art chrétien antique*; and Peter Brown, *The Cult of the Saints: Its Rise and Function in Latin Christianity*. There are also astute comments in Markus, *Ancient Christianity*, pp. 97–106, 139–55.

224. See chapter 1, esp. at nn. 5, 59.

225. *Hom.* 358. 5, a particularly direct statement: ὁ δὲ ἁψάμενος ὀστέων μάρτυρος, λαμβάνει τινὰ μετουσίαν ἁγιασμοῦ ἐκ τῆς τῷ σώματι παρεδρευούσης χάριτος, *PG* 30. 112C. But see also *Hom.* 334. 2 on Julitta: ἁγιάζει μὲν τὸν τόπον, ἁγιάζει δὲ τοὺς εἰς αὐτὸν συνιόντας, *PG* 31. 241B.

226. *Ep.* 240. 2, C 3: 63, D 3: 423.

227. *Ep.* 252, C 3: 93, D 4: 19. This rare association of asceticism and martyrdom is nevertheless very generally expressed: διὰ τὸ συγγενές τι ἔχειν τὸν ἐν ἀκριβείᾳ βίον πρὸς τοὺς διὰ καρτερίας τελειωθέντας. Nor should we imagine that Basil, in his adoption of a local hero like Eupsychius, was attempting to maintain the anti-pagan fervour characteristic

Nevertheless, Basil felt, too few understood the connection. Their ancestors had been persecuted 'by those who worshipped idols'. Now, however, 'to deceive the many', the persecutors 'put forward the name of Christ, that those who are persecuted may not even have the consolation of being confessors'. As a consequence, 'the many and simpler folk ... do not account to us as martyrdom our death for the sake of truth'. The only consolation was that, robbed of 'the openly acknowledged approbation that comes from men', those currently suffering might reasonably expect that 'the recompense which is laid up in the next life for your labours in defence of the true religion is many times greater'.[228] Such a promise might smack of élitism, while remaining despondent: for the reality offered little room for conceit. Basil himself admitted: 'No one of us has been combed with lashes, the home of no one has been confiscated, we have not experienced banishment, we have no knowledge of prison. What terrible thing have we suffered? Unless perhaps this is grievous—that we have suffered nothing, and have not been thought worthy of the sufferings in behalf of Christ'.[229] Martyrdom was used, therefore, as a rallying point for the whole community, not simply to encourage individual self-improvement through ascetic discipline but rather to awaken the Church to the danger of civil and heretical authority masquerading as the instrument of a Christian establishment.

Basil preached four sermons on specific martyrs, which reward close attention.[230] Almost all the heroes involved had been associated with Caesarea, and all had met their deaths within the last century, one as recently as 321.[231] In these sermons, Basil was explicitly anxious to repudiate the principles of traditional public speaking. He did so in order to arouse his audience to an appropriate pitch of celebration and, most important, to the imitation of his subjects' virtues. The mode of

---

of Julian's reign (see Brennecke, *Geschichte der Homöer*, pp. 52f.). He was always more concerned with the development of the inner lives of his people.

228. *Ep.* 257. 1, C 3: 98f., D 4: 31/33.

229. *Ep.* 240. 2, C 3: 63, D 3: 425.

230. See Bernardi, *Prédication*, pp. 77f., although my interests are not his. Mario Girardi, 'Bibbia e agiografia nell'omiletica sui martiri di Basilio di Cesarea', shows how much one can miss in this material if one concentrates merely on literary aspects. Of course, others of Basil's surviving sermons may have been preached on occasions that focussed on martyrdom, without being so specific in their reference. *Hom.* 357, for example, ostensibly on Psalm 116a (V 114), was clearly such and warns us that there may be others.

231. Gordius (*Hom.* 327) was executed under Licinius, Julitta (*Hom.* 334) met her death in 304, Mamas (*Hom.* 337) his in 274. The sermon on the Forty Martyrs is *Hom.* 338. Association with Caesarea was no accident, for the cult of the martyrs was in part an exercise in creating a sense of Christian history within a city, and exalting its status *vis-à-vis* rival centres of cult and authority.

address was carefully tailored to making the martyrs genuine models for the behaviour of the community.[232] Two points recur consistently. First, Christians should be led by recollection to imitation: indeed, imitation was the best form that recollection could take. That was why a simple historical account, ἱστορία, was more valuable than panegyric, ἐγκώμιον. The historical account dealt with things actually done. The celebration of the feast itself was panegyric enough. On such an occasion, all those with memories, either inherited or their own, would pool them in the ceremonies themselves as they gathered about their bishop.[233] Second, family and ancestry (traditionally explored in formal rhetoric of this sort) mattered nothing in comparison with what a holy one had achieved in life and death (although it helped that those men and women were local figures: the sources of their formation and inspiration were the same as those of Basil's audience).[234]

It was the relationship between martyr and audience that mattered most. How were such people to be seen as models for the Christians of Caesarea? The sermon on Julitta was a vignette (only half a sermon, really, since Basil passed on to other matters); but it made important points. Her martyrdom happened almost by accident. She was being quite outrageously (and unsuccessfully) pursued by her husband through the courts; but then she suddenly declared that her religious scruples prevented her from benefitting from the law of a pagan state. Her implication was that those who were not prepared to offer sacrifice should not lay claim to civil rights. Persecution forced one to take a moral stand of that sort, even in what might have appeared to be the neutral territory of civil litigation. Julitta charged the atmosphere of the court with religious sensibilities that others present would not even recognize. When she rejected, therefore, in abstract terms, the material world in favour of the spiritual, she rejected the civil sphere as well. Under Christian emperors, one might presume, such a gesture would have been out of place. What were Christians after Constantine supposed to do with such a woman? Admiration was no simple matter; imitation even more problematic. So a particular type of historical relationship had to be set in place. Basil focussed attention on the spring of water that now flowed from Julitta's tomb: 'So the martyr

232. For the broader pedagogic and homiletic context, see chapter 2, at nn. 79f., 114f., and chapter 4, at nn. 69f., 71f.

233. *Hom.* 327. 1f., 337. 1f., 338. 40. The last assertion is particularly striking: πάντα μοι συναγαγόντες, ἐγκώμιον ἐκ κοινοῦ ἐράνου πονήσατε, *Hom.* 337. 1, *PG* 31. 589C. The process is akin to that recommended to the church at Ancyra, mourning the death of its bishop: see above, at n. 91.

234. *Hom.* 327. 1, 337. 2.

has become, as it were, our mother, suckling with a sort of communal milk those who live in the city'.[235]

Another sermon celebrated Mamas. In his case, the mechanics of recollection defined in a particular way the corporate nature of the festival. It was not like raising a statue to some otherwise forgotten worthy: 'In remembering the martyr, the whole countryside is on the move, the whole city sets itself to celebrate'.[236] Mamas had been a shepherd. That enabled Basil to set him up as the complete antithesis of civic life. He had fled from the agora, the law courts, the sycophancy of city life, wealth, property, even communion with others. He lived alone under the stars, lost in wonder at their maker. He was, in that regard, like many figures of the Old Testament, from Abel onwards. Basil listed his archetypes, until he came to David, who was called, of course, from his task as a shepherd to the exercise of kingship itself: 'For the spheres of the shepherd and the king are akin to one another. The first is entrusted with authority over creatures lacking in intelligence, the second over creatures empowered with reason'.[237] The notion was far from original. What strikes one here is that the martyr, having been rescued, so to speak, from one pattern of 'political' life, was promptly associated with another.[238]

Basil's sermon in honour of Gordius was a more polished piece. He started by describing the persecution period (still, for some, a living memory). It was, he said, a perversion of that civic order which, in the Christian empire, they now enjoyed. The policies of the 'tyrant' Licinius had brought 'confusion and upheaval throughout the city', leading to a disrespect for proper social hierarchy and a subversion of the rule of law.[239] Because of that breakdown, Gordius had decided to leave the city, and to take to remoter regions (as some of Basil's family had done in the same circumstances). As in the sermon on Mamas, the bishop provided a long list of those civic qualities one might happily do without: trade, litigation, sycophancy (again), the misuse of language—all the inevitable consequences of living together in a city.[240] Then Gordius came back from

---

235. *Hom.* 334. 1f., *PG* 31. 241B.

236. *Hom.* 337. 2: πᾶσα μὲν χώρα ... πᾶσα δὲ πόλις, *PG* 31. 592B.

237. *Hom.* 337. 3: ἀδελφαὶ γὰρ ποιμαντικὴ καὶ βασιλική· παρ' ὅσον ἡ μὲν τῶν ἀλό-γων, ἡ δὲ τῶν λογικῶν τὴν ἐπιστασίαν ἐπεπίστευτο, *PG* 31. 593B. Basil cannot have been unaware that Julian and Gallus had built a *martyrium* in honour of Mamas; and his exegesis may have included a savouring of the irony: see Bernardi, *Prédication*, p. 19.

238. *Hom.* 337. 4. For considerations on the dating of this sermon (perhaps before 373), see Marina Silvia Troiano, 'L'*Omelia* XXIII *in Mamantum Martyrem* di Basilio di Cesarea'.

239. *Hom.* 327. 2.

240. Τἆλλα ὅσα, ὥσπερ ἐφόλκια, αἱ πολυάνθρωποι τῶν πόλεων ἐπισύρονται, *Hom.* 327. 3.

his retreat (like David and Mamas from their flocks). He walked right into the hippodrome, one of the great foci of city life, a symbol of urban unity. There he faced his questioners. He began his defence with what were essentially secular points. He specified his place of birth, his family, his social rank, the reasons for his 'flight', and for his return. He also levelled a specific accusation against the archon: 'I have heard that you have been treating many with cruelty [τῇ ἀγριότητι]', implying not mere brutality but conduct against reason, and therefore inimical to law.[241] Just like Mamas, therefore, although here at a real rather than at an allegorical level, Gordius was able to assert an alternative view of correct polity. His fellow citizens, when it came to the moment of his death, travelled symbolically out of the city, leaving behind them all the normal pursuits of their life (Basil was at great pains to make this point). So also those who now celebrated the feast had assembled at the very same place. They had followed the same path of withdrawal. The moral was not overstressed. Each person in the congregation should now proclaim and live to the full what he or she believed within. Eternal good should not be sacrificed for short-term advantage. Once the celebration was over, of course, the audience of the 370s returned to the city, vividly aware of what it once had wrongly represented, and of what it might now become.[242]

There was a common thread to all three addresses. Confrontation began within the city, the sphere of authority and law, flawed by an incorrect attitude to religion and to the common life. The hero or heroine then, in one way or another, rejected that system of values—legally, symbolically, even literally. Yet that was only so that they could 'return'—in Gordius's case as a flesh-and-blood critic—to assert an alternative image of collaboration and authority. The later audience of the sermons themselves, under the impulse of Basil's oratory, made a similar pilgrimage from one polity to another, not withdrawing permanently from the necessary opportunities of city life, but pausing for a moment apart, in order to appreciate more

241. *Hom.* 327. 4, *PG* 31. 500A.
242. *Hom.* 327. 6–8. See Markus, *Ancient Christianity*, pp. 151f.; but he overlooks the significance of the return journey. For a subversion of current institutional expectations in favour of a Christian sense of unity and shared charisma, see Fedwick, *Charisma*, p. 31. Having formulated this argument, I was much struck by Averil Cameron's quotation, *Rhetoric of Empire*, p. 46, from W. Booth, *The Rhetoric of Fiction*: the writer (like the preacher) 'makes [his readers] see what they have never seen before, moves them into a new order of perception and experience altogether'. Her own judgement is even more directly apposite to much that we have discussed in this chapter: 'In the spreading of ideas there is a tension between the need to show compatibility with an existing framework [see above, at n. 127] and the attraction of a complete change', p. 130.

fully the moral contours that were to be imposed upon the civic landscape by subscription to the Gospel.

Basil could be ambiguous and hesitant, even so. His sermon on the Forty Martyrs made that clear also. Having described the way in which Christians were to eschew the traditional laws of secular rhetoric, Basil examined other definitions of πατρίς, of fatherland and place of origin (which would normally form one of the elements in a panegyric):

> The holy ones do not all belong to one country: each is venerated in a different place. So what does that imply? Should we call them city-less, or citizens of the whole world [ἀπόλιδας αὐτοὺς εἴπωμεν, ἢ τῆς οἰκουμένης πολίτας]? Just as at a common meal those things laid before the group by each are regarded as available to all who meet together, so among those holy ones, the homeland of each is common to all, and they give to each other everywhere whatever they have to hand.[243]

That was rather different from being simply 'citizens of the whole world', for it meant, so to speak, 'When I am with you, I am at home; and when you are with me, you are at home'. The notion followed closely Basil's views on the association of churches (that is to say, cult centres).[244] But then he suddenly broadened the canvas again: 'The city of the martyrs is the city of God'. Now the audience had been carried to a new level, transcendent and eschatological. In the very process their individuality, their loneliness, was brought home to them in a new way, as they faced a common Father in the moment of judgement.[245]

It would be foolish to summarize so complex a series of observations, with the intention of attributing to Basil a coherent theory, either about the nature of the Christian community or about the terms in which its destiny could be expressed or about the authority that was exercised within it. What we can and must carry away is the clear impression of two sets of tension, built up over a period of several years. The first was between civic life, as he and his flock would have been accustomed to define it, and the ultimately desirable community that one might label 'Church'. The second was between the corporate ideal, which talk of 'Church' might seem to suggest, and which certainly encouraged in Basil a social morality, and

---

243. *Hom.* 338. 2, *PG* 31. 509B.

244. See, for example, above, at n. 160.

245. *Hom.* 338. 2 (*PG* 31. 509B), 8. For the circumstances see Bernardi, *Prédication*, p. 85. The conclusion of the sermon was rather bland: Christians should regard holy men and women as their intercessors in heaven, and they should not be afraid to ask them for such 'bourgeois' advantages as a happy family life, and the bearing of children no less virtuous than themselves.

the feeling that salvation was ultimately an individual experience, striven for often in the face of social circumstance, and enjoyed most tangibly within the confines of one's own 'soul'. Those tensions had something to do with the frustration and failure in Basil's own career and may even have been their cause. They helped him to create, nevertheless, a moral theory and a religious anthropology that were most exalted in their finest expressions.

· CHAPTER VI ·

THE ASCETIC WRITINGS

During his years of 'philosophical' experiment in Pontus, Basil had begun to draw up a series of texts devoted to the encouragement and ordering of the ascetic life. These constituted the first stage in the creation of what is perhaps his most famous legacy. Once established in Caesarea, he undertook tasks—the setting up of the *Basileiados*, for example—that depended on the continuing support of an ascetic group and catered in part for their specific needs. His correspondence included detailed discussions of ascetic practice. There was, in other words, an 'ascetic history' in his life, to be placed alongside the 'pastoral history', and related closely to it. The one provides us with the moral and interior dimension of the other. The steady flow of ascetic documents is no less essential, say, than the homilies in helping us to understand Basil's vision of the Church, and indeed his personal development, with all its variety and indecision.

In no way did Basil develop a monastic system as an incidental exercise. His very search for models and mentors, in the period immediately following his departure from Athens, shows that he was not content merely to respond to, let alone cater for, existing forms of ascetic life. His most characteristic inclination was to interweave the moral with the social and practical aspects of Christianity. Whatever decisions he made at an ascetic level were part of the broader task of defining his proper audience and the very Church itself. And he wished, as a pastor, to achieve an interior effect. The industry and rhetoric that he brought to bear upon cultic practice, upon the social, economic, and political experiences of his fellow Christians, and upon the secular institutions within which they had to survive, were clearly intended also to touch his audience at the level of motive, self-image, guilt, and confidence; to awaken in them a desire for spiritual and moral growth.

So the homilies form only a small proportion of the sources available to us. Unfortunately, many of Basil's other writings have been labelled 'monastic'—some of them during his lifetime, rather more by later association—as if to make them wholly separate and exclusive in character. Yet serious difficulties are raised by the 'rules' of Basil, together with his *Moralia*, and other examples of spiritual direction.[1] Two sets of questions present themselves. The first concerns breadth of appeal. Here we have a series of documents that frequently recommend a finely disciplined way of life, and very high moral and spiritual ideals and goals. Are we to suppose that they were addressed only to a narrow group of enthusiasts, while Basil contented himself with lower standards when addressing Christians more generally? Quite the contrary. His homiletic address, we have already seen, was by no means content with banality or compromise. Indeed, the homilies deserve the title 'ascetic writings' almost as much as anything else from his pen.

Σπουδή, enthusiasm and dedication, was the mark of any authentic Christian; σπουδαῖος was the title to which he or she could most justly lay claim.[2] We cannot assume, in other words, without extended argument, that a document with an ascetic component, even if it makes reference to patterns of organization that look distinctly 'monastic', was addressed only to a spiritual minority or élite; for another striking point soon emerges: Basil never used the word 'monk' or, in the 'rules' ascribed to him, any obvious synonym.[3]

The second set of questions has already been described: what was the proper or possible relationship between individuals and groups in the life of the Church? Did Basil consistently subscribe to the notion that a life led in common would both sustain and represent at its best the proper spiritual development of the individual? If we do discover such consistent espousal of community life, is it to be taken, again, as referring to a segregated group, or was community in that sense,

---

1. I describe the material in detail in appendix 2. I consistently place 'rules' in quotation marks, for none of the texts so described was called such originally. *Asceticon* is a more authentic title for what is in essence a collection of answers to questions. See Gribomont, *Histoire*, p. 4; Clarke, *Basil*, pp. 114f.

2. Gribomont, *Histoire*, p. 190, commenting on his own B 315; see n. 6 below and appendix 2, n. 8.

3. Gribomont, *Histoire*, pp. 186f.

at least at the level of ideal and theory, coterminous with the Church itself?[4]

Answers to such questions are governed inevitably by the nature of the specifically ascetic documents themselves. We need to remain sensitive not only to their mode of address but also to the variety of dates at which they appear to have been produced, and to the adaptations and interpretations imposed upon them later. The thrust of research over the past fifty years or so has made it all but certain that only over a period of time did Basil adopt anything later generations would recognize as formal monastic institutions. Even as he did so, he maintained his conviction that the ideals he defended were suited to all Christians, to be fulfilled within the Church in the broadest sense, rather than simply within more limited and segregated communities.[5] So the 'rules' that have survived, the *Long Rules* and the *Short Rules*, together with the *Moralia*, have to be regarded as the results of a long process, reaching well beyond Basil's own lifetime. They cannot be taken as symptomatic of some ordered and completed monastic system, presided over by the bishop himself.[6]

―――――――――――

Basil tells us surprisingly little about the processes whereby he began to create that ascetic corpus. Some of his letters found their way into the

4. Fedwick, *Charisma*, chap. 3, is particularly skilful in interweaving church life and asceticism, an approach I wholly support. Piero Scazzoso, *Reminiscenze della Polis Platonica nel Cenobio di S. Basilio*, makes too forceful a distinction between ascetic and civic models and ends by trying to solve a false problem (while finding it hard to detect, in any case, such direct influences as his title suggests). Oddly enough, his later work, *Introduzione alla ecclesiologia di San Basilio*, moves differently in the other direction, asserting the importance of ecclesiology for an understanding of Basil's monasticism. Amand de Mendieta, *Ascèse*, pp. 3, 12f., 29, made the same general point, but with the effect that the Church shrinks: 'La morale que Basile préconise pour les gens du monde, nous paraîtra rigoureuse et ennemie de tout accommodement', p. 13.

5. Such a point of view is maintained most notably by Gribomont and is summed up in his *Histoire*, to which one should add the judgements of Rudberg, *Études*, pp. 121f. Fedwick, *Charisma*, pp. 12–23, has followed in that tradition with many references to dating and the implications of the texts—most of them dependent on Gribomont himself. A detailed account of developments and controversies is provided in appendix 2, pp. 352–357.

6. For the *Long Rules*, see *Regulae fusius tractatae* [henceforward F], *PG* 31. 889–1052; and for the *Short Rules*, *Regulae brevius tractatae* [henceforward B], *PG* 31. 1080A–1305B. The Latin translation by Rufinus, the significance of which is explained in appendix 2, is best edited in *Basili regula a Rufino latine versa* [henceforward R] by Klaus Zelzer. For the *Moralia*, see below, at n. 211. For English translations, see *The Ascetic Works of Saint Basil* by W. K. Lowther Clarke, and *Basil of Caesarea, Ascetical Works*, by M. Monica Wagner.

formal collection, but that reflects only the significance attached to them by later compilers.[7] Additional information is furnished, for example, by *Letter* 223;[8] but it says nothing of 'rules' in any sense. *Letter* 150 emphasizes recollection of the spoken word—'guarding his words carefully in your memory [ἵνα καὶ τῇ μνήμῃ ἀκριβῶς φυλάξας τὰ λεχθέντα]'; but here, too, we find nothing about written prescriptions or advice.[9] *Letter* 2 has been proposed as a species of 'proto-rule', but its place in relation to *Letter* 14 and to the correspondence of Gregory of Nazianzus makes it a predominantly personal and ad hoc document.[10]

Letters 22 and 173 gained a more formal place in the ascetic collections. The first, which is difficult to date, certainly has the look of a 'mini-rule', with carefully listed instructions on moral attitudes and religious behaviour.[11] It is important, therefore, to note the terms in which Basil introduced those instructions:

> Since in the divinely inspired Scriptures many directions[12] are set forth which must be strictly observed by all who wish earnestly to please God, I desire to say, necessarily in the form of a brief reminder [ἐν συντόμῳ ὑπομνήσει], a few words based upon the knowledge which I have derived from the divinely inspired Scriptures themselves, regarding for the present merely those questions which have at this present time

7. See appendix 2, nn. 7 and 25.

8. See chapter 1, at nn. 69f., and chapter 3, at nn. 35f., 58f.

9. *Ep.* 150. 4, C 2: 75, D 2: 371. See chapter 5, at nn. 23, 41f., 85.

10. Amand de Mendieta, *Ascèse*, linked it with *Ep.* 22, describing the two as 'des esquisses, déjà très poussées, d'une doctrine ascétique qui trouvera enfin, dans les Règles, sa forme littéraire', p. 86, and commented on *Ep.* 2 more generally: '[Elle] se tient presque exclusivement sur le plan théorique des principes', p. 94. See chapter 3, at nn. 19f.

11. Fedwick, *Basil*, 1: 8 n. 29, argues, like Maran, for an early date, on the basis of the letter's less sophisticated exegesis; but I would agree with Jean Gribomont, 'Les Règles épistolaires de saint Basile: Lettres 173 et 22', p. 266 (quoted by Fedwick), that the text is remarkably free, both in its sense of dependence upon the opinions and practices of others and in its principles of interpretation. It is instructive to compare what Basil actually wrote with the scriptural texts to which he appears to allude: the 'match' is by no means always evident. Amand de Mendieta, *Ascèse*, pp. 94f., thought the letter was addressed to superiors, and wrote of 'un degré plus développé d'organisation' (even though on p. 86 he appears to have thought that it represented a more preliminary stage). Clarke, *Basil*, p. 53, also placed it early : 'a first sketch'. One has to admit that one passage, in § 3, does point to a degree of organization, although very obscurely: 'No one of those who enter into positions of authority [τῶν ἐπεισερχομένων τινὰ ἐπ' ἐξουσίας] should approach or speak with one of the brothers [ἀδελφῶν], before those charged with the general discipline [οἱ ἐπιτεταγμένοι τὴν φροντίδα τῆς ἐν πᾶσιν εὐταξίας] shall examine how this is pleasing to God, with an eye to the common good', C 1: 54, D 1: 133. We shall examine below, at nn. 105f., such vagueness of terminology in respect of those in authority.

12. Δηλουμένων: perhaps better, just 'pointers'.

been stirred up among you.[13] By so doing I shall leave behind me, in
a form easy to apprehend [εὔληπτον οὖσαν], their testimony on every
point for those to observe who are too much occupied for reading; these
will then be competent to recall the truth to others.[14]

The centrality of Scripture is the first obvious point. Basil's predilection is
brought out beautifully in another letter, to a religious woman living in
her own home: 'If you possess the consolation of the divine Scriptures,
you will need neither us nor anyone else to help you see your duty, for
sufficient is the counsel and guidance to what is expedient which you
receive from the Holy Spirit'.[15] Also important, again, is the ad hoc nature
of the letter. Basil was responding only to inquiries that had arisen at the
time. Finally, the purpose of the letter was to be a reminder, a short cut
in relation to the use of Scripture itself. The concept of 'aid to recollection'
is characteristic. The whole paragraph evokes very clearly a piecemeal
process of admonitory bequest.

Letter 173 is much less helpful. 'Choosing the evangelical life', Basil
wrote, 'is in the power of anyone, but carrying out its observance even
to the smallest details, and overlooking none of the written rules[16]—this
has been accomplished successfully by very few who have come to our
knowledge'. The letter gives no indication of what those 'writings' might
have been, although the phrase 'according to the intent of the Gospel
[κατὰ τὸ βούλημα τοῦ Εὐαγγελίου]' may offer a clue.[17] A similar problem
arises in Letter 23, where Basil used the phrases 'that he be grounded in
the precepts of the holy Fathers as set forth by them in writing [κατὰ τὰ
δόξαντα τοῖς ἁγίοις Πατράσι καὶ ἐγγράφως ὑπ' αὐτῶν ἐκτεθέντα]' and
'that there be laid before him straightway all such rules as are approved by
the strict ascetic discipline [ἅπαντα ὅσα τῇ ἀκριβείᾳ δοκεῖ τῇ ἀσκητικῇ]'.[18]

---

13. Περὶ μόνων τέως τῶν ἐπὶ τοῦ παρόντος κινηθέντων παρ' ὑμῖν; and we should
note that the Greek says, literally: 'Of the many pointers . . . I shall speak only . . .', emphasizing more clearly that what he does say is taken from those pointers.

14. Ep. 22. 1, C 1: 52, D 1: 129/131. Note the phrase σύντομον ὑπόμνησιν in F 2. 4 = R
2. 57. I have tried to avoid in this chapter a lack of balance, in spite of the temptation to discuss
in detail the frequent and interesting contrasts between the Greek and Latin texts. At the
same time, for the reader who may be more of a specialist I have tried to signal where I think
such contrasts occur and briefly in what I think they consist; and I hope that anyone with
time to explore further in each case will discover, as I have, sufficient material for reflection
to fill at least another book. My use of the symbol = need not imply more than general
correspondence between R and F (although equivalence is often precise).

15. Ep. 283, C 3: 154f., D 4: 173.

16. So Deferrari; but καὶ μηδὲν τῶν ἐκεῖ γεγραμμένων παρορᾶν says nothing of
'rules'.

17. Ep. 173, C 2: 109, D 2: 451.

18. Ep. 23, C 1: 58, D 1: 143. Again, 'rules' does not appear in the Greek.

The two phrases appear to make separate references; and it is not wholly clear who the 'Fathers' were.

The witness of the two Gregorys is often obscure and may be misleading. Gregory of Nazianzus, in his funeral oration on Basil, certainly spoke of 'written and unwritten legislation for monks [νομοθεσίαι μοναστῶν, ἔγγραφοί τε καὶ ἄγραφοι]', and of 'written rules [τὰ ἔγγραφα διατάγματα]' designed to encourage bodily purity and spiritual vision.[19] Such allusions included, almost certainly, wisdom after the event and may reflect a different and certainly a highly personalized, if not more institutional, set of preoccupations, characteristic of Gregory himself rather than, necessarily, of Basil.[20] In an early letter to his friend, referring to the time of their joint withdrawal to Pontus, Gregory wrote of their desire for virtue, 'which we made secure by written principles and regulations [ὅροις γραπτοῖς καὶ κανόσιν]'; a phrase often taken to refer to an early attempt at formal legislation but quite possibly related more to the *Moralia* than to the *Asceticon*.[21] Gregory of Nyssa's probable allusion to early work on the *Asceticon* itself, in the period after 362, was precise in pointing to the effect of those 'written instructions [ἔγγραφοι διδασκαλίαι]', namely, their power to carry one from word to deed.[22] Basil's own *Letter* 295 made the same point: 'The things which were spoken by us were not mere words [ῥήματα] but teachings [διδάγματα] which were due to pass into deeds [εἰς ἔργον προελθεῖν ὀφείλοντα] for the benefit of you who submissively accepted them'.[23] The fundamental emphasis remained the living relationship between a teacher and his immediate audience.

We gain the impression, therefore, of gradual development, of minimal structure, of varied practice over a wide territory, and of constant

19. This last in a famous section of great formality: GNaz *Orat.* 43. 34, *PG* 36. 541C, tr. p. 56; and 62, *PG* 36. 577A, tr. p. 79. See Clarke, *Basil*, pp. 111f.

20. Fedwick, *Charisma*, p. xvi n. 15; Gribomont, *Histoire*, pp. 258f.

21. GNaz *Ep.* 6. 4; ed. Gallay, 1: 7. Contrast Clarke, *Basil*, p. 55 ('some rules for the monastic life') with Gribomont, *Histoire*, pp. 257f., followed by Aubineau, *Virginité*, p. 60. It is worth being as literal as possible in interpreting Gregory's famous phrase. First, 'written' *may* (although there must remain some doubt) apply to both elements ('principles and regulations'). Second, ὅροι (here translated 'principles') implies defining limits, while κανών (translated 'regulation') evokes some constant against which to measure other behaviour (a 'rule' in the very literal sense).

22. GNyss *De virginitate* 23. 1; ed. Aubineau, p. 522. See appendix 2, at n. 19.

23. *Ep.* 295, C 3: 170, D 4: 207.

dependence on the personal presence and supervision of Basil himself. Yet it is impossible to deny that the *Asceticon* contains many references to what can only be described as an institutionalized form of the ascetic life. In other texts, such as the *Letters*, there are unambiguous assertions that ascetics formed a recognizable group in the Christian community, with an identity separate from that of the clergy or laity.[24] By the 360s and 370s, it would have been impossible to suggest otherwise: that was the situation Basil inherited. One could question, perhaps, how far beyond the bounds of Egypt one might find during those years the visibly segregated monastery of a 'Pachomian' type; but 'monk', or one of a variety of associated terms, had come to be widely applied to the members of what was considered a distinct class of Christian, regardless of how they organized their lives in detail.[25] All that has to be granted. What is less clear is whether Basil accepted those trends—towards a visible distinction of person and dwelling—and whether he did so quickly or gradually, suddenly or over a period of time. One must ask also whether the principles defended in his ascetic writings were dependent upon, or in any way contributed to, such distinctiveness.

It is worth reminding ourselves, therefore, what a varied picture Basil's *Letters* do present. *Letter* 22, full of ascetic exhortations based on a catena of scriptural allusions, is nevertheless addressed to 'the Christian'.[26] Even a Christian broadly defined needed, of course, ideally, to embark upon a changed way of life; but Basil associated any serious rejection of one's past very closely with baptism.[27] There were plenty of lay people who could nevertheless 'preserve the perfection of love for God', proving that 'a Christian should be marked, not by the fashion of his clothing, but by the disposition of his soul'.[28] And yet we know that Basil thought of himself as in some sense the leader, the guide, the guardian of ascetics in his own community:

---

24. For example, *Ep.* 200. That is not to imply that Basil approved of such distinctions.

25. For the 'Pachomian' type (which took time, in any case, to develop), see the historical stages described in my own *Pachomius*. The variety characteristic of fourth-century asceticism more generally is evident from the examples I explored in *Ascetics*, esp. pp. 33–55; and see also my 'Christian Asceticism and the Early Monks'. For the ambiguities that characterized the earliest well-documented phase of monastic history, the best studies are still E. A. Judge, 'The Earliest Use of Monachos for "Monk" (P. Coll. Youtie 77) and the Origins of Monasticism', and Françoise-E. Morard, 'Monachos, moine: Histoire du terme grec jusqu'au 4ᵉ siècle, Influences bibliques et gnostiques'.

26. *Ep.* 22. 1, C 1: 52, D 1: 131. Basil was explicit—ὅτι δεῖ τὸν χριστιανόν—only in the first few sections; but the constantly repeated phrase ὅτι δεῖ or οὐ δεῖ clearly supposes association with a similarly designated person.

27. *DSS* 15 (§ 35). See chapter 1, at n. 47.

28. *Ep.* 106, C 2: 7, D 2: 203.

> I desire you to know that we boast of having a body of men and women whose conversation is in heaven, who have crucified their flesh with its affections and desires, who do not concern themselves with food and clothing, but, being undistracted and in constant attendance upon the Lord, remain night and day in prayer.... They sing hymns to our God unceasingly, while they work with their own hands that they may have something to share with those who have need.

Those are words written as late as 376. Yet they are marked much more by their allusion to Scripture than by any reference to a segregated régime. Indeed, Basil admitted, just a few sentences earlier: 'Among us these instances are few [μικρὰ ταῦτα], because mankind is still learning and being introduced to piety'.[29]

Nevertheless, to undertake so dedicated a life was undoubtedly to cross some discernible threshold, 'to abandon the pleasures of the flesh, and to follow henceforth the path which leads to the mansions of the Lord'. Of anyone who took that step, Basil would demand 'renunciation of the world' and, as we have seen, adherence to 'the precepts of the holy Fathers as set forth by them in writing', and to 'all such rules as are approved by the strict ascetic discipline'.[30] He would also wish 'to place over him as anointer [ἀλείπτην] ... one who would train him well and make of him, by his unremitting and blessed care, an approved wrestler, to wound and overthrow the universal lord of the darkness of this world and the spirits of iniquity'.[31]

Those words occur in a letter we cannot date; and its stipulations are vague. Certainly, the implication that a single master would train a single disciple does not immediately conjure up a monastic community. Yet there is no doubt that, with time, Basil felt the ascetic life was developing in such a way that its boundaries needed more careful definition. This sense of a 'frontier', however vague, between dedicated religiosity and a less energetic attachment to spiritual growth was probably the first and perhaps the most important step towards the establishment of independent monasticism. In what was certainly a late and carefully constructed letter to Amphilochius of Iconium, devoted entirely to a discussion of church discipline, Basil insisted on a careful process of examination, in all cases where men and women declared a wish to embrace the ascetic life (which

29. He meant in Cappadocia: the contrast was with other parts of the East. *Ep.* 207. 2, C 2: 185f., D 3: 185/187.

30. *Ep.* 23, C 1: 58, D 1: 143. See above, at n. 18.

31. *Ep.* 23, C 1: 58f., D 1: 141/145. For the 'anointer' image, see also *Ep.* 155 and 164. 1; *Hom.* 331. 1. The analogy of wrestling recalls its frequent use by Theodoret in his *Historia religiosa*.

was interpreted in this instance as being made visible above all by the adoption of virginity).[32]

Even here we need to remain hesitant. The very terms of Basil's anxiety betray the fact that men and women were passing in and out of the ascetic profession; and while in the case of women he was concerned most with what we might call an order of virgins (which was long established in the Church, and which was not in any way monastic in character),[33] he seems to have implied that men could embrace a life of radical renunciation without necessarily thinking of themselves (although some did) as monks.[34] It was to such a man that he wrote on another occasion, exhorting him to return to his 'practice of asceticism', and to abandon in the process the perils of a military career; and we may well possess the man's reply, in which he wrote that the 'goodly practice of asceticism ... alone leads to salvation', referring later to 'the keeping of our celibacy [τῆς παρθενίας ἡ φυλακή]'.[35] Such indeterminacy needs to be borne in mind when we come across apparent instances of clearer demarcation. Basil no doubt found it useful, for instance, to insist upon distinctions, when fiscal or legal privileges were at stake. Μονάζοντες had rights he was not ashamed to protect; but to describe them as 'having spent [their 'money'] for the general needs of the poor and having consumed [their 'bodies'] in fasting and prayer' was not to imply necessarily a high degree of organization.[36]

Such glimpses of variety and ambiguity should prepare us for a careful reading of more specifically ascetic texts. If we take, for example, the earliest version of the Preface to the Asceticon, we see at once how easy

32. Ep. 199. 18f.

33. A feature examined at many points in Brown, Body and Society. He discusses this very text on p. 274.

34. The syntax of Ep. 199. 19, as we have it in our surviving texts, still seems to me far from self-evident: long reflection, and conversations with those whose Greek is much better than mine, have left implications ill defined. It is a question of whether we can be sure that οἵ (in οἱ κατὰ τὸ σιωπώμενον δοκοῦσι ...) refers back to εἰ μή τινες (which presents difficulties beyond the merely linguistic, although both Courtonne and Deferrari follow that line of interpretation), or whether Basil was referring to two categories of men: those who were clearly in some sort of 'monastic order', and those who had yet to declare themselves (which seems to make more sense, both of the section as a whole and of its context within the letter, although it implies, perhaps, some lacuna before the οἵ). Amand de Mendieta, Ascèse, p. 238, was certain—and his confidence has reinforced an influential view—that the passage proves the use of a formal vow at that time.

35. Ep. 116, C 2: 21, D 2: 233; 117, C 2: 22f., D 2: 237/239.

36. Ep. 284, C 3: 155, D 4: 173/175. They were supposedly living, however, κατὰ τὸ ἐπάγγελμα and κατὰ τὸ Εὐαγγέλιον, but with the implication that variations from that ideal were possible. They were also in Basil's charge—'thinking it to be incumbent upon me, in so far as I can, to care for such men'—but he may have been speaking there more as a patron than as a spiritual adviser.

it can be to jump to conclusions.[37] Basil was addressing an audience that took its religion seriously. A group had withdrawn to a place of quiet in the later hours of the day, to ask him further questions (following some more public occasion). They did so, however, for one evening only, escaping from the 'hustle' of an 'outside world' to which they were obviously going to return.[38] Rufinus, in his Latin translation, created a misleadingly intimate air and suggested that those listening were more advanced in spirituality.[39] The purpose of the occasion, however, as described in the Greek, was not particularly monastic but designed simply 'to encourage a healthier belief and the adoption of a way of life in accord with the Gospel'.[40]

Even by the time of Rufinus, therefore, a specifically monastic, indeed élitist, interpretation was being placed upon Basil's more open text. We have to measure carefully, therefore, the fact that some of the later sections are addressed to 'the Christian' (as in the letter referred to above), which is far too glibly assumed to mean 'monk'.[41] In what was beyond doubt a public homily, Basil was unperturbed by the thought that all his listeners might renounce property in response to the counsels of the Gospel: 'He who gave the law knows how to reconcile with the law our inabilities'; and that would apply even to those who were married and had families.[42]

37. For this Preface, see appendix 2, at n. 16. In the sections that follow, I take Amand de Mendieta's point that Basil remained ambiguous in his handling of the concept of 'community', although I find it hard to attribute consistency to his own words, Ascèse, pp. 109f.

38. See Fedwick, Charisma, p. 6. This vocabulary, ἀπὸ τῶν ἔξωθεν θορύβων, is strikingly echoed in Hom. 351. 3, which emphasizes the need for a common effort towards the perception of truth ἐν τῷ κρυπτῷ τῆς καρδίας, PG 29. 357B.

39. The audience, he said, was addressed secretius, a word obscure in itself, but not the same as ἰδίᾳ ἑκάστῳ (which should be translated, perhaps, 'to each one individually', meaning simply that Basil had agreed to answer questions). Rufinus also suggested that Basil was speaking 'to the more perfect [perfectioribus quibusque]', which certainly reinforces the impression of a special group; but no corresponding phrase occurs in the Greek (or in the Syriac tradition). R Preface, 4–5; ed. Zelzer, p. 5. For the Greek, see PG 31. 1080A.

40. PG 31. 1080A. Observe Rufinus's gloss, that the discussion was 'concerning the faith [de fide]', R Preface, 5; ed. Zelzer, p. 5. One should avoid, therefore, associating this audience with the one adduced by Amand de Mendieta, 'ΚΗΡΥΓΜΑ and ΔΟΓΜΑ', p. 136: 'an élite, . . . a few people particularly versed in theological studies, and living a quiet and pious life in silence, in σιωπή'. I doubt whether Basil ever addressed such a group.

41. Clarke, Basil, did so constantly. R 2 is wholly uninstitutional in its emphasis, having much more say about inner withdrawal (a point pursued below). Even when Basil appears to have had something more 'monastic' in mind, the ideal was presented still as available to everyone: F 34.

42. Hom. 323. 3, 7. The priority of law over expectation is remarkable. See also 344. 4 (one should not be scared by the assumptions of the Gospel) and 351. 10 (on the transition from bustle to peace).

In relation to the Preface of the *Asceticon,* therefore, we may picture the circumstances as follows: Basil presented to communities in Caesarea and elsewhere principles that he considered were applicable to all; he then asked who among them would take the matter seriously; finally, in response to what was inevitably a smaller group, he gave special advice, which eventually included advice on organization.[43]

A gradual development of such a sort can be illustrated more particularly. Where there appears to be, in some texts, an emphasis on the segregation of ascetics from the wider community, we have to read without presupposition. What was being recommended (and here we may be guided, first, by the Latin of Rufinus) was that one should keep company with those who believed and practised as one did oneself. To live with people who 'take lightly the fear of God', 'unlike us in their way of life or their moral principles', was naturally 'harmful'. Alternative ideals, however, were very generally described: avoid temptation, and adopt a régime of work and prayer. If an element of withdrawal was involved, it was an interior movement, away from 'our own confused and disordered and inconsistent habits [*a nostris ipsis inordinatis et incompositis moribus*]';[44] and Basil could recommend just as much in a public homily.[45] A species of renunciation was certainly involved; but it was a long process and began simply enough with the repudiation of Satan—although once the first step had been taken, the committed devotee was drawn onwards without a break. So the distinction was not between classes of person within the Church but between Christians at differing stages of spiritual development.[46] Perhaps the most visible symptom of more

---

43. This process of increasing definition over time is clear even in the stipulations about seating in R 10. R 11 suggests that *Christians* should all dress in the same way, simply to prove their commitment to belief, although the ones who took the suggestion seriously would inevitably become in the process a visible minority.

44. R 2. 94, 101, 105; ed. Zelzer, pp. 22f. The Greek equivalents, F 5 and 6 especially, are more discursive and more literal, but still with an underlying interior theme: 'forgetfulness of former habits' and 'migrating as it were to another world in our habit of mind [πρὸς ἕτερον κόσμον διὰ τῆς σχέσεως μεταβαίνοντες]' (5. 2) seem important points (though not reproduced in R), *PG* 31. 921A, tr. Clarke, p. 159. Gribomont, *Histoire,* pp. 240f., made important reflections on these passages. A careful comparison of R and F undermines some of the points emphasized by Amand de Mendieta, *Ascèse,* pp. 109f.; and his attempt, p. 89 n. 4, to link the 'withdrawal' here advocated in F with ἡ ἐρημία in *Ep.* 2. 2 (C 1: 7, D 1: 12) was both simplistic and problematic. R 3 reinforces these impressions, although it makes the even more positive recommendation that one should seek the company of those 'with the same purpose and cast of mind [*eiusdem propositi et eiusdem animi*]', ed. Zelzer, pp. 25f. = F 7 at *PG* 31. 928C.

45. *Hom.* 324. 8.

46. R 4 = F 8. Amand de Mendieta, *Ascèse,* p. 191, seems to have confused priority of order in the text with priority of importance on the scale of renunciation. Gribomont, *Histoire,*

serious devotion, eventually, was renunciation of property, to which we shall return, and which became a hallmark of the monastic vocation in a stricter sense. Nevertheless, even when prescriptions became more detailed, and a higher degree of institutionalization was required, the original preoccupation with a change of inner attitude was always maintained.[47] The very word *saecularis*, for example, applied to a person involved in the affairs of this world, hinted most at a wrongly directed *sollicitudo* or μέριμνα—that is to say, a shortcoming in attitude.[48] Similarly, the definition of ἐγκράτεια, one of the fundamental terms for the ascetic life, consisted in 'complete withdrawal from one's own wishes [ἐν τελείᾳ ἀναχωρήσει τῶν ἰδίων θελημάτων]'.[49]

Those points were made, for the most part, in the introductory sections of the *Asceticon*, where theoretical arguments were being set in place. Not yet capable of presenting the picture of a separate institution, they brought into play metaphors of threshold and frontier. Basil recognized he was catering for an audience that had reached a point of no return, an audience for whom retreat would undermine a new sense of social unity, of corporate purpose. How were the borders between themselves and other Christians now patrolled, and what traffic passed back and forth across them?

There came a time when the frontier was almost legal in character, or rather a challenge to the law: for ascetic communities would often provide a haven, in which the disadvantaged could seek refuge.[50] Concern for the poor one might expect, and a special person was carefully appointed to supervise their reception; but slaves, and even married men, could be welcomed as refugees from injustice.[51] We observe also the development

---

pp. 244f., made important points about Basil's 'failure' here to make a sharp distinction between the baptized and the ascetically committed; see also p. 135. See also Antoine Guillaumont, 'Esquisse d'une phénoménologie du monachisme', pp. 42f.

47. In the matter of property, see, for example, R 185 = B 101. Graham E. Gould, 'Basil of Caesarea and the Problem of the Wealth of Monasteries', offers reflections that give credit to the underlying breadth of Basil's principles.

48. R 54 = B 88 (where the equivalent adjective is βιωτική).

49. R 88 = B 128. R has omitted (or perhaps was never faced with) the force of ἀναχωρήσει at *PG* 31. 1168D.

50. The *Basileiados* anticipated such developments, as revealed in *Ep.* 150 and discussed in chapter 5, at nn. 23f.

51. The poor, R 98 = B 100; slaves, F 11; married men, F 12—but these last two sections are part of an elaborate expansion and reworking of the much briefer prescriptions in R 6. See

of a period of probation. The postulant was to be given a forceful impression of what he was letting himself in for, in order that he might prove the seriousness of his intentions.[52] Such prescriptions sprang from an unwillingness to exclude. Basil was happy that the community should receive visitors: they might stay for quite a while, even if they then left. People in that way would find out what the community did, and what ideals it represented. A few might then stay permanently.[53] Openness was extended to relatives, who were to be regarded as 'our common fathers, or fellow members of our household [ὡς κοινοὶ πατέρες ἢ οἰκεῖοι]'.[54] Indeed, hospitality was an essential feature of the ascetic community, closely related to the recommended frugality of its members (which ensured their ability to share with others).[55] That generosity, we must remember, was the enduring context within which apparently contrasting expressions of caution or prohibition—about visits, and about journeys generally—are to be understood.[56]

Gribomont, 'Aristocrate révolutionnaire', p. 186: 'Esclaves, soldats, débiteurs, colons fatigués du travail constituaient une multitude d'aspirants à la vie contemplative et au paradis sur terre; fils et filles en contestation, époux lassés par leur conjoint montraient que le menace [!] touchait non seulement l'ordre social, mais la famille'. Recall the caution expressed in the face of similar exaggeration, chapter 5, n. 11.

52. R 6. 1. Note the concomitant breadth of appeal: 'God in his mercy calls everyone'; and F 10 is expansive. Clarke's phrase 'outside the community', tr. p. 172, is a risky gloss on ἔξω ὄντας at PG 31. 945B. One should respect the generality of 'corpori fraternitatis', R 6. 9; ed. Zelzer, p. 38 = τῇ ἀδελφότητι at PG 31. 945B. These texts betray some connection with the opening section of Ep. 23.

53. R 87 = B 97. F 35. 1 alludes to the same situation.

54. F 32. 1 at PG 31. 996A.

55. F 20. There is certainly no question of excluding those who 'come from the life of the world [ἐκ τοῦ ἔξωθεν βίου]', PG 31. 972C; tr. Clarke, p. 185. Note the use of the term χριστιανός. Amand de Mendieta, Ascèse, pp. 231f., overlooked completely the main point of this passage. Κοσμικοί are not scorned in F 21 at PG 31. 976B (R 10 is less clear in its vocabulary), nor peregrini in R 101; ed Zelzer, p. 131 = B 141.

56. R 32, 33 = B 188, 189; F 44 (and F 39 and 40 offer useful comment on the final sections of this passage). B 107 and 112 may represent later types of caution, with openness being still defended nevertheless. For anxiety about heretical infection (surprisingly rare), see R 139 (B 240 is slightly less explicit), R 147 = B 53 (although the Greek distinction between τὸ ἀναμίγνυσθαι and τὸ ἀδιαφορεῖν at PG 31. 1117BC is not quite as 'social' as the point made in R, § 1), and R 171 = B 250. By continuing to embrace as wide a community as possible, Basil felt his way also towards a new definition of kinship (recall points made in chapter 5, at nn. 121f., 154f.): 'One born of the Spirit, as the Lord put it, and empowered to become a child of God, will allow the sense of kinship according to the flesh to weaken, and regard as fellows those in the household of the faith [οἰκείους δὲ γνωρίζει τοὺς οἰκείους τῆς πίστεως]'. Those reflections lead him to brood on the phrase 'according to the flesh' in Paul's Letter to the Romans, and on the apostle's willingness to accept some sense of Jewish kinship, 'not because the Israelites were his kinsmen but because his kinsmen according to the flesh were Israelites, and were counted worthy of receiving such great and excellent benefits from God. For the adoption [ἡ υἱοθεσία] was theirs and the glory [ἡ δόξα], and theirs was the

If there was a sense of a frontier to be defined and patrolled, it was formed in response to other anxieties, connected chiefly with property and labour. Anxiety in relation to property arose from the desire to be rid of possessions: for the question followed at once, to whom should those possessions be given, and what of the legal obligations normally associated with property—towards family and neighbours, and towards the state? In the earliest versions of the discussion, the problem was handled by Basil as one that arose within a single community of believers; and he recommended that the redistribution of property, and the associated defusing of potential legal difficulties, should be left in the hands of local ecclesiastical authorities.[57] Only later was the situation more narrowly conceived, so that we begin to find a distinction between giving away property once for all and the normal acts of generosity that should distinguish the propertied Christian.[58] Basil insisted also that people outside the ascetic community had obligations in the other direction, towards the community itself, particularly if they were kindred.[59]

As for labour, Basil recommended always that Christians should work for the benefit of others; and that immediately set up an economic relationship between ascetics and the surrounding community. The very fact that Jesus had exhorted people to pray for their daily bread showed, in Basil's

---

giving of the law and the *cultus* [ἡ νομοθεσία καὶ ἡ λατρεία]: they had the covenants and the promises [αἱ διαθῆκαι, καὶ αἱ ἐπαγγελίαι], and theirs were the fathers [οἱ πατέρες, i.e., the patriarchs]'. The elements that constituted for Paul that Jewish 'family' bear very obvious comparison with the qualities of the Church as Basil conceived it. See B 190 (not in R). Gribomont, *Histoire*, p. 169, noted the narrowness of the tradition that has preserved this passage. The translation of the second section, paraphrasing Romans 9.1–5, is that of Clarke, p. 301; Greek text at *PG* 31. 1209BC.

57. R 5 = F 9 (which is more formal; and note the comments of Gribomont, *Histoire*, p. 246: 'des formes organisées de pauvreté religieuse'), R 31 = B 187 (in relation to which, Zelzer's edition, pp. 77f., makes comparison more straightforward; but there are still signs of an ecclesial situation being overlaid by prescriptions more suitable to a separate community). B 304 (not in R) seems simpler. Basil wished to avoid liability in relation to the taxation difficulties of postulants, R 196 = B 94. Zeno of Pontus—influenced, according to Theodoret, by Basil—recommended exactly the same course, *Hist. relig.* 12. 1, 7.

58. R 185 = B 101: the best course is to sell all at the outset of one's dedicated life. R 5 = F 9 shows exactly why!

59. R 31 = B 187. See n. 57 above, and Clarke, *Basil*, p. 82. In making the point, he was anxious in part to exclude from the community the economic and social divisions that operated outside it. One should recall again the discussion by Gould, 'Wealth of Monasteries'. Pachomius and Augustine both insisted on not allowing divisions in society more generally to affect relations within their communities. For the Pachomian texts, see my *Pachomius*, esp. pp. 68f., 149f., 158f.; and, more generally, my 'Blood-relationships among Early Eastern Ascetics'. For Augustine, see the key passages in his *Praeceptum* 1. 6–8, 3. 3f. The *Praeceptum* was an early version of his famous *Ep.* 211. See Luc Verheijen, *La Règle de saint Augustin;* and more recently, George Lawless, *Augustine of Hippo and His Monastic Rule.*

eyes, that any bread produced by labour (as opposed to prayer) should be given away, while the labourers awaited their own sustenance from the hand of God.[60] The ideal community, therefore, would be at once a hive of industry and an oasis of quiet. Members would adapt their activities to the local market. There would be weaving, shoemaking, building, carpentry, metalwork, and above all agriculture. At the same time (in the same passage), Basil rejoiced in 'the peaceable and untroubled nature of our life', 'a life undistracted and waiting continually on the Lord'.[61]

None of that was excluded from the more general addresses of the homilist. Generosity and a sense of responsible stewardship in relation to those less fortunate was, as we have seen, proclaimed very forcibly during the 369 famine.[62] Generosity was also an important antidote to the jealousy and hypocrisy that were such destructive influences in city life.[63] Generosity, above all, authenticated other aspects of religious fervour and commitment, the very life of prayer and fasting that was supposedly so characteristic of the μονάζοντες.[64] It should flow from and support a personal poverty freely adopted in the spirit of the Gospel, and not merely put up with as an unavoidable misfortune.[65] And what Basil emphasized most was the inner dimension. To boast of economic independence—'I owe to no man, and no man owes to me'—was to remain beyond the Christian pale.[66] The proper principle was that one had more obligations towards others than towards oneself—indeed, it could be said that 'existing for others' was part of the basic definition of a human being.[67] In practice, one should rest content with what was needed for survival, and devote all else (both energy and property) to what might be useful for others.[68] In theory, the greatest preoccupation was to avoid distraction, and to make poverty and the associated insecurity inseparable from one's surrender of

60. For the last point, R 173 = B 252 (which goes on to include allusion to the common life reported in Acts).

61. F 38. One is reminded, again, of the complex activities of the *Basileiados*. Basil was aware that application to work on this scale offered a strong incentive to settled residence, *Ep.* 259. See Clarke, *Basil*, p. 91. For various references to the necessary selflessness of Christian labour, see R 118 = B 89; R 127 = B 207; B 272 (not in R); F 37. 1, 42.

62. *Hom.* 322. 1f. See chapter 5, at nn. 14f.

63. *Hom.* 332. 5. See chapter 3, at n. 86, and chapter 5, at nn. 189, 237 (and for contrasting realism, n. 126).

64. *Hom.* 323. 3, which puts *Ep.* 284 in its proper context: see above at n. 36. Almsgiving was also the surest release from sin, *Hom.* 324.8.

65. *Hom.* 351. 5, exactly echoed in R 125 = B 205. See Graham E. Gould, 'Basil of Caesarea and Gregory of Nyssa on the Beatitudes', p. 14.

66. R 30 = B 86.

67. Compare R 141 = B 48 with *Hom.* 354. 2.

68. B 70, 92; see *Hom.* 339. 6.

self into the hands of God. The Lord gave up his *anima,* his very life, for his friends: how could anyone else lay claim to external things?[69]

In this matter of the frontier, therefore, three features stand out. There were groups of enthusiasts, or exceptionally committed Christians, who may even have seemed at times, to themselves and to others, through circumstance or prejudice, a radical and arcane élite;[70] but they remained in many ways open to the rest of the community, inviting guests, and offering service. The spiritual guidance considered necessary by Basil for groups of that sort (and this is the second feature) was provided in a variety of texts: in his letters and homilies, as well as in more specifically ascetic documents. It was provided, in other words, for people well beyond the boundaries of ascetic groups themselves. Finally, the heart of Basil's message was concerned with the inner life of the serious Christian, rather than with the institutions whereby that life might be encouraged and protected.

With time, nevertheless, a more segregated ascetic régime did develop. In the process, a second principle emerged; like inclusiveness, at once fundamental and problematic. At the root of the ascetic, enthusiastic, committed Christianity defended by Basil was love of God and one's neighbour. The *Asceticon* opens with that emphasis, giving it priority, and making it clear that other aspects of a devoted religious life mattered proportionately less.[71] The priority was based on natural human qualities: on an inclination towards goodness, and the ability and desire to communicate with others. Yet Basil betrayed a caution that provides the most reliable clue to his eventual espousal of separate organization. The issue was how to guarantee genuine union among human beings; and the key to success lay in each person's desire to please God. Given that prior inclination, harmony with others would inevitably follow. Authentic community was a product of the individual's genuine love for God.[72] For that reason, however, the experience

------

69. '*Ea quae extra animam sunt*', R 29. 4; ed. Zelzer, p. 76 = B 85. Avoiding distraction, B 263 (not in R).

70. Fedwick, *Charisma,* p. 19.

71. R 1. 5.

72. R 38 = B 162 (although the Greek may suggest that a desire to please God was a means or a motive, rather than a result: see B 225). See also B 93, 139 (neither in R).

of community life could not remain haphazard. Not all neighbours were necessarily the best neighbours. The anxiety was clearly related to other recommendations: that one should avoid the company of the less dedicated and seek out those who thought like oneself.[73] Basil could be surprisingly harsh. We have noted elsewhere how severely he censored those who accepted too readily the charity of the Church.[74] In the 'rules', he even warned his questioners not to take for granted the worthiness of the sick: one should make investigations first; and if worthiness was found lacking, the sick could be dismissed.[75] A similarly exclusive note was struck in *Letter* 22: 'Each one should remain where he has been placed, and not transgress his own bounds [τὸ ἴδιον μέτρον] to enter upon unbidden places [τοῖς μὴ ἐπιτεταγμένοις], unless those entrusted with these matters [οἱ ταῦτα πεπιστευμένοι] judge one to be in need of aid [τινα χρῄζοντα βοηθείας]'.[76] Such supervision operated within the Church more broadly conceived. Basil was disinclined to favour mere cripples who complained, at the expense of honest misfortune bravely borne.[77] One gains the impression that a pool of people existed in whose favour one might exercise goodwill, but with unashamed selectivity.[78]

If he had doubts about indiscriminate neighbourliness, Basil also suspected self-reliance. The explicit and specific demands of Scripture were to be the first criterion for moral action. Where Scripture was less prescriptive, one should take as one's guide the good of one's neighbour. Such principles remained beyond challenge.[79] But one could not regard society as an open field, in which to indulge a personal taste for altruism. Αὐταρεσκεία, a readiness merely to please oneself, was the danger here. It could be countered reliably only by a willingness to heed the advice

73. See above, at n. 44.

74. See chapter 5, at n. 197.

75. R 36 = B 160. See Clarke, *Basil*, p. 100. B 155 (not in R) seems even to suggest that malingerers should be expelled (just from their sickbeds, or from the community?). B 214 provides a theoretical background, with emphasis on the need for justice, as well as for generosity.

76. *Ep.* 22, C 1: 55, D 1: 137. See n. 11 above. The vocabulary of command and authority will be examined below at nn. 105f. For doubts about extending charity beyond ascetic circles, see Karl Holl, *Enthusiasmus und Bußgewalt beim griechischen Mönchtum: Eine Studie zu Symeon dem neuen Theologen*, pp. 168f. Those unfamiliar with this wonderful book should not allow its subtitle to mislead them about the generous breadth of its learning.

77. *Hom.* 346. 6.

78. B 257 (not in R).

79. R 12 = B 1, R 141 = B 48.

or commands of others.[80] Behind that sentiment lay Basil's more general fear of vainglory, his sense that the wider community, the city, although obviously suffering needs that the devout might assuage, was nevertheless prone to hypocrisy, sycophancy, and undisciplined openhandedness in the cause of personal esteem.[81] Even the desire for spiritual growth, the desire to do more in the name of religion, was best fostered under the guidance of others.[82] So the quest was for authenticity in one's relations with others, and in the associated movement towards union with God. Because of the taint of self-will and a desire to impress others, it was all too easy to make use of God's gifts in a way that was 'estranged from God's love [alienum ... a caritate dei]'.[83] Yet one could not simply remove oneself from society and bury one's talent: the presence of others was a necessary condition for the exercise of virtue.[84]

We come now to more developed expressions of ascetic principle. The clearest statements occur early in the Asceticon, as part of a gradually developed argument.[85] People needed others to support them in their material needs; to stimulate their charity and point out their failings; to enable them to carry out the obligations of hospitality and visitation. The image of the many-membered body was the norm. No one could receive all the gifts of the Spirit: according, rather, to a variety of levels in faith, each would receive an appropriate gift, to be shared joyfully with others. The point was repeated elsewhere. Letter 22 is filled with a sense of mutual obligation and dependence: '[The Christian] should not consider himself as his own master, but as having been delivered by God into servitude to his brethren of like spirit [τοῖς ὁμοψύχοις ἀδελφοῖς]'.[86] In an undated letter to 'monks [μονάζουσι]', Basil displayed the same theoretical bias:

80. R 81 = B 96, taking its cue from the longer reflections of R 80 = B 120. For αὐταρεσκεία specifically, B 118 = R 68. See also R 70 = B 38.

81. See n. 63. Vainglory was a fundamental sin, R 22 = B 289; B 298, 299. B 282 alludes much more clearly to the 'secular' associations (none of these last in R).

82. R 82 = B 121, R 151 = B 211.

83. R 187. 3; ed. Zelzer, p. 208 = B 179.

84. R 188 = B 62.

85. R 3 = F 7. For general comments, see Amand de Mendieta, Ascèse, pp. 134f. Gribomont, Histoire, p. 255, suggested a link with Ep. 295: the address to monks alluded to there resembles F 7.

86. Ep. 22. 1, C 1: 54, D 1: 133.

Great is our desire both to see you brought together, and to hear concerning you that you do not favour the life that lacks witnesses, but rather
that you all consent to be both guardians of each other's diligence and
witnesses of each other's success. For thus each one will receive both the
perfect reward given on his own account and that given on account of his
brother's progress; which reward it is fitting that you should supply to
one another by both word and deed through constant intercourse and
encouragement.[87]

Behind such statements lay recollection of the community described in
Acts, which in turn could be presented as an ideal for the Church as a
whole. The allusion is made in the early sections of the *Asceticon*; it recurs
when surrender of property is discussed; and the unity of the apostolic
community ('*illorum in omnibus unanimitas et consonantia*') is made to imply
a standard of morality and observance common to all.[88]

In the same context, a need for obedience was suggested: 'He eats
what is given him by the man who has been charged, after testing, with
the task of carrying out the words: "Distribution was made unto each,
according as any man had need" '.[89] Obedience, or at least the regulation
by others of the impulses of one's own devotion, would have encouraged
a narrower sense of community. And discipline in relation to food was not
the only factor.[90] How did such a narrowing take place? Scripture, after
all, provided overriding and sufficient authority in moral matters, binding
upon everyone without distinction.[91] Nor did it preempt the dignity of
the individual's intelligence. One treated the prescriptions of the Bible
with respect, because guidance was provided within it by the Holy Spirit,
and by the illuminating force of the commandments of Jesus. That was,
nevertheless, a shared blessing: Scripture was always consulted within

87. *Ep.* 295, C 3: 170, D 4: 209. See n. 85 above. Μονάζουσι, in the letter's superscription,
may not, of course, reflect Basil's usage.

88. R 3 = F 7; R 29 (with some reference to Acts) = B 85; R 89. 2, ed. Zelzer, p. 123 (wholly
explicit, and more so than B) = B 129. (B 252, however, is capable of 'adding' an allusion
to Acts, compared with R 173: see n. 60 above.) Holl, *Enthusiasmus*, pp. 156f., pointed out
that reference to the Pauline image of the body is equally important.

89. B 252, again 'adding' to R 173; tr. Clarke, p. 322.

90. In that one regard, there seem to have been two sets of principles at work. First,
there was a norm in relation to eating and fasting, to be defined by superiors and adhered
to trustingly by the majority, exceptions being carefully controlled—so R 9 = F 19, R 91–92
= B 131–32. Second, not everyone was capable of achieving the same level of self-denial,
and superiors should check that no one was exceeding their capacity—so R 114 = B 203,
R 131 = B 152, and B 138 (not in R). F 18 opposes in a special way false attitudes to food: see
Gribomont, *Histoire*, p. 250. The fact that R does not reproduce the passage makes heavy
dependence upon it unwise: contrast Amand de Mendieta, *Ascèse*, pp. 225–31.

91. *Ep.* 283, quoted above at n. 15, provides a clear example of that emphasis.

the context of a believing community. The book by itself might provide an adequate theory; but consulting an architect's plan, for example, was not the same as erecting a stable building.[92] It was the keeping of the commandments that assured one of inspiration by the Spirit; and that in turn afforded insight into Scripture.[93] The real problems arose when Scripture appeared to be silent. Basil appealed first, in that instance, to Paul's First Letter to the Corinthians: "We are free to do anything", you say. Yes, but is everything good for us? "We are free to do anything", but does everything help the building of the community? Each of you must regard, not his own interests, but the other man's'. The good, the constructive, the selfless: those were to be the guiding principles.[94] Yet one could not leave a reader alone to draw his own conclusions. Everyone appeared to know what the Gospel demanded; but someone had to make sure that they knew—implying, of course, that a fair number did not.[95] As soon as that point was made, the notion of hierarchy was introduced: 'The brethren fall into two general divisions, those who are entrusted with leadership and those whose duty it is to defer and obey [εἰς εὐπείθειαν καὶ ὑπακοήν], according to their several gifts [ἐν διαφόροις χαρίσμασι]'. The divisions were characterized by varying relationships with the text of Scripture itself. Superiors should know and understand it all: their subjects should do so only so as to 'learn [their] own duty diligently and practise it, not being curious about anything else'.[96]

It was logical enough to extend such supervision to education in general. Education, after all, was based on Scripture.[97] So superiors were invited to bring within the scope of their jurisdiction all decisions regarding

92. R 3 = F 7. For the earlier point, see the careful arguments in R 12, which significantly = B 1.

93. R 124–25 = B 204–5. There was a certain circularity to the argument; and only with time did Basil attribute unrestricted priority to the influence of the Spirit in the life of the baptized Christian. So there were often ambiguities in his writings about the relation between faith and baptism: see chapter 1, at nn. 46f., chapter 4, at nn. 149f., and chapter 7, at nn. 161f. Holl, *Enthusiasmus*, pp. 165f., is helpful. Points made below at n. 183 are related.

94. R 12 = B 1, reflecting on 1 Cor. 10.23–24.

95. R 119 = B 45—one of those passages in which the vocabulary of authority is applicable within the Church more generally: 'qui ... verbi dei ministerium exhibet', § 5; ed. Zelzer, p. 146. See below, at n. 110.

96. B 235 (not in R); tr. Clarke, pp. 316f. B 64 (not in R) spells out the difficulties that resulted for superiors as well as for subjects. B 254 (not in R) suggests that a superior was above all one who created opportunities for the talents of others. The fact that none of these texts appears in R suggests we are reading later attempts to make the distinctions that seemed necessary in the light of more complex institutionalization.

97. So some references in the *Asceticon* seem to imply, although we have to read them in the broader context of Basil's attitude to learning and to the intellectual basis of theology and religious life. See F 15 (apparently expanding upon R 7), and the characteristic opposition

'the learning of letters'.[98]   Basil betrayed characteristic misgivings: he valued silence; defended the need for discipline, if questions were to be asked correctly; and implied the repudiation of older cultural values. What was required was the controlled adoption of a wholly new style of address: 'for there is a tone of voice and symmetry of language and appropriateness of occasion and special vocabulary which are peculiar to the religious, and can only be learned by the man who has unlearned his former habits'.[99]

Once one had set in place that degree of discipline, it was but a short step to a supervision that covered all aspects of life, particularly when it came to weighing up the suitability of developing other talents that might be calculated to help one's neighbour. All those carpenters and shoemakers had to come from somewhere. Many of those who were members of a strictly ascetic community could have developed such skills before their incorporation; and whether they should continue to exercise them was a matter for group discussion and judgement.[100] Some regulations could be even tighter than that, subjecting the exercise of any talent to the judgement of superiors, particularly in the interests of humility: indeed, to make use of a skill without that authority was a species of theft, since the skill itself was not, as it were, an item of personal property, but bestowed by God for the benefit of others.[101]

There is a certain sequence to what has been said so far. First, we have the question of breadth of address: how many were being called to serious religious dedication?   The very raising of that issue made a species of demarcation between the serious and the indifferent

---

to 'the traditions of men [ἀνθρωπίναις παραδόσεσιν]', B 95 at PG 31. 1149A; tr. Clarke, p. 266. Also R 167–68 = B 218, 248.

98. R 80–81 = B 120, 96.

99. F 13 (not in R, and surely late): καὶ τόνος φωνῆς, καὶ συμμετρία λόγου, καὶ καιροῦ ἐπιτηδειότης, καὶ ῥημάτων ἰδιότης, οἰκεία καὶ διαφέρουσα τοῖς εὐσεβέσιν, PG 31. 949B; tr. Clarke, p. 174.   Clarke noted the absence of scriptural support in this and other passages, which seems to have aroused his suspicions, p. 174 n. 1. The passage bears comparison with Ep. 135, discussed in chapter 2, at n. 77.

100. F 41 (which clarifies points made in F 38): note the phrases 'by the common verdict [ὑπὸ τοῦ κοινοῦ]', 'by the majority [παρὰ τῶν μειζόνων]', 'does not please the brotherhood [τῇ ἀδελφότητι]', at PG 31. 1021C; tr. Clarke, p. 213. Neither passage is in R.

101. R 67 = B 117, and R 102 = B 142. R 192 = B 105 appears to demean the skills of craftsmen in the interests of more spiritual gifts; but B is more laconic, and Zelzer, p. 211, considers the existing Latin an unreliable reflection of the Greek original.

unavoidable. How effectively, then, might one fulfil one's obligations towards one's neighbours, especially the less committed? Should one not seek advice, follow counsel, and conform to policy? If one did, a more restricted notion of community could result, with superiors, obedience, and hierarchy. Yet the sequence is not simple and does not bring us immediately to the threshold of organized monasticism. Formal notions about the structure of an ascetic community did not call into question the fundamental belief in a devout life open to all. Intense attachment to God would inevitably mark one off from one's fellows but would expose one also to the dangers of selfishness or pride. One had to be careful in defining the social circumstances within which intensity was allowed to develop and to support an appropriate concern for others. Frontiers had to be constructed, and decisions made about whom to include. The resulting narrower community had also to develop safeguards within itself, governing the enthusiasm and collaboration of its members. Yet such a community had to remain open to anyone willing to abide by its principles—principles that were, after all, still identifiably related to the characteristic features of the Church itself.

We can see how the tensions were at once recognized and resolved, when we look more closely at Basil's treatment of superiors. They were indisputably persons of importance; but he was cautious in describing the honour due to them: it was to be enjoyed in a context of mutual humility, which would oblige superiors as much as their subjects.[102] While one might regard a superior as the mouthpiece of God, the authority of Scripture and one's own rational judgement had to be allowed full play. 'Reasonable service [λογικὴ λατρεία]' (Paul's phrase in Romans 12.1) had to be preserved. To govern one's own actions was as important to Basil as submitting to the governance of others. It was 'irrational' to follow impulse, emotion, or mere command, without 'the guidance of reason', for one's actions no longer reflected one's wishes. 'But when a man in sound reason and good counsel accompanied by much thought always and everywhere intends and accomplishes what is pleasing to God he fulfils the commandment of a reasonable service'. The effect of such injunctions was beyond doubt to defend values independent of and prior to the practice of obedience: there was no suggestion that obedience

102. R 63 = B 36. See also R 115 = B 170. R 170 = B 249 illustrates the caution; and the Latin is charged with the vocabulary of the grace and freedom conflict. Basil maintained his sense of humour: 'No one who is in possession of his mind', he wrote, would wish to be 'established in some power', *Ep.* 236. 7, C 3: 55, D 3: 405.

would either induce or guarantee the attitudes desired.[103] That explains why 'reasonable servants', in Basil's eyes, were entitled to subject their superiors to careful criticism—or at least some in the community enjoyed that right. Scripture, certainly, and a shrewd assessment of human nature, were canons against which to measure the advice or instructions of those in authority.[104]

The very vocabulary of authority was marked, in addition, by vagueness and variety.[105] The commonest and simplest term for 'superior' was ὁ προεστώς, normally translated by Rufinus as 'is qui praeest'.[106] The term also occurs in plural forms. In some of the instances one is dealing with observations about 'superiors' in general; but in others it does seem to have been suggested that there might be more than one 'superior' within a community.[107] Another pair of terms used frequently was πεπιστευμένος and ἐπιτεταγμένος; and it is tempting to think that a distinction was being made between persons 'entrusted' and persons 'appointed', respectively, with the notion of trust carrying greater authority. In this case, also, the situation is complicated by the occasional use of the plural; and, furthermore, there is no doubt that at times each term could mean 'superior' in exactly the same way as προεστώς.[108]

---

103. B 230 (not in R) at PG 31. 1236BC; tr. Clarke, p. 314. The superior as the mouthpiece of God, not a common emphasis, is perhaps implied in R 70 = B 38.

104. For the last point, see R 13 (especially §§ 6–7) = B 114. Note that R 13 follows upon other reflections on the authority of Scripture, whereas B 114 opens a section on obedience (which R picks up in 64f.). On passing judgement upon superiors, F 27 is cautious but explicit (and see also B 103). F 47–49 emphasize Scripture as the measure and limit the privilege even more. These passages are later than the text translated in R and reflect a degree of balanced authority within the community only possible with more formal development: see Gribomont, Histoire, p. 253; and Clarke, Basil, p. 93.

105. Fedwick, Charisma, pp. 47f., is shrewd on this point. See also Margaret Gertrude Murphy, St. Basil and Monasticism, pp. 35f.

106. For straightforward examples in Greek, without equivalents in R, see F 27, 30, 48; B 303. In R nothing is simple. R 44 = B 27 seems uncomplicated. R 69, however, finds a corresponding plural form in B 119. R 119 has no exact equivalent in B 45. R 192 = B 105 is singular in some MSS, plural in others: see Gribomont, Histoire, p. 106.

107. Other plurals: R 9 = F 19, R 94 (but not in B 135). For a plurality of superiors in some sense, F 35. The hierarchy implied in R 31 = B 187 may offer some explanation. Authority limited in some cases to one narrow sphere may also have allowed apparent duplication: R 9 = F 19, R 10 = F 21, R 131 = B 152.

108. Ambiguity: B 235 (not in R). Singulars and plurals: R 21 = B 288; R 94 = B 135; R 173 = B 252; F 43 (not in R); B 138 (not in R). But these last two suggest strongly a reference, even in the plural, to the major superior of each community. In R 92 the equivalence is beyond doubt: 'is qui praeest' in §§ 1 and 3 represents first πεπιστευμένος at PG 31. 1169D, and second ἐπιτεταγμένος at 1172A. The vocabulary of Ep. 22. 1 is worth quoting at length:

The Christian . . . must not talk idly, prattling of things which neither conduce to the benefit of his listeners nor to the activities that are indispensable and permitted

What one can detect, in relation to πεπιστευμένος and ἐπιτεταγμένος, is a more specific reference to task or responsibility. We gain, in those instances, a clearer picture of what superiors were actually supposed to do. An important notion was 'the care of all'.[109] It was in that context, also, that connections were made with 'the ministry of the word', which is perhaps the clearest indication of a link between authority in the ascetic community and authority in the Church more generally.[110] Although a hierarchy might often be visible, therefore, responsibilities were spread out across a spectrum of skill and authority, all subject to criticism, and having the same terminology at its base; and so there was a less obvious distinction at times between the major superior and a range of other persons with commanding duties beneath him.

Basil was much more concerned with the relationship between superior and subject than with the structure of authority itself. In a superior's life there were, so to speak, two axes of spiritual and emotional intensity. On the one hand, he looked towards God: he acted, in the spirit of Paul, as one of Christ's underlings, and as a steward of the secrets of God.[111] On the other hand, he looked towards his subjects, as a 'nurse' (in the sense of one who offered nourishment: a *nutrix* or τροφός). He would open for them not only the Scriptures but his very soul, bearing in mind the command of Jesus that his followers should love one another and be ready to lay down their lives for their friends.[112] Subordinate officials were also invited

---

us by God; so that both the workers may as far as possible have silence in which to apply themselves zealously to their work, and they themselves, who have been entrusted after trial with the dispensation of the word for the upbuilding of the faith [τοὺς πεπιστευμένους μετὰ δοκιμασίας οἰκονομεῖν τὸν λόγον πρὸς οἰκοδομὴν τῆς πίστεως: every phrase is typical], may speak only good words to the workers, lest God's Holy Spirit be grieved', C 1: 53, D 1: 131/133.

See also *Ep.* 199, intro. (applied to the bishop Amphilochius: τὴν τοῦ διδάσκειν τάξιν πεπιστευμένος, C 2: 154).

109. F 24–25, 43; B 19, 138 (none in R). B 254 (not in R) may have similar notions in mind: see above, at n. 96.

110. For a general statement, F 25. More particular connections: R 15 = B 184 (or perhaps 98), R 21 = B 288, R 119 = B 45. See also F 45.

111. For example, *Hom.* 354. 2. The same point is made in F 43. 1. A broad 'presence' was implied thereby: a superior's influence was not limited to what he said—which confirms Basil's characteristic attachment to the importance of example in a teacher.

112. The key text is R 15 (= B 184, according to Clarke; but 98 offers a closer parallel). For the dispenser of God's mysteries, see n. 110, especially in relation to R 21 = B 288. A connection with R 23–24 = B 99, 158, is discussed below at n. 162. For the νομοθέτης having to be conscious of his own faults, see *Hom.* 319. 5. R 15 concludes a series of reflections on obedience, which Basil then reworked in F 24–32 (section 13 in the 'Y' series). It may not be insignificant that R 12–15 come, in the Vulgate, at either the beginning or the end of sections in the 'X' series. For explanation, see appendix 2, at nn. 28, 31f.

to think in the same way.[113] The subject, meanwhile, was placed in exactly the same pattern of relationships: the one who obeyed was responding like a hungry child to the breast, drawing in this case spiritual food by accepting the commands of those in authority.[114]

The mutual responsibilities were worked out by Basil with considerable subtlety. By doing the will of another, one became in some sense his 'partner' and then, as a consequence, accepted him as 'lord' and 'father'.[115] There was a deep theological conviction at work in this 'surrender', based on the sense of one's inadequacy as a creature.[116] Hierarchy was created by a voluntary act of submission, displacing the natural equality one might otherwise expect to find. Disobedience, in such circumstances, was thought of as a loss of faith, the repudiation of a contract one had entered into with one's accepted superior. The point was echoed in a number of texts.[117] It is essential that we make full use of these images of obedience in action. They represent a lively and constantly reaffirmed principle of cohesion within ascetic society and provide us with the necessary context in which to place more formal and theological reflections.[118]

Why were superiors thought necessary? What lay behind the acceptance of such relationships of trust? Let us recall the point made above: the development of structures associated with obedience and hierarchy depended on the willingness of individuals to harness for their own purposes all the resources available that would help them to overcome, by the exercise of their God-given reason (their λόγος), the influence of passion

113. R 111 = B 148: the cellarer, in this instance, looks towards the superior, thinking, I am not my own master, and towards his fellows, thinking, What does each one need?

114. R 84 = B 166.

115. R 120 = B 283: 'partner' = *socius* and *particeps* in R, κοινωνός in B; 'lord' and 'father' = *dominus* and *pater* in R (*pater* occurring only in some R MSS), κύριος and πατήρ in B: ed. Zelzer (§ 2), p. 146; *PG* 31. 1281B.

116. *DSS* 20 (§ 51). Compare the status of the 'anointer' at n. 31.

117. F 28. 2 (not in R). Although it occurs in section 13 of the 'Y' series, the passage follows immediately upon sections that are reproduced in R (see n. 112), and is faithful to the spirit of R elsewhere: see R 36, 111–13 = B 160, 148–50. More generally, see R 16, 25, 28, 65, 71, 82, 106 = B 3, 159, 9, 116, 39, 121, 146.

118. Which are, in any case, surprisingly rare. Later sections of F are the most obvious examples, 24–32. R 65 = B 116 is characteristically reticent, faced with the opportunity to comment on Phil. 2.8—'obedient unto death'. It would seem that R 64–66 = B 115–16, 37, have maintained the sequence of 'X' and 'Y'; in which case it matters more that the allusion to Philippians is enfolded within a context focussed upon humility and a sense of the presence of God. R 126 = B 206 makes comparable adjustments, in relation to the same text. We have commented already on R 70 = B 38 at n. 103 above.

and sin.[119] A central requirement was the opportunity to discuss one's spiritual progress, which, after all, lay at the heart of the ascetic life. There were instances of formality, of course, which led to an emphasis on certain qualities in a superior at the expense of less institutional talents and dignities. But even the confession of sin (an occasion never strictly defined) was staged on the border between the ascetic community and the Church.[120] Among Christians more generally, the formal correction of the sinner took place against a broader background of shared obligations. Basil took very much to heart and described in sensitive detail the usefulness of such sympathy: one's own tears, cautiously indulged, would lead others to repentance; and a visible capacity for sorrow on one's own part would support and assuage the grief of others.[121]

We find scattered throughout the *Asceticon* examples of even more loosely structured spiritual dialogue. The principles applied are sometimes hard to pin down;[122] but a mechanism of mutual help was consistently appealed to, operating within a community where correction was achieved by exhortation. First came the sense of repentance; and then 'the weaker will be cured by the *constantia* and *integritas* of the stronger' (two simple words surprisingly difficult to translate in their richness, implying as they do a steadiness of character and a high degree of moral consistency and self-possession). The 'cure' was achieved by more than mere example. These *fortiores* were men of experience, skilled in the art of spiritual healing.[123] The weak were set apart, separated like the sick from the circumstances of their disease; and the strong then exhorted them to a change of attitude and behaviour. That was what it meant to 'bear one another's burdens'.[124] One is reminded of the exhortation in *Letter* 285: 'You all consent to be both guardians of each other's diligence and witnesses of each other's success'.[125]

119. See *Hom.* 320. 5. The mechanics of the process carry us to the heart of Basil's anthropology, which we shall explore more fully in chapter 9. See also *Hom.* 319. 7, and 333 passim.

120. R 12 = B 288. See also R 119 = B 45; Holl, *Enthusiasmus*, pp. 261f.; Clarke, *Basil*, pp. 95f.

121. *Hom.* 328. 4, 334. 7, 339. 9.

122. We can sometimes compare, for example, the terminology of Rufinus with that of the existing Greek (which is often, strikingly enough, less rigid in its categories): see, for example, R 193–94 = B 73, 106, where the subsequent editing of B has scattered what R may have found combined.

123. R 200 = B 229 (which is rather more brief), without any implication of specific office.

124. R 177–78 = B 177–78. R 200, above, makes the same allusion to Gal. 6.2.

125. *Ep.* 295, C 3: 170, D 4: 209. The note of mutual agreement is important: καταδέχεσθε. See n. 87 above.

It was only later that such general obligations towards fellow Christians were carried across to coincide with a more formal relationship between superiors and subjects in the ascetic community itself.[126] Even then, the whole process remained consciously open to the less predictable impact of God's presence.[127]

Behind that disciplined system of mutual correction and guidance, over which superiors came eventually to preside, there lay a specific sense of urgency no less characteristic of Basil, his sense of God's judgement. 'God is good', he said, 'but he is also just'—as if to include, in the latter phrase, a contrasting threat.[128] The anxiety reached far beyond the bounds of the *Asceticon:* 'Take note that the soul is blessed which by night and day revolves no other anxiety than how on the great day, on which all creation shall stand about the Judge and give an account of its deeds, it also shall be able easily to discharge the reckoning of the life it has lived'.[129] In *Letter* 173, Basil wrote of 'never letting pass from our minds the remembrance of the awful and inexorable tribunal, towards which we all indeed are hastening, though very few are mindful of it or solicitous about what the issue therefrom shall be'.[130] It was not just that God's justice was likely to cause a sinner distress: it should prompt in everyone a sense of obligation towards other people. ' "Judge a just judgment" is one of the precepts most necessary for salvation'.[131] The task of judging and correcting others was unavoidable: the very integrity of the community as a whole might sometimes depend on it. The sins of the few could so easily bring down upon all the anger of God.[132] And the social effect of disobedience was not the only issue at stake:[133] to remain silent in the face of sin was to run the risk of sharing in its condemnation.[134]

For that reason, some form of excommunication was thought necessary and acceptable. It was a sanction that already operated within the Church more generally. Yet Basil would always allow repentance greater scope than punishment.[135] Within the ascetic community, therefore, 'excommunication' took the form of temporary ostracism, rather than of

---

126. F 43. 1.
127. B 15, 261 (neither in R). The notion will be explored more below.
128. Preface to F, § 4.
129. *Ep.* 174, C 2: 110, D 2: 453/455.
130. *Ep.* 173, C 2: 109, D 2: 453.
131. *Ep.* 204. 2, C 2: 174f., D 3: 159.
132. We have seen the idea at work in *Hom.* 325. 4, preached during the 369 famine: see chapter 5, at n. 16.
133. Although discussed in R 69 = B 119.
134. R 122 (at some length) = B 47.
135. *Ep.* 287, 288; and note the long wait recommended in *Ep.* 188. 4, 7.

expulsion in a literal sense; and it was a punishment meted out to those who defended sinners, just as much as to the sinners themselves.[136] The very style of spiritual direction gave pride of place to repentance. The punishments inflicted during this life were directed towards a change of heart within the sinner.[137] Even fear of judgement was not untempered by hope: 'Hope, then, in the goodness of God, and expect His help, knowing that, if we turn to Him rightly and sincerely, not only will He not cast us off utterly, but will say even as we are uttering the words of our prayer: "Behold, I am with you" '.[138]

Two important theological convictions were at work here: one concerned with the nature of sin, the other with the nature of fear. Basil taught again and again that sins varied in seriousness, and that forgiveness always followed repentance.[139] That message was broadcast very generally. Of course, human beings could not redeem themselves,[140] but the very slightest sign of regret would bring to bear the full mercy of God.[141] Even a little goodness in one's life would immediately outweigh in God's eyes a great amount of evil, for he recognized without hesitation, hidden among its failings, the beauty of human nature as intended in the creation.[142] Because of that divine generosity, creatures should be no less ready to hold out a helping hand towards those who repented.[143] So the virtue of hope

136. So R 26, 28, 43, 76 = B 7, 9, 26, 44. F 28 (not in R) does appear to demand literal expulsion.

137. Very forcefully expressed, for example, in *Ep.* 112. 3; 260 passim. It is worth noting that the formal sanctions of canon law were subject to the same modification: 'if, however, each of those who have been guilty of the aforesaid sins be earnest in preferring penance, he who has been entrusted by the mercy of God in loosing and binding, if he should become more merciful in diminishing the time of punishment on seeing the magnitude of the sinner's penance, shall not be worthy of condemnation; ... for we do not judge things entirely by time, but we attend to the manner of the repentance', *Ep.* 217. 74, 84; C 2: 213, 216; D 3: 257, 265.

138. *Ep.* 174, C 2: 111, D 2: 455.

139. Here I take very forceful issue with Amand de Mendieta. He listed texts that he thought supported his dark and narrow view, *Ascèse*, pp. 152–63, and then commented upon them, pp. 164–79. His most brutal judgement against Basil appears on p. 172. His sense of source dependence was woefully inadequate (his failure to make proper use of Basil's homilies was particularly reprehensible): see pp. 103f. especially. He finally managed to contradict himself, anyway, pp. 271–72. Compare the careful judgements of Holl, *Enthusiasmus*, pp. 261f. (Amand de Mendieta, pp. 164f., offers a particularly illuminating contrast). In addition to texts cited below, *Ep.* 260 provides a long and optimistic treatise on the possibility of forgiveness.

140. *Hom.* 354. 3 puts succinctly what is implied in many passages.

141. *Hom.* 350. 3. Amand de Mendieta, *Ascèse*, pp. 172, 346, tried without success to make sense of the passage, but hopelessly in the face of his own prejudice.

142. *Hom.* 356. 5, 357. 3. See B 84 (not in R).

143. *Hom.* 324. 8.

had a social dimension: the willingness of each to hope for the best in the other. And for oneself, nothing did more than hope to protect the soul of the religious enthusiast.[144]

As for fear, it was regarded as part of a process, designed to encourage the development of motives less dramatic, less sharply felt. Human beings changed by growing, achieving greater potential; and they did so 'day by day', over long periods of time.[145] Fear, therefore, was always associated with a range of other equally emotive concepts, all of which created momentum in a religious life. Hope, love, perfection—these were never far distant, when there was reference to fear. Fear, like hope, was regarded as an aid.[146] It seized upon one suddenly, preventing evil deeds;[147] but then it took one by the hand, leading one forward to a life of piety and affection.[148] There was no question of resting content with the mere fear of death, any more than of authority.[149] Rather one would regard fear as another ἀγαθὸν ἐφόδιον, a species of nourishment on the journey towards eternity; and that journey was not made alone but constituted 'a goodly life [pursued] with those who fear the Lord'.[150]

Those were points made to the Church at large, an exhortation and a philosophy of amendment that was thought suitable for all who were willing to hear it. Basil's advice to the more committed was of exactly the same character. Repentance was a reality, and its encouragement brought spiritual progress. Perhaps he had to make that emphasis because there were some in his audience who found it hard to accept.[151] The opening sections of the *Regulae brevius tractatae* explore the matter at length. First comes what can only be described as the drama of conversion. The enthusiast rejects what may have been a previous life of even scandalous perversity. Then one experiences the fear of eternal fire, albeit cast in

144. *Hom.* 328. 3. See 356. 5.
145. *Hom.* 352. 2. There is an allusion to 2 Cor. 4.16: 'Though our outer nature is wasting away, our inner nature is being renewed every day [ἀνακαινοῦται ἡμέρᾳ καὶ ἡμέρᾳ]'. The matter will be discussed further in chapter 9, at nn. 94 and 144.
146. *Ep.* 174, referred to above at n. 129; *DSS* 20 (§ 51).
147. *Hom.* 340. 2, 351. 6.
148. *Hom.* 350. 6; *Ep.* 26.
149. *Hom.* 351. 8.
150. *Ep.* 249, C 3: 87, D 4: 3.
151. R 27 = B 8, in which Basil alludes at once to the happy shepherd of Luke 15.6: 'He calls together his friends and his neighbours, saying to them, "Rejoice with me, for I have found my sheep which was lost" '. Amand de Mendieta, *Ascèse*, p. 160, was tortuous in his contrasting interpretations. On the effectiveness of repentance, R 182 = B 58: '*ubique tamen digne gesta paenitentia veniae spem praesumit*', § 2; ed. Zelzer, p. 203 = πανταχοῦ δὲ ἡ ἀξιόλογος μετάνοια βεβαίαν ἔχει τὴν ἐλπίδα τῆς ἀφέσεως, PG 31. 1121C. Contrast *Ascèse*, p. 165 and n. 91.

the guise of a teacher (φόβου μὲν διδάσκαλον). Finally, the tears of the penitent, which move God to mercy, are changed to joy, and one receives the 'power to please God'.[152]

There follow more formal reflections, which were not reproduced by Rufinus. The coming of God's Son into the world was to be identified totally with the forgiveness of sin as an historical reality. The phenomenon of individual repentance in the face of that event was at once a manifestation of God's judgement and the perfection of his mercy; and both judgement and mercy were always available: sin, even after baptism, could never outstrip the capacity of God's mercy to bring forgiveness.[153] The implications of that theology were not left to the imagination. Mastery of sin was possible: 'For each man that sin is great which has the mastery of him and that is little of which he is the master [ἑκάστῳ μέγα εἶναι τὸ ἑκάστου κρατοῦν, καὶ μικρὸν τοῦτο, οὗ ἕκαστος κρατεῖ]'.[154]

What was also implied by the theology was that spiritual dedication was a process: it defined one's whole life and committed one to gradual improvement over a number of years, which were likely to be marked by regular failure as well as by success. One had to grapple with disappointment. One had to acknowledge that impediments to progress might be deeply rooted, and that their connection with more immediate problems might not always be apparent.[155] No wonder a constant programme of consultation, encouragement, and advice was central to Basil's view of what the ascetic community was for. A whole series of techniques was developed, based above all on the notion that evil was best countered by the cultivation in each case of its opposite.[156]

Basil's caution did not stop there. While the passing of judgement upon others was legitimate, it had to be exercised with extreme care. It was best to express such opinions only when it was clear that one was

---

152. R 117 = B 10—τὴν ἐξουσίαν καὶ τὴν δύναμιν λαβοῦσα τῆς πρὸς Θεὸν εὐαρεστή-σεως, PG 31. 1088D; tr. Clarke, p. 234; faithfully reproduced in R, § 6. Here, at least, Amand de Mendieta, Ascèse, p. 172, could not deny the importance of the emphasis.

153. B 12, 13 (neither in R). Note, however, the context R (149) provides for the associated B 11: one will find sin odious, immediately its character has been recognized (that is to say, when seen from the point of view of God's judgement); and one will naturally thereafter desire the good that is promised by God, R 159 = B 174.

154. B 293 (not in R); PG 31. 1288D; tr. Clarke, p. 342. Moreover, another graded scale of sinfulness is hereby admitted. The passage (because it may be late) seems to undermine the rigorism imputed by Amand de Mendieta, Ascèse, pp. 103, 159, 162, 165f. See also F. Laun, 'Die beiden Regeln des Basilius, ihre Echtheit und Entstehung', p. 36.

155. R 22, 123 = B 289, 16.

156. R 18, 19, 22, 49 = B 5, 287, 289, 30; F 51 (not in R). See also Hom. 324. 8, referring to advice proffered in what was obviously a very public arena.

corroborating the judgement of God (as opposed to prescriptions imposed by oneself). Even then, one needed to hesitate, if an infringement seemed out of character with the miscreant's normal disposition.[157] Compassion was of the essence, even though the one who rebuked might show it more genuinely than the one who kept silent.[158] Compassion was clearly distinguishable from anger or indignation, and closely conjoined with pity.[159] It was an attitude dependent entirely on the development of genuine sympathy. It was not enough to serve others: one should feel sad at their failure and joyful at their success.[160] So deeply felt a response was the least one's fellows could expect.[161]

It all came back to the theory of mutual trust. Ascetics corrected one another as doctors corrected the misfortunes of their patients (here a medical analogy was substituted for that of nursing and suckling). The healer felt genuine concern, and the patient trusted even the bitterest medicine. Once again, Basil was chiefly concerned with the inner attitudes that were to accompany the cure.[162]

The final segment of the *Regulae fusius tractatae*, picking up an earlier emphasis ('Rebuke is a doctoring of the soul [ἰατρεία ψυχῆς ἐστιν ἡ ἐπιτίμησις]'), develops at considerable length (thus creating its closing impression) the way in which the art of medicine is the model of spiritual guidance.[163] Given Basil's own constant experience of ill health, such a conclusion to his theology of ascesis is not without its pathos.[164]

---

157. R 77–78 = B 164–65. Those were the moments when serious defamation might be more likely, R 42 = B 25: compare the 'evil suspicions' of B 19 (not in R); tr. Clarke, p. 237. Basil was exercising the same hopeful tolerance he would show towards heretics, as in *Ep.* 113, 210. 4.

158. R 17 = B 4. There was at work here just as much a theology of compassion as of sin: compare Amand de Mendieta, *Ascèse*, pp. 161f., and see B 232 (not in R).

159. R 46 = B 29: one was to be moved '*miseratione et compassione*' = οἴκτου καὶ συμ-παθείας, § 4; ed. Zelzer, p. 90; *PG* 31. 1104A.

160. R 155 = B 175.

161. R 191 = B 182: again, συμπάθεια, *PG* 31. 1204C; but the *patientia* of § 4, ed. Zelzer, p. 211, is not in B. See the 'fearful sympathy' of B 296 (not in R); tr. Clarke, p. 343; and note Holl, *Enthusiasmus*, pp. 162f. Gould, 'Beatitudes', p. 17, is too harsh.

162. R 23–24 = B 99, 158 (B separates what R connects). See above, at n. 112.

163. The quotation is from F 53; *PG* 31. 1044A; tr. Clarke, p. 224. The analogy is already made in F 52. For medicine as a type, see F 55 (which constitutes the final section of 'Y'). None of these F passages, of course, is in R. The same theme is handled in B 301 (not in R), and in Gribomont's B 314, *Histoire*, pp. 177f., 182f., 207.

164. Basil may have studied medicine, if we can trust GNaz *Orat.* 43. 23; but not at Athens, according to Ruether, *Gregory*, p. 29. See *Adul.* 10. 7; *Hom.* 349. 5.

So much for the ways in which different types of authority worked in practice. The investigation has carried us far beyond structure and discipline. The texts consulted contain, often at a highly theoretical level, many statements about intimacy, sympathy, patience, and progress. It was theory, in the end, that counted for most. Basil's asceticism was firmly based on philosophical and theological considerations, sustained by deep reflection over a number of years. Above all other notions, the key to his thought is probably the concept of 'nature', φύσις. It is striking that, in the opening discussion on the Great Commandment, his handling of the twin themes of love of God and love of neighbour began with that essentially 'Stoic' emphasis.[165] Of course, 'natural' tendencies could 'produce' evil, as well as good, and could be subverted by other influences.[166] They needed schooling, and assessing in the light of God's revealed commandments.[167] Just occasionally, 'nature' could mean, for Basil, that rougher potential, which needed still the control of a disciplined life.[168] However, not only in his ascetic writings but in all his pastoral teaching, Basil was firm in his commitment to the naturalness of a serious devotion to Christian values. He simply could not believe (and this surely was a strength) that God demanded a moral régime at odds with the essential qualities of creation—even though human beings were compelled to discover those qualities and bring them to destined fulfilment within a framework of experience marred by sin. So it was by nature that people desired to open their hearts to one another, and to develop the gift of

165. Throughout R 2 = F 2–6. The Greek was characterized by Gribomont, *Histoire*, p. 240, as 'un exposé, mûrement réfléchi, des fondements de l'ascèse chrétienne' (his reflections continue in the pages that follow). See also Amand de Mendieta, *Ascèse*, pp. 17, 66 (slightly contradictory), with qualifications pp. 69f.; by p. 171, nature and sin have coalesced (but *Ep.* 4 by itself is not enough to build on). Clarke was peculiar in his translations—of B 75 = R 195, for example, in which φυσικοῖς κινήμασι scarcely justifies 'physical emotions', *PG* 31. 1136A, tr. p. 258 (by the time he had reached B 224, they had become 'physical impulses', p. 311: compare 1232A).

166. *Ep.* 25. 1, 261; *Hom.* 319. 1. R 195 = B 75 is cautious, if not pessimistic, about the usefulness of 'natural' tendencies; R 161 = B 216 suggests, however, that natural goodness (of children, for example) is just as likely to be subverted by bad training.

167. R 203 = B 274 works out the matter fully, with interesting shifts of emphasis between Latin and Greek. Clarke's translation, p. 333, is not entirely helpful. The main conclusion, of both versions, is that the acceptance of guidance within an ascetic régime will ensure fulfilment of God's will, thus justifying a sense that one has achieved a natural goodness. See also R 135 = B 239; and B 230 (not in R), discussed above at n. 103.

168. B 224 (not in R).

language. It was by nature that they brought their λόγος, their reason, to bear upon the passions, schooling them to a life of virtue.[169] It was by nature that they wished to lead a common life, as did so many of the animals with whom they shared the privilege of creation.[170] Human nature, in both its potential and its destiny, should make a life of virtue easy.[171] Basil's portrait of a virtuous man shows a being who achieved no more than should be expected of a creature with human characteristics: liberated from the demands of the body, assessing accurately his own worth, understanding the world around him and the way in which God created and sustained it, he was constantly inspired by generosity towards his friends and those in need.[172] All those convictions, scattered through Basil's sermons, were expressed in the same terms in the introductory sections of the *Asceticon*.

Yet Basil seems to have felt that such a 'scientific' approach might seem too cold to his audience. For him, the social and emotional bonds brought into play by observance of the Great Commandment were based, inevitably, on something else that was natural, albeit more intensely felt by the moral Christian, namely, a capacity for love. It was a truth that Basil thought suitable for the widest audience. Even a short letter to an obscure friend could become incandescent with affection: 'I had conceived with respect to your holy and guileless soul what I may call an amatory disposition [a charmingly reticent rendering of τις διάθεσις ... ἵν' οὕτως εἴπω, ἐρωτική]'; and he continued:

> For this I have thanked the holy God, and I pray, if any period of life be yet left to me, that my life be made sweet through you [γενέσθαι μοι διὰ σοῦ τὴν ζωὴν ἡδεῖαν], since for the present, at least, I consider life a wretched thing and to be avoided, separated as it is from association with those most dear [τῆς τῶν φιλτάτων συνουσίας]. For in my opinion, there is nothing for which a man may be joyful if he be separated from those who truly love him [τῶν ἀληθῶς ἀγαπώντων].[173]

Joy in the face of creation and God's goodness was also a natural state. Basil did not hesitate to encourage in his people generally the ability to recognize and the willingness to welcome the frisson of joy that came with the approach of God within the soul: then they would know what

---

169. *Hom.* 319. 1.
170. *Hom.* 325. 8.
171. *Hom.* 352. 8. See R 150, 152 = B 174, 212.
172. Splendidly expressed in *Hom.* 348. 4.
173. *Ep.* 124, C 2: 29f., D 2: 257/259.

those who were really just felt every moment of their lives.[174] And all those intensities of feeling were reproduced in the more specifically ascetic corpus. The love of God was considered beyond words, 'easier to feel than to describe'.[175] The desire to please God should be *'vehemens et inexplebile'*, a violent thrust, set in motion by contemplation and the recollection of God's goodness.[176] It is by such urgent movements of the inner self that one brought to a fitting peak one's capacity to meet the demands of the religious ideal, 'the observance of the commandment to the point of death'.[177]

Basil did not simply allow such feelings to well up indiscriminately: they were to be fostered and channelled by careful discipline. Matters proceeded by clear stages. Renunciation itself provided the paradigm: first one renounced the devil and then, by a series of logical steps, found oneself committed more and more to a serious interpretation of religious obligation.[178] Those passages concerning a transition from fear to perfection made the same point. The Preface to the *Regulae fusius tractatae* is worth quoting in full:

> I perceive three different dispositions which by inevitable necessity lead us to obey. Either through fear of punishment we turn away from that which is evil, and so are of a slavish disposition [ἐν τῇ διαθέσει τῇ δουλικῇ]; or, seeking to profit by the reward, we fulfil the commandments for the sake of our own benefit, and are accordingly like hirelings [προσεοίκαμεν τοῖς μισθίοις]; or else we do good for the sake of the good itself and firm love of Him who gave us the law [τὸν νόμον], rejoicing that we are thus thought worthy to serve the glorious and great God, and so we have the disposition of sons [ἐν τῇ τῶν υἱῶν διαθέσει].[179]

He was also careful to identify the inner pathways along which it was possible for a soul to move in that way, and the changing qualities of the

174. *Hom.* 328. 2f., 350. 1. Such joy at union with God should then lead to joyous action, *Hom.* 334. 3.

175. R 2. 18: '*ineffabilem . . . sentiri magis quam dici possit*', ed. Zelzer, p. 11. The existing F 2 at *PG* 31. 909C does not quite echo the distinction; but see Gribomont, *Histoire*, p. 241.

176. R 14. 1; ed. Zelzer, p. 63 = B 157. Note the simple but fundamental interpretation of *affectus* in R 156 = B 176: '*nemo dubitat quod caritas in affectu sita sit*', § 4; ed. Zelzer, p. 180.

177. R 126. 1; ed. Zelzer, p. 155 = B 206; echoing R 14, referred to just above. R 49 = B 30 is crucial on the religious function of 'desire [*desiderium*, ἐπιθυμία]'. Zelzer, p. 92, points out how we need the Greek to make sense of the Latin; Clarke's translation, p. 241, is not completely reliable. The chief point is that desire enables one to reject lesser goods. See also B 259 (not in R). Quite measured observations can suddenly burst into flame, so to speak: R 90, slightly weaker than B 130. See Amand de Mendieta, *Ascèse*, pp. 17f.

178. R 4 = F 8, to be read in the context of points made above at n. 46.

179. Preface to F, § 3; *PG* 31. 896B; tr. Clarke, p. 148. For a similar series of images, resulting in sonship achieved by the sealing of the Spirit, see *Hom.* 356. 4.

movement itself.[180] We have mentioned already the built-in shift from contemplation to desire.[181] Something similar was implied in the movement from *meditatio* to purification of soul.[182] Perhaps most important are the movements that start with, or depend upon, belief. They clarify, among other things, the relationship Basil perceived between nature and the religious life, and the associated transition to an economy of redemption, within which nature was elevated, or restored, to its true dignity. First, as we have said already, a just assessment of the nature of sin was expected to induce a sense of aversion. That then prompted belief in God's promises; and the very act of hope generated *affectus* and *desiderium*, which in themselves (and again we have seen the opinion expressed elsewhere) would make possible whatever was desired.[183]

Those movements also reached outwards, beyond the individual. Basil was not just searching, in a familiar way, for an antidote to hypocrisy—that carefully preserved correspondence between inner and outer disposition (although such discussion occurred, as we would expect).[184] What mattered more was that a person should know how to capitalize on interior intensity so that it could be expressed usefully in visible behaviour. Basil's understanding of *affectus*, διάθεσις (a word that implies intensity of feeling but denotes also a lasting disposition), shows how that process of authentic expression was expected to take place. Almost all the relevant texts have been touched upon already. External discipline was not the remote product of some inwardly acknowledged principle of morality, but burgeoned to the accompaniment of a whole range of sentiments (couched equally in theoretical terms):[185] 'Love consists in a disposition of

180. Details of such a sort are contained also in the homilies: for example, 319. 7, or more generally 320. 7.

181. In R 14 = B 157, at n. 176 above.

182. R 35 = B 22. Clarke's translation suggests a weakening of the Latin '*per meditationem*' (§ 2; ed. Zelzer, p. 81), with his phrases 'occupied in' and 'practises continually', p. 239; but there is enough *meditatio* in ἐν τῇ σχολῇ and ἐν μελέτῃ, PG 31. 1097C.

183. R 149–50 = B 11, 174—and again, the Greek divides what R combines: 'X' and 'Y' evidence gives greater authority to the latter; see Gribomont, *Histoire*, p. 207. A whole series of similar observations carry through to R 156. B 174 shows interesting variations, undermining the priority of belief. For further reflections on belief and understanding, see R 167 = B 218, and B 260 (not in R); also above, at n. 93. B 20 (not in R) plots the moral results of disbelief.

184. R 45 = B 28; but R trusts appearances—an evil heart cannot speak good—whereas B, agreeing that good men are inevitably honest, warns that evil men may deceive (surely, a more coherent view). *Hom.* 319. 8 and 350. 2 offer more broadly disseminated reflections; 351. 1 and 352. 3 impinge only less directly on the same point of interest. See Amand de Mendieta, *Ascèse*, pp. 192f.

185. R 23 = B 99; R 15 = B 184, or B 98.

the mind [ἡ ἀγάπη ἐν διαθέσει ἐστί]';[186] 'Love of the brethren should not be superficial but innate and fervent [μὴ ἐπιπόλαιος ἡ φιλαδελφία, ἐνδιάθετος δὲ καὶ διάπυρος]'.[187]

To some extent, it was a matter of distinguishing between intention and fulfilment;[188] but virtue itself was marked by its own duality—the control of qualities at once interior and exterior. Basil was very good at defining these. What was the difference, he asked, for example, between θυμός and ὀργή (both of which we might translate as 'anger')? Θυμός, he said, referred to that stage of emotional disturbance when a person experienced indignation; ὀργή, on the other hand, referred to the moment when something was actually done about it.[189] We find several examples of that subtlety, which pointed also to a distinction between what might affect only the individual and what was likely to impinge upon the community.[190] The same careful analysis occurs in Basil's sermons.[191] It was wholly characteristic of his moral theory that he should highlight the social impact of personal qualities in such a careful way.

There was, finally, an even deeper theme in Basil's ascetic teaching that may bring us closest to the heart of his conception of the religious life. It concerned, again, a pathway, an axis of discipline, which ran from the recollection of God's goodness (in creation, in history, and in one's own life) to the experience of God's presence. The expression of that movement, in Basil's own words, revolved around two notions: that of μνήμη, of recollection or remembrance in some special sense; and that of God seeing into one's heart—'Whether on a journey or at work, whether in darkness or the light of day, the eye of God is watching you'.[192] The two ideas were not disconnected. Meditation in the presence of God enabled one more surely to recollect God at other times; and recollection in its turn would bring a secure sense of his abiding presence.[193]

186. B 176; PG 31. 1200B; tr. Clarke, p. 295 ('of the mind' is a slight gloss) = R 156, already quoted above in n. 176.
187. B 242; PG 31. 1244CD; tr. Clarke, p. 318: 'innate' is not exactly right; perhaps 'deeply and consistently rooted within one's character'.
188. R 202 = B 275, making it almost a distinction between *anima* and *corpus*, ψυχή and σῶμα. See again R 195 = B 75, as at n. 167 above.
189. R 159 (with *ira* and *furor*) = B 55; and see R 190 = B 68.
190. R 147 = B 53; R 164 = B 56; B 66, 77 (neither in R).
191. *Hom.* 349. 4, clarified further by 333. 6; 346. 2; to some extent also 345. 2 and 354. 2, 6. Note how often anger was the issue.
192. *Hom.* 350. 8.
193. R 2. 74f. = F 5. 3 (the Greek is interestingly more expansive); R 109 = B 202. The classic treatment of μνήμη is John Eudes Bamberger, 'Μνήμη-Διάθεσις: The Psychic Dynamisms in the Ascetical Theology of St. Basil'. His title shows how we should link this point with the meanings already attached to διάθεσις. He stresses the *active* quality of

The theme of memory occurs, perhaps, less frequently than that of presence, although we find it in the sermons also, and in the letters.[194] Where it does occur, however, the associated reflections are fundamental in character. It affects the progressive drama of conversion that culminates in fulfilment of the Great Commandment.[195] It governs the famous *exemplum* of the true craftsman, who follows faithfully the model of his master—not only remembering what the master said, but retaining a vivid image of how he demonstrated his craft, leaving the artefacts for his pupil's guidance.[196] Such statements are easy to connect with the passages already noted, presenting recollection as crucial to the momentum of the spiritual life.[197]

More common, perhaps, was the notion of the watchful God. One has to admit that it was frequently deployed in the guise of a method, an inducement, with slightly threatening overtones. It is easy to imagine the processes involved. Wandering thoughts at prayer, for example, were best countered by a sense of God's presence.[198] We may associate that reflection with Basil's more formal teaching on the Trinity, and on the Holy Spirit in particular: his notion of the human heart as the place par excellence where worship of God, of that God who is truly present, might most properly be conducted.[199] But he used the figure also in relation to anger, for example: an awareness of the God who watched was a strong antidote to such emotion and encouraged humility also.[200]

The sense of God's presence provided the environment for religious action—indeed, it became the source of such action. One should do everything 'as if God were beholding',[201] trusting that that awareness would prompt correct behaviour.[202] The implication was that, even amidst great activity, there would be some abiding stillness. Such a belief, like many others we have discussed, is firmly embedded in the homilies also.

μνήμη, which in turn brings it to bear as a force for the long-term development of character, understood partly as διάθεσις (perhaps 'disposition'), esp. pp. 238f.

194. *Hom.* 352. 11. See below at nn. 208f., concerning *Ep.* 2, 22, 146.

195. R 2. 74 again, and R 14 = B 157.

196. R 55f. = B 32, 195–97, echoing points made in R 2. 87. B 32 does not specifically mirror the *memoria* of R 55; but the parallels are there in the other passages. R 58 is more detailed than B 197. R 2. 87 is (in relation to this issue) exactly parallel to F 5. 3.

197. R 2. 74f. = F 5. 2f. R 152 = B 212 shows recollection releasing natural springs of action.

198. R 34 = B 21 provides the most obvious example. R 108 is similar, but B 201 shows interesting variations. B 306 (not in R) brings in the whole Trinity. B 80 (not in R) for the slumber of the soul that impedes illumination.

199. *DSS* 6 (§ 15), 26 (§ 62). See chapter 5, at n. 188.

200. R 46 = B 29, R 79 = B 127. Humility: R 60 = B 34.

201. F 41 (not in R); tr. Clarke, p. 213.

202. B 294 (not in R).

Basil had nothing but praise for the person who was ὅμοιος ἀεὶ αὐτὸς ἑαυτῷ διαμένων (which sounds somewhat weaker in English: 'always remaining the same in himself'). Exactly the same idea recurs in the *Asceticon*, in the phrase '*semper utique et in omni loco idem esset*'.[203] Achieving such stillness depended to some extent on the ability to focus one's life, just as one focussed one's attention on the text of a psalm.[204] 'Neither losses nor illness nor the other inconveniences of life shall touch the virtuous man [τοῦ σπουδαίου], so long as he keeps his mind on God'.[205] That atmosphere of concentrated stillness built about oneself came to constitute a place of sanctification, the preservation of which consisted in 'clinging wholly to God without interruption at all times, and studying to please him'.[206] It represented the inner citadel defended by that paler prescription (in the Preface to Rufinus's translation) that one should remain quiet in the company of fellow dedicatees. It was, therefore, a quiet to be shared: it had a social effect, and the closeness of God's presence was thus made visible to all.[207]

Letters, ascetic and otherwise, defended the same doctrine. We have seen already how *Letter* 2 soars to a full theology of prayer:

> Prayer is to be commended, for it engenders in the soul a distinct conception of God. And the indwelling of God is this—to hold God ever in memory, His shrine established within us. We thus become temples of God whenever earthly cares cease to interrupt the continuity of our memory of Him, whenever unforeseen passions cease to disturb our minds, and the lover of God, escaping them all, retires to God, driving out the passions which tempt him to incontinence, and abides in the practices which conduce to virtue.[208]

In *Letter* 22 Basil warns 'the Christian' not to be 'easily drawn away by anything from the remembrance of God and from His will and judgments', and charges him later: 'There should be no clamour, or any scene or

203. *Hom.* 340. 15, *PG* 31. 420A—an early statement, according to Fedwick, *Basil*, 1: 10 n. 50. R 59. 2; ed. Zelzer, p. 97 = B 33.

204. See R 110 = B 279 in the context of *Hom.* 319. 5. Note the sentiment expressed to correspondents in Neocaesarea: 'We do not consider the past, if only the present be sound', *Ep.* 210. 4, C 2: 194, D 3: 207.

205. *Ep.* 293, C 3: 167, D 4: 201.

206. R 147. 5 = B 53: '*adhaerere deo ex integro et sine aliqua intermissione in omni tempore sollicitum esse et studium gerere placendi ei*', ed. Zelzer, p. 173. See Gribomont, *Histoire*, pp. 135f.

207. R 86 = B 200, which adds the pregnant phrase καὶ τῆς τοῦ Κυρίου παρουσίας, *PG* 31. 1216B.

208. *Ep.* 2. 4, C 1: 10, D 1: 17/19. The passage comes immediately after use of the image of concentrating on a model, found also in R (see above, at n. 196); the letter then returns to practicalities: see chapter 3, at n. 80.

commotion wherein anger is expressed, or any other elation of the mind which draws us away from the full assurance of God's presence'.[209] Perhaps in a chance and brief message to a distant friend we find the most startling summary:

> I exhort you to cleave zealously to the salvation of your soul, moderating all the affections of the flesh by reason, and constantly keeping the thought of God firmly established in your soul, as in a most holy temple; and in every word and in every deed hold before your eyes the judgment of Christ, so that, when all your several activities have been brought before that strict and terrible scrutiny, they may bring you glory on the day of reward, when you are accounted worthy of praise in the presence of every creature.[210]

One text we have so far left aside, the *Moralia*, and for special reasons. The first is related to its date, which may be early; and the second is related to its character, which is that of an address to the widest possible audience.[211] Gregory of Nazianzus's phrase ὅροις γραπτοῖς καὶ κανόσιν, 'written rules and regulations', could have referred at least to a draft of the *Moralia*,[212] placing the work in the period of Basil's sojourn with Gregory in Pontus between 359 and 361. It was then, we know, that he shrewdly assessed the correct relationship between his own desire for a more philosophical life and the opportunities presented by a clerical career and a pastoral concern for the religious development of the Christian

209. *Ep.* 22. 1f.; C 1: 153f., D 1: 131, 133/135.
210. *Ep.* 146, C 2: 67f., D 2: 353.
211. For the text of the *Moralia* itself, see *PG* 31. 700B–869C. English translation by Clarke, pp. 101–31. For the first Preface, *De iudicio dei*, see *PG* 31. 653A–676C. English translation by Clarke, pp. 77–89. Amand de Mendieta, *Ascèse*, pp. 152–58, 265–67, placed great weight on this piece. For the second Preface, *De fide*, see *PG* 31. 676C–692C. English translation by Clarke, pp. 90–99. *Scholion* 2 of the 'Vulgate' (one of the marginal comments, explained in detail in appendix 2, inscribed in the later compilation that brought together earlier scattered ascetic texts) describes how Basil 'sent away' ascetic material after he became a bishop, and mentions that this material included the *Moralia*; but that need not imply that he first *wrote* it after 370: so Gribomont, *Histoire*, pp. 159f.; and I remain unconvinced by the arguments of Léon Lèbe, 'S. Basile et ses *Règles Morales*'. An analysis of the two Prefaces to the *Moralia* (only one of which is clearly later) suggests an earlier period, with the added possibility that the *Moralia* proper could be even earlier than either of its Prefaces: Gribomont, *Histoire*, pp. 257f., together with p. 231 n. 27; and, for numbering, pp. 7f. See also Clarke, *Basil*, pp. 67f.
212. GNaz *Ep.* 6. See chapter 3, at n. 38.

community more generally. He was also aware of, and was adopting with some caution, the principles of Eustathius.[213]

Those possibilities should govern our attitude to this fascinating document. It betrays the conviction that the preacher has the task of summoning all people to a following of the Gospel (§ 70. 13). Yet it concerns also σπουδή, the dedicated seriousness that was taken to be the mark of the true Christian (§ 13). We are dealing first, therefore, with the proper process of engagement with Christianity, namely, conversion (§ 1),[214] which must display itself in action, in detachment from the world (§ 2), and in acceptance of the Great Commandment (§ 3).[215]

Other ideas, dominant also in the *Asceticon*, soon unfold in what follows. One should be bold in one's proclamation and acknowledgement of Jesus (ὁμολογία, § 6), which will demand above all obedience to his commandments (§§ 7, 29). One should place faith above argument (§ 8) and reject the παράδοσις ἀνθρώπων, the traditions that pass merely through human hands (§ 12). Community life is to be recommended, although one should not suppose too readily that the virtue of others will bring one salvation (§§ 15, 16). Sin, and the judgement of sin, are nevertheless everyone's affair, since the moral state of each will affect all (§§ 11, 15, 19). Scripture is the key to the understanding of one's own epoch (§ 17), and the criterion against which to measure the worthiness and effectiveness of other people's religious behaviour (§§ 28, 72). Obedience is mentioned, but chiefly as a guarantee of true illumination (§ 18).

The emphases picked out so far were entirely in keeping with the spirit, and often with the letter, of the *Asceticon*. They sum up in the broadest manner the thrust of Basil's later teaching on a range of topics, which we have already extracted in earlier chapters from his letters, treatises, and sermons. They acquire their cohesion in the *Moralia* by their relationship to the section on baptism (§ 20), which stresses in familiar terms that the sacrament should follow upon belief, leading to a restoration of one's true nature. The impression given is that the previous sections have commented on various principles that governed the lead-up to baptism—conversion, belief, the search for the company of others, the consciousness of sin, the discovery of Scripture, the longing for enlightenment. After the reference to baptism, Basil returned, in the sections that follow, to

213. Gribomont, *Histoire*, pp. 323f. For Eustathius, see chapters 3 and 4.

214. Compare the treatment of 'profession [ἐπάγγελμα]' in § 29. 1 (*PG* 31. 748B; tr. Clarke, p. 109), which was to display itself immediately at a practical level.

215. This reflects exactly the opening sentiments of R and F. Note, however, what is excluded: 'les idées de pénitence et d'isolement du monde', Gribomont, *Histoire*, p. 243.

some of those same principles, suggesting how they might be carried to
a new level by the baptismal experience itself; that is to say, by one's
formal incorporation into the body of the Church. The obligation to
proclaim Jesus, the act of ὁμολογία, is now provided with more detailed
associations—attachment to truth (§ 24), rejection of useless inquiry (§
25), avoidance of heresy (§§ 39–41)—and there are later, more detailed
instructions on the correct way to preach (§ 70. 23, 26f.).

Community life is treated at considerable length. Christians have,
in this matter, models of behaviour entirely proper to themselves, both
living and dead (§ 27). The community is a sacred place, created by the
willingness of its members to discover and follow the will of God (§ 30).
Members will be careful not to give each other offence, offering a carefully
controlled example (§§ 33, 34). In particular, one should be cautious not to
hurry forward in virtue too quickly, in such a way as to imply judgement
upon those less able (§§ 46, 70. 22); for in an important sense all are equals
(§ 45). The gifts of the Spirit displayed in the community have to be
exercised in harmony one with another (§ 60), a matter to be supervised by
the bishop especially (§ 70. 31). The resources of the community are to
be separated from the society around it with great care (§ 31) (suggesting
an élite consisting of those who really understood religion and virtue,
§ 36); but (hand in hand with that tendency towards élitist segregation)
Basil allowed that even a small level of achievement (even by a woman!)
was worthy of admiration (§ 37), and the obligations of hospitality and
generosity overruled, in any case, the sense of separateness (§§ 38, 48).
Christians exist for other people (§ 48) (and that was the principle, also, that
should govern the attitude of the bishop to his own vocation, § 70. 21). The
community hoped for had a clear history of its own. Christians of Basil's
generation had left behind them the era of promise and lived in a period
of open and serious dedication (§§ 42–44).[216] It was the accompanying
sense of progress and fulfilment that assured members of any Christian
community that God's providence still governed their lives, and that they
could look forward to the final resurrection (§§ 42f., 67f.).

Finally, the topic of authority is handled in terms that recall with
startling precision the prescriptions of the *Asceticon*. There is the same
vocabulary of trust and service, related to the word and grace of God

216. We have noted such a sense in the homilies already: see chapter 2, at nn. 91f., and
chapter 5, at nn. 188f. In *Hom.* 355. 2, the transition from ancestral lore to the ἀκρίβεια
of the Gospel is echoed exactly in the Preface to F—'Shall we not recall ourselves from
our accustomed manner of life to the careful life of the Gospel [πρὸς τὴν ἀκρίβειαν τοῦ
Εὐαγγελίου]?', *PG* 30. 892B; tr. Clarke, p. 146.

(§§ 56, 61); and ministers of that word are subject to the judgement of those whom they address (§ 70. 37). We have already had occasion to refer to some of those sections; and this is the moment to concentrate particularly on a long passage devoted to the proper conduct of the bishop and his clergy. It will be no surprise to find that Basil was already beginning to map out a system of responsibilities, as he watched for his own opportunity to seize upon a public role. Bishop and priest are discussed in exactly the same terms as those with authority in the *Asceticon*. We have mentioned the vocabulary of trust. Basil asserted also the priority of Scripture, when it came to formulating a personal view of discipline and morality. The clergy must teach by example; they must show affection and sympathy; they must practise humility and poverty. Every element of significance that we discovered in the *Asceticon* has its brief and succinct counterpart in the *Moralia*.

It ends with a summary that reinforces our impressions (§ 80). First, the Christian is defined by a series of images—a disciple, a sheep, a branch, a member, a bride, a temple, a living sacrifice, a child 'formed after the likeness of God, according to the measure granted to men', a light, salt, a word of life pointing others to the world to come (§ 80. 1–11).[217] Then the process of definition is applied to the preachers in the Church. They are apostles and stewards, heralds, 'a type or rule of piety [τύπον ἢ κανόνα τῆς εὐσεβείας]', an eye for the body, 'since they discern between good and evil, and guide the members of Christ', shepherds, doctors, fathers and nurses, fellow workers with God, planters and builders (§ 80. 12–21).[218] There follows a series of questions, asking what is the specific 'mark [τὸ ἴδιον]' of a Christian? The answers seem to be built around a formula of commitment and sacramental engagement—almost a vow or promise. Faith 'working by love' comes first, leading to a deep sense of conviction, which leads to a readiness to hold exclusively to the word of Scripture. Then comes acceptance of the Great Commandment, submission to baptism, the experience of communion (both sacramental and social), and the adoption of a moral life marked by more than (as Basil described it) the superficiality and dishonesty of the Pharisees. The process follows the structure of the *Moralia* more broadly, making one sharply aware that it is indeed a document of engagement, of commitment, which then proceeds to describe the fulfilment implied. It concludes by returning to fundamentals: love, the sense of God's presence, the expectation of judgement, the experience of nature's restoration in paradise.

217. Tr. Clarke (§ 80. 8), p. 128.
218. The quoted phrases are in § 80. 14 and 15; *PG* 31. 864D; tr. Clarke, p. 128.

There are a number of points to be made about this remarkable document. The chief one is that we have here a blueprint for the life of the Church as a whole.[219] The point is universally acknowledged: the *Moralia* provides us with the essence of Basil's ecclesiology. By studying the work as a unit, and by doing so when we have already seen Basil the churchman in action, and when we have studied his more specifically ascetic writings, a second point becomes equally clear: the Church is coterminous with the community of Christians committed to a serious response to the commands and recommendations of the Gospel. Not all may make that response; but all are called, and are called under the inspiration and supervision of bishops and clergy. So all the 'ascetic' reflections and recommendations that we find in Basil's works were designed to provide an inner and more enlivened dimension to carefully defended ecclesial structures. Whatever distinctions may have been accepted in time (between the dedicated and the indifferent), and whatever visibly separate institution may eventually have been thought necessary for the security of the former, there was at the root of Basil's thought an inseparable conjunction of visible Church and inner devotion, 'an idea bearing fruit in every department of life and spirit'.[220] A third point is perhaps the most stimulating of all. Basil had developed his image of the Christian life during those watchful years in Pontus, when he seemed to have withdrawn from all publicity and responsibility, but when in fact he was clearly at work defining the kind of Church over which he would eventually preside.

219. So we return to the emphasis of Fedwick, *Charisma*, p. 98: 'the most representative work of Basil dealing with the Christian church and its members'; but he may be too narrow in referring to it also as 'the manual for ascetics living in the world', p. 22. Holl, *Enthuisasmus*, pp. 166f., delivered crucial judgements. See also Clarke, *Basil*, p. 68. Amand de Mendieta, *Ascèse*, p. 13 n. 13, was broad at first—'un code de vie évangélique à l'usage de tous les chrétiens'.—but hesitated on pp. 134f. and by p. 158 was sure that only a monk could fulfil the work's prescriptions.

220. Clarke, *Basil*, p. 123.

CHAPTER VII

EUSTATHIUS AND OTHER FRIENDS

'The friend refrains from nothing, even that which gives pain'. So Basil recalled his Plutarch, writing to the sophist Leontius.[1] It was easy, perhaps, to be so stylishly allusive, when the truth of the dictum had yet to hit home. In a condescending and insensitive letter, written some years later to an allegedly offensive layman, Basil, now a bishop, betrayed more pain on his own part: 'for "forgetfulness of friends", and that "haughtiness which is engendered by power" [such, presumably, had been the phrases used by his correspondent], embraces all the crimes there are'. His own capacity for friendship, therefore, had now been called into question.[2] The two quotations sum up the irony of Basil's experience: that of a man dependent at all times on the affection of others, deeply hurt when they failed to match his expectations and demands, and frequently unaware of the pain he inflicted himself through indifference or conceit.

Friendship in his own life was rather like the curve of a rocket in the sky: initial vigour, brief explosions, and the longer and darker path of disappointment. His relationships with Gregory of Nazianzus and Eustathius of Sebaste gave him assurance and a sense of direction as he moved from the experiments and watchfulness of Pontus to the ecclesial commitments of Caesarea. Then followed bitterness and estrangement in regard to both men during the early 370s, an eruption of recrimination

---

1. *Ep.* 20, C 1: 51, D 1: 127. For the circumstances, see chapter 2, at n. 64, and chapter 4, at nn. 20, 25f.
2. *Ep.* 56, C 1: 143, D 1: 353.

and resentment that pressed ever outwards, to impact upon innumerable aspects of church life in Cappadocia and beyond. In his final years, Basil fell back upon important but less spectacular associations—with Amphilochius of Iconium, for example, and Eusebius of Samosata. By following that curve in his life, we discover at once a motive power at the heart of his personality and a clue to his constant and inevitable dissatisfaction.

That is not to attempt some fragile psychoanalysis. It is simply to admit that his view of the Church, his understanding of the moral programme proper to Christianity, and his mode of engagement with his audience all reflected convictions shared with others, convictions that in many cases others had encouraged in him. It is not enough to point to family background, to the character of education in his time, to long-term trends in the development of the Church or the ascetic life: Basil does not merely illustrate the larger scene. If it is at all possible, we should wish to know what drove him as an individual. His dependence upon friends reflected the combination of many habits, none of them mysterious or hidden from view. He drew those friends constantly into his own enterprises, even against their will. He used them as sounding boards for some of his most important theological ideas. He built up a network of contacts, acquaintances, relatives, clients, and of friends in the richest sense; a network that represented, for him at least, the universality of the social ideals and moral principles he held most dear. Such people were also talismans against his fears, his sense of danger and frustration, his dread of judgement, pain, victorious enemies, sheer pointlessness in life. They were the antidote to a recurrent suspicion that a shared life, an affectionate life, was beyond human power. Only around the notion of friendship do the themes of his biography so coherently cluster.

———————

The story has to begin with Gregory of Nazianzus. We have discussed already the major moments in their relations with each other: the years at Athens, the joys and doubts of Pontus, their first ordination to the priesthood, the circumstances of Basil's consecration in 370. The latter experience had already provoked some estrangement or had at least revealed divergent opinions on the nature of the episcopate.[3] Not long afterwards, a

3. See chapter 5, at nn. 46f., together with chapter 3, at nn. 25, 93.

major breakdown occurred in their friendship, one from which they never entirely recovered.[4]

The events did neither of them credit. Cappadocia as an administrative unit had been subdivided early in 372, Tyana being made the centre of the new western portion. The bishop of Tyana, Anthimus, promptly claimed metropolitan status within the new area, formerly under Basil's sway. Basil objected (largely, by Gregory's account, in the interests of status and revenue)[5] and tried to regain a degree of control by insinuating into sees both new and old candidates who would favour his own cause. It was in that connection that he set up his own brother as bishop of Nyssa; and, with the aid of his old ally Gregory the Elder, he more or less forcibly consecrated his friend bishop of the little hamlet of Sasima, 'a thoroughly deplorable and cramped little village', as Gregory later described it.[6]

We are entitled to be rather hard on Basil here. Quite apart from the fact that he was extraordinarily silly to have thought such conduct could gain him his end, he seems to have taken every step to prevent subsequent reconciliation. Gregory's behaviour was also odd, to say the least; but then, in relation to the priestly vocation generally, it had been before and would be again. Not only did he refuse to collaborate with Basil's ill-disciplined scheme: he ran away, characteristically, into the hills, pleading the demands of true philosophy, only returning to Nazianzus (he never went near Sasima!) at the entreaty of his father. Yet he never ceased to admire Basil and took several steps to smooth matters between them, with little obvious response.

Gregory's letters deserve careful reading. We are perfectly entitled to ask why he let himself be consecrated in the first place: there is a limit to what can be included under the heading of compulsion. Probably no other event tells us as much about his capacity for muddled thinking,

4. I have found useful the summary of events in Ruether, *Gregory*, pp. 35f. Stanislas Giet, *Sasimes: Une méprise de saint Basile*, has long been regarded as the classic account and is referred to in monograph after monograph. Certainly, although slim, the book summarizes and discusses the texts concerned and examines the relationship between the two men exhaustively; but it was designed to exonerate Basil, in the guise of confessional hagiography, rescuing him from temperamental and canonical improprieties that might reflect upon his sanctity, while indulging a Catholic and anachronistic anxiety about his attitudes to the bishop of Rome. More is to be gained by direct and easy reference to the primary material.

5. GNaz *De vita sua*, lines 460f.

6. GNaz *De vita sua*, line 442; tr. p. 89. Valens had first chosen Podandus as the centre of new Cappadocia II (which rules out any supposed collusion with a major episcopal rival of Basil), but Tyana quickly became a more obviously suitable choice. The division left Caesarea the only urban centre in Cappadocia I, which explains Basil's dependence on *chorepiscopoi* and his corresponding desire to make as firm a contact as possible with the urban (and episcopal) centres of Cappadocia II. See chapter 2, at nn. 66f., and chapter 5, at nn. 24f., 173f.

and about his remarkably subservient attitude to his own father. Basil may have taken advantage of those weaknesses, but he did not create them. Moreover, Gregory's sense of grievance was, at first, irresponsibly unrestrained. No doubt he had just brought himself round to accepting the implications of Basil's new role as a bishop, agreeing at last to offer him support against his critics, though sadly overestimating his friend's attachment to the philosophic life as he himself understood it.[7] Suddenly to bear the full brunt of Basil's episcopal pretentiousness was probably more than he could endure:

> As for you, play the man, be tough, drag everything into the service of your own glory, just as rivers in winter draw into themselves the smaller streams. Why honour friendship, that shared appreciation of goodness and piety? Why worry what sort of person you seem to be, behaving in this way? Content yourself with the solitude of your own spirit. As for me, I have gained one thing from your friendship: I shall not trust friends.[8]

Basil seems to have accused him, in reply, of not being willing to pull his weight as a churchman, of espousing instead ἀπραξία—little short of irresponsible idleness. Gregory decided to turn the accusation around, elevating the word virtually to the level of ecclesiological theory. Such 'inactivity', he wrote, should be the norm. If everyone threw themselves less into a hubbub of affairs, the Church might have fewer problems. In particular, the faith might suffer less of a strain from being made a mere instrument in the cause of this or that petty victory—a very specific barb.[9]

At that point, Gregory literally headed for the hills. By the time he returned to Nazianzus, a different atmosphere seems to have developed. Anthimus of Tyana was willing to open negotiations with the still distant Basil. He had failed to wean the two Gregorys, father and son, away from their allegiance to the bishop of Caesarea. He even accused them of 'Basilism [Βασιλισμός]', suggesting that, in spite of his sense of grievance, Gregory had taken Basil's side.[10] As a result, a degree of harmony was achieved between the rival metropolitans.[11] Basil seems to have acknowledged Gregory's part, recognizing that he deserved greater leniency. When Gregory wrote to him, not long after, reporting criticisms of his teaching

7. GNaz *Ep.* 47. 2f.
8. GNaz *Ep.* 48. 9f.; ed. Gallay, 1: 63.
9. GNaz *Ep.* 49. 1–3.
10. GNaz *Ep.* 50 (Βασιλισμός, § 5).
11. Until a subsequent and unrelated dispute arose between them. See *Ep.* 122—'he who long ago made his peace with us', C 2: 27, D 2: 253—and *Ep.* 210. 5.

on the Holy Spirit, he was unwilling to make any formal response, even in a form that Gregory could use more privately;[12] but he does seem to have warmed to his friend's politeness—expressed, for example, in the admission that 'from the very beginning, and now, I have regarded you as my leader in life, as my teacher in matters of doctrine, indeed as everything gracious that one might say of another'. He made the point that they ought to collaborate more than they had done recently.[13] Gregory, while still showing signs of pique, agreed to do so.[14] Eighteen months or so after the event, probably during his mother's final illness, he felt able to write a perfectly friendly letter to Basil, asking for his prayers, and promising a visit.[15]

That period of cautious re-engagement is important. It would be wrong to imagine that so long-standing and fundamental a friendship could be destroyed completely, even by insensitive ineptitude. It was Gregory, however, who did most to heal the breach; and that willingness allows us to interpret more justly the subsequent rumblings of indignation that surface here and there in his writings. What the whole incident had made clear was that the two men had drawn apart in their interpretation of the priestly vocation and, correspondingly, of the philosophic life. For Basil the twin aspirations were compatible, in that within the priesthood itself the most precious components of φιλοσοφία could reach fulfilment. For Gregory there remained a constant sense of divergence, in that the priesthood, 'this mean and treacherous mart of souls', presented a constant threat to the philosophic way of life.[16]

The rumblings of indignation are themselves in need of careful reading. To Amphilochius of Iconium, shortly after his consecration, Gregory was party to suggesting that they had 'suffered the same tyranny at the hands of common friends, whom you think of only as benefactors'. Perhaps Amphilochius thought Basil had done Gregory a favour.[17] It would have been about the same time, in his funeral oration for his father, that Gregory made his comment about the 'mart of souls', still bemoaning his

12. That was certainly what Gregory wanted: 'so that we might have these resources to use against those who argue with us', Ep. 58. 14; ed. Gallay, 1: 76. The incident concerned may well have prompted in Basil thoughts that led eventually to the composition of the De spiritu sancto: See below, at nn. 146f.

13. Ep. 71. 2. See GNaz Ep. 58. 1; ed. Gallay, 1: 73.

14. GNaz Ep. 59.

15. GNaz Ep. 60.

16. GNaz Orat. 18. 37—according to the translation, p. 152; but, in the phrase τῇ φορτικῇ καὶ ἐπιβούλῳ τῶν ψυχῶν ἀγορᾷ, we should read something akin to 'burdensome, and liable to lay one open to the devices of others'.

17. GNaz Ep. 63. 6; ed. Gallay, 1: 83, as from Gregory the Elder.

elevation just at the time 'when I was disgusted with the evils of this life, and filled with a passionate desire for solitude, . . . when I strove eagerly to avoid the surge and dust of public life and escape to a place of safety'.[18] Events, of course, were still fresh in his mind. Once Basil had died, it was entirely proper that Gregory should have seen the antagonism of 372 within the context of his friend's life as a whole: not to be exaggerated but nevertheless a revealing incident. Strikingly enough, in his immediate grief, revealed to us in a letter to Gregory of Nyssa, Gregory seems to have said much less about Basil himself than about the demands and supports of φιλοσοφία in such circumstances, about the gap Basil had left at Caesarea, and about the way in which his brother might now stand in his stead: 'Seeing him in yourself, as in a mirror fine and clear, we shall think we have him still'.[19] Yet Basil remained in his eyes 'a spiritual brother'.[20] In his poem De vita sua, written probably in 382, there does seem to be enduring bitterness. He wrote of 'the high-handed style you acquired with the throne', suggesting that the experience gave the lie to all that had lain between them during the previous years:

> Athens, our studies together, our sharing of root and hearth, the single spirit animating two people, the marvel of Greece, the pledge that we made that we would cast aside absolutely the world and live the coenobitic life for God, placing our words in the service of the one wise Word! This was the outcome of it all![21]

But Gregory was thinking more about the shape of his own life; and the harmony he recalled was depicted as coming to an end around 360, rather than suddenly in 372. When it came to giving shape to Basil's life, in his funeral oration, he was more balanced and gracious. He placed most of the blame for the estrangement on the shoulders of Anthimus, mentioning in particular his greed; and he actually praised Basil for multiplying bishoprics in the interests of the orthodox party. Certainly, he mentioned 'his strangeness and distrust toward me, a cause of pain which not even time has effaced'; but he admitted that he himself had been no more than an 'appendage [πάρεργον]' to the enterprise, and that the Sasima incident was the 'one thing I cannot approve [i.e., the only thing, ἓν τοῦτο]'. He was willing enough to conclude that Basil 'recognised the respect due to friendship and he disregarded

18. GNaz Orat. 18. 37, tr. p. 152.
19. GNaz Ep. 76. 5; ed. Gallay, 1: 94.
20. GNaz Ep. 80. 1; ed. Gallay, 1: 103.
21. GNaz De vita sua, lines 388f.; tr. p. 88; and line 476, tr. p. 90.

it only where the honor of God had prior claim and when he had to esteem the object of our hopes as more important than what he set aside'.[22]

In spite of all that he owed to his friendship with Gregory, to his example, advice, and support, Basil felt that he was the dominant party in their relationship, and that he was entitled to adapt that relationship to the changing circumstances of his own career without any sense of injustice or threat. It was quite otherwise in regard to his association with Eustathius of Sebaste. Here was a man who really had inspired Basil at the deepest level, shaping his sense of churchmanship. The feeling that his model had betrayed him cut far more dangerously close to the heart than any disagreement with Gregory could ever have done.

The course of their dispute is confused, interwoven with other preoccupations.[23] Basil's disenchantment with Eustathius focussed on his Trinitarian theology, and in particular on his attitude to the Holy Spirit, whose divinity he seemed to oppose. Misgivings probably began to surface in 372, adding to the distress of opposition from Anthimus and Gregory. Basil did not, however, break with Eustathius entirely until the middle of 375. The delay caused an important rift between himself and two other figures of consequence: Meletius, the exiled bishop of Antioch, and Theodotus, the bishop of Nicopolis in Armenia Minor. Basil felt an increasing need to retain the support of these two men; and that, in the end, may have done most to steel him against his old mentor. At the same time, he was just as often the object of suspicion, the defensive party—a point he took pains to play down.

In 371, relations between master and disciple were amicable still. Eustathius had written to Basil, asking how he was standing up under the pressure of his Arian opponents; and Basil in reply referred to Eustathius still as a champion in the struggle. There was every reason why he should have recalled with satisfaction the part that Eustathius had played in the years before his return to Asia in 367, leaving Lampsacus to plead the cause against the Anomoeans at the court of the new emperor of the West,

---

22. GNaz Orat. 43. 58f., PG 36. 573AB, tr. p. 77.
23. In this as in other matters, I have found particularly useful Yves Courtonne, Un Témoin du IVe siècle oriental: Saint Basile et son temps d'après sa correspondance.

Valentinian, and taking his place among those bishops who returned with support from Liberius, bishop of Rome.[24]

Then, suddenly, Basil found himself at a disadvantage. Meletius of Antioch (who was living in exile in Getasa) and Theodotus of Nicopolis demanded a visit from the bishop of Caesarea, 'desiring that some amendment might be formed of the things which now trouble them'. They suggested making use of the annual gathering in honour of the local martyrs at nearby Phargamos.[25] What provoked this turn of events is perhaps revealed in another letter to Eustathius himself, which Basil must have written around the same time. He described how two clerics, Basil and Sophronius, the first of whom 'I received from your Reverence as a guard of my life [ἀντὶ φυλακτηρίου τῆς ἐμῆς ζωῆς]', had left Caesarea, probably for Sebaste, laying charges against Basil connected partly with some 'fault', partly with his interpretation of asceticism.[26] The 'fault' was almost certainly to do with his theology of the Holy Spirit and would have involved an accusation of Sabellian tendencies.[27] Basil and Sophronius seem to have been associates of Eustathius in former years, whom our Basil had welcomed to Caesarea for the help they could offer him in setting up the *Basileiados* and a local 'Eustathian' programme generally. Such a combination of misunderstandings and soured memories would have made the subsequent collapse of friendship doubly hurtful, since it publicly involved other close colleagues, and not just Eustathius alone.[28]

On his way to face his accusers, Basil held a meeting with Eustathius. (He reported events to the *comes* Terentius at the end of the summer of 373, and it is widely agreed that the meeting and its sequel took place

24. *Ep.* 79. He ended the letter with what might have seemed later an ironic touch: 'So far we have fearlessly sustained every attack through God's mercy, which is blessing us with the assistance of the Spirit, and through Him has strengthened our weakness', C 1: 181, D 2: 89. For the circumstances, see chapter 4, at n. 17.

25. *Ep.* 95, C 1: 208, D 2: 155/157—actually dispatched to his friend Eusebius of Samosata via Eustathius, showing that Basil was still willing to keep in touch with his 'most reverend brother and fellow-worker'. Courtonne dated the letter to 372. So did Fedwick in *Charisma*, p. 145, but changed his mind without explanation in *Basil*, 1: 16 (there 373), perhaps in relation to his opinions about *Ep.* 98 and 99 (see below). Gain, *Église*, p. 394, opted for 373. Note also his comments there on Phargamos, at the end of § 11. It seems unlikely that Basil ever made such a journey on any occasion separate from his visit to Armenia in 373.

26. *Ep.* 119, C 2: 24, D 2: 241/243.

27. We must place the incident in the wider context of opposition to Basil in the period following his consecration, and of the accusations brought against him by an acquaintance of Gregory of Nazianzus: see GNaz *Ep.* 58; n. 12 above; and chapter 5, at nn. 44f.

28. See Gribomont, 'Eustathe', *Dictionnaire de spiritualité*, col. 1709. By the time Basil came to write *Ep.* 223. 3, he saw Basil and Sophronius as 'given to us as sentinels and spies of our life, under pretext forsooth of assistance and affectionate communion', C 3: 11, D 3: 297. See chapter 5, at n. 65.

during a visit he made to Armenia in that year.)[29] A declaration of orthodoxy was drafted, which Eustathius was persuaded to sign.[30] There was already proof, however, that Basil was also 'on trial': one Poimenius 'began vigorously to press the opposing doctrine against us'; and Basil was obliged to refute 'the charges upon the strength of which they seemed to accuse us'.[31] The outcome of the confrontation appears, nevertheless, to have been satisfactory, to Basil at least: Eustathius made sufficient avowal of orthodoxy, and he himself cleared his name with his Armenian opponents.

What happened next is impossible to decide. The planned meeting with Theodotus and others appears to have been cancelled; but whether that was due to second thoughts on their part or caution, even pique, on Basil's remains obscure.[32] Matters, in any case, were hurried forward by their own momentum. Basil began to have doubts, or at least acquiesced in the doubts of others, agreeing that Eustathius should be questioned further.[33] He suspected dishonesty in the signed declaration of orthodoxy

29. *Ep.* 99. The journey will be discussed further in the next chapter. Fedwick, *Charisma*, p. 145, and *Basil*, 1: 16, followed Hauschild in dating the letter to 373. Gain, *Église*, wanted it late in the year, which seems necessary. Courtonne, however, favoured 372, both in his edition, 1: 214, and in *Témoin*, pp. 184f. It has to be admitted that there are difficulties in placing all these events in 373. Possible solutions will emerge below and in chapter 8.

30. The document has been preserved in Basil's correspondence, *Ep.* 125, and the occasion is mentioned in *Ep.* 99. 2. See also *Ep.* 98. 2 and 244. 2.

31. *Ep.* 99. 2, C 1: 215, D 2: 175. This was not, as we have said, the Poimenius whom Basil later appointed bishop of Satala; see chapter 1, at n. 14, and chapter 8, at n. 62. In a later account, he wrote of his wish to 'stop the mouths of those who were slandering us', *Ep.* 244. 2, C 3: 75, D 2: 453.

32. The cancellation of a 'synod' was reported to Terentius, perhaps the proposed assembly at Phargamos: *Ep.* 99. 2, C 1: 216, D 2: 177. Basil referred also to a 'second synod', to be held at a place described as 'ours' (meaning, probably, that its bishop was sympathetic): *Ep.* 244. 2, C 3: 75, D 3: 453/455. Finally, to Eusebius of Samosata, he mentioned 'a passing invitation' from Nicopolis, which he had turned down, partly because Eusebius was not going to be there, partly because the people at Nicopolis had been offhand in their approach. That invitation had been to a 'festival [πανηγύρις]', which recalls the planned gathering at Phargamos; but Basil explained his failure to attend in different terms and mentioned his meeting with Eustathius as occurring afterwards: *Ep.* 98. 1, C 1: 212, D 2: 165/167. (Fedwick, *Basil*, 1: 16, dated this letter to 373; Courtonne to 372, both in his edition, 1: 211, and in *Témoin*, p. 184.) The letter to Terentius proceeds to confuse matters further. Basil described how Theodotus had invited him to come from Getasa to Nicopolis, had spurned him on arrival, and had forced him to go on his way—all after the meeting with Eustathius, and after the abortive 'synod'. This phase of his account is introduced with the words 'after this, therefore, when the necessity of a journey to Armenia fell upon us', as if to suggest that everything mentioned hitherto had taken place before Basil had set out on that journey: *Ep.* 99. 3, C 1: 216f., D 2: 177/179. It seems impossible to unravel these contradictions.

33. He hinted as much in the letter to Terentius, although he gave no indication there (in late 373) that the doubts had been acted upon: *Ep.* 99. 3, C 1: 216f., D 2: 177/179.

he had earlier extracted: he now demanded a more 'succinct' statement.[34] Someone in Sebaste seems to have produced fresh evidence of Eustathius's opinions, laying bare 'the festering ulcer' of his 'evil doctrine', and hoping to attract Basil's 'ecclesiastical attention'.[35] Eustathius did not oblige. By the summer of 374, Basil appears to have reached a new accord with Theodotus, to whom he denounced his former hero in bitter tones: 'He set forth ... a creed to which only an Arius could subscribe or a real disciple of Arius [γνήσιος μαθητής]'; 'In truth were we more strongly confirmed in our separation from him, ... [for] a man who has been nourished on perverted doctrines [ὁ ἐν διαστρόφοις δόγμασι συντραφείς] [cannot] rid himself of the evil of heresy [τὸ κακὸν τῆς αἱρέσεως]'.[36]

Such statements were, of course, *ad hominem*, addressed to a desired ally. They remind us that the dispute revolved around more than Basil's personal association with Eustathius, deep and long-lasting though that may have been. Eustathius had brought accusations of his own, criticizing Basil for his friendship with Apollinarius of Laodicea, regarded by that time as a leading exponent of the Sabellian tradition. Basil was forced to admit the broader doctrinal implications of the whole affair; and that was why he began to associate Eustathius's views on the Holy Spirit with the doctrines of Arius and his followers.[37] The extension of the debate persisted in his climactic letter to Eustathius, written in 375.[38] The fact that he had been an object of suspicion, that he had found it necessary to work carefully with Armenian bishops and with the exiled Meletius, and that

34. Σύντομον ... λόγον: *Ep.* 128. 2, C 2: 38, D 2: 279, written to Eusebius of Samosata, probably in 373 also. Ironically, it was in this same letter that he warned against too heavy a pressure being brought to bear upon those who seemed in error.

35. *Ep.* 138. 2, C 2: 56, D 2: 323.

36. *Ep.* 130. 1, C 2: 43, D 2: 293. The 'last piece of audacity', inspiring 'a chill of horror and a complete aversion for the man', was Eustathius's decision to 're-ordain certain clerics'. 'I do not recall', continued Basil, 'having ever received such deep grief in my soul as at this moment, when I have heard of the confusion in the ecclesiastical laws': § 2, C 2: 43, D 2: 295. Gregory of Nazianzus would no doubt have had his comment to make on such a reduction of friendship to canonical etiquette. Suggestions about the date of this letter are widely divergent. Fedwick, *Charisma*, p. 148, first opted for 375, following Loofs and others, but then changed to the summer of 374, *Basil*, 1: 16. Courtonne, in his edition, 1: 42, suggested 373, which would be difficult.

37. The association affected in the end even letters Basil wrote on the subject to the bishops of the West. Other examples: *Ep.* 212. 2, 250, 251. 2f., 263. 2f—addressed to a layman (the 'truth-loving soul possessed of a sound judgment' discussed in chapter 5, at n. 139), a bishop (thus reinforcing the vigour of *Ep.* 244), a whole community (giving almost a complete history of the Arian controversy), and the West (showing how the more general account became clearer to him with time). Such was the careful breadth of his defence: on which more is to follow, both here and in chapter 8. See also *Ep.* 216.

38. *Ep.* 223. There is no dispute about the date.

he had felt a need to make meticulous reports to lay and civil figures all coloured the tone of the letter and made it much more than the aggrieved outpouring of a betrayed friend. Considerable time was taken in refuting the charge of association with Apollinarius. Basil's more general plea was that he had been theologically consistent throughout his life.[39] Eustathius, on the other hand (and this would become the theme of several letters), had shifted his position considerably over the years, even while trying to disguise the fact.

Basil, as we know, was taking the opportunity to place new constructions on his own life, not to mention the history of the times. He had come to realize, not least in the face of other people's suspicions, that he had adopted a less than conveniently defined theological position during the years since the synod at Constantinople in 360. It was now necessary to revise the account of those years, in such a way as to make certain distinctions clearer. As in his dealings with Gregory of Nazianzus, personal loyalties, even when they sprang from the recognition of fundamental influences in his life, could be sacrificed in the interest of church politics. In the process, his friendship with Eustathius was reduced to a 'semblance of intimacy [τι ... σχῆμα τῆς πρὸς αὐτοὺς συνηθείας]'. He had been misled, thinking that 'lowliness of dress was sufficient evidence of lowliness of mind': for, as he reflected, 'the secret thoughts of each of us are unknown'.[40] So he justified his averred blindness at the time. 'I did not even admit', he continued, 'the accusations about their teachings, although many had insisted that they had no orthodox conceptions about God, but being made disciples by the champion of the present heresy, they were covertly disseminating his teachings'. This sudden discovery of an erroneous past arouses one's suspicions. Basil was suggesting a long-standing motive for Eustathius's current opposition (for he had to be presented as the instigator of the rupture). The business about Apollinarius had been dragged in, he said, only so that Eustathius's party could ingratiate themselves with 'those now in power'.[41]

The 'rewriting of history' persisted throughout the coming year.[42] Basil sought allies even among the friends of Eustathius himself, bemoaning the effects of the rift on his own capacity for trust and affection generally. 'Men of every character', he wrote, 'were regarded with suspicion by me, and

39. See chapter 1, at nn. 69f., 75f.
40. *Ep.* 223. 3, C 3: 11f., D 3: 295/297.
41. *Ep.* 223. 7, C 3: 17, D 3: 311. A later allusion suggests that Basil had in mind the Arian party at Antioch—yet another reminder that his personal dispute was being played out against a wider background of ecclesiastical politics: *Ep.* 226. 2f.
42. See, for example, *Ep.* 224, to a priest, Genethlius.

I thought that the virtue of charity did not exist in man's nature. . . . For if the man who seemed to have kept watch over himself from childhood to late old age was so easily enraged on pretexts so trivial, ... what was I to conjecture about the rest?'[43]   More important, of course, was his varying success in cultivating the support of Eustathius's opponents. When Theodotus died in 375, Basil tried to secure the see for his own cause by transferring Euphronius from Colonia.[44] The notorious *vicarius* Demosthenes, meanwhile, with support from Valens no doubt, strove to maintain an Arian alliance among the churches in the same area.[45] Basil does not seem to have made up his mind about Demosthenes' motives, although he had few doubts about their effect: 'Whether the man is at heart inclined to heresy I am not sure (for I think that he is inexperienced in all reasoning, and has neither interest nor practice in such things . . .), but yet he is friendly to heretics, and . . . full of hate toward us'.[46] It soon became clear that Euphronius had been thrust aside in favour of the Arian Fronto, and his supporters were forced out of Nicopolis and obliged to worship in the open air.[47] That was a victory, not only for Demosthenes and the Arian party generally but also for the supporters of Eustathius, who had taken Fronto's side.[48] The *vicarius* certainly knew that Basil was the influential enemy to be dealt with: it can be no accident that precisely at that moment he attacked Gregory of Nyssa on a charge of financial malpractice.[49] In Nicopolis itself, Basil could do no more than exhort the local Christians to optimism in the light of history, a history of ultimately fruitless persecution. Meanwhile he asked his friend Eusebius for 'more intense prayer on behalf of the churches'.[50] At Sebaste, victory came too late for Basil personally. Eustathius appears to have died around 377, which must have brought relief to Basil's supporters, of whom there had been a number in the city.[51] Later, the see was administered by Basil's

---

43. *Ep.* 244. 4, to Patrophilus of Aegae: C 3: 77f., D 3: 459. See n. 31. The same point was admitted to Eustathius himself in *Ep.* 223. 3. See also the account given in *Ep.* 226.

44. We have already examined his letters on that subject, although from a different perspective: see chapter 5, at nn. 145f.

45. See *Ep.* 227. For Demosthenes, see chapter 5, at n. 160, and appendix 1, at nn. 2 and 6. *Ep.* 229 shows Basil attempting to stiffen morale at Nicopolis precisely against such pressure. Note also the attack on ἄρχοντες in *Ep.* 230, C 3: 35.

46. *Ep.* 237. 2, C 3: 56, D 3: 409.

47. *Ep.* 238, 240.

48. See *Ep.* 237. 2.

49. See chapter 5, at n. 184.

50. See *Ep.* 240. 1, 241 (C 3: 65, D 3: 427 for the last quotation). *Ep.* 246 and 247 add little. For a succinct account, see Courtonne, *Témoin*, pp. 120f.

51. *Ep.* 138. 2. They had still been a sufficiently significant force in 376 to attract further vengeful attentions from Demosthenes, *Ep.* 237. 2.

two brothers, Gregory and Peter, Peter eventually becoming resident bishop.[52]

When we bring together the two sets of events examined so far—the estrangement from Gregory of Nazianzus and the breakdown of all relations with Eustathius of Sebaste—an ominous shift in Basil's conduct is easy to observe. It is not just that he felt happy to repudiate and reinterpret the past: his priorities changed also, when it came to balancing personal relationships against the interests of churches generally and of his own status as a bishop. Bonds between people were put now at the service of bonds between churches. The shift was not accompanied, however, by happiness or success: the pursuit of so heartless a policy coincided with a growing sense of failure and personal inadequacy.[53]

Does the problematic association with Apollinarius, exploited by Eustathius, throw any additional light on Basil's changing attitudes? Was he another friend of significance, later cast aside with skilful apology? We have discussed already the evidence for their acquaintance, during Basil's first ventures into ecclesiastical politics. The later criticism he faced as a result meant simply that positions adopted in the *Contra Eunomium*, and during the period that witnessed its production, had come back to haunt him.[54]

By the time of the controversy with Eustathius, Apollinarius had come to be regarded as a proponent of Sabellianism—that tendency in Trinitarian theology that overemphasized the unity of God and therefore undervalued the distinction of persons that had come to be characteristic of orthodox thought. The imputation was largely false (such would now be the scholarly consensus); and opponents were taking up arms for other reasons.[55] Basil, like anyone seriously engaged by the Trinitarian issue, had for a long time taken Sabellius into account and unhesitatingly rejected any attempt to blur the distinction of persons. Apollinarius would have shared that view: he was more concerned to support and develop what he regarded as an Athanasian insistence on a unity of substance.

52. For useful details, see May, 'Chronologie'.
53. See chapter 5, at nn. 73f., 92f., and chapter 3, at nn. 107f.
54. See chapter 4, at nn. 18f., 95f.
55. In what follows I have depended heavily on Prestige, *Basil and Apollinaris*, and his 'Apollinaris: or, Divine Irruption'.

So there was no reason why Basil, however cautious, should have been suspicious of Apollinarius on those grounds—certainly not at the time he succeeded Basil's old patron, George of Laodicea, after the 360 synod at Constantinople. Indeed, at that time, Basil had felt it was dangerous to be too forceful in one's opposition to Sabellius, since one might become exposed as a result to errors at the other end of the theological spectrum, where subordination of Son to Father, for example, could play into Arian hands.[56]

Basil became much more obviously anxious about Marcellus of Ancyra.[57] Marcellus had not been able to occupy his see since 339; but he did not die until (at the earliest) 374 and thus remained for a long time a thorn in the side of several parties. In the face of much eastern suspicion, he attracted support in the West. The strength of feeling against him elsewhere might seem odd. He maintained to the end, and with some justice, that he was a staunch supporter of the Nicene position. His opponents felt, however, that his exaggerated opposition to the Arians had carried him too far in a Sabellian direction (which had been indirectly the excuse for his first exile in 336); and it is true that he did question the need for a *permanent* distinction of persons, after the redemption of the human race had been achieved and the temporal order had passed away. His successor, Basil of Ancyra, espoused a more moderate position; and this was happily adopted by our own Basil in his early church career. He did not feel that either he or his namesake was moving, in their moderation, towards the Arian parties, but simply making it more likely that the decrees of Nicaea would win eventual acceptance.

How quickly Basil developed more precise misgivings about Marcellus is difficult to judge. His willingness to identify with the somewhat different emphases of Basil of Ancyra might suggest an early date. His own more sharpened opposition, however, does not surface in his writings until as late, perhaps, as 371, when he began to make contact with Athanasius. His indignation was reserved in particular for what he regarded as the shortsightedness of the support that Marcellus had gained among western churchmen.[58] Very quickly the presumed heretic became a *bête*

---

56. *Ep.* 9. 2: it was enough to say simply that Father and Son were οὐ ταὐτὸν τῷ ὑποκειμένῳ, C 1: 38. Note the associated fear of Origenism; and see Prestige, *Basil and Apollinaris*, pp. 17f.

57. See Lienhard, 'Basil of Caesarea'.

58. *Ep.* 69. 2. See also *Ep.* 239. 2. Following the death of Athanasius of Ancyra in 371, Basil had already feared the possibility of new divisions: see *Ep.* 30 to Eusebius of Samosata. The flattery of his consolation addressed to the city, *Ep.* 29, contrasts with the bitterness of *Ep.* 25, which hints at some dispute over his *Contra Eunomium.*

noire pursued by Basil in letter after letter.[59] Sermons also began to address the Sabellian issue.[60] In the very declaration of orthodoxy agreed upon by Eustathius and Basil, Marcellus was singled out for attack. The point was made that supporters of Sabellius had taken new heart from the formulae of Nicaea, allowing them to suggest doctrines that were never intended. That was why Basil felt that Nicaea needed further precise interpretation. In that sense he now felt forced to carry one stage further his cautious adhesion to Nicaea in younger days; to move from understatement to the more explicit exploration of consequences. So he would make more obvious, to us at least, his previous willingness to regard Nicaea as conveniently vague rather than ruthlessly exclusive.[61]

The sense that Nicaea was no longer enough lasted several years, well past the high point of the confrontations that had prompted it.[62] The generosity of his position in the early 360s still needed defence; and the easiest defence seemed to be redefinition. Anxiety about Marcellus became interwoven with other issues; and those included Apollinarius, now presented as the chief exponent of a new Sabellianism. 'Since by his facility in writing he has a tongue that suffices him for every subject, he has', Basil wrote, with solemn disdain, 'filled the world with his books'. Old bugbears were rehearsed as a result: 'human arguments', 'innovations', 'inquiries and contentious investigations', as well as an overall imputation of Judaism.[63] To allies in Egypt, Basil had even more to say and betrayed how the matter had taken on in his mind the guise of a breakdown in personal relations. Once again, we have the 'multitude of books', the 'subtlety of sophisms', and 'innovations'; but now there was also an admission that Apollinarius

> has distressed us so much the more in that in the beginning he seemed to be one of us [ὅσῳ ἔδοξεν εἶναι ἐξ ἡμῶν τὸ ἐξ ἀρχῆς]. For while any suffering inflicted by an open enemy, even if it is excessive in painfulness,

---

59. *Ep.* 125. 1, 207. 1, 263. 5, 265. 3, 266. 1.

60. *Hom.* 321 (especially § 2), 341 passim, and 343 (especially § 4). I would support, for *Hom.* 341, a date around 372, rather than Bernardi's late suggestion (see Fedwick, *Charisma*, p. 153): its treatment of the Holy Spirit looks more like a build-up towards the *De spiritu sancto* than something subsequent to so assured a formulation.

61. See *Ep.* 125. 3. For the background, see chapter 4, at nn. 8f.

62. See *Ep.* 52, esp. § 4, dated to 376 by Hermann Dörries, *De spiritu sancto: Der Beitrag des Basilius zum Abschluß des trinitarischen Dogmas*, p. 115 n. 1. We should probably associate this letter with *Ep.* 51, that is to say, with difficulties surrounding Dianius, which means, further, that Basil was still defending positions adopted in 360.

63. *Ep.* 263. 4, C 3: 124f., D 4: 97/99. Part of his anxiety may have been related to Apollinarius's potential influence as an instructor of the clergy: see G. L. Prestige, *Fathers and Heretics: Six Studies in Dogmatic Faith with Prologue and Epilogue*, p. 213.

is somehow endurable to the sufferer, . . . to experience injury at the hands
of one of like mind and a close friend [παρ' ὁμοψύχου καὶ οἰκείου], this is
altogether hard to bear and admits of no consolation.[64]

Basil had plenty to say of a theological nature also—not least about the supposedly Judaizing tendency of Apollinarius's exegesis[65]—but the sentence
just quoted reduces the matter to personal grievance. As with Eustathius
and others, friendship had been soured by deceit and betrayal.

And it is true that there was more than theological disagreement at
stake. It would be facile to suggest (as Basil sometimes did) that Apollinarius simply let drop his guard, betrayed a long-nurtured error, and thus
outraged those of a more orthodox and steady disposition. What rankled
equally, if not more, was that he had begun to involve himself closely in
the tangled affairs of nearby Antioch.[66] There he had dared to teach.[67]
There he had supported Paulinus and opposed Meletius and his friend
Eusebius of Samosata. That would have been enough to arouse Basil's ire.
Perhaps equally humiliating, Apollinarius might have seemed less eccentric than Basil himself, supporting the cause of Nicaea, of Athanasius, and
of their local champions. Nor was his sympathy for Paulinus unnatural:
he occupied a similar position in Laodicea, where he was opposed by the
more moderate Pelagius.[68] Apollinarius was above all consistent. His
attachment to Athanasius had induced him, many years before, to wean
Basil away from his confusions towards a clearer support for Nicaea.[69]
Basil was being forced, in other words, to face up to the fact that it was
he who had shifted ground, and at the expense of old associations.

Overlap with affairs at Antioch was not the only complication. The
Sabellian anxiety was also connected with developments at Neocaesarea
(a sensitive venue for Basil, of course, enshrining the traditions of Gregory
Thaumaturgus, and presided over by his own distant relative Atarbius).
Just after the initial phase of confrontation with Eustathius, Basil accused

64. *Ep.* 265. 2, C 3: 128f., D 4: 107/109.
65. Which tended, perhaps, only towards a different symbolism of final fulfilment. This
letter will be discussed further in chapter 8, at nn. 191f.
66. Prestige, *Fathers and Heretics*, p. 199; *Basil and Apollinaris*, pp. 13f.
67. So Jerome informs us, *Ep.* 84. 3.
68. Not surprisingly, Pelagius was Basil's preferred ally, *Ep.* 254—a circumspect little
note, nevertheless.
69. As he, Apollinarius, understood it. See his letter, numbered as *Ep.* 364 in the Basil
collection (this correspondence will be discussed more fully below at nn. 93f.). In the matter
of dating (namely, 363 or later), I am inclined to follow De Riedmatten, 'Correspondance',
rather than Henry Chadwick, in his introduction to Prestige, *Basil and Apollinaris*, p. viii. See
also below, at n. 90.

Atarbius of Sabellianism, albeit with cautious grace.[70] One suspects the move was designed in part to bolster himself against the accusations of heresy we have already seen launched by the supporters of Eustathius. Over the next year or so, he subjected Neocaesarea to further instruction, related to a variety of preoccupations.[71] The two letters concerned, written to the clergy and to 'the learned [λογιωτάτοις]'[72] in the city, are masterly examples of Basil's ability to interrelate his own misgivings and the indignation of others. We have noted elsewhere his allusions to nearby relatives, to his early ascetical efforts, and to the memory and teaching of Gregory.[73] He was, in addition, critical of the Eustathian party—'certain newsmongers, fabricators of falsehood, hired for this very purpose';[74] he brought the Sabellian issue into the centre of the discussion; and he mentioned both the Antiochene schism and the evil influence of Marcellus. As matters unfolded, Basil obviously indulged his suspicions of Apollinarius within a broad polemical framework.

There was an even more specific connection between Apollinarius and the Eustathian affair. At precisely the time Basil was beginning to feel a clean break was called for, and a more thorough pursuit of the heretic, Eustathius and his party produced a new weapon in their struggle against him. The rather contorted events unfolded in three stages. Basil wrote first to Meletius, probably in 375, making reference to 'a document [σύνταγμα]' emanating from Sebaste, on the basis of which the Eustathians had begun to level fresh accusations against him.[75] He must have had precise information about the document (although, as we shall see in a moment, he may not actually have seen it). And he did not believe it was a forgery. His opponents at Sebaste, however, were suggesting that Basil was its 'author'. He was confident it had been written by Apollinarius, whom he described as 'approaching [ὡς προσεγγίζοντος] the impiety of Sabellius'.[76] One asks, of course, how he could have known: his defence involved an admission (hardly surprising) that he was familiar with Apollinarius's ideas.

---

70. *Ep.* 126. There is the now familiar confusion over dating, Courtonne opting for 373, while Fedwick followed Hauschild in favour of 375. There had already been some anxious coolness in 373, as revealed in *Ep.* 65: Atarbius seems to have been suspicious and withdrawn.

71. *Ep.* 207, 210.

72. The word occurs only in the later title but represents accurately the character of the contents, addressed to an educated lay élite.

73. See chapter 1, at nn. 36f., 66f.

74. *Ep.* 210. 1, C 2: 190, D 3: 197.

75. *Ep.* 129. 1. For this and what follows, C 2: 39f., D 2: 283f.

76. Basil certainly exaggerated: De Riedmatten, 'Correspondance', p. 63.

At a second stage, still in the same year, Basil wrote to Olympius, one of his supporters in Neocaesarea. He mentioned 'writings which are being circulated against us' and more specifically 'the letter addressed to our very reverend brother Dazinas'. In this last text, ostensibly, were arguments 'drawn from a work written by someone, I know not whom'. He went on to assert that 'parts' of the letter were written by Apollinarius—he knew as much not because he had ever read anything by Apollinarius but because he had heard others talk of his teachings. 'Certain other things written therein', however, he had 'never read nor heard anybody else state'.[77] It looks as if, in his earlier letter to Meletius, Basil had been drawing upon this 'letter to Dazinas' and had still not seen the actual σύνταγμα being circulated by his enemies.[78] A new element, however, had by this time been introduced. Even if he had written, 'many years ago', to Apollinarius, he could not be blamed, he said, simply because the man had now lapsed into error.[79] So the possibility that he had communicated with Apollinarius had obviously come more into the open and could no longer be denied. His response—that one should not be blamed for the subsequent failings of one's old friends—had obvious associations with the problem presented by Eustathius.

At a third stage, the imputed correspondence with Apollinarius took the centre of the stage.[80] Basil's approach now was to insist that his contact with Apollinarius in former years had been superficial and unimportant. It may have been true that he 'forgot or concealed' what letters there might have been;[81] but he continued to avoid a full admission, because he knew that Eustathius and his friends did not possess the original correspondence (which implied, of course, that he knew very well what the original correspondence had said).[82] By the middle of 375, when Basil wrote his definitive letter of repudiation against Eustathius, he simply taunted him on the subject of Apollinarius. Could he produce letters? Could he point convincingly to any link between them at a time when

77. *Ep.* 131. 1, C 2: 44, D 2: 297/299.

78. So I feel, in the face of several complexities; but there has to be a little doubt: see Prestige, *Basil and Apollinaris*, pp. 27f. There is the sudden allusion to τὸν ἀποσταλέντα τόμον, 'the book that was sent', § 2, C 2: 46, D 2: 301. What was this 'book' (which seems distinct from the letter to Dazinas), and to whom was it 'sent'? It cannot be certain that the phrase ἐξ ἔργου, § 1, means 'in his book', C 2: 44, D 2: 299, as if to suggest that it was the *only* book, which Basil had now seen.

79. *Ep.* 131. 2, C 2: 45, D 2: 299.

80. See *Ep.* 223, 224, 226, 244.

81. As Prestige, *Fathers and Heretics*, p. 202, puts it.

82. De Riedmatten, 'Correspondance', pp. 55f. Prestige, in *Basil and Apollinaris*, made the point continuously that Basil never denied outright that such correspondence existed.

Apollinarius's views were suspect? Could he prove that the writings he now possessed were indeed written by Apollinarius? Basil knew that the answer to all those questions was almost certainly no.

He contented himself with this absence of proof, without proving directly an absence of guilt, because he still rallied, in some degree, to Apollinarius's defence: 'Pardon must be granted me if I disbelieve what is said against [him]'.[83] In an associated letter, he described in detail the sleight of hand he considered to have been at work. First, 'these men have introduced in the document against us[84] heretical expressions', which they then cleverly suggested were those of Basil himself. Second, they appeared to be flaunting 'a letter which was written to him [Apollinarius] now twenty-five years ago, ... and not even this as it was written by me, but altered (though by whom God knows)'.[85] Two embarrassments were implied: Basil *had* written to Apollinarius; and an adaptation of his letter had been 'introduced in the document against us'. Now we can begin to see the danger of the situation: somebody had indeed gained possession of written 'evidence', however deviously and with whatever intention to falsify. Basil was unavoidably associated with a man from whom he now wished to keep his distance.

The reality of the original letter continued to be an excuse for bluster.[86] Basil now poured cold water on the significance of *any* old letters. They certainly did not imply an acknowledgement of communion: one did not have to agree with everyone one wrote to (which was fair enough).[87] Beyond that, however, Eustathius was proffering the wrong sort of evidence. He needed 'either a canonical letter [κανονικὰ γράμματα] sent by me to him [Apollinarius] or by him to me, or the association of his clergy with us'.[88] Basil went on to describe two quite separate spheres of contact. His letter to Apollinarius had been 'by a layman to a layman [παρὰ λαϊκοῦ πρὸς λαϊκόν]'; and he continued: 'No one while in the episcopate [οὐδεὶς ἐν ἐπισκοπῇ ὤν] is accused, if through indifference [κατὰ ἀδιαφορίαν] he wrote anything inadvertently [ἀπαρατηρήτως] while in the lay state [ἐν τῷ λαϊκῷ βίῳ], and that too not even on faith [περὶ πίστεως], but a simple

83. *Ep.* 223. 4f, C 3: 13f., D 3: 301f.
84. Here τοῖς καθ' ἡμῶν γράμμασιν, and elsewhere 'the document [τὸ βιβλίον]'—that is to say, the σύνταγμα mentioned in the letter to Meletius, rather than the 'letter to Dazinas' described to Olympius.
85. *Ep.* 224. 1f.; C 3: 17f.; D 3: 313, 317.
86. And the 'letter' would later become 'letters [τὰς ... γραφείσας παρ' ἡμῶν ἐπιστολάς]', *Ep.* 226. 4, C 3: 28, D 3: 339.
87. See *Ep.* 224. 2, 226. 4.
88. *Ep.* 224. 2, C 3: 19, D 3: 317.

letter with a friendly greeting'.[89]   In other words, his association with
Apollinarius, whatever form it had taken, now lay on the other side of
a clear boundary in his life. The dignity and responsibility of episcopal
office demanded a fresh assessment of personal associations. Gregory of
Nazianzus and Eustathius of Sebaste, each in their own way, had already
suffered from that sense of changed circumstance.

A year or so later, in a letter to Patrophilus of Aegae,[90] Basil continued
to worry at the issue. A chief cause of Eustathius's enmity had been the
fact that 'we wrote to Apollinarius'; but, Basil added: 'I never did consider
Apollinarius as an enemy; ... I even respect the man; however, I have
not so united myself to him as to receive upon myself the charges brought
against him'. He admitted to 'reading certain of his works', although 'few';
and some of them 'more recent'. All he denied was 'either asking him for
a book about the Holy Spirit or receiving one sent by him'. He went so
far as to resurrect an older and potentially more favourable view of the
man, suggesting that his opponents should look to their own Arianism.
He simply insisted, otherwise, that 'we have neither been the pupil nor
have been taught anything by the man'.[91] About the letter to Dazinas,
Basil said very little: it had been widely circulated; it contained a variety
of accusations (not all of them theological); he had gone to Nicopolis to
defend himself against deceit. As for letters to Apollinarius, he let slip
not a word.[92] There can be only one conclusion: although Basil continued
to regard the relationship he may have had with Apollinarius as distant
and insignificant, his anxieties came to a head in relation to the advantage
he felt Eustathius might be able to take of it; and they persisted less for
theological reasons than because of the connection between Apollinarius
and his own opponents at Antioch.

The question remains, of course, what was the truth of the matter?
How close had been the connection between Basil and Apollinarius, and
of what character? We possess four letters, two attributed to each of them,
which may fall conveniently into two sets of exchanges. Are they genuine?
Are they the ones referred to in the controversy we have described? The

---

89. *Ep.* 224. 2, C 3: 19, D 3: 317. *Ep.* 226. 4 makes a similar point: λαϊκοὶ ὄντες πρὸς
λαϊκούς, C 3: 28. The 'layman' emphasis argues for an early date, since Apollinarius became
bishop of Laodicea in 360: see n. 69. The question is whether Basil was here telling the truth.

90. Which, as we have seen, had allowed him to draw up a full but slightly less
impassioned history of the whole conflict with Eustathius: see above, at n. 43.

91. *Ep.* 244. 3, C 3: 76f., D 3: 457.

92. Except perhaps in the vague phrase 'They were in such a state of disagreement that
they mixed things both true and false into the information given for those that accuse them',
Ep. 244. 5, C 3: 78f., D 4: 461/463.

answer to both questions is almost certainly yes.[93] We also have a document, the Περὶ τῆς θείας οὐσίας, attributed to Apollinarius, which includes some altered sections of the first of Basil's letters to him. Perhaps in this we have something akin to Eustathius's σύνταγμα.[94] The arguments are more complex than we need rehearse, but the conclusions are important. First, the epistolary association with Apollinarius was closer than Basil had been willing to admit. Although he might not have agreed with Apollinarius's replies, he asked him extensive theological questions and was obviously interested to have them answered. Second, discussion *was* about the faith and extended well beyond friendly greetings. Basil's first approach, and Apollinarius's first reply, undoubtedly date from the time between the 360 synod at Constantinople and the writing of the *Contra Eunomium*.[95] What Basil received from Apollinarius, as we have already suggested and as the existing letter confirms, was a very clear defence of Nicaea (which, of course, we need not suppose he welcomed without reserve: the *Contra Eunomium* deliberately steered what seemed to Basil a more moderate path). The second of Apollinarius's letters (which was not necessarily a reply to Basil's second letter to him) appears to be a reaction to the *Contra Eunomium*, attempting to bring Basil more clearly into line with the Athanasian view.[96]

Given the generosity of his letter to Patrophilus, we should not be surprised to find traces of Apollinarius's influence in Basil's later work. All the anti-Sabellian care in the homilies, for example, seems directed much more against Marcellus. As we have seen, Basil long retained the feeling that Nicaea was by no means self-explanatory; but, in resisting the Sabellian emphasis, one could not afford to call too much into question the ὁμοουσία, the likeness in substance, at stake. In working out the necessary gloss upon Nicaea, Basil seems at times to have been

93. So both Prestige, *Basil and Apollinaris*, pp. 6, 12f., 19f., and De Riedmatten, 'Correspondance', pp. 67f. De Riedmatten's accompanying edition is therefore the best. The letters are numbered as *Ep.* 361–64 in the Basil collection.

94. Here again I follow De Riedmatten. Prestige, *Basil and Apollinaris*, pp. 9, 37, made other suggestions.

95. De Riedmatten, 'Correspondance', pp. 59f. Prestige, *Basil and Apollinaris*, pp. 6f., preferred a date of 359 and closer association with George of Laodicea; but he agreed that the correspondence was prior to, and in many ways anticipatory of, the *Contra Eunomium*, pp. 24f. References to Gregory of Nazianzus and Basil's family would fit either date. See also above, at nn. 69, 89.

96. Prestige, *Basil and Apollinaris*, p. 37, made this point strongly. See also his *Fathers and Heretics*, p. 203, and, for Basil's supposed weakness on the meaning to be attached to οὐσία (compared with Apollinarius), p. 212. Even after the emperor Jovian had begun to give new direction to church policy, Basil had maintained his conservative caution.

guided by the vocabulary of a younger Apollinarius, at least as displayed in the two letters under discussion.[97] We are certainly entitled to suppose, therefore, that here was another friendship, which later controversy and ecclesial loyalties forced Basil at least to reassess, if not altogether dismiss.

———

Basil was coming to feel that places mattered more than people: his own see, of course; but also centres like Neocaesarea and Nicopolis; and above all Antioch. Before we pursue that point of view, we need to ask whether he had begun to lose his capacity for friendship altogether. Several figures that have already emerged upon the scene suggest that such was not the case. We learn a great deal by focussing upon two of them in particular, Eusebius of Samosata and Amphilochius of Iconium.

Eusebius of Samosata had been placed, since 361, at the rim of a circle of churches around Syrian Antioch, which claimed more and more of Basil's attention. Samosata was the leading city of old Commagene, now Euphratensis, strategically placed on the upper Euphrates, south of Melitene and north of Edessa. It had recently witnessed important military events, during confrontations with Persia under Constantius and Julian; and it was to experience further tension during the 370s, when Valens was strengthening his own position *vis-à-vis* the empire's great neighbour.[98] It was, in other words, a city of significance.

Basil had personal reasons, also, for seeking its bishop's patronage. Eusebius had been a supporter of Basil of Ancyra: a reassuring exponent, in other words, of the middle road that Basil so long favoured. By the time of Basil's consecration, Eusebius was considered a man of such reputation that Gregory of Nazianzus and his father were anxious to gain his support and presence, when their protégé was installed in Caesarea.[99] Gregory wrote three admiring letters to Eusebius, after the latter's exile to Thrace

---

97. De Riedmatten, 'Correspondance', p. 67. See, for example, *Ep.* 52; *Hom.* 337, 341. The dating of the letter (to 376: see n. 62) would suggest that even the *De spiritu sancto* had this revised defence of Nicaea in view. It is noteworthy how, in later letters, when he was attacking what were clearly Sabellian positions, Basil did not mention Apollinarius by name. Nor did he rush to make more explicit 'the simplicity of the Creed [τὴν ἁπλότητα τῆς πίστεως; but he was talking about Nicaea]', *Ep.* 258. 2, C 3: 102, D 4: 41. See also *Ep.* 261, 262.

98. See Ammianus Marcellinus 18, 8; 20, 11. 4; 30, 2; and Zosimus 3, 12. 1.

99. GNaz *Ep.* 42, 44. See chapter 5, at n. 55.

in 374.[100] It is ironic that Basil's own acquaintance with the man may have been set in motion by the friend he was about to estrange.

The first phase of Basil's association with Eusebius was in some ways quite formal. Two letters simply mention problems arising at the time—the situation at Antioch, the implications of Demophilus having succeeded Eudoxius at Constantinople (in 370),[101] reasonably stable successions to the episcopate at Neocaesarea and Ancyra, and the 'condition' of the churches generally.[102] So Basil neatly identified the coordinates of his ecclesial map. Those letters date from 371. Eusebius's replies, perhaps, and certainly the recollection of his support in 370, quickly introduced a note of warmth into Basil's subsequent letters: 'We enjoy one single consolation—that we can contemplate your kindness, and alleviate the ferment of our soul by thinking of you and remembering you ... your gentleness and sense of fitness like a gentle touch that dispels all sign of pain'.[103] In another letter, of 374, Basil may well have been referring back to that period (one of pressing difficulty in his own city). He suggested it was hardly necessary to say much about current affairs 'to a man like you who, foreseeing everything long in advance, made protest and issued proclamation beforehand, and not only was the first to rise up yourself, but also helped to rouse the rest, writing them letters, visiting them in person, omitting what act, leaving what word unspoken!' He added with obvious feeling: 'These things we do indeed remember'.[104] He admitted that at one stage he had even thought of taking refuge with Eusebius, 'not lending you any aid in the common cause, but deriving great gain for myself from your company. For I had decided to get out of the way of the missiles of the ecclesiastics because I had no means of protecting myself against the contrivances of my adversaries'.[105] All of which suggests high regard over a number of years.

The second phase of their association was prompted precisely by the events of 373. It was to Eusebius that Basil wrote, mentioning the

100. GNaz Ep. 44–46. The first could almost have come from the pen of Basil himself.

101. Ep. 48, C 1: 129, D 1: 317: 'A certain simulation of orthodoxy and piety on his part [τι περὶ αὐτὸν πλάσμα ὀρθότητος καὶ εὐλαβείας] is uniformly noised abroad by all who come from there. The result is that even the parts of the city that had been divided by schism have come together, and even some of the neighbouring bishops have accepted the union'. So might vagueness and tolerance still produce desired results!

102. Ep. 30, C 1: 72f., D 1: 175. The two letters were probably written in this order. Some impression has already been given of Basil's dependence on Eusebius at this time: see chapter 5, at nn. 73, 99.

103. Ep. 34, C 1: 77, D 1: 189.

104. Ep. 136. 2, C 2: 52, D 2: 315.

105. Ep. 136. 2, C 2: 52, D 2: 315.

anxieties of Meletius and Theodotus, and betraying the fact that Eusebius's absence was the main reason for his calling off an initial confrontation. He wanted Eusebius as an ally then, as he had been in 370—and not just against Eustathius, for he mentioned also the division of his own province and its attendant crises: 'Our situation needs your presence exceedingly, and you must bestir your venerable age once again, that you may give support to Cappadocia, which is even now tottering and near its fall'.[106] Most of their letters, however, were concerned with the Eustathian and Armenian issues.[107] At precisely what stage Eusebius became involved (for he certainly seems to have taken a direct hand in trying to draw some statement from Eustathius)[108] is not clear. Basil soon had reason to express gratitude. A letter from Eusebius had been, in one instance, like 'a beacon fire shining from afar upon the deep ... naturally possessing sweetness and great consolation'.[109] He now needed help on every front, particularly over 'the question of establishing bishops':[110]

> Because of other pressing matters as well I wanted to meet with your Holiness and both to consult with you about many things and to learn many things from you. For here it is not possible to meet with even genuine charity. But though one may at times find a person who shows even very great charity, there exists no one who is able, in a manner comparable with your perfect wisdom and the experience which you have gathered from your many labours for the churches, to offer advice on the matters which lie before us.[111]

Faced subsequently with some earlier, more slowly delivered letters from Eusebius, he was anxious to reassure him that he was being as forceful as possible in maintaining the orthodox cause among the churches open to his influence.[112]

The third stage covers the years of Eusebius's exile. We can detect in Basil's letters an increasing sense of the pressure that Valens was bringing

---

106. *Ep.* 95, 98. The quotation is from the latter, § 2, C 1: 213, D 2: 171.

107. The letters are difficult to order chronologically. The following is possible: *Ep.* 128, 100, 127, 145, 138, 141.

108. *Ep.* 128. 2: 'So do not let him outwit us, and do not let him deceive your wisdom as he has done with the rest; but let him send us a succinct answer to the question', C 2: 38, D 2: 279. See above, at n. 34.

109. *Ep.* 100, C 1: 218f., D 2: 183. *Ep.* 127 is similar in tone.

110. *Ep.* 100, C 1: 219, D 2: 185.

111. *Ep.* 138. 2, C 2: 55, D 2: 321/323. He went on to make reference to the West, Antioch, and more local problems.

112. *Ep.* 141. 2.

to bear towards the end of 373 and into 374.[113] At the beginning of that period, Eusebius had already been driven into some sort of hiding.[114] Early in 374, Basil still thought it might be possible for him to visit Caesarea.[115] Later, news was more definite: Eusebius was banished. Basil wrote to his new friend's nephew, Antiochus, congratulating him on sharing with his uncle so noble a contest, and being able 'to enjoy now in profound peace a man who has accumulated both so much from his learning and so much from his experience in affairs'.[116]

While Eusebius was in Thrace, Basil seems to have taken on the role (although not single-handedly) of envoy or clearinghouse between Samosata and its distant bishop.[117] For that reason he wrote several letters to the Christians there, encouraging them to maintain their considerable loyalty (for Eusebius's Arian rivals received very short shrift).[118]   He also continued to write to Antiochus.[119] During 376, he gave Eusebius a full account of his current woes—the depredations of Demosthenes, the continuing favour shown to Eustathius and his party, the negotiations in train with potential western allies.[120] Basil was no doubt inspired by a sense of responsibility to his former patron and adviser; but in many ways he was talking to himself, or at least to a correspondent to whom he could confide his closest anxieties and frustrations. Eventually, he said as much:

> Not that we may make your distress greater do we often pour out our troubles unsparingly in our letters to your Honour, but that we may grant ourselves some consolation through the lamentations which somehow, when indulged are wont to break up one's deep-seated grief; and so that we may stir your Magnanimity to more intense prayer on behalf of the churches.

Eusebius was like Moses, standing with hands raised, 'from dawn until evening', waiting for the defeat of the Amalekites.[121]   A final letter,

---

113. See the account provided by Theodoret *HE* 4, 15; 5, 4.

114. See *Ep.* 145.

115. *Ep.* 162.

116. *Ep.* 168, C 2: 103, D 2: 437.

117. So much is clear from *Ep.* 181 (late 374) and 198. 1 (375). Eusebius remained interested in a range of issues: see Basil's comments to Meletius about negotiations with the West in *Ep.* 120.

118. *Ep.* 182, 183, 219.

119. *Ep.* 146, 157, 158.

120. *Ep.* 237, 239.

121. *Ep.* 241, C 3: 64f., D 3: 427/429. He had made the same point in *Ep.* 127, three years before.

written towards the very end of Basil's life, pictures Eusebius beset by the increasing chaos of Gothic rebellion in the Balkans.[122]

Here, then, was a mentor totally engaged in what Basil had come to regard as the major issues; a well-established bishop and a proven champion of the Nicene cause; but a friend, also, with whom Basil could exchange genuinely warm feelings, and to whom he could usefully confide his hopes and fears. His other close associate of those years was Amphilochius of Iconium. Basil had actually mentioned him to Eusebius, explaining that Iconium had recently lost its pastor and now 'urges me to make it a visit, that we may give it a bishop'. He was worried 'whether, therefore, I should not decline these ordinations beyond our borders'; but he undoubtedly had a hand in the choice of Amphilochius shortly afterwards.[123]

There was an irony in their friendship, for Amphilochius was a maternal cousin to Gregory of Nazianzus. He leaps up fully armed, so to speak, in the pages of Basil's correspondence. The letter from 'Heracleidas' attempted to attract him to Caesarea in 372. By the end of 373, when Basil wrote to him next, he was already a bishop. Yet the letter from 'Heracleidas' hints at a longer past, which Gregory of Nazianzus allows us to observe in greater detail.[124] Amphilochius was another young rhetor, a pupil of Libanius, with experience in Constantinople, who had decided in the company of a friend with similar background (the real Heracleidas) to embrace the 'philosophic' life. The parallels with Basil and Gregory are obvious to us and must have been so to them as well. The opening sections of Basil's invitation were little more than a reminder of his own experience during the late 350s and early 360s. The release from 'public life', the need for 'someone to lead us by the hand', for 'a great and experienced teacher', the struggle between 'reason' and 'habit', 'the task of cleansing the eye of the soul'—all recall the excitements and anxieties of those years, shared, of course, with Gregory.[125]

---

122. *Ep.* 268. Theodoret appreciated the irony of his survival there, compared with his subsequent murder after his return home: καὶ τοὺς ἐν τῇ Θράκῃ βαρβάρους διαφυγών, τὰς τῶν δυσσεβῶν αἱρετικῶν οὐ διέφυγε χεῖρας, *HE* 5, 4. 9; ed. Parmentier, p. 284.

123. *Ep.* 138. 2, C 2: 56, D 2: 325. *Ep.* 62 exemplifies his practical lack of scruple. Iconium was in Lycaonia, although Basil here placed it in 'Pisidia'.

124. Essential background to all that follows is provided by Karl Holl, *Amphilochius von Ikonium in seinem Verhältnis zu den großen Kappadoziern*.

125. *Ep.* 150. 1, C 2: 71f., D 2: 361/363.

The main purpose of the letter, however, was to draw Amphilochius to a different style of asceticism.[126] He had been living more remotely: hence the allusion to 'wandering in the desert [εἰς ἐρημίας πλανᾶσθαι]' and to 'the caves and the rocks'.[127] Basil was anxious to gain his adhesion now to the style of religious commitment represented by the charitable work of the *Basileiados*. He was not only extending a firm invitation to submit to his own spiritual guidance: the whole régime at Caesarea was held up as a proper model for the fulfilment of Christian obligations—'the way that is in accordance with Christ's polity [τῆς ὁδοῦ τῆς κατὰ Χριστὸν πολιτείας]', 'the life that is in accordance with God', summed up in a crucial phrase: 'There is only one way leading to the Lord, and all who travel toward Him are companions of one another and travel according to one agreement as to life [καὶ κατὰ μίαν συνθήκην τοῦ βίου πορεύεσθαι]'.[128]

All that was written at the time when Basil had become estranged from Gregory himself. Was he, perhaps, indulging in a little spiteful poaching, robbing Gregory of a sympathetic supporter? Gregory reacted in a telling way to the consecration of Amphilochius, suggesting to his uncle that he and his cousin had been victims of one and the same 'tyranny'.[129] Yet Gregory was, as we know, constantly confused about the relationship between priesthood and philosophy; and that contributed to his unease as much as any resentment towards Basil. In the same letter to his uncle, he suggested that, while Amphilochius's episcopate represented a departure from a philosophic ideal, there was no need to indulge too much a father's grief.[130] Long before Amphilochius had made his first gesture of ascetic renunciation (around 362), Gregory congratulated him on his religious devotion but promptly advised him to associate with churchmen: 'How shall you honour [God and things divine], and what shall you do to show that honour? In this way only: by associating with those who stand close to God and serve at his altar [λειτουργούντων τοῦ βήματος]'. He then recommended the cause of a friend, the deacon Euthalios, who was being embarrassed by secular responsibilities.[131] It was just the sort of letter one wrote to relatives with influence in the capital, whether they were pious or

126. See chapter 5, after n. 26 and at nn. 41f., 85; and chapter 3, at n. 57.
127. *Ep.* 150. 4, C 2: 75, D 2: 371.
128. *Ep.* 150. 1, 2; C 2: 71f.; D 2: 361, 365.
129. See above, at n. 17. Amphilochius may have felt that way, too. Basil later suggested that he had been 'trying to escape, not us, but the expected call through us', *Ep.* 161. 1, C 2: 93, D 2: 411.
130. GNaz *Ep.* 63. 3f. No doubt he had half an eye on the demands imposed by his own father.
131. GNaz *Ep.* 9. 2f.; ed. Gallay, 1: 12.

not; but it shows also how principles could waver, when the advantage of the Church was at stake.

Once Amphilochius was established in Iconium, towards the end of 373, he entered upon a very special relationship with Basil. It was obviously important to the bishop of Caesarea to have a sympathetic and orthodox bishop in a neighbouring see; but Amphilochius was also a younger man, still in his thirties; and that allowed Basil to adopt a paternal role: 'To a father's heart every occasion is good for the embracing of a well-beloved child'.[132] Amphilochius was also a disciple and had the grace to seek advice and ask questions.[133] More than all else, he represented an ideal fulfilled: he was a man pleasing to God, a vessel of election.[134] Basil's letters habitually ended with a formula of special affection: 'In good health and joyful in the Lord, praying for me, may you be preserved to me and to the Church of God by the grace of the Lord'.[135]

There followed a great outpouring of advice, ecclesiastical prescription, and theological reflection. Just as Eusebius seemed eventually to take on the role of safety valve, a man to whom Basil could betray his sense of frustration and despondency, so Amphilochius became the one to whom he expressed his convictions and ambitions about the development of church life, and his more speculative thoughts. The 'canonical' letters are the most famous examples of communication between them. Just as, in the *Asceticon*, Basil created ad hoc 'rules' for ascetic disciples, so, in these letters, he gave advice on the church order to be followed in Iconium. While he appealed characteristically to the broader traditions of the Church, he applied his principles in a precise way to the needs of the church under Amphilochius's care, with its peculiar difficulties.[136] In the process, formal advice on the courses to be followed was packed

132. *Ep.* 161. 2, C 2: 94, D 2: 415. See also *Ep.* 176.
133. See the short bursts of exegesis he had already enticed from Basil in 374, *Ep.* 190. 3.
134. *Ep.* 161. 1—Basil's first letter to the new bishop.
135. So here *Ep.* 176, C 2: 113, D 2: 461. See also *Ep.* 200, 231, 202, 248 (probably in that order). Similar phrases occur in *Ep.* 191, which may not have been addressed to Amphilochius (although Courtonne is happy to think so).
136. Holl, *Amphilochius*, pp. 17f., 20f., identified well the particular needs of the Church in that area, beset as it was by civil unrest and a long tradition of radical heterodoxy (in no way immediately associated with Arianism). For a vigorous description of contemporary events in Isauria, see John Matthews, *The Roman Empire of Ammianus*, pp. 355f. A longer period is covered in Keith Hopwood, 'Policing the Hinterland: Rough Cilicia and Isauria'. Brennecke, *Geschichte der Homöer*, p. 191, notes how the appointment of Amphilochus represented a new phase in the establishment of Nicene supporters in this neighbouring province. The letters concerned are *Ep.* 188, 199, and 217. The division into 'canons' occurred later; and they were therefore really no different from, for example, *Ep.* 233. For Basil's interpretations of the episcopate, addressed to Amphilochius, see chapter 5, at nn. 82f., 86, 161.

about with phrases of affection. Amphilochius had asked the questions of a wise man, encouraging Basil to learn more himself.[137] He showed a 'zeal for knowledge ... in that you not only consent to learn, although you have been entrusted with the office of teaching, but also to learn from us, in whom there is nothing great in the way of knowledge'.[138] After his long journey to Pontus in 376,[139] Basil was 'considerably afflicted in soul'; but 'when I took into my hands the letter of your Piety', he wrote, 'I straightway became forgetful of everything, since I had received symbols of both the sweetest voice of all to me and also of the dearest hand'.[140]

Because of that intimacy, Basil felt able to share with his new protégé the religious ideas that lay deepest in his heart. Some of his letters are little more than brief greetings;[141] but four longer ones sum up in a remarkable and unusual way his theological position on almost every fundamental point he ever addressed. To no one else did he write with such consistent deliberation.[142] The last of the four long letters is the least cohesive (their current order tells us little about their dating, or about the lapse of time between them). It covers a variety of issues with varying detail but is devoted mainly to the sensitive issue of whether Jesus knew as much as his Father, and includes a useful summary of the distinction between οὐσία and ὑπόστασις. The other three, however, are brilliant vignettes of theological inquiry. They reach back very clearly to the *Contra Eunomium* and forward to the *De spiritu sancto*.

The first is probably the most carefully structured. It sets out to define the character of 'mind [νοῦς]' and 'the activity of the mind [τοῦ νοῦ ἡ ἐνέργεια]'. That activity can move in two directions, towards fantasy and towards truth; and it is the movement towards truth that leads 'to the likeness of God [πρὸς τὴν τοῦ Θεοῦ ὁμοίωσιν]'. The letter then describes three 'states of life' (to which there correspond three 'activities of our mind'): wickedness, virtue, and an 'intermediate' state, which consists in activities and skills that are 'inclining in no way either to virtue or to

---

137. *Ep.* 188, intro.
138. *Ep.* 199, intro.; C 2: 154; D 3: 105.
139. See Gain, *Église*, pp. 395f.
140. *Ep.* 217, intro.; C 2: 208f.; D 3: 241/243.
141. *Ep.* 200–202, 232.
142. *Ep.* 233–236. See Holl, *Amphilochius*, pp. 24f. Note, however, the splendid passage in *Ep.* 226. 3 (to ascetics): 'Our mind being enlightened by the Spirit looks up at the Son, and in Him as in an image beholds the Father', C 3: 27, D 3: 339. *Ep.* 52 (to religious women), associated by Dörries with the productivity of 376, rises also to some height but is rather more historical and akin to other more mundane letters on the Arian issue, displaying in the end a different attitude to its audience and a different tone in the handling of its content. So we see correlated a scale of intimacy and an intensity of theological reflection.

wickedness'. In regard to these last, the mind must make a 'choice'. At this point, the ideal ἐνέργεια is defined:

> The mind that is tempered with the divinity of the Spirit [τῇ θεότητι τοῦ Πνεύματος ἀναχραθείς] is at last initiated into the great speculations [τῶν μεγάλων ... θεωρημάτων], and observes the divine beauties, but only to the extent that grace allows and its constitution [κατασκευή] admits.

It is not, however, the function of the mind to pose, in the process, 'dialectical questions', but to 'inquire into the truth, not mischievously, but reverently'. It will do so by observing in the correct light the wonders of the created world. It cannot do that on its own, nor can it range beyond its nature; 'but if it gives itself up to the assistance of the Spirit, it will know the truth and recognize God'.[143]

Such ideas are entirely familiar to us now. One notes, even so, the brilliance and brevity, and the person of the recipient. The other two letters of the series expand upon the first. The second is very close to the teaching of the *Contra Eunomium*. Here, as in the other letters, Basil was suggesting to Amphilochius what he should say when faced with heretical challenge: even at his most profound, he remained thoroughly practical. When enemies ask, therefore, whether you worship what you know, and whether you pretend as a consequence to know the substance, the οὐσία of God, you say: 'Of course not; what we know are the actions and attributes of God, his ἐνέργειαι'. That assertion allowed Basil to describe the distinction between act and substance. Can one be saved, therefore, having such imperfect knowledge? Yes: through faith; through knowing *that* God exists, rather than *what* God is. And from that knowledge will flow a desire to worship. Basil ended with a characteristically dynamic image:

> Therefore from the activities is the knowledge, and from the knowledge is the worship [προσκύνησις].... Thus worship follows faith, and faith is strengthened by power.... We understand God from his power. Therefore we believe in Him whom we understand, and we worship Him in whom we believe.[144]

The third of the four letters explains at greater length the relationship between knowledge and belief. Πίστις, paradoxically, is more necessary at first 'in the sciences [ἐπὶ τῶν μαθημάτων]', for one has to take on faith principles that only later become fully intelligible. In 'our own teaching',

---

143. So *Ep.* 233 in a number of passages, C 3: 39f., D 3: 365f.
144. *Ep.* 234, C 3: 41f., D 3: 371f.

also, Christians can admit to the priority of knowledge, so long as they admit that such knowledge is limited by nature (τῇ ἀνθρωπίνῃ καταλήψει σύμμετρον). Knowledge is dependent, further, on the observance of God's works in creation: one cannot know the substance, the οὐσία of God. 'And faith follows this knowledge, and worship [προσκύνησις] follows such faith'. Basil ended this letter by allowing the momentum of his imagery to carry much more obviously into the daily experience of religious life: ' "Knowledge" is manifold, as we have said. For it is the apprehension of Him who has created us, and the understanding of His wonders, and the keeping of His commandments, and intimacy with Him [ἡ οἰκείωσις ἡ πρὸς αὐτόν]'—a neat 'salvation history', reaching from Genesis to Paradise. Religious opponents, by contrast, 'pushing all these things aside, reduce "knowledge" to one significance, the contemplation of the very substance of God [τὴν θεωρίαν αὐτῆς τοῦ Θεοῦ τῆς οὐσίας]'.[145]

How much more easily we can read the *Contra Eunomium*, having these brilliant texts at hand. The reminiscence, of course, was not accidental. Fresh developments had by now made it clear to Basil that his old essay was no longer adequate. The central problem was the Holy Spirit. We have seen how misgivings had built up over the previous few years: the slur upon his preaching at Gregory's dinner table, suspicions at Ancyra about the hidden implications of his earlier treatise, the accusations of Eustathius and the anxieties of Meletius and Theodotus, even the pressure of the audience at his own homilies.[146] The wonderfully clear expositions now provoked by the friendship and curiosity of Amphilochius heralded, and in some instances may have accompanied, the production of the *De spiritu sancto*, dedicated also to the young bishop of Iconium.[147]

145. *Ep.* 235, C 3: 44f., D 3: 377f.
146. In addition to the Eustathian issue, see GNaz *Ep.* 58. 4 (referred to briefly at nn. 12, 27), his own *Ep.* 25 (for which see n. 58), and *Hom.* 341 (nn. 60, 97). If, as suggested earlier, Gregory's warnings had done much to start a theological hare, one might usefully speculate whether Basil's *Ep.* 7 was not a reply to his friend's *Ep.* 58. One sentence seems particularly apposite: 'My previous discussion, then, whether it is regarded as adequate or whether it needs a supplement to make it more accurate, calls for a special opportunity for revision', C 1: 22, D 1: 47. (This brief letter is full of Basil's character.)
147. Dörries, *De spiritu sancto*, provides essential background. There is some difficulty in judging how public the work was supposed to be. Basil ended with references to a need for silence and to the error of casting pearls before swine, even though he regretted the restrictions thus placed upon 'the tradition of the fathers'. Amphilochius provided an

That work did not appear accidentally, therefore: it marked a moment of new assurance, of self-definition, of choice in Basil's life. The turmoil of the years since 370 was now made sense of. Friendships had been lost or modified, opportunities rejected or forgotten. Challenges had been faced—not just those of the Arians but those mounted by Eustathius, and by those opposed to his style of episcopacy, his asceticism, his notion of what 'Church' should mean. He had faced also a crisis in his health, and a decline of confidence. The bitterness of those experiences might now be dispelled by this new young friend, with whom he had so much in common—family, education, ascetic enthusiasm—and who was ready to applaud, indeed to imitate, his ideas and way of life. Upon Amphilochius, therefore, he now focussed a fatherly affection. In collaboration with him, he saw the potential fulfilment of his own vision of the community of churches. From his loyalty, his orthodoxy, his effectiveness, Basil would draw fresh strength. The *De spiritu sancto* was the chief fruit of these new blessings.

For that reason it is necessary to observe its tone. The importance of the treatise does not reside simply in its theology; in the fact that it made the teaching of the Holy Spirit more explicit and presented at last, in its fullest form, the necessary gloss upon Nicaea. In many ways, it says no more than the letters we have just examined, and repeats a great deal of the *Contra Eunomium*; but it does so with a tone of confidence more dependent on a deep sense of what religion means. Not only had the pain of divorce from Eustathius been assuaged, but Basil's understanding of the 'place' where human beings meet their God had shifted inwards. The work marks a clear step towards the great sermons on the creation with which he ended his life.

On the subjects of knowledge and the development of human argument, the treatise adopts very much the standpoint of the *Contra Eunomium*. Arians sought constantly for proof, which carried more weight with them than Scripture.[148] They appealed uselessly to ancient philosophy (to Aristotle especially) for an understanding of prepositions and relationships (which loomed large when it came to expressing the dependence or otherwise of the Spirit upon both Father and Son). They failed to realize that

---

alternative haven of intimate discussion: 'Your sober and reticent character ensures that what we say to one another will not be broadcast among larger numbers [τὸ τοῦ τρόπου ἐμβριθὲς καὶ ἡσύχιον, ἐγγυώμενον μὴ εἰς πολλοὺς ἐξοίσειν τὰ ῥηθησόμενα]', DSS 30 (§ 79); ed. Pruche, p. 530 (translation mine). The matter is touched upon again at n. 152. Other letters cluster around the year 376, associating Amphilochius with the reflections that produced the treatise: *Ep.* 202, 231, 248.

148. *DSS* 10 (§ 25).

Scripture did not depend upon that kind of logic, that sterile exactitude. They were led, also, into a misunderstanding of cause and instrumentality, which encouraged a false view, not only of creation and the Trinity but also of relation.[149] It was the corresponding task of Christian leaders to protect their people from the allurements of heretical logic.[150] Faced with the taunts and threats of their opponents, the best reaction from the orthodox was silence: the 'silence of which wise Solomon speaks; for what is the good of crying to the wind when life is swept by so fierce a storm that there is not a man instructed in the word whose mind is not clouded with fallacious reasoning?'.[151]

What the Church had lost above all was ἀγαπητικαὶ νουθεσίαι: the capacity to think aloud in a loving way.[152] This is almost the final sentence of the treatise. The difference from statements of earlier years is marked. Silence was best, not because it did fullest justice to the limits of human understanding but because the social complexion of the Church itself had rendered argument ineffective and antagonistic. With characteristic skill, Basil recalled his opening point. One should not ask questions merely to test the adversary, score points, provoke conflict. The ideal inquirer was one whose love of learning was a quality of soul, who saw ignorance as a failing in need of cure. Such, of course, was Amphilochius.[153] Basil invited him to the closest possible scrutiny of God's word, of each syllable of Scripture; to a mental posture of keenly focussed attention, protected by that other silence, the presence of God. 'To track down the hidden meaning—that is impossible to those sluggish in their piety, and open only to those who know the purpose of our calling, for it is our destiny to become like God ... and there is no likeness without knowledge'.[154] Indeed, to draw close to God and close to the truth were one and the same.[155]

The source of authority best calculated to supply the deficiencies of false logic was tradition. An ability to appreciate the history of salvation

149. For Basil, naturally, the dynamism of one was revealed in the momentum of the other: DSS 3f. (§§ 5f.), 17 (§§ 41f.), 25 (§§ 58f.).

150. DSS 7 (§ 16), 17 (§ 41).

151. DSS 29 (§ 75), tr. p. 143.

152. DSS 30 (§ 78); ed. Pruche, pp. 526/528. That was why one should not cast pearls (see n. 147).

153. DSS 1 (§ 1).

154. DSS 1(§ 2): κεκρυμμένον νοῦν ἐξιχνεύειν, οὐκ ἀργῶν εἰς εὐσέβειαν, ἀλλὰ γνωριζόντων τὸν σκοπὸν τῆς κλήσεως ἡμῶν· ὅτι πρόκειται ἡμῖν ὁμοιωθῆναι Θεῷ, ... ὁμοίωσις δέ, οὐκ ἄνευ γνώσεως, ed. Pruche, p. 252 (translation mine).

155. DSS 7 (§ 16), 21 (§ 52), 26 (§ 61).

was in itself the mark of an educated person.[156] Even from a human point of view, it was clear that Greek polytheism had given way before the force of Christian theology.[157] Central to tradition were the verbal usages of the Church and the Scriptures themselves.[158] Each Christian, in an intimate way, was made to share in that tradition by the 'life-giving charity' of the Spirit himself.[159] Like Basil, he or she could draw together three sources of instruction: the common understanding of words, the witness of Scripture, and the teaching handed down within the Church.[160]

The shift from argument to tradition provided a setting within which to gain a correct understanding of the distinction between knowledge and belief. The result (echoing once again the letters to Amphilochius and the *Contra Eunomium*) was an inspired awareness of God's works, especially of the gifts represented and guaranteed by the life of Jesus—all signs of God's providential care for his creation.[161] The inevitable response was the act of worship. The modes of worship were central components of the unwritten tradition of the Church, 'those things given us by the tradition of the apostles ἐν μυστηρίῳ [which does not mean in a 'hidden' or 'secret' way, but in the cultic practice of the Church, as the sequel makes clear]'. The genius of such a species of silence (for such it was) lay in translating truth into action so as to make it available to believers, while rendering it incomprehensible to those without belief.[162] For a supposed Christian to question the divinity of the Spirit was to repudiate the very engagement entered into at baptism (ὡς τὰς πρὸς Θεὸν παραβάντι συνθήκας): 'Such a person is excluded from true worship [ἄμοιρός ... τῆς ἀληθινῆς προσκυνήσεως]'.[163]

None of this is unexpected, given earlier declarations. Greater concentration on the action of the Spirit, however, gave that final stage of Trinitarian and salvific drama a more intimate quality and allowed Basil

---

156. *DSS* 24 (§ 33).

157. *DSS* 18 (§ 47).

158. *DSS* 7 (§ 16), 12 (§ 28).

159. *DSS* 12 (§ 28).

160. *DSS* 9 (§ 22). The last element we may associate with the famous distinction between δόγματα and κηρύγματα, 27 (§§ 66f.). See Amand de Mendieta, 'ΚΗΡΥΓΜΑ and ΔΟΓΜΑ', and *'Unwritten' and 'Secret' Apostolic Traditions*; also Georges Florovsky, 'The Function of Tradition in the Ancient Church', particularly p. 194. A similar distinction is alluded to in *Ep.* 240. 1.

161. *DSS* 8 (§§ 17f.).

162. *DSS* 27 (§§ 66f.). See also 7 (§ 16) on the current use of 'with' and 'through' in relation to Jesus and the notion of glory, and 26 (§§ 61f.) on the similar issue of 'in' in relation to the Spirit.

163. *DSS* 11 (§ 27); ed. Pruche, pp. 340, 342 (translation mine).

to reflect more explicitly upon the personal experience of the worshipper. He made a heavy moral emphasis as well. To be baptized was to undertake a lifetime's imitation of Jesus. One identified with his death, the model for one's own death to sin, and the guarantee that one would enjoy, under the impact of the Spirit's power, that life promised to humanity 'from the beginning'. One rejected, also, 'the life that went before', by imitating the humility of Jesus, his gentleness, his generosity of spirit:

> So the Lord is preparing us for the risen life by placing before us in the Gospel a whole régime [τὴν εὐαγγελικὴν πᾶσαν ... πολιτείαν], prescribing for us gentleness, patience, a manner of life unsullied by the love of pleasure or of wealth. So we shall come to possess through our own choice [ἐκ προαιρέσεως] all that the [coming] age possesses by nature [κατὰ τὴν φύσιν].[164]

Basil made it clear that the holiness, the ἁγιασμός, achieved with the aid of the Spirit, was not automatic, or achieved at the expense of individual freedom and commitment. Holiness was an enduring state, which depended upon a constant association, a κοινωνία, with the Spirit, leading to an ordered life governed by declared principle.[165]

So, from the very beginning of his new account of the Spirit's character and role, Basil emphasized the intimacy of the relationship that might result. Here were the firstfruits of οἰκείωσις, of human restoration to the close friendship of God. As in the *Contra Eunomium*, the relationship between the Spirit and the other persons of the Trinity was seen as akin to the relationship between spirit and self in human experience. Human beings were already structured in such a way as to take in their stride, so to speak, the infused bonding of divine person with divine person.[166] The capacity for οἰκείωσις, which reflected at one and the same time the nature of God's creative act and the enduring patience of his salvific will, implied a tension, an expectation, a sense of being always on the verge of a change that would reduce the distance between creature and God.

164. *DSS* 15 (§ 35); ed. Pruche, p. 370 (translation mine).
165. *DSS* 16 (§ 38). The alternative would be that ἀνομοθέτητος, ἄτακτος, ἀόριστος αὐτῶν ἡ ζωή, ed. Pruche, p. 382. *DSS* 16 (§ 40) makes it clear that people's actions would determine the readiness of the Spirit on Judgement Day to recognize those close to him. Points made in chapter 1, at nn. 46f., in chapter 2, at nn. 80f., and in chapter 4, at nn. 133f., have some bearing on the matter.
166. *DSS* 16 (§ 40).

The matter is captured brilliantly in a central passage of the treatise.[167] 'Who', Basil began, 'on hearing the titles of the Spirit, does not experience an elevation of soul and rise in thought to the supreme nature?' That was not due merely to the thrill of the sacred text: 'Towards this Spirit all those turn who have need of holiness, and who live according to virtue:[168] they are refreshed by his breath, and helped towards that end which is proper to themselves and in accordance with their nature [πρὸς τὸ οἰκεῖον ἑαυτοῖς καὶ κατὰ φύσιν τέλος]'. The new sense of fulfilment was experienced most, perhaps, in the mind: 'Since he is the source of holiness, an intelligible light [φῶς νοητόν], he is able from his own resources to supply to every rational power [πάσῃ δυνάμει λογικῇ] a certain enlightenment [τινα καταφάνειαν], which will enable them to discover the truth'. Yet that elevation and illumination of spirit and of mind was not, once again, automatic but depended upon the worthiness and faith of the creature (bestowed τοῖς ἀξίοις, and κατ' ἀναλογίαν τῆς πίστεως). Nor was Basil thinking of some vague seizure or gratuitous ecstasy. The Spirit would come to each person in exact proportion to their freedom from passion (that freedom being not merely the result or symptom of the Spirit's closeness, but the very closeness itself). The rejection of vice; the regaining of a natural beauty [τὸ ἐκ φύσεως κάλλος]; the restoration, by purification, of 'that ancient form proper to the royal image [of God]': that was what it meant to draw near to the Spirit.[169] Then one would see the Image itself, the archetype of one's own nature.[170]

The process was spread out over time, nevertheless: hearts were stirred, then the weak were to be taken by the hand, and at last those firmly on the path were led to perfection, to the status of being 'spiritual', πνευματικοί. Eternal fulfilment would follow, the consequence of all that had been achieved through moral progress in the company of the Spirit (τῇ πρὸς ἑαυτὸ κοινωνίᾳ): 'foreknowledge of the future, an understanding of mysteries, the grasp of hidden things, the bestowal of spiritual gifts, the citizenship of heaven, singing with the angels, unending joy, resting in God's company, likeness to God, and that crowning of all desires, becoming a god [θεὸν γενέσθαι]'.

---

167. For all that follows, DSS 9 (§§ 22f.); ed. Pruche, pp. 322f. Some of the translations are by Blonfield Jackson, pp. 51f. (see Bibliography under Basil, De spiritu sancto); some are my own.

168. Ἁγιασμός, 'holiness', as we shall see, might therefore be the reward for, as much as the result of, ἀρετή, 'virtue'.

169. For the Spirit's impact on the passions, see DSS 14 (§ 31).

170. For even greater emphasis on the intimacy involved, see DSS 18 (§ 47).

A thread of logic runs right through the passage. The achievement was a gift, unfolding in the secret interstices of the self; but it was based on a visible, moral commitment. Basil would later expand upon the point:

> The cosmos, that is to say all life that is enslaved to the passions of the flesh, cannot receive the gift of the Spirit. But to his disciples the Lord bore witness that they could purify their lives by following his teachings, and that they were already capable of contemplating the mysteries of the Spirit: 'You have already been cleansed by the word that I spoke to you'.

So moral commitment was proof of worthiness: by treading underfoot all earthly things, by living at a higher level, by achieving purity of heart, one opened oneself to the gift of the Spirit.[171]

It is immensely important to weigh correctly the implications of the fact that Basil wrote such a work as this amidst the difficulties of the 370s. It was not wholly original: its dependence on Origen is particularly marked. Nor is it surprising, in that it stands quite logically between the *Contra Eunomium* and the sermons of the *Hexaemeron*. That in itself has some significance: Basil's ideas did take shape in stages. It matters, too, that the treatise was, in a sense, 'post-Arian'. By 376, Basil felt that arguments against Arianism had been sufficiently rehearsed: there was little to do but repeat, albeit more clearly, positions already worked out. He had entered a new phase of debate, bringing to the surface of his mind theological riches far in excess of what Eunomius had inspired.[172] The treatise also marked, as we have said, a new curve on the changing graph of friendship. The verve of expression, the intensity, the exalted descriptions of inspiration and eternal destiny, owed less to his sources than to the warmth of his relationship with Amphilochius. Basil had found a refuge from earlier turmoil; and his religious confidence, from now on, would be safer from pettiness and persecution.

171. *DSS* 22 (§ 53); ed. Pruche, p. 442 (translation mine).
172. *DSS* 18 (§ 43) provides fine illustration of the point.

· CHAPTER VIII ·

BASIL ON THE WORLD STAGE

'Lifting his head high and casting the eye of his soul in every direction, he obtained a mental vision of the whole world through which the word of salvation had been spread'.[1] So Gregory of Nazianzus described his friend. 'A trumpet penetrating the immensity of space, or a voice of God encompassing the world, or a universal earthquake resulting from some new wonder or miracle, his voice and mind were all of these'.[2] Praise, indeed; and so it may have seemed in later years, with Basil's old enemies in retreat. But just what broader significance did he acquire during his struggles on behalf of orthodoxy? For he knew well enough that success would depend on carrying to the furthest possible limits the battle against error: 'Who will allow me to step upon the stage of the wide world? Who will give me a voice clear and penetrating like a trumpet?'.[3]

Correspondence examined in previous chapters—about the division of Cappadocia, about Eustathius, and about Antioch—points to a growing awareness of place. Basil's failure with Gregory and success with Amphilochius included an element of purely territorial interest. Once he had become a bishop, he began to develop a clear sense of the geography of his world; a geography that allowed him not only to pinpoint interests rivalling his own but also to associate with different localities—different

---

1. GNaz Orat. 43. 41, tr. p. 62.
2. GNaz Orat. 43. 65, tr. p. 83. The same sentiment occurs in GNaz Ep. 46. 2: ὁ τῆς οἰκουμένης ὀφθαλμός, ed. Gallay, 1: 59.
3. Hom. 342. 1. Could Gregory have known of this sermon?

sees, different groups of supporters and antagonists—the varying components of his own theology, the theology not only of the Trinity but also
of human nature and the community within which that nature had to
operate.

Antioch occupied a central place in that network;[4] Neocaesarea, and
Armenia beyond it, also loomed large. A connection with Neocaesarea was
only to be expected, given its prominence in Pontus, and the proximity of
Basil's family property, some fifty kilometres to the west. We have already
mentioned most of the important letters connected with the region. First
came Basil's response to the death of the bishop Musonius, near the end
of 371. He naturally recalled the heritage of Gregory, Neocaesarea's first
bishop; but he betrayed anxiety also that a change of leaders might rob
him of a potential ally and generally weaken the city's resistance to error in
those trying days. He hoped for 'a token either of neighbourly sympathy,
or of the fellowship of men of like faith, or, more truly, of the fellowship
of men who obey the law of love and shun the peril of silence'.[5] So he
recalled the city's more recent resistance to error—'amid this great storm
and tempest of affairs ... unshaken by the waves'—and urged its people
quickly to unite in their own defence around a new leader.[6]

The need to build up a community of churchmen who could present
a common face against the forces that threatened them—the hope invested
in Amphilochius not long afterwards—was felt most acutely at those
moments when leaders died, and when the quality of their successors
was uncertain. Basil struck the same note in a letter to Ancyra, following
the death of its bishop Athanasius at around the same time: 'To whom
shall we now transfer the cares of the churches? Whom now shall I take
as partner in my sorrows? Whom as a sharer in my joy?'[7] 'There is no
little danger', he continued with some pointedness, 'that many will fall
together with this support which has now been taken from under them
[i.e., Athanasius], and that the rottenness of certain persons will be laid
bare'. 'The struggle', he concluded, 'is not slight, that we may prevent the
springing up again, over the election of a superintendent, of strifes and
dissensions, and the utter overturning, as the result of a petty quarrel, of
all our labours'.[8]

---

4. The connection was emphasized strongly by Fedwick, *Charisma*, p. 102.
5. *Ep.* 28. 3, C 1: 69f., D 1: 169. See chapter 3, at n. 102, and chapter 4, at n. 33.
6. *Ep.* 28. 1, C 1: 67, D 1: 163.
7. *Ep.* 29, C 1: 71, D 1: 173. Not that Athanasius had been the warmest of colleagues:
see *Ep.* 25. Indeed, Musonius could have been placed in the same category: see *Ep.* 28. 3.
8. *Ep.* 29; C 1: 71; D 1: 171/173, 173/175.

At Neocaesarea, Musonius was succeeded by Atarbius, a distant relative of Basil. The man was not inspired thereby with automatic affection; and he seems to have made no move to acknowledge either Basil's anxieties or his sense of loyalty to Neocaesarea itself. Eventually, Basil decided to open communications himself, in 373. He was anxious still that Atarbius should bestir himself more effectively in the dangerous struggle against the enemies of orthodoxy:

> Unless we assume a labour on behalf of the churches equal to that which the enemies of sound doctrine have taken upon themselves for their ruin and total obliteration, nothing will prevent truth from being swept away to destruction by our enemies, and ourselves also from sharing in the condemnation, unless with all good zeal and good will, in harmony with one another and in unison with God, we show the greatest possible solicitude for the unity of the churches.

That was where Amphilochius had scored points, and where Atarbius had been particularly remiss:

> Cast from your mind the thought that you have no need of communion with another.... Consider this—that if the evil of war which now goes on all about us should sometime come upon ourselves likewise ... we shall find none to sympathize with us, because in the season of our tranquillity we failed to pay betimes our contribution of sympathy [τὸν τῆς συμπαθείας ἔρανον] to the victims of injustice.[9]

It was a theme very much to the fore at that moment, when not only was the policy of Valens, from a religious point of view, most oppressive, but also the division of the province had created new occasions for disunity. To the curia of Tyana, the see of his new rival, Anthimus, Basil wrote: 'We would never attribute so much to ourselves as to consider that single-handed we could surmount our difficulties, for we know very clearly that we need the help of each and every brother more than one hand needs the other'.[10]

Because of the way in which the controversy with Eustathius developed, Basil eventually accused Atarbius of Sabellianism. That represented, of course, a careful attempt to defend himself, and to preserve what allies he could, within the orbit of Neocaesarea itself. It is likely, however, that the opinions of Atarbius seemed bad enough in themselves, and deserving of censure, 'lest perchance, in addition to the countless wounds which the Church has suffered at the hands of those who have erred against the

9. *Ep.* 65, C 1: 156, D 2: 25/27.
10. *Ep.* 97, C 1: 210, D 2: 163.

truth of the Gospel, still another evil may spring up'.[11] So he went about building up a wider circle of potential supporters. An obvious example was Olympius, a friend of long standing,[12] to whom he wrote about many aspects of the controversy, 'in order that you yourself may know the truth, and may make it clear to those eager not to let it suffer in the grip of injustice'.[13] The cultivation of locally influential lay persons, even in letters not explicitly theological in content, was an important means of maintaining one's position among ecclesiastical peers and rivals.[14] Nor was Olympius his only friend in the city.[15]

Basil actually travelled to Pontus in 376: so in a sense the letters discussed so far had been preparing the soil. The process continued in a long letter to the bishops of the coastal region. To some extent like Atarbius, they had been disturbingly quiet, slow to send either letters or envoys to comfort the embattled bishop of Caesarea. By this stage, several more reflective themes were beginning to come together in Basil's mind, following the breakdown with Eustathius and the continuing controversy over Apollinarius; and he now saw himself as the leader of the orthodox cause in Asia Minor generally: 'We, being publicly exposed to all, like headlands jutting out into the sea, receive the fury of the heretical waves'.[16] Such a sense of destiny had already been hinted at in his earliest correspondence with the newly consecrated Amphilochius—'awaiting the calm which the Lord will cause as soon as a voice is found worthy of rousing Him to rebuke the winds and the sea'[17]—and it seems confirmed in his letter to the curia at Tyana: 'If anyone follows us who are leading the way in this matter [κἂν μὲν ἕπηταί τις ταῦτα καθηγουμένοις ἡμῖν], that is excellent, and my prayer

11. *Ep.* 126, C 2: 36, D 2: 273.
12. See *Ep.* 4, 12, 13.
13. *Ep.* 131. 2, C 2: 46, D 2: 301; but Deferrari's slightly different text ends with obscurity; Courtonne reads: ἵνα αὐτός τε εἰδείης τὴν ἀλήθειαν καὶ τοῖς βουλομένοις μὴ κατέχειν ἐν ἀδικίᾳ τὴν ἀλήθειαν φανερὰν καταστήσεις. See also *Ep.* 211.
14. See *Ep.* 63 to a ἡγεμών at Neocaesarea (not datable). It refers to news carried by one Elpidius (not the bishop mentioned below in n. 15), who fulfilled a similar function in *Ep.* 64 (more closely concerned with affairs in Cappadocia itself: see *Ep.* 72), and was associated with the disgraced official Therasius of *Ep.* 77 and 78. Compare the letter to the ἡγεμών of Sebaste (similarly not datable), *Ep.* 306.
15. See *Ep.* 208 and (perhaps) 209. In pursuit of the same general cause, he wrote assiduously to a bishop Elpidius, no friend of Eustathius (see *Ep.* 251. 3). He wanted above all, with Elpidius's help, to bring the bishops of the region together, 'to uproot the troubles which arise from our present suspicions of one another, and strengthen the love without which the Lord Himself has declared to us that the performance of every commandment is incomplete', *Ep.* 205, C 2: 182, D 3: 177.
16. *Ep.* 203. 1, C 2: 168, D 3: 145.
17. *Ep.* 161. 2, C 2: 93f., D 2: 415.

is fulfilled'.[18] The same sense of changed circumstance was expressed quite clearly in his long, self-justificatory letter to Patrophilus, written also in 376 (the moment when he rose to new heights of self-confidence in the *De spiritu sancto*):

> Last year, having become ill with a most violent fever, and having approached the very gates of death, then being recalled by God's mercy, I was dissatisfied at my return, considering the evils upon which I was again entering; and by myself I inquired what in the world it was that lay in the depths of God's wisdom, whereby days of life in the flesh had again been granted to me. But when I understood these things, I considered that the Lord wished us to see the churches resting from the storm which they had experienced before this.[19]

Such was the spirit in which he wrote to his colleagues in Pontus. Yet Eustathius, Apollinarius, and Atarbius were never far from his mind: Basil wanted a local synod, in which he could be formally accused, instead of slandered behind his back, and where others could examine evidence, instead of merely listening to abuse.[20] He then went on to repeat, virtually, the imagery of his letter to Tyana, emphasizing the need for unity, just as limbs and organs in a body are in need of one another; and he repeated his warning to Atarbius not to think 'we who inhabit the sea-coast are outside of the suffering of the many, and have no necessity at all of aid from others'. He lamented the fact, as he had to Amphilochius, that no one felt shame in their being cut off from one another. The contrast was with that older model, represented by 'those fathers who decreed that by small signs the tokens of communion should be carried about from one end of the earth to the other, and that all should be fellow-citizens and neighbours to all'.[21]

From his temporary retreat in Pontus, Basil wrote three more long letters to Neocaesarea itself; and they probably represent the most carefully thought-out description of his state of mind on a number of issues

---

18. *Ep.* 97, C 1: 211, D 2: 165.

19. *Ep.* 244. 8, C 3: 81, D 3: 469. The extent to which he now felt that the hopes of earlier years were closer to fulfilment may be revealed by another comparison with that letter to Tyana: 'We ourselves, nevertheless, neither see nor hear anything but the peace of God and whatsoever leads to it. For even if others are powerful, and great, and confident in themselves, we, on the contrary, are nothing, and worth nothing', *Ep.* 97, C 1: 210, D 2: 161/163. His own confidence, if not self-piteous, would seem to have been bought at the cost of esteem and status.

20. *Ep.* 203. 2.

21. *Ep.* 203. 3, C 2: 170f., D 3: 149/151. Deferrari, with 'tokens of communion', is translating τὰ τῆς κοινωνίας σύμβολα, where Courtonne has ἐπιμιξίας.

beyond the immediate dissension.[22] Writing to the clergy of the city, Basil addressed the question of Sabellianism, making little attempt to hide the fact (for it would have been obvious) that he was attacking Atarbius. Yet the letter hints at other disputes, which may have been going on for a long time, and which probably do more to explain the atmosphere of sourness and suspicion in which recent misunderstandings had been able to flourish. There seems to have been division, in the first place, over the liturgy; the complaint being that, in singing the psalms, Basil and his congregation were departing from the practice inherited from Gregory Thaumaturgus. There had also been misgiving over Basil's asceticism; in particular over the way in which he had introduced it into the very heart of his church. Such misgiving dated back, perhaps, to the early 360s, when Basil had made his choice between remote self-denial and involvement in church affairs. It reminds us not to expect total or automatic agreement among Basil's critics (in this case, between Atarbius and Eustathius).[23] In the second of the two later letters, Basil addressed the educated élite of Neocaesarea: that wider circle of potential allies from whom, for example, Olympius may have been drawn. To them he mentioned, as possible bases for sympathy, his family connections in the area, and the many years he had spent pursuing the ascetic life nearby.[24] He also recalled, as even more likely to awaken their sympathy, the way in which the city had tried to entice him there permanently, as a resident rhetor. The suspicions and disappointments of those years could now be forgotten: 'We do not consider the past, if only the present be sound'.[25] What mattered was to warn the informed and influential laity of the danger they faced: 'A subversion of faith is being contemplated among you, hostile to both apostolic and evangelical doctrines, and hostile to the tradition of the truly great Gregory and of those who followed after him up to the blessed Musonius, whose teachings are of course still fresh in your minds even now'.[26] He was referring to 'the evil of Sabellius'; but once again he became usefully specific: for the problem seems not to have been simply a general acceptance of the Sabellian tradition, but a debate within the city partly about the significance of not being able to 'name' the second person of

22. The two later letters appear to have responded to a silence that had greeted the first; and they did so by attending to quite particular points.

23. *Ep.* 207 passim.

24. This was the letter he wrote while staying with his brother Peter: see *Ep.* 216 and chapter 3, n. 18.

25. *Ep.* 210. 4, C 2: 194, D 3: 207.

26. *Ep.* 210. 3, C 2: 191f., D 3: 201. 'Even now [ἔτι καὶ νῦν]' was a nice touch: it was still possible for them to segregate Atarbius from that respectable genealogy.

the Trinity (for 'Only-begotten', was not, strictly speaking, a name), partly about supposedly ambiguous or obscure writings left behind by Gregory Thaumaturgus himself (writings that we no longer possess in full). So some of the philosophical and historical anxieties abroad in the region were quite specific, and older than any disagreement with Atarbius.[27]

Basil's first letter to the city (by a slight margin the longest of the three) was broader in its reference and implication. As we would expect from his contemporary letters to others in the region, he wanted above all a just hearing, which meant open confrontation with his accusers; and he wanted (since the current dispute was over matters of faith and doctrine) an examination of his suspect writings (if they could find any!) by competent critics.[28] He did not disguise, however, his genuine affection for the community: it was among 'the greatest of the churches', 'the church most dear to us'; and he implied sadly that its antagonism towards him had lasted 'for almost a whole generation'.[29] Against that coldness he asserted the rights of his own historical association with the city.

The thrust of his argument has been already discussed—the early allusion to 'blood relationships'; the fact that 'both you and we have not only the same teachers of God's mysteries, but also the same spiritual fathers who from the beginning have laid the foundation of your church'; the evocation of 'the famous Gregory and all who ... succeeded in turn to his chair'—preparing the way for the crucial passages, later in the letter, where he discussed both his family history and its relationship to, indeed its total involvement in, the ecclesial history of the region.[30] Now we can see the wider significance of his careful description of development— the development, as explained to Eustathius in the previous year, of the teachings of his grandmother Macrina.[31] His more explicit understanding of the doctrine of the Spirit, and his associated move away from any middle-of-the-road theological party towards a careful and limited gloss upon the simple teaching in Nicaea, were precisely the issues at stake; and they contributed to a new sense of where he stood, doctrinally, as well as to a new acceptance of the paths he had followed in his career to date. 'We

27. The 'naming' anxiety was closely associated with central points of debate in the Arian dispute: for the ability to name, in a purely logical sense, the three persons of the Trinity was closely connected with the ability to distinguish characteristics of each one of them (characteristics descriptive of three ὑποστάσεις), while safeguarding a unity of οὐσία.

28. On the importance of limiting disputes to written statements, see chapter 4, at nn. 94f.

29. *Ep.* 204. 1, 7; C 2: 172f., 180; D 3: 155, 173.

30. *Ep.* 204. 2, C 2: 173f., D 3: 157.

31. *Ep.* 223. 3. For all these points, see chapter 1, at nn. 69f.

are conscious', he wrote, 'of having received into our hearts no doctrine inimical to sound teaching, nor of having at any time defiled our souls by the abominable blasphemy of the Arians'. So he felt able to excuse any association he may have at one time countenanced between himself and churchmen who were later exposed as suspect in their theology (thinking, no doubt, of Apollinarius, but also of his old 'semi-Arian' friends): 'If we ever received into communion anyone who came from that teacher, they concealed the malady deep in their hearts and uttered pious words or at least did not oppose what was expressed by us, and thus we received them'.[32]

The last point embodied a principle he defended elsewhere: that one should not press too hard upon those in theological error, if they showed signs of repentance. Churchmen should ostracize and stigmatize as few as possible, enter into the warmest collegiality with the rest, and only then, when harmony had begun to do its work, press for additional 'clarification [τράνωσιν]'.[33] He also brought to his defence a letter from Athanasius (not extant), 'in which he has clearly ordered that, if anyone wish to come over from the heresy of the Arians by confessing the faith of Nicaea, we should receive him without making any discrimination in his case'.[34] To that extent Basil had now carried the dispute onto a broader plane.

He continued in that vein, demanding nothing less (even *vis-à-vis* Neocaesarea) than a universal council, brought together simply (so it would seem) to discuss the matters at issue between them. It was more likely that he wished, even if only in passing, to draw Neocaesarea into his wider plans for church unity: it seems scarcely credible that Atarbius alone could have been the excuse for so momentous a congregation. Basil's true purpose was to bring home the isolation Neocaesarea threatened to bring upon itself:

> From the letters which are being conveyed from those regions [he listed more or less the provinces of the whole empire!], and from those which are being sent back to them from here, it is possible for you to learn that we are all of one mind, having the same ideas [τὸ ἓν φρονοῦντες]. So let him who flees communion with us, who cuts himself off from the whole Church, not escape the notice of your keen mind. Look around

32. *Ep.* 204. 6, C 2: 179, D 3: 169/171.
33. *Ep.* 113 to Tarsus, C 2: 17, D 2: 225. See Fedwick, *Charisma*, p. 74 and n. 170. See also *Ep.* 114. For a fuller analysis of these letters, see Michael A. G. Haykin, 'And Who Is the Spirit? Basil of Caesarea's Letters to the Church at Tarsus'.
34. *Ep.* 204. 6, C 2: 179, D 3: 171.

you, brethren, and see with whom you are in communion; once you are not received by us, who henceforth will acknowledge you?[35]

So he ended the letter bemoaning 'the wickedness of the age', which he contrasted, as on other occasions, with the practice of earlier days (thus clearly associating his programme for unity with an ancient model of the Church):

> Question your fathers and they will tell you that even if the parishes seemed to be divided by geographic position, they were yet one in mind and were governed by one counsel. Continuous was association among the people, continuous was mutual visiting among the clergy; and among the pastors themselves there was such love for one another that each used the other as a teacher and guide in matters pertaining to the Lord.[36]

The confrontation with Neocaesarea tells us a great deal about Basil's view of his own task and standing. It does so partly because it helps us to tie up loose ends in relation to Eustathius and Apollinarius, but mainly because it places firmly in its context the great exercise in self-definition *vis-à-vis* his own family, studied in the opening chapter. It also shows the extent to which, by 376, almost all the issues Basil faced were being drawn into the orbit of a universal ambition in the face of the Arian dispute. The ripples now covered the whole surface of the pond. We can see to what broader level of self-confidence he had now been able to raise himself— finding new friends, describing to his own satisfaction the path he had followed in life, articulating more clearly the principles he felt governed the inner lives of Christians, and identifying a single challenge and a single model within the Church, to which he might dedicate the energy of spirit miraculously reserved to him after so much sickness and disappointment. The sense of purpose is beyond doubt. Its fulfilment, as we shall see, was another matter.

————

Basil's activities in Armenia are no less difficult to disengage from his personal alarm, as he was faced with the errors of Eustathius and the suspicions of Theodotus of Nicopolis (a man with whom he had closely to

35. *Ep.* 204. 7, C 2: 180, D 3: 173.
36. *Ep.* 204. 7, C 2: 180, D 3: 173/175.

work in his Armenian mission). Yet the circumstances were obviously of an importance far greater than could be encompassed by Basil's biography.[37]

The unity, independence, and eventually Christian character of the kingdom of Armenia, following the Roman defeat of Persia in 298, had made the area a sensitive buffer zone, and a scene of contentious struggle for influence, between the two rival empires. 'Unity' calls for some clarification. Armenia fell into at least three regions, which seem naturally divided one from another in the light of history and as a result of geography: the west, Armenia Minor, exposed to Hellenistic, Roman, and ultimately Christian influence; the north, more remote from both its powerful neighbours; and the south, adjacent to Syria, where local governors and aristocrats had long been susceptible to Roman influence, and where cities and peoples were naturally absorbed into Roman strategy, based upon Antioch, and reaching north as well as east.[38] Nor is 'independence' entirely appropriate. When Persian pressure induced fresh division, Constantine had been happy to appoint his nephew, Hannibalianus, king of what area he could control.[39] From then until 358, Rome demanded tax. During the middle years of the century, the interests of Armenia were easily sacrificed when it suited the emperors in Constantinople.

Events came to a new head in 363. Cut down unexpectedly in his grandiose war against Shapur II, and leaving no obvious successor, Julian bequeathed to the empire the need for a swift and bitter choice. War had to be abandoned, and a new emperor secured. Persia naturally took advantage of Roman embarrassment. Among the provisions of the treaty forced upon the empire, as Jovian strove to establish his authority, was an agreement (binding on both parties) not to interfere in the affairs of Armenia.[40] The result in practice was that the kingdom fell apart, to everyone's advantage but its own.

Arshak, the king, experienced particular humiliation. He had been, in latter years at least, a loyal friend to Rome. He had come to power around 350, when both Romans and Persians were preoccupied on other

37. Two general surveys have proved particularly useful: R. H. Hewsen, 'The Successors of Tiridates the Great: A Contribution to the History of Armenia in the Fourth Century'; and Roger C. Blockley, 'The Division of Armenia between the Romans and the Persians at the End of the Fourth Century A.D.'. Much can still be gained from Norman H. Baynes, 'Rome and Armenia in the Fourth Century': clarity and grace compensate for the imperfections of an older scholarship.

38. See Matthews, *Ammianus*, p. 53.

39. Matthews, *Ammianus*, pp. 136, 499 n. 14, with cautious comment on the nevertheless invaluable article by T. D. Barnes, 'Constantine and the Christians of Persia'.

40. Ammianus Marcellinus 25, 7. 12f.

fronts—Constantius with the usurper Magnentius, and the Persians with frontier raids.[41] As time went by, he found it either useful or attractive to adopt a religious position more favourable to the Arianism espoused by Constantius. Inclination to the Roman cause brought tax relief in 358, and an arranged marriage with Olympias, daughter of Ablabius, Constantine's great Praetorian Prefect.[42] It also led soon after to the exile from Armenia of Nerses, the orthodox *catholicos*.[43] Nerses had been educated in Caesarea. His relationship with Gregory the Illuminator had made his succession as Christian leader in Armenia (after a period in the service of the king) impossible to challenge. He had been consecrated, also in Caesarea, in 353. It is not unlikely, therefore, that Basil, after his return from Athens to Cappadocia three years or so later, would have learned of this distinguished figure and might have begun to follow his career with some interest. Seeking the tax relief of 358, the successful Armenian embassy, led by the *catholicos*, may have met the emperor in Caesarea itself.[44] Finally, Nerses had known, and had been influenced by, Eustathius of Sebaste, making it a mark of his administration to encourage both the ascetic life and the care of the poor and sick. All those associations would have encouraged the interest and admiration of Caesarea's future bishop.[45]

Nerses was not able to regain his see until 368 or 369. Arshak, meanwhile, fell victim to changed circumstance. As soon as Jovian had made his enforced peace, Shapur invaded Armenia, captured and imprisoned Arshak, and may have been directly responsible for his death soon after. The king's son, Pap, took refuge in Neocaesarea.[46] Gradually, Roman

41. Ammianus Marcellinus 14, 3. 1; 14, 5.

42. Ammianus Marcellinus 20, 11. 1f.; *Cod. Theod.* 11, 1. 1. For the date (358 rather than 360), see Nina G. Garsoïan, 'Politique ou orthodoxie? L'Arménie au quatrième siècle', p. 305. On Ablabius, see Eunapius *Lives* B 463f. in W 384f.

43. Nerses did not have a metropolitan see, as was normal for church leaders within the empire, but exercised a wandering authority over bishops he had appointed.

44. Ammianus Marcellinus 20, 9. 1, 11. 1–4. For Nerses' involvement, see Nina G. Garsoïan, 'Quidam Narseus? A Note on the Mission of St. Nerses the Great'.

45. Nina Garsoïan, 'Nerses le Grand, Basile de Césarée et Eustathe de Sébaste', pp. 148f., was of the opinion that the connections dawned on Basil only later—perhaps an unnecessary caution: albeit 'remote' in Pontus, Basil could easily have heard reports. (I am much less open to Garsoïan's suggestion, p. 149, that the 'Narses' of *Ep.* 92 was the Armenian prelate.) For Nerses' own relations with Eustathius, see the same article, esp. pp. 164f., and her 'Sur le titre de *protecteur des pauvres*', esp. p. 29. The plentiful references to Basil in Armenian sources are frequently unreliable; but see Faustus of Byzantium 4, 3f.; 5, 24. For Faustus, I have relied on the French translation of Jean Baptiste Emine.

46. Ammianus Marcellinus 27, 12. 9. For Pap specifically, see Roger C. Blockley, *Ammianus Marcellinus: A Study of His Historiography and Political Thought*.

interest encouraged and supported Pap in a reclamation of his heritage. By the time Valens had completed his campaigns against the Goths in 369, Pap was on the path to full kingship. The *comes* Terentius was appointed *dux Armeniae* in that year and took a direct hand in regaining for Pap his royal authority.[47]

Nerses had not been idle since 359, cultivating his friends among the Armenian aristocracy. He returned to the kingdom in triumph on the back of Pap's own success, representing once again a temporarily welcome alliance with Rome. The visibly ad hoc friendship of emperor, king, and *catholicos*, however, could not last. Nerses had never been able to reserve his criticism—'Those whom he blessed were blessed, and those whom he cursed were cursed'[48]—and Pap resented his resistance to immorality and persecution.

Valens, meanwhile, found Pap difficult to keep in place. The Persians had not viewed recent events with equanimity; and in 371 it proved necessary to forestall, with a considerable show of strength, a Persian attack. Roman forces penetrated far to the east, to Bagravand, the high country between the upper valleys of the Aras and the Murat. It was what Themistius called 'saving Armenia'.[49]

Basil, in a sense, travelled in their wake, for it was in the context of that 'settlement' that he received the command from Valens to put in order the affairs of the churches in Armenia.[50] Judging by his subsequent correspondence, his responsibility (or at least his successful influence) was restricted to Armenia Minor in the west: he does not seem to have played any part in affairs further east than Satala, barely a hundred kilometres up the Lykos (Kelkit) valley from Nicopolis. It may seem unnecessary, therefore, to speculate about further relations with Nerses at that late stage; but one incident is bound to awaken our curiosity. At some point in 373, relations between Nerses and Pap reached breaking point, and Nerses was murdered at the command of the king himself.[51] Surely such an event would have coloured Basil's view of affairs, even in Armenia Minor, had he known of it. He did not make his journey until the middle months of the year and seems to have been back in Caesarea during August. Nerses may not have died

47. See *PLRE* 1: 881f., s.v. Terentius 2.
48. Faustus of Byzantium 5, 21; tr. p. 289.
49. Themistius *Orat.* 11, 149B (ἀνασῴζεται Ἀρμενίους); ed. Schenkl and Downey, 1: 224. See also Ammianus Marcellinus 29, 1. 2.
50. *Ep.* 99. 1, C 1: 214, with its phrases τῷ βασιλικῷ προστάγματι and τῇ κοινῇ καταστάσει τῶν Ἐκκλησιῶν. See the points already made in chapter 5, at nn. 178f.
51. The Armenian sources give wonderfully full accounts. See n. 45 above and n. 53 below.

until the end of July.[52] It leaves little time for an overlap. However, there is no way of telling whether Basil heard of the death of the *catholicos* while he was away from home, or whether he received the news of the funeral (conducted amidst Pap's carefully expressed grief) just across the border south of Satala, where Nerses had once resided and Pap had a fortified lodge.[53]

Pap continued to claim his attention. Before we examine what Basil actually did in Armenia, we should therefore pursue the more general story just a little further. Still within the context of the most recent Roman intervention, Pap himself was murdered, either in 374 or 375. Valens's long-term plan was to transfer support to his cousin Varazdat, who reigned until 378. Much more was involved, however, than simple dynastic strategy. The murder itself, ostensibly committed on the spur of the moment at a banquet, was the work of Traianus, *comes rei militaris* in the East since 371 and Roman commander in Armenia. Basil may have been his correspondent.[54] The deed seems likely to have won the approval, if not to have sprung from the intrigue, of Valens himself.[55] Terentius, no lover of Pap, and similarly in touch with Basil, may also have been involved. He had his connections with Samosata, where his daughters were deaconesses, and maintained friendships with orthodox aristocrats in the south of the kingdom (naturally aggrieved by, among other things, the treatment of Nerses). He had actually accused Pap to Valens's face and thereby engineered the king's virtual arrest for a time in Tarsus, from which he escaped only with some difficulty. His murder would have seemed no more than an astute alternative.[56] In the aftermath, Rome mounted a great

52. *PLRE* 1: 666, s.v. Papa, suggests with apparent confidence 25 July 373; but I have been unable to discover on what authority. Faustus and Moses (on whom see the following note) appear to be silent. The tenth-century *Généalogie de la famille de saint Grégoire et Vie de saint Narse*, 14, has the phrase (in the French translation, which I have been given no reason to doubt) 'dans le mois de hroditz [more properly, Hrotic'], le jour de jeudi', in *Collection des historiens anciens et modernes de l'Arménie*, ed. Victor Langlois, 2: 41. 'Hrotic' ran from early July to early August: V. Grumel, *La Chronologie* = *Traité d'études byzantines*, 1: 301. J. R. Russell was kind but equally at a loss.

53. At Khakh and Til respectively. See Moses of Chorene (Moses Khorenats'i), *History of the Armenians*, 3. 38, tr. Robert S. Thompson, pp. 298f.

54. See *Ep.* 148 and 149. *PLRE* 1: 921f., s.v. Traianus 2, seems assured, as is Garsoïan, 'Politique', 316f. See also Treucker, *Studien*, pp. 47, 51. Yet we cannot be completely certain that we are dealing with the same man.

55. Ammianus Marcellinus was appalled, 30, 1. 18f., and one detects irony (obvious also to Traianus) in his phrase '*modo serenae mentis Valentis indices litteras tradens*', § 19, in Rolfe, 3: 304. Traianus remained in favour, acting as *magister peditum* in Thrace in 377; but he was killed at Hadrianople.

56. Ammianus Marcellinus 30, 1. 2f. Compared with Traianus, Terentius may have experienced more censure (as much in relation to his own orthodoxy): *PLRE* 1: 881f., s.v. Terentius 2.

drive in 377, to confirm its support of Varazdat. However, the Gothic revolt in the Balkans demanded a sudden and massive redeployment of troops. That could have opened the way for a significant reassertion of Persian might; but by one of those remarkable accidents of history, just in the year when Valens was meeting his death at Hadrianople, Shapur II died also. Armenia, divided now between two kings, was able to enjoy a brief period of fragmented independence.

With this survey of events, we seem to have thrust Basil onto the 'world stage' with a vengeance. It was, indeed, a moment of some importance for our understanding of his career and personal development. On the one hand, far from disappearing into the mountains on some obscure mission, he was thrust into the heart of a political and military situation crucial to the survival of the empire. On the other hand, many different incidents in his life were now given new significance by conjunction: the division of Cappadocia, the confrontation with Valens, the estrangement from the two Gregorys and other bishops, the enmity of Demosthenes, the confrontation with Eustathius, the involvement with Neocaesarea, the correspondence with high officials, and the interest in Antioch. It has often seemed difficult to explain why Valens, so much a villain in sources closely associated with Basil himself, should have appointed him for a mission of such delicacy.[57] Yet Valens knew that he could not afford to sacrifice strategic security to theological passion, and that any potential division in Armenia was dangerous to the wider interest. The natural association of Caesarea with the Armenian church and Basil's personal connections around Neocaesarea would have made him an attractive envoy. Their meeting in 372 could not have disguised from Valens Basil's reputation and personal authority and may even have awakened his reluctant admiration. He knew, on the other hand, that the division of Cappadocia had clipped the bishop's wings a little, even if that had not been its direct intention. He knew that Basil's orthodoxy was still a relatively isolated and threatened advantage. He knew that lesser officials like Demosthenes could be relied on to keep the man in his place. He may even have known that Basil

---

57. Fedwick, *Charisma*, makes little reference; and the reasons adduced on p. 104 n. 9 are not corroborated. Gain's allusions are scattered in pursuit of other interests: 'ce qui ne manque pas de piquant, vu leur affrontement', *Église*, p. 81; and 's'explique par des raisons politiques', p. 322 n. 148. Courtonne, *Témoin*, esp. pp. 120f., places matters firmly in the context of the Arian controversy. Brennecke, *Geschichte der Homöer*, p. 195, may overestimate Basil's success ('im Auftrage des Kaisers, doch eigentlich gegen seinen Willen'), and he is surprisingly vague in assessing Valens's motives, picking out, as I would, Basil's impressive personality, and adding his friendships with those in high places and his reluctance to indulge in the fiery excommunication of Homoeans.

badly needed to maintain the friendship of bishops further east, not least Theodotus of Nicopolis himself, in order to gain the upper hand against Eustathius and to defend his own theological position. He was useful, in other words, but unlikely to prove offensive. It is sobering to observe how Basil might be thought of when viewed from such a height!

Setting out in June 373, Basil appears to have returned to Caesarea by August. It was from there that he sent a report of his conduct to Terentius, a personal friend, but, as we have seen, closely interested in Armenian affairs.[58] The *comes* had had a hand in transmitting to Basil the emperor's original wishes.[59] What Basil had to report was that 'I was not permitted to turn my desire into action', thanks to the unfriendly attitude of Theodotus, 'the bishop assigned to co-operate with us'. As we know, the cause of that problem was Eustathius. The letter proceeds to offer a long description of their dispute; but one new point commands attention: Basil seems to have travelled first, or certainly at a very early stage of his trip, to Getasa, where Meletius of Antioch was residing. His first significant port of call, in other words, in fulfilment of a government commission, was the temporary home of his Antiochene hero. That tells us something about the context in which Basil viewed his opportunity in Armenia, even if relations with Eustathius had also been at issue. However, Theodotus was there as well (it was at Getasa that he and Meletius taxed Basil further on the reliability of Eustathius's declarations to date). The plan was that they should travel on together to Satala. Theodotus did not do so. It is likely that Basil did, and that he received his rebuff at Nicopolis after that. He certainly went to Satala; and he described to Terentius what he achieved there: he 'established peace among the bishops of Armenia', urged them 'to put aside their habitual discord',[60] and supplied certain disciplinary 'rules [τύπους]'. The Christians in Satala then asked him to appoint a bishop; and he reconciled their community with 'Cyril, the bishop of Armenia', against whom slander had been 'falsely fomented by the calumny of his enemies'. Basil was well aware that, beside his own difficulties, those achievements were 'trivial and of no importance' (for once, tactful humility was near the mark), and therefore not up to the emperor's expectations.[61]

Filling the bishopric at Satala seems not to have been an easy matter, nor swiftly accomplished: Basil had to make his eventual plans known

---

58. *Ep.* 99. See also his earlier report concerning Apollinarius, *Ep.* 214.

59. 'Both the Imperial ordinance and the friendly letter of your Honour': *Ep.* 99. 1, C 1: 214, D 2: 171/173.

60. Τὴν συνήθη διαφοράν, which is not quite Deferrari's 'customary indifference'.

61. *Ep.* 99. 4, C 1: 217f., D 2: 181/183.

by a later letter. The man chosen was a certain Poimenius, a long-standing friend and distant relative. His own city and family were very reluctant to see him go, and the probability is that Basil had drawn upon personal connections further west in making his choice.[62] When problems recurred in the region, Basil continued to address Poimenius with complete trust.[63]

He maintained his interest in Armenian affairs[64]—hence his anxiety in the face of a new problem that surfaced the following year (Poimenius may have been the first to hear of his complaints). 'Armenians', he warned, would be travelling through Satala, escorting one Faustus, consecrated (as *catholicos* of Armenia) by Anthimus of Tyana in direct opposition to Basil, who traditionally had that right, and who was reluctant for the moment to have anything to do with the man. A letter from Poimenius, however, would satisfy Basil that Faustus was orthodox; and he was prepared to overlook Anthimus's slight if Poimenius would speak on behalf of the new *catholicos*, 'bearing witness for him, if you see that the life of the man is good'. He could, moreover, if such were the case, 'urge the rest to do likewise'. Poimenius was thus authorized to exercise at least moral authority on Basil's behalf over the church in Armenia.[65] Basil sent a letter on the same topic to Theodotus of Nicopolis, expressing dismay that Faustus should have demanded consecration, when he had been unable to produce a reassuring letter 'from your Reverence and from the rest of the bishops'.[66] He also wrote finally to Meletius. He regarded the consecration of Faustus not only as an example of arrogance on the part of Anthimus but also as further evidence of opposition in Armenia to the Cyril mentioned in the letter to Terentius; 'In consequence Armenia has become filled with schisms'.[67]

Behind these developments lay the increasing estrangement of Pap from policies favourable to the empire, in church affairs as elsewhere. Rejection of Cyril was hardly likely to endear the king to such advocates of the orthodox cause as Terentius and Traianus. The events do show, moreover, that Basil's association with Armenia proper was not just a consequence of his status as bishop of Caesarea but was directly connected with his responsibilities (albeit ad hoc) in Armenia Minor, and with his

---

62. *Ep.* 102, with confirmation in 103.

63. See *Ep.* 122, to be discussed shortly.

64. Hence his improving relationship with Theodotus (*Ep.* 130), and other letters (now lost) addressed to the region (see *Ep.* 195).

65. *Ep.* 122, C 2: 28, D 2: 251/253.

66. *Ep.* 121, C 2: 27, D 2: 251.

67. *Ep.* 120, C 2: 26, D 2: 249. See Gain, *Église*, pp. 77 (with n. 71), 81.

ability to place in a strategic frontier see a childhood friend who was also a member of his own family.

Events took another turn in the following year: Theodotus of Nicopolis died. Basil, with other bishops, was faced with the task of filling another vacancy. His solution was to recommend the transfer of Euphronius from his 'distant spot' at Colonia. The first task was to assuage natural dissatisfaction in Colonia itself (whose Christian citizens even threatened legal proceedings). Basil did so by recommending to the clergy of the city the broadest principles of church government. The decision had been no 'human arrangement ... prompted by the reasoning of men' but had been made, rather, by 'those who are committed with the care of the churches of God' through their 'union with the Spirit'. The clergy of Colonia were exhorted, moreover, to 'impress this source of their action upon [their own] minds, and strive to perfect it [καὶ ἐμβάλλεσθε τῇ διανοίᾳ τὴν ὁρμὴν ταύτην, καὶ σπουδάσατε αὐτὴν τελειῶσαι]'.[68] Distrust of 'the reasoning of men [ἐκ λογισμῶν ... φρονούντων ἀνθρώπων]' dated back several years; but the reference to the Spirit was characteristic of Basil's more recent interests, with its accompanying exhortation to an inner change, and to moral improvement. He also wished to make it clear that Colonia was part of a wider world and would benefit from a secure succession at Nicopolis, whereas weakness in the mother church would undermine all efforts elsewhere. An accompanying letter to the leading citizens of Colonia was less intense in its address, asking more for 'pardon' than for ecstatic insight; but it did impress upon them, 'situated on the outskirts of Armenia', that they needed to take account of dangers and advantages just a little more distant than their own preoccupations.[69]

Then Basil had to assuage, for different reasons, the people of Nicopolis itself, where he had never found an easy reception. To the clergy he repeated his conviction that a task undertaken by 'pious persons' was pursued 'with the counsel of the Spirit': 'no human consideration is present', and 'it is the Lord who is directing their hearts'.[70] He was specific about the identity of those 'pious persons': chief initiator was no less a person than Poimenius of Satala. The plans set in motion in 373 were still having their effect. Nor was he the mere instrument of Basil's distant wishes: 'He did not resort to postponements of the matter and thus give an opportunity for defence to those who are opposing, ... but he immediately

68. *Ep.* 227, C 3: 30, D 3: 345. This letter was discussed in chapter 5, at n. 182.
69. *Ep.* 228, C 3: 33, D 3: 351.
70. *Ep.* 229. 1, C 3: 33f., D 3: 353.

brought his excellent plan to fulfilment'.[71] To the laity of the city, Basil was briefer in his comments, exhorting them to support in their own way the task of the new bishop.[72]

The outcome, perhaps predictably, was not a success. Eustathius in particular had seen the death of his old critic too good an opportunity to be missed. Not without the support of Demosthenes, he and others had intruded another candidate against Euphronius, named Fronto; and they proceeded to consecrate him as a rival bishop.[73] Fronto had at first succeeded in creating the impression of unsullied theological respectability, employing 'both words of faith and affectation of piety all for the deception of those who met him'.[74] Once he had emerged in his true colours, he became 'a common abomination to all Armenia'; but he could still muster enough accomplices to force those more amenable to Basil's viewpoint out of the city, at least to the extent that they were denied the use of the church and forced to worship in the open air.[75] That may call into question Basil's own assertion that Fronto's party represented only a minority, although it may also demonstrate how little a community could do, when faced with Arians confident of government support.[76] Other letters written later in that year continued to describe the depredations of Demosthenes.[77] All Basil was able to do was impress upon the clergy at Nicopolis that their misfortune was not unique in history. They should see themselves in a tradition of martyrs and confessors, whose enemies had not been able to triumph in the long run.[78]

71. *Ep.* 229.1, C 3: 34, D 3: 353/355.

72. *Ep.* 230. See chapter 5, at nn. 145f. It would seem that *Ep.* 127 and 128 to Eusebius of Samosata were written in 373 rather than in 375, which would bring all the Colonia and Nicopolis involvements closer together. *Ep.* 128 in particular is filled with reference to the Spirit and 'the old laws of charity'—matters touched upon already and to be touched upon again.

73. *Ep.* 237. 2.

74. *Ep.* 238, C 3: 58, D 3: 413. The same point is made in *Ep.* 239. 1.

75. *Ep.* 239. 1, C 3: 60, D 3: 417. For other references to enforced worship in the open, see *Ep.* 238, 240. 2. Theodoret corroborates these other instances, *Hist. relig.* 2 (Julian). 15.

76. See *Ep.* 238 at C 3: 58, lines 16f.; and 240. 3: 'Now that they have seen that the laity are provoked they are again pretending orthodoxy', C 3: 64, D 3: 425; although 'laity' may be a tendentiously specific rendering of τοὺς λαούς (Courtonne has 'les peuples').

77. *Ep.* 246, 247.

78. *Ep.* 240. 1; but the whole letter makes the point.

By that time, Pap was dead. Although, for another year or so, Rome continued to play a forceful role in Armenian affairs, the diplomatic subtleties that may have seemed relevant in 373 might now have proved less useful. Failure at Nicopolis, and in the kingdom of Armenia itself (given the difficulties of Cyril), was a disappointing conclusion to Basil's efforts. Other preoccupations, however, had already begun to override the significance of the area in his mind. In the midst of his Armenian involvements, Eusebius of Samosata had been exiled, imparting a new emotional intensity to events in Syria. The need to maintain pressure on the Arian party had also drawn Basil further afield, at least in his correspondence. This is the moment, therefore, to marshal together the references, first to Antioch and its schism, and then to the Arian conflict, as fought out on a wider field. The question still remains, however: was Basil driven more by the fortunes of his own friends, and by a need to vindicate himself in the face of personal enemies, than by any elevated concern with ideological debate in the empire more generally? Was it possible for *any* bishop of the time to rise above divisions of language, cultural history, and political convenience, and to think in anything approaching 'universal' terms?

In the first place, the Arian conflict was consistently associated in Basil's mind with conflict in the church of Antioch itself. That conflict had been a feature of the city's life for decades already.[79] Eustathius had been

---

79. In what follows I have depended heavily on the clear and detailed account given by Courtonne, *Témoin*, and, with slightly more caution, the older study by Robert Devreesse, *Le Patriarcat d'Antioche, depuis le paix de l'Église jusqu'à la conquête arabe*. Behind both works stands F. Cavallera, *Le Schisme d'Antioche (IVe–Ve siècles)*. Of comparable importance are the references to Antioch in Brennecke, *Geschichte der Homöer*. Note also his convincing scepticism about a persecution in Syria under Valens, pp. 233f. Basil's heroes and friends did most to isolate themselves from the mainstream of church opinion. Fedwick's chronology, *Charisma*, pp. 108f., is different from older works, but his narrative no less useful. Lukas Vischer, *Basilius der Große: Untersuchungen zu einem Kirchenvater des 4. Jahrhunderts*, is also particularly clear. A focus on Antioch is central to the argument of E. Amand de Mendieta, in an excellent and indispensable study, 'Basile de Césarée et Damase de Rome: Les causes de l'échec de leurs négociations', marred only by confessional anxieties over the status of the bishop of Rome (see, for example, nn. 126, 158 below). More balanced is the useful account by Justin Taylor, 'St. Basil the Great and Pope St. Damasus I'. He is content to leave Basil at once orthodox and indignant, while showing a shrewd sympathy for Damasus's difficulties. His dating, however, is open to revision. Important criticisms are levelled on Basil's behalf by Wilhelm de Vries, 'Die Ostkirche und die Cathedra Petri'. Reference back to the early sections of chapter 4 may sometimes prove helpful.

chosen its bishop in 325; and for more than fifty years loyalty or opposition to his name and policy lay at the heart of the city's divisions. At Nicaea, he had been a clear opponent of Arius; but he subsequently tangled both with Eusebius of Caesarea (who accused him of too forceful a condemnation of Sabellius) and with Eusebius of Nicomedia (whom he accused in his turn of undermining all that Nicaea had attempted to achieve). Mostly as a result of that perceived impudence, Eustathius was deposed at a synod in Antioch in 330 and exiled to Thrace.

Not surprisingly, given the passions that Arius had aroused, and the accusations that had been bandied about between Eustathius and his immediate enemies, there followed a turmoil of succession to the see. Some of the effects we have noted already. The council held at Sardica in 343 calmed matters somewhat, largely because it made very clear the division of opinion (on Arianism as on other matters) between the eastern and western sectors of the empire (a division exacerbated by the shared rule and divergent opinions of Constans and Constantius, lasting until 350). Leontius, bishop from approximately 344 until 357, gained for Antioch a long and relatively stable period of church government, a period marked also by Constantius's engagements with Persia (always important for the city), and by the violent administration of the Caesar Gallus from 351. It was also the period during which Aetius began to come to prominence.[80] In 357, Leontius was succeeded by Eudoxius. The latter's appointment was not regular, and he maintained his position only with government support. In return, he agreed to the formula of Sirmium in 357, then supported more openly the Anomoean party, and maintained friendly relations with Aetius. It was after his deposition at Seleucia in 359 that the see passed to Meletius, whose position was confirmed at Constantinople in 360.[81]

Meletius, who maintained his rights in the see of Antioch for the rest of Basil's life and for a short while thereafter, and who will claim most of our attention, came originally from Melitene. He had been appointed formerly to the see of Sebaste in 358, in place of the other Eustathius; but he failed to gain acceptance there and lived at Beroea. In 359, at Caesarea in Palestine, he had signed the formula of Acacius, confirmed at Seleucia, which specified only that the Son was ὅμοιος. Evidently he came

---

80. See chapter 4, at nn. 5f.

81. The circumstances of those events, and the startling transfer of Eudoxius to the see of Constantinople, have all been discussed in chapter 4, as just noted above. It is important to stress the association of Meletius with the synod of Constantinople. Whatever move towards a clearer espousal of Nicaea he may have made, it happened gradually and later. See Brennecke, *Geschichte der Homöer*, pp. 69f.

to regret the move. He later made a declaration of his revised opinions to Constantius, which represented certainly greater caution and probably orthodoxy.[82] Not surprisingly, he was exiled from Antioch (to Armenia Minor). His place was taken by Euzoius (who would later baptize the emperor Constantius as he headed north and west to meet the challenge of Julian).

At that point, matters became complicated in ways that would not be unravelled for at least two generations. With the pagan Julian in power (and it would not be unjust to describe his approach to Christian episcopal politics as meddlesome), Meletius was allowed back to Antioch. The city now had two bishops. Very shortly afterwards, a third appeared: Paulinus, consecrated in 362, with no respect for canonical regularity, by the unsavoury Lucifer of Cagliari. As a priest, Paulinus had long provided a focus in the city for those faithful to the memory of Eustathius himself. Consequently, he and his supporters were thought by others to incline towards Sabellianism. They had, nevertheless, the possibly dubious advantage of having been encouraged in their loyalties by Athanasius himself, who visited Antioch in 346. Yet they remained a minority. Most of the orthodox in Antioch had gathered around two other clerics, Diodorus and Flavianus, who had been unswerving in their opposition to Leontius and his immediate successor. They now transferred their allegiance to Meletius and were explicitly careful to avoid Sabellianist positions.

The confusing turn of events naturally caused concern elsewhere, not least in Alexandria (where Athanasius had also benefitted from Julian's 'tolerance'). A meeting of bishops was held there in 362; and part of the resulting synodal letter, which was widely addressed, attempted to wean some of Meletius's supporters away and awaken greater loyalty towards Paulinus. The document emphasized the formula of Nicaea and the belief that the Holy Spirit was not a creature. Its chief appeal was to the ideas of the Antiochene Eustathius, as expressed at the time of Nicaea itself; and it paid much less attention to the tangled legalities (or more often illegalities) of subsequent episcopal succession in the city.[83]

An embassy travelled to Antioch to announce the decisions reached at Alexandria. Perhaps fortunately, the churchmen involved were chary about the rights of Paulinus, for they soon discovered that matters were even more complicated than Athanasius and his immediate associates

---

82. See Epiphanius *Panarion* 70. 3. 29f. Courtonne, *Témoin*, p. 248, observes: 'Le discours de Mélèce était d'un homme attaché à l'orthodoxie'.

83. Athanasius *Tom. ad Ant.* 3f., *PG* 26. 798f.

might have supposed. The two Apollinarii, father and son, at Laodicea had been firm supporters of Athanasius for many years; and the younger Apollinarius had sent a representative to Alexandria. He also had a finger in the Antiochene pie, bringing his influence to bear in the cause of the priest Vitalis, who was a firm adherent to the traditions of Nicaea and headed what was virtually a fourth party in the city. (More than ten years later, he managed to gain episcopal consecration also, although Damasus of Rome had eventually come to suspect his orthodoxy.)[84] The reputation of Apollinarius in the early 360s, and the seeming orthodoxy of his protégé, may have made Paulinus less obviously acceptable in the eyes of the delegates from Egypt. Later, when Apollinarius himself had become more compromised and western support for Paulinus more entrenched, Vitalis was less able to maintain his claims.

The accession of Valens in 364 brought to an end the chaotic fruits of Julian's cynical indifference. Antioch's strategic position made its social stability important to the emperor; and he was bound to defuse tensions as far as he could. Meletius once again attracted censure and was exiled.[85] Collaboration with the West seemed to moderate parties the best way of strengthening their position against an emperor of uncertain orthodoxy. It was at that point that supporters of Basil of Ancyra, with Eustathius of Sebaste, went to the West, gained communion with Liberius of Rome, and returned in triumph to their synod at Tyana early in 367.[86] Yet endeavours of that sort were soon under serious threat. Meletius may have been able to return to Antioch briefly, while Valens was preoccupied with the revolt of Procopius and with his campaigns against the Goths in the late 360s; but he was certainly absent from the city again by 370.[87] The tone of eastern church affairs at that stage was best symbolized by the ambiguities and ill-defined promises of Demophilus, recently

84. Vitalis actually went to Rome in 375 and gained some favour; but that ebbed with time. See Damasus's letter to Paulinus, Per filium (his Ep. 3), PL 13. 356f., together with his Ep. 7 against Apollinarius, PL 13. 369f. Also Epiphanius Panarion 77. 20f.; and Basil's Ep. 258, to which we shall return. Behind more recent accounts of the relations between Damasus and Basil lies the important textual study of E. Schwartz, 'Über die Sammlung des Cod. Veronensis LX'. See also his 'Zur Kirchengeschichte des vierten Jahrhunderts'.

85. See Rochelle Snee, 'Valens' Recall of the Nicene Exiles and Anti-Arian Propaganda', p. 414. Jovian's brief reign had encouraged Meletius and his supporters to move closer to a Nicene position, chiefly because of their alarm at the conduct of Eunomius. Valens, restoring churchmen to the positions they had enjoyed under Constantius, simply (and successfully) ignored the intervening confusions caused by Julian and Jovian. See Brennecke, Geschichte der Homöer, pp. 173f., 209.

86. See chapter 4, at n. 17, and chapter 7, at n. 24.

87. Snee, 'Recall of the Exiles', p. 413 n. 103, following Gwatkin, is happy to think so. Brennecke, Geschichte der Homöer, p. 233 n. 64, implies as much.

appointed to the see of Constantinople, and by the growing ambition and influence of Euzoius, even closer to Valens (who had soon moved to Antioch).[88]

We have come now to the beginning of Basil's own episcopate. It should be clear that the whole Antiochene saga had close connections with the Arian controversy. Eustathius of Antioch's original stand had been taken in that context; and successors and rivals had benefitted or suffered from the patronage or misfortune of conflicting parties in the dispute. There were elements, nevertheless, peculiar to Antioch itself. The clerical body in particular was obviously fractured by intense and local loyalties, which may have had little to do with the major theological issues of the day. As Basil put it, the city was not only 'completely divided by heretics' but also 'torn asunder by those who affirm that they hold identical opinions with one another'.[89] The support of great sees, such as Alexandria and Rome, or the shifting favour of the government of the day, may have been no more than opportunistic interference (when viewed from outside) or convenient but temporary reinforcement (when viewed from within).

We can avoid an extensive history of Antioch itself;[90] but it has to be added that its status in other respects had a direct effect on the course and variety of its religious difficulties. For the pagan Julian, it symbolized the vitality, cultic as well as political, of the traditional Hellenic *polis*. The degree to which he underestimated the strength of its ancient Christian traditions was revealed both in his own petulant comments and in the social unrest his intransigence appeared to unleash.[91] Like any great city in the empire, Antioch, with its large population, was always potentially volatile, making any tendency to faction a dangerous

---

88. For Demophilus, see *Ep.* 48; for Euzoius, see Snee, 'Recall of the Exiles', pp. 414f. According to Brennecke, *Geschichte der Homöer*, p. 232, Valens's final settlement in Antioch ensured that Meletius would find no place in the city.

89. *Ep.* 66. 2, C 1: 158, D 2: 33.

90. See Glanville Downey, *A History of Antioch in Syria from Seleucus to the Arab Conquest*; A. M. J. Festugière, *Antioche païenne et chrétienne: Libanius, Chrysostome et les moines de Syrie*; Jones, *Cities*; J. H. W. G. Liebeschuetz, *Antioch: City and Imperial Administration in the Later Roman Empire*; Petit, *Libanius et la vie municipale à Antioche* (see chapter 2, n. 31); and D. S. Wallace-Hadrill, *Christian Antioch: A Study of Early Christian Thought in the East*. Recall the point made in chapter 3, n. 54, about Basil's early interest in Syria generally, and the usefulness of Theodoret's *Historia religiosa* (extensively quoted by several of the authors referred to above).

91. His *Misopogon* gives the fullest impression. See especially the accounts of Bowersock and Browning, and Maude W. Gleason, 'Festive Satire: Julian's *Misopogon* and the New Year at Antioch'.

indulgence in the government's eyes.[92] Caution was increased by the fact that, from 371, Valens made the city his place of residence. Also established there, as a permanent feature, was the residence of the Praetorian Prefect of the East. Basil, as we have seen, was related to Antioch at that level also, in his dealings with Modestus.[93] The added presence of the emperor probably explains the vicious 'treason trials' that took place in Antioch, vividly described by Ammianus Marcellinus, and proof of the intrigue and paranoia that had infected the community at many social levels.[94]

Antioch was also the city of Chrysostom. It was there he developed his views of theology, discipline, and ecclesial order, long before he achieved prominence as the patriarch of Constantinople at the end of the century.[95] The city produced great literary figures also. There was Ammianus Marcellinus, already mentioned, whose view of the empire as a whole, of Valens, and of political ideology has done so much to colour our own interpretations of the age and springs so directly from much that is recognizably Antiochene.[96] There was Libanius, a correspondent of Basil himself, perhaps the greatest orator of the age, a loyal chronicler of the city he loved, and among the most vivid symbols of pagan literary and religious survival in a Christian empire.[97]

Finally, Antioch was, for Rome, the gateway to Persia. It was always the imperial headquarters in any military confrontation; and the significance of such confrontation would always dwarf (fatally, no doubt), in the imaginations of those in power, any threat or chance of glory on the Danube or the Rhine.[98] So the emperor was a frequent and sometimes lengthy visitor, and the army a constant presence.

---

92. In addition to the general material listed in n. 90, the following add useful reflections (even if dated) and references to sources: Glanville Downey, 'The Economic Crisis at Antioch under Julian the Apostate'; Robert Browning, 'The Riot of A.D. 387 in Antioch: The Role of the Theatrical Claques in the Later Empire'; and Timothy E. Gregory, 'Urban Violence in Late Antiquity'. The necessary caution had governed the imperial handling of church affairs in Antioch since the early days of Constantius's reign. See Brennecke, *Geschichte der Homöer*, pp. 66f.

93. For Modestus, see appendix 2, at nn. 1f.

94. See Ammianus Marcellinus 29, 1f.

95. In addition to the study by Festugière mentioned in n. 90, see J. C. Baur, *John Chrysostom and His Time*; and Matthews, *Western Aristocracies*, pp. 121–45.

96. See Matthews, *Ammianus*, esp. chaps. 2 and 18. Some excellent points are succinctly presented in his 'Ammianus' Historical Evolution'.

97. For Libanius, see n. 90 and chapter 2, nn. 6, 16, 31.

98. Julian's dismissive comment that the Goths were a less worthy enemy, for an emperor, than the Persians, may not have been idiosyncratic: Ammianus Marcellinus 22, 7. 8.

In all those respects, Antioch was a microcosm of Roman society at the time; culturally, politically, religiously, and strategically. It set its face boldly against the Syrian interior and against Mesopotamia beyond, declaring itself the best symbol of all that was precious in the Hellenic past and of all that challenged the alternative polities of the Orient. How much less central, therefore, but how much more dangerous might its little schism now appear! How much easier it is to understand why Basil, placed midway at Caesarea on the major route between Antioch and the capital, would have found its affairs of importance in his provincial life.

Let us examine, therefore, in more detail the phases of his involvement. They related chiefly to embassies, sent or encouraged by Basil, to Alexandria and Rome; and to that extent they followed the major shifts of the Arian dispute itself. The first phase began in 371—almost at the beginning of Basil's episcopate.[99] Dorotheus, a deacon of Meletius (now in exile again), was sent with a letter to Athanasius.[100] Basil had in mind at that stage a broad campaign: 'I recognize but one avenue of assistance to the churches in our part of the world—agreement with the bishops of the West'. Athanasius would be crucial in making such an appeal: 'What is more venerated in the entire West than the white hair of your majestic head?' So Basil exhorted the patriarch to send a deputation from Alexandria itself, 'a number of men who are mighty in the true doctrine'.

He also had much to say about Antioch. Athanasius should have a special sense of responsibility towards that church (Basil would have known, of course, of his earlier interventions), not least because unity achieved there would 'calm the confusion of the people, put an end to factional usurpations of authority, subject all men to one another in charity, and restore to the Church her pristine strength'.

Dorotheus carried also a letter to Meletius, to be delivered en route. In that note, Basil presented the embassy to the West as his own idea, designed to bring pressure to bear on the eastern government to rescind the various decrees of exile then current. He asked Meletius to

99. Considerable difficulties attach to the dating of the various embassies between East and West. On the whole I have followed Fedwick, Charisma. Detailed variations very rarely affect my own argument; but a few alternatives will be noted as we proceed. I have numbered my phases simply in the interests of clarity. Different divisions are used by Courtonne, Témoin, Fedwick, Charisma, and Amand de Mendieta, 'Basile de Césarée et Damase de Rome'. A detailed account is contained in Charles Pietri, Roma Christiana: Recherches sur l'Église de Rome, son organisation, sa politique, son idéologie de Mithrade à Sixte III (311–440), esp. 1: 791–872. In spite of the fact that Basil's involvement was evident from 371, I question Taylor's view, 'Basil and Damasus', p. 187, that 'he came to his episcopal office with a grand strategy already worked out'.

100. For what follows, Ep. 66, C 1: 156f., D 2: 27f.

prepare letters of his own, for Dorotheus to take to Italy, hoping that their western colleagues would then mount an embassy in the reverse direction.[101]

All those plans were apparently set awry by the arrival of a messenger from Alexandria. The news he brought prompted Basil to write instead a longer letter to Athanasius.[102] He still wanted the patriarch to provide companions for Dorotheus from his own church; but he now decided that they should carry a letter from himself to Damasus. Again, he wanted the West to send an embassy in return. He described his motives in cryptic terms: 'When all this has been done without the knowledge of any one [his chief hope being that they would formally reverse the compromises of Ariminum], our thought is that the bishop of Rome shall quietly, through a mission sent by sea, assume charge of affairs here so as to escape the notice of the enemies of peace'. Quite what species of unobtrusive infiltration he had in mind is hard to judge: presumably an attempt to persuade churchmen one by one, rather than to direct their address to the secular authorities, since the hoped-for ambassadors were to be 'capable, by the gentleness and vigour of their character, of admonishing those among us who are perverted'.[103]

There were other issues to be addressed. Basil hoped that such an embassy would declare itself strongly against Marcellus of Ancyra. His error (being, in Basil's eyes, at the other extreme from that of Arius) had escaped the desirable degree of censure in the West. 'Above all they must be solicitous for the Church at Antioch'.[104] There was a particular twist to those expectations, which we shall come across again. 'The result will be that henceforth we shall be able to recognize those who are of one mind with us, instead of being like those who fight a battle at night—unable

101. *Ep.* 68. The reference to Euippius brings the letter within the context of Arian conflict more generally but also relates to the growing dispute with Eustathius. See also *Ep.* 128.

102. *Ep.* 69. I take it that this letter was to be carried by Dorotheus on the same first-planned journey: it appears from the text that he was still considered to need a full introduction; and Deferrari's 'we have *again* sent to your Piety' (2: 41) is an unjustified gloss on the Greek.

103. *Ep.* 69. 1, C 1: 162, D 2: 43. One does need to keep constantly in mind the question of what Basil wanted from Damasus specifically: his early intentions must have coloured his later disappointment. The phrases δοῦναι γνώμην and αὐτὸν αὐθεντῆσαι περὶ τὸ πρᾶγμα are by no means insipid. Concerning Basil's relations with the bishop of Rome, in addition to the material cited above in n. 79, see Perikles-Petros Joannou, *Die Ostkirche und die Cathedra Petri im 4. Jahrhundert*—a book useful for bringing together documents and references, but lacking in overall judgement of any significance.

104. *Ep.* 69. 2, C 1: 164, D 2: 47. On the prolonged and central attention to Marcellus, see Amand de Mendieta, 'Basile de Césarée et Damase de Rome', p. 144.

to distinguish between friends and foes'.[105]   That was a further hint of Basil's feeling that doctrinal division was often a front for more serious disloyalties, which raises at once the question of what he thought *were* the issues that divided him from other churchmen.

What Basil intended to say to Damasus himself we shall come to shortly. Unfortunately, yet another interruption postponed his plans. A certain Silvanus arrived from the West, with a letter; and this prompted Basil to write yet a third message to Athanasius, presumably to be substituted for the two already penned. It seems, in any case, that Dorotheus was not entirely happy with what Basil had said so far, demanding perhaps that he should make absolutely clear, both to Athanasius and to the West, that he was in favour of Meletius and confident that he could bring together the various factions in his city: 'He stands at the head of the whole body of the Church, so to speak, while the residue are, as it were, segments of its limbs'. Basil claimed (what is not altogether easy to believe) that Silvanus had brought a similar opinion from 'your co-religionists in the West'.[106]

Basil's drafted letter to Damasus gave central place to the Arian debate: 'The heresy, sown long ago by Arius, the enemy of truth, and now already grown up into shamelessness, and, like a bitter root, producing a deadly fruit, at last prevails'. What was required, therefore, was a delegation from the West: 'Send us men of like mind with us'. One should note the scale of anticipated achievements: the westerners 'will either reconcile the dissenters, or restore the churches of God to friendship, or will at least make more manifest to you those who are responsible for the confusion'. The last ambition may have been the most realistic, and the closest to Basil's heart: 'It will thus be clear to you also for the future, with what men it is proper to have communion'. Meletius was not mentioned by name; but what we know of the accompanying messages would have made that point entirely in his favour.[107]

Thanks to the many interruptions and delays, it is quite possible that none of that correspondence was carried further than Antioch—certainly no further than Alexandria.[108] A third visitor now arrived, calling into question the viability of the whole exercise: Sabinus of Milan, bringing with him a letter from Damasus, *Confidimus quidem*, which recounted

105. *Ep.* 69. 2, C 1: 163, D 2: 47. See below, at nn. 122, 131.

106. *Ep.* 67, C 1: 159f., D 2: 35. See chapter 4, n. 17.

107. *Ep.* 70, C 1: 164f., D 2: 49f. This was the only letter Basil ever tried to write to Damasus personally.

108. Fedwick, *Basil*, 1: 12 n. 72.

decisions made at a synod in Rome in 368.[109] Amidst many other disappointments, the written material made no mention of Antioch. Basil decided to rethink his plans and wrote to Meletius, bringing him up to date (by this time it was early 372). Once again, Meletius was to write his own letters to the West, to accompany what were now several from Basil, so that they could take advantage of Sabinus's return (although Dorotheus was to go as well). Nor had Basil lost all hope that Athanasius would help, even though communion between Alexandria and Meletius had not yet been achieved.[110] Yet it was the interests of Meletius that Basil had at heart, far more than any international front that might be mounted on the basis of Athanasius's reputation. It was loyalty to Meletius that now drove him to greater initiative and leadership, not any sense that he was about to take up the mantle of the great champion of orthodoxy (who was, after all, still very much alive).[111]

So, from that first phase, we have a series of letters that started and finished with a concern for Antioch and for the fortunes of its exiled bishop. Alexandria was drawn into play but then faded again. Relations with the West were yet to take on a clear form. The truth is that the issues at stake had engaged Basil's attention for some time before he hatched his plan to invite wider authorities to his aid. In a letter to Eusebius of Samosata, written early in 371, before the correspondence with Athanasius, he referred to 'the affairs of Antioch'.[112] A letter to Meletius himself may have been earlier again and hinted at some scheme that extended further in scope than his own troubles in Caesarea.[113] So the letters to Athanasius have to be read with some care, if we are to make correct sense of what Basil valued most in the eastern church, and of what he hoped might be achieved by an approach to Damasus and the bishops of the West.

Basil recognized in Athanasius a 'great solicitude for all the churches', as great as 'for the one especially entrusted to you'; and this at a time when 'most men deem it sufficient to look each to his own particular charge'.[114] The compliment summed up both his hopes and his convictions.

109. Following Fedwick, *Charisma*, p. 109 n. 29. This is Damasus's *Ep.* 1, *PL* 13. 347–349, also edited by Schwartz, 'Sammlung'. Amand de Mendieta, 'Basile de Césarée et Damase de Rome', p. 127, follows Schwartz in dating the synod concerned to 372. Basil acknowledged receipt of the material in *Ep.* 90.

110. We can almost certainly catch the final cadence of his optimism in another, vaguely expressed and vaguely dated, letter to the patriarch, *Ep.* 82.

111. *Ep.* 89. 2.

112. *Ep.* 48, C 1: 128f., D 1: 315.

113. *Ep.* 57.

114. *Ep.* 69. 1, C 1: 161, D 2: 39.

Athanasius also possessed 'beyond the rest of us the guidance of the Spirit [τὴν ἐκ τοῦ Πνεύματος συμβουλίαν]', which made his 'counsels ... more nearly unerring [ἀσφαλεστέρας]'. 'Your years and your experience in affairs' also carried weight.[115] Soon Basil was able to feel that 'the Lord has appointed you the physician to heal the maladies of the churches'. 'You assuredly can see', he added, 'from the lofty watch-tower, so to speak, of your mental vision, what is happening on every hand'.[116] That was partly because Athanasius had been at the centre of the Arian dispute for so long—indeed, since Nicaea itself. He was a man 'who from childhood has struggled in the contests in defence of the faith',[117] a man 'who has experienced the pristine tranquillity and concord of the churches of the Lord touching the faith'.[118] 'Just as greater sorrow devolves upon your Excellency', Basil wrote, 'so we hold that it is proper for your prudence also to bear a greater solicitude for the churches'. The intensity of those appeals, and the broad theological terms in which they were expressed, make it all the more striking that Basil should have abandoned his appeal, as soon as he saw that antagonism between Alexandria and Antioch might render his efforts useless, if not disadvantageous.

Yet the correspondence of the first phase had afforded him an opportunity to express his views on the nature of the Church, seen now as extending beyond the confines of his recently acquired diocese. We find emphases already touched upon: in particular, that the laity were the chief victims of disunity, either docile in the face of confused leadership or enslaved by the enemies of orthodoxy.[119] We have also mentioned Basil's fear that apparent doctrinal division could overlay and even obscure the more fundamental problem of disloyalty to friends. Conveniently labelled factions set at odds with one another churchmen who should have been more effectively united against their true theological enemies. Petty, private scores were also being settled in the name of religion.[120] The central

---

115. *Ep.* 69. 1, C 1: 162, D 2: 41.
116. *Ep.* 82, C 1: 184, D 2: 97.
117. *Ep.* 82, C 1: 185, D 2: 99.
118. *Ep.* 66. 1, C 1: 157, D 2: 27.
119. The slavery image occurs at the beginning and end of *Ep.* 70: τοῖς αἰχμαλωτίζουσι τὰς ψυχάς, ἐκ τῆς αἰχμαλωσίας, and αἰχμαλωσίαν ψυχῶν, C 1: 165f. Thus heretics were given satanic status: see *Hom.* 354. 3. In *Ep.* 66, it is not certain whether τῶν τε κρατούντων refers to bishops, C 1: 157; but episcopal leadership seems to be implied somewhere in the sentence, as the translations of Deferrari and Courtonne both suggest. For the associated misfortune of the laity see chapter 4, at n. 121, and, for the corresponding bond between clergy and laity, chapter 5, at nn. 126f.
120. *Ep.* 69. 2. See above, n. 105. The theme was developed very fully in *Ep.* 92. 2, discussed below.

concept, which occurs significantly enough in his letter to Damasus, was that of an 'ancient love [ἀρχαία ἀγάπη]', which had characterized in better days the life of the Church and relationships among its leaders.[121] As in the letters to Athanasius, appeal was made to a sense of shared destiny and mutual responsibility. That counted for more than (though it did not exclude) the seniority or reputation of this churchman or that. Basil was now applying on a world scale the principle of collegiality that had inspired him in his relations with bishops in Cappadocia and Armenia, joined with the same sense of history.

The second phase opened in 372 with the return journey of Sabinus to the West, accompanied by Dorotheus. They carried with them letters to churchmen in the West generally, to Valerian of Aquileia, and to bishops in Italy and Gaul. There were no doubt other letters in their baggage— from Meletius, for example, as Basil had requested.[122] No reply was received until the following year. Basil should have known, from the very character of Sabinus's original embassy, that his overtures were likely to fail. Damasus and his colleagues were working to different agenda. For them, Arianism had entered its final phase. Valentinian was proving a tolerant emperor favourable to the Nicene cause—which in itself raises the question of whether principles of church unity could be applied in a divided empire.[123] It was now possible to appoint orthodox bishops quite easily to vacant sees, and doctrinal positions and opponents were

121. *Ep.* 70, C 1: 164, D 2: 49. Deferrari's phrase '*an* old affection' appears to limit it to a description of the relationship between Basil and Damasus. The letter as a whole, however, makes clear reference to an ecclesiology, which 'we know through a continuous tradition [μνήμης ἀκολουθίᾳ]', C 1: 165, D 2: 51. Amand de Mendieta, 'Basile de Césarée et Damase de Rome', stresses with justice the importance of this ἀγάπη but is less successful in presenting it as a species of *history* (although note his discussion of 'la conception primitive', pp. 148f.). It is a major point in Pietri, *Roma Christiana*, that two different views of the Church were being stressed one against the other.

122. It is difficult to decide who wrote what. Amand de Mendieta, 'Basile de Césarée et Damase de Rome', p. 127, follows Lietzmann in suggesting that *Ep.* 92 was written by Meletius, while 90 represented Basil's additional thoughts; but both letters bear Basil's mark.

123. Snee, 'Recall of the Exiles', p. 415. I am not sure that Amand de Mendieta, however, makes suitable contrasts. Damasus was just as concerned as Basil with maintaining ecclesial alliances—as Amand de Mendieta, 'Basile de Césarée et Damase de Rome', p. 136, admits. 'Attention aux problèmes moraux et humains ainsi qu'à leurs solutions pratiques', p. 135, was not an attitude exclusive to the West! Nor should it be considered grounds for criticism, if Basil and his colleagues were 'imbus d'hellénisme et épris de liberté intellectuelle', p. 158.

more clear-cut. As for Antioch, the position of Paulinus would be hard to undermine, in the face of what had been from the beginning a western commitment to his episcopacy.

For us, therefore, the chief interest attaching to the doomed missives carried by Dorotheus and his companion will continue to be the image of the Church that they so forcefully projected. Central still was the notion of the 'ancient love', hallmark of earlier days.[124] The vocabulary of admired antiquity was repeated elsewhere—'the old order of things [τῆς παλαιᾶς καταστάσεως]', the 'ancient glory of orthodoxy [τὸ ἀρχαῖον καύχημα τῆς ὀρθοδοξίας]'.[125] To accompany that clear historical appeal, Basil and his colleagues seem now to have acquired a broader sense of geography also. The crisis afflicted the whole of the East, 'from the borders of Illyricum to the Thebaid'; 'half the world [was] swallowed up by error'.[126] The West was seen as a contrasting territorial unit, where harmony and fearless proclamation of the truth were safely established. On the basis of that security, the West should now be able to come to the easterners' aid. History was still of relevance in that territorial contrast. A debt was about to be repaid, in return for the ancient expansion of the faith: 'There must come from you a renewal of the faith for the East, and in due time you must render her a recompense for the blessings which you have received from her';[127] 'Do not allow the faith to be extinguished in those lands where it first flashed forth'.[128]

In order to arouse further the sympathy of his readers, Basil and Meletius presented two pictures: one institutional, outlining the effect of error on the fabric of religious society; the other theological, describing the false formulae and the methods of argument now widely favoured among their enemies. In his general letter to the West, Basil complained that 'the shepherds are driven away, and in their places are introduced troublesome wolves who tear asunder the flock of Christ. The houses of prayer are bereft of those wont to assemble therein; the solitudes are filled with those who weep'. Again, an historical note was struck: 'The elders weep, comparing the past with the present; the young are more

---

124. In the opening phrase of *Ep.* 91.
125. *Ep.* 92. 3; C 1: 201, 203; D 2: 141/143.
126. *Ep.* 92. 2f., C 1: 201f., D 2: 137/141.
127. *Ep.* 91, C 1: 198, D 2: 131.
128. *Ep.* 92. 3, C 1: 202, D 2: 141. Concrete evidence that Damasus appreciated the point, while pleading more local preoccupations of his own, may be supplied in the inscription discussed by Henry Chadwick, 'Pope Damasus and the Peculiar Claim of Rome to St. Peter and St. Paul': 'Discipulos Oriens misit, quod sponte fatemur; ... Roma suos potius meruit defendere cives'.

to be pitied, since they know not of what they have been deprived'.[129] In the more detailed letter to the bishops of Italy and Gaul, those points were expanded and more vividly expressed. 'Lust for office [φιλαρχίαι]' had taken possession of the Church. 'Those who have obtained power for themselves through the favour of men are the slaves of those who have conferred the favour'. As a result, church leaders no longer dared to say publicly what the laity had grown unaccustomed to hearing. They were eager, rather, to score points against one another, using 'the vindication of orthodoxy [ἡ ἐκδίκησις ... τῆς ὀρθοδοξίας]' to further their 'private enmities [τὰς ἰδίας ἔχθρας]'.[130] Meanwhile, 'the laity who are sound in faith flee the houses of prayer as schools of impiety' and, 'having poured forth in front of the walls, offer up their prayers under the open sky, enduring all the discomforts of the weather with great patience, while they await assistance from the Lord'.[131]

When it came to theological method, the emphasis made was what we would expect of Basil himself: 'None are left to tend the flock of the Lord with knowledge [μετ' ἐπιστήμης]'.[132] In his general letter to the West, he lamented the casting aside of 'the teachings of the Fathers' and 'the apostolic traditions'. In their place 'the fabrications of innovators are in force in the churches', produced by men who 'train themselves in rhetorical quibbling and not in theology; the wisdom of the world takes first place to itself, having thrust aside the glory of the Cross'.[133] It was the language entirely of the *Contra Eunomium* and of its time,[134] and it included a characteristic reference to baptism: 'May the good teaching of our fathers who met at Nicaea shine forth again, so that the doxology in harmony with saving baptism [σύμφωνον τῷ σωτηρίῳ βαπτίσματι τὴν δοξολογίαν] may be duly rendered to the Blessed Trinity'.[135]

What strikes one most in these letters is their intensity and logical rigour. Great stress was laid on consolation and hope, entirely in the spirit and with the same vocabulary we find in letters more technically designed to express sympathy. Basil was making those statements to western churchmen at exactly the time he was bringing such sentiments

---

129. *Ep.* 90. 2, C 1: 196, D 2: 125/127. See n. 119 above.
130. *Ep.* 92. 2, C 1: 200, D 2: 137/139. See above, at nn. 105, 121.
131. *Ep.* 92. 2, C 1: 201, D 2: 139/141. The same emphasis was made in the earlier draft of this letter (*Ep.* 242. 2)—see Fedwick, *Basil*, 1: 13. Similar events had been witnessed in Armenia: see above, at n. 75.
132. *Ep.* 92. 2, C 1: 200, D 2: 137.
133. *Ep.* 90. 2, C 1: 195f., D 2: 125.
134. See chapter 4, esp. at nn. 97f., 125f.
135. *Ep.* 91, C 1: 198, D 2: 131.

to bear upon his more personal sense of sinfulness, misfortune, isolation, and ineptitude.[136] 'The tempest-tossing and confusion in which we now find ourselves' would be calmed, he felt, by the prayers and intervention of the West. Their 'strict harmony and unity with one another' was at once a cause of hope and an assurance of healing and peace.[137] There was a melding, in other words, of various elements—the ancient love, the effect of unity, the contrasting 'famine of love' that afflicted the East. The very intensity of feeling with which anguish was betrayed and optimism asserted became, as it were, a model of the order and orthodoxy hoped for. Indeed, it made the Church most obviously and intimately present within the individual (in this case, Basil himself): 'Embracing us with your spiritual and holy yearning [τῷ πνευματικῷ σου καὶ ἁγίῳ πόθῳ] you have engendered in our souls an ineffable affection [ἀμύθητόν τι φίλτρον]'.[138]

And what would that lead to? What was the outcome Basil hoped for? Here logic came into force. A series of steps was suggested, a recipe that would provide the ferment of a new church order. One of the fruits of western unity, so Basil wrote to Valerian, was 'that without hindrance the proclamation of the true faith is being made among you'.[139] Κήρυγμα, 'proclamation', was the crucial word. Basil expanded the argument in his general letter to the West:

> Let us also pronounce with boldness [μετὰ παρρησίας] that good dogma of the Fathers [again, κήρυγμα: the translation is confusing], which overwhelms the accursed heresy of Arius, and builds the churches on the sound doctrine [διδασκαλίᾳ], wherein the Son is confessed to be consubstantial with the Father, and the Holy Spirit is numbered with them in like honour and so adored; in order that the Lord through your prayers and your co-operation may also bestow upon us that fearlessness in the cause of truth [ἣν ... ὑπὲρ τῆς ἀληθείας παρρησίαν], and that glory in the confession [τὸ ἐπὶ τῇ ὁμολογίᾳ ... καύχημα] of the divine and saving Trinity, which He has given to you.[140]

Κήρυγμα, therefore, and the acccompanying παρρησία, represented a free-flowing clarity of expression among Christians, which was the only guarantee of sound structure, of that combination of healthy discussion,

---

136. As discussed in chapter 5, at nn. 73f.

137. So Ep. 91, C 1: 197, D 2: 131; but the point was made extensively in the opening sections of Ep. 90, 92 (and 242), all with reference to storm and calm.

138. Ep. 91, C 1: 197, D 2: 129.

139. Ep. 91, C 1: 197, D 2: 131. See chapter 7, at nn. 160f.

140. Ep. 90. 2, C 1: 196, D 2: 127. The contrast is with οἱ προεστῶτες ἀπαρρησίαστοι of Ep. 92. 2. There, οἱ λαοὶ ἀνουθέτητοι are to be judged by οἱ ὑγιαίνοντες τῶν λαῶν, C 1: 200f. The civic echoes of such vocabulary should never be overlooked.

domestic balance, and simple adoration, which summed up for Basil the essence of the Church. Behind that conviction there lay, moreover, a traditional association between openness and order in ancient society.[141]

In these three letters, therefore, Basil achieved, with the support of his allies, a full and satisfying synthesis of ideas on the nature of the Church. Particularly impressive, in only the third year of his episcopate, was his ability to combine historical, geographical, theological, and personal elements in one ecclesial vision. Nor were his immediate ambitions petty in scale. It may even have been another council of the Church he had in mind:

> Remember that there is need of haste, if those who are still left are to be saved, and of the presence of several brethren, that they in visiting us may complete the number of the synod [πλήρωμα εἶναι συνόδου], so that by reason not only of the high standing of those who have sent them, but also of the number of the delegates they themselves constitute, they may have the prestige [τὸ ἀξιόπιστον] to effect a reform; and may restore the creed which was written by our fathers at Nicaea, may banish the heresy, and may speak to the churches a message of peace by bringing those of like convictions into unity.[142]

In his lifetime and on his terms, that was not to be; but the patterns of thought reflected in his letters to the West were equally prominent in correspondence of a more limited scale. His attachment to Athanasius continued to wane. In a letter to Ascholius of Thessalonica, he acknowledged that 'zeal . . . for the most blessed Athanasius gives the clearest possible evidence of your soundness in the matters of greatest importance'.[143] He was still recalling the patriarch's authority in 376, in his long letter to the people of Neocaesarea.[144] The new association with Ascholius led, however, to more protracted reflections, incorporating the broad view of church affairs that Basil had now developed. Reading Ascholius's letter,

> we thought that we were back in the olden times [ἐπὶ τῶν ἀρχαίων καιρῶν], when the churches of God flourished, taking root in the faith, united by charity, there being, as in a single body, a single harmony of the various members; when the persecutors indeed were in the open, but in the open were also the persecuted; when the laity, though harassed,

141. See chapter 5, after n. 43 and at nn. 187f.

142. *Ep.* 92. 3, C 1: 202, D 2: 141; but there is no hint of this in the draft, *Ep.* 242; which may support the view that a general council was Meletius's idea only (since *Ep.* 92 may have been his reworking of the original text). See Taylor, 'Basil and Damasus', 196f. Basil did, however, entertain the notion eventually: see n. 186 below.

143. *Ep.* 154, C 2: 79, D 2: 379.

144. *Ep.* 204. 6. See above, at nn. 29f.

became more numerous, and the blood of the martyrs watering the churches nurtured many times as many champions of religion, later generations stripping themselves for combat in emulation of their predecessors. Then we Christians had peace among ourselves, that peace which the Lord left to us, of which now not even a trace any longer remains to us, so ruthlessly have we driven it away from one another.[145]

The theme was now familiar. In that period of 'old-time happiness [τὴν παλαιὰν ἐκείνην μακαριότητα]', one knew who was enemy and who was friend. Basil feared cautious deceit and a false sense of party almost as much as he feared error itself. How much more reassuring had been the conflicts of the martyrs, now no more than a memory. Their herosim had allowed issues to remain clear, whereas now the obscure and shifting intensities of schism made resolution all the harder.

Athanasius died at the beginning of May 373, having dominated the Arian debate for half a century. Basil felt obliged to build a new relationship with his successor, Peter. His first attempt was cautious. Gone was 'the intimacy engendered through long association' (which was an exaggeration, anyway): one had to fall back on 'true love ... formed by the gift of the Spirit'. He hoped that Peter, 'having been the spiritual nursling of so great a man', would 'walk in the same spirit' as Athanasius, 'guided by the same dictates of piety'; but he took nothing for granted, asking simply for regular news and continued regard.[146] The sequel would prove that his caution had been justified.

He also kept in touch with Meletius, chiefly in connection with events in Armenia.[147] He maintained contact with Antioch, too. A letter on Christian style to Diodorus, written in late 372, we have examined elsewhere.[148] Now, towards the end of 373, he wrote a long and important letter on more specifically ecclesial matters to the whole community at Antioch, over which Diodorus, together with Flavianus, presided in Meletius's name. The themes of sin, trial, hope, and consolation were repeated once more. There was a hint that the end of suffering might be in sight: 'Presently He will come who will take our part; He will come and not delay. For

---

145. *Ep.* 164. 1, C 2: 97f., D 2: 423.

146. *Ep.* 133, C 2: 47, D 2: 303. *Ep.* 139 was also addressed to Alexandria and made the same points as the letter to Ascholius quoted above, *Ep.* 154. This seems an odd letter to have sent to Egypt, in that it suggests that, in better health, Basil would have travelled there; but we have no reason to doubt its editorial title, ᾿Αλεξανδρεῦσιν.

147. It is useful to recall here *Ep.* 99 to Terentius, and events discussed above, at nn. 58f.

148. *Ep.* 135. See chapter 2, at nn. 67, 76f.

you must look forward to affliction upon affliction, hope upon hope, for yet a little while, yet a little while'.[149]

The third phase began when at last news was brought back from the West. Evagrius (the later friend of Jerome, and translator of the *Life of Antony*) delivered (in 373) a specific request that Basil and other bishops should endorse *Confidimus quidem* and send a new delegation to Rome.[150] Basil relayed the news, together with his own misgivings, to Eusebius of Samosata.[151] With his close friend he was able to share a rather different view of how embassies should be conducted, both locally and further afield:

> And yet it does not seem best to me to estrange ourselves entirely from those who do not accept the faith, but we should show some concern for these men according to the old laws of charity [κατὰ τοὺς παλαιοὺς θεσμοὺς τῆς ἀγάπης] and should with one accord write letters to them, offering every exhortation to kindliness, and proffering to them the faith of the Fathers we should invite them to join us [demanding, in other words, as little as possible, fearing to drive them otherwise into intransigent opposition]; and if we convince them, we should be united with them in communion; but if we fail, we should ourselves be content with one another, and should remove this present uncertainty from our way of life,

149. *Ep.* 140. 1, C 2: 61, D 2: 335. The importance of Flavianus and Diodorus (see above, after n. 82) was stressed by Theodoret *Hist. relig.* 8. 7. The vocabulary recurs in *Ep.* 238 of the year 376. We shall have occasion to discuss the theme further at n. 195 below. For other points connected with *Ep.* 140, see chapter 4, at n. 110, and chapter 5, at n. 98. *Ep.* 113 and 114 to Tarsus show how Basil thought open unity was best achieved: do not press those in error further than necessary. That point is well handled by Fedwick, *Charisma*, pp. 73f., and has occurred already in chapter 4, at n. 112 (and see chapter 6, n. 157).

150. For Evagrius, see the several useful references made throughout his work by Kelly, *Jerome.* That one should have some sympathy for Damasus is a point made by Joannou, *Ostkirche*, pp. 14f.: he was caught between Liberius's earlier recognition of Meletius and Athanasius's persistent resistance. He also felt the need for a signed declaration of orthodoxy, as had been forthcoming from eastern delegates to Julius and Liberius before him. Basil, on the other hand, remembered such incidents precisely for their hidden tolerance of Marcellus of Ancyra and their encouragement of Eustathius's deceit. See Pietri, *Roma Christiana*, 1: 801f.

151. *Ep.* 138. 2: 'Our own letter he has brought back to us again on the ground that it was not pleasing to the more strict of the people there', C 2: 55f., D 2: 323. There was some irony in this attempt by Damasus to gain a clearer picture of Basil's theology: he may have remembered how Eustathius had fooled Liberius some ten years before—a point made, of course, by Basil himself! See n. 86 above, and Taylor, 'Basil and Damasus', p. 199.

taking up again that evangelical and guiltless polity in which they lived who from the beginning adhered to the Word.[152]

That was still how he felt the Arian dispute should be resolved, as also the schism at Antioch. Even more fundamental was the principle of consulting 'the good of our neighbours', since otherwise 'the ruin of each of us is involved in the common disaster'.[153] It was becoming clear, perhaps, that Damasus and his colleagues had rather more peremptory procedures in mind, which were likely to cause as much dissension as they relieved.

Even more shattering, however, was the news that Damasus had decided to give his unqualified support to Paulinus. Writing to Evagrius himself, Basil made no attempt to hide his dismay, or to play down his contrasting principles of mediation. The hope was still the same: that 'all those who are not divided from one another in mind [and that was the important point, so often obscured by the follies of party] shall fill the same assembly'.[154] Such an achievement would depend on delicacies of policy that Damasus, by implication, had failed to preserve: 'Evils which have been strengthened by time need time first of all for their correction'. Then 'the complete elimination of suspicions and of the clashes arising from controversies is impossible, unless there be some trustworthy man to act as a mediator in the interest of peace'.[155] Moreover, mediation had to be conducted face to face: letters were not enough. Basil took it also as a personal slight, not unnaturally, that in the midst of other tensions and disappointments Evagrius had seen fit not to share communion with Dorotheus—anticipating, of course, the sharper lines that were about to be drawn in Antioch.

As for setting up yet another embassy to the West, Basil was strikingly hesitant. He left it very much to Evagrius, saying that he could not think of anyone among his own circle who could either lead or take part in such a venture. Whether that arose from pique, which is far from impossible, or whether it reflected a sense of isolation on Basil's part, is hard to say. It may have been simply the result of his embroilments elsewhere: that was the year, after all, of his trip to Armenia. Subsequent journeys were undertaken, as we shall see, and may suggest that Basil had not lost hope in the West completely, as he had been forced to do in relation to Alexandria;

---

152. *Ep.* 128. 3, C 2: 39, D 2: 281/283. One should notice, again, how much interwoven with other concerns the point was: in this instance, affairs at Colonia, and Eustathius, discussed in the previous chapter. Compare the letters to Tarsus mentioned above in n. 149.

153. *Ep.* 136. 2, C 2: 52, D 2: 315, also discussed in chapter 7, at n. 104.

154. *Ep.* 156. 1, C 2: 82, D 2: 385.

155. *Ep.* 156. 1f., C 2: 82, D 2: 387.

but there is no doubt that the setback represented by Evagrius's mission seriously modified his view of what could be achieved in collaboration with Rome.

During the next two years Basil continued to afflict himself with indignation over the recognition of Paulinus. He also directed a number of letters to church communities in Syria, bemoaning above all the success of Valens in controlling their affairs. No doubt he saw a connection between the two problems.

In regard to the first preoccupation, a letter to the *comes* Terentius (appointed once again to a position of responsibility in Antioch) expressed his chief misgivings.[156] Paulinus and his followers had apparently received further written encouragement from Rome (this letter to Terentius was written towards the end of 376). Basil did not mince his words. The fresh correspondence from the West, he said, 'entrusts to them the episcopate of the church at Antioch' but also 'misrepresents the most admirable bishop of the true church of God, Meletius'. He asserted without hesitation that western churchmen were 'absolutely ignorant of affairs here [ἀγνοοῦσι παντελῶς τὰ ἐνταῦθα]'. He wasted little time in pretending to respect opinions held in Rome: 'This is my position: not only shall I never consent to dissemble just because somebody has received a letter from human beings and is elated over it; nay, not even if it came from the very heavens but does not agree with the sound doctrine of faith, can I regard him as sharing in communion with the saints'.[157] He was careful to follow up this letter with shorter messages to Meletius and to Dorotheus.[158] In a slightly earlier letter to a community of ascetics, Basil showed how readily he connected affairs at Antioch with his own difficulties in relation to Eustathius of Sebaste. His more local opponents had begun to feel by this time that their interests might be additionally served if they sought an alliance with Euzoius in Antioch. In the process, therefore, they had

156. *Ep.* 214. We have already examined this letter as an example both of theological advice to a layman and of Basil's wish that matters of discipline associated with heresy should be left to churchmen: see chapter 5, at nn. 151, 183 (and see chapter 3, at n. 47).

157. *Ep.* 214. 2, C 2: 203f., D 3: 229/231. Here is perhaps the clearest indication that Basil rejected Damasus's point of view. It is probably true, however, that he did not fully understand the chief anxieties of the bishop of Rome; in which case, it is anachronistic to suppose he was preoccupied with the confessional issues that might later focus on papal expectations—see Amand de Mendieta, 'Basile de Césarée et Damase de Rome', p. 149. We are dealing here simply with his reaction to Vitalis's attempt to curry favour in the West, and to Damasus's *Ep.* 3: see n. 84 above.

158. *Ep.* 214 and 215 (probably in that order, although any lapse of time between them would have been insignificant). It was in the latter that Basil criticized Gregory of Nyssa as a potential diplomat: see chapter 1, at n. 20.

begun to express more explicitly Arian doctrines, thus undermining, of course, the achievements they had boasted of, and the western support to which they had laid claim, at the synod of Tyana.[159]

As for his Syrian connections, Basil had been careful from the beginning of his episcopate to keep in touch with Christian communities in various parts of the region.[160] We have already discussed his long and cautious letter to the community at Chalcis, written in 375.[161] He also continued to encourage the church at Beroea: having received news of their 'daily struggle and vigorous opposition on behalf of religion', he was able to assure them that 'your example has set many churches aright'.[162] Contacts of that sort continued during the next phase of events. The priest Sanctissimus (of whom we shall say more below) brought Basil news of the dispersal of some at least of the orthodox community at Beroea, and of similar disruptions in the church of Batnae.[163] All his letters of that period testify not only to continuing anxiety and involvement but also to the success that Valens and the Arian party generally were enjoying in the churches of the region. Heroism and the postponement of hope were all that Basil now could bank on: 'In this we rejoice with you, and pray that the God of all, Whose is the struggle, Whose is the arena, and through Whom are the crowns, may create eagerness, may supply strength of spirit, and may bring your work to complete approval in His sight'.[164]

_____

The fourth phase is represented by the preparations for, and the results of, a third journey undertaken to the West.[165] Events may have been

159. *Ep.* 226. It is not clear whereabouts this community was situated. Later editors have entitled the letter τοῖς ὑφ' ἑαυτὸν ἀσκηταῖς; but the content does not immediately suggest Basil was addressing people well known to him.

160. For example, *Ep.* 184 to Eustathius of Himmeria, and *Ep.* 185 to Theodotus of Beroea.

161. *Ep.* 222. See chapter 5, n. 89, and at n. 144, and chapter 7, at n. 37.

162. *Ep.* 220, C 3: 4, D 3: 277/279. The Acacius mentioned here was later bishop of Beroea, which links this correspondence with that addressed to Dorotheus and Meletius, mentioned at n. 158 above. See Theodoret *Hist. relig.* 2 (Julian). 9. *Ep.* 221, also written in 375, makes the same points.

163. See *Ep.* 256 (which also mentions Acacius). *Ep.* 132 was addressed to Abramius, bishop of Batnae, but then resident in Antioch.

164. *Ep.* 221, C 3: 5, D 3: 281.

165. Dating problems are numerous. I have accepted 376, taking into account the narratives of Devreesse and Courtonne and points made more recently by Fedwick, *Basil*, 1: 16, and Gain, *Église*, pp. 374f. This does not mean that I have unravelled the obscurities to my own satisfaction; and I have had to rest content with the ambition of describing ideas

precipitated by the exile of Eusebius of Samosata in 374. It was Eusebius who recognized, at the latest by 375, that some response would have to be made to the demands brought back by Evagrius in 373. That prompted Basil, early in 375, to write to Meletius, saddling him in effect with the responsibility of acting upon Eusebius's advice.[166] He suggested using the services of Sanctissimus, a priest from Antioch loyal to Meletius. The idea was that Sanctissimus would travel around various communities, seeking ideas and support for a new embassy. Basil's recent letters to Beroea and to Abramius of Batnae may be seen, therefore, as having taken the first steps; and Sanctissimus also carried back to Syria this very letter to Meletius.[167] A letter to Eusebius of Samosata, written towards the end of the process, shows us what Basil continued to regard as the important issues.[168] There is, it has to be said, more than a hint of confusion in his mind, which may explain why he passed on Eusebius's idea so quickly to Meletius in the first place: 'What message, then, I ought to send through them [Dorotheus and Sanctissimus], or how I am to come to an agreement with those who write, I myself am at a loss'. His enduring pessimism in regard to the bishop of Rome may be reflected in his observation that 'proud characters, when courted, naturally become more disdainful than usual'. After all, he said, 'if the Lord has been reconciled to us, what further assistance do we need? But if God's anger abides, what assistance can we have from the supercilious attitude of the West?' He did make a passing reference to Marcellus of Ancyra, which no doubt points to associations that endured in his mind; but otherwise all he could think of doing was sending a covering letter with Sanctissimus's eventual document, making the point that 'they should not attack those who have been brought low by trials nor judge self-respect to be arrogance'. His loss of confidence could not have been more clearly expressed.

Sanctissimus, meanwhile, had gathered together the threads of a new declaration to the West and had developed his own ideas about what should be emphasized. Basil betrayed once again that he was slightly

---

rehearsed by Basil over the course of a year or so. Note that this 'fourth' phase corresponds to Lietzmann's third—a solo journey by Dorotheus, made in 374—as described by Amand de Mendieta, 'Basile de Césarée et Damase de Rome', pp. 128f.

166. *Ep.* 120. The move may have been associated with the burst of frustrated correspondence between Basil and Eusebius himself, discussed in *Ep.* 198 (of the same year).

167. There is further confusion over dating. Fedwick, *Basil*, 1: 16, suggests, contrary to the accounts of Devreesse and Courtonne, that *Ep.* 253, 254, and 255, to Antioch, Laodicea, and Carrhae respectively, were also written at this juncture. The alternative suggestion is that they were written *after* the next journey to the West, announcing its success. Given the several references to recent western experience, I am inclined to agree with that view.

168. For what follows, *Ep.* 239. 2, C 3: 60f., D 3: 419/421.

out of touch with what was afoot: 'If the letter to the people of the West appears to contain anything that is important for us, be pleased to draft it and send it to us'.[169] There was only one point that he himself felt obliged to emphasize, and it had much more to do with his vision of church order than with the intricacies of the Arian controversy itself. He wanted to urge western churchmen

> not to receive indiscriminately [ἀκρίτως] the communion of those coming from the East, but after once choosing a single portion of them [ἅπαξ μίαν μερίδα ἐκλεξαμένους], to accept the rest on the testimony of these already in communion; and ... not to take into communion everyone who writes down the Creed as a supposed proof of orthodoxy.[170]

In this way, presumably, he hoped that authorities in the West would not be able to ignore (as they seemed to have done in the case of Paulinus) a carefully prepared consensus, such as Sanctissimus and Dorotheus were about to present. Basil's motives were once again ecclesial rather than strictly doctrinal. He was dealing still with the old and different problem of people who opposed one another, even though they appeared to subscribe to the same doctrines. If the westerners did not follow his advice, they would 'find themselves to be in communion with men prone to fight, who often put forward statements of doctrine which are identical, but then proceed to fight with one another as violently as the men who are of opposite opinions'.[171]

As soon as the spring or early summer of 376 advanced, Sanctissimus and Dorotheus set out. Exactly what they carried with them, in the way of documentation, is not entirely clear from the surviving writings of Basil himself. Of the two letters that occur in the relevant section of his correspondence, one is clearly a draft of a letter already taken to the West by Dorotheus in 372. It is unlikely that it was taken again. The other is almost certainly a personal letter from Basil, designed to accompany and to endorse whatever documents Sanctissimus had been able to collect during his journey seeking support in the previous year.[172]

This second letter was filled with characteristic anxieties. It included a fairly mild version of his habitual grouse: some westerners with authority

---

169. *Ep.* 129. 3 (to Meletius, the year before), C 2: 41, D 2: 287.
170. *Ep.* 129. 3, C 2: 41, D 2: 289.
171. *Ep.* 129. 3, C 2: 41, D 2: 289.
172. *Ep.* 242 and 243. The first is a draft of *Ep.* 92 (see nn. 125f. above). The detailed list of bishops at the beginning of *Ep.* 92 describes, no doubt, Sanctissimus's careful itinerary through Syria. The second reflects Basil's correspondence with Eusebius of Samosata, *Ep.* 239 (see n. 167 above).

should come on a visit, 'in order that they may see with their own eyes the sufferings of the East, which it is impossible to learn by report, since no words can be found that can set forth our situation clearly to you'.[173] He then expressed a more fundamental misgiving: 'The most oppressive part of this is, that neither do those who are being wronged accept their sufferings in the certainty of martyrdom, nor do the laity reverence their athletes as being in the class of martyrs, because the persecutors are cloaked with the name of Christians'.[174] The lines of division, in other words, were obscured by the apparent theological unity of those in conflict.

A clear policy among the persecutors was laid bare by Basil's plea: 'Shepherds are being persecuted that their flocks may be scattered'. As a result, whole communities were torn apart. Basil described the destruction not in terms of theological argument but of decay in the conduct of cult. To begin with, 'the pious are driven from their native places, and are exiled to desert regions'. The results were quite specific:

> Our feasts have been turned into mourning; houses of prayer have been closed; idle are the altars of spiritual service. No longer are there gatherings of Christians, no longer precedence of teachers, no teachings of salvation, no assemblies, no evening singing of hymns, nor that blessed joy of souls which arises in the souls of those who believe in the Lord at the gatherings for Holy Communion and when the spiritual blessings are partaken of. It is fitting for us to say: 'neither is there at this time prince, or prophet, or leader, or oblation, or incense, or place of first-fruits before the Lord and no place to find mercy'.[175]

There was a frank admission, therefore, that theological oppression, so to speak, was in no way so powerful a weapon as manipulation of cultic practice:

> The ears of the more simple-minded ... have become accustomed to the heretical impiety. The nurslings of the Church are being brought up in the doctrines of ungodliness. For what are they indeed to do? Baptisms are in the heretics' hands, attendance upon those who are departing this life, visits to the sick, the consolation of those who grieve, the assisting of those who are in distress, succour of all kinds, communion of the mysteries; all of these things, being performed by them, become a bond of agreement between them and the laity. Consequently after a little time has passed, not even if all fear should be removed, would there then be hope of

---

173. *Ep.* 243. 1, C 3: 69, D 3: 437.
174. *Ep.* 243. 2, C 3: 69, D 3: 437.
175. *Ep.* 243. 2, C 3: 70, D 3: 437/439, 441.

recalling those held by a long-standing deception back to the recognition of the truth.[176]

Those emphases count for much more, in the letter as a whole, than do the half dozen or so sentences that make more explicit reference to theological argument.

There was also a specific point being made *ad hominem*, tailored, as Basil must have thought, to the prevailing indifference of the western church. 'Consider', he wrote, 'that our sufferings are yours'. Here he was recalling a point made in earlier correspondence with the West:

> Since the gospel of the kingdom, having begun in our region, has gone forth to the whole world, on this account the common enemy of our souls strives that the seeds of apostasy, having taken their beginning in the same region, may be distributed to the whole world. For upon whom the light of the knowledge of Christ has shone, upon these the darkness of impiety also contrives to come.[177]

The struggle was above all in defence of history, of tradition, of what Basil called 'our common possession—our treasure, inherited from our fathers, of the sound faith'.[178] Everything expressed here had already coloured entirely his conduct and attitude within the local church.

While the ambassadors were absent in the West, Basil had occasion to write to Epiphanius of Salamis. He refused to be drawn into a detailed discussion of the Arian issue, falling back in his characteristic way on the belief that 'we can add nothing to the Creed of Nicaea, not even the slightest thing, except the glorification of the Holy Spirit'.[179] He did have more to say about the situation at Antioch. He lamented once again the way in which 'orthodoxy has itself also been divided against itself'. He reasserted his support for Meletius, on the significant grounds of his 'great affection for him because of that steadfast and unyielding stand he made' (during 'that noble contest in the reign of Constantius'). He insisted that Athanasius had desired communion with Meletius at heart and had simply been misled 'through malice of counsellors'. As for himself, 'we have never accepted communion with any one of those who entered the see thereafter [including Paulinus, of course, as well as Euzoius], not because

---

176. *Ep.* 243. 4, C 3: 72f., D 3: 447. This preoccupation with cultic control was much more important to Basil than any sense of moral failing on the part of Arians: compare Amand de Mendieta, *Ascèse*, p. 175; and see chapter 4, at n. 121.

177. *Ep.* 243. 3, C 3: 71, D 3: 443/445. See above, at nn. 127f.

178. *Ep.* 243. 4, C 3: 71, D 3: 445.

179. *Ep.* 258. 2, C 3: 101f., D 4: 41.

we considered them unworthy, but because we were unable to condemn Meletius in anything'. He recommended that Epiphanius should avoid taking sides and should concentrate more on effecting a reconciliation.[180] Basil was digging in his toes, in other words, and allowing himself to say less and less.

That brings us in effect to the fifth and final phase of Basil's 'international' career. Sometime in 377, Dorotheus and Sanctissimus came back from the West. They brought with them a letter from Damasus condemning Arianism in general terms, and also Apollinarius.[181] It was scarcely satisfactory; and the two long-suffering ambassadors were soon on their way to the West again, carrying a precise set of demands from Basil. Arianism, he said, was no longer the issue. That 'reckless and impudent heresy ... being plainly cut off from the body of the Church, remains in its own error, and harms us but little [ὀλίγα ἡμᾶς λυμαίνεται] because their impiety is evident to all'.[182] Once again, it was internal enemies, appearing to share with him a common belief, who caused him most concern. He wanted them exposed, named formally, condemned explicitly by a general declaration from the West, so that they would no longer be able 'through an unguarded communion to share their own disease with their neighbours'.[183]

Who were those villains? They are by now familiar enough to us: Eustathius, Apollinarius, and Paulinus. Basil's portrayal of Eustathius was particularly skilful, given the diplomatic context. He had been able, as Basil put it, to gain acceptance at the hands of the unsuspecting

180. *Ep.* 258. 3, C 3: 102f., D 4: 43/45. Basil was gaining much greater confidence in the face of the ambiguities involved. *Ep.* 257 was the herald, perhaps, of a new sense of release.

181. According to Fedwick, *Charisma*, p. 110 and n. 33, this was *Ea gratia*. According to an older account, reflected in Amand de Mendieta, 'Basile de Césarée et Damase de Rome', p. 130, it was *Illud sane miramur*. Schwartz, 'Sammlung', considered these, along with *Non nobis*, to be fragments of separable letters, although they are presented as Damasus *Ep.* 2 in *PL* 13: 350–354. By this time, Damasus had had second thoughts about Vitalis and had committed himself much more to Paulinus (witness his *Per filium*): see n. 84 above. Taylor, 'Basil and Damasus', pp. 262f., may have a point in suggesting the influence of Jerome at this point; but other forces were sufficient to explain the hardening of western attitudes.

182. *Ep.* 263. 2, C 3: 122, D 4: 91. If Basil died later in 377 (a possibility to be discussed in the next chapter and in appendix 3), this and associated letters can still easily be dated to the early months of that year.

183. *Ep.* 263. 2, C 3: 122, D 4: 93.

Hermogenes of Caesarea. He had then proceeded to undermine the purity of Nicaea at the various gatherings at Ancyra, Seleucia, and Constantinople. Then came his journey to the West, his favourable consultation with Liberius in Rome, and his triumphant return to Tyana. Basil implied, without much attempt at subtlety, that Liberius had been fooled. Certainly, 'this man now tries to destroy that creed on the basis of which he was received'. The bishops of the West had helped to create that situation: they should now take steps to correct it:

> Since, then, his power to harm the churches came from your quarter, and since he has used the privilege granted him by you for the downfall of the many, from you must come also his correction, and you should write to the churches what the conditions are on which he was received, and how now, having undergone a change, he nullifies the favour that was granted to him by the fathers of that time.[184]

Apollinarius, meanwhile, was having a pernicious effect, largely through the widespread distribution of his many writings, remarkable above all for their misleading obscurity. Finally, their protégé in Antioch, Paulinus, was 'inclined towards the teachings of Marcellus [of Ancyra: τοῖς Μαρχέλλου προσπεπονθὼς δόγμασι]'.[185]

Basil concluded that ideally a council of East and West together should expose those individuals once and for all, so that they would either seek communion on orthodox terms or find themselves publicly excluded from the unity of the Church.[186] Yet now, he said, was not the moment. That feeling may have been connected with his earlier admission that he currently lacked the authority to take part in such a gathering: 'Statements made by us are suspected by the many, on the ground that we perhaps, through certain personal quarrels, hold ill-will towards them'.[187] Quite frankly, Basil gave little sign here that he had made any attempt to extend himself beyond the orbit of his personal relationships and their attendant antagonisms.

---

184. *Ep.* 263. 3, C 3: 124, D 4: 97.

185. *Ep.* 263. 5, C 3: 125, D 4: 99.

186. A universal council seems implied by Basil's phraseology: ἔδει ἡμᾶς συνεδρεύοντας μετὰ τῆς ὑμετέρας φρονήσεως ἐν κοινῇ σκέψει τὰ περὶ τούτων διαλαβεῖν, *Ep.* 263. 5, C 3: 125. On a smaller scale, he had used the same technique against Neocaesarea in *Ep.* 204. 7: see above, at n. 35.

187. *Ep.* 263. 2, C 3: 122, D 4: 93. Fedwick, *Charisma*, p. 65 n. 134, is anxious to stress that Basil did not wish to see Paulinus explicitly condemned, and that this was the first time the possibility of his heresy was raised. See also Gain, *Église*, pp. 371f.; Taylor, 'Basil and Damasus', pp. 192, 268. Amand de Mendieta, 'Basile de Césarée et Damase de Rome', p. 124, highlights the importance of Basil's perceived lack of authority.

The final embassy to the West had not been, in any case, a great success. All it managed to bring back was a deep sense of grievance and another ineffectual letter from the bishop of Rome.[188] It seems that the frustration of Dorotheus's hopes had been due to the intervention of Peter of Alexandria, who was in Rome at the time, and who commanded much more respect in western eyes, both because of the status of his see and because of his natural association with the reputation of Athanasius.[189] Peter had gone so far as to accuse Meletius and Eusebius of Samosata of Arian sympathies. The suggestion was, quite frankly, ridiculous and irresponsible; and Basil showed remarkable self-control in his subsequent letter to Peter himself. While continuing to defend his colleague in Antioch, he also warned the patriarch to tread more cautiously, if he wished to help in the achievement of any harmony among the eastern churches:

> We all need each other in the communion of our members, and especially now, when the churches of the East look to us, and will take your harmony as a start towards firmness and strength; but if they perceive that you are somewhat suspicious of each other, they will relax and will slacken their hands, so that they should not raise them against enemies of the faith.[190]

Basil seems to have reconciled himself, in any case, to the fact that authoritative aid from the West was no longer to be hoped for. He began, in his correspondence, to clarify for his own sake how matters now stood generally. Eustathius and Apollinarius still occupied the centre of the stage; but two other points made greater sense in relation to Antioch. First, Basil continued to associate Paulinus and his party with the teachings of Marcellus of Ancyra.[191] Second, he wished at least to create the impression that communication with the West had reinforced the weight of opinion against his own adversaries and had made more obvious their geographical isolation: 'Look about on the world, and observe that this portion which is unsound is small, but that all the rest of the Church, which from one end to the other has received the Gospel, abides by this sound and unchanged doctrine'.[192] He was still attempting to encourage his scattered allies to see themselves as belonging to a

---

188. Probably *Non nobis quidquam* and *Illud sane miramur*: Fedwick, *Charisma*, p. 112 n. 43. See nn. 84 and 181 above.

189. He had become, in Amand de Mendieta's words, 'Basile de Césarée et Damase de Rome', p. 127, 'le conseiller attrité pour les affaires d'Orient'. According to his account, all this would have predated the first journey made by Dorotheus and Sanctissimus.

190. *Ep.* 266. 2, C 3: 135f., D 4: 127. On dating, see n. 182 above.

191. *Ep.* 265. 3. See n. 104 above.

192. *Ep.* 251. 4, C 3: 93, D 4: 17. See also *Ep.* 265. 3.

larger party, whose interests and beliefs they should take more carefully into account, before they accepted or rejected the leaders of this group or that.[193]

Conflict within Antioch itself did not end at that point. After the death of Valens at the battle of Hadrianople in 378, Meletius and Eusebius were able to return from exile. In the following year, Meletius held a synod at Antioch and seems to have gained recognition in the West. Certainly in 381, he presided over the Council of Constantinople, a vindication of his perseverance and perhaps the peak of his career. He lived long enough to see Gregory of Nazianzus briefly installed as bishop of the eastern capital; but he died shortly afterwards. It is a great sorrow that Gregory's funeral oration has not survived. Paulinus was still alive, and this might have been taken as the opportunity to settle matters once and for all; but a Meletian rival, Flavianus, was also installed as bishop, and the schism continued for many years yet.[194]

By that time, Basil was dead. His final letters hint in several ways that he may have felt his enemies' days were numbered, and that the end of the Arian controversy was now in sight.[195] To Peter of Alexandria, he was willing to admit (and it may not have been merely self-deluding consolation) that the Church possessed strengths scarcely affected by mere theological discord: 'We have given thanks to the Lord, that a remnant of the ancient good discipline [τῆς παλαιᾶς εὐταξίας] is being preserved in you and that the Church has not lost her strength in our persecution. For the canons [οἱ κανόνες] have not also been persecuted along with us'.[196] Yet he admitted also to a certain numbness of spirit, after so much struggle:

> But be informed, our most honoured and beloved brother, that continuous afflictions, and this great tumult which is now shaking the Churches, cause us to be astonished at nothing that takes place. For just as workers in smithies, whose ears are struck with a din, become inured to the noise, so we by the frequency of strange reports have at length become accustomed to keep our heart unmoved and undismayed at unexpected events. Therefore the charges that have from of old been fabricated by

193. Very much the point of *Ep.* 265, esp. § 3. We have already touched upon this and *Ep.* 251 in chapter 7, at n. 37, and in chapter 4, at n. 98.

194. The dating of these events will be discussed at the beginning of the next chapter and in appendix 3, in the light of Snee, 'Recall of the Exiles'.

195. See *Ep.* 264 to Barses of Edessa. *Ep.* 267 suggests that this letter may not have reached its destination.

196. *Ep.* 266. 1, C 3: 134, D 4: 123.

the Arians against the Church, although many and great and noised throughout the whole world, can nevertheless be endured by us.[197]

As usual, it was the hidden enemies, 'men of like mind and opinion with ourselves', that caused him more anxiety. Those remained much more closely associated in his eyes with the narrow arena of his own experience and preoccupation. The letter to Peter is the last from his pen that we can clearly date—in the moving words of one historian, 'le dernier écho qui nous soit parvenu de sa noble voix'.[198] It was the voice, we have to admit, of a man by now weary, isolated, and robbed of many hopes.

197. *Ep.* 266. 1, C 3: 133, D 4: 121. The sentiment was in some ways analogous to the calculated humility of his letter to Tyana: see n. 19 above. Yet scarcely months before he had considered himself 'a byword all over the earth, and, I shall add, even over the sea', *Ep.* 212. 2, C 2: 199, D 3: 221. The resignation of tone in the letter quoted here seems the jaundiced successor of what might earlier have been taken as spirited confidence: 'The topsy-turvy condition of the times has taught us to be vexed at nothing', *Ep.* 71. 1, C 1: 167, D 2: 55.

198. Devreesse, *Patriarcat*, p. 34; but Pierre Maraval, 'La Date de la mort de Basile de Césarée', p. 34, may reserve that distinction for *Ep.* 267. Fedwick, *Basil*, 1: 18, places *Ep.* 268, 269, and 196 in the year 378; but that must now be questioned in the light of the recent controversy over the date of Basil's death, to be discussed in the next chapter and in appendix 3.

· CHAPTER IX ·

'WE SEEK
THE ANCIENT FATHERLAND'

Fortunately, we do not have to part company with Basil in so disengaged or despondent a mood. His importance—indeed, the meaning he himself was able to give to his life—extended well beyond his success or failure as a polemicist. In the subsequent period (for which we have no surviving documents), he undoubtedly continued to preach sermons, write letters, and work further on his ascetic endeavours. More than that, however, we have good reason to believe that the optimism of 376, visible in his friendship with Amphilochius and the writing of the *De spiritu sancto*, reflected a persistent sense of worthwhile endeavour at the deepest levels of his personality.

Such an enduring capacity for elevated and self-confident argument displayed itself above all in his *Hexaemeron*, eleven great sermons on the creation of the world.[1] To read such works, wrote Gregory of Nazianzus,

---

1. *Basile de Césarée, Homélies sur l'Hexaéméron*, edited, with introduction and French translation, by Stanislas Giet; and *Basile de Césarée, Sur l'origine de l'homme (Homélies X et XI de l'Hexaéméron)*, edited, with introduction and French translation, by Alexis Smets and Michel van Esbroeck. There is an English translation of sermons 1–9 by Agnes Clare Way in *Saint Basil, Exegetic Homilies*, pp. 3–150. I regard 10 and 11 as essentially the work of Basil (a view fully defended by the editors), although they are clearly less finished. For the role of Gregory of Nazianzus in polishing the work after Basil's death, see Socrates *HE* 4. 26. I have relied heavily on the introductions to the 'Sources chrétiennes' editions for Basil's sources, Christian and non-Christian alike. See also Yves Courtonne, *Saint Basile et l'Hellénisme*. Useful reflections are contained also in E. Amand de Mendieta, 'The Official

was to be 'purified, soul and body', to become 'a temple ready to receive God, and an instrument struck by the Spirit, chanting hymns to the glory and power of God'.[2] If they were not the crowning achievement of his last years (although that is still not impossible to believe), they may certainly be regarded with justice as the clearest expression of his mature thought.[3]

A sense of drama, of course, makes it attractive to imagine Basil at work on these sermons just as the world of Valens was about to crumble in the face of Gothic victory. Their optimism, therefore, is all the more significant. There is no morbid sense of doom, of imminent failure or destruction. Yet they are possessed of urgency. They reflect on the questions that Basil thought most fitting in a Christian: 'whence he arose and whither he is going'.[4] A demand for clarity about human origins (which the Hexaemeron attempted to provide) would lead naturally to excitement about human destiny. The σπουδαῖος, the person of genuine religious and moral commitment, 'keeps his mind on God, keeps it moving onward, gazing steadily upon the future [τὴν διάνοιαν Θεῷ συμπορευομένην καὶ τὸ μέλλον ἀποσκοποῦσαν]'.[5] The momentum of the Hexaemeron, therefore, had little to do with circumstance, whether Arian or Gothic, and more to do with Basil's understanding of what drew the Christian along the path from creation to fulfilment. The lack of finish typical of human experience gave one the right to cast one's eye forward with assurance, even possessiveness. The gift of knowledge—knowledge of how the future was to be defined, and in that sense controlled—was the legitimate reward of hope and faith. Hence Basil's feeling that controversy would wane, that error was the symptom only of some more basic failing in the Church: it was natural, by contrast, to invest a greater passion in longer-term convictions that escaped the pressure of event. And if sermons and ascetic reflections, for example, seem likely to have appealed to a smaller group (which the learning and spiritual exaltation of the Hexaemeron might certainly imply),[6] that should

---

Attitude of Basil of Caesarea as a Christian Bishop towards Greek Philosophy and Science'. The paper as a whole, however, imposes too marked a distinction between public ecclesial caution and personal acceptance of classical learning: Basil achieved a far greater integration of ideas.

2. GNaz Orat. 43. 67, tr. p. 85. Leo McCauley must have felt simply unable to translate the next sentence (and who can blame him!): τούτῳ μεθαρμόζομαι, καὶ ῥυθμίζομαι, καὶ ἄλλος ἐξ ἄλλου γίνομαι, τὴν θείαν ἀλλοίωσιν ἀλλοιούμενος, PG 36. 585C.

3. For the dating of the Hexaemeron, and of Basil's death, see appendix 3, pp. 358–361.

4. Ep. 277, C 3: 150, D 4: 161.

5. Ep. 293, C 3: 167, D 4: 201.

6. Bernardi, Prédication, pp. 48f., was confident that the Hexaemeron had in mind, in fact, the general audience of the church of Caesarea. That impression is reinforced by the observations of Lim, 'Politics of Interpretation': see below, at n. 57.

not be taken as the unwelcome symptom of limitation or failure: to tap a deeper and richer vein of thought in the company of intimate devotees was no more than the natural mark of an older man. If the address appears withdrawn—in the spirit, say, of the Preface to the *Asceticon*[7]—the stamp of Basil's personality was undiminished in its clarity and consistent strength. As he wrote himself, one should not take 'a man's preoccupation with affairs' as the 'sign of his character [σημεῖον τρόπου]'.[8] All of which explains, of course, what we have already discovered: that his attention to the doctrine of the Trinity, for example, was simply one facet of his fundamental attachment to personal loyalty and friendship and helped to underwrite a much broader picture of human potential and destiny.

Basil's chief purpose in the *Hexaemeron*, as we have already hinted, was to present a complete cosmology. He did not shrink from the associated task, speculation on the origin, structure, and function of the visible world.[9] More important, however, was his account of humanity's place in that world, and of humanity's destiny. The central theme in that account—with obvious debts to both Plato and Origen—was that the genuine beauty and fascinating intricacy of creation found its meaning and fulfilment in a return to a world that was invisible and eternal. In relation to human beings, as we shall see, such a theory of 'return'—to the 'ancient fatherland'[10]—demanded reflection on both morality and the mechanisms of the psyche. The sense of history provoked by examination of the external world was thus allowed to affect the realm of individual self-knowledge.[11]

7. See chapter 6, at n. 37; but bearing in mind the point made there: that a 'special occasion' need not point to a privileged or restricted group.

8. *Ep.* 56, C 1: 143, D 1: 353. See chapter 5, at n. 60.

9. The sermons are full of learning on these matters; and allusions to older theories are fully documented in the more recent editions: an aspect I have taken largely for granted, concentrating on the moral thrust of the work.

10. The phrase from which this chapter takes its title occurs in the *De spiritu sancto*, in the course of an explanation as to why one faced east in prayer: ὀλίγοι δὲ ἴσμεν ὅτι τὴν ἀρχαίαν ἐπιζητοῦμεν πατρίδα, τὸν παράδεισον, DSS 27 (§ 66); ed. Pruche, p. 484. It can be found also at *Hex.* 6. 1. See below, at n. 81

11. A vivid example of Basil's enduring preoccupation is provided in *Hom.* 351. 1, which describes a cycle of return within the individual: God's providential inspiration ('the bread that comes down from heaven') creates an 'inner voice [νοητὸν στόμα τοῦ ἔνδον ἀνθρώπου]', which pours forth unending praise in return, PG 29. 355BC. *Hex.* 9. 6 provides a vivid example of how historical inquiry and self-analysis were wholly interwoven. We shall return to the theme.

Such a shift, from the broad level of human development through time to the recesses of the individual soul, was far from rare in the philosophical, and specifically the patristic, literature of the period. One thinks of Augustine, perhaps, as culminating that tradition. Treatises on the Trinity and Genesis provided perfect opportunities for such an emphasis and became, therefore, almost a necessary qualification for leadership in the Church. In the *Hexaemeron*, Basil came closest to a *De Genesi ad litteram*; perhaps even to a *City of God*. In his case, however, the invitation was to a reverse transition: from a knowledge of self to a full understanding of human progress through time.

The work was also a study of salvation—the salvation of the individual, but also of the whole human community. The notion of salvation endowed the process of return with a specifically Christian quality.[12] It represented a response, not just to the potential of the created order, but also to the promises of the New Testament.[13] It brought together two principles of belief: that God was merciful in the face of sin, and that 'life in paradise' had always been his intended goal for the human race.[14] Seen in that light, the work also continued to make a point against the Arian position, which, in the hands of Eunomius, had made the creator (as Basil saw it) more remote from creation and had undermined the relationship of dependence and gratitude proper to those redeemed by an incarnate saviour; a people, moreover, who discovered their need of help and their capacity for worship within an historical community, the Church.

For Basil, the perceptible nature and destiny of the visible world and the paradise promised to the human race were both aspects of objective reality. He realized, nevertheless, as he had done before, that such a confident assessment of experience depended on a theory of knowledge. How reliable were the impressions that contributed to his cosmology? Two characteristic emphases, closely connected, and made in the opening section of the *Hexaemeron* itself, reiterated positions adopted in previous

12. Reference to the Spirit and use of the word 'salvation [σωτηρία]' already occurs in *Hex.* 1. 1. As we shall see, many fundamental points were anticipated in Basil's other sermons. In this instance, compare *Hom.* 354. 1, where goals desired by pagans (ἐπιστήμη, πρακτικὴ ἐνέργεια, ἡδονή) are contrasted with the achievement promised to Christians: 'a happy life in the age to come [ἡ μακαρία διαγωγὴ ἐν τῷ μέλλοντι αἰώνι]', *PG* 29. 432B.

13. See *Hom.* 328. 2: τὰς ψυχὰς ἡμῶν πειρωμένου [sc. Ἀποστόλου, i.e., Paul] χαμόθεν πρὸς ὕψος μετεωρίζειν, καὶ ἐπὶ τὸ οὐράνιον μετατιθέναι πολίτευμα, *PG* 31. 220D. The Church represented an anticipation of that πολίτευμα: *Hom.* 353. 4.

14. See *Hom.* 357. 3: 'We were once considered worthy of life in paradise, ... so God has mercy on us, seeing us as we once used to be [ὀρῶν ἡμᾶς οἷοι ἀνθ' οἵων γεγόναμεν]', *PG* 29. 489B.

works: the human mind, he felt, was weak; and it was foolish, therefore, to rely on 'worldly wisdom'.

The weakness of human perception, of διάνοια, was revealed largely by its inadequate achievements. Human beings were constantly the victims of their own instability. Even those who reached apparently firm conclusions would rarely rest content for long with their opinion. Not surprisingly, as a consequence, they found it hard to reach agreement with others (agreement being, for Basil, an essential characteristic of any healthy community).[15] There was also the problem of limited imagination: Basil brought to bear, at this point, quite human arguments, pointing to the difficulty most people experienced, when faced with the 'scientific' paradoxes and obscurities of time and space.[16]

As for secular learning, the 'wisdom of the world', Basil maintained the suspicions we have already detected, particularly in the *Contra Eunomium*.[17] The distinction between 'us' and 'them', between Christians and those 'outside', was now much sharper.[18] The chief shortcoming of the educated élite was that it devoted too much attention to attracting the admiration of others.[19] Even worse, its members seemed to think that the purpose of learning was to provoke and support argument, and to sharpen skills in effective contradiction. No one could formulate a position that someone else did not instantly attack.[20]

The antidote to those failings was to develop an alternative mode of understanding—and it was still to be thought of as understanding, even though Basil called it 'faith'.[21] Faith in this sense depended in its turn on a particular form of exegesis, the strict and literal interpretation of the

15. These points, adumbrated in *Hex*. 1. 1, will recur below. Instability of opinion is to be set in the wider context of human instability generally: see *Hex*. 9. 4.

16. *Hex*. 1. 9.

17. As discussed in chapter 4. In addition to the passages in *Hex*. 1. 1, see also 3. 6 and 8; 6. 1.

18. *Hex*. 1. 2, 3. 3.

19. *Hex*. 1. 1. The criticism featured prominently in Christian commentary; perhaps, in this period, most famously in John Chrysostom's *On Vainglory*. Basil certainly contributed to the corpus: see, for example, chapter 4, at nn. 105, 122f. It was, however, an attitude not wholly foreign to pagan commentators, as we saw briefly in chapter 2, at nn. 31f.

20. *Hex*. 1. 2, 3. 3. The point is made again in 1. 8, with the consequent assertion that one should not inquire into every οὐσία. A. H. Armstrong was alarmed by so un-Plotinian a view of διάνοια and λογισμός. See his 'Plotinus's Doctrine of the Infinite and Its Significance for Christian Thought', p. 55.

21. It is important to stress that, for all his hesitations, Basil never lost sight of knowledge in some better sense as a fundamental goal, 'by the grace of Him who summoned us with a holy calling to the knowledge of Himself [εἰς τὴν ἑαυτοῦ ἐπίγνωσιν]', *Ep*. 204. 6, C 2: 178f., D 3: 169. See n. 59 below.

text of Scripture.[22] First, one had to take the text at face value, ἁπλῶς, simply, without burrowing away to find difficulties and complexities that were not there.[23] The truth, Basil felt, was by its nature 'naked', and therefore easily discovered.[24] Included in the theory was the conviction that words should be taken according to their common use (ἡ κοινὴ χρῆσις)—a point already made in the *Contra Eunomium*.[25] Only on the basis of that humility, so to speak, would one gain access to deeper knowledge. There was an important motive behind such insistence: Scripture was indeed a message, a series of moral instructions, directed to its readers by the Spirit; and for that reason every phrase was to be accorded its just weight.[26]

Priority was to be given, therefore, to faith and Scripture; but once that priority was conceded, all other sources of knowledge could be harnessed to 'that highest of all goods', the contemplation of God, 'to which every rational nature [λογικὴ φύσις] aspires'.[27] The world of nature was chief among those sources, and human nature at its heart. Basil had long developed a careful respect for 'nature'. We have seen how it affected his ascetic teaching.[28] It appeared also in his sermons. There was the simple image of Mamas, the future martyr, segregated as a shepherd from the iniquities of civic life, gazing at the night sky, and recognizing in the beauty of the stars the wonder of their creator.[29] Others were encouraged

22. The historical roots of Basil's exegetical method form too large a topic to be treated here. In what follows, the influence of Theophilus, and of Antioch generally, is not unlikely. See Smets and van Esbroeck in their introduction to *Hex.* 10 and 11, pp. 95f.; balanced by Lim, 'Politics of Interpretation'. The latter's allusions extend usefully beyond his specific interest. Passages that appear particularly to focus on the dangers of allegory (and therefore, perhaps, of 'Origenism' generally) are *Hex.* 3. 9, 9. 1. Analogy, as we shall see, is preferred. This inclination to the straightforward was obviously not seen by Basil as a dangerous concession to Arians: compare Young, 'God of the Greeks', p. 49. Gribomont, 'Origénisme', has much to the point.

23. *Hex.* 2. 5, 9. 1.

24. *Hex.* 3. 8. Note the praise of simple truth in 7. 3.

25. *Hex.* 8. 3, ed. Giet, p. 442. The contrast here is with Aristotle. It is probably fair to say that Basil promptly failed to follow his own advice. Note also the phrase in 9. 1, τὰς κοινὰς τῶν γεγραμμένων ἐννοίας, ed. Giet, p. 480.

26. *Hex.* 8. 8; for the last point, 6. 11.

27. *Hom.* 334. 7, *PG* 31. 256A. There was still some correlation between the way the mind functioned and the structure of the created world itself: the human ability to distinguish mentally what could not be separated physically pointed to the stages whereby the creator actually progressed from conception to creation, *Hex.* 6. 3. It will be useful to refer back to the vocabulary later: ὅτι ἃ ἡμῖν τῇ ἐπινοίᾳ ἐστὶ χωριστά, ταῦτα δύναται καὶ αὐτῇ τῇ ἐνεργείᾳ παρὰ τοῦ ποιητοῦ τῆς φύσεως αὐτῶν διαστῆναι, p. 336.

28. See chapter 6, at nn. 71, 142, and esp. 165f.

29. *Hom.* 337. 3. See chapter 5, at nn. 236f.

to follow the same avenues of discovery.[30] They would find themselves in the process blessed with a fuller understanding that was justly called faith:

> If, says the psalmist, you look at the heavens and observe their order, you are on the road to faith: for they show forth the one who shaped them. And if you open your eyes to the beauties of the earth, they in their turn will augment your belief in God. For our belief in him does not depend on a knowledge that comes merely through the eyes of the flesh: it is the power of the mind [τῇ τοῦ νοῦ δυνάμει] that makes visible for us, through what we see, the things we cannot see.[31]

Now, Basil confirmed that view in detail. Moses (naturally, being the author of Genesis!) led the way: he spent a period of retreat in Ethiopia τῇ θεωρίᾳ τῶν ὄντων, 'contemplating existence'; and that provided him with the basis for his later vision of God.[32] So Christians should wean themselves from the superficial amazement induced by urban life and open themselves to the genuinely instructive wonder prompted by sight of the natural world.[33] They would also, by analogy, draw moral fruit from the experience. As the sun gave light, so the holy ones of ancient times dispelled the shadows of ignorance.[34] As the moon waxed and waned, so human fortune and progress in virtue succeeded and failed by turns.[35] Big fish ate little fish: so the rich consumed the poor.[36] Animals detected the coming seasons: Christians should anticipate eternity.[37] Animals also walked bowed to the ground: men and women, naturally erect, should set their sights on heaven.[38] The connections were laborious; but the usefulness of the exercise depended on a certain exactness of observation. Moreover, the various aspects of nature were seen to form a whole, which was at once abundant and social: the order and affection of family life, the adequate support of simple nourishment, the advantage of harmony with neighbours—all were aspects of the system Basil wished his audience to admire and imitate.[39]

One could learn also from oneself. That, too, was a point that Basil had made before (as, of course, had any number of reflective people in

---

30. *Hom.* 324. 6.
31. *Hom.* 350. 3, *PG* 29. 329B. The allusion is to Psalm 33 (V 32).
32. *Hex.* 1. 1, p. 90.
33. *Hex.* 4. 1 makes the point with particular force. For nature as a book, see 11. 4.
34. *Hex.* 6. 2.
35. *Hex.* 6. 10f.
36. *Hex.* 7. 3.
37. *Hex.* 9. 3.
38. *Hex.* 9. 2, 11. 15. Less complimentary analogies are presented in 10. 19.
39. *Hex.* 9. 4, 7. 3, 8. 5 respectively.

antiquity before him):[40] 'Do not search about outside ... but pass within, to the hidden places of your own soul; and there you will learn that in the beginning God was'; 'In yourself, as in a miniature world [οἱονεὶ μικρῷ τινι διακόσμῳ], you will discover the great wisdom of the one who made you'.[41] Once again, this 'power of the mind' was rooted in the intimate connection between God and creature. It meant that one recognized at once 'the very hallmarks of a human being [τὰ τοῦ ἀνθρώπου ἐξαίρετα]'; and those were 'a thorough understanding of God the Father, the received tradition [παραδοχή] concerning the Word who was in the beginning with God, and the enlightenment brought about by the Holy Spirit'. The Trinity, in its literal guise, created by its interior impact another trinity— of knowledge, tradition, and enlightenment—which reached outwards to colour one's vision of the world and embraced history as well as the individual's perfection.[42] So one was faced with the translucent overlay of different planes of perception: the self, the world, and the drama of God's action:[43]

> Heaven and earth, the vasty deep and living creatures which move in the waters, animals of the dry land, and plants, stars, air, seasons, and the manifold evidence of design which meets us everywhere [ἡ ποικίλη τοῦ παντὸς διακόσμησις], do not so vividly impress with the sense of transcendent power [τὸ ὑπερέχον τῆς ἰσχύος συνίστησιν], as the fact that God, who is incomprehensible, should impassibly by means of flesh be in conflict with death, so that by His own suffering He might set us free from all suffering.[44]

In the *Hexaemeron*, Basil confirmed those convictions. Knowledge of self was difficult, he conceded: 'We are more likely to understand the

40. It would be laboriously pedantic to document at length the philosophical tradition based on the ancient command γνῶθι σεαυτόν. Particularly helpful to me has been Pierre Courcelle, *Connais-toi toi-même, de Socrate à saint Bernard*.

41. *Hom.* 343. 4, *PG* 31. 481AB; *Hom.* 319. 7, ed. Rudberg, p. 35. It is striking that, in the first text, the result of such understanding was thought to be sound theology and devout adoration—as in the *Contra Eunomium*.

42. *Hom.* 354. 6, *PG* 29. 445B. For earlier discussion of the passage and its implications, see chapter 4, at nn. 152f., and also, for more general reflections, at nn. 75f.

43. See the phrase of Averil Cameron, *Rhetoric of Empire*, p. 69, 'a totally integrated rhetoric of God, community, and individual', in what is perhaps the most exciting passage of her book.

44. *DSS* 8 (§ 18); ed. Pruche, p. 308; tr. p. 44. 'Incomprehensible' may now appear misleading for ἀχώρητον, meaning 'not contained by space'. 'Suffering' is ambiguous. God is, paradoxically, in conflict with death ἀπαθῶς διὰ σαρκός: paradoxically, because it is τῷ ἰδίῳ πάθει that he gains for mankind the gift of ἀπάθεια, which is not so much freedom from suffering in the modern sense as freedom from passivity, especially exposure to passion.

heavens than we are to understand ourselves'.[45] Yet the self was no more, once again, than a world in miniature.[46] The cosmic analogy endowed the inner life of the individual with a broad scale of its own, with height and depth; and each person was invited to range over the levels and surfaces of that private universe, penetrating ever inwards.[47] Only when one had reached the most secret, hidden level could one begin to grow in the knowledge of God.[48]

Success in such a task was impossible without an appreciation of the Bible: 'Our minds have no other way of seeing themselves, unless they attend closely to the Scriptures'.[49] As in the *Contra Eunomium*, only Scripture could provide the categories of thought, indeed the very vocabulary, upon which to base an accurate psychology.[50] To that extent, Basil's solution to the weakness of the unaided mind and the futility of secular learning was religious in character. Disenchantment with mere argument led to a notion of understanding based more on faith.[51] He was precise in describing the mechanics of the alternative style of inquiry. When διάνοια, a person's natural understanding, was no longer able, for example, to imagine how the visible world could be supported in space (and that was the kind of mental failure Basil meant by weakness), then one should shift to a new level of language, specifically religious and figurative in character. All things, one should say, are in the hand of God (without supposing, in other words, that this was what we, in our own age, might call a 'scientific' statement).[52] The shift was based on analogy (he used the word ἀναλογιζώμεθα): a shift from the grandeur that one could observe to the grandeur of God, which 'outstripped all understanding in the fullness of its power'.[53] Such a change in the level or mode of discourse

45. *Hex.* 10. 2: εὔκολοί ἐσμεν γνῶναι οὐρανὸν μᾶλλον ἢ ἑαυτούς, p. 168. The point is adumbrated in 6. 1.

46. Μικρὸς διάκοσμος, the phrase used in the sermon quoted above at n. 41: see *Hex.* 11. 14, p. 266.

47. There was some paradox in this command to delve deeper, ἐπὶ τὸ βάθος ... ἔνδοθεν, p. 266 (as in the previous note); but it reminds us that the exterior inversion—to lift one's eyes from the ground and look up to the heavens—was always conceived as a moral rather than a literal exercise.

48. *Hex.* 9. 6.

49. *Hex.* 10. 1: ὁ νοῦς ὁ ἡμέτερος ἄλλως ἑαυτὸν οὐ βλέπει, ἐὰν μὴ ταῖς Γραφαῖς ἐγκύψῃ, p. 166.

50. *Hex.* 10. 1. See chapter 4, at nn. 70f., 141f.

51. *Hex.* 1. 10, 10. 3, 11. 1. By the time Basil came to the final sermon, the Spirit, as teacher of the mind, with Solomon as the exemplar, dominated the discourse.

52. *Hex.* 1. 9.

53. *Hex.* 1. 11: πᾶσαν διάνοιαν ἐν τῷ πλήθει τῆς ἑαυτοῦ δυνάμεως ὑπερβαίνοντα, p. 134.

was justified because it occurred in Scripture. The author of the sacred text (in this case, supposedly, Moses) was considered 'trustworthy' (possessing ἀξιοπιστία), or, more exactly, worthy of belief; a conviction on the reader's part based on a recognition that Scripture's purpose was, as we have said, moral rather than 'scientific'.[54]

The very reading of Scripture, therefore, was a moral rather than a merely intellectual endeavour. The attitude of trust, of belief, had to come first, before one considered the exact meaning of this or that passage. A complete ascetic programme was the inescapable prerequisite: purification from passion, escape from the distractions of ordinary life, a readiness for hard work, a heightened desire for things spiritual.[55] Above all, the person of true understanding would depend on a constant sense of God's presence within.[56] Parallels with Basil's ascetic exhortations are easy to discern; and yet he made explicit his awareness that, in the *Hexaemeron*, he was addressing 'ordinary' people with many other preoccupations.[57] It was to this audience that he presented the very highest ideal, an intimate dialogue with God: for in the straightforward words of the sacred text, he said, it was ultimately God himself who was revealed to the true exegete.[58]

To present Scripture in that way was to move inevitably towards an overriding emphasis on reverent cult within a believing community. The concepts involved, of authority and moral discipline, demanded an exercise of faith and ascetic rigour entirely dependent on the guidance and support of other people. The whole of this study has witnessed Basil's movement in that direction. His engagement with an ecclesial 'family'; his encouragement of a new community in Caesarea, with its own sense of cohesion and corporate responsibility; his conception of the institutions necessary for ascetic progress; and his own dependence on colleagues in the eastern church all represented a move from individual ideals, albeit high-minded, to the shared experience encapsulated by his understanding of the word 'Church'.

Even in the field of natural talent, that habit of mind had displayed itself constantly. When he asserted, for example, that 'this is the height of human achievement; this is our glory and our greatness: to understand

54. *Hex.* 1. 1 and 11.
55. All in *Hex.* 1. 1.
56. *Hex.* 3. 10: διὰ τῆς συνεχοῦς μνήμης ἔνοικον ἔχοντες ἑαυτῶν τὸν Θεόν, p. 242.
57. See chapter 6, esp. at nn. 37f., 201f. Lim, 'Politics of Interpretation', emphasizes the 'ordinariness' of the audience and links it specifically with the simplicity of exegesis recommended by Basil: see above, at n. 6.
58. *Hex.* 6. 1.

genuinely what matters most, and cling to that',[59] he was not congratulating his audience person by person, but rejoicing in a shared endowment. When he spoke of the moral control necessary to true understanding—stillness, withdrawal, an inner steadiness of mind untouched by passion, open to the peace of God's presence in the soul—he could adopt a singleness of tone and create the impression of addressing one person only (displaying, perhaps, no more than a preacher's dramatic skill).[60] Yet his audience would have recalled other occasions, when the same achievement was presented in more social terms. Fasting, for example, would bring a peace that spilled out beyond the individual's heart: 'The whole city generally, and all its people, are brought together in well-ordered harmony: raucous voices put to rest, strife banished, insults hushed'.[61] Of course the Church was made up of individuals.[62] The goal of each one's life was pursued in some sense independently of others; and the death at its close was a unique experience, symbolizing some inevitable isolation, and subjecting one to a judgement based on individual acts.[63]

59. *Hom.* 329. 3: τοῦτο ὕψος ἀνθρώπου, τοῦτο δόξα καὶ μεγαλειότης, ἀληθῶς γνῶναι τὸ μέγα, καὶ τούτῳ προσφύεσθαι, *PG* 31. 529BC. Attention to vocabulary is important. Γνῶναι here is richer, perhaps, than the language of διάνοια and reminds us that Basil was moving constantly towards a definition of knowledge that involved inextricably the indwelling action of God (a point adumbrated above in n. 21). See, for example, the status of νοῦς and λόγος in relation to the creature's being made 'in the image of the creator' (a matter to which we shall return), *Hom.* 328. 2; or the juxtaposition of ἔννοια with words like περιέλαμψε, καταφρονῆσαι and εὐφροσύνη, and γνώρισον, *Hom.* 350. 1. *Hom.* 353. 7 is worth quoting more fully: 'So it is with those things contemplated by the mind: anyone who does not attain, by his own works, a fellowship, an intimate association with God, is unable to see the works of God himself with the pure eyes of understanding [οὕτω καὶ ἐπὶ τῶν κατὰ νοῦν θεωρημάτων, ὁ μὴ διὰ τῶν ἔργων οἰκειωθεὶς καὶ πλησιάσας Θεῷ ἰδεῖν τὰ ἔργα αὐτοῦ καθαροῖς τῆς διανοίας ὀφθαλμοῖς οὐ δύναται]', *PG* 29. 428A. This variety of terminology was deployed in the service of subtle but important distinctions.

60. *Hom.* 351. 10 provides a particularly fine example, with phrases that themselves progress from achievement to achievement: κτῆσαι γαληνιῶντα νοῦν ... κτήσῃ τὴν εἰρήνην τοῦ Θεοῦ τὴν ὑπερέχουσαν πάντα νοῦν, φρουροῦσαν τὴν καρδίαν σου, *PG* 29. 376BC.

61. *Hom.* 331. 5: πᾶσαν ἀθρόως τὴν πόλιν, καὶ πάντα τὸν δῆμον μεθαρμόζει πρὸς εὐταξίαν, κοιμίζει κραυγὴν, ἐξορίζει μάχην, λοιδορίαν κατασιγάζει, *PG* 31. 192B. There were individual advantages, of course: 'Nothing can prevent us [as a result] from passing our lives in profound peace and tranquillity of soul [οὐδὲν ἐκώλυεν ἐν εἰρήνῃ βαθείᾳ καὶ ἀταραξίᾳ ψυχῶν τὴν ζωὴν ἡμᾶς παραπέμπειν]', 192D/193A. *Hom.* 330. 10 makes the same point, with the same conjunction of individual and community. One discovers, anyway, that *Hom.* 351 just quoted goes on to make similarly social statements, § 13. For the broader context of all these sermons, see chapter 5, at nn. 129f., 215.

62. Καθ' ἕκαστον, *Hom.* 325. 8: see chapter 5, at nn. 213f., and below, at n. 75.

63. *Hom.* 334. 5, 338. 2. Note his allusion to what he thought was the Jewish custom of naming persons after their most characteristic virtues (in contrast to a more 'social' concentration on genealogy), *Hom.* 345. 1.

Nevertheless, pursuit of any spiritual goal brought one inevitably into alliance with those of similar purpose:

> A single mind, the efforts of a single person, are far from sufficient to grasp the great works of God. So, together, we devote all our modest talents to achieving that power in common. We need complete freedom from labour, away from the turmoil of the outside world. Imposing complete silence within the hidden chamber of the heart, we thus apply ourselves to the contemplation of the truth.[64]

In the *Hexaemeron* itself, perception based on faith was supposed to lead to an attitude of wonder—to generate, in other words, a response characteristic of the worshipper.[65] Engagement with Scripture had its part to play: the sacred text was itself a temple, into which the reader as worshipper penetrated.[66] That specifically religious act took place within a wider context still: for the worshipper joined with nature itself, offering a harmonious hymn to the creator.[67]

The importance of community was underlined by frequent reference to 'the building up of the Church [ἡ τῆς ἐκκλησίας οἰκοδομή]'.[68] Pastoral considerations had taken over from simple images of civic order. In that respect, the social emphasis was conjoined with a move from text to action, so central to Basil's cast of mind.[69] A range of psychological reflections mapped the paths along which one might make such a move. Christians were marked by their attachment to word, to law, to the Gospel, and to the Spirit—a chain of concepts that represented in its way the passage from

64. *Hom.* 351. 3: ἐπεὶ οὖν εἷς νοῦς καὶ ἑνὸς ἀνδρὸς μελέτη, οὐδὲ πρὸς βραχὺ αὐταρκεῖ πρὸς τὴν τῶν μεγαλείων τοῦ Θεοῦ κατάληψιν, πάντας ὁμοῦ τοὺς πραεῖς εἰς τὴν κοινωνίαν ταύτης τῆς ἐνεργείας παραλαμβάνει. δεῖ γὰρ πᾶσαν σχολὴν ἄγειν ἀπὸ θορύβων τῶν ἔξωθεν, καὶ πᾶσαν ἡσυχίαν ἐν τῷ κρυπτῷ τῆς καρδίας βουλευτηρίῳ [a very civic 'chamber'!] ποιήσαντα, οὕτως ἐπιβάλλειν τῇ θεωρίᾳ τῆς ἀληθείας, *PG* 29. 357B. For another fine conjunction of themes, see *Hom.* 348. 4, which encourages freedom from the flesh (the soul of the virtuous Christian is ἀδούλωτος ... τῷ φρονήματι τῆς σαρκὸς), an accurate assessment of one's own worth (μέγεθος δὲ καὶ ἀξίωμα πρέπον ἑαυτῇ ἐκ τῆς συναισθήσεως τῶν προσόντων αὐτῇ ἀπὸ Θεοῦ ἀναλάβῃ), an understanding of creation and providence (e.g., ὑψηλῶς δὲ τεθεωρηκότες τοὺς περὶ κτίσεως λόγους), and a spirit of generosity towards both friends and those in need (καὶ προσέτι ἐν ταῖς δαπάναις ἀφειδεῖς, καὶ μεγαλόδωροι ἐν τῷ τὰς τῶν ἀδελφῶν χρείας ἐπανορθοῦσθαι), *PG* 29. 293A. Bernardi, *Prédication*, p. 43, linked this sermon with the *Hexaemeron*.

65. The point was essential to the argument of the *Contra Eunomium*, as examined in chapter 4. See, for example, *Hex.* 2. 7 for the expected response to the beauty of light: the note of joy carries the passage well beyond a Stoic appreciation of order.

66. The atmosphere of 'mystery' is very marked: *Hex.* 2. 1.

67. *Hex.* 3. 9, 4. 5.

68. *Hex.* 1. 8, 2. 1, 4. 7, 9. 1, 11. 8.

69. We noted its early roots in the opening paragraph of chapter 2.

thought to deed.[70] More specifically, in relation to Scripture, one weighed up, first, the intentions of the writer; and then, with help from the Spirit and with the co-operation of God's grace, one would be in a position to 'build up the Church'.[71]

We seem to have come a long way from a mere theory of knowledge or exegesis. The increased distance from secular learning and the corresponding shift in the meaning of διάνοια, coupled with an emphasis on faith and a strict interpretation of the sacred text, carried with them unavoidable consequences, in social as well as moral attitudes, for the believer. Admiration for one form of wisdom over another underpinned the recommendation of a new society.

In this we detect one of Basil's major skills: his ability to use the images of secular life, no longer as a series of goals but rather as starting points for a journey, a journey first of the imagination, carrying his audience towards the experience of what he regarded as genuine community life. We began to explore elsewhere this transference, as it were, from fatherland to fatherland.[72] The process was bound to be slow; but it was based on a belief that, once distracted by such an act of the imagination, the 'disposition [διάθεσις] of [the] soul' could veer away from the traditional patterns of life that appeared otherwise to persist on the surface.[73] Basil continued, therefore, to address his message to people whom he knew would return to the practical task of gaining their living in a compromised community.[74] He himself made use of traditional forms: his definition of πολιτεία continued to honour the expositions of Aristotle.[75] Yet he presented powerful and negative portraits of the 'men of power' typical of late Roman society, thus identifying clearly the long-standing habits

70. *Hex.* 7. 5: οἱ λόγῳ τετιμημένοι, καὶ νόμῳ πεπαιδευμένοι, ἐπαγγελίας προτραπέντες, πνεύματι σοφισθέντες, p. 414.

71. *Hex.* 2. 1: τοῦ βουλήματος τῆς Γραφῆς ... τῇ βοηθείᾳ τοῦ Πνεύματος ... τῇ συνεργίᾳ τῆς χάριτος οἰκοδομήν τινα τῇ ἐκκλησίᾳ, p. 140.

72. *Hom.* 346. 1, within the general context of embarking upon a new life (ἐπείγεσθαι δὲ πρὸς ἑτέραν ζωήν), uses the image of exile from a purely 'natural' πατρίς as the starting point for return to something better, *PG* 29. 252AB. See especially the final sections of chapter 5.

73. *Ep.* 106 provides a perfect instance—'a man who proves that even in military life one may preserve the perfection of love for God', C 2: 7, D 2: 203. See chapter 6, at n. 28.

74. *Hex.* 3. 1 and 10 make the most explicit references to the accepted preoccupations of the audience.

75. *Hex.* 8. 4, with reference to *Hist. an.* 1. 1: τὸ πρὸς ἓν πέρας κοινὸν συννεύειν τὴν ἐνέργειαν τῶν καθ' ἕκαστον. His acceptance of this vocabulary throws further light on the tension between individual and community already referred to above at n. 62, and in chapter 5, at nn. 213f.

that he wished to supersede.[76] The Church, by contrast, as a paradigm of social perfection, was built upon a unity of thought, mirroring that of nature itself.[77] Christians were grafted by their faith into a single vine (that faith being inspired by the ancient tradition of teaching within the Church).[78]

It was the movement from one to the other that demanded attention. One rejected, for example, the theatre of classical drama, so destructive of the imagination, preferring the theatre of nature, in which one could achieve understanding of the creator.[79] One rejected the arena of cruel conflict and short-lived victory, entering upon the struggle of exegesis itself, becoming with Basil a συναγωνιστής as he grappled with the sacred text.[80] One left the city of daily experience and entered the city of hidden mysteries. One returned to the ἀρχαία πατρίς, the ancient fatherland from which one had been driven out by sin; one moved forward, also, to the fatherland of the heavenly Jerusalem promised in the writings of the New Testament.[81]

So much for the prerequisites of true understanding, and the social setting within which it was best achieved—for Basil was asking about the status of the tangible, created world, and about the reliability of 'knowledge', faced with that world. He moved quickly, in reply, to the realm of faith, morality, and religious community (matters to which we shall return); but he pleaded, also, for exact observance and an ordered mind.

His conclusions had their effects at the level of individual experience, particularly in the matter of freedom. One point he stressed above others: there was a single and total explanation for everything, and there had been from the beginning—God. That meant, among other things, that God was in control: there was no need to fear that any aspect of creation escaped

76. *Hex.* 5. 2, 11. 13. The latter is a particularly striking passage, full of detail, ending with the ringing phrase 'When you see [such people], do not let the sight cause you fear [for they have much more to fear themselves!]'. The contrast is with a natural desire for neighbourliness, as in 8. 5.

77. *Hex.* 4. 7.

78. *Hex.* 5. 6.

79. *Hex.* 4. 1.

80. *Hex.* 6. 1.

81. *Hex.* 6. 1, and, for the final point, 9. 2.

his mastering hand. Fatalism was ruled out by faith.[82] The simplicity of the theory was not new. Evident normality and apparent disorder had always been seen by Basil as equally parts of God's plan: the one inspired faith, the other put faith to the test.[83] A good deal was thereby taken for granted. The visible order of the universe, its διακόσμησις, was presumed to have come about either αὐτομάτως, without the involvement of any external agency, or under the influence of God: no other explanations were admitted.[84] Pagans did not know about God: therefore they started off on the wrong foot, with only the self-sufficiency of the visible world at their disposal.[85] It followed that an admission of God's influence necessarily came before any process of understanding. Christians were lucky: they had had imprinted upon their souls (by Moses, apparently, as author of Genesis) the safeguarding seal of the name of God.[86] Consequently, they were better placed to recognize defensible theories of creation.

Confidence in God's control demanded reflection on human freedom, even where the argument had yet to take into account the specific creation of men and women, and the particular characteristics of the human psyche. The Fall, which represented at once a squandering of freedom and a punishment for its misuse, was the result, after all, of an arrogant trust in human shrewdness[87]—that is to say, the rejection of understanding in a truer sense.[88] So the human race had passed from simplicity of heart to the chaotic divisiveness of passion.[89] However, God had left his mark

82. *Hex.* 5. 8, 7. 5, 8. 7, 9. 4f. (three times!). The contrast was with a pagan resignation to fate and chaos: 1. 2, 5. 8.

83. *Hom.* 325. 5f. See the reference (at n. 31 above) to *Hom.* 350. 3, which was designed to assuage the fear that God was not wholly master of circumstance.

84. *Hex.* 1. 1, p. 86.

85. *Hex.* 1. 2, with the assertion that their atheism was almost innate: ὑπὸ τῆς ἐνοικούσης αὐτοῖς ἀθεότητος, p. 94.

86. *Hex.* 1. 2: οἱονεὶ σφραγῖδα καὶ φυλακτήριον ταῖς ψυχαῖς ἡμῶν ἐμβαλὼν τὸ πολυτίμητον ὄνομα τοῦ Θεοῦ, p. 96. The use of the word 'seal [σφραγίς]' connects the statement with baptism: see *Hex.* 10. 17; the references below to *Hom.* 356 at nn. 116, 155; and chapter 4, at nn. 149f. Here, perhaps, one stumbles upon an important view of conversion. The list of qualities attached to the Mosaic conception of God is at once charged with emotion—μακαρία, ἄφθονος, ἀγαπητόν, πολυπόθητον—and acceptable to any pagan with philosophical training.

87. *Hom.* 329. 1f. For the link between knowledge and humility, see *Ep.* 277.

88. *Hom.* 336. 7: Adam had simply shifted value from the invisible to the visible; 'Evil does not arise out of necessity, but from a lack of thought [ἐξ ἀβουλίας]', *PG* 31. 345A. The whole sermon reflects, with some cruelty, on the nature of the Fall: see chapter 5, at n. 15. The *Hexaemeron* reproduces the element of carelessness: 'a falling away from goodness sparked off by heedless indifference [διὰ τὴν ἀπὸ τοῦ καλοῦ ἀπόπτωσιν τοῖς ῥᾳθύμοις ἐγγινομένη (sc. διάθεσις)]', *Hex.* 2. 4, p. 158.

89. *Hom.* 350. 8.

upon all natural inclinations: they were given rather than learned; and they contained within themselves the possibility of their salvation.[90] It was within that framework that freedom had to operate. Astrology, for example, or the activity of demons had no place in honest explanations of human circumstance; nor were human wills imprisoned at some clouded level of the cosmos.[91] Basil presented a clear and contrasting picture of the controls he thought imposed themselves on individual liberty: nature itself, with its heritage of sickness and senility; accidents, in the normal sense of the word; and the influences each person brought to bear, τὰ δὲ ἐφ' ἡμῖν τυγχάνει—particularly the decision to control passion.[92]

Making clear the relationship between cosmic theory and a belief in freedom was perhaps one of the most important tasks for a man in Basil's position. His own solution to the philosophical problems involved was based on the belief that the cosmos itself was on the move, anticipating and guaranteeing the change, the choice, the self-improvement open to human beings within that cosmic system.[93] He thus provided a broad context for the belief in moral progress apparent in his ascetic teaching.[94] He had long made the point in a variety of circumstances. The fruits of repentance were not postponed but visible within the body that had first experienced sin and its frustrations.[95] The common and corporeal ground thus occupied, as it were, by both sin and redemption controlled any tendency to limit

90. *Hex.* 9. 4 is particularly emphatic. We shall explore the themes again below. We have already noted the theory in the context of Basil's ascetic works: see chapter 6, at nn. 165f. It recurs in the sermons. *Hom.* 340. 9 and 345. 5 even use the same phrase to make the point: (in *Hom.* 340) 'the basis of salvation implanted within the very process of our understanding [ταῖς κατεσπαρμέναις ἐν ταῖς ἐννοίαις ἡμῶν σωτηρίοις ἀφορμαῖς]', *PG* 31. 404C; *PG* 29. 240B is virtually identical. It was on that basis that 'the coming of the Lord' could be 'stimulative of the special qualities of the soul [τῶν τῆς ψυχῆς ἰδιωμάτων]', *Ep.* 260. 7, C 3: 113, D 4: 69.

91. See, respectively, *Hex.* 6. 5f., 9. 6, 3. 9.

92. *Hex.* 2. 5. *Hex.* 6. 7 stresses the importance of choice, which makes us subject to judgement by God. A full treatment of freedom was naturally postponed until the creation of the human race, described in *Hex.* 10 and 11 and examined below.

93. The sense of momentum is very marked in *Hex.* 5. 10—ἀκολουθία, διεξέρχεται, πρὸς ... συντέλειαν, p. 322. See also 1. 4f.

94. See chapter 6, at nn. 137f. (the theme is treated at some length). Particularly striking is the recollection of Paul in *Hom.* 352. 2, ἀλλοίωσις οὖν ἐστι τοῦ ἔσω ἀνθρώπου ἀνακαινουμένου ἡμέρᾳ καὶ ἡμέρᾳ, *PG* 29. 389C (for which refer to chapter 6, n. 145). The same text is recalled in *Hex.* 10. 7 (emphasizing in that instance the *inner* renewal). See also n. 144 below.

95. *Hom.* 350. 2: 'Since it is in the body that we sin, ... so shall we show honour and gratitude to that body, as to the very instrument by which we obtain release from sin [ἐπειδὴ γὰρ ἐν τῷ σώματι ἡμάρτομεν, ... τῷ σώματι καὶ ἐξομολογησώμεθα, τῷ αὐτῷ κεχρημένοι ὀργάνῳ πρὸς τὴν ἀνάλυσιν τῆς ἁμαρτίας]', *PG* 29. 325C. A similar position was defended in *Ep.* 261. 3: 'We in the resurrection resume the flesh that is neither liable to death nor subject to sin', C 3: 118, D 4: 83. Hence virtue will be visible: compare the important

self-mastery to some spiritual future, or to misplace the significance of the mind's conquest of passion.[96] By the very complexity of his vocabulary, Basil avoided any simple distinctions between soul and body, between mind, flesh, and spirit.[97]

So we are presented, in the *Hexaemeron*, with two arcs of natural movement. On the grand scale, creation proceeded from its beginnings to its great fulfilment; and men and women were invited to share in that drama.[98] On a smaller scale, each creature must either grow or decline. Suspension within the flow of time was, in that regard, at once an opportunity and a threat.[99] Yet time and the natural world provided an atmosphere in which change became possible, and an environment in which human beings could learn, a διδασκαλεῖον καὶ παιδευτήριον; learn above all how to grow morally.[100] Moral change was genuinely possible, as nature demonstrated; and one was thinking of a change (μεταβολή) in one's very disposition (διάθεσις), even though the human species remained unchanged over time (for creation in that sense was indeed 'given').[101] Visible growth (in height, for example) was genetic, beyond one's control; but within, one was capable of learning, and thus moving forward.[102] An inbuilt power—the gift of reason—gave each person mastery over self.[103]

---

phrase in *Hom.* 349. 5: διαβαινούσης μέχρι τῶν περάτων τοῦ σώματος τῆς κατὰ ψυχὴν διαθέσεως, *PG* 29. 317C.

96. One can see temptations (largely the product of cultural heritage) both exposed and resisted throughout the sermons and letters: see *Ep.* 260. 6 (particularly tortuous in its account of falling and rising), 261. 3 (which speaks of resurrection, but the resurrection of what is still σάρξ, the flesh), 277 (where 'making the passions of the flesh subservient to reason' is still 'a pleasant sight [ἥδιστον δὲ θεαμάτων]', C 3: 149f., D 4: 163), and 293 (with its emphasis on the masterly stillness of the virtuous mind); and then *Hom.* 330. 10, 340. 15 (this last an extensive treatment of the calm government of ordered reason, touched upon in *Ep.* 293).

97. For examples of cautious interchange (between ψυχή and νοῦς, for example), see *Hom.* 328. 2, 330. 9, 331. 1f., 339. 5 (with masterly sleight of hand in this last instance: having discussed ψυχή and σῶμα at some length, Basil ended the passage with a definition of ἄνθρωπος: νοῦς (!) ἐνδεδεμένος προσφόρῳ καὶ πρεπούσῃ σαρκί (!), *PG* 31. 549A.

98. *Hex.* 9. 2; and see again, for the last point, 5. 10: ἐφ' ἣν καὶ ἡμεῖς πάντες ... ἐπειγώμεθα, p. 322.

99. *Hex.* 1. 5, 11. 5 (with greater allusion to Scripture).

100. *Hex.* 1. 5. The vocabulary recurs in § 6.

101. *Hex.* 2. 4, 9. 1.

102. *Hex.* 11. 5. Learning was what made the difference, ἡ διὰ τῶν μαθημάτων εἰς τελείωσιν προσθήκη, pp. 234/236. The point is adumbrated in 5. 7.

103. *Hex.* 10. 6f. Possession of an inner life is what makes the difference. There was a paradoxically negative aspect of the matter. The ability to change was what distinguished human corruptibility from the incorruptibility of God. Yet the gift of reason was based in its turn on the fact that men and women were made in God's image, a theme that we shall examine later.

Since growth was understood chiefly as moral growth, all movement in the cosmos, human or otherwise, was regarded as a movement towards judgement. God was a judge before all else. Nature, freedom, growth—all were to be interpreted in such a way as to safeguard that inescapable quality of the creator. Both nature and the lives of individual souls would retain, even beyond the end of time, an affinity with the character of the first creation: in no other way could the intentions of the creator be fulfilled with justice. That desired concordance explains, of course, why Basil was anxious to assess correctly the form and implication of God's final judgement, while discussing ostensibly the beginnings of the universe. Christian preoccupation with 'the last things' exerted perhaps the most obvious pressure on classical theories concerning the origins of the world.[104] Therefore law, rewards for the observance of law, and the freedom to choose observance were all demanded by reason itself.[105] Basil was in no way morose in making such an emphasis: each person should feel drawn back to that everlasting day of creation, in which the human creature could enjoy true freedom in the company of the angels.[106]

In making such points, he was rejecting fashionable alternatives. The cycle he described—from the creator's intention that human beings should make moral progress to his equally firm resolve that associated efforts should gain their reward—would not have coincided with everyone's view of cosmology, history, and individual destiny. We need not describe in full the background to those alternatives; but it is worth noting that Basil did not make his points in a philosophical vacuum, and that he addressed the objections of a range of antagonists known to us from other sources. Gnostics were dismissed, largely because their taste for mythology was at odds with a strict interpretation of the Bible.[107] The notion of pre-existent matter, entirely respectable within the classical tradition, was equally abhorrent: Basil's creator did not inherit his materials.[108] A great

104. *Hex.* 1. 3f., 3. 10. Compare the phrase in *Hom.* 353. 5: οὕτω γὰρ τὸ δίκαιον τοῦ Θεοῦ διασώζεται, *PG* 29. 424C.
105. *Hex.* 2. 1, 6. 7. 'Law', in this context, was a broad concept: 'a change of life, freedom from lawlessness, progress towards justice, intimacy with God, good order in the world, and the regulation of life's necessary tasks [μεταβολὴ βίου, ἀνομίας ἀνάλυσις, δικαιοσύνης εἴσοδος, Θεοῦ ἐπιδημία, εὐταξία εἰς κόσμον, νομοθέτησις τῶν πρακτέων]', p. 250. The same point is made forcefully in *Hom.* 336. 1, 344. 4f. Because God is a judge, human beings must become judges also—choosing courses of action according to a 'natural criterion', the sense of justice implanted within them, *Hom.* 340. 9. See also 356. 4.
106. *Hex.* 11. 7; but the point had been made already in 2. 8.
107. *Hex.* 2. 1f. and 4.
108. *Hex.* 1. 8. Note how the Spirit was protected against diminished status in that context, 2. 6. See Armstrong, 'Plotinus's Doctrine of the Infinite', esp. pp. 55f.—although

deal of energy was devoted to the topic of the sun: no one should imagine, in Basil's opinion, that the sun was in any way, or at any stage in time, the source of life.[109] Manichees were subject to predictable attack, although Basil's disquiet was, perhaps, less usual in countering mainly their view that 'soul' was locked into the material world, awaiting release.[110]

He tried also to develop a theory of evil that avoided attributing it to God, or indeed to anything other than human choice. The issue was closely connected with his understanding of freedom and judgement. It has to be said that the *Hexaemeron* was not entirely successful in overcoming the problems involved. Human beings were seen, eventually, as in some sense the 'creators' of evil—a view at once pessimistic and contradictory.[111] These sermons were not by any means Basil's first attempt to grapple with the difficulties; and the possibly earlier versions of his argument betrayed the same failure.[112] In one sermon devoted specifically to the causes of evil, he was driven to suggest that the very gift of freedom meant that a natural inclination to goodness was necessarily exposed to the danger of corruption—for corruption could be deliberately chosen. That, surely, implied a freedom to reject 'nature'. The question then was, what made a choice of corruption likely? Excessive identification with the body? Was the 'body', then, outside the pale of 'nature'? Such difficulties, let us remember, were tolerated in the cause of answering others—doubts about God's providence, for example. Basil accepted the logic of his own argument, as we have seen: evil arose, he said, because thought was sacrificed to the whims of the flesh.[113] Yet that led to yet another paradox: for he had to admit in the end that the human mind could not always make

---

the author's surprise at Basil's supposed philosophical idiosyncrasy has to be read in the light of Rist, 'Basil's "Neoplatonism" '.

109. *Hex.* 5. 1, 6. 2f. For further technicalities, see 3. 7, 4. 5.

110. *Hex.* 8. 1. For Manichees and the primal 'darkness', see 2. 4.

111. *Hex.* 2. 4f. So the διάθεσις of the soul might incline just as easily to vice as to virtue, § 4, p. 158; and one had to face up to the fact that one was the ἀρχηγός, the originator of any evil in one's life, § 5, p. 160.

112. Optimism won the day: it was just that premonitions of success were not always expressed in passages concerned with the Fall. Obviously optimistic statements, some of which will be discussed further below, can be found in *Hom.* 319. 6, 320. 5, 328. 2, 334. 6f., 335. 8, 357. 3, 358. 3. *Hom.* 354. 3 seems to present a particularly black picture of the Fall (everyone loses freedom and is forced to submit to the yoke of Satan); but the resulting weakness means only that redemption cannot be achieved unaided (rather than, for example, that human nature is essentially vitiated). Meredith, 'Asceticism', p. 327, refers to Basil's 'basic belief in the uncorrupted character of the human soul or heart', which need not lead us to suppose that he espoused 'a weak doctrine of grace and an absence of a doctrine of original sin'.

113. See above, at n. 88.

sense of the evil in the world—so much, therefore, for the usefulness of the mind! Only a general assertion remained: evil could not come from good.[114] As for the Fall itself, by the end of the argument it was seen to result merely from a necessary trick of Satan, without which it would have been impossible to put human beings to the test.

Basil appeared to concentrate most on making clear what he did not wish to say; and that probably explains why he was less successful in achieving a true synthesis of his more positive convictions. Most of his remarks on the Fall occurred when he was discussing providence, fate, or the inevitability of evil and misfortune. They should be related, in other words, to his characteristic habit of accepting life as a test of faith.[115] He did not think that the Fall had destroyed nature in any fundamental way. Nor did he think that God required some ransom, or some satisfaction for anger. The process of redemption, and in particular the role of Jesus, were to be seen in many ways as quite separate from the circumstances of the Fall. They did not simply reverse, according to some tidy irony, the fatal incidents of Genesis. Jesus was not intent upon a fresh creation but came to reawaken nature to its destiny. 'Redemption', therefore, occupied a separate theological niche. It was achieved by the liberation of the mind, the gift of enlightenment, the safeguarding of God's image in each person, the establishment of genuine fellowship with the divine. Those in turn were brought about most obviously by the action of the Holy Spirit, and bound up with a theology of baptism. Sinful weakness, natural imperfection, and the experience of failure or loss were no more than trials that ushered in, through hope and faith, a promised enlightenment of the mind, and intimacy with God.[116]

We confront, therefore, two contrasting components of Basil's argument: he thought human understanding, carefully defined, capable of

114. It was a δόγμα (which here must mean something like an unquestionable truth) 'inherent in our souls [ταῖς ψυχαῖς ἡμῶν ἐνυπαρχέτω—which last word implies all the force of inescapable logic]', *Hom.* 336. 7, *PG* 31. 345C. Amand de Mendieta, *Ascèse*, pp. 146f., placed great weight on the bleakness of this sermon.

115. So we recall the observations on fate made in the final section of chapter 3, and his inability to cope with apparent failure, chapter 5, at nn. 73f.

116. The traces of those distinctions are scattered throughout Basil's work and are not even treated in one place within the *Hexaemeron*. *Hom.* 356, however, provides a concise treatment of most of the themes.

recognizing the intended structure and momentum of the created universe; and yet the shortcomings of experience and the perceived divorce between destiny and weakness were themselves, he felt, the results of the mind's inadequacy. Resolution of the tension between those two views would depend on a more detailed account of how the psyche 'worked'; and that could be presented only when the creation of man and woman occupied the centre of the stage. The modern reader, therefore, is also obliged to grasp the work as a whole. The two final sermons in particular provide a necessary sense of harmony and balance. We have to read each part with the knowledge of what is to come: for every aspect of the material creation found its fullest meaning in the nature of Adam and Eve.

The first act of God in Genesis was speech: 'And God said, "Let there be light" '. What did it mean, asked Basil, to say that God 'spoke' (given the fact that vibrations in the created air were not as yet possible)?[117] In a series of passages, he proceeded to present pictures of powerful movements or impulses within the mind and will of God: his thought itself was power.[118] That Basil should have focussed at once on God's mind should not be surprising (although he may seem guileless in taking for granted that God had a mind: only his 'voice' appeared a problem). Thought, intelligence, understanding, had all seemed sources of difficulty, when it came to the creature's awareness of what the visible world might signify. So the same ideas, more properly understood, might offer some clue to the redemption of human failure.[119] God knew the world, obviously, before the world knew him; and it was by maintaining that priority, as we shall see, that a true pathway back to God could be opened for the human race. Nor did Basil miss the opportunity to link God's 'voice', φωνή, with his λόγος or word, and therefore with the Word, his Son, essential partner in the creative act.[120]

Once there was something created, and once a creature had begun to grow, an even more difficult question arose. How was one to interrelate the inner surges of divine power with the qualities of nature that contributed to growth? As one observed organic changes in the material world, was one witness to the action of the mind of God itself? Simple assertions of conjunction were not enough—'The voice of God is the source of nature', for example, or 'The slightest command becomes suddenly a great natural

---

117. *Hex.* 2. 7, 3. 2, 7. 1.
118. *Hex.* 2. 2.
119. See above, at n. 21.
120. *Hex.* 3. 2, 6. 2—both of which carry further the points made above.

phenomenon'.[121] Basil needed a concept more akin to collaboration. Water, for example, had in itself the capacity to give life, which came into action as God gave his command. God was, in that instance, a demiurge (Basil used the word, albeit adjectivally), channelling as he chose the tendencies of the material at hand.[122] That material, however, was also his own creation; and one had to be more subtle yet. Basil described (while attacking the Manichees) what happened when 'the earth brought forth a living soul'. The nature, the φύσις, of all that came into being was contained ultimately in the divine word. It was not, therefore, that the earth produced something it already possessed: it witnessed the creation from within itself of something it did not possess, because God gave it the power (so, yes, it did have the power) to be active in that way.[123]

One gained a clearer idea, therefore, of what an innate and natural capacity might mean: 'nature' was the hidden presence of God's creative word, initiating constantly the familiar and apparently predictable movements of the observable world: 'The Lord has placed within the smallest living creature the visible traces of his own great wisdom'.[124] Matters became more complicated, however, when one introduced the notion of 'soul' (more or less as one passed, in Genesis, from the sea to dry land). Fish, according to Basil, lacked memory and imagination; and whatever 'psychic' movements one might like to suppose they enjoyed were entirely the result of their bodily processes. Among land creatures, on the other hand, 'the soul exercises mastery in all things'.[125] The apparently self-sufficient force of habit and immediate inclination in an animal made the process of cooperation with an immanent divinity considerably more problematic. The soul's mastery was not, of course, by any means complete. In an animal, it remained 'of the earth', condemned to a cycle of

121. *Hex.* 4. 2: Θεοῦ φωνὴ φύσεώς ἐστι ποιητική, p. 250; *Hex.* 5. 10: τὸ μικρὸν τοῦτο πρόσταγμα εὐθὺς φύσις μεγάλη, p. 322.

122. *Hex.* 7. 1. The phrases are very cautious in their tightness of expression: 'So the water was eager to assist the demiurgic command [οὕτω πᾶν ὕδωρ ἠπείγετο τῷ δημιουργικῷ προστάγματι ὑπουργεῖν]', p. 392; and 'The great and unutterable power of God was displayed in the very command that brought into being in the waters their capacity to nurture life [ἀπέδειξεν ἡ μεγάλη καὶ ἄφατος τοῦ Θεοῦ δύναμις, ὁμοῦ τῷ προστάγματι τῆς πρὸς τὸ ζωογονεῖν ἐπιτηδειότητος ἐγγενομένης τοῖς ὕδασιν]', p. 392.

123. *Hex.* 8. 1. Note the phrase Θεοῦ δωρουμένου τῆς ἐνεργείας τὴν δύναμιν, p. 430; and see above and below, at nn. 27, 135.

124. *Hex.* 7. 5: τῷ μικρῷ ζώῳ τῆς μεγάλης ἑαυτοῦ σοφίας ἐναργὲς ἴχνος ἐνέθηκεν, p. 416. The same vocabulary is used with force in 9. 4. Since it is there applied to human beings, it affects considerably the possible understanding of freedom, as we shall see below. See the related conviction that all future potentiality is present in the unborn foetus, 10. 13.

125. *Hex.* 8. 1f. For the quoted phrase, see § 1: ἡ ψυχὴ τὴν ἡγεμονίαν ἐπιτέτραπται πᾶσαν, p. 432.

corruption and dissolution. Even human beings shared in that humiliation: their φύσις was also of the earth (though God—a point to be dealt
with shortly—had honoured them in compensating ways, by the very
mode of their creation).[126] As one comes to the end of the first nine sermons, therefore, one can sense the approach both of human dignity as a
free collaborator with God and of human weakness as an earthly creature
enfolded in the processes of change and decay.

Freedom, as Basil was prepared to admit, was going to pose the
ultimate problem. How was it to be squared with the inbuilt tendencies of
nature? Was 'freedom to reject nature', hinted at above, the only logical
path to a resolution of the difficulty?[127] It seemed easy to say that men and
women made their choices 'according to the unlearned law of nature',[128]
or that to pursue goodness was analogous to enjoying sound health—
something entirely natural to the soul.[129] Such insouciance was proper,
surely, to any animal. Yet human freedom implied an element of command;
and that could spring only from the fact that each person was made κατ'
εἰκόνα ... τοῦ κτίσαντος, in the image of the creator. In a sense, therefore,
men and women acquired a power characteristic of God, the power to
initiate action within themselves and the world around them.[130] There
was, however, danger in such a theory: one might suppose that they
acquired thereby a degree of perfection or fulfilment akin to that of God.
Basil solved the difficulty by introducing the notion that, while each person
possessed the status of one made in the *image* (εἰκών) of God, that was not
the same as *likeness* (ὁμοίωσις) to God, which had yet to be striven for.
Only the Son was like God by nature. For a human being, made in the
image of God, likeness came only through grace. Freedom, in other words,
did not possess within itself a guarantee of persistently sound choice or
final achievement.[131]

126. *Hex.* 8. 2; but see the more optimistic handling of the theme in 11. 12.
127. See above, at nn. 112f.
128. *Hex.* 9. 3: τῷ ἀδιδάκτῳ τῆς φύσεως νόμῳ, p. 496. The contrast was with a morality
based on bookish learning.
129. *Hex.* 9. 4. The emphasis on avoidance of a learned response is repeated here—
ἀδιδάκτως, p. 498; more positively, κατὰ φύσιν, a phrase used several times in this section,
pp. 496/498.
130. *Hex.* 9. 5, anticipating a much fuller treatment in 10f., explored below. The visible
traces within them of God's wisdom (see above, at n. 90) serve to show that they are 'equipped
to safeguard their personal salvation [ἐμπαράσκευα πρὸς τὴν φυλακὴν τῆς οἰκείας αὐτῶν
σωτηρίας]', p. 500. The conjunction of this point with references to 'unlearned' nature makes
it clear that Basil was arguing chiefly against a sense of dependence on fate or necessity—see
esp. p. 504.
131. *Hex.* 9. 6. In the way he made the distinction, Basil pursued a different line of
argument from that of his brother: see the comments of Smets and van Esbroeck in their

Many a clue, therefore, had been set in place by the end of the first nine sermons. When Basil analyzed specifically, however, the passages of Genesis devoted to the creation of the first man and woman, he expressed himself with more coherence and carried matters into new realms of salvation, ascesis, and ecclesiology. On the threshold of the great event, God entered into a dialogue with himself: ' "Let *us* make man in *our* image" '.[132]   That turning of the Father towards the Son (for so Basil interpreted the verse) presaged the bestowal of a special honour.   In the process, the creative act of God moved to a new level, where φύσις, 'nature', was enfolded by the concept εἰκών, 'image'.   The paradoxes that had afflicted φύσις when left to itself, particularly in the realm of freedom, were now to be more successfully resolved: 'If you look only at nature [τὴν φύσιν], then a human being seems nothing, and worthy of nothing.   If you look, however, at the high regard with which we have been honoured [τὴν τιμὴν ἣν ἐτιμήθη], then humanity is great indeed'.[133] So it was the honour (that is, the status of being made in God's image, κατ' εἰκόνα) that now controlled human potential and development and defined in particular the scope of human freedom. This 'image' of God, as stated before, was displayed, according to Basil, in a human ability to command, which rested in turn on the possession of reason: '[Human] nature has within itself, in unwritten form, the spoken word of God, "Have dominion" [as in Genesis 1.28]'. Command over the passions was the most obvious example of that rational power: it was in the mastery of passion that human nature expressed itself most fully, collaborating with the creative power of God.[134]   Likeness to God, ὁμοίωσις, was similarly acquired by choice (that is, through mastery of self under the command of reason); but here Basil made room for a further distinction: humans had the δύναμις or power to acquire likeness, as part of their created nature,

introduction to *Hex.* 10 and 11, pp. 24f., 112f. Once again, that limitation was natural, not the result of sin. See n. 112 above. But it was real enough: see *Hom.* 349. 3. The concept of 'likeness to God' was not, of course, original to Basil. For an introduction to the broader philosophical tradition, see Dillon, 'Self-Definition', pp. 65f.; and Whittaker, 'Christianity and Morality', pp. 219f., and 'Plutarch, Platonism, and Christianity', p. 56.

132. The point had already been made in *Hex.* 9. 6; and recall those passages in which God's 'speaking' had invited reflection on the role of the Son in creation, above at n. 120.

133. *Hex.* 11. 2, p. 228. For the wider context, 10. 3.

134. *Hex.* 10. 6f. For the quotation, see § 8: ἀνάγραπτον ἡ φύσις ἔχει τὴν θείαν φωνήν: "ἀρχέτωσαν", p. 184; and note the immediately associated phrase 'Reason is the master of the passions [ὁ λογισμὸς τῶν παθῶν δεσπότης]', p. 184.

but would depend also on ἐνέργεια, their readiness to carry that power into effect. So he reserved an element in the process for the prior creative influence of God, while making the acquisition of the likeness a truly human achievement, deserving an eternal reward.[135]

Those ideas were not limited to the *Hexaemeron*, and statements made elsewhere in Basil's work help to fill out the picture. 'There is no likeness without knowledge [ὁμοίωσις δέ, οὐκ ἄνευ γνώσεως]': so he declared at an early point in the *De spiritu sancto*.[136] The point was, of course, that humans were not only capable of knowledge *because* they were made in God's image and possessed of reason; they were capable of knowing *that* they were made in God's image. Such reflective power was due only to the fact that God had known them (in the very act of creating them) first. Nor was it a matter of mere knowledge: the awakening of self-understanding (which was what, for human beings, creation involved) set in motion the very processes by which they might achieve their destined union with their creator.[137] The whole pattern of return and fulfilment was thus contained in the very first moment of God's action: 'He breathed on [Adam's] face— that is to say, he instilled in man some part of his own love, so that like might come to recognize like'.[138]

For that reason, the δύναμις mentioned above, the power to achieve likeness, was a power exercised within the context of redemption: for it was genuinely 'a power of renewal [δύναμιν ... ἀνακαινώσεως], bringing to our souls the great boon of salvation [μεγάλην ... τὴν σωτηρίαν]'.[139] That many of these ideas should have been stated most forcefully in the *De spiritu sancto* shows how far beyond a 'natural anthropology' Basil's inquiry had reached. The knowledge he valued most was wholly inspired by the Spirit's presence, a genuine enlightenment. The fundamental ἐνέργεια at work in human lives was that of the Spirit himself, enabling each person to 'gain insight into the divine mysteries'.[140] As a result, the whole process of recognition and return was given a more elevated and theological character.

---

135. *Hex.* 10. 15f. On the importance of the distinction between δύναμις and ἐνέργεια, refer also to the point made in 6. 3, discussed above in n. 27, and see also above, at n. 123.

136. *DSS* 1 (§ 2); ed. Pruche, p. 252.

137. See *Hom.* 329. 4.

138. *Hom.* 354. 8: ἐνεφύσησε γὰρ εἰς τὸ πρόσωπον· τουτέστι, μοιράν τινα τῆς ἰδίας χάριτος ἐναπέθετο τῷ ἀνθρώπῳ, ἵνα τῷ ὁμοίῳ ἐπιγινώσκῃ τὸ ὅμοιον, PG 29. 449C.

139. *DSS* 12 (§ 28); ed. Pruche, p. 346. The atmosphere of the passage is vague with mystery. 'Renewal' must recall the emphasis on the genuine possibility of moral progress: see above, at nn. 94f.

140. *Hom.* 353. 1: ὥστε ... κινεῖσθαι αὐτοῦ τὴν ψυχὴν ὑπὸ τοῦ ἐνεργοῦντος αὐτῇ ἁγίου Πνεύματος, and ἐνιδεῖν τοῖς θείοις μυστηρίοις, PG 29. 416C.

The distinction between image and likeness, between εἰκών and ὁμοίωσις, was concerned as much as anything with the identification of a social framework within which ὁμοίωσις could be acquired. One might be able to say that one was made 'in the image of God' simply because one saw oneself as endowed with reason; but one became 'like' God—and here Basil wasted no breath—by becoming a Christian, by entering into the community of the Church and adopting its moral programme.[141] Just as εἰκών had defined a human being, so now ὁμοίωσις defined Christianity itself—'likeness to God, in so far as that is allowed to human nature [Θεοῦ ὁμοίωσις κατὰ τὸ ἐνδεχόμενον ἀνθρώπου φύσει]'.[142] All the instruments and goals of evangelization were therefore reaffirmed. One should overcome passion; one should avoid anger and enmity; one should love others and forgive them; one should, like God, show mercy.[143] That was what it meant to 'put on Christ'. Recognizing in oneself the image of God and recognizing obligations that flowed from the fact were now more than 'natural' responses: they were touched in new ways by the initiative of God; and they depended on the influence of the Gospel and the ministrations of the Church:

[The figures of the Old Testament] did not die with Christ, and so they shall not rise with him. They did not bear the image of the heavenly one. They did not carry in their bodies the death of Jesus. They did not put off the old man, nor put on the new—the renewal that brings full knowledge, in accordance with the image of one's creator.[144]

The role of Jesus in the process was thereby made clear. It was not enough to say that by drawing near to Jesus one drew near to God, even with the added assurance that such intimacy was confirmed by the 'seal' of baptism: it was the role of the Spirit that provided the necessary explanations. Jesus had assured his followers that his own teaching had brought them 'purity of life', making them capable of the highest contemplation the Spirit could grant. The ' "word which I have spoken to you" ', therefore, had inspired them to rise above earthly matters; but union with the Spirit

141. *Hex.* 10. 16.
142. *Hex.* 10. 17, p. 210. Notice how φύσις has now become restrictive.
143. A similar 'evangelical' list is presented in § 18.
144. *DSS* 14 (§ 32): οὐ συναπέθανον ἐκεῖνοι Χριστῷ· διόπερ οὐδὲ συνηγέρθησαν. οὐκ ἐφόρεσαν τὴν εἰκόνα τοῦ ἐπουρανίου, οὐ τὴν νέκρωσιν τοῦ Ἰησοῦ ἐν τῷ σώματι περιήνεγκαν, οὐκ ἀπεδύσαντο τὸν παλαιὸν ἄνθρωπον, οὐκ ἐνεδύσαντο τὸν νέον, τὸν ἀνακαινούμενον εἰς ἐπίγνωσιν κατ' εἰκόνα τοῦ κτίσαντος αὐτόν, ed. Pruche, pp. 358/360. The phraseology is directly comparable to that of *Hex.* 10 generally.

was the goal.[145] It was achieved, nevertheless, by divine rather than by human initiative. Just as God knew his creatures before they knew him, so Jesus generously intervened in human lives before human beings could aspire to the virtue he recommended.[146] Incarnate, he was able to appreciate human weakness and bring tranquillity to the soul.[147] Because he had experienced 'passivity', the unavoidable pressures of the flesh itself, he was able to bring the human race a freedom from that enslavement:[148]

> The plan that God and our Saviour have for humankind is to recall us from exile and set us on the upward path back to intimacy with God, overcoming the estrangement that followed upon disobedience. In that cause Christ dwelt in the flesh and gave us for a model the Gospel way of life—suffering, the cross, the tomb, the resurrection—so that, saved by the imitation of Christ, we might regain the ancient state of adopted sonship.... So that he might prepare us for the risen life, the Lord has placed before us the whole of the Gospel way of life, commanding us to eschew anger, to remain patient in the face of evil, untarnished by the love of pleasure or of wealth. In that way we may seize in advance, through our own choice, and with assured success, those things which, in the age to come, are more naturally possessed.

The Spirit, however, remained central: 'It is through the Holy Spirit that we achieve our re-establishment in paradise'; and so for every other eternal reward, including υἱοθεσία, adopted sonship.[149]

Two sets of demands were set in place, therefore. First, each Christian would have to engage in a lifetime of ascesis, of personal discipline in the cause of moral progress.[150] Only in that way could one avoid clouding

---

145. *DSS* 22 (§ 53); ed. Pruche, p. 442. The allusion is to John 15.3.

146. *Hom.* 329. 4.

147. *Hom.* 356. 2.

148. *DSS* 8 (§ 18) is thus made clearer: see n. 44 above.

149. *DSS* 15 (§ 35): ἡ τοῦ Θεοῦ καὶ Σωτῆρος ἡμῶν περὶ τὸν ἄνθρωπον οἰκονομία ἀνάκλησίς ἐστιν ἀπὸ τῆς ἐκπτώσεως, καὶ ἐπάνοδος εἰς οἰκείωσιν Θεοῦ ἀπὸ τῆς διὰ τὴν παρακοὴν γενομένης ἀλλοτριώσεως. διὰ τοῦτο ἡ μετὰ σαρκὸς ἐπιδημία Χριστοῦ· αἱ τῶν εὐαγγελικῶν πολιτευμάτων ὑποτυπώσεις· τὰ πάθη· ὁ σταυρός· ἡ ταφή· ἡ ἀνάστασις· ὥστε τὸν σωζόμενον ἄνθρωπον διὰ μιμήσεως Χριστοῦ, τὴν ἀρχαίαν ἐκείνην υἱοθεσίαν ἀπολαβεῖν, ed. Pruche, p. 364; and πρὸς οὖν τὸν ἐξ ἀναστάσεως βίον καταρτίζων ἡμᾶς ὁ Κύριος, τὴν εὐαγγελικὴν πᾶσαν ἐκτίθεται πολιτείαν, τὸ ἀόργητον, τὸ ἀνεξίκακον, τὸ φιληδονίας ἀρρύπωτον, τὸ ἀφιλάργυρον τοῦ τρόπου νομοθετῶν· ὥστε ἅπερ ὁ αἰὼν ἐκεῖνος κατὰ τὴν φύσιν κέκτηται, ταῦτα προλαβόντας ἡμᾶς ἐκ προαιρέσεως κατορθοῦν, ed. Pruche, p. 370. The final distinction, between κατὰ τὴν φύσιν and ἐκ προαιρέσεως, illustrates clearly the point made above at n. 149. For the centrality of the Spirit, see § 36.

150. That much would be intelligible, even to a sympathetic pagan; and it was to a pagan that Basil expressed himself in entirely similar terms, speaking of 'the uniting of [oneself] with God [οἰκειωθῆναι Θεῷ] through the true knowledge [τῆς ἀληθοῦς ἐπιγνώσεως] and

over in the mind the enlightenment of the Spirit,[151] and denying him the space he justly claimed within oneself.[152] Second, one did so under the aegis of baptism, which brought with it membership of the Church, but also a lasting state of knowledge, illumination, and renewal.[153] So one 'submitted oneself to the yoke of Christ';[154] but the promised rewards were of the most exalted nature: 'You are a slave of the great king, called by him to the highest companionship. Accept the Spirit who is promised, so that sealed in him you may be revealed as a son of God'.[155]

The eleventh sermon is much less polished. Basil was clearly working towards some account of the eternal vision of God: as it stands, the piece ends with a rough and lengthy reflection on the wonders of ordinary sight.[156] In another revealing moment, however, when he reached the verse 'Be fruitful and multiply, and fill the earth' (Genesis 1.28), Basil reinforced even more the points we have just examined. 'Here', he said, 'praise is bestowed upon the Church. Theology is never limited to the individual'.[157] Few words could have summed up more clearly his constant espousal of community life. All the instructions for acquiring 'likeness' were relentlessly transposed into a social programme. Basil's conception of religion carried one inevitably into a crowded history of human endeavour.[158] Participation in that history, however, and achievement of the natural moral destiny that lay at its heart, were now offered only to those who were willing to live by the Gospel, and could be guaranteed only by a life led within the Church. In that sense, history had now become theology: the account of creation, progress, and fulfilment *looked* like history; but the power at work within it demanded an altogether higher level of analysis

---

the life which is according to virtue', *Ep.* 276, C 3: 149, D 4: 159. For the background to the letter, see chapter 5, at n. 158.

151. *Hom.* 330. 9. See also 353. 8. Both passages use the crucial word ἔλλαμψις.

152. *Hom.* 333. 7.

153. The vocabulary of *Hom.* 320 (*exhortatoria ad sanctum baptismum*) is succinct: '[Without baptism] you will not know [γνωριζούσῃ] your creator', 'He who is not baptized is not enlightened [πεφώτισται]', '[Baptism] will carry you back to the true flowering of youth [τῆς νεότητος]' (you having previously 'grown old [ἐπαλαίωσας]' in wrongdoing), §§ 1, 5; *PG* 31. 423C, 433A.

154. *Hom.* 320. 1: γενοῦ ὑποζύγιον τοῦ Χριστοῦ, *PG* 31. 425D.

155. *Hom.* 356. 4: ὅτι δοῦλος εἶ τοῦ μεγάλου βασιλέως, προσκληθεὶς παρ' αὐτοῦ εἰς τὴν ἄκραν οἰκείωσιν, λαβὼν τὸ Πνεῦμα τῆς ἐπαγγελίας, ὥστε σφραγισθεὶς ἐν αὐτῷ υἱὸς ἀποδειχθῆναι Θεοῦ, *PG* 29. 477AB. For other comment on the passage see n. 105 above. Σφραγίς, once again, evokes baptism: see above, at nn. 86, 116.

156. *Hex.* 11. 16f.

157. *Hex.* 11. 5: ἐκκλησίας ἡ εὐλογία. μὴ ἐν ἑνὶ περιγραφήτω ἡ θεολογία, p. 238.

158. In the *De spiritu sancto*, transcendence to the level of illumination had also been made part of an historical process, the passage from letter to spirit, 21 (§ 52). See Averil Cameron, *Rhetoric of Empire*, p. 116.

and articulation:[159] 'The teachings of theology are scattered like mystical seeds throughout the historical account'.[160] History, therefore, could now be projected forward in an unbroken line, so that paradise itself was seen as waiting to be peopled, according to God's earliest command. The defeat of passion, the exercise of liberty, the enjoyment of likeness to God—all were to be shared, and shared ultimately in the company of the angels.[161]

The essence of Basil's philosophy lay in exploring the scope and nature of self-knowledge, making the self demonstrably part of an historical tradition (both natural and religious), and drawing each person into conscious association with a biological and spiritual community, in this life and in the next. Each step in the process depended on the security of the last. Every chapter in this book has been concerned, in one way or another, with the interplay between individual and community; and the problems and solutions presented sprang inevitably from the essential emphasis on the inner life, on history, and on shared fulfilment.

There is no doubt that the *Hexaemeron* confirmed and in some ways summarized Basil's convictions. Yet it would be a mistake to see either the work itself or our analysis of it as a mere appendix to his life. Rather, it brings to the surface of the historical record, in the richest possible form, the beliefs, the habits of thought and expression, that lay beneath everything else he wrote, and inspired his every action. The *Hexaemeron* is a psychological paradigm in the strictest sense, governing the logic of his life. That is why it has been important to allude to earlier works, to the homilies in particular. They provide the most striking instances of a constant anthropological undercurrent in Basil's thought—that on the text *Attende tibi ipsi* in particular: its treatment of 'nature' and the image of God; its exploration of knowledge and wisdom; its conviction that the approach to God lay in an accurate awareness of one's inner nature, transforming knowledge into faith.[162]

159. *Hex.* 10. 4: ὅρα ἱστορίαν μὲν σχήματι, θεολογίαν δὲ δυνάμει, p. 174.
160. *Hex.* 6. 2: πανταχοῦ τῇ ἱστορίᾳ τὸ δόγμα τῆς θεολογίας μυστικῶς συμπαρέσπαρται, p. 332.
161. *Hex.* 11. 7. So, too, the history of the inner life had its theological fulfilment: self-knowledge, under the Spirit's guidance, was the best key to history itself, 9. 6.
162. *Hom.* 319 passim. We have made several references to this text: see chapter 4, at nn. 55f.; chapter 5, at nn. 127f., 209; chapter 6, at nn. 112, 119, 166, 169, 180, 186, and 204; and in this chapter, at nn. 41 and 112.

It is the homilies and letters we have referred to most, although echoes of the *Contra Eunomium* and the *De spiritu sancto* are naturally important. Basil was most urgent in his defence of human nature when he was speaking and writing as a pastor. The maintenance of a sound and progressive relationship between individual and community was, not least, a matter of conversion: persuading an audience to embrace a particular pattern of adhesion, which was constituted not only by personal enthusiasm but also by the readiness of the convert to join with others in the acting out of new religious convictions. The key to successful persuasion lay in convincing people that their natural expectations, in regard both to their inner lives and to their social experience, were part of God's plan in creation, and best sustained and fulfilled within the framework of Christianity, presented as an historical community and a pathway to personal moral and spiritual development. What gave that pastoral emphasis a character proper to Basil himself was the adoption of the concept of community life as both a means and a goal. He lived and wrote at a time when corporate Christianity, as inspired by the dispensation of Constantine and his successors, still seemed a viable ideal, respectful of classical antecedent, but inspired by a Christian sense of form and destiny. Very soon, within less than a generation, that confidence would be seriously undermined, and the Christian future (in the West, perhaps, more) would appear potentially a more lonely experience.

It may well be Basil's optimism that strikes us most. There is something pathetic, in the theatrical sense, associated with the image of a dying man, encompassed still by government intransigence, ecclesial isolation, and the preliminaries of a fateful war, preaching to a limited entourage of puzzled and anxious devotees these eloquent exercises in learning, suffused with the confidence of an ancient culture, exalted in their dependence on the Christian Scriptures, and promising each of his hearers a destined, natural, and everlasting intimacy with God. The scale of circumstance seems so out of keeping with the scale of expectation. Yet Basil was immensely cautious in identifying the bases of his self-assurance. He was not just the child of παιδεία and πόλις, content with the privilege of an urban and aristocratic élite. He was not even the unquestioning disciple of his Christian forebears: his deference to Origen in particular was always tempered by a distaste for forced exegesis and overblown eschatology. It was his attachment to the text of Scripture that always asserted itself in the end. Scripture provided the framework for understanding and moral achievement, based on a careful, straightforward interpretation and the safeguarding of theological tradition. And Basil also kept his eye firmly fixed on social realities. By cleaving to the biblical heritage, Christians protected themselves from fragmentation and isolation: they preserved their links with the past and with those who held common beliefs within the Church of their own time. That mattered more than novel speculation, more even than the most respectable mysticism.[163]

We discover, therefore, the genuine antidote to the inadequacies of Basil's career. It is not just that we, in our own age, achieve a more rounded portrait: he himself was able to balance against passing dissatisfaction the heavier weight of his essential philosophy. His tendency to élitist arrogance, the doubtful advantage of his eccentric loyalties, opposition to his ascetic goals, the pressure of heresy, the weakness of his 'international' diplomacy, and the draining effect of his own disease: those were trials challenged constantly by the principles embedded in the *Hexaemeron*. If previous chapters have concentrated more on making clear just how pressing the difficulties were, this one provides an invitation to read the account again, detecting a measured and harmonious bourdon beneath the more strident orchestration of conflict and disappointing reverse. The *Hexaemeron* provides us also with a tone of voice, almost a facial expression, to attach to more disjointed or formal declarations in earlier years—supplying to some extent a loss lamented in the funeral *oratio* of Gregory his friend.[164]

Outstanding talent will often find itself suspended between haughtiness and self-doubt. It may be Basil's chief claim to our admiration that he mastered his own temperament in that regard. The struggle was a personal one but played out on the stage of his public career; and that gave his seizure and exercise of episcopal authority an altogether idiosyncratic quality. We might find ourselves obliged to say much the same of many bishops in his time. To have achieved the vision he did in a cruel and uncertain age was no small victory. The circumstances of his own formation did not encourage originality; and he himself was often suspicious of passion. Yet he was able to express beliefs that were widely intelligible, not least because of their compatibility with rhetorical convention and their affinity with an ancient culture; and he did so with a forcefulness that betrayed genuine feeling. Above all, he was clear and simple. The unvarnished triad at this chapter's head is a typical example—'We seek the

163. Compare the (for him, paradoxical) assertion of Amand de Mendieta, *Ascèse*, p. 335. Here is another instance of our need to respect Basil's particular interests, and to avoid a hasty association with Gregory of Nyssa in particular.
164. See in particular GNaz *Orat.* 43. 64.

ancient fatherland [ἀρχαίαν ἐπιζητοῦμεν πατρίδα]'—evoking the models of the past, the desires of the heart, and a lasting and familiar community. The prejudices of his peers allowed such skills and sentiments the title of sanctity. Would we begrudge him the compliment of humanity and courage?

· APPENDIX I ·

VALENS'S VISITS TO CAESAREA

The main events seem clear enough. Basil had had one or two brushes with the Praetorian Prefect Modestus,[1] who had hoped to win him to the Arian cause. There had also been some confrontation with an imperial official named Demosthenes.[2] Valens then visited Caesarea, at Epiphany 372.[3] He was to some extent won over by Basil's impressive manner and obvious authority. Vaguely associated with those events were the illness and death of Valens's son, and an abortive attempt to have Basil exiled.

Details are more confused. Gregory of Nazianzus arranged matters as follows. Modestus confronted Basil.[4] The Prefect then reported to Valens; and the emperor came to Caesarea at Epiphany, when he was impressed by the conduct of the liturgy, had private discussions with the bishop, and displayed 'kindly feeling'.[5] Oblique reference to Demosthenes comes before this account;[6] and the abandoned attempt to exile Basil, together with allusion to the illness of Valens's son, occurs later in the narrative.[7]

1. Modestus was Praetorian Prefect for most of Basil's ecclesiastical career, from 369 to 377; and several letters were addressed to him. See *PLRE* 1: 605f., s.v. Modestus 2.

2. There are some doubts about his role and identity. See *PLRE* 1: 249.

3. Marie-Madeleine Hauser-Meury, *Prosopographie zu den Schriften Gregors von Nazianz*, p. 41 n. 47.

4. On a single occasion: GNaz *Orat*. 43. 48–50.

5. *Orat*. 43. 51–53.

6. *Orat*. 43. 47. We take this to refer to Demosthenes, because both Gregorys referred to Nebuzaradan in this context (see 2 Kings 25.8), and Gregory of Nyssa then made the connection with Demosthenes, *Contra Eunomium* 1. 139.

7. GNaz *Orat*. 43. 54.

Gregory of Nyssa, who must also be a reasonably reliable witness, presents us with two confrontations with Modestus.[8] He placed the first meeting soon after what appears to be a reference to Valens's success against the Goths in 369. In his report to the emperor, Modestus implied clearly that Basil was not yet a bishop: the Prefect had promised him the emperor's help in gaining the government of the church. But Modestus had come to Caesarea to prepare the way for an imperial visit; and that cannot have been, therefore, the visit of 372.[9]

Clearly, the two accounts cannot be reconciled; but, taken together, they suggest very strongly that the events described could have covered a period of at least two years, including a visit by Valens in the spring of 370, and his attendance at the celebration of the Epiphany in 372. When we turn to later accounts, particularly that of Theodoret, the relevance of those obscurities to the development of the *Basileiados* becomes more obvious.[10] It is Theodoret who tells us that Valens gave the revenues of nearby estates towards the upkeep of the needy whom Basil cared for. He mentions the sick in particular. The gesture follows, in his account, the description of what is obviously the Epiphany celebrations of

8. The first bears most resemblance to that described by Gregory of Nazianzus. It includes a threat of exile, if not worse. See generally GNyss *Contra Eunomium* 1. 119–46; ed. Jaeger, 1: 62–71. In the first confrontation, both he and Gregory of Nazianzus have Basil saying that he escaped those civil threats by being a citizen of the world: *Contra Eunomium* 1. 134; *Orat.* 43. 49.

9. Gregory of Nazianzus, in spite of his placing on Basil's lips the famous dictum 'Perhaps you have never met a bishop', may also have been describing in part events that took place before Basil's consecration (although in the Epiphany celebrations themselves he was certainly a bishop). Note Gregory's precise words, in *Orat.* 43. 50: 'Perhaps you have never met a bishop . . . or he *would have* spoken in exactly the same way [ἢ πάντως ἂν τοῦτον διειλέχθη τὸν τρόπον]', PG 36. 561A. Modestus's complaint to Valens, § 51, should not be translated 'We have been worsted by the head of this church [ἡττήμεθα, Βασιλεῦ, ... τοῦ τῆσδε προβεβλημένου τῆς ἐκκλησίας]', PG 36. 561B, as if, again, to imply that Basil was bishop. The phrase is sufficiently oblique to suggest Basil's position under Eusebius, perhaps as a sort of 'heir apparent'. Indeed, when Modestus says, § 51: 'Some other more ignoble person must be tried [ἄλλον δεῖ τινα πειρᾶν τῶν ἀγενεστέρων]', PG 36. 561B, bearing in mind the promise reported by Gregory of Nyssa, he may have been implying that they should seek out another candidate to succeed, eventually, Eusebius. In *Orat.* 43. 48, Gregory of Nazianzus used the phrase οὔπω γὰρ ἐπίσκοπον ἠξίου καλεῖν, PG 36. 560A, which in the context can mean only that Modestus was not polite enough to address Basil as a bishop deserved. Here is a passage that may reflect, but may also have caused, confusion about the number of conversations held with Modestus and the times when they occurred. Gregory of Nyssa did not mention any face-to-face meeting with Valens; and he placed his discussion of the enmity of Demosthenes between the two meetings with Modestus: *Contra Eunomium* 1. 139. Behind these confusions, there may be allusion to Valens's visit of 365: see chapter 3, at n. 28.

10. See Theodoret HE 4. 16; ed. Parmentier (where it occurs as §19), pp. 242–46. See also the general references to the *Basileiados* made by Sozomen HE 6, 34. 9. His account of Valens's visit is quite separate, in 6, 15. Another account of the confrontation, even more confused, but in any case less circumstantial, is offered by Socrates HE 4. 26 (PG 67. 533A).

372.[11] We are led to wonder, of course, whether that generosity had any connection with what Gregory of Nazianzus had described more vaguely as the emperor's 'kindly feeling'.

In relation to Basil's letter to Elias, therefore, he could easily have been describing an enterprise that had already attracted the patronage of the emperor. Even if we continue to link the donation firmly with a visit by Valens to Caesarea in 372, it is still permissible to suppose that that development had been under way for some time—long enough for the emperor's curiosity and admiration to be aroused: the signs of conflation and gloss that characterize the available accounts mean that imperial involvement might have dated from as early as 370.

11. His ordering of events is otherwise rather different. We have one visit by the Prefect, followed immediately by Valens's arrival. Then comes an account of the illness of the emperor's son and (rather more explicitly than in Gregory of Nazianzus) of the boy's death. Attendance at the liturgy comes next (as also in Sozomen: so both writers could have been placing the death of the son before 372—see Van Dam, 'Emperor, Bishops, and Friends', p. 75), and discussions with Basil. Note that reference to Demosthenes is subsequent. There is also a later confrontation with Valens, followed by an attempt to exile Basil.

THE FORMATION
OF THE *ASCETICON*

The published components of Basil's ascetic writings have been familiar for generations and consist for the most part of two series of 'rules' in Greek (one 'long', one 'short'),[1] and one in a Latin translation made by Rufinus towards the end of the 390s.[2] These do not constitute a monastic *Rule* in any strict sense, and take the form of relatively short (often very short) answers to specific questions.[3] To that extent they are much closer, in terms of genre, to the *Sayings of the Fathers* than they are, for example, to the *Rule* of Benedict.

There are other documents to be associated with those basic texts. The *Moralia* is dealt with in some detail at the end of chapter 6 and is to be regarded as an early work. It has what are in effect two Prefaces, the *De iudicio dei* and the *De fide*.[4] There is a *Sermo asceticus* (Λόγος ἀσκητικός), which was written either by Basil very late in his life or by a close disciple, possibly a person in charge of ascetics in Caesarea.[5] We may now accept as genuine a letter that probably introduced a late compilation

---

1. *Regulae fusius tractatae* (F), *PG* 31. 889–1052; and *Regulae brevius tractatae* (B), *PG* 31. 1080A–1305B.

2. *Basili regula a Rufino latine versa* (R), edited by Klaus Zelzer.

3. Gribomont, *Histoire*, p. 4. Clarke, *Basil*, pp. 114f., made the same point, although without being able to explain why Basil should have made that sort of choice. It is one of the merits of Margaret Gertrude Murphy's *St. Basil and Monasticism* that she emphasized this point at Clarke's expense, pp. 35f., 94f. See Amand de Mendieta, *Ascèse*, p. 327.

4. *PG* 31. 653A–676C and 676C–692C respectively.

5. *PG* 31. 881B–888D. This was called by Gribomont Preface 5: see *Histoire*, pp. 7f., 295f.

of texts made towards the end of Basil's life.[6] A conflation of *Letters* 22 and 173 was also included in many collections, almost certainly from an early date. Indeed, several other letters found their way at one time or another into manuscripts of Basil's ascetic works.[7] Finally, we should add the *Extravagantes*, five short pieces in the style of the *Regulae brevius tractatae*, which come to us through a manuscript tradition independent of that of the main collection.[8]

About other pieces to be found in the printed editions, we have to be rather more hesitant. They include most importantly the *Praevia institutio ascetica*,[9] the *De renuntiatione saeculi*,[10] the *De ascetica disciplina*,[11] another *Sermo asceticus*,[12] and some of the *Epitimia*.[13]

It will be necessary to remember also that there is an unpublished Syriac manuscript, which appears to resemble very closely the (certainly Greek) text translated by Rufinus.[14] There is also an independent (and unpublished) Greek tradition, known as the Studite text, which contains 350 'rules' in a single series. The manuscript we possess is dated to the 880s but almost certainly reproduces a much older tradition.[15]

The printed texts of the main 'rules', when taken together, present us at once with problems, the chief of which concern the relationship between the Latin translation by Rufinus and the Greek versions as we now have them. Rufinus's

6. *PG* 31. 1509D–1513A. This was called by Gribomont Preface 6, which he also edited, *Histoire*, pp. 279–82; and see pp. 8, 282f., 301.

7. *Ep.* 2, 23, 42–44, 150. An edition of *Ep.* 173 is printed in Rudberg, *Études*. For the dubious status of *Ep.* 42–44 (as well as others), see Anders Cavallin, *Studien zu den Briefen des hl. Basilius*; and Emmanuel Amand de Mendieta, 'L'Authenticité des lettres ascétiques 42 à 45 de la correspondance de Saint Basile de Césarée'.

8. Gribomont numbered these B 314–18. Text, translation, and commentary, *Histoire*, pp. 180–92; and see n. 2 above. I have already indicated my respect for the *De baptismo*, and for the judgements of Gribomont upon it: see chapter 4, n. 148. In the context of this chapter, the main point to note is that the work, obviously, concerns initiation into the Christian community, the Church, in the broadest sense, and yet, as Gribomont made clear, presents the clearest possible summary of Basil's ascetic ideals. A correlation between the two could hardly be more forcefully maintained.

9. *PG* 31. 620A–625B.

10. *PG* 31. 625C–648C. See Jean Gribomont, 'L'*Exhortation au renoncement* attribué à saint Basile'. Those doubts seriously undermine the use Amand de Mendieta, *Ascèse*, pp. 222f., 243f., 246f., attempted to make of the text, in relation to gluttony, women, and homosexuality.

11. *PG* 31. 648C–652D. Gribomont, *Histoire*, pp. 8f. (and see p. 312), thought this a prologue to the 'Caesarea collection' (about which we shall discover more in a moment), written by a disciple of Basil.

12. *PG* 31. 869D–881B.

13. I have thought it best to make no use of these. For all these caveats, see Gribomont, *Histoire*, pp. 8f.

14. On the witness of this MS to even fifth-century developments, see Gribomont, *Histoire*, pp. 13, 108f., 144.

15. For the date, comparisons with the 'Vulgate' tradition (to be discussed shortly), and probable earlier sources, see Gribomont, *Histoire*, pp. 26, 163, 172f. Fedwick, *Basil*, 1: 15 n. 82, supposes the relevant tradition to have developed between 372 and 375.

text contains some elements (only some) from both the 'long' and the 'short' Greek series; but it presents them in a single series, and in a very different order. Moreover, when we match each Latin 'rule' with its corresponding Greek 'rule' (for the correspondences are normally clear enough), there are variations that cannot be attributed merely to the licence of the translator. Finally, the main Preface to the Latin version (that which translates Basil himself—for Rufinus added a Preface of his own) finds the bulk of its Greek equivalent in the Preface to the 'short' series: the much fuller Preface to the 'long' series in Greek makes only a truncated appearance in the Latin.[16]

So we have differences in order, differences in content, and differences in prefatory material. The solution to those oddities is now thought to lie along the following lines. The Latin of Rufinus has preserved for us an early version of the 'rules', which, in the original Greek, was also drawn up as a single series. From that 'primitive' version, our existing Greek series, both 'long' and 'short', subsequently developed. The earlier version (which no longer survives) is referred to as the *Small Asceticon*, to distinguish it from the existing Greek 'rules', referred to as the *Great Asceticon*.[17]

Two questions remain, however. When and how did the development of the two surviving Greek series take place; and is it possible to identify within the surviving Greek the elements translated by Rufinus?

The chief clues in relation to those issues are contained in the *scholia* to the 'Vulgate' edition—that is to say, in the editorial comments made by the compiler of the sixth-century manuscript upon which subsequent tradition and our own printed versions are based. These *scholia* have now been edited and printed.[18]

They provide three important sets of information. First, in *scholion* 2, the compiler distinguishes between two classes of material: a μικρὸν ἀσκητικόν (precisely, a 'small *asceticon*'), which was drawn up by Basil before he was a bishop, for ascetics with whom he had personal contact (and this has now been taken to be the Greek upon which Rufinus drew);[19] and another collection, which Basil 'sent' somewhere, after 370. Second, in *scholion* 3, the compiler tells us that he had at his disposal a collection of material from Pontus, another Caesarea, and a third from elsewhere.[20] The Pontus collection, known to the compiler as

---

16. The Latin Preface to R was called by Gribomont Preface 1, its Greek equivalent Preface 3 (*PG* 31. 1080), and the Preface to F Preface 4 (*PG* 31. 889–901). The section of the 'long' series reproduced by Rufinus runs from ὥσπερ to ἔρχεται, 900C–901A. For further complexities, see Gribomont, *Histoire*, pp. 7f.

17. Compare the superseded suppositions of Clarke, *Basil*, p. 65, for whom Rufinus 'abbreviated and adapted' an F+B collection 'so as to form one composite work'; see also pp. 69f., 166f.

18. Text, translation, and commentary in Gribomont, *Histoire*, pp. 151–64. They supply much better information than Photius, used by Clarke, *Basil*, p. 66.

19. Gribomont, *Histoire*, pp. 156f., followed by Aubineau, *Virginité*, p. 78, who says that Gregory of Nyssa was referring to such a compilation in *De virginitate* 23. 1—placing it, therefore, after 362, during Basil's second withdrawal to Pontus.

20. On these last, see Gribomont, *Histoire*, pp. 53, 163f., 267f.

the ὑποτύπωσις ἀσκήσεως (now referred to generally as the *Hypotyposis*), ended at *Regulae brevius tractatae* 286, perhaps with the addition of the conflation of *Letters* 22 and 173,[21] and was considered by him to be early. We learn from *scholion* 6 that the Caesarea collection was in a single series, while the Pontus collection was divided into two, 'long rules' and 'short rules';[22] and the 'long' section of the latter was devoted to broader issues. Further, in *scholion* 7, he says that *Regulae brevius tractatae* 287–313 occurred only in the Caesarea collection, which was to be associated with the *Basileiados* and did not represent a primitive tradition. The Pontus material, on the other hand (which constituted for him the main collection), was associated with a region where Basil had actually practised the ascetic life.

Putting those first two sets of information together, we should note that the Pontus collection, as known to the compiler, and called by him ὑποτύπωσις ἀσκήσεως, was not necessarily identical with the μικρὸν ἀσκητικόν he also mentions (and which Rufinus, perhaps, translated): the latter would have been marked, almost certainly, by additions and rearrangements.[23]

The third set of information concerns the variations (that is to say, even within the Greek tradition) faced by the compiler. He suggests that Basil had his own copy, so to speak, which he no doubt modified and added to, and which he then adapted further, during travels here and there, in the course of which he faced questions from ascetics in a variety of circumstances. His answers, therefore, were copied down differently in different places.[24] That would be to suggest, therefore, that the 'rules' did not have in mind a single community, intimately associated with Basil himself, but reflected a much broader sense of responsibility that he felt towards religious enthusiasts of very varied types.[25]

We can make certain reflections at this point. First, there were obviously phases in the development of the corpus—first in Pontus, and then at Caesarea—and we must bear in mind a difference of circumstance, as well as of locality. Second, the corpus did develop, and it developed in both places. Third, Rufinus caught the process of development at an early stage (hence his version has a single series), but at a stage when there was a visible collection in place (with the core of the broader and more theoretical sections, which would eventually contribute to the 'long' series, already written). That means, further, that the existing 'long' sections with no equivalent in Rufinus's version must represent later theory (and, as we suggest in chapter 6, a more institutional phase), although they could still have been the work of Basil himself. We should bear in mind, however, that Rufinus himself was also 'late' in a sense, working some twenty years after Basil's death,

21. Gribomont, *Histoire*, pp. 161, 300f.

22. Although there is reason to suppose that the Pontus material, too, had originally been in a single series: Gribomont, *Histoire*, p. 256.

23. Fedwick, *Basil*, 1: 17, nn. 94f., dates the *Hypotyposis* to 376/377.

24. Gribomont, *Histoire*, pp. 160, 323f., agreed.

25. Gribomont, *Histoire*, pp. 255f., with reflections on *Ep.* 223 and 295.

and viewing his material through the haze, as it were, of institutional development made during that time.

A final set of questions remains. Can we actually detect how the collections were constructed, before the compiler of the Vulgate brought them all together?[26] The *scholia*, again, offer clues. *Scholion* 4 tells us that, of the fifty-five 'long rules', only eighteen occurred in the oldest manuscripts: the rest were added gradually. The division into fifty-five 'rules' was, in any case, the scholiast's own work;[27] and we can now detect signs of an earlier division of the 'long' material into twenty sections.[28] Armed with that insight, we can see that §§ 1–11 of Rufinus's text follow almost exactly the first twelve of those older divisions; and the subdivisions of that set of twelve enable us to see how our existing 'long' version has added to the texts available to Rufinus.[29] As for the portion of the 'long' Greek 'rules' with no equivalent in the Latin, the rest of the older subdivisions mark the subsequent stages of addition to the primitive core.[30]

Scholion 7, as we have seen, reveals that *Regulae brevius tractatae* 287–313 occurred only in the Caesarea material: those were late in date and included by the compiler at the end of his 'edition'. *Scholion* 6 adds the important information that he interwove Pontus and Caesarea 'rules' throughout his 'short' series, placing (in blocks) Pontus material first and Caesarea additions afterwards. A complex series of collations, made in the light of this statement, shows that the *Regulae brevius tractatae* do indeed fall into sections, twelve in number,[31] and that the equivalents in Rufinus, where they exist, instead of being (as they might seem in our eyes) scattered at random, run within each section in a strict numerical order.[32]

From those two *scholia*, 4 and 6, two implications may be drawn. The first 'short rules' within each section of the *Regulae brevius tractatae*, for many of which there will be equivalents in Rufinus, come from the Pontus material, whereas those at the end of each section, for which there is never any equivalent in Rufinus, come

26. Here comparison with the 'Studite' version is helpful, because it seems to have been closely associated with the Caesarea material. See n. 15 above.

27. Gribomont, *Histoire*, p. 157.

28. This is the so-called Y series: see Gribomont, *Histoire*, pp. 55, 172f.

29. Compare the methodology of Clarke, *Basil*, p. 166.

30. Namely, F 24–32, 33–34, 35–36, 37, 38–42, 43–45, 46–54, and 55.

31. Or rather, to be precise, ten plus a small supplement (B 279–86) plus the Caesarea additions at the end (B 287f.). This is the so-called X series: see Gribomont, *Histoire*, pp. 166–78, 193–208.

32. For example, section 5 of 'X' contains B 114–23, which are equivalent to R 13, 64, 65, 67, 68, 69, 80, 82, 133, 176 (in numerical order), and then B 124–25, which do not have equivalents in R. But this is an unusual section, in that a complete run of B, 114–23, has equivalents in R. In other sections, the opening run of B will, here and there, lack equivalents in R. For example, in section 4 of 'X' we have a run of B, 96–111, with some equivalents in R, followed by a 'tail', 112–13, without such equivalents; but, in the main run, B 98, 102–4, and 107 have no equivalents in R. The full significance of this pattern will appear in the immediately following paragraph.

from the Caesarea material. It is clear, second, that someone rearranged the Pontus material, after the time Rufinus had access to it, largely in the interest of thematic clarity.[33]

So the straightforward conclusion stands: Rufinus has preserved for us a 'primitive' version of Basil's 'rules'. But we can understand more clearly the ways in which he does not tell us about developments in Caesarea.[34] We can also appreciate, on the basis of what has been discovered about the composition of the material between the time of Basil himself and the creation of the Vulgate, how the *Regulae fusius tractatae* developed, and what Caesarea added to Pontus, especially in the *Regulae brevius tractatae*.

33. Clarke, *Basil*, p. 64, attempted to describe this phase. It will be worthwhile listing these thematic sections of 'X': 1 = B 3–20, repentance and conversion; 2 = B 21–84, sin; 3 = B 85–95, poverty; 4 = B 96–113, the duties of superiors; 5 = B 114–25, obedience; 6 = B 126–40, fasting; 7 = B 141–56, work; 8 = B 157–86, the interior life; 9 = B 187–90, family, and 191–238, virtue generally, particularly as based on Scripture; 10 = B 239–78, further reflections on morality; 11 = B 279–86, a less coherent supplement; and 12 = B 287f., the 'Caesarea addition'.

34. One small note of caution: the first three items of section 12 of 'X', namely, B 287–89, which are presumably 'Caesarea pieces', do have equivalents in R (19, and 21–22). They appear to contain more advanced reflection on repentance, the subject of R 20 (B 6): an interesting puzzle.

THE DATE OF BASIL'S DEATH AND OF THE *HEXAEMERON*

Traditionally, Basil's death has been dated 1 January 379. More recently, important doubt has been cast upon that suggestion, bringing in its train the need for many readjustments, not only in chronology but also in assessment of character and motive.[1] Argument for the new dating takes as its starting point the possibility that Valens recalled from exile the leading opponents of his religious policy in the East (including, therefore, Meletius of Antioch and Eusebius of Samosata) prior to his departure for the Balkans to settle finally the challenge of the Gothic revolt. (Some sources assert that such a rescript was issued; others are silent or obscure.) It is then supposed that preparations necessary for the eventual campaign of 378 would place such a rescript as early as September 377. The point is, of course, that such an unpredictable victory for the orthodox cause would surely have awakened surviving cries of triumph in the writings of Basil. There is, so to speak, not a sound: therefore he was dead.[2]

Several difficulties undermine the simplicity of the thesis. First, while it is likely, in relation to the campaign against the Goths, that strategy and supplies would have absorbed a great deal of attention in the final months of 377, it does not follow that a recall of the exiles would have been considered only at a similarly early stage. Second and more important, why did Gratian find it necessary to

---

1. See Maraval, 'Date'. As will be explained, much of the argument depends on the implications of Snee, 'Recall of the Exiles'. The debate was set in train well before, by Alan D. Booth, 'The Chronology of Jerome's Early Years'. Brennecke, *Geschichte der Homöer*, p. 241, makes no attempt to explain the supposed change of heart on the emperor's part.
2. Snee does not relate her argument to the chronology of Basil's life specifically.

issue a similar decree in 378, after Valens's defeat and death? The explanatory suggestion that Valens's own rescript may not have been widely broadcast or acted upon with any speed could explain, surely, why a Basil still alive might have remained in silent ignorance of the event. It certainly supports the view that, whatever Valens did, he did it hastily and at the last moment. Third, those sources that mention explicitly a recall of exiles by Valens emphasize also that the step was taken in the cause of tolerance and plurality (somewhat in the tradition of Julian or Valentinian). Accounts, on the other hand, that describe directly the return of the exiles themselves make it a matter of total victory, the irreversible defeat of everything the emperor had striven for. That Valens should have made such a complete volte-face at a moment of crisis, even under the impulse of extreme remorse, is not easy to believe.

If one accepts, however, a recall of the exiles in 377, the implications in relation to Basil are by no means certain either. Gregory of Nyssa described a synod held at Antioch some nine or ten months after Basil's death. (The synod has been traditionally dated, therefore, to September or October 379).[3] A list of those present, led by Meletius, describes them as churchmen previously exiled by Valens. One is invited to suppose, therefore (and it is a supposition), that such a synod would have been held soon after their return from exile.[4] If that return is dated to 377, various arguments can be produced that place the synod of Antioch in the middle of 378; which allows one to judge, further (on the strength of Gregory's reference to nine or ten months), that Basil died perhaps as early as August 377.

The revision has important consequences. It means, for example, that Basil may have become bishop of Caesarea in 369.[5] It also affects the dating of some of his final letters.[6] One, addressed to Eusebius of Samosata, implying that he was still in exile, would have to be brought forward from 378 to 377; and its allusion to army movements—'The war has spread, as I hear, round about on every side', and 'We hear of the arrival of the army [that is, in Thrace: ἀκούομεν τοῦ στρατοπέδου τὴν πάροδον]'—must be made to refer to the recall of troops from Armenia under Profuturus and Traianus, as described by Ammianus Marcellinus.[7] Another letter, consoling the widow of the *magister peditum* Arinthaeus, seems now less likely to have been written after Hadrianople.[8] More problematic is the necessary redating

---

3. GNyss *VMac.* 15. 1–6. The arguments now described are those of Maraval.

4. 'On peut raisonnablement estimer que l'évêque d'Antioch n'a pas attendu très longtemps, après son retour d'exil, pour la convoquer': Maraval, 'Date', p. 28. Maybe; but a great deal hangs upon that 'estimer', as we shall see.

5. Maraval, 'Date', 31f. Such an adjustment makes little difference, however, to one's assessment of the character of Basil's early episcopal career.

6. As we have seen in the final sections of chapter 8: see there nn. 182f., 190, 196f.

7. *Ep.* 268, C 3: 138, D 4: 131/133. See Ammianus Marcellinus 31, 6f. For one of Basil's rare reflections on barbarians, see *Hom.* 345. 5, where, characteristically, their supposedly rare demonstrations of peaceable generosity induce moral guilt.

8. *Ep.* 269. Compare Maraval, 'Date', pp. 34f., with *PLRE* 1: 102f., s.v. Flavius Arinthaeus. Yet the letter was late enough to bring us a sense of Basil's mature sentiments,

of Basil's letter to the Praetorian Prefect Aburgius. All hinges on the implications
of its phraseology:

> That you are darting hither and yon like a star, arising now here now
> there in the barbarian land, now furnishing provisions to the army [νῦν
> μὲν σιτηρέσια τῷ στρατιωτικῷ παρέχοντα], and now appearing before
> the Emperor in resplendent array [μετὰ λαμπροῦ τοῦ σχήματος], fame,
> the messenger of good tidings, does not cease to announce to us. And
> we pray God that, with your enterprise proceeding in accordance with
> your plan, you may approach very near [ἐπὶ μέγα σε προελθεῖν], and
> may show yourself at some time in our native land, while we are above
> the earth and breathe this air. For the only part we have in life is that
> we still breathe.[9]

There is no doubt that the activities described were those proper to a Praetorian
Prefect. We know that Modestus still held that office on 20 November 377.[10] For
those who wish to date the letter earlier, the only solution is to suppose that Basil
was anticipating Aburgius's promotion (without any explanation as to why he
should have thought it likely); and hopes are pinned on the phrase ἐπὶ μέγα
σε προελθεῖν. Certainly, this is unlikely to mean 'that ... you may approach very
near'; but nor does it suggest a comparative statement, as if to express hope of some
higher office. 'That you may do well' is the least one could offer in translation, and
'that you may go on to great things' is probably nearer the mark; but neither implies
a specific and further promotion.[11] Both obscurities and suppositions abound; and
one has to retain the feeling that an earlier date for Basil's death is by no means
finally established.

-----

even within the bounds of the *consolatio*. There is a special tranquillity in its genuine
penetration of a widow's feelings, and in its acceptance that sorrow was not easily dispelled
but was not overwhelming of hope either. For the literary conventions, see chapter 3, at
nn. 108f.

9. *Ep.* 196, C 2: 149, D 3: 89/91. For Aburgius, see *PLRE* 1: 5.

10. He is named in *Cod. Iust.* 8, 10. 8 of that date; see *PLRE* 1: 607.

11. I see no reason why the phrase should mean 'd'avancer jusqu'à une haute dignité'
(Maraval, 'Date', p. 34). (Courtonne is only slightly less specific with 'que tu parviennes ainsi
à une haute situation'.) No one to my knowledge has weighed the implications of the letter's
opening phrases. Ἄλλοτε κατ' ἄλλο, 'now here now there', is all subsumed under 'in the
barbarian land [μέρος τῆς βαρβαρικῆς]'; and that implies further (given the force of νῦν μὲν
... νῦν δὲ) that both the supplying of the army *and* the appearing before the emperor were
taking place in that 'barbarian' area—surely, the Balkans. In which case, Basil was writing
after Valens had arrived in Thrace to conduct his final campaign. *Ep.* 196 has been attributed
to Gregory of Nazianzus; but Gallay is sure that the attribution is false. Maraval, 'Date',
p. 34 and n. 52, presents no argument against Gregory's editor, although he allows himself
the observation that the letter 'semble davantage dans son [i.e., Gregory's] style'. I am not
equipped to judge that opinion; but the closing complaint of the letter is entirely typical of
Basil (and used accordingly as an argument by Maraval himself!), while no other evidence
suggests why Gregory should have felt the same at such a time.

Where does that place the *Hexaemeron*? One may still contend with justice that all eleven sermons formed a closely knit and calculated unit; and the quality of their style and perception makes them arguably a product of Basil's mature years, both as theologian and as bishop.[12] The recently revised chronology, however, may suggest that a late date for the *Hexaemeron* is no longer defensible. The older view led to a precise judgement: Basil preached these sermons between Monday 12 and Friday 16 March 378.[13] If 378 is ruled out, the arguments for so exact a calculation are valid next (moving backwards) in 374. Those arguments, however, were already insecure in relation to 378, and there seems little point in attaching them with equal insecurity to some other period in Basil's life.[14] Moreover, a perceived connection between the *Hexaemeron* and early sermons, for example, does not mean it has to be considered contemporary with them: reaffirmation in the longer work of points made constantly in Basil's career is precisely one of the characteristics that supports its later composition.[15] The only remaining argument against, say, 377 is that Basil, about to die, must have been too ill to undertake such a task.[16] Of that we could never be certain, of course; but it bears saying that Basil's constant reference to his own illness makes it surprising that he ever wrote anything! While it would be foolish, therefore, to insist that the *Hexaemeron* was composed in Basil's final year (whether 377 or 378), there is little compulsion to believe that it was not.

12. Such is the opinion of the most recent editors, reflecting an even broader and long-standing tradition, to which they make extensive reference.

13. Bernardi, *Prédication*, pp. 44f., relaxes slightly his earlier rigour but still thinks of 378.

14. Maraval, 'Date', p. 36. I cannot think of the year 374 as 'un moment assez paisible de la vie de Basile et de sa communauté': serious illness, frustration over Armenia, and growing confrontation with Eustathius had already taken their toll. Only a few weeks before Lent that year, Basil had felt himself to be at 'the very gates of death', and filled with despair, *Ep.* 141. 1, C 2: 63, D 2: 341. See chapter 5, nn. 73f., 94f.

15. Maraval, 'Date', pp. 36f., feels that the *Hexaemeron* must predate the theological precision of the *De spiritu sancto*. I find less than convincing his sparsely documented assertion that the *Hexaemeron* is 'timide' on the subject of the Holy Spirit. Bernardi, *Prédication*, p. 43, pointed out long ago a clear connection with the manifestly early *Hom.* 348; but he felt, surely rightly, that such an echo was entirely compatible with a long period of gestation for the more extensive work. Maraval is prepared to accept, however, that *Hex.* 10 and 11 were completed in 377.

16. Maraval, 'Date', p. 36.

BIBLIOGRAPHY

This bibliography does not set out to exhaust the material on Basil. It contains only items referred to in the text and notes, or works that have contributed substantially to the construction of my argument. General surveys of the period and standard works of reference have been omitted. Collections of papers are listed under the names of their editor(s).

SOURCES

Where editions contain important or frequently quoted introductions and commentaries, they are listed also in the section 'Secondary Works', under the name of the editor.

Ammianus Marcellinus. The most convenient edition is the revised three-volume edition in the Loeb Classical Library, with an English translation by John C. Rolfe (London and Cambridge, Mass.: Heinemann and Harvard University Press, 1950, 1952).

Basil of Caesarea. *Ad adulescentes*. PG 31. 563–590. *Basilio di Cesarea, Discorso ai Giovani (Oratio ad adolescentes), con la versione latina di Leonardo Bruni*, ed. Mario Naldini (Florence: Nardini editore, 1984). See also *Saint Basil on the Value of Greek Literature*, ed. N. G. Wilson (London: Duckworth, 1975); and *Saint Basile, Aux jeunes gens sur la manière de tirer profit des lettres helléniques*, ed. and tr. Fernand Boulenger, Collection Guillaume Budé (Paris: Les Belles Lettres, 1952). English translation in *Saint Basil, The Letters*, 4: 379–435.

——— . *Ascetica. Long Rules = Regulae fusius tractatae.* PG 31. 889–1052. *Short Rules = Regulae brevius tractatae.* PG 31. 1080A–1305B. Latin translation by Rufinus: *Basili regula a Rufino latine versa,* ed. Klaus Zelzer, Corpus scriptorum ecclesiasticorum Latinorum 86 (Vienna: Hoelder-Pichter-Tempsky, 1986). English translations: *The Ascetic Works of Saint Basil,* tr., with intro. and notes, W. K. Lowther Clarke (London: S.P.C.K., 1925); and *Basil of Caesarea, Ascetical Works,* tr. M. Monica Wagner, Fathers of the Church 9 (Washington, D.C.: Catholic University of America Press, 1950).

——— . *Contra Eunomium.* PG 29. 497–670. *Basile de Césarée, Contre Eunome, suivi de Eunome, Apologie,* 2 vols., tr., with intro. and notes, Bernard Sesboüé, with Georges-Matthieu de Durand and Louis Doutreleau, Sources chrétiennes 299, 305 (Paris: Éditions du Cerf, 1982, 1983).

——— . *De baptismo. Basile de Césarée, Sur le baptême,* ed. U. Neri and tr., with intro. and notes, Jeanne Ducatillon, Sources chrétiennes 357 (Paris: Éditions du Cerf, 1989).

——— . *De spiritu sancto.* PG 32. 67–218. *Basile de Césarée, Sur le Saint-Esprit,* ed. and tr., with intro. and notes, Benoît Pruche, Sources chrétiennes 17 bis, 2d ed. (Paris: Éditions du Cerf, 1968). English translation: *St. Basil the Great on the Holy Spirit,* tr. Blonfield Jackson, rev. David Anderson (Crestwood, N.Y.: St Vladimir's Seminary Press, 1980).

——— . *Epistulae.* PG 32. 219–1112. *Saint Basile, Lettres,* 3 vols., ed. and tr. Yves Courtonne, Collection Guillaume Budé (Paris: Les Belles Lettres, 1957, 1961, 1966). English translation: *Saint Basil, The Letters,* 4 vols., tr. Roy J. Deferrari, Loeb Classical Library (reprint, London and Cambridge, Mass.: Heinemann and Harvard University Press, 1950–53). See also *Saint Basil, Letters,* 2 vols., tr. Sister Agnes Clare Way, Fathers of the Church 13, 28 (Washington, D.C.: Catholic University of America Press, 1951, 1955; reprint, 1965, 1969).

——— . *Hexaemeron 1–9.* PG 29. 4–208. *Basile de Césarée, Homélies sur l'Hexaéméron,* ed. and tr., with intro., Stanislas Giet, 2d ed., revised and expanded, Sources chrétiennes 26 bis (Paris: Éditions du Cerf, 1968). English translation: *Saint Basil, Exegetic Homilies,* tr. Agnes Clare Way, pp. 3–150, Fathers of the Church 46 (Washington, D.C.: Catholic University of America Press, 1963).

——— . *Hexaemeron 10 and 11. Basile de Césarée, Sur l'origine de l'homme (Homélies X et XI de l'Hexaéméron),* ed. and tr., with intro. and notes, Alexis Smets and Michel van Esbroeck, Sources chrétiennes 160 (Paris: Éditions du Cerf, 1970).

——— . *Homilia(e).* PG 29. 209–494; 31. 163–618, 1429–1514. English translations of homilies on the Psalms by Agnes Clare Way in *Saint Basil, Exegetic Homilies,* Fathers of the Church 46 (Washington, D.C.: Catholic University of America Press, 1963). (For the numbering used, see the supplement to the Bibliography.)

——— . *Hom. 319. L'Homélie de Basile de Césarée sur le mot "Observe-toi toi-même",* ed. Stig Y. Rudberg, Acta Universitatis Stockholmiensis, Studia Graeca Stockholmiensa, 2 (Stockholm: Almqvist & Wiksell, 1962).

———. (with Gregory of Nazianzus). *Philocalia. The Philocalia of Origen*, ed., with critical intro. and indices, J. Armitage Robinson (Cambridge: Cambridge University Press, 1893). English translation by George Lewis, *The Philocalia of Origen* (Edinburgh: Clark, 1911). See also *Origène, Philocalie 21–27, Sur le libre arbitre*, ed. and tr., with intro. and notes, Éric Junod, Sources chrétiennes 226 (Paris: Éditions du Cerf, 1976).

Epiphanius. *Panarion* ['The Refutation of All Heresies']. *Epiphanius (Ancoratus und Panarion)*, ed. Karl Holl, vol. 3, GCS 37 (Leipzig: J. C. Hinrichs'sche Buchhandlung, 1933).

Eunapius. *Lives of the Philosophers and Sophists. Philostratus and Eunapius, The Lives of the Sophists*, tr. Wilmer Cave Wright, Loeb Classical Library, rev. ed. (London: Heinemann; Cambridge, Mass.: Harvard University Press, 1952).

Eunomius. *Apology*. See Basil of Caesarea, *Contra Eunomium*. Also *Eunomius: The Extant Works*, ed. Richard Paul Vaggione (Oxford: Clarendon Press, 1987).

Faustus of Byzantium. French translation by Jean Baptiste Emine in *Collection des historiens anciens et modernes de l'Arménie*, ed. Victor Langlois, 1: 209f. (Paris: Firmin-Didot, 1880).

Firmus of Caesarea. *Firmus de Césarée, Lettres*, ed. and tr., with intro. and index, Marie-Ange Calvet-Sebasti and Pierre-Louis Gatier, Sources chrétiennes 350 (Paris: Éditions du Cerf, 1989).

Gangra, Council of. Canons. *Histoire des conciles, d'après les documents originaux*, by Carl Joseph Hefele, tr. H. Leclercq, vol. 1, pt. 2, pp. 1029–45 (Paris: Letouzey et Ané, 1907; reissue, Hildesheim: Olms, 1973).

Gregory of Nazianzus. *Contra Julianum. Grégoire de Nazianze, Discours 4–5, Contre Julien*, ed. and tr., with intro. and notes, Jean Bernardi, Sources chrétiennes 309 (Paris: Éditions du Cerf, 1983).

———. *De rebus suis = Carmina de seipso 1*. PG 37. 969–1017. English translation by Denis Molaise Meehan in *Gregory of Nazianzus, Three Poems*, Fathers of the Church 75 (Washington, D.C.: Catholic University of America Press, 1987).

———. *De seipso et de episcopis = Carmina de seipso 12*. PG 37. 1166–1227. English translation by Denis Molaise Meehan in *Gregory of Nazianzus, Three Poems*, Fathers of the Church 75 (Washington, D.C.: Catholic University of America Press, 1987).

———. *De vita sua = Carmina de seipso 11*. PG 37. 1029–1166. English translation by Denis Molaise Meehan in *Gregory of Nazianzus, Three Poems*, Fathers of the Church 75 (Washington, D.C.: Catholic University of America Press, 1987). See also *Gregor von Naziaz, De vita sua*, ed. and tr., with intro. and notes, Christoph Jungck (Heidelberg: Carl Winter, 1974).

———. *Epistulae. Saint Grégoire de Nazianze, Lettres*, 2 vols., ed. and tr. Paul Gallay, Collection Guillaume Budé (Paris: Les Belles Lettres, 1964, 1967). See also *Gregor von Nazianz, Briefe*, ed. Paul Gallay, GCS 53 (Berlin: Akademie-Verlag, 1969).

———. *Oratio 2*. PG 35. 408–513.

———. *Oratio 3*. PG 35. 517–525.

——— . *Oratio* 7 (on his brother Caesarius). *PG* 35. 756–787. English translation by Leo P. McCauley in *Funeral Orations*, pp. 5–25 (see below, under *Orationes*).

——— . *Oratio* 8 (on his sister Gorgonia). *PG* 35. 789–817. English translation by Leo P. McCauley in *Funeral Orations*, pp. 101–18.

——— . *Oratio* 18 (on his father). *PG* 35. 985–1044. English translation by Leo P. McCauley in *Funeral Orations*, pp. 119–56.

——— . *Oratio* 43 (on Basil). *PG* 36. 493–605. English translation by Leo P. McCauley in *Funeral Orations*, pp. 27–99.

——— . *Orationes*. English translations of *Orationes* 7, 8, 18, and 43 by Leo P. McCauley in *Funeral Orations by Saint Gregory Nazianzen and Saint Ambrose*, Fathers of the Church 22 (New York: Fathers of the Church, Inc., 1953).

Gregory of Nyssa. *Contra Eunomium*. *Gregorii Nysseni opera*, ed. Werner Jaeger, vols. 1 and 2 (Leiden: Brill, 1960).

——— . *De virginitate*. *Grégoire de Nysse, Traité de la virginité*, ed. and tr., with intro., notes, and index, Michel Aubineau, Sources chrétiennes 119 (Paris: Éditions du Cerf, 1966). Also in *Gregorii Nysseni opera ascetica*, ed. Johannes P. Cavarnos (see following entry). English translation by Virginia Woods Callahan in *Saint Gregory of Nyssa, Ascetical Works*, pp. 6–75 (see following entry).

——— . *Gregorii Nysseni epistulae*, ed. G. Pasquali. In *Gregorii Nysseni opera*, ed. Werner Jaeger, vol. 8, pt. 2, 2d ed. (Leiden: Brill, 1959).

——— . *Gregorii Nysseni opera ascetica*, ed. Werner Jaeger, Johannes P. Cavarnos, Virginia Woods Callahan. *Gregorii Nysseni opera*, ed. Werner Jaeger, with others, 8:1 (1951; Leiden: Brill, 1963). English translations by Virginia Woods Callahan in *Saint Gregory of Nyssa, Ascetical Works*, Fathers of the Church 58 (Washington, D.C.: Catholic University of America Press, 1967).

——— . *In laudem fratris Basilii*. *PG* 46. 788–817. English translation: *Encomium of Saint Gregory Bishop of Nyssa on His Brother Saint Basil Archbishop of Caesarea*, ed. and tr., with intro. and notes, Sister James Aloysius Stein, A.M., Catholic University of America Patristic Studies 17 (Washington, D.C.: Catholic University of America Press, 1928).

——— . *In quadraginta martyres* 2. *PG* 46. 773–788.

——— . *In suam ordinationem*. *PG* 46. 544–553.

——— . *Vita s. Macrinae*. *Grégoire de Nysse, Vie de sainte Macrine*, ed. and tr., with intro., notes, and index, Pierre Maraval, Sources chrétiennes 178 (Paris: Éditions du Cerf, 1971). Also in *Gregorii Nysseni opera ascetica*, ed. Virginia Woods Callahan, pp. 370–414; and *Vita di S. Macrina*, ed. E. Gianarelli, Letture cristiane del primo millenio 4 (Turin: Ed. Paoline, 1988). English translation by Virginia Woods Callahan in *Saint Gregory of Nyssa, Ascetical Works*, pp. 163–191.

Gregory Thaumaturgus. *Grégoire le Thaumaturge, Remerciement à Origène, suivi de la Lettre d'Origène à Grégoire*, ed. and tr., with intro. and notes, Henri Crouzel, Sources chrétiennes 148 (Paris: Éditions du Cerf, 1969). English translation of the former by W. Metcalfe, *Address to Origen* (London: S.P.C.K., 1920).

Himerius. *Himerii declamationes et orationes cum deperditarum fragmentis*, ed. Aristides Colonna (Rome: Typis publicae officinae polygraphicae, 1951).

Julian. *The Works of the Emperor Julian*, 3 vols., tr. (from Hertlein's edition, revised) Wilmer Cave Wright, Loeb Classical Library, new ed. (London: Heinemann; Cambridge, Mass.: Harvard University Press, 1954, 1949, 1953).

Libanius. *Epistulae. Libanii opera*, ed. R. Foerster, vols. 10–11 (Leipzig: Teubner, 1871–72; reprint, Hildesheim: Olms, 1963).

———. *Libanius' Autobiography (Oration I)*, ed. and tr., with intro. and notes, A. F. Norman (London: Oxford University Press, 1965).

———. *Libanius, Selected Works*, ed. A. F. Norman, vol. 1, *The Julianic Orations*, Loeb Classical Library (Cambridge, Mass., and London: Heinemann and Harvard University Press, 1969).

Moses of Chorene (Moses Khorenats'i). *History of the Armenians*, tr., with notes, Robert S. Thompson (Cambridge, Mass.: Harvard University Press, 1978).

Palladius. *Historia Lausiaca. The Lausiac History of Palladius: A Critical Discussion, together with Notes on Early Monachism*, ed. with intro., Cuthbert Butler, Texts and Studies, vol. 6, pts. 1 and 2 (Cambridge: Cambridge University Press, 1898–1904; reprint, Hildesheim: Olms, 1967). English translation: *The Lausiac History*, tr., with notes, Robert T. Meyer, Ancient Christian Writers 34 (Westminster, Md., and London: Newman Press, 1965).

Porphyry. *Vita Plotini*. In *Plotini opera*, ed. Paul Henry and Hans-Rudolf Schwyzer, 1: 1–38 (Oxford: Clarendon Press, 1964). English translation by Arthur Hilary Armstrong in *Plotinus: The Enneads*, vol. 1, Loeb Classical Library (London: Heinemann; Cambridge, Mass.: Harvard University Press, 1966).

Socrates. *Historia ecclesiastica*. PG 67. 9–842. English translation: *Socrates, The Ecclesiastical History*, tr., with notes, Valesius (London: Bohn, 1853).

Sozomen. *Historia ecclesiastica*. In *Sozomenus, Kirchengeschichte*, ed. Joseph Bidez, GCS 50 (Berlin: Akademie-Verlag, 1960).

Themistius. *Themistii orationes quae supersunt*, 3 vols., ed. Heinrich Schenkl, completed by Glanville Downey (Leipzig: Teubner, 1965–74).

Theodoret of Cyrrhus. *Epistulae. Théodoret de Cyr, Correspondance*, ed. and tr., with intro. and notes, Yvan Azéma, Sources chrétiennes 40, 98, 111 (Paris: Éditions du Cerf, 1955, 1964, 1965).

———. *Historia ecclesiastica. Theodoret, Kirchengeschichte*, ed. Léon Parmentier, with 2d ed. by Felix Scheidweiler, GCS 44 (19) (Berlin: Akademie-Verlag, 1954). English translation: *Ecclesiastical History: A History of the Church in Five Books, from A.D. 322 to the Death of Theodore of Mopsuestia, A.D. 427, by Theodoretus, Bishop of Cyrus*, Greek Ecclesiastical Historians of the First Six Centuries of the Christian Era 5 (London: Samuel Bagster and Sons, 1843).

———. *Historia religiosa. Théodoret de Cyr, Histoire des moines de Syrie: 'Histoire Philothée' I–XIII*, 2 vols., ed. and tr., with intro. and notes, Pierre Canivet and Alice Leroy-Molinghen, Sources chrétiennes 234, 257 (Paris: Éditions du Cerf, 1977, 1979). English translation: *A History of the Monks of Syria by Theodoret of Cyrrhus*, tr., with intro. and notes, R. M. Price, Cistercian Studies 88 (Kalamazoo, Mich.: Cistercian Publications, 1985).

Zosimus. *Historia nova. Zosime, Histoire nouvelle*, 6 vols., ed. and tr. François Paschoud, Collection Guillaume Budé (Paris: Les Belles Lettres, 1971–89). English translation: *Zosimus, New History*, tr., with notes, Ronald T. Ridley, Byzantina Australiensia 2 (Sydney: Australian Association for Byzantine Studies, 1982).

SECONDARY WORKS

Aland, Kurt, and F. L. Cross, eds. *Studia patristica*, vol. 2. *Texte und Untersuchungen* 64. Berlin: Akademie Verlag, 1957.

Amand, David. See Amand de Mendieta, Emmanuel.

Amand de Mendieta, Emmanuel (David Amand). *L'Ascèse monastique de saint Basile: Essai historique*. N.p.: Éditions de Maredsous, 1949.

———. 'L'Authenticité des lettres ascétiques 42 à 45 de la correspondance de Saint Basile de Césarée'. *Recherches de science religieuse* 56 (1968): 241–64.

———. 'Basile de Césarée et Damase de Rome: Les causes de l'échec de leurs négociations'. In *Biblical and Patristic Studies*, edited by Birdsall and Thomson, pp. 122–66.

———. 'Essai d'une histoire critique des éditions générales grecques et gréco-latines de s. Basile de Césarée'. *Revue Bénédictine* 52 (1940): 141–61; 53 (1941): 119–51; 54 (1942): 124–44; 56 (1944–45): 126–53.

———. 'The Official Attitude of Basil of Caesarea as a Christian Bishop towards Greek Philosophy and Science'. In *The Orthodox Churches and the West*, edited by Baker, pp. 25–49.

———. 'The Pair ΚΗΡΥΓΜΑ and ΔΟΓΜΑ in the Theological Thought of St. Basil of Caesarea'. *Journal of Theological Studies*, n.s. 16 (1965): 129–42.

———. 'La Tradition manuscrite des œuvres de saint Basile'. *Revue d'histoire ecclésiastique* 49 (1954): 507–21.

———. *The 'Unwritten' and 'Secret' Apostolic Traditions in the Theological Thought of St. Basil of Caesarea*. Scottish Journal of Theology, Occasional Papers, 13. Edinburgh: Oliver & Boyd, 1965.

Anastos, Milton V. 'Basil's Κατὰ Εὐνομίου, a Critical Analysis'. In *Basil of Caesarea*, edited by Fedwick, 1: 67–136.

Armstrong, Arthur Hilary. 'Man in the Cosmos: A Study of Some Differences between Pagan Neoplatonism and Christianity'. In *Romanitas et Christianitas*, edited by den Boer, pp. 5–14. Reprinted in his *Plotinian and Christian Studies*.

———. *Plotinian and Christian Studies*. Collected Studies 102. London: Variorum, 1979.

BIBLIOGRAPHY 371

——— . 'Plotinus's Doctrine of the Infinite and Its Significance for Christian Thought'. *Downside Review* 73 (1955): 47–58. Reprinted in his *Plotinian and Christian Studies*.

Athanassiadi-Fowden, Polymnia. *Julian and Hellenism*. Oxford: Oxford University Press, 1981. Reprint. 1992.

Aubin, P. *Le Problème de la conversion*. Théologie historique 1. Paris: Beauchesne, 1963.

Aubineau, Michel. *Grégoire de Nysse, Traité de la virginité*. Sources chrétiennes 119. Paris: Éditions du Cerf, 1966.

Baker, Derek, ed. *The Orthodox Churches and the West*. Studies in Church History 13. Oxford: Blackwell, 1976.

Bamberger, John Eudes. 'Μνήμη-Διάθεσις: The Psychic Dynamisms in the Ascetical Theology of St. Basil'. *Orientalia Christiana periodica* 34 (1968): 233–51.

Bardy, Gustave. *Recherches sur Saint Lucien d'Antioche et son école*. Paris: Beauchesne, 1936.

Barnard, Leslie William. 'The Antecedents of Arius'. In his *Studies in Church History*, pp. 289–311. Conflates two earlier articles in *Vigiliae Christianae* 24 (1970): 172–88, and *Theologische Zeitschrift* 28 (1972): 110–17.

——— . 'East-West Conciliatory Moves and Their Outcome in the Period 341–351 A.D.'. *Heythrop Journal* 20 (1979): 243–56.

——— . 'Pope Julius, Marcellus of Ancyra, and the Council of Sardica—A Reconsideration'. *Recherches de théologie ancienne et médiévale* 38 (1971): 69–79. Reprinted in his *Studies in Church History*, pp. 341–53.

——— . *Studies in Church History and Patristics*. Thessalonica: Patriarchal Institute for Patristic Studies, 1978.

Barnes, T. D. *Athanasius and Constantius: Theology and Politics in the Constantinian Empire*. Cambridge, Mass., and London: Harvard University Press, 1993.

——— . 'Constantine and the Christians of Persia'. *Journal of Roman Studies* 75 (1985): 126–36.

——— . *Constantine and Eusebius*. Cambridge, Mass.: Harvard University Press, 1981.

——— . 'A Correspondent of Iamblichus'. *Greek, Roman and Byzantine Studies* 19 (1978): 99–106.

——— . 'The Date of the Council of Gangra'. *Journal of Theological Studies*, n.s. 40 (1989): 121–24.

——— . 'Himerius and the Fourth Century'. *Classical Philology* 82 (1987): 206–25.

Baur, J. C. *John Chrysostom and His Time*. Translated by M. Gonzaga. 2d ed. Vaduz: Buchervertriebanstalt, 1988.

Bayet, Jean. *Mélanges de littérature latine*. Storia e letteratura, raccolta di Studi e Testi, 110. Rome: Edizioni di storia e letteratura, 1967.

——— . 'Science cosmique et sagesse dans la philosophie antique'. *Diogène* 6 (1954): 41–72. Reprinted in his *Mélanges*, pp. 499–528.

Baynes, Norman H. *Byzantine Studies and Other Essays*. London: University of London Athlone Press, 1955.

―――. 'Rome and Armenia in the Fourth Century'. *English Historical Review* 25 (1910): 625–43. Reprinted in his *Byzantine Studies and Other Essays*, pp. 186–208.

Bernardi, Jean. *La Prédication des pères cappadociens: Le Prédicateur et son auditoire.* Publications de la Faculté des lettres et sciences humaines de l'Université de Montpellier 30. Marseille: Presses universitaires de France, 1968.

Bessières, Marius. *La Tradition manuscrite de la correspondance de s. Basile.* Reprint. Oxford: Clarendon Press, 1923. For an earlier version, see *Journal of Theological Studies* 21 (1919–20): 1–50, 289–310; 22 (1920–21): 105–37; 23 (1921–22): 113–33, 225–49, 337–58.

Birdsall, J. Neville, and Robert W. Thomson, eds. *Biblical and Patristic Studies in Memory of Robert Pierce Casey.* Freiburg: Herder, 1963.

Blockley, Roger C. *Ammianus Marcellinus: A Study of His Historiography and Political Thought.* Collection Latomus 141. Brussels, 1975.

―――. The Division of Armenia between the Romans and the Persians at the End of the Fourth Century A.D.'. *Historia* 36 (1987): 222–34.

Blumenthal, H. J., and Robert A. Markus, eds. *Neoplatonism and Early Christian Thought: Essays in Honour of A. H. Armstrong.* London: Variorum, 1981.

Bonner, Gerald. 'The Extinction of Paganism and the Church Historian'. *Journal of Ecclesiastical History* 35 (1984): 339–57.

Booth, Alan D. 'The Chronology of Jerome's Early Years'. *Phoenix* 35 (1981): 237–59.

Boulenger, Fernand. *Saint Basile, Aux jeunes gens sur la manière de tirer profit des lettres helléniques.* Collection Guillaume Budé. Paris: Les Belles Lettres, 1952.

Bowersock, Glen W. 'From Emperor to Bishop: The Self-Conscious Transformation of Political Power in the Fourth Century A.D.'. *Classical Philology* 81 (1986): 298–307.

―――. *Hellenism in Late Antiquity.* Jerome Lectures 18. Ann Arbor: University of Michigan Press, 1990.

―――. *Julian the Apostate.* Cambridge, Mass.: Harvard University Press, 1978.

Bowie, Ewen Lyall. 'Apollonius of Tyana: Tradition and Reality'. In *Aufstieg und Niedergang der römischen Welt* II. 16. 2, edited by Wolfgang Haase, pp. 1652–99. Berlin and New York: Walter de Gruyter, 1978.

Brennecke, Hanns Christof. *Studien zur Geschichte der Homöer: Der Osten bis zum Ende der homöischen Reichskirche.* Beiträge zur historischen Theologie 73. Tübingen: Mohr (Siebeck), 1988.

Brown, Peter. *The Body and Society: Men, Women, and Sexual Renunciation in Early Christianity.* Lectures on the History of Religions, n.s. 13. New York: Columbia University Press, 1988.

―――. *The Cult of the Saints: Its Rise and Function in Latin Christianity.* The Haskell Lectures on History of Religions, n.s. 2. Chicago: University of Chicago Press, 1981.

Browning, Robert. *The Emperor Julian.* London: Weidenfeld and Nicolson, 1975.

―――. 'The Riot of A.D. 387 in Antioch: The Role of the Theatrical Claques in the Later Empire'. *Journal of Roman Studies* 42 (1952): 13–20.

Cadiou, R. 'Le Problème des relations scolaires entre saint Basile et Libanios'. *Revue des études grecques* 79 (1966): 89–98.

Cameron, Alan. 'Iamblichus at Athens'. *Athenaeum*, n.s. 45 (1967): 143–53. Reprinted in his *Literature and Society*.

———. *Literature and Society in the Early Byzantine World*. Collected Studies 209. London: Variorum, 1985.

Cameron, Averil. *Christianity and the Rhetoric of Empire: The Development of Christian Discourse*. Sather Classical Lectures 55. Berkeley: University of California Press, 1991.

Campbell, James Marshall. *The Influence of the Second Sophistic on the Style of the Sermons of St. Basil the Great*. Catholic University of America Patristic Studies 2. Washington, D.C.: Catholic University of America Press, 1922.

Canivet, Pierre. *Histoire d'une entreprise apologétique au Ve siècle*. Paris: Blond & Gay, 1958.

Carpenter, H. J. 'Creeds and Baptismal Rites in the First Four Centuries'. *Journal of Theological Studies* 44 (1943): 1–11.

Casevitz, Michel. 'Basile, le grec et les grecques: Réflexions linguistiques'. *Vigiliae Christianae* 35 (1981): 315–20.

Cavallera, F. *Le Schisme d'Antioche (IVe–Ve siècles)*. Paris: Picard, 1905.

Cavallin, Anders. *Studien zu den Briefen des hl. Basilius*. Lund: Gleerupska Universitetsbokhandeln, 1944.

Cazeaux, Jacques. *Les Échos de la sophistique autour de Libanios, ou le style 'simple' dans un traité de Basile de Césarée*. Collection Guillaume Budé. Paris: Les Belles Lettres, 1980.

Chadwick, Henry. *Heresy and Orthodoxy in the Early Church*. Collected Studies 342. Aldershot: Variorum, 1991.

———. *History and Thought of the Early Church*. Collected Studies 164. London: Variorum, 1982.

———. 'Pope Damasus and the Peculiar Claim of Rome to St. Peter and St. Paul'. In *Neotestamentica et patristica*, edited by Van Unnik, pp. 313–18. Reprinted in his *History and Thought*.

———. 'The Role of the Christian Bishop in Ancient Society'. *Center for Hermeneutical Studies, Protocol of the 35th Colloquy (February, 1979)* 35 (1979): 1–14. Reprinted in his *Heresy and Orthodoxy in the Early Church*.

Clarke, Graeme, with Brian Croke, Alanna Emmett Nobbs, and Raoul Mortley. *Reading the Past in Late Antiquity*. Rushcutters Bay, N.S.W.: Pergamon Press for Australian National University Press, 1990.

Clarke, W. K. Lowther, tr. *The Ascetic Works of Saint Basil*. London: S.P.C.K., 1925.

———. *St. Basil the Great: A Study in Monasticism*. Cambridge: Cambridge University Press, 1913.

Clover, F. M., and R. S. Humphreys, eds. *Tradition and Innovation in Late Antiquity*. Madison, Wis.: University of Wisconsin Press, 1989.

Coleman-Norton, P. R., ed. *Studies in Roman Economic and Social History in Honor of Allan Chester Johnson*. Princeton: Princeton University Press, 1951.

Courcelle, Pierre. *Les Confessions de saint Augustin dans la tradition littéraire: Anté-cédents et posterité*. Paris: Études augustiniennes, 1963.

——. *Connais-toi toi-même, de Socrate à saint Bernard*. 2 vols. Paris: Études augustiniennes, 1974, 1975.

Courtonne, Yves. *Saint Basile et l'Hellénisme: Étude sur la rencontre de la pensée chrétienne avec la sagesse antique dans l'Hexaméron de Basile le Grand*. Paris: Firmin Didot, 1934.

——. *Un Témoin du IVe siècle oriental: Saint Basile et son temps d'après sa correspondance*. Paris: Les Belles Lettres, 1973.

——, ed. *Saint Basile, Lettres*. 3 vols. Collection Guillaume Budé. Paris: Les Belles Lettres, 1957, 1961, 1966.

Cox, Patricia L. *Biography in Late Antiquity: A Quest for the Holy Man*. Transformation of the Classical Heritage 5. Berkeley: University of California Press, 1983.

Cramer, J. A. *A Geographical and Historical Description of Asia Minor*. 2 vols. 1832. Reprint (2 vols. in 1). Amsterdam: Hakkert, 1971.

Croke, Brian, and Alanna Emmett, eds. *History and Historians in Late Antiquity*. Sydney: Pergamon Press, 1983.

Crouzel, Henri, Gennaro Lomiento, and Josep Rius-Camps, eds. *Origeniana*. Premier colloque international des études origéniennes, 18–21 Septembre 1973. Bari: Università di Bari, Istituto di letteratura cristiana antica, 1975.

Cuming, G. J., and Derek Baker, eds. *Popular Belief and Practice*. Studies in Church History 8. Cambridge: Cambridge University Press, 1972.

Dagron, G. *L'Empire romain d'Orient au IVe siècle et les traditions politiques d'hellénisme: Le Témoignage de Thémistios*, Centre de recherche d'histoire et civilisation byzantines, Travaux et mémoires, 3. Paris: de Boccard, 1968.

Daly, Lawrence J. 'Themistius' Concept of *Philanthropia*'. *Byzantion* 45 (1975): 22–40.

——. 'Themistius' Plea for Religious Tolerance'. *Greek, Roman and Byzantine Studies* 12 (1971): 65–79.

Daniélou, Jean. 'Grégoire de Nysse à travers les lettres de saint Basile et de saint Grégoire de Nazianze'. *Vigiliae Christianae* 19 (1965): 31–41.

——. 'Le Mariage de Grégoire de Nysse et la chronologie de sa vie'. *Revue des études augustiniennes* 2 (1956): 71–78.

Deferrari, Roy J. *Saint Basil, The Letters*. 4 vols. Loeb Classical Library. Reprint. London and Cambridge, Mass.: Heinemann and Harvard University Press, 1950–53.

Delehaye, Hippolyte. *Les Passions des martyres et les genres littéraires*. Subsidia hagiographica 13b. 2d and rev. ed. Brussels: Société des Bollandistes, 1966.

Den Boer, W., ed. *Romanitas et Christianitas*. London and Amsterdam: North Holland Publishing, 1973.

De Riedmatten, Henri. 'La Correspondance entre Basile de Césarée et Apollinaire de Laodicée'. *Journal of Theological Studies*, n.s. 7 (1956): 199–210; n.s. 8 (1957): 53–70.

Devos, Paul. 'Saint Grégoire de Nazianze et Hellade de Césarée en Cappadoce'. *Analecta Bollandiana* 79 (1961): 91–101.

Devreesse, Robert. *Le Patriarcat d'Antioche, depuis le paix de l'Église jusqu'à la conquête arabe.* Paris: Gabalda, 1945.

De Vries, Wilhelm. 'Die Ostkirche und die Cathedra Petri'. *Orientalia Christiana periodica* 40 (1974): 114–44.

Dihle, Albrecht, ed. *L'Église et l'empire au IVe siècle.* Entretiens sur l'antiquité classique 34. Vandœuvres-Genève: Fondation Hardt, 1989.

Dillon, John M. 'Self-Definition in Later Platonism'. In *Jewish and Christian Self-Definition,* vol. 3, edited by Meyer and Sanders, pp. 60–75.

Dockrill, D. W., and R. G. Tanner. *The Idea of Salvation.* Prudentia suppl. Armidale, N.S.W.: University of Newcastle, 1988.

Dörries, Hermann. *De spiritu sancto: Der Beitrag des Basilius zum Abschluß des trinitarischen Dogmas.* Abhandlungen der Akademie der Wissenschaften in Göttingen, Philologisch-historisch Klasse 3, ser. 39. Göttingen: Vandenhoeck & Ruprecht, 1956.

Downey, Glanville. 'The Economic Crisis at Antioch under Julian the Apostate'. In *Studies in Roman Economic and Social History,* edited by Coleman-Norton, pp. 312–21.

———. 'Education and Public Problems as Seen by Themistius'. *Transactions of the American Philological Association* 86 (1955): 291–307.

———. 'Education in the Christian Roman Empire: Christian and Pagan Theories under Constantine and His Successors'. *Speculum* 32 (1957): 48–61.

———. *A History of Antioch in Syria from Seleucus to the Arab Conquest.* Princeton: Princeton University Press, 1961.

———. 'Philanthropia in Religion and Statecraft in the Fourth Century after Christ'. *Historia* 4 (1955): 199–208.

Ducatillon, Jeanne, tr. *Basile de Césarée, Sur le baptême.* Sources chrétiennes 357. Paris: Éditions du Cerf, 1989.

Duncan-Jones, Richard P. 'City Population in Roman Africa'. *Journal of Roman Studies* 53 (1963): 85–90.

———. *Structure and Scale in the Roman Economy.* Cambridge: Cambridge University Press, 1990.

Eadie, John W., and Josiah Ober, eds. *The Craft of the Ancient Historian: Essays in Honor of Chester G. Starr.* Lanham, Md.: University Press of America, 1985.

Fedwick, Paul Jonathan, ed. *Basil of Caesarea: Christian, Humanist, Ascetic, A Sixteen-hundredth Anniversary Symposium.* 2 vols. Toronto: Pontifical Institute of Mediaeval Studies, 1981.

———. *The Church and the Charisma of Leadership in Basil of Caesarea.* Studies and Texts 45. Toronto: Pontifical Institute of Mediaeval Studies, 1979.

Festugière, A. M. J. *Antioche païenne et chrétienne: Libanius, Chrysostome et les moines de Syrie.* Bibliothèque des Écoles françaises d'Athènes et de Rome 194. Paris: Boccard, 1959.

Florovsky, Georges. 'The Function of Tradition in the Ancient Church'. *Greek Orthodox Theological Review* 9 (1963): 181–200.

Fontaine, Jacques, and Charles Kannengiesser, eds. *Epektasis: Mélanges patristiques offerts au Cardinal Jean Daniélou*. Paris: Beauchesne, 1972.

Forrat, Marguerite. Introduction to *Eusèbe de Césarée, Contre Hiéroclès*. Sources chrétiennes 333. Paris: Éditions du Cerf, 1986.

Fortin, Ernest L. 'Christianity and Hellenism in Basil the Great's Address *Ad Adulescentes*'. In *Neoplatonism and Early Christian Thought*, edited by Blumenthal and Markus, pp. 189–203.

Fowden, Garth. 'The Athenian Agora and the Progress of Christianity'. *Journal of Roman Archaeology* 3 (1990): 494–501.

———. 'Bishops and Temples in the Eastern Roman Empire, A.D. 320–435'. *Journal of Theological Studies*, n.s. 29 (1978): 53–78.

———. 'The Pagan Holy Man in Late Antique Society'. *Journal of Hellenic Studies* 102 (1982): 33–59.

Frantz, Alison, with contributions by Homer A. Thompson and John Travlos. *The Athenian Agora: Results of Excavations Conducted by the American School of Classical Studies at Athens*. Vol. 24, *Late Antiquity: A.D. 267–700*. Princeton: The American School of Classical Studies at Athens, 1988.

———. 'From Paganism to Christianity in the Temples of Athens'. *Dumbarton Oaks Papers* 19 (1965): 185–205.

———. 'Pagan Philosophers in Christian Athens'. *Proceedings of the American Philosophical Society* 119 (1975): 29–38.

Frazee, Charles A. 'Anatolian Asceticism in the Fourth Century: Eustathios of Sebastea and Basil of Caesarea'. *Catholic Historical Review* 66 (1981): 16–33.

French, D. H. 'The Roman Road-system of Asia Minor'. In *Aufstieg und Niedergang der römischen Welt* II. 7. 2, edited by Hildegard Temporini, pp. 698–729. Berlin and New York: Walter de Gruyter, 1980.

Gain, Benoît. *L'Église de Cappadoce au IV*e *siècle d'après la correspondance de Basile de Césarée*. Orientalia Christiana analecta 225. Rome: Pontificium institutum Orientale, 1985.

Gallay, Paul. *Grégoire de Nazianze*. Paris: Les Éditions ouvrières, 1959.

———. *La Vie de saint Grégoire de Nazianze*. Lyon: E. Vitte, 1943.

———, ed. *Saint Grégoire de Nazianze, Lettres*. 2 vols. Collection Guillaume Budé. Paris: Les Belles Lettres, 1964, 1967.

Gallicet, Ezio. 'Osservazioni sul "De virginitate" di Gregorio di Nissa'. *Civiltà classica e cristiana* 3 (1982): 119–51.

Garsoïan, Nina G. *Armenia between Byzantium and the Sasanians*. Collected Studies 218. London: Variorum, 1985.

———. 'Armenia in the Fourth Century: An Attempt to Re-define the Concepts "Armenia" and "Loyalty"'. *Revue des études arméniennes*, n.s. 8 (1971): 341–52. Reprinted in her *Armenia between Byzantium and the Sasanians*.

————. 'Nerses le Grand, Basile de Césarée et Eustathe de Sébaste'. *Revue des études arméniennes*, n.s. 17 (1983): 145–69. Reprinted in her *Armenia between Byzantium and the Sasanians*.

————. 'Politique ou orthodoxie? L'Arménie au quatrième siècle'. *Revue des études arméniennes*, n.s. 4 (1967): 297–320. Reprinted in her *Armenia between Byzantium and the Sasanians*.

————. 'Quidam Narseus? A Note on the Mission of St. Nerses the Great'. In *Armeniaca: Mélanges d'études arméniennes*, pp. 148–64. Ile de Saint Lazare - Venise, 1969. Reprinted in her *Armenia between Byzantium and the Sasanians*.

————. 'Sur le titre de *protecteur des pauvres*'. *Revue des études arméniennes*, n.s. 15 (1981): 21–32. Reprinted in her *Armenia between Byzantium and the Sasanians*.

Garstang, John, and O. R. Gurney. *The Geography of the Hittite Empire*. London: British Institute of Archaeology at Ankara, 1959.

Giet, Stanislas. *Les Idées et l'action sociales de s. Basile*. Paris: Gabalda, 1941.

————. 'S. Basile et le concile de Constantinople de 360'. *Journal of Theological Studies*, n.s. 6 (1955): 94–99.

————. *Sasimes: Une méprise de saint Basile*. Paris: Gabalda, 1941.

————, ed. *Basile de Césarée, Homélies sur l'Hexaéméron*. 2d ed., revised and expanded. Sources chrétiennes 26 bis. Paris: Éditions du Cerf, 1968.

Girardi, Mario. 'Bibbia e agiografia nell'omiletica sui martiri di Basilio di Cesarea'. *Vetera Christianorum* 25 (1988): 451–86.

Gleason, Maude W. 'Festive Satire: Julian's *Misopogon* and the New Year at Antioch'. *Journal of Roman Studies* 76 (1986): 106–19.

Gould, Graham E. 'Basil of Caesarea and Gregory of Nyssa on the Beatitudes'. *Studia patristica*, vol. 22, edited by Livingstone, pp. 14–22.

————. 'Basil of Caesarea and the Problem of the Wealth of Monasteries'. In *The Church and Wealth*, edited by Sheils and Wood, pp. 15–24.

Grabar, André. *Martyrium: Recherches sur le culte des reliques et l'art chrétien antique*. London: Variorum, 1972.

Gregg, Robert Clark. *Consolation Philosophy: Greek and Christian Paideia in Basil and the Two Gregories*. Patristic Monograph Series 3. Cambridge, Mass.: Philadelphia Patristic Foundation, 1975.

————. Review of *Arius*, by Rowan Williams. *Journal of Theological Studies*, n.s. 40 (1989): 247–54.

————, ed. *Arianism: Historical and Theological Reassessments*. Papers from the Ninth International Conference on Patristic Studies, September 5–10, 1983, Oxford, England. Patristic Monograph Series 11. Philadelphia: Philadelphia Patristic Foundation, 1985.

Gregg, Robert Clark, and Dennis E. Groh. *Early Arianism—A View of Salvation*. Philadelphia: Fortress Press, 1981.

Gregory, Timothy E. 'Urban Violence in Late Antiquity'. In *Aspects of Graeco-Roman Urbanism*, edited by Marchese, pp. 138–61.

Gribomont, Jean. 'À propos du rigorisme de saint Basile: Gravité du péché, libération du pécheur' (Note additionelle 3). In *Commandements*, edited by Gribomont, pp. 139–73.

———. 'Un Aristocrate révolutionnaire, évêque et moine: S. Basile'. *Augustinianum* 17 (1977): 179–91. Reprinted in his *Saint Basile*, 1: 65–77.

———. 'Études sur l'histoire du texte de saint Basile'. *Scriptorium* 8 (1954): 298–304.

———. 'Eustathe de Sébaste'. *Dictionnaire de spiritualité*, vol. 4, pt. 2, cols. 1708–12. Paris: Beauchesne, 1961. Reprinted (with the following) in his *Saint Basile*, 1: 95–106.

———. 'Eustathe de Sébaste'. *Dictionnaire d'histoire et de géographie ecclésiastiques*, vol. 16, cols. 26–33. Paris: Letouzey et Ané, 1967. Reprinted (with the above) in his *Saint Basile*, 1: 95–106.

———. 'Eustathe le philosophe et les voyages du jeune Basile de Césarée'. *Revue d'histoire ecclésiastique* 54 (1959): 115–24. Reprinted in his *Saint Basile*, 1: 107–16.

———. 'L'*Exhortation au renoncement* attribué à saint Basile'. *Orientalia Christiana periodica* 21 (1955): 375–98. Reprinted in his *Saint Basile*, 2: 365–88.

———. *Histoire du texte des Ascétiques de s. Basile*. Bibliothèque du *Muséon* 32. Louvain: Publications universitaires/Institut orientaliste, 1953.

———. 'Il monachesimo orientale'. In *Dall'eremio al cenobio: La civiltà monastica in Italia dalle origini all'età di Dante*, edited by Giovanni Pugliese Carratelli, pp. 127–52. Milan: Collana antica madre Milano libri Scheiwiller, 1987.

———. 'Le monachisme au IVe siècle en Asie Mineure: De Gangres au Messalianisme'. *Studia patristica*, vol. 2, edited by Aland and Cross, pp. 400–415. Reprinted in his *Saint Basile*, 1: 26–41.

———. 'Le monachisme au sein de l'église en Syrie et en Cappadoce'. *Studia monastica* 7 (1965): 7–24. Reprinted in his *Saint Basile*, 1: 3–20.

———. 'Mystique et orthodoxie' (Note additionelle 1). In *Commandements*, edited by Gribomont, pp. 106–19. Reprinted in his *Saint Basile*, 1: 78–91.

———. 'Notes biographiques sur s. Basile le Grand'. In *Basil of Caesarea*, edited by Fedwick, 1: 21–48. Reprinted in his *Saint Basile*, 1: 117–44.

———. 'Obéissance de charité et liberté envers l'église de Rome' (Note additionelle 2). In *Commandements*, edited by Gribomont, pp. 120–38. Reprinted in his *Saint Basile*, 2: 502–20.

———. 'Obéissance et évangile selon saint Basile le Grand'. *Supplément de La Vie spirituelle* 5 (1952): 192–215. Reprinted in his *Saint Basile*, 2: 270–93.

———. 'L'Origénisme de saint Basile'. In *L'Homme devant Dieu: Mélanges Henri de Lubac*, 1: 281–94. Paris: Aubier, 1963. Reprinted in his *Saint Basile*, 1: 229–42.

———. 'Le Panégyrique de la virginité, œuvre de jeunesse de Grégoire de Nysse'. *Revue d'ascétique et de mystique* 43 (1967): 249–66.

———. 'Les Règles épistolaires de saint Basile: Lettres 173 et 22'. *Antonianum* 54 (1979): 255–89. Reprinted in his *Saint Basile*, 1: 157–89.

——— . 'Les Règles morales de s. Basile et le Nouveau Testament'. *Studia patristica*, vol. 2, edited by Aland and Cross, pp. 416–26. Reprinted in his *Saint Basile*, 1: 146–56.

——— . 'Le Renoncement au monde dans l'idéal ascétique de saint Basile'. *Irenikon* 31 (1958): 282–307, 460–75. Reprinted in his *Saint Basile*, 2: 322–63.

——— . 'Saint Basile'. In *Commandements*, edited by Gribomont, pp. 81–105. Reprinted as 'Commandements du seigneur et libération évangélique: Saint Basile' in his *Saint Basile*, 2: 295–319.

——— . 'Saint Basile'. In *Théologie de la vie monastique: Études sur la tradition patristique*, pp. 99–113. Théologie 49. Paris: Aubier, 1961.

——— . *Saint Basile: Évangile et église. Mélanges*. 2 vols. Spiritualité orientale et vie monastique 36–37. Bégrolles-en-Mauges: Abbaye de Bellefontaine, 1984.

——— . 'Saint Basile, le Protreptique au baptême'. In *Lex orandi, lex credendi: Miscellanea Vagaggini*, pp. 71–92. Studia Anselmiana 79. Rome: Editrice Anselmiana, 1980. Reprinted in his *Saint Basile*, 2: 391–412.

——— , ed. *Commandements du seigneur et libération évangélique*. Études monastiques proposées et discutées à Saint-Anselme, 15–17 Février 1976. Studia Anselmiana 70. Rome: Editrice Anselmiana, 1977.

Grumel, V., ed. *La Chronologie*. Traité d'études byzantines, vol. 1, edited by Paul Lemerle. Paris: Presses universitaires de France, 1958.

Guillaumont, Antoine. 'Esquisse d'une phénoménologie du monachisme'. *Numen* 25 (1978): 40–51.

Hanson, R. P. C. 'The Achievement of Orthodoxy in the Fourth Century A.D.' In *The Making of Orthodoxy*, edited by Williams, pp. 142–56.

Harl, Marguerite, ed. *Écriture et culture philosophique dans la pensée de Grégoire de Nysse*. Actes du Colloque de Chevetogne, 22–26 Septembre 1969. Leiden: Brill, 1971.

Hauser-Meury, Marie-Madeleine. *Prosopographie zu den Schriften Gregors von Nazianz*. Theophaneia 13. Bonn: Hanstein, 1960.

Haykin, Michael A. G. 'And Who Is the Spirit? Basil of Caesarea's Letters to the Church at Tarsus'. *Vigiliae Christianae* 41 (1987): 377–85.

Hazlett, Ian, ed. *Early Christianity: Origins and Evolution to A.D. 600, In Honour of W. H. C. Frend*. London: S.P.C.K., 1990.

Heather, Peter, and John Matthews. *The Goths in the Fourth Century*. Translated Texts for Historians 11. Liverpool: Liverpool University Press, 1991.

Hengel, Martin. *Acts and the History of Earliest Christianity*. Translated by John Bowden. Philadelphia: Fortress Press, 1980. First published as *Zur urchristlichen Geschichtsschreibung* (Stuttgart: Calmer, 1979).

Hewsen, R. H. 'The Successors of Tiridates the Great: A Contribution to the History of Armenia in the Fourth Century'. *Revue des études arméniennes*, n.s. 13 (1978–79): 99–126.

Holl, Karl. *Amphilochius von Ikonium in seinem Verhältnis zu den großen Kappadoziern*. Tübingen and Leipzig: J. C. B. Mohr (Paul Siebeck), 1904.

———. *Enthusiasmus und Bußgewalt beim griechischen Mönchtum: Eine Studie zu Symeon dem neuen Theologen.* Leipzig: J. C. Hinrichs, 1898.

Hopwood, Keith. 'Policing the Hinterland: Rough Cilicia and Isauria'. In *Armies and Frontiers*, edited by Mitchell, pp. 173–81.

Hunt, E. D. 'Did Constantius II Have "Court Bishops"?' In *Studia patristica*, vol. 19, edited by Livingstone, pp. 86–90. Louvain: Peeters Press, 1989.

———. *Holy Land Pilgrimage in the Later Roman Empire, A.D. 312–460.* Oxford: Clarendon Press, 1982.

Isaac, Benjamin H. *The Limits of Empire: The Roman Army in the East.* Oxford: Clarendon Press, 1990.

Jackson, Blonfield, tr. *St. Basil the Great on the Holy Spirit.* Revised by David Anderson. Crestwood, N.Y.: St Vladimir's Seminary Press, 1980.

———. English translation of sermons 1–9 of Basil's *Hexaemeron.* In *Nicene and Post-Nicene Fathers*, 2d ser. Vol. 8, *St. Basil, Letters and Selected Works.* New York: Christian Literature Co.; Oxford and London: Parker and Co., 1895.

Jaeger, Werner. *Early Christianity and Greek Paideia.* Cambridge, Mass.: Harvard University Press, 1961.

———. *Paideia: The Ideals of Greek Culture.* A translation by Gilbert Highet of the 2d German ed. 3 vols. Oxford: Blackwell, 1939–47.

Joannou, Perikles-Petros. *Die Ostkirche und die Cathedra Petri im 4. Jahrhundert.* Päpste und Papsttum 3. Stuttgart: Anton Hiersemann, 1972.

Jones, A. H. M. *The Cities of the East Roman Provinces.* 2d ed. Oxford: Clarendon Press, 1971.

Jones, A. H. M., J. R. Martindale, and J. Morris, eds. *The Prosopography of the Later Roman Empire.* Vol. 1, *A.D. 260–395.* Cambridge: Cambridge University Press, 1971.

Judge, E. A. 'The Earliest Use of Monachos for "Monk" (P. Coll. Youtie 77) and the Origins of Monasticism'. *Jahrbuch für Antike und Christentum* 20 (1977): 72–89.

Junod, Éric. 'Particularités de la Philocalie'. In *Origeniana*, edited by Crouzel, Lomiento, and Rius-Camps, pp. 181–97.

———. 'Remarques sur la composition de la "Philocalie" d'Origène par Basile de Césarée et Grégoire de Nazianze'. *Revue d'histoire et de philosophie religieuses* 52 (1972): 149–56.

———, ed. *Origène, Philocalie 21–27, Sur le libre arbitre.* Introduction, texte, traduction, et notes par Éric Junod. Sources chrétiennes 226. Paris: Éditions du Cerf, 1976.

Kelly, J. N. D. *Early Christian Creeds.* 3d ed. London: Longman, 1972.

———. *Jerome, His Life, Writings, and Controversies.* London: Duckworth, 1975.

Kennedy, George Alexander. *Greek Rhetoric under Christian Emperors.* Princeton: Princeton University Press, 1983.

Klein, Richard. *Constantius II und die christliche Kirche.* Darmstadt: Wissenschaftliche Buchgesellschaft, 1977.

Klock, Christoph. *Untersuchungen zu Stil und Rhythmus bei Gregor von Nyssa: Ein Beitrag zum Rhetorikverständnis der griechischen Väter.* Beiträge zur klassischen Philologie 173. Frankfurt am Main: Athenäum, 1987.

Kopecek, Thomas A. 'The Cappadocian Fathers and Civic Patriotism'. *Church History* 43 (1974): 293–303.

———. *A History of Neo-Arianism.* 2 vols. Patristic Monograph Series 8. Philadelphia: Philadelphia Patristic Foundation, 1979.

———. 'The Social Class of the Cappadocian Fathers'. *Church History* 42 (1973): 453–66.

Koschorke, Klaus. *Spuren der alten Liebe: Studien zum Kirchenbegriff des Basilius von Caesarea.* Paradosis 32. Freiburg: Universitätsverlag Freiburg Schweiz, 1991.

Kurmann, Alois. *Gregor von Nazianz, Oratio 4, Gegen Julian: Ein Kommentar.* Schweizerische Beiträge zur Altertumswissenschaft 19. Basel: Friedrich Reinhardt, 1988.

Lamberz, Erich. 'Zum Verständnis von Basileios' Schrift, "Ad Adolescentes"'. *Zeitschrift für Kirchengeschichte* 90 (1979): 75–95.

Lane Fox, Robin. *Pagans and Christians.* Harmondsworth and New York: Penguin Books, Viking, 1986.

Langlois, Victor, ed. *Collection des historiens anciens et modernes de l'Arménie.* 2 vols. Paris: Firmin-Didot, 1880.

Laun, F. 'Die beiden Regeln des Basilius, ihre Echtheit und Entstehung'. *Zeitschrift für Kirchengeschichte* 44 (1925): 1–61.

Lawless, George. *Augustine of Hippo and His Monastic Rule.* Oxford: Oxford University Press, 1987.

Lèbe, Léon. 'S. Basile et ses *Règles Morales*'. *Revue Bénédictine* 75 (1965): 193–200.

———. 'S. Basile: Notes à propos des règles monastiques'. *Revue Bénédictine* 76 (1966): 116–19.

Leclercq, H. 'Ibora'. *Dictionnaire d'archéologie chrétienne et de liturgie* 7, 1: 4–9. Paris: Letouzey et Ané, 1926.

Lewis, George, tr. *The Philocalia of Origen.* Edinburgh: Clark, 1911.

Liebeschuetz, J. H. W. G. *Antioch: City and Imperial Administration in the Later Roman Empire.* Oxford: Clarendon Press, 1972.

Lienhard, Joseph T. 'Basil of Caesarea, Marcellus of Ancyra, and "Sabellius"'. *Church History* 58 (1989): 157–67.

———. 'The Epistle of the Synod of Ancrya, 358: A Reconsideration'. In *Arianism,* edited by Gregg, pp. 313–19.

Lim, Richard. 'The Politics of Interpretation in Basil of Caesarea's *Hexaemeron*'. *Vigiliae Christianae* 44 (1990): 351–70.

Livingstone, Elizabeth A., ed. *Studia patristica.* Vol. 22 (= Papers Presented to the Tenth International Conference on Patristic Studies, Oxford, 1987). Louvain: Peeters Press, 1989.

Loofs, F. *Eustathius von Sebaste und die Chronologie der Basilius-Briefe: Eine patristische Studie.* Halle: Niemeyer, 1898.

MacMullen, Ramsay. *Christianizing the Roman Empire (A.D. 100–400)*. New Haven: Yale University Press, 1984.

———. 'The Preacher's Audience'. *Journal of Theological Studies*, n.s. 40 (1989): 503–11.

Macro, Anthony D. 'The Cities of Asia Minor under the Roman Imperium'. In *Aufstieg und Niedergang der römischen Welt* II. 7. 2, edited by Hildegard Temporini, pp. 658–97. Berlin and New York: Walter de Gruyter, 1980.

Magie, David. *Roman Rule in Asia Minor to the End of the Third Century after Christ*. 2 vols. Princeton: Princeton University Press, 1950.

Malingrey, A.-M. *'Philosophia': Étude d'un groupe de mots dans la littérature grecque, des Présocratiques au IVe siècle après J.-C.* Paris: C. Klincksieck, 1961.

Maran, P. *Vita Basilii. PG* 29. 5–177.

Maraval, Pierre. 'La Date de la mort de Basile de Césarée'. *Revue des études augustiniennes* 34 (1988): 25–38.

———. 'Encore les frères et soeurs de Grégoire de Nysse'. *Revue d'histoire et de philosophie religieuses* 60 (1980): 161–66.

———, ed. *Grégoire de Nysse, Vie de sainte Macrine*. Sources chrétiennes 178. Paris: Éditions du Cerf, 1971.

Marchese, Ronald T., ed. *Aspects of Graeco-Roman Urbanism: Essays on the Classical City*. British Archaeological Reports, international ser., 188. Oxford, 1983.

Markus, Robert. *The End of Ancient Christianity*. Cambridge: Cambridge University Press, 1990.

Marrou, Henri-Irénée. *A History of Education in Antiquity*. A translation of the 3d French ed. by George Lamb. London: Sheed and Ward, 1956.

Matthews, John. 'Ammianus' Historical Evolution'. In *History and Historians in Late Antiquity*, edited by Croke and Emmett, pp. 30–41. Reprinted in his *Political Life and Culture*.

———. 'Hostages, Philosophers, Pilgrims, and the Diffusion of Ideas in the Late Roman Mediterranean and Near East'. In *Tradition and Innovation*, edited by Clover and Humphreys, pp. 29–49.

———. *Political Life and Culture in Late Roman Society*. Collected Studies 217. London: Variorum, 1985.

———. *The Roman Empire of Ammianus*. London: Duckworth, 1989.

———. *Western Aristocracies and Imperial Court, A.D. 364–425*. Oxford: Clarendon Press, 1975.

May, Gerhard. 'Die Chronologie des Lebens und der Werke des Gregor von Nyssa'. In *Écriture et culture philosophique*, edited by Harl, pp. 53–63.

Meeks, Wayne A., and Robert L. Wilken. *Jews and Christians in Antioch in the First Four Centuries of the Common Era*. Society of Biblical Literature, Sources for Biblical Study, 13. Missoula, Mont.: Scholars Press, 1978.

Meredith, Anthony. 'Asceticism—Christian and Greek'. *Journal of Theological Studies*, n.s. 27 (1976): 312–32.

———. Review of *Untersuchungen zu Stil und Rhythmus bei Gregor von Nyssa*, by Christoph Klock. *Journal of Theological Studies*, n.s. 40 (1989): 256–57.

Meyendorff, John. 'St. Basil, Messalianism, and Byzantine Christianity'. *St Vladimir's Theological Quarterly* 24 (1980): 219–34.

Meyer, Ben F., and E. P. Sanders. *Jewish and Christian Self-Definition*. Vol. 3, *Self-Definition in the Greco-Roman World*. Philadelphia: Fortress Press, 1982.

Millar, Fergus. 'Empire and City, Augustus to Julian: Obligations, Excuses, and Status'. *Journal of Roman Studies* 73 (1983): 76–96.

——. 'P. Herennius Dexippus: The Greek World and the Third-Century Invasions'. *Journal of Roman Studies* 59 (1969): 12–29.

Mitchell, Stephen. 'The Balkans, Anatolia, and Roman Armies across Asia Minor'. In *Armies and Frontiers*, edited by Mitchell, pp. 131–45.

——, ed. *Armies and Frontiers in Roman and Byzantine Anatolia*. Proceedings of a Colloquium Held at University College, Swansea, April 1981. British Archaeological Reports, international ser., 156. Oxford, 1983.

Moffatt, Ann. 'The Occasion of St. Basil's *Address to Young Men*'. *Antichthon* 6 (1972): 74–86.

Momigliano, Arnaldo. 'Ancient Biography and the Study of Religion in the Roman Empire'. *Annali della Scuola superiore di Pisa*, ser. 3, vol. 15, fasc. 2 (1985). Reprinted in his *On Pagans, Jews, and Christians*, pp. 159–77.

——. 'The Life of St. Macrina by Gregory of Nyssa'. In *The Craft of the Ancient Historian*, edited by Eadie and Ober, pp. 443–58. Reprinted in his *On Pagans, Jews, and Christians*, pp. 206–21.

——. *On Pagans, Jews, and Christians*. Middletown, Conn.: Wesleyan University Press, 1987.

——. 'Popular Religious Beliefs and the Late Roman Historians'. In *Popular Belief and Practice*, edited by Cuming and Baker, pp. 1–18.

Morard, Françoise-E. 'Monachos, moine: Histoire du terme grec jusqu'au 4ᵉ siècle, Influences bibliques et gnostiques'. *Freiburger Zeitschrift für Philosophie und Theologie* 20 (1973): 325–425.

Morison, Ernest Frederick. *St. Basil and His Rule: A Study in Early Monasticism*. London: Frowde, 1912.

Murphy, Margaret Gertrude. *St. Basil and Monasticism*. Catholic University of America Patristic Studies 25. Washington, D.C.: Catholic University of America Press, 1930.

Naldini, Mario. 'Paideia origeniana nella "Oratio ad adolescentes" di Basilio Magno'. *Vetera Christianorum* 13 (1976): 297–318.

——. 'Sulla "Oratio ad adolescentes" di Basilio Magno'. *Prometheus* 4 (1978): 36–44.

——, ed. *Basilio di Cesarea, Discorso ai Giovani (Oratio ad adolescentes), con la versione latina di Leonardo Bruni*. Florence: Nardini editore, 1984.

Nautin, P. 'Epiphane'. *Dictionnaire d'histoire et de géographie ecclésiastiques*, vol. 15, cols. 617–31. Paris: Letouzey et Ané, 1963.

——. *Origène, sa vie et son œuvre*. Christianisme antique 1. Paris: Beauchesne, 1977.

Nikolaou, Th. 'Der Mensch als politisches Lebewesen bei Basilios dem Großen'. *Vigiliae Christianae* 35 (1981): 24–31.

Nock, A. D. *Conversion.* Reprint. Oxford: Clarendon Press, 1952.

Norman, A. F., ed. *Libanius' Autobiography (Oration I).* London: Oxford University Press, 1965.

Patlagean, Evelyne. *Pauvreté économique et pauvreté sociale à Byzance, 4ᵉ–7ᵉ siècles.* Civilisations et sociétés 48. Paris: Mouton, 1977.

Penella, Robert J. *Greek Philosophers and Sophists in the Fourth Century A.D.: Studies in Eunapius of Sardis.* Leeds: Francis Cairns, 1990.

Petit, Paul. *Les Étudiants de Libanius.* Études prosopographiques 1. Paris: Nouvelles éditions latines, 1957.

———. *Libanius et la vie municipale à Antioche au IVᵉ siècle après J.-C.* Paris: Geuthner, 1955.

Pietri, Charles. *Roma Christiana: Recherches sur l'Église de Rome, son organisation, sa politique, son idéologie de Mithrade à Sixte III (311–440).* Bibliothèque des Écoles françaises d'Athènes et de Rome 224. Rome: Palais Farnèse, 1976.

Pollard, T. E. 'Marcellus of Ancyra: A Neglected Father'. In *Epektasis,* edited by Fontaine and Kannengiesser, pp. 187–96.

Prestige, G. L. 'Apollinaris: or, Divine Irruption'. In his *Fathers and Heretics,* pp. 195–246.

———. *Fathers and Heretics: Six Studies in Dogmatic Faith with Prologue and Epilogue.* Bampton Lectures for 1940. London: S.P.C.K, 1940.

———. *St. Basil the Great and Apollinaris of Laodicea.* Edited by Henry Chadwick. London: S.P.C.K., 1956.

Pruche, Benoît. *Basile de Césarée, Sur le Saint-Esprit.* Sources chrétiennes 17 bis. 2d ed. Paris: Éditions du Cerf, 1968.

Puech, Aimé. *Histoire de la littérature grecque chrétienne.* 3 vols. Paris: Les Belles Lettres, 1928–30. For Basil, see 3: 235–317.

Ramsay, William Mitchell. *The Historical Geography of Asia Minor.* Royal Geographical Society, Supplementary Papers, 4. 1890. Reissue. New York: Cooper Square Publishers, 1972.

Rist, John M. 'Basil's "Neoplatonism": Its Background and Nature'. In *Basil of Caesarea,* edited by Fedwick, 1: 137–220. Reprinted in his *Platonism.*

———. *Platonism and Its Christian Heritage.* Collected Studies 221. London: Variorum, 1985.

Robinson, J. Armitage. *The Philocalia of Origen.* Cambridge: Cambridge University Press, 1893.

Rousseau, Philip. *Ascetics, Authority, and the Church in the Age of Jerome and Cassian.* Oxford: Oxford University Press, 1978.

———. 'Basil of Caesarea: Choosing a Past'. In *Reading the Past in Late Antiquity,* edited by Clarke et al., pp. 37–58.

———. 'Basil of Caesarea, *Contra Eunomium:* The Main Preoccupations'. In *The Idea of Salvation,* edited by Dockrill and Tanner, pp. 77–94.

――――. 'Blood-relationships among Early Eastern Ascetics'. *Journal of Theological Studies*, n.s. 23 (1972): 135–44.

――――. 'Christian Asceticism and the Early Monks'. In *Early Christianity*, edited by Hazlett, pp. 112–22.

――――. *Pachomius: The Making of a Community in Fourth-Century Egypt*. Transformation of the Classical Heritage 6. Berkeley: University of California Press, 1985.

Rudberg, Stig Y. *Études sur la tradition manuscrite de saint Basile*. Lund: Håkan Ohlssons Boktryckeri, 1953.

――――. *L'Homélie de Basile de Césarée sur le mot "Observe-toi toi-même"*. Acta Universitatis Stockholmiensis, Studia Graeca Stockholmiensa, 2. Stockholm: Almqvist & Wiksell, 1962.

Ruether, Rosemary Radford. *Gregory of Nazianzus, Rhetor and Philosopher*. Oxford: Clarendon Press, 1969.

Saffrey, H. D., and L. G. Westerink. 'L'École d'Athènes au IVᵉ siècle'. In their *Proclus, Théologie Platonicienne*, 1: 35–48. Collection Guillaume Budé. Paris: Les Belles Lettres, 1968.

Salzman, Michele R. '"*Superstitio*" in the *Codex Theodosianus* and the Persecution of Pagans'. *Vigiliae Christianae* 41 (1987): 172–88.

Scazzoso, Piero. *Introduzione alla ecclesiologia di San Basilio*. Milan: Publicazzioni della Università cattolica del Sacro Cuore, 1975.

――――. *Reminiscenze della Polis platonica nel Cenobio di S. Basilio*. Milan: Istituto editoriale italiano, 1970.

Schlumberger, Jörg A. '*Potentes* and *potentia* in the Social Thought of Late Antiquity'. In *Tradition and Innovation*, edited by Clover and Humphreys, pp. 89–104.

Schneemelcher, Wilhelm. *Kirche und Staat im 4. Jahrhundert*. Bonner Akademische Reden 37. Bonn: Hanstein, 1970.

Schoedel, William R., and Robert L. Wilken, eds. *Early Christian Literature and the Classical Intellectual Tradition: In Honorem Robert M. Grant*. Théologie historique 54. Paris: Beauchesne, 1979.

Schucan, Luzi. *Das Nachleben von Basilius Magnus 'ad adolescentes': Ein Beitrag zur Geschichte des christlichen Humanismus*. Travaux d'humanisme et renaissance 133. Geneva: Droz, 1973.

Schwartz, E. 'Über die Sammlung des *Cod. Veronensis* LX'. *Zeitschrift für die neutestamentliche Wissenschaft* 35 (1936): 1–23.

――――. 'Zur Kirchengeschichte des vierten Jahrhunderts'. *Zeitschrift für die neutestamentliche Wissenschaft* 34 (1935): 129–213.

Scicolone, Stefania. 'Basilio e la sua organizzazione dell'attività assistenziale a Cesarea'. *Civiltà classica e cristiana* 3 (1982): 353–72.

Sesboüé, Bernard, with Georges-Matthieu de Durand and Louis Doutreleau. *Basile de Césarée, Contre Eunome, suivi de Eunome, Apologie*. 2 vols. Sources chrétiennes 299, 305. Paris: Éditions du Cerf, 1982, 1983.

Sheils, W. J., and Diana Wood, eds. *The Church and Wealth*. Studies in Church History 24. Oxford: Blackwell, 1987.

Simonetti, Manlio. *La crisi ariana nel IV secolo*. Studia ephemeredis 'Augustinianum' 11. Rome: Institutum patristicum Augustinianum, 1975.

Smets, Alexis, and Michel van Esbroeck. *Basile de Césarée, Sur l'origine de l'homme (Homélies X et XI de l'Hexaéméron)*. Sources chrétiennes 160. Paris: Éditions du Cerf, 1970.

Snee, Rochelle. 'Valens' Recall of the Nicene Exiles and Anti-Arian Propaganda'. *Greek, Roman and Byzantine Studies* 26 (1985): 395–419.

Spanneut, M. 'Eunomius de Cyzique'. *Dictionnaire d'histoire et de géographie ecclésiastiques*, vol. 15, cols. 1399–1405. Paris: Letouzey et Ané, 1963.

Staats, Reinhart. 'Basilius als lebende Mönchsregel in Gregors von Nyssa "De virginitate" '. *Vigiliae Christianae* 39 (1985): 228–55.

Stead, Christopher (G. C.). *Substance and Illusion in the Christian Fathers*. Collected Studies 224. London: Variorum, 1985.

———. 'The *Thalia* of Arius and the Testimony of Athanasius'. *Journal of Theological Studies*, n.s. 19 (1978): 20–52. Reprinted as paper X in his *Substance and Illusion*.

Taylor, Justin. 'St. Basil the Great and Pope St. Damasus I'. *Downside Review* 91 (1973): 186–203, 262–74.

Thébert, Yvon. 'À propos du "Triomphe du Christianisme" '. *Dialogues d'histoire ancienne* 14 (1988): 277–345.

Thompson, Homer A. 'Athenian Twilight: A.D. 267–600'. *Journal of Roman Studies* 49 (1959): 61–72.

Treucker, Barnim. *Politische und sozialgeschichtliche Studien zu den Basilius-Briefen*. Bonn: Habelt, 1961.

Troiano, Marina Silvia. 'L'*Omelia* XXIII *in Mamantem Martyrem* di Basilio di Cesarea'. *Vetera Christianorum* 24 (1987): 147–57.

Van Dam, Raymond. 'Emperor, Bishops, and Friends in Late Antique Cappadocia'. *Journal of Theological Studies*, n.s. 37 (1986): 53–76.

———. 'Hagiography and History: The Life of Gregory Thaumaturgus'. *Classical Antiquity* 1 (1982): 272–308.

———. Review of *Gregor von Nazianz, Oratio 4, Gegen Julian*, by Alois Kurmann. *Journal of Theological Studies*, n.s. 40 (1989): 618–20.

Van Eijk, Ton H. C. 'Marriage and Virginity, Death and Immortality'. In *Epektasis*, edited by Fontaine and Kannengiesser, pp. 209–35.

Van Unnik, W. C., ed. *Neotestamentica et patristica: Eine Freundesgabe Herrn Prof. Dr. Oscar Cullmann zu seinem 60. Geburtstag überreicht*. Leiden: Brill, 1962.

Verheijen, Luc. *La Règle de saint Augustin*. 2 vols. Paris: Études augustiniennes, 1967.

Vernant, Jean Pierre. 'The Individual within the City-State'. In *Mortals and Immortals*, edited by Zeitlin, pp. 318–33.

Vischer, Lukas. *Basilius der Große: Untersuchungen zu einem Kirchenvater des 4. Jahrhunderts*. Basel: Reinhardt, 1953.

Wagner, M. Monica, tr. *Basil of Caesarea, Ascetical Works*. Fathers of the Church 9. Washington, D.C.: Catholic University of America Press, 1950.

Walker, Peter W. L. *Holy City, Holy Places: Christian Attitudes to Jerusalem and the Holy Land in the Fourth Century A.D.* Oxford: Clarendon Press, 1990.

Wallace-Hadrill, D. S. *Christian Antioch: A Study of Early Christian Thought in the East*. Cambridge: Cambridge University Press, 1982.

Way, Agnes Clare, tr. *Saint Basil, Letters*. 2 vols. Fathers of the Church, 13, 28. Washington, D.C.: Catholic University of America Press, 1951, 1955. Reprint. 1965, 1969.

Whittaker, John. 'Christianity and Morality in the Roman Empire'. *Vigiliae Christianae* 33 (1979): 209–25. Reprinted in his *Studies*.

——— . 'Plutarch, Platonism, and Christianity'. In *Neoplatonism and Early Christian Thought*, edited by Blumenthal and Markus, pp. 50–63. Reprinted in his *Studies*.

——— . *Studies in Platonism and Patristic Thought*. Collected Studies 201. London: Variorum, 1984.

Wickham, L. R. 'The Date of Eunomius's *Apology*: A Reconsideration'. *Journal of Theological Studies*, n.s. 20 (1969): 231–40.

Wiles, Maurice. 'Eunomius: Hair-splitting Dialectician or Defender of the Accessibility of Salvation?' In *The Making of Orthodoxy*, edited by Williams, pp. 157–72.

Williams, Rowan. *Arius: Heresy and Tradition*. London: Darton, Longman, and Todd, 1987.

——— , ed. *The Making of Orthodoxy: Essays in Honour of Henry Chadwick*. Cambridge: Cambridge University Press, 1989.

Wilson, N. G., ed. *Saint Basil on the Value of Greek Literature*. London: Duckworth, 1975.

Young, Frances M. *From Nicaea to Chalcedon: A Guide to the Literature and Its Background*. Philadelphia: Fortress Press, 1983.

——— . 'The God of the Greeks and the Nature of Religious Language'. In *Early Christian Literature*, edited by Schoedel and Wilken, pp. 45–74.

Zeitlin, Froma I., ed. *Mortals and Immortals, Collected Essays*. Princeton: Princeton University Press, 1991.

Zelzer, Klaus, ed. *Basili regula a Rufino latine versa*. Corpus scriptorum ecclesiasticorum Latinorum 86. Vienna: Hoelder-Pichter-Tempsky, 1986.

SUPPLEMENT: THE NUMBERING OF THE HOMILIES

To make reference as simple as possible, I have used the numbering printed by Fedwick in *Basil*, 1: xxvii–xxviii; and I add below the traditional numbers and names, and the corresponding references to *PG*. Note the more modern edition of *Hom.* 319 (details in the section 'Sources'). The English translations used in this book are all my own. Some of the homilies have been translated into English by Agnes Clare Way (see, again, the section 'Sources'), as I indicate below also.

319   3   *Homilia in illud: 'Attende tibi ipsi'. PG* 31. 197–217.

320   13   *Homilia exhortatoria ad sanctum baptismum. PG* 31. 424–444.

321   27   *Homilia in sanctam Christi generationem. PG* 31. 1457–1476.

322   6   *In illud dictum evangelii secundum Lucam: 'Destruam horrea mea, et maiora aedificabo': itemque de avaritia. PG* 31: 261–277.

323   7   *Homilia in divites. PG* 31. 277–304.

324   14   *Homilia in ebriosos. PG* 31. 444–464.

325   8   *Homilia dicta tempore famis et siccitatis. PG* 31. 304–328.

326   15   *Homilia de fide. PG* 31. 676–692. English translation: Clarke, *Ascetic Works*, pp. 90–99.

327   18   *Homilia in Gordium martyrem. PG* 31. 489–508.

328   4   *Homilia de gratiarum actione. PG* 31. 217–237.

329   20   *Homilia de humilitate. PG* 31. 525–540.

330   *De ieiunio, homilia I. PG* 31. 164–184.

331   *De ieiunio, homilia II. PG* 31. 185–197.

332   11   *Homilia de invidia. PG* 31. 372–385.

333   10   *Homilia adversus eos qui irascuntur. PG* 31. 353–372.

334   5   *Homilia in martyrem Iulittam et in ea quae superfuerant dicenda in prius habita concione de gratiarum actione. PG* 31. 237–261.

335   26   *Homilia dicta in Lacizis. PG* 31. 1437–1457.

336   9   *Homilia quod deus non est auctor malorum. PG* 31. 329–353.

337   23   *Homilia in sanctum martyrem Mamantem. PG* 31. 589–600.

338   19   *Homilia in sanctos quadraginta martyres. PG* 31. 508–525.

339 21 *Homilia quod rebus mundanis adhaerendum non sit, et de incendio extra ecclesiam facto.* PG 31. 540–564.

340 12 *Homilia in principium proverbiorum.* PG 31. 385–424.

341 24 *Homilia contra Sabellianos, et Arium, et Anomoeos.* PG 31. 600–617.

342 29 *Homilia adversus eos qui per calumniam dicunt dici a nobis deos tres.* PG 31. 1488–1496.

343 16 *Homilia in illud: 'In principio erat verbum'.* PG 31. 472–481.

344   *Homilia in psalmum 1.* PG 29. 209–228. Tr. Way, pp. 151f.

345   *Homilia in psalmum 7.* PG 29. 228–249. Tr. Way, pp. 165f.

346   *Homilia in psalmum 14a.* PG 29. 249–264. Tr. Way (with the following), pp. 181f.

347   *Eiusdem homilia.* PG 29. 264–280. Tr. Way (with the above), pp. 181f.

348   *Homilia in psalmum 28.* PG 29. 280–305. Tr. Way, pp. 193f.

349   *Homilia in psalmum 29.* PG 29. 305–324. Tr. Way, pp. 213f.

350   *Homilia in psalmum 32.* PG 29. 324–349. Tr. Way, pp. 227f.

351   *Homilia in psalmum 33.* PG 29. 349–385. Tr. Way, pp. 247f.

352   *Homilia in psalmum 44.* PG 29. 388–413. Tr. Way, pp. 275f.

353   *Homilia in psalmum 45.* PG 29. 416–432. Tr. Way, pp. 297f.

354   *Homilia in psalmum 48.* PG 29. 432–460. Tr. Way, pp. 311f.

355   *Homilia in psalmum 59.* PG 29. 460–469. Tr. Way, pp. 333f.

356   *Homilia in psalmum 61.* PG 29. 469–484. Tr. Way, pp. 341f.

357   *Homilia in psalmum 114.* PG 29. 484–493. Tr. Way, pp. 351f.

358   *Homilia in psalmum 115.* PG 30. 104–116.

GENERAL INDEX

INDEX OF CITATIONS
from the Works of Basil, Gregory of Nazianzus, and Gregory of Nyssa

Designer: Barbara Jellow
Compositor: Theodora S. MacKay
Text: 10/13 Palatino
Display: Palatino
Greek Font: Ibycus by Silvio Levy
Printer: Edwards Brothers, Inc.
Binder: Edwards Brothers, Inc.